POPE: THE CRITICAL HERITAGE

THE CRITICAL HERITAGE SERIES

GENERAL EDITOR: B. C. SOUTHAM, M.A., B.LITT. (OXON.)

Formerly Department of English, Westfield College, University of London

For a list of books in the series see the back end paper

POPE

The Critical Heritage

Edited by
JOHN BARNARD
School of English, University of Leeds

ROUTLEDGE & KEGAN PAUL : LONDON AND BOSTON

First published in 1973
by Routledge & Kegan Paul Ltd
Broadway House, 68–74 Carter Lane,
London EC4V 5EL and
9 Park Street,
Boston, Mass. 02108, U.S.A.
© John Barnard 1973
No part of this book may be reproduced in
any form without permission from the
publisher, except for the quotation of brief
passages in criticism
ISBN 0 7100 7390 9

Printed in Great Britain
by Richard Clay (The Chaucer Press), Ltd,
Bungay, Suffolk

General Editor's Preface

The reception given to a writer by his contemporaries and near-contemporaries is evidence of considerable value to the student of literature. On one side we learn a great deal about the state of criticism at large and in particular about the development of critical attitudes towards a single writer; at the same time, through private comments in letters, journals, or marginalia, we gain an insight upon the tastes and literary thought of individual readers of the period. Evidence of this kind helps us to understand the writer's historical situation, the nature of his immediate reading-public, and his response to these pressures.

The separate volumes in the *Critical Heritage Series* present a record of this early criticism. Clearly, for many of the highly productive and lengthily reviewed nineteenth- and twentieth-century writers, there exists an enormous body of material; and in these cases the volume editors have made a selection of the most important views, significant for their intrinsic critical worth or for their representative quality—perhaps even registering incomprehension!

For earlier writers, notably pre-eighteenth century, the materials are much scarcer and the historical period has been extended, sometimes far beyond the writer's lifetime, in order to show the inception and growth of critical views which were initially slow to appear.

In each volume the documents are headed by an Introduction, discussing the material assembled and relating the early stages of the author's reception to what we have come to identify as the critical tradition. The volumes will make available much material which would otherwise be difficult of access and it is hoped that the modern reader will be thereby helped towards an informed understanding of the ways in which literature has been read and judged.

B.C.S.

Acknowledgments

Like all recent work on Pope, this volume owes a profound debt to George Sherburn and the editors of the Twickenham Pope, without whose foundations the work would hardly have been possible. James M. Osborn's definitive edition of Spence has been a constant source of information, and J. V. Guerinot's *Pamphlet Attacks on Pope* provided a very valuable account of the Dunces' vociferous ridicule.

I would like to thank Mr David Berry for his help in checking the French translations, Dr T. Benn for information about the French translations, Dr B. Moloney for references to Pope's Italian reputation, Mr D. V. Reidy for translating the Italian passages, Professor Christopher Ricks for his early advice, and Dr E. T. Webb for his help with the Latin and Greek references. I am very grateful for the generous assistance given me by the staffs of the Bodleian Library and the British Museum, and for the kindness shown by Mr David Masson of the Brotherton Library, University of Leeds, and Mr Robert Kenedy of the Victoria & Albert Museum. Finally, I would like to thank Miss Audrey Stead of the School of English, University of Leeds, for her invaluable help with the typescript.

Contents

vii

CONTENTS

xi

PART II

LATER CRITICISM 1745–82

CONTENTS

xiii

Abbreviations

The following abbreviations are used throughout:

Corresp.: *The Correspondence of Alexander Pope*, ed. G. Sherburn (Oxford, 1956).

Dennis, *Critical Works*: *The Critical Works of John Dennis*, ed. E. N. Hooker (Baltimore, 1939–43).

PMLA: *Publications of the Modern Language Association of America*.

Spence, *Anecdotes*: Spence, Joseph, *Observations, Anecdotes and Characters of Books and Men*, ed. James M. Osborn (Oxford, 1966).

Twickenham: *The Twickenham Edition of the Poems of Alexander Pope* (London and New Haven, 1939–69). For full details, see the bibliography.

Preface

Critics of Pope's work have always found it difficult to separate the man from the poet. It is a confusion most apparent in Pope's lifetime. His critics, like his own satires, were dominated by the Augustan interest in personality. In England, the often hectic interest in Pope's character and writings was fed by a rapid accumulation of pamphlets and other trivia. Well over two hundred separate pamphlets for and against Pope were published between 1711 and 1744, the year of his death. To these publications must be added the frequent outbreaks of journalistic warfare, as well as a multiplicity of comments in letters and diaries. On the Continent, a stream of translations quickly spread Pope's fame, creating further detractors and supporters, who made their own substantial addition to eighteenth-century criticism of Pope.

The great difficulty in selecting from this mass of material was to balance the conflicting demands of criticism, literary history, and biography. Most of Pope's contemporaries were too close to their subject to see the larger issues clearly, if they could see them at all, and most of them are of little critical stature. In choosing passages from criticism written in Pope's lifetime, I have attempted to show its effect upon Pope's development as well as the critical positions taken. Much of this ephemeral material is now hard to come by, even with the publication of J. V. Guerinot's *Pamphlet Attacks on Alexander Pope 1711–1744* (1969). Consequently, Pope's own comments on poetry, though throwing more light on his work than any other contemporary critic, have been largely omitted since they are easily available.

A few pamphlets and poems from both sides are given in their entirety, but most of the documents are extracted from larger works. Private letters and informal comments are an important subsidiary source of information. Substantial passages are taken from John Dennis's frequently shrewd but always one-sided attacks, and from Joseph Spence's sympathetic critique of *The Odyssey*. The criticism written after Pope's death is of a much higher standard than the first phase, and gives a valuable index of the development of eighteenth-century critical thinking. The publication of the second volume of Joseph Warton's *Essay on the Genius and Writings of Pope* in 1782 provides a convenient stopping-point, since it allows for the inclusion of Johnson's *Life*, and much of the significant reassessment given Pope's work by his younger contemporaries.

This volume, then, falls into two main divisions. Part I (1705–44) covers Pope's lifetime. It is arranged in three sections, which reflect the main periods apparent in contemporary reactions. The first covers the years 1705–20, spanning Pope's early career up to the completion of the *Iliad*: the second runs from 1721 to 1729, when the edition of Shakespeare, the translation of the *Odyssey*, and the first version of the *Dunciad* all appeared; the final period, between 1730 and 1744, saw the publication of *An Essay on Man*, the Horatian satires, and *The Dunciad* in four books. Each of these sections is headed by a collection of general responses to Pope's poetry over the period. Within the sections themselves, comments made during Pope's lifetime on individual poems are placed according to the work's publication date.

Part II (1745–82) follows a straightforward chronological arrangement, giving an index of the widely divergent assessments of Pope's work in these years.

Comments on Pope's physique, sexual proclivities, politics, religion, and morals loom large in the attacks. They are mainly omitted here in favour of directly critical remarks. Nor does the volume give any record of the reactions to Pope's edition of Shakespeare (1725), his correspondence, the *Peri Bathous*, the miscellaneous prose pieces, or the plays in which he collaborated. The history of Pope's foreign reputation has yet to be written: I have given no more here than a brief indication of its nature. Unfortunately, it has been impossible to include any of the portraits of Pope, which are a primary source of information on his contemporary standing. It is an important omission: the interested reader should consult W. K. Wimsatt's monumental *The Portraits of Alexander Pope* (1965).

Introduction

I

The sharpest outline of Pope's eighteenth-century reputation is given by his portraits. They overwhelmingly present him as a contemporary who had attained classic immortality. Richardson's painting of Pope wearing the 'Critick's *Ivy*', Kneller's drawing of the 'English Homer' wearing the poet's bays, or his painting showing Pope pensively holding the Greek *Iliad*, Roubiliac's sensitive marble busts of the poet as Roman stoic, or Hayman's engraving of the dying Pope in his grotto surrounded by Chaucer, Spenser, Milton, and the Muse, all sought to show him as the crowning glory of English Augustan poetry. Numerous copies, medallions, prints, and even pieces of garden statuary, popularized this picture. Between 1726 and 1729, Voltaire recorded that 'The picture of the prime minister hangs over the chimney of his own closet, but I have seen that of Mr. Pope in twenty noblemen's houses.'[1] Pope's poetry was the literary equivalent of the extraordinary burst of creative energy which spread the orders of classical architecture throughout eighteenth-century England.

The serene confidence with which Pope stood alongside Homer in the libraries and gardens of great country houses was offset by bitter attacks. Dahl's portrait of the great writer in the act of composition was crudely travestied by a print published in 1729, which depicts Pope as an ape wearing a papal crown, and accompanied by an ass. Michael Rysbrack's bust met with swift abuse in the newspapers:[2]

To. Mr. REISBRANK, on his Carving A POPE'S Busto

REISBRANK, no longer let thy Art be shown
In forming Monsters from the *Parian* Stone;
Chuse for this Work a Stump of crooked Thorn,
Or Logg of Poyson-Tree, from *India* born,
There carve a *Pert*, but yet a *Rueful Face*,
Half Man, half Monkey, own'd by neither Race . . .

The frontispiece to *Ingratitude* (1733), abandoning any pretence to satire, showed the diminutive Pope held down by a nobleman, while another stands by laughing, and a third urinates on the poet. With more pertinence, a print of 1732 attacking the Palladian taste of the connoisseurs, presents Pope as a workman, splattering passers-by as he plasters the façade of Lord Burlington's town house.[3] The attempts to discredit Pope were, however, coarsely executed: the literary genius celebrated by the painters and sculptors dominated the public imagination.

Criticism written during Pope's lifetime presents the same violent dichotomy, but with a great difference in emphasis. Grub Street's assaults on the deformed poet overshadowed the constant stream of adulation: whereas the artists' likeness of Pope could fuse the actual man with the metaphoric references in a single image, the same idea put into words degenerated into unsubstantiated flattery. Even at its best, criticism in these years is marred either by blind prejudice, as in John Dennis's tirades, or restricted to a limited area of Pope's work, like Spence's *Essay* on the *Odyssey*.

If it were not for the particular nature of Pope's genius much of the repetitive and fragmentary comment between 1705 and 1782 could be ignored. Unlike the great Romantics, whose imaginations are intensely subjective, Pope's voice, themes, and structures are public. More than any other major English poet, his work is rooted in the immediate facts, personalities, and literary tastes of his time. A sense of the intellectual and social fabric of early eighteenth-century London is important to an understanding of his work in a way in which a knowledge of Regency London is irrelevant to Keats's major poetry. Pope's profoundest imaginative values and characteristic techniques were conceived within the cross-currents of a period determining its literary standards.

It is more than giving a face and shape to Pope's targets, though this is important—even at the time Swift complained the satires were obscure to anyone outside London (No. 54). There is a symbiotic relationship between Pope's ambitions, his art, and his public's response. Without his audience's financial support he could not have translated Homer: without the Dunces there would be no *Dunciad*. His satiric *persona*, essential to his later poetry, was shaped in the course of the pamphlet wars. If the Dunces' merciless caricature of Pope as a malevolent hunchback, more closely related to an ape than to a human being, forced him to sharpen his role as urbane man of sense, his supporters' flattery encouraged him to assume the mantle of Augustan poet-hero. The development of Pope's youthful idealism into an aristocratic humanism, conservative in its literary preferences and Tory in its political sympathies, owes much to his opposition to the world typified by Grub Street in which, according to Pope's analysis, commercialism and a corrupt taste were subverting civilized values. Pope's poetry sought to annihilate the critical pretensions of his detractors and to fulfil the cultural aspirations of his 'polite' audience.

The virulence of the War of the Dunces, inevitable in a society caring excessively for 'Reputation', has obscured the substantial issues involved. The early complaints against the facile smoothness of his versification, too-slavish imitation of the ancients in the *Pastorals*, his lack of invention or sublimity, and the running battle against the topicality and grossness of the satires, were as much issues for Warton as they had been forty years earlier for John Dennis.

On the other side, Pope's supporters reflected with great fidelity the image which he hoped to leave to posterity. For Swift, Gay, Arbuthnot, Fielding, and later Dr Johnson, Pope stood for an Augustanism opposed to the rising tide of sentimentality and sensibility. Like theirs, Pope's ideals were embedded in the humane and literary values of the classical world and deeply antipathetic to the venality and political jobbing of Hanoverian England. Those who shared his cultural values saw in his poetry the recrudescence of the virtues of the Augustan age, and thought the variety of his genius no less remarkable than his mastery of the couplet. The heroic simplicity and nervous energy of the Homer translations proved English poetry capable of epic grandeur, *The Rape of the Lock* was at once remarkable for its elegant satire and its knowledge of women, the pathos of *Eloisa to Abelard* explored the extreme reaches of passion, and the 'sublime' philosophy of *An Essay on Man* represented a bold attempt to reconcile religious divisions. The satires, though they inspired unease among otherwise friendly critics like Lord Lyttelton (No. 62), were generally seen as a necessary corrective, written by a man of moral integrity driven to the defence of virtue by the age's degeneracy.

Pope's early ambition to establish neoclassical correctness in English poetry, a task he believed Dryden had left incomplete, was realized with remarkable speed. Only twenty years after publishing his first work he was widely recognized on the Continent. By the mid-eighteenth century his stature seemed obvious to most cultured readers. In 1752 Lord Chesterfield wrote to his son, 'A gentleman should know those which I call classical works, in every language—such as Boileau, Corneille, Racine, Molière, etc., in French; Milton, Dryden, Pope, Swift, etc., in English. . . .'[4]

3

Too schematic an account of Pope's admirers and detractors over-simplifies the picture. They did not form two homogeneous groups. Dennis's position was very close to Pope's own and in many ways opposed to that of Addison's literary group, yet both attacked Pope. Spence, a devoted admirer, nevertheless questioned the appropriateness of heroic couplets in a translation of Homer. Augustanism meant different things to different writers, and the prolonged disagreement over Pope's merits is a forcible reminder that his version did not enjoy a monolithic victory.

As Pope was the only major Augustan whose primary medium was poetry, any debate on the nature of poetry was forced to centre on his work. A prolonged attempt to define the nature, scope and, for some critics, the limitations of neoclassical poetry is the overriding theme of the eighteenth-century criticism of Pope. During his lifetime the issues were discussed, largely ineffectually, within a neoclassical framework. Pope's death ended this unfruitful battle, leaving room for a more balanced approach. Joseph Warton's painstaking *An Essay on the Genius and Writings of Pope* (1756, 1782) was the first serious challenge to the hegemony of Pope's correctness. The growing emphasis upon the primacy of feeling, originality, and imagination made the ordered control of Pope's work seem constricting or uninspired. Warton, William Cowper, and Edward Young all relegated him to the second rank of poets, and there were some who denied he was a poet at all (No. 126a). This confrontation between the new attitudes of the Age of Sensibility and established neoclassical values was resolved by Johnson's reaffirmation of Pope's genius in his *Life of Pope* (1781). There the greatest Augustan critic encounters the greatest eighteenth-century poet, and until the end of the century the common reader could take Pope's mastery for granted. Indeed, his perfection almost denied the possibility of further development in English poetry. As Goldsmith wrote, 'Mr. Pope has somewhere named himself the last English Muse; and, indeed, since his time, we have scarce seen any production that can justly lay claim to immortality. . . .' (No. 120a).

II

Throughout his career Pope could rely upon an extraordinary degree of public interest. In 1698 the traveller, Henri Misson, had observed: 'The *English* have a mighty Value for their Poetry. If they believe that their

Language is the finest in the whole World, tho' spoken no where but in their own Island; they have proportionably a much higher Idea of their Verses.'⁵ This cultural chauvinism was as strong in the early eighteenth century as it had been in Dryden's London. It echoed the nation's growing awareness of its economic and military power, and its pride in the international reputation of thinkers like Locke and Newton. In 1724 Bolingbroke urged Pope to write 'what will deserve to be translated three Thousand years hence into Languages as yet perhaps unform'd. . . . Whilst you translate [Homer] therefore you neglect to propagate the English Tongue. . . .' (No. 39). The vociferous response generated by Pope's poetry testifies to English audiences' very real involvement in the achievements of contemporary poetry.

Unfortunately this widespread concern could not be supported by a critical response equal to the sophistication of Pope's art. The practice of criticism had long been in disrepute, and Pope's *An Essay on Criticism* (1711), which called for informed responsiveness in place of myopic fault-finding, had little perceptible effect. In 1728 John Oldmixon described the shortcomings of contemporary critics: 'Criticism is so far from being well understood by us *Englishmen*, that it is generally mistaken to be an Effect of Envy, Jealousy, and Spleen; an invidious Desire to find Faults only to discredit the Author, and build a Reputation on the Ruin of his.'⁶ These faults were encouraged and to some extent caused by the publishing conditions of the times. Pope's singular abilities, allied with shrewd business sense, brought him a modest fortune, but he was the exception. Less able writers were forced to fight for their living in the new era of popular journalism. A writer with literary aspirations might hope for a small return from a book or a play, but his livelihood came from hack-work, from pamphlets, or from the growing number of periodicals. In this world Defoe not Pope was the typical figure. Writers were at the mercy of the booksellers or in the pay of government or opposition factions. This sub-literary world was openly commercial, and in addition to older and unsuccessful authors like Dennis and Charles Gildon it attracted a new breed of writers who were characteristically ill-educated with little interest in literature.

By default Pope's early reputation was largely left in their hands. Periodicals like *The Tatler* or *The Spectator* devoted too little space to contemporary literature to establish an alternative forum, while men like Swift or Bolingbroke, who might have provided an Augustan Coleridge to Pope's Wordsworth, were driven by a sense of urgency which precluded the diversion of their energies into criticism. Pope's poetry frequently suffered from the envy of second-rate minds, whose native inability was exaggerated by economic or political considerations. Even if, like Dennis, they had pretensions to critical seriousness, their major vehicle, the Grub Street pamphlet, whose literary antecedents were the lampoon and libel, was not conducive to measured evaluation. For many hacks an anti-Pope pamphlet was simply a quick way of turning a dubious penny.

At worst Pope's supporters retaliated with the Dunces' weapons. Others, like Lord Lyttelton (No. 62), ignored the opposition and turned to panegyric. A few like Walter Harte in *An Essay upon Satire* (No. 59) attempted a genuine critical defence, but efforts to raise the level of discussion were hampered by the pamphlet format and by a predilection for clumsy rhyming couplets. The single exception is Joseph Spence's *An Essay on Pope's Odyssey* (Nos 49, 50) whose detailed prose analysis proved that the critical tradition exemplified by Dryden's *Essay of Dramatic Poesy* was not entirely defunct.

Pope's relationship with the booksellers and Grub Street was a complicated one. Although he despised the treatment of literature as a commodity, he was obliged to take an active and often devious part in the publication of his works. A flair for publicity, a jealous concern for his reputation, and an intimate knowledge of the publishing trade, allowed him to turn Grub Street to advantage. The frenetic attacks and counter-attacks on his religion, personality, and poetry kept him constantly in the public eye. With careful management Pope was able to make the appearance of a new work into a public event. When *The Dunciad* appeared in 1728, '. . . a Crowd of Authors besieg'd the Shop; Entreaties, Advices, Threats of Law, and Battery, nay Cries of Treason were all employ'd, to hinder the coming out of the *Dunciad*: On the other Side, the Booksellers and Hawkers made as great Efforts to procure it. . . .'[7]

Pope's worldly success was a source of deep irritation to the Dunces. Condemned to poverty and obscurity they were not only satirized by Pope, but their failure was mocked by his success. Professional envy and jealousy were powerful factors in their rejection of Pope.

The criticism which undoubtedly had the greatest effect upon Pope's work was given in private, and little has survived. Even as a youth his translations had benefited from the detailed comments of Sir William Trumbull and Ralph Bridges.[8] The versification and diction of the *Pastorals* were subjected to the close criticism of William Walsh, a widely admired but unproductive critic, and Pope's own letters to

Walsh and Cromwell gave detailed analyses of his ideas on correctness (Appendix A). Throughout his life Pope paid careful attention to informed criticism of his poetry's verbal texture, whether the source was Dennis or Bishop Atterbury.[9] Conversation with like-minded friends like Gay, Arbuthnot, Swift, and Bolingbroke must have ranged beyond minute stylistic matters, but unfortunately led to no critical formulation. The nearest thing to a record of this kind of dialogue is Spence's *Essay*. Otherwise the exigencies of polemic and the generalizing tendencies of Augustan critics excluded this very important area from the pamphlets.

The conditions which crippled Pope criticism in the first part of the century gradually altered. Literary journalism became an increasingly reputable profession, and the considered essay or book replaced the pamphlet as the main channel of literary criticism. Periodicals like *The Rambler* (1750–2) and *The Adventurer* (1752–4) gave Johnson and Warton the opportunity to discuss literature in detail and with independence. It was a form which encouraged the eighteenth-century writer to unite the bare assertions of earlier neoclassical literary discussion with his informal passion for the minute analysis of beauties and faults. The growing respect for criticism was accompanied by the beginnings of literary history, and in the best writers of this period critical argument is joined to a sense of Pope's place in English literature. Johnson's progress from Grub Street hack to a widely respected position as moralist and arbiter of taste is symptomatic of the establishment of a cultured middle-class audience, confident of the greatness of English literature. That Johnson's *Lives of the Poets* originated in a bookseller's enterprise is the clearest indication of the profound alteration in the literary climate.

III

EARLY CAREER (1705–20)

In 1705 Pope arrived in London, a precociously brilliant seventeen-year-old. Between his arrival and the publication of the *Pastorals* in 1709, he cultivated the acquaintance of the group of writers and noblemen surrounding the Kit Kat Club. Wycherley promptly accepted the young man on equal terms (No. 1), and he was further encouraged by the praise of men like Lord Lansdowne and William Walsh. When Pope ventured into print, first with the *Pastorals* and, more confidently, with *An Essay on Criticism* (1711), response was prompt. In 1712 Addison spoke of his 'rising Genius' in *The Spectator*, while John Gay described him in God-like terms (No. 2). Praise of his Augustan virtues was a major theme, and in 1717 his friend Parnell hailed Pope as a 'Bard triumphant in immortal bays', calling upon Callimachus, Homer, Virgil, and Horace to pay their homage to the English poet.

This chorus of praise was answered by irate condemnation. John Dennis delivered his first attack in 1711 (No. 10) and followed it up in 1716 with the virulent *True Character of Mr. Pope and his Writings* (No. 3), given here in full as the earliest example of the Dunces' image of Pope. Gildon's 'venal quill' quickly gave Dennis support (Nos 12, 19). Other attacks were less prejudiced. Neither the *Pastorals* nor the *Iliad* translation received universal praise, and Leonard Welsted's accusation that Pope's 'numbers smooth' lacked 'the spirit and informing flame, / Which breathes divine, and gives a Poet's name' (No. 4), was echoed through the next two centuries. But the overall reaction was closer to that voiced in Giles Jacob's *Poetical Register* (No. 6), which claimed Pope's poetry united 'Ease' to 'Strength' and 'sublime' thought, and concluded that his widely applauded work was 'equal to any of this Age'. Only twelve years after reaching London Pope could publish a handsome edition of his *Works*, including the *Pastorals*, *An Essay on Criticism*, *Windsor Forest*, the 'romantic' poems, and *The Rape of the Lock*. The completion of the *Iliad* translation in May 1720 clearly established Pope's rights as the major living Augustan poet.

Early poems

Pope's early poetry is conservative rather than innovative. It worked towards the perfection of the neoclassical art of poetry through well-established forms. The promise of his *Pastorals* was swiftly discerned by the like-minded Kit Kat group. Congreve, Garth, Lord Halifax, Lord Sheffield, and others all read and approved the poems in manuscript. In 1705 or 1706 Lord Lansdowne prophesied, 'If he goes on as he has begun, in the Pastoral way, as *Virgil*, first try'd his Strength, we may hope to see *English* Poetry vie with the Roman, and this Swan of Windsor sing as sweetly as the *Mantuan*' (No. 7a). Wycherley and William Walsh foresaw the same future, and with the *Pastorals'* publication in 1709 Wycherley gave public expression to his feelings (No. 8).

The heady praise of eminent men, coupled with the naïvety of youthful ambition, led Pope to expect the applause of the whole nation, regardless of political or literary affiliations. He was deeply affronted when Thomas Tickell, writing in *The Guardian*, pointedly ignored his poems in favour of Ambrose Philips's pastorals, which had appeared in the same volume of Tonson's *Miscellanies*. Since both Tickell and Philips were Addison's protégés, Pope suspected a petty conspiracy. In this he was probably wrong. Addison and his sympathizers, with their emphasis upon simplicity and their interest in unsophisticated forms like the ballad, found Pope's strict neoclassical imitations, which imposed an artificial Golden Age upon their English setting, unduly limited. Philips's poetry was flaccid, but his notions of pastoral were more progressive than Pope's: he replaced classical mythology with the superstitions of the English countryside and injected a measure of realism into the genre's stiffly formal conventions. Pope retaliated with an essay giving ironic praise to Philips, which he successfully foisted on Steele who published it as *Guardian* no. 40. Although his *jeu d'esprit* created a legacy of ill-will between Pope and Addison's camp, its mockery of Philips's attempts to achieve rustic artlessness (No. 9) gives a witty account of the issues involved in this minor skirmish between the Ancients and the Moderns.[10]

The disagreement over the *Pastorals* stemmed from the way in which the Augustans, though looking to apparently similar values, could draw very dissimilar conclusions. John Dennis, an irascible critic and friend of Dryden and Congreve, had for years battled with more intelligence than tact for neoclassical standards, for the dignity of criticism, and for the moral imperatives of good taste. Pope's *An Essay on Criticism* (1711) argued the same case with moderation and urbanity, but at the same time satirized Dennis as a representative of the bad critic. The response was immediate and virulent (No. 10). Dennis was not only enraged by what he regarded as a pretentious upstart, but his emphasis upon the 'terrific' or Longinian sublime, elements little apparent in the *Pastorals* or the *Essay*, led him to regard Pope as a mere versifier, who did not even understand the ideas he purported to discuss. Dennis quite rightly saw that Pope's use of his key term, 'wit', was elusive, but what Dennis castigated as confused thinking was a supple attempt to synthesize the conflicting elements of neoclassical theory. As so often Dennis had serious points to make, but his chop-logic argumentation and his intemperate lampoon of Pope as a 'hunch-back'd Toad' are more suggestive of paranoia than critical shrewdness. Pope's reaction was dignified. He quietly altered the poem to meet Dennis's occasionally valid objections.[11] He wrote to Caryll, 'I will make my enemy do me a kindness where he meant an injury, and so serve instead of a friend.'[12]

In December 1711 Dennis's assault was offset by Addison's praise in *The Spectator* (No. 11), which compared Pope's *Essay* with Horace's *Ars Poetica*, unhesitatingly placing it in the same rank as the two peaks of 'polite' criticism, Sheffield's *Essay on Poetry* (1682) and Roscommon's *Essay on Translated Verse* (1684). Addison also acclaimed his masterly ability to make 'the sound an echo to the sense', initiating what became a favourite topic among Pope's eighteenth-century critics. Aaron Hill's prolix corrections in 1738 of Pope's examples of this art (No. 13) indicate the subject's absorbing appeal, though Hill's pedantic solemnity compares poorly with the later discussions of Johnson, Kames, or Campbell. Addison's recognition of Pope's achievement, though it echoed public sentiment, could not go unchallenged in the prevailing atmosphere of jealous rivalry. Four days later Charles Gildon made his first appearance among the prospective Dunces, and heaped scorn on the suggestion that Pope and Horace had anything in common (No. 12).

The episodic structure and conversational manner of *An Essay on Criticism*, though lacking Dryden's ratiocinative energy, admirably suited Pope's genius and his audience's taste. But poems like *Windsor Forest* (1713) and *The Temple of Fame* (1715), standing at the end of allegorical traditions going back to the Renaissance, puzzled the Augustan reader. Dennis used the similarity between *Windsor Forest* and Denham's *Cooper's Hill* to condemn Pope (No. 16), but was blind to the continuity of genre which does much to explain the later poem. William Bond did little more than damn the poem's versification (No. 17). *The Temple of Fame* suffered from similar incomprehension. Dennis condemned it as 'one long Chain of Blunders and Boggisms' (No. 44), Johnson and Joseph Warton thought Pope had 'improved' Chaucer, while in 1774 Thomas Warton, reacting strongly in favour of the Gothic, found Pope's neat Palladian structure betrayed the original (No. 123). Both poems, with their weight of learning and allusion, fell outside the mainstream of eighteenth-century poetry: only recently have their literary origins and intentions been sympathetically explored.[13]

No difficulties of this kind affected *The Rape of the Lock* (1714),[14] Pope's most universally admired poem in all periods. Three thousand copies were bought in the four days following publication, and by September 1715 six thousand copies had been sold. Favourable comparisons with Boileau's mock-heroic *Le Lutrin* were swift (No. 18), and in 1726–9 Voltaire ranked Pope above Boileau (No. 42). French readers, like the Abbé Guyot (No. 23), admired Pope's delicacy and wit, qualities European audiences had found lacking in other English literature, and the same was true of Italian readers (No. 24). *The Rape of the Lock*'s tightly shaped perfection, its sharp commentary on contemporary manners, and its poise, ensured its popularity. Thomas Blackwell spoke for most eighteenth-century readers when he asked, 'can anything in its kind surpass the *Rape of the Lock?*'[15]

Adverse criticism raised no serious issues. Charles Gildon's *New Rehearsal* (No. 19), portrays Pope as Sawney Dapper, 'a young poet of the modern stamp, an easy versifier, and a contemner secretly of all others', and used the poem's sexual puns to fabricate a charge of obscenity. Six years later William Bond was still repeating these feeble charges (No. 21). John Dennis, in a series of letters written in 1714 but unpublished till 1728, perversely deployed his learning to argue that the poem disobeys epic rules (No. 20).

If *The Rape of the Lock* showed an intimate knowledge of women in an affectionately satiric vein, *Eloisa to Abelard* and *An Elegy to an Unfortunate Young Lady* were, for eighteenth-century readers, deeply moving portrayals of womanly feeling. Although the poems depict extreme emotional situations within a highly artificial form, both were prized for their truth to life. Mrs Thrale reported in 1782: 'I have heard that all the kept Mistresses read Pope's Eloisa with singular delight—'tis a great Testimony to its Ingenuity; they are commonly very ignorant Women, & can only be pleased with it as it expresses the strong Feelings of Nature & Passion'.[16] The *Elegy* not only threw the blind poet, Thomas Blacklock, into physical agitation, but served as a touchstone of true feeling for the sceptical David Hume (No. 36). *Eloisa to Abelard* aroused equally strong feelings. Prior quickly praised its delicate pathos (No. 35a). Some years later James Delacour, author of one of the many imitations of and replies to Pope's poem,[17] celebrated the 'gloomy Horrors, and mournful Images . . . soften'd with [Pope's] all-tender Expressions' (No. 35b) which were to excite readers throughout the century, and satisfy Warton's taste for the 'Gothic'.

Perhaps the oddest example of the Augustan divorce between reality and these poetic surrogates for feeling occurs in the three widely differing versions of Pope's epitaphs on John Hewet and Sarah Drew, two farmhands struck by lightning. Bishop Atterbury's solemnity before the sublime version is neatly punctured by Lady Mary Wortley Montagu's common-sense awareness of the gap between Pope's inflated memorial and the couple's prosaic virtues (No. 37). The eighteenth century simultaneously believed and disbelieved in these 'ingenious' fictions. Physical and emotional passion were too dangerous to indulge without the distancing of appropriate theatrical devices.

The *Iliad*

For Pope's audience the most substantial achievement of his early career was the translation of the *Iliad*. It attracted more comment than any poem before *The Dunciad*, cost six years of Pope's working life, and was published over five years (June 1715 to May 1720). the *Iliad* and his subsequent translation of the *Odyssey* were central to Pope's eighteenth-century reputation. Without them Pope is only half the poet read by his contemporaries. When Warton asked 'What is there very Sublime or very Pathetic in POPE', earlier readers would have pointed to the 'romantic' poems and the 'sublimity' of *An Essay on Man*, but above all to the Homer (see Nos 28d and 33 for instance). Spence's sense of the greatness of the *Odyssey* translation is only equalled by Johnson's admiration for the *Iliad*, which he thought a 'poetical wonder'. Pope's translations expressed the high ideals and passion which Augustan literature found it impossible to realize successfully in any other literary form. The *Iliad*'s intellectual energy, its heroic scope, and its epic grandeur provide the positive scale in Pope's imaginative world.[18] Warton was to ignore them for the same reason that much later criticism did—namely, that they are not original. It is a comment both on our distance from Pope and upon the limitations of his genius and age.

The 'English Homer''s early reception is entangled with the events surrounding its publication in 1715. After Pope had invited the public to subscribe to his translation, a rival version by Thomas Tickell was announced. Tickell's earlier part in the rivalry between Philips's and Pope's pastorals made Pope fearful of an attempt to undermine his venture. Certainly Addison, though later to praise the *Iliad* (No. 28g), was guilty of collusion in the first Homerides pamphlet (No. 26), which attacked Pope's translation even before its appearance. On the other hand, Richard Fiddes had offered homage as early as 1714 (No. 25), and Pope had powerful and active supporters. As publication approached excitement reached such a pitch that the newspapers reported the rivalry (No. 27). Once books i–iv were in public hands Pope gradually gained the ascendancy (No. 28). For a later reader the passions stimulated by this literary fracas seem astonishing, but the Augustan audience felt the honour of the nation involved.

Those who admired Pope's *Iliad* easily agreed with one another. Lewis Theobald, later to be numbered among the Dunces, believed Pope had caught the 'Spirit of *Homer*' (No. 29). Lady Mary Wortley Montagu thought he had 'touched the mantle of the divine Bard, and imbibed his spirit' (No. 31), as did William Melmoth (No. 33). Its detractors charged that Pope did not know Greek,[19] that he misrepresented Homer, and that he was despicably mercenary, all accusations which pursued Pope for the rest of his career. Dennis's *Remarks on Mr. Pope's Homer* (No. 30), published in 1717, offered more substantial criticism. Although marred by hatred of Pope, it demonstrates the distance of Pope's Homer from the 'Simplicity and Majesty of the Original' by examining particular examples, berating Pope for ignorantly magnifying the Greek army from thousands to 'Millions' (*Iliad*, ii. 109–10). Pope's alteration was deliberate, but Dennis pinpoints the way in which Pope's continuous search for epic scale through multiplication could on occasions result in grandiosity instead of grandeur.[20]

The most serious threat to the translation was posed by Anne Dacier's 'Reflexions' (No. 32), which argued that Pope's Homer obscured the regularity and finish of its original. Both Pope and Mme Dacier agreed that the Homeric world was different from the modern world and not merely barbaric, but where she sentimentalized Homer in an attempt to make him a Christian moralist, Pope saw him more accurately as 'the supreme poet of Manners—that is, nature presented in terms of action'.[21] Pope's translation easily overcame its early opposition, and although the Augustan dress of Pope's *Iliad* was less neoclassical than Mme Dacier could have wished, it remained the definitive English rendering of Homer for several generations. Its effect on subsequent poetry was less fortunate: though Coleridge recognized it as an 'astonishing product of matchless talent and ingenuity', he considered it 'the main source of our pseudo-poetic diction'.

IV

CONSOLIDATION AND COUNTER-OFFENSIVE
(1721–9)

Between 1720 and 1726 Pope, who had now settled at Twickenham, gave most of his energies to the *Odyssey* and his edition of Shakespeare.

Daunted by memories of unremitting labour on the *Iliad*, he employed Elijah Fenton and William Broome as collaborators in the translation, unwisely keeping this fact private. Both enterprises were in part undertaken for money, and the *Odyssey*, which brought Pope about £5,000, capitalized heavily on the *Iliad*'s success.

Friends and critics began to question whether Pope was writing too little original work. Bolingbroke warned him not to regard the Homer as the 'great Work' of his life—'You owe a great deal more to your self, your Country, to the present Age, and to Posterity' (No. 39). More specifically, Edward Young called on Pope to aid the nation by turning to satire (No. 40). Pope, however, was content to rest on his laurels while consolidating his fortune. In the meantime, his reputation grew. In England the young Walter Harte asserted Pope's greatness (No. 41), while Voltaire called Pope 'the best poet in England, and at present in the world' (No. 42). Readers in Massachusetts eagerly sought his poems and portrait, and Harvard College's library acquired his works (No. 43).

However, the revelation of Broome's and Fenton's part in the *Odyssey* and Lewis Theobald's disclosure of the editorial shortcomings of Pope's Shakespeare, exposed him to the rancour of Grub Street. The exultant Dunces accused Pope of shoddy workmanship, dishonesty, and avarice. His long-delayed decision to reply to his enemies through *The Dunciad* channelled Pope's energies back to original work, and into a form which was to dominate the remainder of his writing life.

The *Odyssey*

The *Odyssey*, with *The Dunciad*, is the centre of critical interest in these years. Inevitably the translation invited a repetition of the charges against the *Iliad* (No. 51), to which were added accusations of fraud (No. 47). Pope's use of his collaborators was defended, probably ironically, by Defoe, who saw him as a kind of master-manufacturer, a more accurate description perhaps than Pope would have wished (No. 48).

Then in the summer of 1726 the first part of Joseph Spence's *An Essay on Pope's Odyssey* appeared, followed by a second part in 1727. Pope had at last found a critic free from personal animus prepared to analyse poetry as poetry. Spence's *Essay* is remarkable for its close verbal criticism, and its picture of 'polite' conversation. The dialogue between Antiphaus and Philypsus ranges beyond Pope to discuss the taste of the age, the differences between corrupt and pure diction, and the limitations and advantages of Pope's employment of rhyme. Always sharply aware of the losses in transposing Homer into a neoclassical idiom, Spence nevertheless argues that in some ways Pope has 'improved' upon Homer. He sees the workings of Pope's imagination with the eyes of a sensitive and sympathetic contemporary, an advantage which allows him to point to effects only rediscovered in this century. Spence highlights the way in which the *Odyssey*'s linguistic energy comes from Pope's epithets, which fix the essential properties of the object described in a single word (p. 203), he is able to demonstrate Pope's use of literary allusion, and his constant concern with Pope's pictorial effects underlines a major resource in the poetry of the period.[22] As Johnson remarked, in Spence 'Pope had his first experience of a critick without malevolence, who thought it as much his duty to display beauties as expose faults; who censured with respect, and praised with alacrity.'[23]

The Dunciad (1728) and the nature of satire

Spence's *Essay* is a high point in contemporary criticism of Pope, and offered a brief respite before *The Dunciad* called down a new flood of vilification. In the eyes of his enemies Pope's misshapen form and his initials, A. P—E, revealed his true nature: he was an animal disguised as a man, his physical deformity an outward sign of moral deformity:[24]

> . . . what Art
> Can frame the monst'rous Image of his Heart.
> Composed of *Malice, Envy, Discontent,*
> Like his Limbs crooked, like them impotent.

Pope was a Yahoo, with all that creature's love of excrement (No. 66). As a matter of course, this line of abuse was linked with his supposed sexual shortcomings, while his Catholicism proved him a Jacobite and traitor. Obscenity, blasphemy, and malevolence were all that could be expected of such a creature. His poetry was subjected to the same kind of misrepresentation: imitation was labelled plagiarism, metaphor labelled nonsense, and harmonious versification branded as monotonous. This grotesque portrait was as useful in the Battles of the Dunces as it had been to Dennis in 1711 and was to be for Cibber in 1742.

Until 1728 Pope endured this unremitting fusillade in virtual silence, preferring dignity to revenge, despite the obvious gift for personal satire manifested by the 'Atticus' portrait. This attack on Addison, published without Pope's consent in 1722, led Atterbury to write:

'Since you now therefore know, where you real Strength lyes, I hope you will not suffer that Talent to ly unemploy'd.'[25] Despite continuing provocation, Pope was not yet ready to heed this advice.

Several factors coincided in the years 1725 to 1728 to persuade Pope to write *The Dunciad*. Above all, he was tired of petty attacks. In 1725 he wrote to Swift: 'my Spleen is at the little rogues. . . . It would vexe one more to be knockt o' the Head by a Pisspot, than by a Thunderbolt.'[26] Pope was also encouraged by the example of Swift, at work upon *Gulliver's Travels*, and by the Scriblerus Club, whose most active members were Swift, Gay, Arbuthnot, and Pope himself. In the context of the Scriblerian attacks on 'False Learning' and corrupt taste, Pope could conceive of his attack upon the Dunces as a defence of deeply felt cultural values.[27] Lewis Theobald's *Shakespeare Restored* (1726) provided Pope with an occasion, and *The Dunciad* with its first hero.

Pope organized the publication of *The Dunciad* carefully. The *Peri Bathous* appeared in the Swift–Pope *Miscellanies* in March 1728, and deliberately provoked the hornets' nest by using the writings of the Dunces to illustrate an art of anti-poetry. When the first version of *The Dunciad* appeared in May its Preface claimed, 'every week for these two Months past, the town has been persecuted with Pamphlets, Advertisements, Letters and Weekly Essays, not only against the Wit and Writings, but against the Character and Person of Mr. Pope'. Interest ran high—six editions were published in eleven months—and counter-attacks followed at once (Nos 52–4). In 1729 *The Dunciad Variorum*, with its mock-scholarly annotation, led to a second outburst (Nos 55–60).

One of the earliest replies was written by a 'Club' of Dunces (No. 52). They marshalled most of the usual arguments against Pope, and noted the poem's connection with *MacFlecknoe*. Their main complaint, however, was that Pope 'reproaches his Enemies as poor and dull; and to prove them *poor*, he asserts they are *dull*; and to prove they are *dull*, he asserts they are *poor*'. Unfortunately, they were poor because too dull to achieve independence, which in turn forced them to be mercenary. As Pope said, 'the Poem was not made for these Authors, but these Authors for the Poem'. His enemies showed some awareness of *The Dunciad*'s mock-heroic structure (No. 54), and Dennis, in his last Pope pamphlet, thought the poem deeply flawed by its lack of an epic action (No. 56), an opinion held by Warton (p. 517) and which still finds support.[28]

Among those who had supported Pope earlier there was a rift of opinion. Some were upset by the poem's coarse physical imagery ('obscenity'), its scurrility, and its personal satire. Atterbury ungratefully considered Pope had 'engaged himself in a very improper and trouble-some scuffle, not worthy of his pen at all, which was designed for greater purposes' (No. 57). It is a view which has much in common with the 'Club of Dunces', and both reflect a growing middle-class sense of propriety, whose sensibility was shortly to be typified by Richardson's novels[29].

The literary issue at stake was the nature of satire. All shades of opinion looked to classical precedent and Renaissance theory to support their sharply divergent views. Those opposed to *The Dunciad* thought it mere lampoon: satire should chastise the type not the individual. Traditionally too, satire with its 'low' subject matter was regarded as an inferior genre, a belief with important results in Warton's criticism. At root the Dunces misunderstood the nature of satire, but their misunder-standing is common throughout the period. The mistaken notion that 'satire' was derived from 'satyr' encouraged the assumption that the cragged and harsh licentiousness of Juvenal and Persius was its proper style. Satire of the preceding century, especially political satire, further blurred the distinction between lampoon and true satire.[30] These beliefs encouraged them to label all topical satire as lampoon, and to confuse the satirist's persona with the poet himself. As Pope observed,[31]

. . . there is not in the world a greater Error, than that which Fools are so apt to fall into, and Knaves with good reason to incourage, the mistaking a *Satyrist* for a *Libeller*; whereas to a *true Satyrist* nothing is so odious as a *Libeller*, for the same reason as to a man *truly Virtuous* nothing is so hateful as a *Hypocrite*.

The fullest contemporary attempt to outline a theory sympathetic to Pope's practice was Walter Harte's *An Essay upon Satire, Particularly on the Dunciad* (No. 59). Harte draws from the tradition embodied in Dryden's *Discourse concerning the Original and Progress of Satire*. He insists upon the dignity of satire, which must not only blame vice but must exhort its reader to virtue by giving a positive vision, and is aware that Pope uses parody not, as the Dunces argued, to demean epic, but to establish a scale of values. His classification of *The Dunciad* as 'Epic Satire' builds on Dryden's argument that some satire was a 'species' of heroic poetry. Unlike many eighteenth-century critics Harte shows a grasp of the oblique methods of satire, and by appending to his work a translation of Boileau's *Discourse of Satires Arraigning Persons by Name*[32]

17

gave authoritative support to Pope's practice of tying his satire to the visible facts of society. Other critics, like the author of *The Satirist* (No. 64), could see the need for Pope to hunt individuals from the herd, but Harte's is the only coherent and developed justification of Pope written before 1744.

V

LATER CAREER (1730–44)

After *The Dunciad* Pope turned to his most ambitious poetic enterprise, the 'Ethic Epistles', which he described to Swift as 'a system of Ethics in the Horatian way'.[33] From 1729 until 1734 he struggled to realize his grandiose plan, but by 1736 his interest had slackened. As it is, *An Essay on Man* (1733), intended as no more than 'what a scale is to a book of maps', stands on its own, while the four 'Moral Essays' (1731–5), meant at one time as part of the larger work, are really four Horatian satires. After the *Essay* Pope tended to depart from his grand plan in favour of the more manageable *Imitations of Horace* (1733–8). Finally he returned to *The Dunciad*, enlarged it to four books in 1742, and enthroned Cibber as hero in place of Theobald the following year.

Over this period three basic attitudes to Pope are apparent. Eulogy of Pope's classic stature is the basis of Lord Lyttelton's *Epistle* (No. 62), Thomas Dale's *Epistle from South Carolina* (No. 67), and Henry Brooke's fulsome letter of 1739 (No. 69). Pope continued to rely heavily upon the advice of friends like Swift (No. 86). For them Pope's satire was motivated by what Arbuthnot called a 'noble *Disdain* and *Abhorence* of Vice'.[34] Meanwhile Pope's Continental reputation grew (No. 63).

In sharp contrast, Grub Street's blind antipathy continued (Nos 65, 66). Pope was increasingly attacked for his friendship with Bolingbroke, who was cast in the role of the poet's evil genius (No. 87). The controversy over *An Essay on Man* gave new force to the charge of irreligion, and Pope's growing tendency to widen his satire beyond the literary world gave an increasingly political bias to the attacks. A measure of his position in these years is that aristocrats like Lord Hervey and Lady Mary Wortley Montagu entered the lists against him, adding their voices to the well-established ranks of hacks. This running battle culminated in an outburst against the final version of *The Dunciad* in 1742 and 1743. *Sawney and Colley* (No. 72) provides a vigorous example of this last phase, summing up the common objections to Pope's success.

Atterbury's earlier reaction against *The Dunciad* marked the beginning of a new attitude, which became stronger in the last decade of his career, though largely confined to private letters and conversation. Samuel Richardson (Nos 61, 93, 95) and the 'blue-stockings', Elizabeth Rowe and the Countess of Hertford (Nos 68, 88a), felt that satire was a betrayal of Pope's genius, and deplored the lack of charity and 'tender sentiments of nature' which allowed Pope to give 'Anguish and Confusion to Beings of his own kind. Slander and Invective is an Injury never to be repair'd, & by consequence is an unpardonable sin' (No. 88a). Isaac Watts, though he had no doubts of the magnitude of Pope's genius, objected to *The Dunciad*'s obscurity for the same reasons (No. 68a). These readers' evangelical strain of Christianity, and their strong preference for poetry marked by feeling and pure religion, announce the growth of a view of literature differing radically from neoclassical attitudes.

Moral Essays and *Imitations of Horace* (1731–8)

Taken together, the *Imitations of Horace* and the 'Moral Essays' are a major expression of Pope's mature satiric power. The contemporary response to this surge of creativity is feeble, partly because the poems appeared sporadically and partly because the imitations were not taken as seriously as his original work. Most writers concentrated on the furores caused by *An Essay on Man* and *The Dunciad* of 1742 and 1743.

The artistic power of the *Imitations* was further obscured by political considerations. Pope's portrait of 'Timon's villa' in the *Epistle to Burlington* (1731) was, it now seems, a satiric attack upon Walpole himself. Leonard Welsted, a government creature, diverted the shaft by spreading the lie that Lord Chandos was Pope's target, at the same time pretending Chandos to have been one of Pope's benefactors.[35] These fabrications were completely successful. Pope could not openly admit to satirizing Walpole, and Welsted was able to indict the poet for his supposed ingratitude (No. 75). Chandos himself exculpated Pope (No. 74), but Welsted's slander was quickly repeated (No. 77). This politically inspired effort to blunt Pope's satire suggests both the government's sensitivity to his poetry and Pope's increasingly open opposition to Walpole's England. Seven years later the political overtones of *Epilogue to the Satires II* were to bring him close to punishment by the House of Lords. Only then did Pope muzzle his satire: 'Could he have hoped,' he said of himself, 'to have amended any, he had continued those attacks; but bad men were grown so shameless and so powerful, that Ridicule was become unsafe as it was ineffectual.'[36] That the political factors in the outcry over the *Epistle to Burlington* were not discovered until very recently testifies to Pope's mastery of a technique of satiric allusion, sufficiently oblique to avoid the law but still recognizable to his contemporaries.

Response to the other 'Moral Essays' and *Imitations* was equally partial and intermittent. *Satire* II. i (1733) drew the fire of Lord Hervey and Lady Mary Wortley Montagu (No. 77), as well as the anonymous *An Epistle to the Little Satyrist of Twickenham* (No. 78). *Sober Advice from Horace* (1734) was countered by a scurrilous broadside (No. 87) from Thomas Bentley, nephew of the scholar Richard Bentley. The following year, *An Epistle to Dr. Arbuthnot* was rejected as mere lampoon (No. 88). Despite this persecution the satires sold well, and the praise given by Swift and Aaron Hill to the *Epilogue to the Satires* II (No. 89) is proof of the *Imitations*' effectiveness for at least one part of Pope's audience.

An Essay on Man (1733)

These intermittent reactions were overshadowed by the controversy over the supposed heterodoxy of *An Essay on Man*. The poem was published anonymously, and at first attracted universal praise (Nos 79, 80), including that of the unsuspecting Welsted. Pope's sublimity and purity of religion were the main themes of this enthusiastic welcome. William Somervile wrote:[37]

> Was ever work to such perfection wrought;
> How elegant the diction! pure the thought! . . .
> So breaks the day upon the shades of night,
> Enlivening all with one unbounded light.

Even Mr Bridges's *Divine Wisdom* (No. 81), published three years after Pope's poem, does no more than suggest that the poem is capable of Deistic misinterpretation. The French found its style vigorous and concise—'never has a poet been more sparing of words and more generous with meaning. Any paraphrase enervates its vigour, slackens and, so to speak, dissolves a completely solid and compact body.'[38] The Abbé du Resnel made the remarkable claim that the *Essay* gave 'all the necessary Rules which Morality lays down for the Practice of our Duty to God and Man' (No. 82).

This remarkable unanimity was short-lived. French savants were worried by the poem's tendencies,[39] and in 1757 a Swiss professor, J. P. de Crousaz, brought the argument into the open. The Protestant theologian's *Examen de l'Essai sur l'Homme* (No. 83) and his *Commentaire* (1738) saw the *Essay* as a dangerously popular version of Spinoza's Deistic notions, and accused Pope of threatening the very basis of Christianity. That Crousaz misrepresented Pope's ideas, since he knew the *Essay* only through Silhouette's inaccurate translation,[40] was immaterial. Pope's attempt at a grand synthesis of the varying strands in Christian belief immediately became an issue in the struggle raging on the Continent between the Church and the *philosophes*. Conservative Catholic theologians attacked Pope as a representative of the heretical beliefs emanating from England. With equal energy the *philosophes* looked for a *système* in the *Essay* sympathetic to their own beliefs. Crousaz's ingenuous misunderstanding of the poem is the mirror-image of Voltaire's certainty that the *Essay* agreed with his ideas, even if Pope did not realize the fact (No. 109). It was left to Lessing and Mendelssohn in their *Pope ein Metaphysiker!* (1755) to demonstrate that Pope was neither a 'Spinozist' or a 'Leibnitzian', and that it was misguided to treat the *Essay* as philosophy.[41]

Crousaz's attacks were promptly translated. The Dunces, while grateful to Crousaz, found it easier to concentrate on Pope's friendship for Bolingbroke, and the *Essay*'s concluding address was proof for them that Bolingbroke, traitor and atheist, was the real source of Pope's ideas. The true extent of Bolingbroke's influence has never been satisfactorily determined.[42] Pope regarded the ideas in the poem as his own, though he clearly did not appreciate the implications of the conclusions he had reached with the encouragement of the free-thinking Bolingbroke.

Surrounded by an international dispute, Pope was delighted by Warburton's unexpected defence of his orthodoxy which appeared in 1738 and 1739 in *The Works of the Learned* (No. 84). Warburton had earlier sided with Theobald and is reputed to have called the *Essay* 'rank atheism'. His *Vindication* clumsily twists the poem towards a literal pietism and imposes a rigorous orthodoxy upon Pope's attempt to steer a middle passage between conflicting dogmas. Even so, Pope was only too glad to accept the shelter offered—'I know I meant just what you explain, but I did not explain my own meaning so well as you.'[43]

In the heat of the controversy few writers recognized the fallacy of treating Pope as a philosopher. The essential question about the poem is not its orthodoxy but its artistic unity. It was posed in passing when Lord Hervey, in *A Letter to Mr. C—b—r* (1742), remarked that the wide variety of 'speculative Books' drawn on by Pope had produced not a poem but an '*Olio, Hodge-Podge Mess of Philosophy*' (No. 85).

The Dunciad (1742, 1743)

The final versions of *The Dunciad* caused a last storm of recrimination. In 1742 Pope added a fourth book, keeping Theobald as his anti-hero. There were some charges of obscurity—the Town thought, according to *The Universal Spectator*, 'that the *Satire* is too *allegorical*, and the *Characters* he has drawn are too *conceal'd*: That *real Names* should have been inserted instead of *fictitious* ones.'[44] Thomas Gray in part agreed, but admired the final book; Shenstone thought it proved Pope in his dotage (No. 90). As might be expected, Richardson was uneasy, thinking mere lack of taste an insufficient crime to excuse the coarseness of the poem's satire (No. 93).

Early in 1742 Pope deliberately provoked Colley Cibber,[45] who attacked Pope in *A Letter from Mr. Cibber, to Mr. Pope* (No. 91). More good-humoured than many of Pope's opponents, he admires the genius but questions the motives of the satirist. Cibber also told for the first time how he had saved the young Pope from catching a clap in a brothel, so saving the English Homer for posterity.[46] This questionable story is given here because it cut Pope to the quick, as well as providing a public excuse for displacing Theobald in Cibber's favour in *The Dunciad* (1743).

Richardson thought the alteration proof that Pope's satire was the child of malice (No. 95). Elizabeth Montagu reacted differently, realizing that in the enlarged satiric world of Book Four, Cibber was a more appropriate hero than the scholarly Theobald: '. . . the new Hero is certainly worthy to have the precedency over all foolish Poets. I like the last Dunciad for exposing more sorts of follies than the first did, which was merely upon bad poets and bad criticks.'[47]

The Cibber–Pope pamphlet war continued vigorously, and other Dunces like John Henley (No. 94) replied as best they could. Their ineptitude and violence only lends support to Fielding's brusque rejection of their claims for sympathy (No. 92). Pope's death in 1744 brought the years of bitter in-fighting to an abrupt end, leaving the field in the possession of Pope's admirers. Several elegies were quickly published, one of which is given in full (No. 96). The writer gives a comprehensive survey of Pope's achievement, repeating his well-established claim to greatness, but places the final emphasis (as Pope would have wished) upon the poet's virtue:

> This then our Poet's Province, this his Art,
> T'awake fair Virtue, and instruct the Heart.

VI

CRITICISM OF POPE (1745–82)

'No authours ever had so much fame in their own life-time as Pope and Voltaire; and Pope's poetry has been as much admired since his death as during his life. . . .'[48] Johnson's remark in 1778 indicates the slight impact of the Dunces' attacks upon Pope's widely acknowledged claims to greatness. The seven months following his death saw the publication of no fewer than three biographies, though only the third, William Ayre's *Memoirs of the Life and Writings of Alexander Pope, Esq.* (1745, No. 97), which faithfully reflects the general admiration, deserves any attention. In 1751 Warburton's edition elevated Pope to the same category as Milton and Shakespeare, the only other native writers paid the honour of properly edited and annotated texts. The critical notes sought to provide a definitive interpretation of Pope's poetry (No. 100), but Warburton's authoritarian arrogance frequently led him to impose his own meaning on the poems. Johnson said that his analysis of *An Essay on Criticism* discloses 'such order and connection as was not perceived by Addison, nor, as is said, intended by the author'.

Warburton's edition is a symptom of the growth of literary scholarship and history in the mid-eighteenth century. This, together with the establishment of biography as an important form, created an atmosphere in which Pope's work could be seen with a degree of objectivity impossible previously. The work of Ayre and Warburton, and the subsequent biographies of Robert Shiels (1753), W. H. Dilworth (1759) and Owen Ruffhead (1769), gradually built up an outline of Pope's life and career which, though perpetuating many errors,[49] attempted to clear away the myths and counter-myths created by the pamphlet wars and by Pope's own intrigues.

Joseph Warton's *Essay on the Writings and Genius of Pope* allied this interest in biography and literary history with a new stress on the importance of originality, sublimity, and feeling in poetry. Warton's

Essay, whose first volume was published in 1756 (No. 106), quickly became a rallying point for the Age of Sensibility. Earlier criticism of Pope had contained intimations of new attitudes to literature. Tickell, Philips, Addison, and the Dunces had reacted against Pope's deep traditionalism, and in the 1740s Richardson, the 'blue-stockings', and younger writers like Shenstone and Gray began to place feeling above judgment. It remained for Warton to develop a critical position from these doubts.

Before publishing his first volume Warton had uncovered new information about Pope, and consulted the manuscript of Spence's *Anecdotes*. He had also written on Pope's poetry. In *The Adventurer*, no. 51 (1753), he used the Bible's sublime style to show the artificiality of Pope's Homer, and in no. 63 (No. 105) he somewhat gingerly opened discussion of Pope's originality. Presenting an impressive list of sources for passages in the poetry, he commented, 'it may appear difficult, to distinguish imitation and plagiarism from necessary resemblance and unavoidable analogy'. Neither Johnson nor Pope, working within neoclassical habits of allusion and imitation, would have found the distinction hard to make.

Warton's *Essay* appeared, significantly, in the same year as Burke's treatise on the sublime. In his dedicatory letter to Edward Young, Warton announces a radical re-orientation of neoclassical ideas, though his tone is moderate:

I revere the memory of POPE, I respect and honour his abilities; but I do not think him at the head of his profession. In other words, in that species of poetry wherein POPE excelled, he is superior to all mankind: and I would only say, that this species of poetry is not the most excellent one of the art.

In Warton's view, 'The Sublime and the Pathetic are the two chief nerves of all genuine poetry'. Pope, as the poet of reason and wit, belongs to the second rank of poets. This subversive conclusion relies in part on an appeal to the traditional neoclassical hierarchy of genres. Pope's major successes were within an inferior genre, satire: he was, therefore, a lesser writer than Milton or Shakespeare.[50] The author of 'The Ballance of the Poets' (Appendix B) would have found agreement easy, and Johnson's review (No. 107) shows that in the context of neoclassical criticism Warton's views could, as yet, be regarded as less than revolutionary.

One of the most remarkable features of Warton's *Essay* is the detail of its attention to Pope's poetry. Although Johnson's 'Dissertation' on

Pope's epitaphs is more vigorous, its subject is confined, and the *Essay* is the only example of a sustained close reading of Pope's major poems by a sensitive eighteenth-century mind. Warton's other great strength is his sense of Pope's place in the tradition of English literature. Johnson, like Pope, considered English poetry prior to Dryden immature, and looked to established classical standards for his norms. Warton was more catholic, measuring Pope not merely against Greek and Roman authors, but against his English forerunners and European rivals. His widening of critical horizons is a refreshing change from the closed world of earlier criticism. Warton claimed that Pope had modelled himself upon French neoclassicism 'as *Milton* formed himself upon the Greek and Italian sons of *Fancy*', and insists that Pope be measured against the sublimity of Milton, and the achievements of contemporaries like Thomson and Gray. Pope, if taken at his own valuation, would deprive the reader of the full riches of English poetry. 'He who would think *Palamon* and *Arcite*, the *Tempest* or *Comus*, childish and romantic, might relish POPE.' His eclectic attitude questions the very basis of Augustan taste.

Warton's search through Pope's poetry revealed little that earned him a place in the first rank of poets. Again and again he finds Pope lacking in originality. The *Pastorals* contain not a 'single rural image that is new', and they confuse Greek scenery with English. Although *The Rape of the Lock* displays 'more imagination than in all his other works taken together', Warton points out that Pope did not invent the sylphs but only 'employed them with singular judgement and art'. He gives high praise to *Eloisa to Abelard* and the *Elegy to an Unfortunate Young Lady* as examples of the pathetic, but discovers Pope's characteristic strength in the 'DIDACTIC and the MORAL' modes of *An Essay on Criticism* and *The Rape of the Lock*. At this point the first volume breaks off.

Warton's search for vividness, his preference for originality over imitation, and for feeling above artifice, is linked to the belief that poetry should particularize. Foreshadowing the Romantics (the poetry of his pupil Bowles influenced Coleridge's early verse), Warton writes, 'Homer and Shakespeare do not give their readers GENERAL ideas: every image is the particular and unalienable property of the person who uses it. . . .' From this standpoint, a 'close and faithful representation of nature' can only be achieved through 'minute and particular enumeration of circumstances'. Pope's generalized description could not meet Warton's criteria for true poetry.

Between 1756 and 1782, when Warton's second volume appeared, the dialogue stirred up by his revaluation continued. Warton himself, judging by the alterations made to the successive editions of the first volume and the much later notes to his edition of Pope's *Works* (1797), constantly reappraised his ideas. Particularly striking is the difficulty he had in ranking the poets into their various classes.[51] The second volume of his *Essay* (No. 128) completed Warton's survey of Pope's canon, and exhibits greater sympathy with Pope than the earlier volume. He finds *An Essay on Man* remarkable for its 'BREVITY OF DICTION'; less expectedly, he thought that at some points it almost reached the 'transcendently sublime'. Of the *Imitations of Horace* Warton says, 'No part of our author's works have been more admired than these imitations', and immediately undertakes a long and sensitive comparison with the originals.[52] When he comes to *The Dunciad*, however, Warton is unwilling to praise Pope. The fourth book's subject is 'foreign and heterogeneous, and the addition of it . . . injudicious, ill-placed, and incongruous'. A more radical charge, and one which articulates clearly the root objection of the Dunces, is that the poem misrepresents the figures and institutions it satirizes. Warton defends Cibber, Bentley, and the universities by arguing that Pope told lies. If *The Dunciad* is guilty of fundamental misrepresentation, then the satire fails because it lacks the basis of truth to fact.

Warton's final position is that '*imagination* was not [Pope's] predominant talent, because he indulged it not': Pope's 'poetical enthusiasm' is continually reined in by the dictates of correctness, reason, and harmony. Warton's admiration for Pope was real, but his literary sympathies lay with the future.

The first volume of the *Essay* was quickly supported in 1759 by Edward Young's *Conjectures on Original Composition* (No. 112). In his earlier manuscript version the *Conjectures* originally paid tribute to Pope's imaginative powers, but, at Richardson's suggestion, the praise was omitted (No. 110). The published text shows no sign of Young's earlier admiration for Pope. Nature not imitation is the source of originality for Young. 'Imitation is inferiority confessed . . . though we stand much obliged for his giving us an *Homer,* yet had he doubled our obligation, by giving us—a *Pope.*' Young's dogmatic ideas are simplistic, and his impercipience is nowhere more evident than when he pronounces: '*Swift* is a singular wit, *Pope* a correct poet, *Addison* a great author.'

The influence of Young's and Warton's ideas is apparent in the popular lectures which Hugh Blair delivered at Edinburgh (No. 116).

Blair's admiration of the *Imitations of Horace* is circumscribed by his preference for original verse over imitation, and his belief that Pope lacked sublimity. Practising poets often reacted against Pope more strongly: Cowper characterized him as a mere 'mechanical maker of verses' (No. 126). For all these readers Shakespeare and Milton were the touchstones of genius: neoclassicism like Pope's no longer dominated creative imagination.

These signs of changing taste were simply ignored by critics like Goldsmith (No. 120) and Lord Lyttelton (No. 115), who remained faithful to the established Augustan case for Pope's poetry. Others replied directly. Dilworth's *Life* (1759, No. 111) attacked Warton by name, but did little more than repeat earlier eulogies of Pope. Owen Ruffhead's 'official' biography (1769, No. 121) does a little better. It makes a few minor hits, but otherwise limits itself to praising those poems praised by Warton. Percival Stockdale's excitable *An Inquiry into the Nature, and Genuine Laws of Poetry* (1778, No. 125), which concludes with a particularly far-fetched example of hagiolatry, persuasively argues the necessity and artistry of Pope's verbal control, shrewdly characterizing Warton as a critic with a 'vitiated' taste for 'Gothick' sublimity.

The most convincing among the early replies to Warton was made by Arthur Murphy in 1762 (No. 118). Identifying himself firmly with Augustan values, Murphy undertakes to show that Warton misunderstood the nature of genius and originality. Pope's handling of the sylphs in *The Rape of the Lock*, Murphy argues, went far beyond its source in *Le Comte de Gabalis*. Pope gave them 'such a ministry, such interests, affections and employments as carried with them sufficient poetical probability, and made very beautiful machinery in his poem, enlarging the main action, and ennobling the trifles, which it celebrates'. The mere fact that a poet borrows material does not deny his originality. As Murphy points out, Warton's argument would reduce Homer, who uses Greek fables, to the rank of a secondary genius. He also claimed that Lucretius had allowed philosophy to be a proper subject for poetry, and that *An Essay on Man* supplies the sublimity which Warton had failed to find in Pope's work. Murphy's ability to perceive the complexities of the subject from within the critical vocabulary of neoclassicism allows him to uncover an essential flaw in Warton's and Young's over-enthusiastic development of their argument. The first is not necessarily the best: tradition and the individual talent are interdependent.

Dr Johnson's *Life of Pope* (No. 127), published in 1781, is the definitive expression of the conservative attitude to Pope. Johnson's magisterial certainty of Pope's genius was united to a conviction, perhaps too complacent, that he spoke for the majority of his contemporaries. When asked why Warton's second volume was so slow in appearing, he answered: 'Why, Sir, I suppose he finds himself a little disappointed, in not having been able to persuade the world to be of his opinion as to Pope.'[53] Johnson, though more deeply moved by Dryden's vitality, was overwhelmed by the perfection of Pope's art: 'New sentiments and new images others may produce; but to attempt any further improvement of versification will be dangerous. Art and diligence have now done their best, and what shall be added will be the effort of tedious toil and needless curiosity.' His answer to critics like Warton and Young is a twin appeal to tradition and to his reader's experience:

If Pope be not a poet, where is poetry to be found? To circumscribe poetry by a definition will only show the narrowness of the definer, though a definition which shall exclude Pope will not easily be made. Let us look round upon the present time, and back upon the past; let us enquire to whom the voice of mankind has decreed the wreath of poetry; let their productions be examined and their claims stated, and the pretensions of Pope will no more be disputed.

Johnson's firm adherence to neoclassical values is filled out by his wide experience of books and men. He invigorates a critical vocabulary, whose prescriptive generalities had blinkered lesser writers, with an alertness and trenchancy unequalled elsewhere in the eighteenth century.

Johnson approached the composition of the *Life* with great advantages. His sympathy with Pope's literary aims was backed by an intimate knowledge of Pope's life and works, and by an interest going back to his translation of Crousaz's *Commentaire* in 1738.[54] His discussion of the relationship of sound and sense in Pope's poetry in 1751 (No. 99) had laid the foundations for subsequent analyses of Lord Kames (No. 117) and George Campbell (No. 124), and his vigorous 'Dissertation on the Epitaphs of Pope' (1756, No. 108) gives the kind of close attention to the words on the page not always associated with eighteenth-century criticism. In *The Idler* no. 77 (No. 114) his discussion of 'easy poetry' based on an examination of examples drawn from Pope's work showed his alertness to lapses in Pope's standards, and he reviewed both Warton's *Essay* (No. 107) and Ruffhead's biography (No. 122). While preparing to write the *Life* itself he consulted Pope's friends and, like Warton, used Spence's record of his conversations with the poet.

Finally, between November 1780 and March 1781, Johnson wrote the *Life of Pope*. When read, as here, separated from the *Life*, his critical remarks show a surprising dependence on earlier writers. Johnson was content to reply to first one and then another of his predecessors, to condense others, and to develop material drawn from his own earlier essays.[55] Dennis, Spence, Warton, Shiels, Murphy, Ruffhead, Kames, and Campbell all contribute to the *Life*, and the argument of Warton's first volume provides the first part of Johnson's analysis with a theme against which he can put his own disagreements and modifications.

To some extent this pattern is a sign of haste and exhaustion. It is, more importantly, part of Johnson's critical strategy in replying to Warton's scepticism. The *Life*, though it assumes aloofness from literary squabbles, attempts to resolve the years of debate over Pope's genius. Johnson's Pope is in essence the poet pictured by his contemporary admirers—the poet who had wrought English versification to its highest pitch, whose *Iliad* was a living proof of his genius and that of the English language, and whose success in widely varied neoclassical idioms placed him above all poets since Milton. Retrospectively, it is clear that Johnson does not deal with Warton's central question. He avoids any open discussion of Pope's relative position among English poets, arguing instead what Warton had never denied, that Pope is unquestionably a poet of genius. Johnson's own 'partial fondness' for Dryden, which might have qualified his acceptance of 'correctness' as an absolute good, is simply thrown at the reader as a self-evident truth. What Johnson gained from his encounter with Warton and other writers on Pope was a sharpened sense of Pope's Augustan virtues. The constant need to test his own experience of Pope's poetry against earlier critics, gives his criticism a notable toughness and incision.

Johnson's pragmatic approach saved him from the excesses of Warton's attachment to theory. Faced, for instance, with Warton's lengthy attack on the *Pastorals*' lack of originality, Johnson briskly replied: 'To charge these Pastorals with want of invention, is to require what was never intended.' He then points out their true importance: they demonstrate Pope's precocious technical gifts and his early grasp of what the classics offered him. In his admiration of *The Rape of the Lock*, Johnson was happy to concur with the common judgment, but the brilliance of *An Essay on Man* did not prevent him from damning its 'penury of knowledge and vulgarity of sentiment'. Nor could *The Dunciad*'s 'beauties' overcome his conviction that Pope took 'an unnatural delight in ideas physically impure'.

The overwhelming superiority of Johnson's *Life* is apparent in an independent vigour of mind which allows him to create a comprehensive account of Pope from the discord of earlier responses. But the foundations of its strength lie in the biographical structure. Recent scholarship may have corrected many points of fact, but the *Life* still has no serious rival as a critical biography. Where the conventionally neoclassical view made Pope into a lifeless paragon of abstractions, Johnson's own experience of Grub Street and his long wait for recognition, placed him in an ideal position to understand the contradictions of Pope's character and career, while perceiving the essential continuity of his development. Johnson's assessment, though often stringent, is shot through with a sympathetic understanding of the literary and social pressures which shaped Pope's poetry. Both as a man and as a poet, Pope is an elusive figure: Johnson's greatest achievement is to make the life and the poetry mutually illuminating.

VII

FOREIGN REPUTATION[56]

Pope was the first English poet to have a substantial foreign audience during his own lifetime. His work was read throughout Europe and in the New World. French translations of his poetry outnumbered even those of the works of Locke or Newton. *An Essay on Man* was translated into at least seventeen languages, including Czech and Icelandic, in the hundred years following its publication: the German versions alone numbered twenty-four.[57]

Pope's Continental reputation began with *An Essay on Criticism*, a manuscript translation of which was in circulation only a couple of years after the poem's first appearance.[58] Of all his works, *The Rape of the Lock* met with most constant approbation, while *An Essay on Man* stirred up the most controversy. In Italy and France his translations of Homer found readers eager to take the measure of the 'English Homer'.[59] *The Dunciad's* coarseness and topicality made it less acceptable to Enlightenment tastes, though German translations began to appear before Pope's death, and in 1764 Palissot felt able to imitate it for a French audience (No. 119). Even the *Pastorals* eventually found a French translator (No. 103).

The swift establishment of Pope's fame abroad is a symptom of the cosmopolitanism of the early Enlightenment. Both Pope and his

Continental reader felt the attraction of the idea of a literature, common
to all Europe, reaching from Homer to the present day. Prior to Pope's
appearance, foreign readers' admiration for the close thinking of Locke
or Newton had been balanced by a conviction that England's literature
was in a state of cultural darkness and Gothic barbarity. Pope changed
this at a stroke. His poetry exhibited the terse reasoning typical of the
English in *An Essay on Criticism* and *An Essay on Man*, but joined this
virtue to wit, elegance, and neoclassical correctness, hitherto regarded
as the preserve of European writers. By 1724, when Bolingbroke urged
Pope to write an original work to make English literature known to
the world (No. 39), his early poetry had already gone a long way
towards establishing English Augustan poetry as equal to that in any
language.

As the century developed, estimates of Pope began to shift. By 1759
Count Algarotti, a weathervane of European taste, found Pope's
compression a sign of harshness (No. 113). He could give wholehearted
approval only to *The Rape of the Lock*. Algarotti reflects the general
turning away from neoclassical standards which marks the middle years
of the century.

VIII

For the rest of the century, and into the early years of the nineteenth
century, Pope belonged among the classics of English poetry. Warton,
though he forecast with remarkable prescience the objections of the
Romantics and Victorians and spoke for the most vital current in
contemporary poetry, did not represent the ordinary reader. In 1796
Gilbert Wakefield could still call Pope 'a poet, for delicacy of feeling,
for accuracy of judgement, poignancy of art, urbanity of humour,
vivacity of fancy, discernment of human character, solemnity of pathos,
pregnancy of sentiment, rectitude of taste, comprehensive diction,
melodious numbers, and dignified morality, without rival in antient or
modern times'.[60] Looking back on his schooldays in the 1790s, Francis
Jeffrey recorded: '. . . every young man was set to read Pope, Swift and
Addison, as regularly as Virgil, Cicero and Horace . . . they and their
contemporaries were universally acknowledged as our great models of
excellence, and placed without challenge at the head of our national
literature.'[61]

The full-scale assault upon Augustan poetic diction in the Preface
to the *Lyrical Ballads* (1798) had little immediate impact upon this

entrenched position—the first edition of five hundred copies had to be disposed of at a loss. Pope's poetry, however, soon became a major issue in the upheavals caused by the growth of Romanticism. In 1806 Warton's disciple, William Lisle Bowles, published an edition of Pope's *Collected Works*, and precipitated a controversy which lasted until 1826. Bowles entirely lacked his old schoolmaster's moderation. Where Warton thought Pope a great poet who had chosen to exploit only the lesser side of his genius, Bowles regarded him as inherently second-rate, deficient in sensibility, and ignorant of nature. This aggressively Romantic interpretation threw Pope's poetry into the midst of an urgent dispute in which it was only the ostensible subject. The Lake Poets, and later Keats and Shelley, were fighting for the overthrow of beliefs which threatened their freedom as writers. Their emphasis upon subjectivity and the visionary world of the imagination, made Pope's conscious artistry, and his public frame of reference, seem the antithesis of poetry. Wordsworth wrote:[62]

To this day I believe I could repeat, with a little previous rummaging of my memory, several thousand lines of Pope. But if the beautiful, the pathetic, and the sublime be what a poet should chiefly aim at, how absurd it is to place those men among the first of poets of this country! Admirable are they in treading their way, but that way lies almost at the foot of Parnassus.

It was inevitable that Pope's reputation should suffer in the reaction against the previous age. Yet it remained possible for writers less committed than Wordsworth and more intelligent than Bowles, to perceive Pope's worth. Byron, Rogers, Campbell, Hazlitt, and De Quincey all came to Pope's defence. Their firm sense of his virtues is tempered by a realization of his limitations. Hazlitt is representative: 'I believe I may date my insight into the mysteries of poetry from the commencement of my acquaintance with the authors of the *Lyrical Ballads*; at least, my discrimination of the higher sorts—not my predilection for writers such as Goldsmith or Pope.'[63]

Throughout the Romantic period the question of Pope's genius was a live conflict. For the Victorians the great Romantic discoveries were established truisms: Pope and Augustanism appeared a temporary aberration in the course of English poetry. By 1880 Matthew Arnold could confidently dispose of Augustan pretensions to greatness: 'Dryden and Pope are not classics of our poetry, they are classics of our prose.' The low rank assigned to Pope's poetry was enforced by a dislike of his satire: he once more became the malicious hunchback portrayed by the Dunces. At best he was regarded as a master of filigree work, written for the complacent world of Queen Anne.

This view was not seriously challenged until 1930, when William Empson's seminal remarks in *Seven Types of Ambiguity* revealed the witty and complex profundity of Pope's verse. Four years later, F. R. Leavis, provoked by T. S. Eliot's *Homage to John Dryden*, sought to reinstate Pope's poetry by demonstrating the continuity of its wit with that of Metaphysical poetry.[64] These critical insights mark the start of a complete revaluation of Pope. This new attention to the texture of the poetry and to the richness of Pope's imaginative world was supported by the scholarly work in eighteenth-century studies which had been in progress for some years, especially in America. George Sherburn's account of Pope's early career, also published in 1934, cleared away many of the slanders surrounding the poet. The subsequent exploration of Pope's mind and art has depended upon an interchange between the literary awareness represented by Empson and Leavis, and the insights which have come from labours of humane scholars like Sherburn. Geoffrey Tillotson's *On the Poetry of Pope* (1938) combined both virtues. His sensitive exposition of Pope's ideals of 'correctness' showed that wit, decorum, and artifice do not disguise feeling, but enable him to achieve an ordered and powerful expression of specific and deeply felt emotions.

This resurgence of interest found its centre from 1939 to 1967 in the Twickenham edition, whose exploration of the way Pope's greatest poetry is deeply embedded in its age is balanced by a sense of its intrinsic merits. Its editors demonstrate conclusively the central place of imitation and allusion in the texture of Pope's poetry, his skill in working within established genres, and the vitality with which he creates a symbolic and moral order from traditional and classical values.[65] In this rehabilitation of Pope the satires, including the Horatian imitations, have formed the foundation of his claims to greatness. At the same time, the serious intellectual ambitions of *An Essay on Man* had been recognized, and the Homer translations once more seen as a crucial part of his Augustan achievement.

Cleanth Brooks, W. K. Wimsatt, and Maynard Mack have shown that Pope's stylistic and metaphoric structures could yield as much to the 'New Criticism' as the Metaphysicals or modern poetry,[66] and Donald Davie has argued that, like Eliot or Pound, Pope's poetry renovates the language of the tribe.[67] This somewhat belated admission of Pope to the ranks of genuine poetry has encouraged discussion of his poems' dominant images and symbolic patterns, enabling a work like Aubrey Williams's thematic analysis (1955) of *The Dunciad* to offer a convincing reply to the long-standing objections to the poem's structure.

The most tireless promoter of Pope's reputation has been Maynard Mack. Like his earlier work on Pope's wit, his analysis of *An Essay on Man*'s Christian framework, or his exhumation of the grandeur of the Homer,[68] Mack's *The Garden and the City* (1969) is a vindication of the union of scholarly and critical intelligence. It explores Pope's growing political motivation in the later satires, and brilliantly reveals how the poet's house and grotto at Twickenham became an integral part of his symbolic world. In all, recent criticism has encouraged a more complete reading of Pope's poetry than any since Johnson's *Life*. Although the relative importance assigned to the various areas of poetry differs radically from that of the eighteenth-century reader, a sympathy with Pope's intentions has disclosed a poet whose artistic mastery is the expression of a coherent attitude to life. Despite a deviousness in his life often approaching downright dishonesty, Pope's embodiment of a humane and conservative 'virtue' in his poetry is now clearly recognizable.

The eighteenth-century reading of Pope obviously supports the historicist elements in this rediscovery. Contemporary emphasis upon the Homer and Pope's classical heritage shows the accuracy of scholarly excavation of these strata in his work, while a reading of the Dunces forces a recognition of the essential truth of Pope's portraits: *The Dunciad* and its apparatus tell us all we need to know. But the variety of reactions between 1705 and 1782 serves as a warning against too easily taking Pope at his own valuation. The inertness of emotion lying behind the clichés which assert his Augustan greatness takes one back to Warton's basic questions with a sense of relief. Translation is not after all original poetry: it is important that Pope failed to write an epic of his own. Satire may not be an inherently inferior genre, but neoclassical praise for Pope's successes in other genres, praise we can no longer endorse, points to a certain narrowness in Pope's range. The kind of excitement stimulated by *Eloisa to Abelard* underlines a straitened responsiveness in Pope's approach to sexuality. The ease with which Crousaz, Voltaire, or Warburton twisted *An Essay on Man* to suit their own interpretations asks whether the poem, though containing passages of Pope's most eloquently fervent poetry, lacks an important measure of intellectual coherence. Dr Johnson, speaking as a strong-minded

34

Christian, certainly found its 'philosophy' pretentious. So too, Johnson's awe before Pope's versification is a reminder that for Pope, and the eighteenth century in general, 'correctness' often dwindled to a matter of style. Nor is it easy to brush aside the recurrent complaints against the satire's obscurity, while the embarrassment of Pope's admirers before his satiric verve stresses the way in which his poetry is often most powerful when its real motives are not fully admitted. Johnson's blunt admission that malice and an attraction to the 'physically impure' are elements in *The Dunciad* would offend some of Pope's modern apologists, but they are undoubtedly present. While they may make judgment difficult, they are a powerful source of the poem's energy.[69]

Pope's idealizing Augustan vision, which dominated his early work and sustained friendly critics throughout his career, has given a framework for much twentieth-century criticism. The Augustan myth was a necessary fiction for Pope and his audience, but how far is its resonance factitious? Now that the recovery work is more or less complete, criticism should perhaps pose the basic issues once more, and the wholeness of Pope's world be measured against the fuller worlds of Swift, Fielding, or Hogarth.

NOTES

1 *Letters Concerning the English Nation* (1732) p. 178. Quoted by W. K. Wimsatt, *The Portraits of Alexander Pope* (New Haven, 1965), p. xvii. For reproductions and discussion of the portraits mentioned in this and the following paragraph, see Wimsatt, *op. cit.*

2 *The Weekly Journal or the British Gazetteer*, 29 March 1729. Quoted Wimsatt, *op. cit.*, p. 101.

3 The print entitled *Taste . . .* is reproduced in Twickenham III, ii. Both W. K. Wimsatt, *op. cit.*, pp. 115–17, and R. B. Paulson, *Hogarth's Complete Graphic Works* (New Haven, 1965), i. 299–300, reject the earlier attribution to Hogarth. The print, however, shares Hogarth's enmity toward Burlington, Kent, and the connoisseurs.

4 *The Letters of Philip Dormer Stanhope, Earl of Chesterfield*, ed. J. Bradshaw (1905), ii. 500.

5 *Memoirs and Observations in His Travels over England* (1719), pp. 220–1. First printed in French (Paris, 1698).

6 *An Essay on Criticism* (1728), pp. 3–4. Reprinted Augustan Reprint Society, nos 107–8 (1964).

7 Richard Savage, *A Collection of Pieces in Verse and Prose* (1732), p. vi.

8 See Twickenham, i. 353–6.

9 See especially Nos 13, 15, 53, and 86.

10 Further, see Twickenham, i. 15–20.

11 See J. V. Guerinot, *Pamphlet Attacks on Pope 1711–44* (1969), pp. 5–11.

12 25 June 1711, *Corresp.*, i. 121. However, in 1713 Pope satirized Dennis in *The Narrative of Dr. Robert Norris*.

13 On *Windsor Forest* see Earl Wasserman, *The Subtler Language* (Baltimore, 1959), chap. iv, and Twickenham, i. 131–44. On *The Temple of Fame* see Twickenham, ii. 215–42.

14 Publication of the five-canto version is treated here as the poem's first appearance. The two-canto version in Lintot's *Miscellany* (1712) was virtually ignored.

15 *An Enquiry into the Life and Writings of Homer* (1735), reprinted in *Eighteenth-Century Critical Essays*, ed. S. Elledge (New York, 1961), i. 446.

16 *Thraliana*, ed. K. C. Balderston (1942), i. 536.

17 See further, L. S. Wright, 'Eighteenth-Century Replies to Pope's *Eloisa*', *Studies in Philology*, xxxi (1934), 519–33, and Twickenham, ii. 414–16.

18 Further, see Maynard Mack's illuminating Introduction, Twickenham, vol. vii.

19 An unjustified charge: see Twickenham, vii, pp. lxxxi–cvii.

20 Pope altered the line to meet Dennis's objection.

21 Norman Callan, Twickenham, vii, p. lxxix. See Callan's discussion for a fuller account of the exchange.

22 For recent discussions of this area see Twickenham, vii, pp. liv–lv, and J. Hagstrum, *The Sister Arts* (Chicago, 1958), pp. 229ff.

23 *Lives of the Poets*, ed. G. B. Hill (1905), iii. 143.

24 29 March 1729, *The Weekly Journal or the British Gazetteer*. For the first lines of this, see p. 1 above. It was reprinted in *Pope Alexander's Supremacy and Infallibility Examin'd* (1729), p. vi.

25 *Corresp.*, ii. 104–5.

26 *Corresp.*, ii. 349–50.

27 For a detailed account of the poem's genesis, see Twickenham, v, pp. xiii–xv.

28 See especially James Sutherland's views, Twickenham, v, pp. xl–xliii, 464–6.

29 See No. 95 for Richardson's reaction to *The Dunciad*'s final version.

30 On earlier notions of satire, see A. Kernan, *The Cankered Muse* (New Haven, 1959).

31 Advertisement to *Imitations of Horace*, *Sat.* II. i (quoted Twickenham, III. i, p. xl).

32 Reprinted in T. B. Gilmore's edition of Harte's *Essay*, Augustan Reprint Society (Los Angeles, 1968).

33 See Twickenham, III. i, pp. xii–xiv, III. ii, pp. xiv–xxv, and Spence, *Anecdotes*, i. 131–4.

34 *Corresp.*, iii. 417.

35 See Maynard Mack, *The Garden and the City* (Toronto, 1969), pp. 122ff., 272–8 and K. Mahaffey, 'Timon's Villa: Walpole's Houghton', *Texas Studies in Language and Literature*, ix (1969), 193–222.

36 Twickenham, iv, p. xl. Further, see *ibid.*, pp. xxxvi–xli.

37 *The Works of the English Poets*, ed. A. Chalmers (1810), xi. 201.

38 E. de Silhouette, *Essais sur la critique et sur l'homme* (Paris, 1741 ed.), pp. 11–12.

39 See Du Resnel's remarks (No. 82), and J. de La Harpe, 'Le *Journal des Savants* et la renommée de Pope en France au xviiie siècle', *University of California Publications in Modern Philology*, xvi (1933), 173–216.

40 As Johnson pointed out in his translation of the *Commentaire* (1739, reissued 1742).

41 See Twickenham, III. i, note p. xli.

42 For two opposed views, see Twickenham, III. i, pp. xxix–xxxi, and I. Kramnick, *Bolingbroke and his Circle* (Cambridge, Mass., 1968), pp. 217–23, 306.

43 *Corresp.*, iv. 171.

44 3 April 1742, quoted Twickenham, v, p. xxxi.

45 Twickenham, v, pp. xxxii–iv, and Spence, *Anecdotes*, i. 111–12.

46 Further see N. Ault, *New Light on Pope* (1949), pp. 298–307, and Spence, *Anecdotes*, i. 110–12.

47 To the Duchess of Portland, 4 December 1743, *Elizabeth Montagu: The Queen of the Bluestockings*, ed. E. J. Climenson (1906), i. 172.

48 *Boswell's Life of Johnson*, ed. G. B. Hill, rev. L. F. Powell (1934–50), iii. 332.

49 W. L. Macdonald, *Pope and his Critics* (1951), pp. 251ff.

50 See J. Pittock, 'Joseph Warton and his Second Volume of the *Essay on Pope*', *Review of English Studies*, xviii (1967), 264–73.

51 For his significant alterations, see p. 382 below; also H. Trowbridge, 'Joseph Warton's Classification of English Poets', *Modern Language Notes*, li (1936), 515–18.

52 *Essay*, ii. 337ff.

53 *Boswell's Life of Johnson*, ed. G. B. Hill, rev. L. F. Powell (1934–50), i. 448.

54 In 1743 he wrote a brief account of the controversy, *Gentleman's Magazine*, xliii (1743), 152, 587–8.

55 See Benjamin Boyce, 'Samuel Johnson's Criticism of Pope in the *Life of Pope*', *Review of English Studies*, v (1954), 37–46. Also F. W. Hilles, 'The Making of *The Life of Pope*' in *New Light on Dr. Johnson*, ed. F. W. Hilles (New Haven, 1959).

56 Pope's foreign reputation has not been systematically explored. See Bibliography for a list of the studies made to date.

57 See Twickenham, III. i, note p. xli.

58 Twickenham, i. 208–9. For examples of French reaction, see Nos 42, 82.

59 *Corresp.*, i. 447.

60 *Observations on Pope* (1796), p. v.

61 *Edinburgh Review* (September 1816), p. 1.

62 *Letters of the Wordsworth Family*, ed. W. Knight (1907), iii. 122.

63 *Collected Works*, ed. A. R. Waller and A. Glover (1902–6), vii. 226.

64 *Scrutiny*, ii (1934); reprinted in *Revaluation* (1935), chap. iii.

65 Ian Jack's *Augustan Satire* (1952), R. Brower's *Pope: the Poetry of Allusion* (1959), Thomas Edward's *This Dark Estate* (Berkeley, 1963), and Peter Dixon's *The World of Pope's Satires* (1968) all illuminate Pope's imaginative world.

66 Cleanth Brooks, 'The Case of Miss Arabella Fermor', *Sewanee Review*, li (1943); reprinted in *The Well Wrought Urn* (New York, 1947). W. K. Wimsatt, 'Rhetoric and Poems: Alexander Pope', *English Institute Essays* (1948); reprinted in *The Verbal Icon* (1954). Maynard Mack, 'Wit and Poetry and Pope' in *Pope and his Contemporaries*, ed. J. L. Clifford and L. Landa (1949).

67 *Purity of Diction in English Verse* (1952, 1967 with postscript), and *Articulate Energy* (1955).

68 See the Introduction to Twickenham, III. i; and the collaborative essay to vol. vii. Mack has also edited *Essential Articles for the Study of Pope* (Hamden, Conn., 1968 enlarged ed.).

69 See Emrys Jones's 'Pope and Dulness', British Academy Chatterton Lecture (1968), for a fresh approach to these (and other) problems.

Note on the Text

The text is normally taken from the first edition when available, or from a definitive modern text. Where a text presents complications, the headnote preceding the item describes the situation. Editorial interference has been kept to a minimum. In some details the text has been normalized to follow modern practice. Texts originally printed in italic are here given in roman, but otherwise contemporary capitalization, punctuation, and italics are retained. Typographical errors are silently corrected, as are quotations and line references, except where the misquotation affects the writer's remarks. The form of footnotes and references has been adapted to suit modern conventions where the original is misleading or obscure. Footnotes added by the editor are in square brackets, as are alterations or explanatory additions to the text. Latin and Greek quotations are given in English, the translation usually being that of the Loeb editions. As far as possible, translations from the French originals are given from eighteenth-century versions: despite their freedom, contemporary translators share their authors' critical vocabulary.

In the case of short excerpts from longer works, page references to the original are given in the headnote; where the selection is more substantial, page references are given in square brackets in the text itself. Long quotations from Pope's poetry used for illustrative rather than critical purposes, are replaced by line references to the Twickenham edition.

The dates of attacks on Pope are normally taken from J. V. Guerinot, *Pamphlet Attacks on Pope 1711–1744* (1969).

Part I

Contemporary Criticism

1705–44

GENERAL REACTIONS

1705–20

1. Wycherley welcomes the young poet

April 1705

William Wycherley, extract from letter to Pope, 7 April 1705, *Corresp.*, i. 6–7.

Wycherley (1640?–1716), the aging poet and dramatist, quickly befriended the young poet. In return Pope helped Wycherley correct his poems, which later led to an estrangement between the two men. On their relationship, see Spence, *Anecdotes*, i. 32–41. Wycherley saw the manuscript version of the *Pastorals*, not published till 1709.

As to my enquiry after your Intrigues with the *Muses*, you may allow me to make it, since no old Man can give so young, so great, so able a Favourite of theirs, Jealousy. I am, in my Enquiry, like old Sir *Bernard Gascoign*,[1] who us'd to say, That when he was grown too old to have his Visits admitted alone by the Ladies, he always took along with him a young Man, to ensure his Welcome to them; who, had he come alone had been rejected, only because his Visits were not scandalous to them. So I am (like an old Rook, who is ruin'd by Gaming) forc'd to live on the good Fortune of the pushing young Man, whose Fancies are so vigorous, that they ensure their Success in their Adventures with the Muses, by the Strength of their Imagination.

[1] [An Italian who served Charles I, and was favoured in Charles II's court]

2. Opinions of Gay and Addison

May, October 1712

Here Gay and Addison give their reactions to Lintot's *Miscellaneous Poems and Translations* (1712), which Pope himself probably edited. It was advertised in *The Spectator* on 20 May 1712, and included *The Rape of the Lock*, along with other of Pope's early poems.

(a) John Gay (1685–1732), extract from 'On a Miscellany of Poems', *Miscellaneous Poems and Translations* (1712). The lines refer to the *Pastorals* and possibly to an early version of *Windsor Forest*:

> When *Pope*'s harmonious Muse with pleasure roves,
> Amidst the Plains, the murm'ring Streams, and Groves,
> Attentive Eccho pleas'd to hear his Songs,
> Thro' the glad Shade each warbling Note prolongs;
> His various Numbers charm our ravish'd Ears,
> His steady Judgment far out-shoots his Years,
> And early in the Youth the God appears.

(b) Joseph Addison (1672–1719), extract from *The Spectator*, no. 523, 30 October 1712, ed. D. F. Bond (1965), iv. 361:

I am always highly delighted with the Discovery of any rising Genius among my Countrymen. For this Reason I have read over, with great Pleasure, the late Miscellany published by Mr. *Pope*, in which there are many Excellent Compositions of that ingenious Gentleman.

3. John Dennis's 'Character' of Pope

May 1716

John Dennis, *A True Character of Mr. Pope, and His Writings* (1716), *Critical Works*, ii. 103–8. *A True Character* is dated 7 May, and was published 31 May 1716.

John Dennis (1657–1734), critic and dramatist, was one of Pope's more persistent butts. For his first attack on Pope see No. 10. E. N. Hooker (ed. cit., ii. 458) accepts *A True Character* as Dennis's, although Pope thought that both Dennis and Charles Gildon were involved. This attack is given in full as an example of one of the more venomous assaults on his name and character, and as one which wounded him particularly. For a fuller discussion of Dennis's authorship, and a defence, see E. N. Hooker, 'Pope and Dennis', *English Literary History*, vii (1940), 188–98.

To Mr. ——

SIR,

I have read over the *Libel*,[1] which I received from you the Day before Yesterday. Yesterday I received the same from another Hand with this Character of the Secret Author of so much stupid Calumny.

That[2] [Pope] is one, whom God and Nature have mark'd for want of Common Honesty, and his own Contemptible Rhimes for want of Common Sense, that those Rhimes have found great Success with the Rabble, which is a Word almost as comprehensive as Mankind; but that the Town, which supports him, will do by him, as the Dolphin did by the Ship-wrack'd *Monkey*, drop him as soon as it finds him out to be a Beast, whom it fondly now mistakes for a Human Creature. 'Tis, *says he*, a very little but very comprehensive Creature, in whom all Contradictions meet, and all Contrarieties are reconcil'd; when at one and the same time, like the Ancient *Centaurs*, he is a Beast and a Man, a Whig and a Tory, a virulent *Papist* and yet forsooth, a Pillar of the Church of *England*,

---

[1] [The 'Libel' was called an 'Imitation of Horace'. It was not in fact by Pope]
[2] [The 'Character' itself was not by Dennis. It may be Gildon's]

45

a Writer at one and the same time, of *GUARDIANS* and of *EXAMINERS*,[1] an assertor of Liberty and of the Dispensing Power of Kings; a Rhimester without Judgment or Reason, and a Critick without Common Sense; a Jesuitical Professor of Truth, a base and foul Pretender to Candour; a Barbarous Wretch, who is perpetually boasting of Humanity and Good Nature, a lurking way-laying Coward, and a Stabber in the Dark; who is always pretending to Magnanimity, and to sum up all Villains in one, a Traytor-Friend, one who has betrayed all Mankind, and seems to have taken his great Rule of Life from the following lines of *Hudibras*.[2]

> For 'tis easier to *Betray*
> Than Ruin any other way,
> As th' Earth is soonest undermin'd,
> By vermin Impotent and Blind.

He is a Professor of the worst Religion, which he laughs at, and yet has most inviolably observ'd the most execrable Maxim in it, *That no Faith is to be kept with Hereticks*. A wretch, whose true Religion is his Interest, and yet so stupidly blind to that Interest, that he often meets her, without knowing her, and very grosly Affronts her. His Villainy is but the natural Effect of his want of Understanding, as the sowerness of Vinegar proceeds from its want of Spirit; and yet, *says My Friend*, notwithstanding that Shape and that Mind of his, some Men of good Understanding, value him for his Rhimes, as they would be fond of an *Asseinego*, that could sing his part in a Catch, or of a *Baboon* that could whistle *Walsingham*. The grosser part of his gentle Readers believe the Beast to be more than Man; as Ancient Rusticks took his Ancestors for those Demy-Gods they call *Fauns and Satyrs*.

This was the Character, which my Friend gave of the Author of this miserable Libel, which immediately made me apprehend that it was the very same Person, who endeavour'd to expose you in a *Billinsgate* Libel, at the very time that you were doing him a Favour at his own earnest Desire, who attempted to undermine Mr. *PHILIPS* in one of his *Guardians*,[3] at the same time that the *Crocodile* smil'd on him, embrac'd him, and called him Friend, who wrote a Prologue in praise of *CATO*, and teaz'd *Lintott* to publish Remarks upon it;[4] who at the same time, that he openly extoll'd Sir *Richard Steele* in the highest manner, secretly publish'd the Infamous Libel of Dr. *Andrew Tripe*[5] upon him;

---

[1] [It is unlikely that Pope wrote for *The Examiner*, though he did of course write for *The Guardian*]

[2] [*Hudibras*, ed. J. Wilders (1967), III. ii. 1469–70, 309–400]

[3] [Pope's ironical tribute to Philips's pastorals in *The Guardian* no. 40 (No. 9)]

[4] [This charge is otherwise unsubstantiated]

[5] [*A Letter from the Facetious Doctor Andrew Tripe* (1714): it was not, however, by Pope]

who, as he is in Shape a *Monkey*, is so in his every Action; in his senseless Chattering, and his merry Grimaces, in his doing hourly Mischief and hiding himself, in the variety of his Ridiculous Postures, and his continual Shiftings, from Place to Place, from Persons to Persons, from Thing to Thing. But whenever he Scribbles, he is emphatically a *Monkey*, in his awkard servile Imitations. For in all his Productions, he has been an *Imitator*, from his Imitation of *VIRGILS Bucolicks*, to this present Imitation of *HORACE*. —— His *Pastorals* were writ in Imitation of *VIRGIL*, —— His *Rape of the Lock* of *BOILEAU*, —— His *Essay on Criticism*, of the Present Duke of *Buckingham*, and of my Lord *Roscommon*, —— His *Windsor-Forest* of Sir *John Denham*, —— His *Ode upon St. Cæcilia* of Mr. *Dryden*, and —— His *Temple of Fame*, of *CHAUCER*.

Thus for fifteen Years together this Ludicrous Animal has been a constant *Imitator*. Yet he has rather mimick'd these great Genius's, than he has Imitated them. He has given a False and a Ridiculous Turn to all their good and their great Qualities, and has, as far as in him lies, Burlesqu'd them without knowing it. But after having been for fifteen Years as it were an *Imitator*, he has made no Proficiency. His first Imitations, tho' bad, are rather better than the Succeeding, and this last Imitation of *HORACE*, the most execrable of them all.

> For as a Dog that turns the Spitt,
> Bestirs himself and plies his Feet
> To climb the Wheel, but all in vain,
> His own Weight brings him down again,
> And still he's in the self same place,
> Where at his setting out he was,
> So in the Circle of the Arts,
> Does he Advance his natural Parts.[1]

If you should chance, Sir, to shew this LETTER to any of your Acquaintance who have perus'd his Senseless Calumnies, they may think perhaps that we follow his Example, and retort Slander upon him. I Desire that you would have the Goodness to assure such, that in the Moral part of his Character, and all that relates to matter of Fact, there is no manner of Rhetorick us'd, all is exactly and litterally true, for which we appeal to those Poetical Persons, with whom we have been most Conversant in *Covent-Garden*. We have always been of Opinion that he who invents, or pretends, or falsifies Matter of Fact, in order to slander

---

[1] [*Hudibras*, ed. J. Wilders (1967), II. iii. 209–16]

any one, deserves an Infamous Punishment, and we have always had before our Eyes the following Verses out of *Horace*,[1]

> —— *Absentem qui rodit amicum,*
> *Qui non defendit alio culpante, solutos*
> *Qui captat risus Hominum, famamq; dicacis,*
> *Fingere qui non visa potest, commissa tacere,*
> *Qui nequit, hic niger est, hunc tu Romane, caveto, &c.*

As to what relates to the *Person* of this wretched Libeller, if in that there may be some trifling Exaggerations, yet even that is not design'd to Deceive or Impose upon any to whom you may happen to shew it, but is intended to lead them to an exact Knowledge of the Truth by a very little enlarging upon it.

But if any one appears to be concern'd at our Upbraiding him with his Natural Deformity, which did not come by his own Fault, but seems to be the Curse of God upon him; we desire that Person to consider, that this little Monster has upbraided People with their Calamities and their Diseases, and Calamities and Diseases, which are either false or past, or which he himself gave them by administring Poison to them; we desire that Person to consider, that Calamities and Diseases, if they are neither false nor past, are common to all Men; that a Man can no more help his Calamities and his Diseases, than a Monster can his Deformity; that there is no Misfortune, but what the Generality of Mankind are liable too, and that there is no one Disease, but what all the rest of Men are subject too; whereas the Deformity of this Libeller, is Visible, Present, Lasting, Unalterable, and Peculiar to himself. 'Tis the mark of God and Nature upon him, to give us warning that we should hold no Society with him, as a Creature not of our Original, nor of our Species. And they who have refus'd to take this Warning which God and Nature have given them, and have in spight of it, by a Senseless Presumption, ventur'd to be familiar with him, have severely suffer'd for it, by his Perfidiousness. They tell me, he has been lately pleas'd to say, *That 'tis Doubtful if the Race of Men are the Offspring of* Adam *or of the* Devil.[2] But if 'tis doubtful as to the Race of Men, 'tis certain at least, that his Original is not from *Adam*, but from

---

[1] [Horace, *Sat.*, I. iv. 81–5: 'The man who backbites an absent friend; who fails to defend him when another finds fault; the man who courts the loud laughter of others, and the reputation of a wit; who can invent what he never saw; who cannot keep a secret—that man is black of heart; of him beware, good Roman']

[2] [The poem referred to is Pope's *To Mr. John Moore, Author of the Celebrated Worm-Powder* (1716). See omitted stanza between ll. 12–13, Twickenham, vi. 161n]

the *Devil*. By his constant and malicious Lying, and by that Angel Face and Form of his, 'tis plain that he wants nothing but Horns and Tayl, to be the exact Resemblance, both in Shape and Mind, of his Infernal Father. Thus, Sir, I return you Truth for Slander, and a just Satire for an Extravagant Libel, which is therefore ridiculously call'd an Imitation of *Horace*. You know very well, Sir, that the Difference between *Horace*, and such an Imitation of him, is almost Infinite; and I leave you to consider what Influence such an Imitation must have upon its Readers of both Kinds, both upon those who are acquainted with that Great Poet, and with those that know him not; how contemptible it must render *Horace* to the latter, and his Imitator to the former, who when they shall behold the Ghost of their old and their valued Friend, raised up before them, by this awkard Conjurer, in a Manner so ridiculously frightful, when they behold him thus miserably mangled, and reflect at once with Contempt and Horrour, upon this Barbarous Usage of him, will not be able to refrain from exclaiming in the most vehement Manner.

Qualis adest, Quantum mutatus ab illo, &c.[1]

They must think that their old and valued Friend had a Prophetick Spirit, and seem'd to foretel the Usage, which he has lately received from this Barbarian and his Brethren, when in the fourth Ode of his Third Book he cryed,

Visam Britannos Hospitibus feros.[2]

But as for the other sorts of Readers, the Readers who have no Knowledge of *Horace*, but from this contemptible Imitation; what must they think, Sir, of those great Men, who extol him, for the second Genius of the *Roman-Empire*. Illustrious for so many great Qualities which are to be found in him alone? Must they not look upon all his Admirers, as so many Learned Idiots, and upon the *Roman-Empire* it self, as a vast Nation of Fools?

You know very well, Sir, that as *Horace* had a firmness of Judgment, and a sureness and truth of Taste; he never once form'd a wrong Judgment to himself, either of the Actions of Men in general, or of the particular Worth and Merit of Authors; he had an Honour and a Rectitude of Soul, that would have oblig'd him to die a thousand times rather than to Write any thing against his Conscience.

[1] [Horace, *Odes*, IV. ix. 50: 'What aspect was his! how changed from that']
[2] [*Ibid.*, IV. iii. 32: 'the Britons, no friends to strangers']

Pejusque letho flagitium timet.[1]

He was capable indeed of being provok'd to expose either a Fool or a Knave, whom otherwise he might have suffer'd to have remain'd in Obscurity; but the most Barbarous Usage of his most Malicious Enemy, could never urge him to Slander that Enemy. From this Force and Clearness of his Understanding, and this Noble Rectitude of his Will, it has proceeded that all his Censures are like so many *Decrees*, that have been all affirm'd by Posterity, the only Supream Court of Judicature, for the Distribution of Fame and Infamy, from which Mankind can have no Appeal. That Supream, Impartial, Incorruptible Judicature, has the same Opinions of Persons and Things, and especially of Authors that he had. The same high Value for *Tibullus*, for *Pollio*, for *Varius*, for *Virgil*; and the same Contempt for *Bavius*, for *Mævius*, for *Crispinus*, for *Alpinus*, for *Fannius*, and for a thousand more.

The same Justness and Fineness of Discernment, and the same noble Rectitude of Will, appear in the *French Satirist*, which make the most considerable Share of his Merit, and the most Distinguishing part of his Character, if we will believe what he says of himself, in his Admirable Epistle to *Monsieur SEIGNELEY*.[2] You know, Sir, that what *Boileau* says there of himself is exactly true in Fact. The Persons whom he has attack'd in his Writings have been for the most part Authors, and most of those Authors Poets. The Censures which he has pass'd on them have been confirm'd by all *Europe*. But at the same time that judicious Poet, has been as liberal of his Praise to his Contemporaries, who were excellent in their Kinds, as *Corneille*, *Racine*, *Moliere*, and *La Fontaine*. Nay, he was generous enough to defend *Racine*, and to support and strengthen him, when a clamorous crou'd of miserable Authors endeavoured to oppress him, as appears by his Admirable Epistle addrest to that Tragick Poet.

You, and I, both know very well, Sir, that there has been never wanting a Floud of such Authors, neither in *England* nor *France*, who being like this Imitator, in ev'ry Respect, the reverse of *Horace*, in Honour, in Discernment, in Genius; have always combin'd to attack any thing that has appear'd above their own dull Level, while they have hug'd and admir'd each other, Authors who have thought to be too hard for their Adversaries by opposing *Billinsgate* to Reason, and Dogmatical Assertion to Moral Demonstration; and who have been Idiots enough

---

[1] [*Ibid.*, IV. ix. 50: 'and fears dishonour worse than death']
[2] [Boileau, *Épître* ix]

to believe that their Noise and Impudence could alter the Nature of Things, and the Notions of Men of Sense.

Of all these Libellers, the present Imitator is the most Impudent, and the most Incorrigible, who has lately pester'd and plagu'd the World with Five or Six Scandalous Libels, in Prose, that are all of them at once so Stupid, and so Malicious, that Men of Sense are Doubtful, if they should attribute them to the Libellers Native Idiotism, or to Accidental Madness.

In all these Libels, the chief Objects of his Scandal and Malice, have been Persons of distinguish'd Merit, and among these he has fallen upon none so foully as his Friends and Benefactors. Among these latter, he has attack'd no one so often, or with so much ridiculous, impotent Malice, as Sir *Richard Blackmore*; who is Estimable for a thousand good and great Qualities. And what time has he chosen to do this? Why, just after that Gentleman had laid very great Obligations on him; and just after he had oblig'd the World with so many Editions of his Excellent *Poem* upon *CREATION*,[1] which *Poem* alone is worth all the *Folios*, that this Libeller will ever write, and which will render its Author the Delight and Admiration of Posterity. So that 'tis hard to determine whether this Libeller is more remarkable for his Judgment or his Gratitude.

I dare venture to affirm, that there is not an Author living so little Qualified for a Censurer as himself. I know nothing for which he is so ill Qualified as he is for Judging, unless it be for Translating *HOMER*. He has neither Taste nor Judgment, but is, if you will pardon a Quibble, the very necessity of *Parnassus*; for he has none of the Poetical Laws; or if he has the Letter of any, He has it without the Spirit. Whenever he pretends to Criticise, I fancy I see *Shamwell* or *Cheatly* in the Squire of *Alsatia*,[2] cutting a Sham or Banter to abuse some Bubble. The *Preface* is full of gross Errours, and he has shewn himself in it, a Dogmatical, Ignorant, Impudent Second-Hand Critick. As for the *Poem*, however he may cry up *HOMER* for being every where a *Græcian-Trumpeter* in the Original, I can see no *Trumpeter* in the *Translator*, but the King of *Spain*'s.[3] But since his Friends will alledge 'tis easie to say this, I desire that it may go for nothing, till I have so plainly prov'd it, that the most Foolish, and the most Partial of them shall not be able to deny it.

As for what they call his *Verses*, he has, like Mr. *Bayes*, got a notable

---

[1] [*The Creation* (1712)]
[2] [Thomas Shadwell, *The Squire of Alsatia* (1688)]
[3] [A hit at Pope's Catholicism]

knack of Rhimeing and Writing smooth Verse, but without either Genius or Good Sense, or any tolerable Knowledge of *English*, as I believe I shall shew plainly, when I come to the rest of his Imitations. As for his Translation of *HOMER*, I could never borrow it, till this very Day, and design to read it over to Morrow; so that shortly you may expect to hear more of it. I will only tell you beforehand, that *HOMER* seems to me to be untranslatable in any Modern Language. That great Poet is just in his Designs, admirable in his Characters, and for the most part exact in his Reasoning, and correct in his Noble Sentiments, but these are Excellencies, which may be already seen in the Prose Translations of Him.[1]

The Qualities which so admirably distinguish *HOMER* from most other Writers, and which therefore a Translator in Verse is particularly oblig'd to show, because they cannot be shown in Prose, are the Beauty of his Diction, and the various Harmony of his Versification. But 'tis as Ridiculous to pretend to make these Shine out in *English* Rhimes, as it would be to emulate upon a *Bag-pipe*, the Solemn and Majestick Thorough Basse of an *Organ*.

But you may suddenly expect more of this, if what I have already said, happens to entertain you.

I am
Sir,
Your, &c.

London
May 7. 1716.

---

[1] [Mme Anne Dacier, *L'Iliade d'Homère* (Paris, 1699), which was translated into English in 1711–12 by John Ozell and others. Dennis later attacked the *Iliad*, No. 30]

4. Welsted on Pope's 'vulgar art'

March 1717

Leonard Welsted, extract from *Palæmon to Cælia, at Bath; or, The Triumvirate* (1717), reprinted in *The Works in Verse and Prose, of Leonard Welsted, Esq.*, ed. J. Nichols (1787), p. 43. (First published 7 March 1717.)

Welsted (1688–1747) was another of Pope's opponents and butts. This pamphlet is his first attack on Pope (see further Nos 75, 80a). Welsted's poem is cast in the form of a letter, which reports the following conversation between 'Sir Harry' and 'Sir Fopling'.

[*Sir Harry*] 'Ev'n Pope (I speak the judgment of his foes)
    The sweets of rhime and easy measures knows.'
    'This,' answered Fopling, 'is a vulgar art,
    Which never wakes the soul, or warms the heart:
    He wants the spirit, and informing flame,
    Which breathes divine, and gives a Poet's name:
    His verse the mind to indolence may sooth;
    The strain is even, and the numbers smooth;
    But 'tis all level plain; no mountains rise,
    No startling line, that's pregnant with surprize.
    Here [in London] some incline to praise what others blame;
    So hard it is to fix Poetic Flame.'

5. Parnell assesses Pope's early career

1717

Thomas Parnell, 'To Mr. Pope', in *The Works of Mr. Alexander Pope* (1717), sig. f1-2.

Parnell (1679–1718) was a minor poet, and friend of Pope and Swift. He had written the 'Essay on the Life Writings and Learning of Homer' for Pope's *Iliad*. He lived mostly in Ireland, and died when returning there from London in 1718. Pope edited his poems for their posthumous publication in 1721.

To praise, and still with just respect to praise
A Bard triumphant in immortal bays,
The Learn'd to show, the Sensible commend,
Yet still preserve the province of the Friend;
What life, what vigour must the lines require?
What Music tune them, what Affection fire?
   O might thy Genius in my bosom shine!
Thou shouldst not fail of numbers worthy thine;
The brightest Ancients might at once agree,
To sing within my lays, and sing of thee.
   Horace himself wou'd own thou dost excell
In candid arts to play the Critic well.
Ovid himself might wish to sing the Dame,
Whom *Windsor*-Forest sees a gliding stream:
On silver feet, with annual Osier crown'd,
She runs for ever thro' Poetic ground.
   How flame the glories of *Belinda*'s Hair,
Made by thy Muse the envy of the Fair?
Less shone the tresses *Ægypt*'s Princess wore,
Which sweet *Callimachus* so sung before.
Here courtly trifles set the world at odds;
Belles war with Beaus, and Whims descend for Gods.

The new Machines, in names of ridicule,
Mock the grave frenzy of the Chimick fool.
But know, ye Fair, a point conceal'd with art,
The Sylphs and Gnomes are but a woman's heart.
The Graces stand in sight; a Satyr-train
Peeps o'er their head, and laughs behind the scene.
    In Fame's fair Temple o'er the boldest wits,
Inshrin'd on high, the sacred *Virgil* sits,
And sits in measures, such as *Virgil*'s Muse,
To place thee near him, might be fond to chuse.
How might he tune th' alternate reed with thee,
Perhaps a *Strephon* thou, a *Daphnis* he;
While some old *Damon*, o'er the vulgar wise,
Thinks he deserves, and thou deserv'st the Prize.
Rapt with the thought, my fancy seeks the plains,
And turns me shepherd while I hear the strains.
Indulgent nurse of ev'ry tender gale,
Parent of flowrets, old *Arcadia*, hail!
Here in the cool my limbs at ease I spread,
Here let they Poplars whisper o'er my head!
Still slide thy waters soft among the trees,
Thy Aspins quiver in a breathing breeze!
Smile, all ye valleys, in eternal spring,
Be hush'd, ye winds! while *Pope* and *Virgil* sing.
    In *English* lays, and all sublimely great,
Thy *Homer* warms with all his ancient heat;
He shines in Council, thunders in the fight,
And flames with ev'ry sense of great delight.
Long has that Poet reign'd, and long unknown,
Like Monarchs sparkling on a distant throne;
In all the Majesty of *Greek* retir'd,
Himself unknown, his mighty name admir'd;
His language failing, wrapt him round with night;
Thine, rais'd by thee, recalls the work to light.
So wealthy Mines, that ages long before
Fed the large realms around with golden Oar,
When choak'd by sinking banks, no more appear,
And Shepherds only say, *The mines were here*:
Should some rich youth (if nature warm his heart,
And all his projects stand inform'd with art)

Here clear the caves, there ope the leading vein;
The mines detected flame with gold again.
　　How vast, how copious are thy new designs!
How ev'ry Music varies in thy lines!
Still, as I read, I feel my bosom beat,
And rise in raptures by another's heat.
Thus in the wood, when summer dress'd the days,
When *Windsor* lent us tuneful hours of ease,
Our ears the lark, the thrush, the turtle blest,
And *Philomela* sweetest o'er the rest:
The shades resound with song—O softly tread,
While a whole season warbles round my head.
　　This to my friend—and when a friend inspires,
My silent harp its master's hand requires,
Shakes off the dust, and makes these rocks resound;
For fortune plac'd me in unfertile ground.[1]
Far from the joys that with my soul agree,
From wit, from learning—very far from thee.
Here moss-grown trees expand the smallest leaf;
Here half an Acre's corn in half a sheaf;
Here hills with naked heads the tempest meet,
Rocks at their sides, and torrents at their feet;
Or lazy lakes, unconscious of a flood,
Whose dull brown *Naiads* ever sleep in mud.
Yet here Content can dwell, and learned Ease,
A Friend delight me, and an Author please;
Ev'n here I sing, when *Pope* supplies the theme,
Shew my own love, tho' not increase his fame.

---

[1] [That is, in Ireland]

6. Two assessments

1718, 1719

(a) Giles Jacob, entry on Pope in *The Poetical Register . . .* (1719-20), ii. 145 (first published 4 December 1718).

The Poetical Register was a biographical dictionary of all the major British writers. It is probable, as Jacob claimed in a letter reprinted in Dennis's *Remarks upon the Dunciad* (1729, pp. 48–9), that this entry was overseen by Pope. For Jacob's later attitude, see No. 58.

This excellent Poet, whose Fame exceeds not his Merit, was born in *London*, the Year 1688. His Parents being of the *Roman* Catholick Persuasion, educated him by a private Tutor, of whom he learned *Latin* and *Greek* at one and the same time. He passed through some Seminaries, with little Improvement, till twelve Years of Age, after which, I have been informed, he perfected his Studies by his own Industry; and so considerable a Progress he made therein, as to be sufficiently qualified for that great Undertaking, the Translation of *Homer*. The celebrated Mr. *Addison* has declared to the Publick, that if Mr. *Pope* should die, and leave his Translation unfinished, there would be found no Successor to compleat it. There appears not only great Ease but Strength in his Compositions; his Numbers flow with great Facility, and his Thoughts are sublime; these with a ready Wit, quick Fancy, and a good Judgment, have deservedly gained him a Reputation equal to any of this Age. Almost all his Pieces are universally applauded, and, tho' some few of them have been cavilled at by the Criticks, what can Criticisms avail when the great *Sheffield*[1] asserts his Work?

(b) Dr Abel Evans, extract from letter to Pope, from Oxford, 26 July 1719, *Corresp.*, ii. 8.

Evans (1679–1737) was a friend of Pope and helped distribute the *Iliad* at Oxford.

---

[1] [John Sheffield, Earl of Mulgrave, author of *An Essay upon Poetry* (1682), contributed the first of the recommendatory poems to Pope's *Works* (1717)]

. . . if wishes had any Power in Medicine I coud soon make you [and your mother] immortal for she very well deserves it for furnishing the world with you, & you have your self made your name immortal enough. I wish only your Body might come in for a small share of that Noble Blessing if it only were for nine hundred & ninety nine years.

PASTORALS

2 May 1709

---

7. Reactions 1705–9

These extracts from private letters testify to the wide impression created by the *Pastorals* prior to their publication and immediately after.

(a) George Granville (1667–1735), later Lord Lansdowne, extract from letter to 'Harry', *c.* 1705 or 1706, *Genuine Works* (1732), i. 437. Granville was a leading Tory as well as a minor poet and patron of the arts.

[Wycherley] shall bring with him, if you will, a young Poet, newly inspir'd, in the Neighbourhood of *Cooper's-Hill*, whom he and *Walsh* have taken under their Wing; his name is *Pope*; he is not above Seventeen or Eighteen Years of Age, and promises Miracles: If he goes on as he has begun, in the Pastoral way, as *Virgil*, first try'd his Strength, we may hope to see *English* Poetry vie with the Roman, and this Swan of Windsor sing as sweetly as the *Mantuan*.

(b) William Walsh, letter to Wycherley, 20 April 1705, *Corresp.*, i. 7. Walsh (1663–1708) was a minor poet and influential critic, though not a productive writer. He had been befriended by Dryden and was a close friend of Congreve.

I return you the Papers[1] you favour'd me with, and had sent them to you yesterday morning, but that I thought to have brought them to you last night my self. I have read them over several times with great satisfaction. The Preface[2] is very judicious and very learned; and the Verses very tender and easy. The Author seems to have a particular Genius for that kind of Poetry, and a Judgment that much exceeds the

---

[1] [I.e., of the *Pastorals*]
[2] [The Preface was not published until it appeared in Pope's *Works* (1717)]

years you told me he was of. He has taken very freely from the Ancients, but what he has mixt of his own with theirs, is no way inferior to what he has taken from them. 'Tis no flattery at all to say, that *Virgil* had written nothing so good at his Age. I shall take it as a favour if you will bring me acquainted with him; and if he will give himself the trouble any morning to call at my House, I shall be very glad to read the Verses over with him, and give him my opinion of the particulars more largely than I can well do in this Letter.

(c) Jacob Tonson, letter to Pope, 20 April 1706, *Corresp.*, i. 17. Tonson (1656?–1736), who had published Dryden's *Virgil*, printed the *Pastorals* in the sixth part of his *Miscellanies* in 1709.

Sir,—I have lately seen a pastoral of yours in mr. Walsh's & mr. Congreve's hands, which is extreamly ffine & is generally approv'd off by the best Judges in poetry. I Remember I have formerly seen you at my shop & am sorry I did not Improve my Acquaintance with you. If you design your Poem for the Press no person shall be more Carefull in the printing of it, nor no one can give a greater Incouragement to it.

(d) William Walsh, extract from letter to Pope, 9 September 1706, *Corresp.*, i. 21.

. . . I read over your Pastorals again, with a great deal of pleasure, and to judge the better read *Virgil*'s Eclogues, and *Spenser*'s Calendar, at the same time; and I assure you I continue the same opinion I had always of them. By the little hints you take upon all occasions to improve them, 'tis probable you will make them yet better against Winter; tho' there is a mean to be kept even in that too, and a Man may correct his Verses till he takes away the true Spirit of them; especially if he submits to the correction of some who pass for great Critics, by mechanical Rules, and never enter into the true Design and Genius of an Author.

(e) William Wycherley, extract from letter to Pope, 17 May 1709, *Corresp.*, i. 59.

. . . I must thank you, for a Book, of your Miscellanies,[1] which Tonson sent me, I suppose, by your Order; and all, I can tell you of it is, that nothing has lately been better received by the Publick than your part of it; so that, you have only displeas'd the Criticks, by pleasing them, too well; having not left them a word to say, for themselves, against

[1] [The sixth part of Tonson's *Miscellanies* (1709), containing the *Pastorals*]

you, and your ingenious Performances; so that, now your Hand is in, you must persever, till my Prophisys of you, be fulfill'd. In earnest all the best Judges, of good Sense, or Poetry are Admirers of Yours; and like your part of the Book so well, that the rest is lik'd the worse; this is true, (upon my word,) without Compliment; so that the first Success will make you, for all your Life a Poet, in spight of your Wit; for a Poets Success at first, like a Gamesters fortune at first, is like to make him a Lover at last, and so to be undone, by his good fortune, and merit, by being drawn to farther Adventures, of his future Credit, by his first Success.

8. Wycherley's public acclamation

1709

William Wycherley, 'To my Friend, Mr. *POPE*, on his Pastorals', *Poetical Miscellanies: the Sixth Part* [i.e., Tonson's *Miscellany*] (1709), pp. 253–6. Reprinted in Pope's *Works* (1717).

Philips's *Pastorals* open this volume and Pope's *Pastorals* are printed as the last poem. Wycherley's poem is given in the middle along with another poem praising Pope. The charge that Pope in fact forged Wycherley's poem seems to lack substance, though it had a certain contemporary currency: see John Dennis, *Reflections Critical and Satyrical, upon a Late Rhapsody, call'd, an Essay upon Criticism* (*Critical Works*, i. 417), and Charles Gildon, *British Mercury*, 21 January 1712.

> In these more dull, as more censorious Days,
> When few dare give, and fewer merit Praise;
> A Muse sincere, that never Flatt'ry knew,
> Pays what to Friendship and Desert is due.
> Young, yet Judicious; in your Verse are found
> Art strengthning Nature, Sense improv'd by Sound:

Unlike those Wits, whose Numbers glide along
So smooth, no Thought e'er interrupts the Song;
Laboriously enervate they appear,
And write not to the Head, but to the Ear;
Our minds unmov'd and unconcern'd, they lull,
And are, at best, most Musically dull.
So purling Streams with even Murmurs creep,
And hush the heavy Hearers into Sleep.
As smoothest Speech is most deceitful found,
The smoothest Numbers oft are empty Sound,
And leave our lab'ring Fancy quite a-ground.
But Wit and Judgment join at once in you,
Sprightly as Youth, as Age consummate too:
Your strains are Regularly Bold, and please
With unforc'd Care, and unaffected Ease,
With proper Thoughts, and lively *Images*:
Such, as by Nature to the Ancients shown,
Fancy improves, and Judgment makes your own;
For great Men's Fashions to be follow'd are,
Altho' disgraceful 'tis their Clothes to wear.
Some in a polish'd Stile write Pastoral,
Arcadia speaks the Language of the *Mall*,
Like some fair Shepherdess, the *Sylvan* Muse
Deck't in those Flow'rs her native Fields produce,
With modest Charms wou'd in plain Neatness please;
But seems a Dowdy in the Courtly Dress,
Whose aukward Finery allures us less:[1]
But the true Measure of the Shepherd's Wit
Shou'd, like his Garb, be for the Country fit;
Yet must his pure and unaffected Thought
More nicely than the common Swain's be wrought.
So, with becoming Art, the Players dress,
In Silks, the Shepherd and the Shepherdess;
Yet still unchang'd the Form and Mode remain,
Shap'd like the homely Russet of the Swain.
Your rural Muse appears, to Justify
The long-lost Graces of Simplicity;

[1] ['With . . . less': these lines occur in the collected edition of 1717, but are omitted in later editions]

So Rural Beauties captivate our Sense
With Virgin Charms, and Nature's[1] Excellence.
Yet long her Modesty those Charms conceal'd,
'Till by Men's Envy to the World reveal'd;
For Wits industrious to their Trouble seem,
And needs will Envy what they must Esteem.
  Live, and enjoy their Spite! nor mourn that Fate
Which wou'd, if *Virgil* liv'd, on *Virgil* wait;
Whose Muse did once, like thine, in Plains delight;
Thine shall, like his, soon take a higher Flight;
So Larks which first from lowly Fields arise,
Mount by degrees, and reach at last the Skies.

9. Pope compares himself with Philips

1713

Alexander Pope (anonymously), *The Guardian*, no. 40, 27 April 1713.

For the background to this witty *jeu' d'esprit*, see Introduction, p. 9.

Compulerantque Greges Corydon & Thyrsis in unum,
Ex illo Corydon, Corydon est tempore nobis.[2]

I Designed to have troubled the Reader with no farther Discourses of
Pastorals, but being informed that I am taxed of Partiality in not mentioning an Author, whose Eclogues are published in the same Volume
with Mr. *Philips*'s; I shall employ this Paper in Observations upon him,

---

[1] ['Nature's' in *Miscellany* (1709) and collected poems of 1717; later editions have 'native']

[2] [Virgil, *Eclogues*, vii. 2 with a line added by Pope: 'Corydon and Thyrsis gathered their flocks together. From that Corydon comes a Corydon of our time']

written in the free Spirit of Criticism, and without Apprehension of offending that Gentleman, whose Character it is, that he takes the greatest Care of his Works before they are published, and has the least Concern for them afterwards.

I have laid it down as the first Rule of Pastoral, that its Idea should be taken from the Manners of the *Golden Age*, and the Moral form'd upon the Representation of Innocence; 'tis therefore plain that any Deviations from that Design degrade a Poem from being true Pastoral. In this view it will appear that *Virgil* can only have two of his Eclogues allowed to be such: His First and Ninth must be rejected because they describe the Ravages of Armies, and Oppressions of the Innocent; *Corydon*'s Criminal Passion for *Alexis* throws out the Second; the Calumny and Railing in the Third are not proper to that State of Concord; the Eighth represents unlawful Ways of procuring Love by Inchantments, and introduces a Shepherd whom an inviting Precipice tempts to Self-Murder. As to the Fourth, Sixth, and Tenth, they are given up by *Heinsius Salmasius, Rapin*,[1] and the Criticks in general. They likewise observe that but eleven of all the *Idyllia* of *Theocritus* are to be admitted as Pastorals; and even out of that Number the greater Part will be excluded for one or other of the Reasons above mentioned. So that when I remark'd in a former Paper, that *Virgil*'s Eclogues, taken all together, are rather *Select Poems* than *Pastorals*; I might have said the same thing, with no less Truth, of *Theocritus*. The Reason of this I take to be yet unobserved by the Criticks, *viz. They never meant them all for Pastorals.* Which it is plain *Philips* hath done, and in that Particular excelled both *Theocritus* and *Virgil*.

As Simplicity is the distinguishing Characteristick of Pastoral, *Virgil* hath been thought guilty of too Courtly a Stile; his Language is perfectly pure, and he often forgets he is among Peasants. I have frequently wonder'd that since he was so conversant in the Writings of *Ennius*, he had not imitated the Rusticity of the *Doric*, as well, by the help of the old obsolete *Roman* Language, as *Philips* hath by the antiquated *English*: For Example, might he not have said *Quoi* instead of *Cui*; *Quoijum* for *Cujum*; *volt* for *vult* &c. as well as our Modern hath *Welladay* for *Alas*, *Whilome* for *of Old*, *make mock* for *deride*, and *witless Younglings* for *simple Lambs*, &c. by which Means he hath attained as much of the Air of *Theocritus*, as *Philips* hath of *Spencer*.

Mr. *Pope* hath fallen into the same Error with *Virgil*. His Clowns do not converse in all the Simplicity proper to the Country: His Names

---

[1] See [René] Rapin *de* Carm[ina] Past[orali] *pars* 3.

are borrow'd from *Theocritus* and *Virgil*, which are improper to the Scene of his Pastorals. He introduces *Daphnis*, *Alexis* and *Thyrsis* on British Plains, as *Virgil* had done before him on the *Mantuan*; whereas *Philips*, who hath the strictest Regard to Propriety, makes choice of Names peculiar to the Country, and more agreeable to a Reader of Delicacy; such as *Hobbinol*, *Lobbin*, *Cuddy*, and *Colin Clout*.

So easie as Pastoral Writing may seem, (in the Simplicity we have described it) yet it requires *great Reading*, both of the *Ancient* and *Moderns*, to be a Master of it. *Philips* hath given us manifest Proofs of his Knowledge of Books; it must be confessed his Competitor hath imitated some single Thoughts of the Ancients well enough, if we consider he had not the Happiness of an University Education; but he hath dispersed them, here and there, without that Order and Method which Mr. *Philips* observes, whose whole third Pastoral is an Instance how well he hath studied the fifth of *Virgil*, and how judiciously reduced *Virgil*'s Thoughts to the Standard of Pastoral; as his Contention of *Colin Clout* and the *Nightingale*, shows with what Exactness he hath imitated *Strada*.

When I remarked it as a principal Fault to introduce Fruits and Flowers of a Foreign Growth, in Descriptions where the Scene lies in our Country, I did not design that Observation should extend also to Animals, or the Sensitive Life; for *Philips* hath with great Judgment described *Wolves* in *England* in his first Pastoral. Nor would I have a Poet slavishly confine himself (as Mr. *Pope* hath done) to one particular Season of the Year, one certain Time of the Day, and one unbroken Scene in each Eclogue. 'Tis plain *Spencer* neglected this Pedantry, who in his Pastoral of *November* mentions the mournful Song of the Nightingale:

Sad Philomel *her Song in Tears doth steep.* [l. 141.]

And Mr. *Philips*, by a Poetical Creation, hath raised up finer Beds of Flowers than the most industrious Gardiner; his Roses, Lillies and Daffadils blow in the same Season.

But the better to discover the Merits of our two Contemporary Pastoral Writers, I shall endeavour to draw a Parallel of them, by setting several of their particular Thoughts in the same light, whereby it will be obvious how much *Philips* hath the Advantage. With what Simplicity he introduces two Shepherds singing alternately:

Hobb. Come, *Rosalind*, O come, for without thee
What Pleasure can the Country have for me:

Come, *Rosalind*, O come; my brinded Kine,
My snowy Sheep, my Farm, and all is thine.
Lanq. Come *Rosalind*, O come; here shady Bowers
Here are cool Fountains, and here springing Flow'rs.
Come, *Rosalind*; Here ever let us stay,
And sweetly waste our live-long Time away.
[Philips, vi. 93–100.]

Our other Pastoral Writer, in expressing the same Thought, deviates
into downright Poetry.

Streph. In Spring the Fields, in Autumn Hills I love,
At Morn the Plains, at Noon the shady Grove,
But *Delia* always; forc'd from *Delia*'s Sight,
Nor Plains at Morn, nor Groves at Noon delight.
Daph.   *Sylvia*'s like Autumn ripe, yet mild as May,
More bright than Noon, yet fresh as early Day;
Ev'n Spring displeases, when she shines not here,
But blest with her, 'tis Spring throughout the Year.
[Pope, i. 77–84.]

In the first of these Authors, two Shepherds thus innocently describe
the Behaviour of their Mistresses.

Hobb. As *Marian* bath'd, by chance I passed by.
She blush'd, and at me cast a side-long Eye:
Then swift beneath the Cristal Wave she try'd
Her beauteous Form, but all in vain, to hide.
Lanq. As I to cool me bath'd one sultry Day,
Fond *Lydia* lurking in the Sedges lay.
The Wanton laugh'd, and seem'd in Haste to fly;
Yet often stopp'd, and often turn'd her Eye.
[Philips, vi. 77–84.]

The other Modern (who it must be confessed hath a knack of Versifying)
hath it as follows.

Streph. Me gentle *Delia* beckons from the Plain,
Then, hid in Shades, eludes her eager Swain;
But feigns a Laugh, to see me search around,
And by that Laugh the willing Fair is found.
Daph.   The sprightly *Sylvia* trips along the Green,
She runs, but hopes she does not run unseen;

> While a kind Glance at her Pursuer flyes,
> How much at Variance are her Feet and Eyes!
>
> [Pope, i. 53–60.]

There is nothing the Writers of this kind of Poetry are fonder of, than Descriptions of Pastoral Presents. *Philips* says thus of a Sheephook.

> Of Season'd Elm; where Studs of Brass appear,
> To speak the Giver's Name, the Month and Year.
> The Hook of polish'd Steel, the Handle turn'd,
> And richly by the Graver's Skill adorn'd.
>
> [Philips, iv. 147–50.]

The other of a Bowl embossed with Figures.

> —— —— where wanton Ivy twines,
> And swelling Clusters bend the curling Vines;
> Four Figures rising from the Work appear,
> The various Seasons of the rolling Year;
> And what is That which binds the radiant Sky,
> Where twelve bright Signs in beauteous Order lie.
>
> [Pope, i. 35–40.]

The Simplicity of the Swain in this Place, who forgets the Name of the *Zodiack*, is no ill Imitation of *Virgil*; but how much more plainly and unaffectedly would *Philips* have dressed this Thought in his *Doric*?

> And what That hight, which girds the Welkin sheen,
> Where twelve gay Signs in meet array are seen.

If the Reader would indulge his Curiosity any farther in the Comparison of Particulars, he may read the first Pastoral of *Philips* with the second of his Contemporary, and the fourth and sixth of the former, with the fourth and first of the latter; where several Parallel Places will occur to every one.

Having now shown some Parts, in which these two Writers may be compared, it is a Justice I owe to Mr. *Philips*, to discover those in which no Man can compare with him. First, that *beautiful Rusticity*, of which I shall only produce two Instances, out of a hundred not yet quoted.

> O woful Day! O Day of Woe, quoth he,
> And woful I, who live the Day to see!

That Simplicity of Diction, the Melancholy Flowing of the Numbers,

the Solemnity of the Sound, and the easie Turn of the Words, in this
Dirge (to make use of our Author's Expression) are extreamly Elegant.
  In another of his Pastorals, a Shepherd utters a *Dirge* not much inferior
to the former, in the following Lines.

> Ah me the while! ah me! the luckless Day,
> Ah luckless Lad! the rather might I say;
> Ah silly I! more silly than my Sheep,
> Which on the flowry Plains I once did keep.
>
> > [Philips, ii. 63–68, abridged.]

How he still Charms the Ear with these artful Repetitions of the
Epithets; and how significant is the last Verse! I defie the most common
Reader to repeat them, without feeling some Motions of Compassion.
  In the next Place I shall rank his *Proverbs*, in which I formerly ob-
served he excels: For Example,

> A rolling Stone is ever bare of Moss;
> And, to their Cost, green Years old Proverbs cross.
>
> > [*Ibid.*, ii. 85–86.]

> —— He that late lyes down, as late will rise,
> And, Sluggard like, till Noon-day snoaring lyes.
>
> > [*Ibid.*, iv. 171–72.]

> Against *Ill-Luck* all cunning Fore-sight fails;
> Whether we sleep or wake it nought avails.   [*Ibid.*, 61–62.]

> ——Nor fear, from *upright* Sentence, *Wrong.*   [*Ibid.*, vi. 16.]

Lastly, His *Elegant Dialect*, which alone might prove him the eldest
Born of *Spencer*, and our only true *Arcadian*; I should think proper for
the several Writers of Pastoral, to confine themselves to their several
Counties. Spencer seems to have been of this Opinion; for he hath laid
the Scene of one of his Pastorals in *Wales*, where with all the Simplicity
natural to that Part of our Island, one Shepherd bids the other *Good-
morrow* in an unusual and elegant Manner.

> *Diggon Davy*, I bid hur God-day:
> Or *Diggon* hur is, or I mis say.

Diggon answers,

> Hur was hur while it was Day-light;
> But now hur is a most wretched Wight, &c.[1]

[1] [*Shepheardes Calendar*, September, ll. 1–4]

But the most beautiful Example of this kind that I ever met with, is in a very valuable Piece, which I chanced to find among some old Manuscripts, entituled, *A Pastoral Ballad*; which I think, for its Nature and Simplicity, may (notwithstanding the Modesty of the Title) be allowed a Perfect Pastoral: It is composed in the *Somersetshire* Dialect, and the Names such as are proper to the Country People. It may be observed, as a further Beauty of this Pastoral, the Words *Nymph, Dryad, Naiad, Fawn, Cupid,* or *Satyr,* are not once mentioned through the whole. I shall make no Apology for inserting some few Lines of this excellent Piece. *Sicily* breaks thus into the Subject, as she is going a Milking;

> Cicily. *Rager* go vetch tha Kee,[1] or else tha Zun,
>   Will quite be go, be vore c'have half a don.
> Roger. Thou shouldst not ax ma tweece, but I've a be
>   To dreave our Bull to Bull tha Parson's Kee.

It is to be observed, that this whole Dialogue is formed upon the Passion of Jealousie; and his mentioning the Parson's Kine naturally revives the Jealousie of the Shepherdess *Sicily,* which she expresses as follows:

> Cicily. Ah *Rager, Rager,* chez was zore avraid
>   Ween in yond Vield you kiss'd tha Parson's Maid:
>   Is this the Love that once to me you zed
>   When from tha Wake thou brought'st me Ginger-bread?
> Roger. *Cicily* thou charg'st me false,——I'll zwear to thee,
>   The Parson's Maid is still a Maid for me.

In which Answer of his are express'd at once that *Spirit of Religion,* and that *Innocence of the Golden Age,* so necessary to be observed by all Writers of Pastoral.

At the Conclusion of this Piece, the Author reconciles the Lovers, and ends the Eclogue the most simply in the World.

> So *Rager* parted vor to vetch tha Kee,
>   And vor her Bucket in went *Cicily.*

I am loth to show my Fondness for Antiquity so far as to prefer this Ancient *British* Author to our present *English* Writers of Pastoral; but I cannot avoid making this obvious Remark, that both *Spencer* and *Philips* have hit into the same Road with this old *West Country* Bard of ours.

[1] That is the *Kine* or *Cows.*

After all that hath been said, I hope none can think it any Injustice to Mr. *Pope*, that I forbore to mention him as a Pastoral Writer; since upon the Whole he is of the same Class with *Moschus* and *Bion*, whom we have excluded that Rank; and of whose Eclogues, as well as some of *Virgil's*, it may be said, that according to the Description we have given of this sort of Poetry, they are by no means *Pastorals*, but *something Better*.

AN ESSAY ON CRITICISM

10. Dennis's first attack on Pope

June 1711

John Dennis, from *Reflections Critical and Satyrical, upon a late Rhapsody, call'd, An Essay upon Criticism* (1711), in *Critical Works*, i. 396–414. The *Reflections* were published 20–9 June.

For Pope's manuscript notes towards revisions of the *Essay* to meet some of Dennis's objections, see Twickenham, i. 482–4. Further see J. V. Guerinot, *Pamphlet Attacks on Alexander Pope 1711–1744* (1969), pp. 5–11.

A most notorious Instance of [contemporary] Depravity of Genius and Tast, is the Essay upon which the following Reflections are writ, and the Approbation which it has met with. I will not deny but that there are two or three Passages in it with which I am not displeas'd; but what are two or three Passages as to the whole? . . . The approving two or Three Passages amongst a multitude of bad ones, is by no means advantageous to an Author. That little that is good in him does but set off its contrary, and make it appear more extravagant. The Thoughts, Expressions, and Numbers of this Essay are for the most part but very indifferent, and indifferent and execrable in Poetry are all one. But what is worse than all the rest, we find throughout the whole a deplorable want of that very Quality, which ought principally to appear in it, which is Judgment; and I have no Notion that where there is so great a want of Judgment, there can be any Genius. . . .

[After an introduction, from which the preceding is taken, Dennis prints a long letter he had written on *An Essay on Criticism* 'To Mr —— at Sunning-Hill, Berks.,' of which the following is part.]

. . . I am inclin'd to believe that it was writ by some young, or some raw Author, for the following Reasons.

First, He discovers in every Page a Sufficiency that is far beyond his little Ability; and hath rashly undertaken a Task which is infinitely above his Force; a Task that is only fit for the Author, with the just Encomium of whose Essay my Lord *Roscommon* begins his own.[1]

> Happy that Author whose correct Essay
> Repairs so well our old *Horatian* way.

There is nothing more wrong, more low, or more incorrect than this Rhapsody upon Criticism. The Author all along taxes others with Faults of which he is more guilty himself. He tells us in the very two first Lines, that

> 'Tis hard to say if greater want of Skill
> Appear in writing, or in judging ill.

Now whereas others have been at some Pains and Thought to shew each of these wants of Skill separately and distinctly, his comprehensive Soul hath most ingeniously contriv'd to shew them both in a supreme Degree together.

Secondly, While this little Author struts and affects the Dictatorian Air, he plainly shews that at the same time he is under the Rod; and that while he pretends to give Laws to others, he is himself a pedantick Slave to Authority and Opinion. . . .

But a third infallible mark of a young Author, is, that he hath done in this Essay what School-boys do by their Exercises, he hath borrow'd both from Living and Dead, and particularly from the Authors of the two famous Essays upon Poetry and Translated Verse; but so borrow'd, that he seems to have the very Reverse of *Midas*'s noble Faculty. For as the coursest and the dullest Metals, were upon the touch of that *Lydian* Monarch immediately chang'd into fine Gold; so the finest Gold upon this Author's handling it, in a moment loses both its lustre and its weight, and is immediately turn'd to Lead.

A fourth thing that shews him a young man, is the not knowing his own mind, and his frequent Contradictions of himself. His Title seems to promise an Essay upon Criticism in general, which afterwards dwindles to an Essay upon Criticism in Poetry. And after all, he is all

[1] [Roscommon's *Essay on Translated Verse* (1684) begins by praising Mulgrave's *Essay upon Poetry* (1682)]

along giving Rules, such as they are, for Writing rather than Judging.
In the beginning of the 8th Page the Rules are nothing but Nature.

> These Rules of old discover'd, not devis'd,
> Are Nature still, but Nature methodiz'd.   [ll. 88–9]

But no sooner is he come to the 10th Page, but the Rules and Nature are
two different things.¹

> When first great *Maro*, in his boundless mind,
> A Work t' outlast immortal *Rome* design'd,
> Perhaps he seem'd above the Critick's Law,
> And but from Nature's Fountains scorn'd to draw.
>
>   [ll. 130–3]

But in the last Line of this very Paragraph they are the same things again.

> Learn hence for ancient Rules a just Esteem,
> To copy Nature is to copy them.   [ll. 139–40]

But to this he will answer, That he is guilty of no Contradiction, that he
is only shewing that *Virgil* was guilty of Error and Ignorance; who first
absurdly began to write his *Æneis*, and afterwards sate down to learn the
Rules of Writing; which when he began to write that Poem, he took to
be things distinct from Nature; but that after he had wrote part of it, he
fell to the reading of *Homer*, and that undeceiv'd him. That while he is
talking of *Virgil*'s Error and Ignorance, he is making a Parade of his
own incomparable Wisdom and Knowledge; and not contradicting
himself, but *Virgil*, or rather making him appear inconsistent with and
contradicting himself: for that tho' *Virgil* took the Rules and Nature to be
distinct from each other, for his own part he is wiser, and knows better
things. Now is not this a very modest and a very judicious Gentleman? . . .

But now, my dear Friend, if I had young Mr. *Bays* here, I would
desire that I might ask him one Question, and he not be angry. And
that is, what he means by

> There are whom Heav'n has bless'd with store of Wit,
> Yet want as much again to manage it.²   [ll. 80–1]

¹ [In 1713 Pope altered the first two lines to meet Dennis's strictures. See Twickenham,
i. 254n, 483. There is a manuscript memorandum by Pope detailing his response to the
strictures of Dennis and others]

² [In 1744 Pope altered this couplet to read: 'Some, to whom Heav'n in wit has been
profuse, / Want as much more, to turn it to its use']

But let us go on, and see if 'tis possible to find it out without him.

> For Wit and Judgment ever are at strife,
> Tho' meant each others, are like Man and Wife.[1]

[ll. 82–3]

That is as much as to say, there are People who have that which they call Wit, without one dram of Judgment. Is not this another wonderful Discovery? But I fancy that Mr. *Bays* has the Misfortune to be wrong in the first Verse of the foresaid Couplet.

> For Wit and Judgment ever are at strife.

What a Devil, Mr. *Bays*, they cannot be at strife sure, after they are parted, after Wit has made an Elopement, or has been barbarously forsaken by Judgment, or turn'd to separate maintenance! Much less can they be at strife where they never came together, which is the Case in the Essay. But now we talk of Man and Wife, let us consider the Yoke-fellow to the former Rhime.

> Tho' meant each others, and like Man and Wife.

Now cannot I for my Soul conceive the reciprocal *Aid* that there is between Wit and Judgment. For tho' I can easily conceive how Judgment may keep Wit in her Senses, yet cannot I possibly understand how Wit can controul, or redress, or be a help to Judgment.

If Mr. *Bays* in that Couplet

> There are whom Heav'n has bless'd with store of Wit,
> Yet want as much again to manage it.

Intended to say that People have sometimes store of false Wit without Judgment to manage it, he intended nothing but what all the World knew before.[2] But if he meant to say this of true Wit, nothing can be more mistaken; for I cannot conceive how any one can have store of Wit without Judgment. I believe that Father *Bouhours* has given a

---

[1] [Dennis misquotes: l. 83 should read 'other's Aid'. A few lines later Dennis gives 'others, *and*'. In 1744 Pope altered l. 82 to read, 'For Wit and Judgment often are at strife'. See J. V. Guerinot, *Pamphlet Attacks on Alexander Pope 1711–1744* (1969), p. 8]

[2] [In the second edition (1713) Pope altered this to read, 'And *speak*, tho' *sure*, with seeming *Diffidence*']

tolerable Description of Wit in his Treatise upon that Subject, *C'es un solide qui brille:* 'Tis a shining Solid, like a Diamond, which the more solid it is, is always the more glittering; and derives its height of Lustre from its perfect Solidity.' Now how any thing in the Works of the Mind can be solid without Judgment, I leave Mr. *Bays* to consider....

In the 20ᵗʰ Page we have another Simile, and consequently another Absurdity.

> But true Expression, like th' unchanging Sun,
> Clears and improves whate'er it shines upon.   [ll. 315–16]

Which is borrow'd from the Essay on Poetry.

> True Wit is everlasting like the Sun,[1]

But awkwardly borrow'd, and utterly spoil'd in the removal. For what can Expression be properly said to shine upon? True Wit, or Genius; for that the noble Author means, as is plain from several parts of his Poem, shines thro' and discovers it self by the Expression; but Expression, at the very best, can but shine with a borrow'd Light, like the Moon and the rest of the Planets, whereas Genius shines and flames with its own Celestial Fire....

Wherever this Gentleman talks of Wit, he is sure to say something that is very foolish, as Page 29.

> What is this Wit that does our Cares employ,
> The Owner's Wife that other Men enjoy?
> The more his Trouble as the more admir'd,
> Where wanted scorn'd, and envy'd where acquir'd.[2]
>
> [ll. 500–3]

Here again I desire leave to ask two or three Questions. First, how can Wit be scorn'd where it is not? Is not this a Figure frequently employ'd in *Hibernian* Land? The Person who wants this Wit may indeed be scorn'd; but such a Contempt declares the Honour that the Contemner has for Wit. But secondly, what does he mean by acquir'd Wit? Does he mean Genius by the word Wit, or Conceit and Point? If he means Genius, that is certainly never to be acquir'd; and the Person who should

---

[1] [Earl of Mulgrave, *Essay on Poetry* (1682), *Critical Essays of the Seventeenth Century*, ed. J. E. Spingarn (1908), ii. 294]

[2] [Pope altered these lines. The 1744 version reads, 'Then most our *Trouble* still when most *admir'd*, / And still the more we *give*, the more *requir'd*'. See Twickenham, i. 295, 483, and J. V. Guerinot, *Pamphlet Attacks on Pope 1711–1744* (1969), pp. 8–9]

pretend to acquire it, would be always secure from Envy. But if by Wit
he means Conceit and Point, those are things that ought never to be in
Poetry, unless by chance sometimes in the Epigram, or in Comedy,
where it is proper to the Character and the Occasion; and ev'n in
Comedy it ought always to give place to Humour, and ev'n to be lost
and absorp'd in that, according to the Precept of the noble Author of the
Essay of Poetry.

> That silly thing Men call sheer Wit avoid,
> With which our Age so nauseously is cloy'd;
> Humour is all, Wit should be only brought
> To turn agreeably some proper Thought.[1]

In the beginning of the 33[d] Page there is a Couplet of Advice, the
first line of which is very impertinent, and the second very wrong.

> Be silent always when you doubt your Sense. [l. 566]

Now who are the Persons to whom he is giving Advice here? Why, to
Poets or Criticks, or both; but the Persons to whom he ought to be
speaking are Criticks, that is, People who pretend to instruct others.
But can any man of common Sense want to be told, that he ought not to
pretend to instruct others, as long as he doubts of the Truth of his own
Precepts?

But what can be more wrong or more absurd than the latter Verse of
the Couplet?

> Speak when you're sure, yet speak with Diffidence.[2] [l. 567]

Now I should think that when a man is sure, 'tis his Duty to speak with a
modest Assurance; since in doing otherwise he betrays the Truth,
especially when he speaks to those who are guided more by Imagination
than they are by Judgment, which is the Case of three parts of the
World, and three parts of the other Part. . . .

Thus are his Assertions, and his Precepts frequently false or trivial, or
both, his Thoughts very often crude and abortive, his Expressions
absurd, his Numbers often harsh and unmusical, without Cadence and
without Variety, his Rhimes trivial and common. He dictates perpetually, and pretends to give Law without any thing of the Simplicity

[1] [Earl of Mulgrave, *Essay upon Poetry, loc. cit.*]
[2] [See Twickenham, i. 305, 483, and J. V. Guerinot, *op. cit.*, p. 9]

or Majesty of a Legislator, and pronounces Sentence without any thing of the Plainness or Clearness, or Gravity of a Judge. Instead of Simplicity we have little Conceit and Epigram, and Affectation. Instead of Majesty we have something that is very mean, and instead of Gravity we have something that is very boyish. And instead of Perspicuity and lucid Order, we have but too often Obscurity and Confusion. . . .

11. Addison on *An Essay on Criticism*

December 1711

Joseph Addison, *The Spectator*, no. 253, 20 December 1711, ed. D. Bond (1965), ii. 481–6.

> *Indignor quicquam reprehendi, non quia crassè*
> *Compositum, illepidève putetur, sed quia nuper.*[1]

THERE is nothing which more denotes a great Mind, than the abhorrence of Envy and Detraction. This Passion reigns more among Bad Poets, than among any other Set of Men.

As there are none more ambitious of Fame, than those who are conversant in Poetry, it is very natural for such as have not succeeded in it to depreciate the Works of those who have. For since they cannot raise themselves to the Reputation of their Fellow-Writers, they must endeavour to sink it to their own Pitch, if they would still keep themselves upon a Level with them.

The greatest Wits that ever were produced in one Age, lived together in so good an Understanding, and celebrated one another with so much Generosity, that each of them receives an additional Lustre from his Contemporaries, and is more famous for having lived with Men of so extraordinary a Genius, than if he had himself been the sole Wonder of

---

[1] [Horace, *Epistles*, II. i. 76–77: 'I hate a Fop should scorn a *faultless* Page,/ Because 'tis *New*, nor yet approv'd by Age' (Creech)]

the Age. I need not tell my Reader, that I here point at the Reign of *Augustus*, and I believe he will be of my Opinion, that neither *Virgil* nor *Horace* would have gained so great a Reputation in the World, had they not been the Friends and Admirers of each other. Indeed all the great Writers of that Age, for whom singly we have so great an Esteem, stand up together as Vouchers for one another's Reputation. But at the same time that *Virgil* was celebrated by *Gallus, Propertius, Horace, Varius, Tucca* and *Ovid*, we know that *Bavius* and *Mævius* were his declared Foes and Calumniators.

In our own Country a Man seldom sets up for a Poet, without attacking the Reputation of all his Brothers in the Art. The Ignorance of the Moderns, the Scriblers of the Age, the Decay of Poetry are the Topicks of Detraction, with which he makes his Entrance into the World: But how much more noble is the Fame that is built on Candour and Ingenuity, according to those Beautiful Lines of Sir *John Denham*, in his Poem on *Fletcher*'s Works.

> But whither am I straid? I need not raise
> Trophies to thee from other Mens Dispraise;
> Nor is thy Fame on lesser Ruins built,
> Nor needs thy juster Title the foul Guilt
> Of Eastern Kings, who to secure their Reign
> Must have their Brothers, Sons, and Kindred Slain.[1]

I am sorry to find that an Author, who is very justly esteemed among the best Judges, has admitted some Stroaks of this Nature into a very fine Poem, I mean *The Art of Criticism*, which was published some Months since, and is a Master-piece in its kind. The Observations follow one another like those in *Horace*'s *Art of Poetry*, without that Methodical Regularity which would have been requisite in a Prose Author. They are some of them uncommon, but such as the Reader must assent to, when he sees them explained with that Elegance and Perspicuity in which they are delivered. As for those which are the most known, and the most received, they are placed in so beautiful a Light, and illustrated with such apt Allusions, that they have in them all the Graces of Novelty, and make the Reader, who was before acquainted with them, still more convinced of their Truth and Solidity. And here give me leave to mention what Monsieur *Boileau* has so very well enlarged upon in the Preface to his Works, that Wit and fine Writing doth not consist so much in advancing things that are new, as in giving things that are known

[1] ['On Mr John Fletcher's Works', ll. 19–24]

an agreeable Turn.[1] It is impossible, for us who live in the later Ages of the World, to make Observations in Criticism, Morality, or in any Art or Science, which have not been touched upon by others. We have little else left us, but to represent the common Sense of Mankind in more strong, more beautiful, or more uncommon Lights. If a Reader examines *Horace*'s Art of Poetry, he will find but very few Precepts in it, which he may not meet with in *Aristotle*, and which were not commonly known by all the Poets of the Augustan Age. His way of Expressing and Applying them, not his Invention of them, is what we are chiefly to admire.

For this reason I think there is nothing in the World so tiresom as the Works of those Criticks, who write in a positive Dogmatick Way, without either Language, Genius or Imagination. If the Reader would see how the best of the *Latin* Criticks writ, he may find their manner very beautifully described in the Characters of *Horace*, *Petronius*, *Quintilian* and *Longinus*, as they are drawn in the Essay of which I am now speaking.

Since I have mentioned *Longinus*, who in his Reflections has given us the same kind of Sublime, which he observes in the several Passages that occasioned them;[2] I cannot but take notice, that our *English* Author has after the same manner exemplified several of his Precepts in the very Precepts themselves. I shall produce two or three Instances of this kind. Speaking of the insipid Smoothness which some Readers are so much in love with, he has the following Verses.

> These *Equal Syllables* alone require,
> Tho' oft the Ear the *open Vowels* tire,
> While *Expletives* their feeble Aid *do* join,
> And ten low Words oft creep in one dull Line.[3]

The gaping of the Vowels in the second Line, the Expletive *do* in the third, and the ten Monosyllables in the fourth, give such a Beauty to this Passage, as would have been very much admired in an Ancient Poet. The Reader may observe the following Lines in the same View.

> A *needless Alexandrine* ends the Song,
> That like a wounded Snake, drags its slow Length along.[4]

[1] [Cf. the Preface to Boileau's *Œuvres* (1701) (*Œuvres*, ed. Berriat-Saint-Prix, [Paris, 1837], i. 19–20)]
[2] [Cf. the Preface to Boileau's translation of Longinus (1674) and *The Spectator*, no. 103]
[3] [*An Essay on Criticism*, ll. 344–7]
[4] [*Ibid.*, ll. 356–7]

And afterwards,

> 'Tis not enough no Harshness gives Offence,
> The *Sound* must seem an *Eccho* to the *Sense*.
> *Soft* is the Strain when *Zephir* gently blows,
> And the *smooth Stream* in *smoother Numbers* flows
> But when loud Surges lash the sounding Shore,
> The *hoarse, rough Verse* shou'd like the *Torrent* roar.
> When *Ajax* strives, some Rock's vast Weight to throw,
> The Line too *labours*, and the Words move *slow*;
> Not so, when swift *Camilla* scours the Plain,
> Flies o'er th'unbending Corn, and skims along the Main.

[ll. 364–73]

The beautiful Distich upon *Ajax* in the foregoing Lines, puts me in mind of a Description in *Homer*'s Odyssey,[1] which none of the Criticks have taken notice of.[2] It is where *Sisiphus* is represented lifting his Stone up the Hill, which is no sooner carried to the Top of it, but it immediately tumbles to the Bottom. This double Motion of the Stone is admirably described in the Numbers of these Verses. As in the four first it is heaved up by several *Spondees*, intermixed with proper Breathing-places, and at last trundles down in a continued Line of *Dactyls*.

[Quotes in Greek, *Odyssey*, xi. 593–8]

It would be endless to quote Verses out of *Virgil* which have this particular kind of Beauty in the Numbers; but I may take an Occasion in a future Paper to shew several of them which have escaped the Observation of others.

I cannot conclude this Paper without taking notice that we have three Poems in our Tongue, which are of the same Nature, and each of them a Master-piece in its kind; the Essay on Translated Verse, the Essay on the Art of Poetry, and the Essay upon Criticism.[3]

---

[1] [This passage, *Odyssey*, xi. 593–8, is discussed by Campbell (No. 124) and Johnson, pp. 495–6]

[2] [Bond points out that Pope wrote to Addison on 10 October 1714, and cited a discussion of the passage by Dion of Halicarnassus]

[3] [I.e. *Essay on Translated Verse* (1684) by Wentworth Dillon, Earl of Roscommon, and the *Essay upon Poetry* (1682) by John Sheffield, Duke of Buckingham]

12. Gildon's first attack on Pope

1711

Charles Gildon, extract from *British Mercury*, 24 December 1711, quoted by J. Honoré, 'Charles Gildon redacteur du *British Mercury* (1711–12): les attaques contre Pope, Swift et les Wits', *Études Anglaises*, xv (1962), 356–7.

Gildon (1665–1724) was a hack writer, whose connection with the *British Mercury* was not known until Honoré discovered manuscript evidence. The 'thing on Wycherley' which started Pope's animosity towards Gildon's 'venal quill' is probably an attack in the issue for 21 January 1712 (see Honoré, *op. cit.*, p. 357).

In the passage given here Gildon replies to Addison's praise of *An Essay on Criticism* (No. 11). For another attack by Gildon, see No. 19.

[Horace is complaining to Apollo of the affront to his art contained in Addison's praise of Pope]

But unweary'd with provoking us, he, with his wonted Air of intimate Acquaintance with us, has drawn me in against my self in the Motto to his last Thursday's Harangue. For whereas I condemn'd those Coxcombs of my Time, who despis'd the best Performances only because new, he, in my Words, would commend a Poem that was read only for being new; and by an overflowing good Nature, stretches the Maxim of speaking well of the Dead, to a Panegyric on the Damn'd. And this, without the Fear either of you his Sovereign Lord, or the Censure of the *Plain-dealer* on my Lord *Plausible*, as being *so fond of Flattery, that rather than not flatter, he would flatter the Poets of the Age, whom no Body else will flatter*.[1] He endeavours, in this Libel on me, to shelter this Poem, call'd *An Essay on Criticism*, under my Protection, for a few good Lines (if we allow those quoted to be so) tho' he might have remembered what I said of Choerilus.

---

[1] [William Wycherley, *The Plain Dealer*, II. i. In fact, spoken by Olivia about Novel]

Sic, mihi qui multum cessat, fit Choerilus *ille*
Quem bis terque bonum, cum Risu miror.[1]

I fear, if his Friend were to stand the Test of that *Poetaster*, the Vanity of this Panegyric would vanish in the Apprehension of the Buffets; which would so vastly outnumber the Pieces of Gold, that these would scarcely pay for the Cure: But the Notions of the *Athenians* and the *Spectator*, seem extreamly unlike. They would not suffer the Number of his ill Verses, to rob him of the Reward of six Pieces of Gold for his six good Verses; nor would they let the six good Verses save the Poem from merited Damnation, or the Poetaster from a Buffet for every bad one. If a few good Lines, among a Crowd of bad ones, made a Poet, why are *Taylor* and *Cleeveland* excluded the Number?

13. Aaron Hill 'improves' *An Essay on Criticism*

1738

Aaron Hill, from a letter to Pope, 11 May 1738, *Corresp.*, iv. 96–9.

See further, Hill to Pope, 28 January 1730/1, and Pope's reply to the quoted letter, 9 June 1738, *Corresp.* Hill (1685–1750), minor poet, essayist, and dramatist, had a long and uneasy relationship with Pope. It started in 1718 when Pope commented adversely on Hill's poem, *The Northern Star*, and followed a pattern of alternative estrangement and friendliness. Hill's friendship, accompanied by his prolix letters, must have been as trying as his enmity. For a later comment by Hill, see No. 89a.

When such a writer as *you*, for example, took a resolution of describing the swiftness of *Camilla*,[2] under the most agile hyperbole of lightness;

[1] [*Ars Poetica*, ll. 357–8: 'so the poet who often defaults, becomes methinks, another Choerilus, whose one or two good lines cause laughter and surprise']
[2] [*An Essay on Criticism*, l. 372]

even to her treading upon *cornstalks*, without *bowing* them; nobody can doubt, but your meaning, in such a description, must have been, that she *skimm'd* the scarce-touch'd plain, she *flew over*;—yet, when, on the contrary, your expression says, that she *scours* it—that unwary mis-use of one word, checks the speed of your airy idea, and presents to the fancy, a quite opposing image of *pressure, attrition*, and *adherence*: And thus, by admitting even a single monosyllable, that concurs not in the general idea, you was so warmly conveying to the *reader*, it arrests the velocity you had in your view, with as sure and as sudden effect, as the *leaden death* did your *larks* in the *forest*, when they so beautifully left their little lives, in air, to the never-dying applause of the marksman who shot them.

You may reply, (I mean, any body, but you might reply) that, by the metaphorical sense of the word *scours*, as applied, in this place to *Camilla*, we ought to understand nothing more, than her rushing violently over the surface: It is true; but in that very violence, you will have discovered, by this time, the disagreement between your intent and expression: Let us only imagine we see her charging, at the head of her squadrons, or pursuing the disarray of an enemy; and, in a moment, it becomes elegant to say, she is *scouring the plain*; because military rapidity, including ideas of insult and hostility, must be supposed to *lay waste*, while it passes; so that what, in one case, is *propriety*, becomes but *obstruction*, in the other, being mis-applied to velocity, independent of force; where it ought to have been simply considered as *swiftness*. A writer of *your* rank, will never be capable of condemning such instances as these, under the thin plausibility of their being trifling, and verbal remarks; for, since your only design, in the place this is drawn from, was to instruct, by an example, how to paint *things* in *words*; such a word as defaces the very idea, you proposed to imprint, was an error, in the actual foundation, and must, in consequence, throw down the building. Besides, as the chief point here in view, was the structure or *sound* of your verse, with purpose to make it, in your own fine expression, an *echo to the sense*; the minutest exactness of choice, in the words, seems to have been of double demand and necessity.

Be so good, therefore, to tell me (and believe I ask it sincerely, for the sake of instruction) whether I am mistaken or not, when I think you rather contented yourself with the general idea, than examined into the coherence of particular parts, in one of the liveliest poetical pictures that ever was drawn; yet, additional whereto, I am under an unlucky necessity of sending you some, still too faint and imperfect new colourings; because, without taking that extraordinary liberty (liable as it is, to the appearance of something the reverse of my modester meaning), I know not, how to explain to you, within any reasonable compass of a letter, in what parts of the piece I was of opinion, so much happier a hand as your own, should have given it a more heightened resemblance than that glowing one, you bestowed on it.

> Soft, breathes the whisp'ring verse—if zephir plays:
> Flows the stream smooth?—still smoother glide the lays,
> Where high-swoln surges sweep the sounding shore,
> Roll the rough verse, hoarse, like the torrent's rore:
> When *Ajax* strives some rock's vast weight to throw,
> The line too lab'ring, each dragg'd word moves slow.
> Livelier, the light *Camilla* skims the plain,
> Shoots o'er th' unbending corn, nor *shakes* th' unconscious grain.[1]

It would be offering an indignity to a temper and genius, like yours, to apprehend (from a freedom I had but only the private curiosity to use) any danger of being mistaken for coxcomb enough, to have thought of so empty a vanity, as that of comparing my numbers. The simple truth is, I amused myself, at that time, for my own satisfaction; but I now recommend to your reconsideration, one of your most admired great master-pieces of poetical harmony, with the honest and friendly intention of convincing you, by an instance, derived from yourself, that there appears still too much room, for a more verbal exactness of propriety, even in the works of our first class of writers.

I am afraid of growing tedious, if I should particularise all my reasons for imagining, you could have carried much farther than you did, the above noble likeness, between your *verse* and your *images*: Such as, that the word *strain*, in your first line, requiring a *stretch'd* and impressive pronunciation, suits not the *softness* of the epithet.—As also, that, both in sound and acceptation there arises, from your expression *blows*, at the end of the verse, a kind of ruffling air of *windyness*, too discomposing for the breath of a *zephyr*.[2]

Add to these, that as, in the fourth line, you seem to have designed, in the first four words, a gloomy picture of high billows, rising, rolling, and swelling, while they are yet in their approach to the strand, the *fifth* word (as it gives beginning to the cadence of that verse) ought to have brought on a *burst*, like the hoarseness of those billows in their

---

[1] [Hill's revision of *An Essay on Criticism*, ll. 366–72]
[2] [*Ibid.*, l. 366]

breaking—The rushing of a watery sound—a kind of hollow, washy murmur, like the workings of a surfy tide, repulsed and struggling amongst pebbles. But, I hope, it may be enough, to acquit me of impertinence, if I only say something more largely, concerning any one verse of the eight; for, while I shall be busy in so doing, I am sure, your apprehension will preclude, and run before my justification, so as to make needless either reasonings or apology.

The line too labours,—and the words move slow.

I have wondered very often, how it happened to be possible, to so cultivated an *ear* as your *own*, not to distinguish, in the second division of this verse, a certain declination to improper *quickness*, that runs down hill, too current, and unincumbered, for the labour and resistance of the image. According to my poor perception, three words, at least of the five (which, I am sure, you must have meant, should move most slowly, because they convey both the *rule* and the *example*) dance away upon the tongue, with a *tripping* and *lyrical* lightness. And if such, in reality, is the case, then, from a want of that unpliant *repugnance*, that *obtundity*, or *bluntness* of structure, which you thought, you had sufficiently given them, and which would have kept them stubbornly distinct and inflexible, they incorporate into a numerous *fluidity*, that expresses not the *idea* in your *precept*. . . .

14. Two contrasting views

1736, 1741

(a) Sir Thomas Hanmer (?), extract from *Some Remarks on the Tragedy of Hamlet* . . . (1736), pp. vi–vii (reprinted with an introduction by C. Thorpe, Augustan Reprint Society, Series III, No. 3 [Los Angeles, 1947]).

Criticism in general, is what few of our Countrymen have succeeded in: In that respect, our Neighbours have got the better of us; altho' we can justly boast of the compleatest Essay on that Subject that has been publish'd in any Language, in which almost every Line, and every Word, convey such Images, and such Beauties, as were never before found in so small a Compass, and of whose Author it may properly be said, in that respect,

> He is himself that great Sublime he draws.

(b) Lady Mary Wortley Montagu, remark made to Rev. Joseph Spence, January–February 1741, *Anecdotes*, i. 304. Lady Mary (1689–1762) and Pope had been on particularly close terms when they first met, but by 1725 their relationship cooled. For the causes of their enmity, see Twickenham, iv. pp. xv–xvi, Robert Halsband, *Life of Lady Mary Wortley Montagu* (1956), pp. 113–14, 129–32, and Peter Quennell, *Alexander Pope* (1968), pp. 136–8, 171–3, 232–4. See also Nos 31, 37b, 77, 88b.

I admired Mr Pope's *Essay on Criticism* at first very much, because I had not then read any of the ancient critics and did not know that it was all stolen.

MESSIAH, A SACRED ECLOGUE

14 May 1712

15. Steele's comments

1712

Sir Richard Steele, extract from letter to Pope, 1 June 1712, *Corresp.*, i. 146.

Steele (1672–1729), essayist and pamphleteer, was friendly towards Pope, and the 'Messiah' first appeared in *The Spectator*, no. 378, which was written by Steele. In response to Steele's comments, Pope revised the couplet,

> Before him Death, the grisly Tyrant flies;
> He wipes the Tears for ever from our Eyes.

It reads as follows in 1717,

> No Sigh, no Murmur the wide World shall hear,
> From ev'ry Face he wipes off ev'ry Tear.
> In adamantine Chains shall Death be bound,
> And Hell's grim Tyrant feel th'eternal Wound.   (ll. 45–8)

See Twickenham, i. 99–100, 117.

. . . I have turn'd to every verse and chapter, and think you have preserv'd the sublime and heavenly spirit throughout the whole, especially at—*Hark a glad voice* [l. 29]—and—*the lamb with wolves shall graze* [l. 77]—There is but one line which I think below the original,

> He wipes the tears for ever from our eyes.

You have express'd it with a good and pious, but not with so exalted and poetical a spirit as the prophet. *The Lord God will wipe away tears from off all faces.* If you agree with me in this, alter it by way of paraphrase or otherwise, that when it comes into a volume it may be amended. Your poem is already better than the *Pollio* [of Virgil].

WINDSOR FOREST

7 March 1713

16. Dennis's opinion

1714

John Dennis, a letter to Barton Booth, dated 18 December 1714, which Dennis did not print until he attacked Pope in *Remarks upon Mr. Pope's . . . Homer* (1717), *Critical Works*, ii. 135–7.

SIR,

You are in the right of it: *Windsor Forest* is a wretched *Rhapsody*, not worthy the Observation of a Man of Sense. I shall only take Occasion from it to display the Beauties of *Cooper's-Hill*, in Emulation of which it was impudently writ. The *Cooper's-Hill* of Sir JOHN DENHAM is a Poem upon the Prospect which that Hill affords us. *Cooper's-Hill*, is a Hill in *Windsor-Forest*, about a Mile from *Egham* in *Surrey*, about Half a Mile from the *Thames*, and Three Miles from *Windsor*.

The Conduct of Sir JOHN DENHAM in his *Cooper's-Hill*, is as admirable, as that of the Author of *Windsor Forest*, is despicable. Sir JOHN DENHAM presents no Object to his Reader, but what is truly in the Compass of his Subject. Whereas Half the Poem of *Windsor Forest* has nothing in it, that is peculiar to *Windsor Forest*. The Objects that are presented to the Reader in this latter Poem, are for the most part trivial and trifling, as Hunting, Fishing, Setting, Shooting, and a thousand common Landskips. Whereas of a thousand Objects that *Cooper's-Hill* presents to the View, Sir JOHN DENHAM chuses only the most Instructive, the most Noble, and the most Magnificent; and which, at the same time, are the most Noble, and most Magnificent, which *Great Britain* can show: As St. *Paul's*, *London*, *Windsor*, *Thames*, the Side of *Cooper's-Hill* that is next to the *Thames*, and *Runny-Mead* between them, ennobled by the Grant of the Great Charter there to the People of *England*.

In *Windsor Forest*, though a Poem of above Four hundred Lines, there is no manner of Design, nor any Artful and Beautiful Disposition of Parts.[1] Whereas Sir JOHN has both an Admirable Design, and a Beautiful Disposition of Parts. . . .

Thus have I endeavour'd to set before you, in a full Light, the admirable Art and Contrivance that are to be found in the *Cooper's-Hill*, in order to make the Rhapsody call'd *Windsor Forest*, appear the more contemptible. I have already exceeded the Bounds which I prescrib'd to my self. Otherwise, I should set several of the Parts of these Two Poems in Parallel against one another; by which it would appear, that the Knight has more the Advantage of this little 'Squire of *Parnassus*, in the Beauty of the Parts, than he has in the Admirable Contrivance of the Whole. I would say something likewise of the Expression and the Harmony, and would pretend to show, that as Sir JOHN DENHAM perpetually thinks clearly, he always expresses himself perspicuously; that the Language in his boldest Flights, is almost always sacred to him; that he is Bold, without Rashness; Plain, without Meanness; High, without Pride; and Charming, without Meretricious Arts: But that the Author of *Windsor Forest* has almost every where,

> Absurd Expressions, crude, abortive Thoughts,
> All the lewd Legion of exploded Faults.[2]

That he is Obscure, Ambiguous, Affected, Temerarious, Barbarous: And, lastly, That there is as much Difference between the Harmony of one Poem, and that of the other Piece, as there is between a Piece of Musick, which is Dead and Flat, and barely Mathematical; and one in which to the Truth of Composition, is added a Fine and a Charming Air. I know not but that I may prevail upon my self to do this another time, provided that you are entertained by what I at present send you.

[1] [See Johnson's reply to this point, p. 492 below]
[2] Roscommon on *Translated Verse*.

17. Another comparison with *Cooper's Hill*

1720

William Bond ('Henry Stanhope'), extract from *The Progress of Dulness. By an Eminent Hand. Which will Serve for an Explanation of the Dunciad* (1728), pp. 5–7. This pamphlet, advertised on 11 June 1728, was a Curll publication occasioned by *The Dunciad*. In the same volume appeared Dennis's attacks upon *Windsor Forest* and *The Temple of Fame*. All three pieces had been written much earlier, and *The Progress of Dulness* bears the date 6 June 1720.

Who hopes to Please, shall strive to Please by Pains,
Shall gaining Fame, earn hard whate'er he gains,
And DENHAM's Morals, join to DENHAM's Strains.
Here Paint the *Thames*[1] When running to the Sea
Like Mortal Life to meet Eternity.
There show both Kings and Subjects one excess,
Makes both, by striving to be Greater, Less.
Shall climb, and sweat, and falling, climb up still,
Before he gains the height of *Cooper's Hill*.

In *Windsor-Forest*,[2] if some trifling Grace,
Gives, at first Blush, the whole a pleasing Face,
'Tis *Wit*, 'tis true; but then 'tis *Common Place*.
The *Landscape-Writer*, branches out a *Wood*,
Then digging hard for't, finds a *Silver Flood*.
Here paints the *Woodcock* quiv'ring in the Air,
And there, the bounding *Stag* and quaking *Hare*.
Describes the *Pheasant*'s Scarlet-circled Eye,
And next the *slaught'ring-Gun*, that makes him Die.
From *common* Epithets that Fame derives,
By which his most *uncommon* Merit lives.

[1] See *Cooper's Hill*.
[2] See, *Pope*'s String of Verses, upon this Subject, without any Connection.

'Tis true! if finest Notes alone could show,
(Tun'd justly high, or regularly low,)
That we should Fame to these mere *Vocals* give,
POPE more, than we can offer, should receive.
For, when some gliding River is his Theme,
His Lines run smoother, than the smoothest Stream;
Not so, when thro' the Trees fierce *Boreas* blows,
The Period blustring with the Tempest grows.
But what Fools Periods read, for Periods sake?
Such Chimes improve not Heads, but make 'em Ach;
Tho' strict in Cadence on the Numbers rub,
Their frothy Substance is Whip-Syllabub;
With most *Seraphic Emptiness* they roll,
Sound without Sense, and Body without Soul.

THE RAPE OF THE LOCK

2 March 1714

The first version of *The Rape of the Lock* which appeared in 1712 consisted of only two cantos and lacked the 'machinery' of the sylphs. It attracted little attention. The publication of the enlarged version in 1714 is treated here as the first appearance of the poem.

---

18. Trumbull's and Berkeley's immediate response

March, May 1714

(a) Sir William Trumbull, extract from letter to Pope, 6 March 1714, *Corresp.*, i. 212. A retired diplomat, Trumbull (1639–1716) had encouraged the young Pope before he came up to London. Their intimacy was a real one, despite the disparity in years, and Pope had dedicated the first *Pastoral* to Trumbull.

. . . I will tell you as fast as I can, that I have receiv'd . . . your kind present of *The Rape of the Lock*. You have given me the truest satisfaction imaginable, not only in making good the just opinion I have ever had of your reach of thought, and my Idea of your comprehensive genius; but likewise in that pleasure I take as an *English* Man to see the *French*, even *Boileau* himself in his *Lutrin*, outdone in your Poem: For you descend, *leviore plectro*,[1] to all the nicer touches, that your own observation and wit furnish, on such a subject as requires the finest strokes, and the liveliest imagination. But I must say no more (tho' I could a great deal) on what pleases me so much: and henceforth I hope you will never condemn me of partiality, since I only swim with the stream, and approve what all men of good taste (notwithstanding the jarring of Parties) must and do universally applaud.

[1] [Horace, *Odes*, II. i. 40: 'with a lighter mood']

(b) Rev. (later Bishop) George Berkeley, extract from letter to Pope, 1 May 1714, *Corresp.*, i. 221. Berkeley (1685–1753) was at this time travelling in Italy, and wrote to Pope from Leghorn. He later reported on the reception of Pope's *Iliad*, see No. 28d.

I have accidentally met with your *Rape of the Lock* here, having never seen it before. Stile, Painting, Judgment, Spirit, I had already admired in others of your Writings; but in this I am charm'd with the magic of your *Invention*, with all those images, allusions, and inexplicable beauties, which you raise so surprizingly and at the same time so naturally, out of a trifle.

19. 'Bawdy' in *The Rape of the Lock*

April 1714

Charles Gildon, *A New Rehearsal, or Bays the Younger* ... (1714), pp. 42–4.

Gildon's pamphlet was published 6 April. His attack has been thought to have been the starting-point of Pope's animosity towards Gildon: but see No. 12. *A New Rehearsal* is cast in dramatic form, with Pope portrayed as Sawney Dapper, 'a young Poet of the Modern stamp, an easy Versifyer, Conceited, and a Contemner secretly of all others'. Truewit has been identified with Steele; see M. Goldstein, 'Gildon's *New Rehearsal*', *Philological Quarterly*, xxxvi (1957), 511–12.

Dapper. Why, Sir, you must know for getting a Reputation for *Poetry*, there are some Qualifications absolutely necessary, as a happy knack at Rhime, and a flowing Versification; but that is so common now that very few do want it; then you must chuse some odd out of the way Subject, some Trifle or other that wou'd surprize the Common Reader that any thing cou'd be written upon it, as a *Fan*,[1] a *Lock of Hair*, or the like.

Truewit. As the *Lutrin* of *Boileau*, or the *Dispensary* of Dr. *Garth* I suppose.

Dapper. Ah, Sir, that won't do; *Boileau* and *Garth* have treated of little things with Magnificence of Verse, as *Homer* did of the Frogs; but that is now Old, we must have something New; Heroic Doggrel is but lately found out, where the Verse and the Subject agree, as

> My Lord, why what the Devil?
> Zounds, Damn the Lock, 'foregad you must be Civil;
> Plague on't 'tis past a Jest; nay prithee, Pox
> Give her the Hair ——   [iv. 127–30]

If a Man wou'd distinguish himself, it must be by something New and Particular. *Boileau* and *Garth* had arriv'd to so much Fame and Reputation in the former way, that there was no coming after them in the same Track; we therefore found out the *Heroic-Comical* way of Writing, that no Man ever thought of before.

Truewit. That I dare swear. True, we have heard of *Tragi-Comical*, a very preposterous and unnatural Mixture, and now I think pretty well exploded; but for this *Heroic-Comical*, I confess it is new and more odd than the other.

Dapper. Ay, Sir, and that makes it do. But, Sir, that is not enough, besides the newness of the Verse, you must have a new manner of Address; you must make the Ladies speak Bawdy, no matter whether they are Women of Honour or not; and then you must dedicate your Poem to the Ladies themselves. Thus a Friend of mine has lately, with admirable Address, made *Arabella F[er]m[o]r* prefer the Locks of her Poll, to her Locks of another more sacred and secret Part.

> Oh! hadst thou Cruel! been content to seize
> Hairs less in Sight—*or any Hairs* but these.   [iv. 175–6]

But this is likewise a Complement to those Parts of the Lady, to let the World know that the Lady had *Hairs* elsewhere, which she valu'd less.

> Nor fear'd the chief th' unequal Fight to try,
> Who sought no more than on his Foe to Die.
>   [v. 77–8]

---

[1] [A reference to Gay's poem]

Admirable Good again, you know what Dying is on a fair Lady Sir *Indolent*,[1] prettily express'd, I vow, *than on his Foe to Die*. But then, Sir, the *Machinary* of this Poem is admirably contriv'd to convey a luscious Hint to the Ladies, by letting them know, that their Nocturnal Pollutions are a Reward of their Chastity, and that when they Dream of the Raptures of Love, they are immortalizing a *Silph* as that Ingenious and Facetious Author sweetly intimates in his Epistle Dedicatory, as the Book of the *Count de Gabalis* recommended explains it.

Truewit. I have seen that most Ingenious Piece, in which I find somewhat extraordinary in the Contrivance of the Author. He Publish'd his Poem first without his *Machinary*, and afterwards with it, this is an extraordinary Method indeed. Now the Poets of Antiquity, founded their Poems on their Machinary; but I find it is the new way of Writing to invent the Machinary, after the Poem is not only Written but Publish'd. . . .

[1] [Another character in the play, satirizing Charles Montagu, Lord Halifax]

20. Dennis's opinion

May 1714ff.

John Dennis, extracts from *Remarks on Mr. Pope's Rape of the Lock* (1728), *Critical Works*, ii. 324, 329–31, 335–9.

The *Remarks* were written as private letters, and not published by Dennis until 1728, after Pope had attacked him in both the *Peri Bathous* and *The Dunciad*. The letters were prefaced by a long introduction, part of which opens the selection given below. In his own copy of the *Remarks* (British Museum, C.116.b.2) Pope made several manuscript comments which are printed in Twickenham, ii. 392–9.

. . . The impartial Reader, who knows the *Rape of the Lock*, and who will read the following *Remarks*, will be able to determine whether *A. P——E* has shewn one Dram of Judgment, either in the Choice of this trifling *Subject*, or of his more senseless *Machinery*, or in the *Manners* and *Behaviour* of his fine Lady, who is so very rampant, and so very a Termagant, that a Lady in the Hundreds of *Drury* [1] would be severely chastis'd, if she had the Impudence in some Company to imitate her in some of her Actions. The impartial Reader is to determine whether the *Sentiments* are not often exceeding poor, and mean, and sometimes ridiculous; and whether the *Diction* is not often impure and ungrammatical.

But if the Author has not shewn one Dram of Judgment in the Piece that has been so much applauded by Readers more light than the Subject, what shall we say of the insipid *Profound*? What shall we say of the fulsome *Dunciad*? Were they not written in perfect Spight to good Sense, to Decency, to Justice, to Gratitude, to Friendship, to Modesty? And can such a Creature as this be deserving of the noble Name of a POET, the Name and Function which he has so much blasphem'd? Nay, can he deserve even the Name of a Versifyer, whose Ear is as injudicious and undistinguishing as the rest of his Head? The Commendation which *Tasso* so justly and so judiciously gave to *Lucretius*,

[1] [A prostitute living off Drury Lane]

is, *Nobilissimo Versificatore*, a *most noble Versifyer*: For *Lucretius* knew all the Variety, the Force, and the Power of Numbers; so that his Harmony in some Parts of him has never been surpass'd, not even by *Virgil* himself. But *A. P——E* has none of these distinguishing Talents, nor Variety, nor Force, nor Power of Numbers, but an eternal Monotony. His *Pegasus* is nothing but a batter'd *Kentish* Jade, that neither ambles, nor paces, nor trots, nor runs, but is always upon the *Canterbury*;[1] and as he never mends, never slackens his Pace, but when he stumbles or falls. So that having neither Judgment nor Numbers, he is neither Poet nor Versifyer, but only an eternal Rhimer, a little conceited incorrigible Creature, that like the Frog in the Fable, swells and is angry because he is not allow'd to be as great as the Ox. . . .

LETTER II.[2]

SIR,   *May* 3. 1714.

I hope mine of the first of this Month came to your Hands, which contain'd some Reflections upon the *Dedication* and *Title-Page* of the *Rape of the Lock*; which latter creates an Expectation of *Pleasantry* in us, when there is not so much as one *Jest* in the Book.

Quanto rectius hic qui nil molitur ineptè?[3]

How much more judiciously does *Boileau* appear in the *Title-Page* of his *Lutrin*? In a sottish Emulation of which, *this* and several late *fantastick Poems* appear both to you and me to have been writ. *Boileau* calls his *Lutrin* an *Heroick Poem*, and he is so far from raising an *Expectation* of Laughter, either in the *Title*, or in the *Beginning of the Poem*, that he tells Monsieur *de Lamoignon*, to whom he addresses it, that 'tis a *grave Subject*, and must be read with a *grave Countenance*.

Garde toy de rire en ce grave sujet.[4]

Lutrin, Chant. I. [16]

Butler modestly calls his *Poem*, by the Name of his Hero, *Hudibras*; and without endeavouring to prepossess his Reader, leaves the *Poem* itself to work its natural Effect upon him.

---

[1] [I.e., at an awkward canter]
[2] [Pope wroter under 'LETTER II.', 'Mr Dennis's positive word that the Rape of ye Lock *can* be nothing but a triffle and that the Lutrin cannot be so, however it may appear']
[3] [Horace, *Ars Poetica*, l. 140: 'How much better he who makes no foolish effort']
[4] ['Keep yourself from laughing at this grave subject']

But now, Sir, since I have said that the *Rape of the Lock* seems to be writ in Imitation of the *Lutrin*, (I mean so far in Imitation, that the Author had a Mind to get Reputation by writing a great many Verses upon an *inconsiderable Subject*, as *Boileau* appears to have done before him;) I believe it will not be disagreeable to you, if I shew the Difference between the *Lutrin* and this *fantastick Poem*.

The *Rape of the Lock* is a very *empty Trifle*, without any *Solidity* or *sensible Meaning*; whereas the *Lutrin* is only a *Trifle* in *Appearance*, but under that Appearance carries a very grave and very important Instruction: For if that *Poem* were only what it appears to be, *Boileau* would run counter to the *fam'd Rule* which he has prescrib'd to others.

> *Auteurs, prêtez l'oreille à mes instructions.*
> *Voulez vous faire aimer vos riches fictions?*
> *Qu'en sçavantes leçons votre muse fertile,*
> *Partout joigne au plaisant le solide & l'utile?*
> *Un lecteur sage fuit un vain amusement,*
> *Et veut mettre à profit son divertissement.*[1]

And which *Horace* has given before him.

> *Centuriæ seniorum agitant expertia frugis:*
> *Celsi prætereunt austera poemata Ramnes.*
> *Omne tulit punctum qui miscuit utile dulci,*
> *Lectorem delectando, pariterque monendo.*[2]

And the Rule which my Lord *Roscommon* has given for *Translations*, is certainly more strong for *Originals*.

> Take then a Subject proper to expound,
> But moral, great, and worth a Poet's Voice,
> For Men of Sense despise a trivial Choice,
> And such Applause it must expect to meet,
> As would some Painter busy'd in a Street
> To copy Bulls, and Bears, and every Sign,
> That calls the staring Sots to nasty Wine.[3]

---

[1] [*Art poetique*, iv. 85–90: 'Authors, give ear to my instructions. Would you like to make you fictions valuable? So that the well-informed lessons of your fertile muse everywhere joins the solid and useful with the pleasing']

[2] [*Ars Poetica*, ll. 341–4: 'The centuries of the elders chase from the stage what is profitless; the proud Ramnes disdains poems devoid of charms. He has won every vote who has blended profit and pleasure, at once delighting and instructing the reader']

[3] [*An Essay on Translated Verse*, *Critical Essays of the Seventeenth Century*, ed. J. E. Spingarn (1908–9), ii. 300]

Now since 'tis impossible that so judicious an Author as *Boileau* should run counter to his own, and to the Instructions of his Master *Horace*, the *Lutrin* at the Bottom cannot be an *empty Trifle*. 'Tis indeed a noble and important satirical Poem, upon the Luxury, the Pride, the Divisions, and Animosities of the Popish Clergy.[1] 'Tis true indeed the *admirable Address* of the Poet has made it in Appearance a *Trifle*; for otherwise it would not have been suffer'd in a bigotted Popish Country. But yet *Boileau* in some Places seems to have given broad Hints at what was his real Meaning; as in the following Passage.[2]

> *La Deesse en entrant, qui voit la nappe mise,*
> *Admire un si bel ordre, & reconnoit l'eglise.*[3]
>
> Lutrin, Chant. I. [69–70]

And this other Passage is still more bold.

> *Pour soûtenir tes droits, que le ciel autorise,*
> *Abîme tout plutôt, c'est l'esprit de l'eglise.*[4]
>
> Lutrin, Chant. I. [185–6]

As the *Rape of the Lock* is an *empty Trifle*, it can have no *Fable* nor any Moral; whereas the *Lutrin* has both *Fable* and *Moral*. 'Tis true, indeed, the *Allegory* under which that *Moral* is conceal'd, is not so perspicuous as *Boileau* would have made it, if it had not been for the Apprehension of provoking the Clergy. But, on the other Side, 'tis not so obscure, but that a penetrating Reader may see through it. The Moral is, *That when Christians, and especially the Clergy, run into great Heats about religious Trifles, their Animosity proceeds from the Want of that Religion which is the Pretence of their Quarrel.*[5] The Fable is this; 'Two Persons being deserted by true Piety, are embroil'd about a religious Trifle, to the Perplexity and Confusion of them and theirs: Upon the Return of Piety, they agree to set aside the Trifle about which they differ'd, and are reconcil'd, to the Quiet and Satisfaction both of themselves and their Partizans.'

[1] [Pope replaced 'Popish Clergy' with 'Female sex', thus replying to Dennis by pointing to the moral of *The Rape of the Lock*]

[2] [Pope added a marginal note, 'Clarissas Speech' (v. 9–34). However, Pope had added the speech only in 1717 'to open more clearly the MORAL of the Poem', Twickenham, ii. 395]

[3] ['The entering Goddess, who sees the placing of the cloth, admires such a smart arrangement, and recognises the church']

[4] ['To maintain your rights, which heaven authorises, damages rather, there is the spirit of the Church']

[5] [Pope altered this sentence in order to reply to Dennis: he probably meant it to read, 'That when Christians, and especially the Ladies, run into great Heats, their Animosity proceeds from Want of sense.' See Twickenham, ii. 395]

If you will be pleased to compare the Beginning of the Sixth *Canto* with the rest of the Poem, you will easily see that this Account which I have given of the *Lutrin* is not without Foundation. But you know very well, Sir, that there is not the least Shadow of a Moral or Fable in the *Rape*.

As nothing could be more ridiculous than the writing a full, an exact, and a regular Criticism upon so empty a Business as this trifling Poem; I will say but a Word or two concerning the *Incidents*, and so have done with what relates immediately to the *Design*. The Intention of the Author in writing this Poem, as we find in the Title-Page, is to raise the Mirth of the Reader; and we find by the Effects which *Hudibras* and the *Lutrin* produce in us, that *Butler* and *Boileau* wrote with the same Intention. Now you know very well, Sir, that in a Poem which is built upon an Action, Mirth is chiefly to be rais'd by the *Incidents*. For Laughter in *Comedy* is chiefly to be excited, like Terror and Compassion in Tragedy, by Surprize, when Things spring from one another against our Expectation. Now whereas there are *several* ridiculous Incidents in the *Lutrin*, as, The Owl in the Pulpit frighting the nocturnal Champions; The Prelate's giving his Benediction to his Adversary, by way of Revenge and Insult; The Battle in the Bookseller's Shop, &c. And whereas there are a thousand such in *Hudibras*; There is not so much as *one*, nor the *Shadow of one*, in the *Rape of the Lock*:[1] Unless the Author's Friends will object here, That his *perpetual Gravity*, after the *Promise* of his Title, makes the whole Poem one continued *Jest*.

I am Your's, &c.

LETTER IV.

SIR,   *May* 9. 1714.
According to the Promise made in my last, I am now to treat of the *Machines*; in the doing of which I shall lie under a great Disadvantage: For before I come to those of the *Rape*, it is necessary to say something of *Machines* in general, of the Reason of introducing them, and of the *Practice* of the greatest and best of the Moderns. 'Tis necessary to say something to all these, in order to shew the Absurdity of our Author's *Machines*, and his utter Ignorance of the Art he pretends to. . . .

The Reasons, that first oblig'd those Poets which are call'd Heroic to introduce *Machines* into their *Poems*, were,

[1] [Pope replied to Dennis interlineally, naming as a ridiculous incident, '[. . .?] of men & women for ye loss of a Lock'.]

First, To make their *Fable* and their *Action* more instructive: For, says *Bossu, Lorsque les poetes sont devenus philosophes moraux, ils n'ont pas cessé d'etre theologiens. Au contraire, la morale qu'ils traitent, les oblige indispensablement, de mêler la divinité dans leurs Ouvrages; parceque la conoissance, la crainte, & l'amour de Dieu, en un mot, la piete, & la religion sont les premiers, & les plus solides fondements, des autres vertus, & de tout la morale.*[1]

By introducing Machines into their Fables, the Epic Poets shew'd two Things, 1. That the great Revolutions in human Affairs are influenc'd by a particular Providence. 2. That the Deity himself promotes the Success of an Action form'd by Virtue, and conducted by Prudence. But,

Secondly, The Heroic Poets introduc'd *Machines* into their Fables in order to make those Fables more *delightful*: For the employing *Machines* made the Actions of those Poems *wonderful*; now every Thing that is *wonderful* is of course *delightful*. . . .

[Dennis quotes Boileau, *Art poétique*, iii. 177–92, in support of his argument]

. . . as the Epic Poets by their *Machines* made the *Actions* of their Fables more *wonderful* and more *delightful*, as well as more *instructive*; they likewise made the *poetical Expression* more *wonderful* and more *delightful*, since 'tis from them that they chiefly derive that Greatness of Expression which renders their Works so Divine.

I shall now come to the Practice of the antient Poets, and the Method which they made use of in introducing their *Machines*, in order to render their Poems more *instructive* and more *delightful*.

1. They took their *Machines* from the Religion of their Country, upon which Account these *Machines* made the stronger Impression, and made their Fables, and the Actions of them, *probable* as well as *wonderful*; for nothing was more natural than for those antient Heathens to believe that the Powers which they ador'd were wont to intermeddle in human Affairs, and to promote the Success of those Designs which they favour'd; and nothing could be more natural for them, than to believe that that Design must prosper which was espous'd by *Jupiter*. But this was not all; for the *Machines*, by making the Actions of their Poems *probable*,

---

[1] [*Traité du pöeme epique*, I. ii: 'When poets became moral philosophers, they did not cease to be theologians. On the contrary, the morality they dealt with, obliged them unavoidably to mix divinity into their works; because the knowledge, the dread, and the love of God, in a word, piety and religion, are the first and most solid foundations for other virtues and for the whole of morality']

made them *wonderful* to Men of Sense, who never can admire any Thing in Humanity which *Reason* will not let them believe. But,

2. The antient Poets made their *Machines* allegorical, as well as their human Persons.

3. They oppos'd them to one another.

4. They shew'd a just Subordination among them, and a just Proportion between their Functions. While one was employ'd about the greatest and the sublimest Things, another was not busied about the most trifling and most contemptible.

5. They always made their *Machines* influence the Actions of their Poems; and some of those *Machines* endeavour'd to *advance* the Action of their respective Poem, and others of them endeavour'd to *retard* it.

6. They made them infinitely more powerful than the human Persons.

But, Secondly, The Practice of the greatest modern Heroic Poets is conformable to that of the antient.

1. They take their *Machines* from the Religion of their Country; witness *Milton, Cowley, Tasso*.

2. They make them Allegorical.

3. They oppose them to one another.

4. They shew a just Subordination among them, and a just Proportion between their Functions.

The Author of the *Rape* has run counter to this Practice both of the Antients and Moderns. He has not taken his *Machines* from the Religion of his Country, nor from any Religion, nor from Morality. His Machines contradict the Doctrines of the Christian Religion, contradict all sound Morality; there is no allegorical nor sensible Meaning in them; and for these Reasons they give no Instruction, make no Impression at all upon the Mind of a sensible Reader. Instead of making the Action wonderful and delightful, they render it extravagant, absurd, and incredible. They do not in the least influence that Action; they neither prevent the Danger of *Belinda*, nor promote it, nor retard it, unless, perhaps, it may be said, for one Moment, which is ridiculous. And if here it be objected, that the Author design'd only to *entertain* and *amuse*; To that I answer, That for that very Reason he ought to have taken the utmost Care to make his Poem *probable*, according to the important Precept of *Horace*.

Ficta voluptatis causâ sint proxima veris.[1]

[1] [*Ars Poetica*, l. 338: 'Fictions meant to please should be close to the real']

And that we may be satisfy'd that this Rule is founded in *Reason* and *Nature*, we find by constant Experience, that any thing that shocks *Probability* is most insufferable in Comedy.

There is no Opposition of the *Machines* to one another in this *Rape o, the Lock. Umbriel* the *Gnome* is not introduc'd till the Action is over, and till *Ariel* and the Spirits under him, have quitted *Belinda*.[1]

There is no just *Subordination* among these *Machines*, nor any just *Proportion* between their *Functions*. *Ariel* summons them together, and talks to them as if he were their Emperor.

> Ye *Sylphs* and *Sylphids*, to your Chief give ear,
> *Fays, Fairies, Genii, Elves,* and *Dæmons*, hear;
> Ye know the Spheres and various Tasks assign'd,
> By Laws eternal, to th' aerial Kind.
> Some in the Fields of purest *Æther* play,
> And bask and whiten in the Blaze of Day.
> Some guide the Course of wandring Orbs on high,
> Or roll the Planets thro' the boundless Sky ——
> Or brew fierce Tempests on the watry Main,
> Or o'er the Glebe distil the kindly Rain.
> Others on Earth o'er human Race preside,
> Watch all their Ways, and all their Actions guide:
> Of these the Chief the Care of Nations own,
> And guard with Arms Divine the *British* Throne.[2]
>
> [ii. 73–80, 85–90]

Now, Sir, give me leave to ask you one Question: Did you ever hear before that the Planets were roll'd by the aerial Kind? We have heard indeed of Angels and Intelligences who have perform'd these Functions: But they are vast glorious Beings, of *Celestial* Kind, and *Machines* of another System. Pray which of the *aerial* Kind have these *sublime* Employments? For nothing can be more ridiculous, or more contemptible, than the Employments of those whom he harangues

> To save the Powder from too rude a Gale,
> Nor let th' imprison'd Essences exhale.   [ii. 93–4]

---

[1] [Pope's comment has been partly cut away. Tillotson, Twickenham, ii. 396, thinks Pope may have written, 'because they send a Gnome & Earthly Lover prevents']

[2] [For Pope's jottings against these lines, and their significance, see Twickenham, ii. 396–7]

There is a Difference almost infinite between these vile Functions and the former sublime ones, and therefore they can never belong to Beings of the same Species. Which of the aerial Kinds are the Movers of Orbs on high, or the Guardians of Empires below; when he who calls himself their Chief, is only the Keeper of a vile *Iseland Cur*, and has not so much as the Intendance of the Lady's *Favourite Lock*, which is the Subject of the Poem? But that is entrusted to an inferior Spirit, contrary to all manner of Judgment and Decorum.

The *Machines* that appear in this Poem are infinitely less considerable than the *human Persons*, which is without Precedent. Nothing can be so contemptible as the *Persons*, or so foolish as the *Understandings* of these *Hobgoblins*. *Ariel's* Speech, for the first thirty Lines, is one continu'd Impertinence: For, if what he says is true, he tells them nothing but what they knew as well as himself before. And when he comes at length to the *Point*, he is full as impertinent as he was in his *Ramble* before; for after he has talk'd to them of *black Omens* and *fire Disasters* that threaten his Heroine, these Bugbears dwindle to the breaking a Piece of *China*, the staining a *Petticoat*, the losing a *Necklace*, a *Fan*, or a Bottle of *Sal Volatile*. But we shall consider this Passage further when we come to examine the *Sentiments*; and then we shall see, that *Sawney* takes the Change here, and 'tis *He*, a little *Lump of Flesh*, that talks; instead of a little *Spirit*.

That which makes this Speech more ridiculous, is the Place where it is spoken, and that is upon the Sails and Cordage of *Belinda's* Barge; which is certainly taken from the two Kings of *Brentford* descending in Clouds, and singing in the Style of our modern Spirits.

> *1 King.* O stay, for you need not as yet go astray,
> The Tide, like a Friend, has brought Ships in our Way,
> And on their high Ropes we will play.

But now, Sir, for the *Persons* of these Sylphs and Sylphids, you see what Ideas the Threats of *Ariel* give us of them, when he threatens them, that for their Neglect they shall

> Be stopt in Vials, or transfix'd with Pins,
> Or plung'd in Lakes of bitter Washes lie,
> Or wedg'd whole Ages in a Bodkin's Eye.   [ii. 126–8]

Discord is describ'd by *Homer* with her Feet upon the Earth, and Head in the Skies: Upon which *Longinus* cries out, That this is not so much the Measure of *Discord*, as of *Homer's Capacity*, and *Elevation* of *Genius*.

Ev'n so these *diminutive Beings* of the intellectual World, may be said to be the *Measure* of Mr. *Pope's Capacity* and *Elevation* of Genius. They are, indeed, Beings so *diminutive*, that they bear the same Proportion to the rest of the intellectual, that Eels in Vinegar do to the rest of the material World. The latter are only to be seen thro' *Microscopes*, and the former only thro' the false Optics of a *Rosycrucian* Understanding.

I shall mention but one or two more of the numerous Defects which are to be found in the *Machines* of this Poem; the one is, The Spirits, which he intends for *benign* ones, are *malignant*, and those, which he designs for *malignant*, are *beneficent* to Mankind. The *Gnomes* he intends for *malignant*, and the *Sylphs* for *beneficent* Spirits. Now the *Sylphs* in this Poem promote that *Female Vanity* which the *Gnomes* mortify. And Vanity is not only a great Defect in Human Nature, but the Mother of a thousand Errors, and a thousand Crimes, and the Cause of most of the Misfortunes which are incident to Humanity.

The last Defect that I shall take notice of, is, That the *Machines* in this Poem are not taken from *one System*, but are *double*, nay *treble* or *quadruple*. In the first *Canto* we hear of nothing but *Sylphs*, and *Gnomes*, and *Salamanders*, which are *Rosycrucian* Visions. In the second we meet with *Fairies*, *Genii*, and *Dæmons*, Beings which are unknown to those *Fanatick Sophisters*. In the fourth, *Spleen* and the *Phantoms* [1] about, are deriv'd from the Powers of *Nature*, and are of a separate System. And *Fate* and *Jove*, which we find in the fifth *Canto*, belong to the Heathen Religion. [2]

But now, Sir, in treating of these Matters, I have, before I perceiv'd it, transgress'd the Bounds which I prescrib'd to my self, which I desire that you would excuse.

I am, SIR,
Yours, &c.

[1] [For Pope's comments, see Twickenham, ii. 397–8]
[2] [See *ibid*]

21. William Bond's opinion

1720

William Bond ('Henry Stanhope'), extract from *The Progress of Dulness* ... (1728), pp. 1–3. Dated 6 June 1720 (for details of this poem, see headnote to No. 17).

Late on Fantastic Cabalistic Schemes,
Of waking Whimsies, or of Fev'rish Dreams,
New Cobweb Threads of *Poetry* were spun,
In gaudy Snares, like Flies, were Witlings won,
Their Brains entangled, and our *Art* undone.
  Pope first descended from a *Monkish* Race,
Cheapens the Charms of Art, and daubs her Face;
From *Gabalis*,[1] his Mushroom Fictions rise,
Lop off his *Sylphs* —— and his *Belinda*[2] dies;
Th' attending Insects hover in the Air,
No longer, than they're present, is She Fair;
Some dart those Eye-beams, which the Youths beguile,
And some sit Conquering in a dimpling Smile.
Some pinch the Tucker, and some smooth the Smock,
Some guard an Upper, some a *Lower* Lock;
But if these truant Body-Guards escape,
In whip the *Gnomes* and strait commit a Rape;
The curling Honours of her Head they seize,
Hairs less in Sight, or any Hairs they please;
But if to angry Frowns, her Brow She bends,
Upon her Front some sullen *Gnome* descends;
Whisks thro' the Furrows, with its Airy Form,
Bristles her Eye-brows, and *directs the Storm*.
  As wide from these, are *Addisonian* Themes,
As Angels Thoughts are from distemper'd Dreams;

---

[1] See, The History of the Count *de Gabalis*, from whence He has taken the Machinery of his *Rape of the Lock*.
[2] Mrs *Arabella Fermor*.

Spenser and *He*, to Image Nature, knew,
Like living Persons, Vice and Virtue drew:
At once instructed and well-pleas'd we read,
While in sweet Morals these two Poets laid,
No less to Wisdom, than to Wit, pretence,
They led *by Music*, but they led to *Sense*.

   But *Pope* scarce ever *Force* to *Fancy* joins,
With *Dancing-Master*'s Feet equips his Lines,
Plumes empty Fancy, and in *Tinsel* shines.
Or, if by chance his Judgment seems to lead,
Where one poor Moral faintly shews its Head;
'Tis like a Judge, that reverendly drest,
Peeps thro' the Pageants, at a Lord May'rs Feast;
By Starts he reasons, and seems Wise by Fits,
Such Wit's call'd *Wisdom, that has lost its Wits*.

22. Concanen's praise

1725

Matthew Concanen, extract from 'Of Modern Poetry', signed 'W. Sharpsight' and dated 13 November 1725 in *The Speculatist. A Collection of Letters and Essays* . . . (1730), p. 40.

Concanen has been talking of the difficulty of using pagan mythology as 'machinery' now that Christianity has replaced the pagan Gods. Matthew Concanen (1701–49) was later suspected by Pope of having a hand in *A Miscellany of Taste* (1732) which ridiculed the *Epistle to Burlington*, and numbered among the Dunces. For further extracts from his remarks on Pope, see Nos 38, 45, and 51.

Mr. *Pope* has struck out a pretty Discovery in the *Rosycrucian* Scheme which he uses in the *Rape of the Lock*, but it's surprizing how the same Writer could stumble upon the School-boy Tale of *Pan* and *Lodona* in *Win[d]sor Forest*. Besides in light Poems, the Fairy Tales are a more amusing and palatable Superstition, that those of the Heathen Gods, better suited for our belief, and affording more Scope for Invention.

23. A French assessment

1728

P.-F. Guyot (1685–1745), Abbé Desfontaines, 'Preface du Tra-
ducteur', *La Boucle de Cheveux Enlevée* (Paris, 1728), sig. Avii-Biv^v.

Here is the translation of a little English poem by the celebrated Mr. Pope,
the best modern poet in English. Among other works which he has given
the public, he is the author of a translation into English verse of Homer's
Iliad, which has been so justly praised by M. Voltaire in his *Essai sur la
Poësie Epique*, recently translated from English into French and printed
in Paris. . . .

The translation of this mock epic poem, entitled the *Rape of the Lock*
in English, will help to show the error into which prejudice can lead
us, namely that the English nation has its part only in the serious and
profound, and cannot aspire as we can to refinement of wit, delicate
satire, and elegant badinage. . . .

I do not believe that there can be found in our language anything more
ingenious, in this playful genre, than Mr. Pope's *Rape of the Lock*, who
when he wrote this poem was only, they say, twenty years old; the only
age at which it is proper to amuse oneself with writing verses of this kind,
and perhaps of any kind at all.

What caused this work to spring forth was an incident which happened in 1712 to Madame Fermor, to whom he dedicated it. The
mediocrity of a subject so sterile in appearance served only to make even
more esteemed the genius and fine wit of the author. Among the English
the poem, the *Rape of the Lock*, is what *Le Lutrin* is among us, if it is not,
as it seems, more sprightly, and more gallant. . . .

We will find in this little poem invention, design, order, the supernatural, fiction, images and thought; in a word, that which constitutes
true poetry. We will notice also a laughing comedy, far removed from
insipid burlesque, satirical allusions which do not offend, forceful
witticisms which are not too free, and a delicate raillery on the fair sex,
perhaps more capable of pleasing them than all the flowerets of our
madrigals and modern bucolics.

We have not yet seen a poem in which the supernatural, which the English call the 'machinery', was taken from the imaginary system of the Cabbalists: the use Mr. Pope has made of this system shows that these ideas are very suitable in poetry: but it is also necessary to admit that it is only in a poem of this genre that it has a place. However, one sees in Mr. Pope's Dedicatory Epistle that on his own confession he has greatly profited from the Abbé Villaro's book, entitled *Le Comte de Gabalis*.

One hopes that this little work will please not only the ladies, but that it will also be valued even by those who only look at vaudeville pieces with critical eyes; they will find here all the proportions observed as in the most serious poem, and all the main principles of the epic faithfully followed.

Whoever publishes this poem in French today, should expect from the public the gratitude due to a traveller who brings into his native land a flower from foreign fields.

24. Two Italian assessments

1739

(a) Andrea Bonducci, extract from his 'Amico Lettore' prefacing his translation, *Il Riccio Rapito Poema Heroicomico* . . . (Florence, 1739), p. 1:

. . . Mr. Pope has made such a way for himself in the world that no one will deny him the esteem of being the greatest poet, not only of England but of all living men.

(b) Abate Giuseppe Buondelmonti, extracts from a letter written on behalf of Andrea Bonducci to serve as an introduction to his Italian translation, *ibid.*, pp. 5–21:

I have read your translation of Mr. Pope's mock-heroic poem entitled

The Rape of the Lock with much delight. I experienced great pleasure in seeing the splendid verses of a happy British wit turned with rare accuracy and charm into our own vernacular. The author merits the praise of supreme poet and of most excellent philosopher, for in several of his works full of sublime philosophy (if one gives a healthy interpretation to some equivocal propositions) he has been able to combine, as far as I am aware, and with more skill than any other author be he ancient or modern, both philosophical precision and clear reasoning with the deceitful dreams and brilliant but often confused and apparently lucid expressions with which a poet should embellish his moral teachings in order that they should stimulate the intellect and appeal to a far wider audience.

Nor can the criticism which has often been levelled at other translators of English—of having translated works of heterodox writers, which are tinged with some of their false creeds—be levelled at you, for Mr. Pope is a Roman Catholic and this fact is to be admired all the more in him than in writers born and raised in countries in which the Catholic religion is the universal and dominant religion. . . .

. . . Tassoni's work [*La Secchia Rapita*] was the model for Boileau's *Le Lutrin*, a very fine poem which by far surpasses the *Secchia Rapita*. Our author has written his poem in a style similar to these two poets equalling *Le Lutrin* in gallantry, but, due to the greater number of fine truths that it contains, deserves to surpass it.

In my opinion the second and fourth cantos of Mr. Pope's poem stand out more than any others, be it for the charming descriptions one finds in the second canto—of Belinda gliding gently down the Thames in a boat, of Ariel, King of the sylphs, haranguing his subordinates, of the punishments he threatens them with should they transgress his royal decrees (punishments entirely unheard of before, yet at the same time ideally proportioned to the nature of these spirits and their crimes).

As for the fourth canto all that concerns the description of the dark cavern of Hypochondria is most beautiful inasmuch as the writer embroiders the most sublime physical and moral truths with the most marvellous and charming poetic images. The same can be said of Umbriel's speech to the sad Goddess, her replies, her resolution promptly executed by the odious Gnome and finally Belinda's pathetic declamation after the fatal cutting of the lock, and it is with such an excellent model of poetic eloquence that the poet concludes this very beautiful canto.

In the first canto the theory of the spirits is explained by Ariel and the description of Belinda's toilet is given, in the third the game of ombre and the end of the canto contains singular beauty which need only be brought to the reader's attention so that by lingering over it he can realise this and appreciate its most high worth. The end of the fifth canto in which Belinda's lock is raised to the highest honour a lock can ascend to—that of being changed into a very luminous star—is similarly fine.

The fact that I have singled out many beautiful episodes from the poem and stated that they are superior to others does not mean that the remaining episodes are not up to the same high standard.

As there are many different forms of poetry, among them the mock-heroic poem, it is necessary that the poet should at times write simply, humbly or in other words not so marvellously all the time, not only with a view to making some beautiful passage stand out all the more, and in order not to be irritatingly witty, poems must have their shadows, just as paintings do, that is, it is necessary for the reader to be transported little by little to what is most splendid and most surprising in some poetic works; but also it is impossible not to do this without falling a prey to the principal defect of false eloquence, which consists of spreading over all the objects of the mind, as the prism does over bodies, the same poetical or rhetorical colours without distinction of the matter, or without that variety and gradation which are sought after in prose works and poetry so that they do not remain confusingly bright and dissimilar to the objects they are meant to represent.

This is what Mr. Pope has achieved in just measure in this poem as in his other poems—this capacity for adapting style to suit different subjects with their varying modifications without ever being prosaic, base, or tedious, and is one of the principal gifts which render his name and works so famous at the present and which will make them above envy and immortal in the future.

ILIAD

Even before the publication of the first four books of Pope's translation, interest was excited by the threat from a rival translation by Thomas Tickell. The three first items (Nos 25–7) represent this hectic pre-publication interest. Since the *Iliad* is one of Pope's most important contemporary achievements, a wide sampling of the critical response from 1715 to 1728 is given here. Further, see Introduction pp. 12–13.

---

25. Preliminary praise

1714

Richard Fiddes, extract from *A Prefatory Epistle Concerning some Remarks to be published on Homer's Iliad: Occasioned by the Proposals of Mr. Pope* ... (1714), pp. 9–10. The pamphlet is dedicated to Swift.

The *Iliad* had been announced in October 1713. Fiddes (1671–1725), who had written some 'Cursory Observations' on the *Iliad*, was prompted by Pope's proposals to put them together as a promissory prolegomena in the hopes of attracting patronage.

The Author of the *Essay* on Criticism, who has a Wit capable of every thing, but what relates to the Controversy betwixt us and the Church of *Rome*, will, it is hop'd, with a fine Version of the *Iliad*, oblige the World with just Remarks upon it. As he has confessedly the most sprightly and easy *Muse*, except perhaps one Person you will not give me leave to Name [i.e. Swift], he will now have a noble Occasion of trying her *Strength*. And there will be a great disappointment of the general Expectation, if he do not at once enrich the Language wherein he writes, and reduce it, which seems very much wanting, still nearer to a *Standard*.

26. Preliminary Censure from 'Sir Iliad Doggrel'

March 1715

Thomas Burnet and George Duckett (under the pseudonym of 'Sir Iliad Doggrel'), extract from *Homerides: or, A Letter to Mr. Pope, Occasion'd by his intended Translation of Homer* (1715), pp. 5–6.

This attempt at a pre-emptive strike appeared on 7 March, more than two months before Pope's translation was published. The authors' place in the Buttonian clique makes it very much a party-piece, if a high-spirited one. There is some evidence that Addison was guilty of collusion in this work: see *The Letters of Thomas Burnet to George Duckett, 1712–1722*, ed. D. N. Smith (1914), p. 81.

SIR

Your ingenious Description of that *Temple of Fame*, in which you are likely to have so large a Place, has been no unhappy Earnest to the Town, of what they may justly expect from your Muse in a Translation of *Homer*. 'Tis indeed somewhat bold, and almost prodigious, for a single Man to undertake a Work, which not all the Poets of our Island durst jointly attempt, and it is what no Man of an Inferior Genius to Mr. *Pope* cou'd even have thought of. But *jacta est alea* ['the die is cast'], it is too late to disswade you, by demonstrating the Madness of your Project. No! not only your attending Subscribers, whose Expectations have been raised in Proportion to what their Pockets have been drained of, but even the industrious, prudent *Bernard* [Lintot],[1] who has advanced no small Sum of Money for the Copy, require the Performance of your Articles.

'Tis too late then to give Advice; and all that we now have left, as good-natur'd Men to do, is to give you all the Assistance imaginable in this great Time of Need. And amidst the Croud of Friends that you

[1] [The publisher of Pope's translation]

may meet with among the Poets, I offer my Service to you, as far as ever I can be able, to help forward, your present Translation.

There are indeed but two things to be considered in every Heroick Poem; first, how to *write* the Poem, secondly, how to make it *sell*.

The Latter of these being without dispute the main and principal Thing about which you and *Bernard* are concern'd, I shall begin with that. . . .

[Sir Iliad goes on to give an 'Epilogue' to drum up trade, and then obligingly translates samples of Homer into burlesque doggerel]

27. The battle between Pope and Tickell begins

June 1715

(a) Anonymous, item from *The Weekly Journal. With fresh advices foreign and domestic*, 4 June 1715; the text is that given by George Sherburn, *The Early Career of Alexander Pope* (1934), p. 142. This and the following item describe the events from the point of view of Pope's camp.

The Discourse at present among the Learned, is upon the Publication of the first Volume of *Homer*, done by the most Ingenious Mr. Pope, who has already given us as Many Testimonies as he has written Poems, that he alone is equal to so great an Undertaking; and this Pleasure is heightened by a Consideration, that those Enemies of Wit who would get a Name by finding Fault with any Perfection that they cannot attain to, are like to meet with as much Discouragement as Mr. Pope will with Honour and Applause: We are however advis'd from *Button's*, That as their Party have engrossed to themselves the whole Art of Politicks, so they will now advance with Vigour and will continue to make violent Incursions into all the Provinces of Literature, till they have laid waste all good Sense as well as Honesty. But as the Fort of *Homer* is the first

Place they set upon, and seems impregnable by Art and Nature, 'tis believ'd the Siege will be razed [sic], and the Besiegers quit with Shame, so heedless a Project, and so umpromising an Undertaking.

(b) Anonymous, item from *ibid.*, 11 June 1715; the text is that given by George Sherburn, *op. cit.*, p. 143.

According as we advised in our last, a Poetical War was openly declar'd on Wednesday, by Mr. *Tickel*, (supported on one Hand by Sir R[ichard] St[ee]le, and on the other by a Person who made his Fortune by one *Campaign*[1]) whose Translation of the first Book of HOMER's Iliad was then publish'd, in Opposition to the first Volume of the same Author translated by Mr. POPE: These Gentlemen have gain'd great Reputation by the Parts they have already perform'd of this Work; for as HOMER was accounted the most ingenious among the Greek Authors, so Mr. POPE's Translation has the Reputation of coming next to it: And as all Authors agree that HOMER was Blind, so Mr. *Tickel* is said to have imitated him in that Respect, which occasion'd the following *Epigram*:

> As some harsh Criticks, who are too severe,
> And verse, by Judgment try, as well as Ear,
> 'Gainst *Tickel* as a *Rhiming Falstaff* plead
> For Murth'ring HOMER, after he was dead;
> And say, our *Isle* could for no Pardon hope,
> Were not th'absolving Words bestow'd by POPE:
> So by more *Civil* Judges it is said,
> That not ev'n POPE could without *Tickel*'s Aid,
> Have rais'd *entire*, HOMER from the Dead.
> 'Tis plain to reconcile the Difference,
> *This* Bard his *Blindness* shews, and *that* his *Sense*.

[1] [That is, Addison, whose *Campaign* (1705) had been a poetic success]

28. The public takes sides

June 1715–March 1717

(a) Thomas Parnell, extract from letter to Pope, 27 June 1715, *Corresp.*, i. 299. For another document by Parnell, see No. 5.

I have here seen [Tickell's] *First Book* of *Homer*, which came out at a time when it cou'd not but appear as a kind of setting up against you. My opinion is, that you may if you please, give *them thanks who writ it*. Neither the numbers nor the spirit have an equal mastery with yours; but what surprises me more is, that, a scholar being concern'd, there should happen to be some mistakes in the author's sense, such as putting the light of *Pallas*'s eyes into the eyes of *Achilles* [i. 268]; and making the taunt of *Achilles* to *Agamemnon*, (that he should have spoils when *Troy* should be taken) to be a cool and serious proposal [i. 163–4]: the translating what you call *ablution* by the word *Offals* [i. 413], and so leaving *Water* out of the rite of lustration, *&c.* but you must have taken notice of all this before.

(b) Jonathan Swift, extract from a letter to Pope, 28 June 1715, *The Correspondence of Jonathan Swift*, ed. Sir H. Williams (1963), ii. 176–7. The letter is written from Dublin.

I borrowed you Homer from the Bishop (mine is not yet landed) and read it out in two evenings. If it pleases others as well as me, you have got your end in profit and reputation: Yet I am angry at some bad Rhymes and Triplets, and pray in your next do not let me have so many unjustifiable Rhymes to *war* and *gods*. I tell you all the faults I know, only in one or two places you are a little obscure; but I expected you to be so in one or two and twenty. I have heard no soul talk of it here, for indeed it is not come over; nor do we very much abound in judges, at least I have not the honour to be acquainted with them. Your Notes are perfectly good, and so are your Preface and Essay.[1] You were pretty bold in mentioning Lord Bolingbroke in that Preface.[2]

[1] [Pope was not altogether satisfied with Parnell's prefatory 'Essay']
[2] [Pope's complimentary references to Bolingbroke were printed when Bolingbroke had fled the country, and might well seem bold. On 28 June, Charles Jervas advised Pope to even the balance by adding a reference to Walpole (*Corresp.*, i. 300)]

(c) Dr Edward Young, letter to Thomas Tickell, written from Oxford on 28 June 1715, R. E. Tickell, *Thomas Tickell and the Eighteenth Century Poets* (1931), pp. 43–4. For the shifts in Young's attitude to Pope, see Nos 40 and 112.

DR TICKELL,

Be assured I want no Inducement to behave myself like your Friend. To be very plain the University almost in general gives the Preference to Popes Translation. They say his is written with more Spirit Ornament & Freedom & has more the air of an Original.

I inclined some, Harrison &^{c}, to compare the Translations with the Greek, which was done; it made some small alteration in their opinions, but still Pope was their Man. The Bottom of the Case is this, they were strongly prepossest in Popes Favour, from a wrong Notion of your Design, before the Poem came down & the Sight of yours has not had Force enough upon them, to make them willing to contradict themselves & own they were in the wrong; but they go far for prejudist Persons & own yours an excellent Translation, nor do I hear any violently affirm it to be worse, but those who look on Pope as a Miracle, & among those to your Comfort, Evans is the first. And even those Zealots allow that you have outdone Pope in some Particulars. E.G. The Speech beginning

Oh sunk in Avarice &^{c}
And leave a naked &^{c1}

Upon the whole I affirm your Performance has gained you much Reputation & when they compare you with what they sh^d compare you, with Homer only, you are much admired. It has given many of the best Judges a Desire to see the Odyssey by the same Hand, which they talk of with Pleasure & I seriously believe your first Piece of that will quite break this Partiality for Pope, which your Iliad has weakened & secure your Success. Nor think my opinion groundlessly swayd, by my Wishes, for I observe as Prejudice cools, you grow in Favour & you are a better Poet now, than when your Homer first came down. I am persuaded fully your Design cannot but succeed here, & it shall be my hearty desire & Endeavour that it may.

(d) Rev. (later Bishop) George Berkeley, extract from a letter to Pope, 7 July 1715, *Corresp.*, i. 304. (See note on following item.)

¹ [Tickell's translation of Book i of *Iliad* (1715), pp. 10, 23]

—Some days ago, three or four Gentlemen and my self exerting that right which all readers pretend to over Authors, sate in judgement upon the two new Translations of the first *Iliad*. Without partiality to my country-men, I assure you they all gave the preference where it was due; being unanimously of opinion that yours was equally just to the sense with Mr. [Tickell]'s, and without comparison more easy, more poetical, and more sublime. But I will say no more on such a threadbare subject, as your late performance is at this time.

(e) John Gay, extract from a letter to Pope, 8 July 1715, *Corresp.*, i. 305. This, with the preceding, was one of three 'extracts' which Pope printed in all editions of his *Letters* except the 'authorized' quarto and folio of 1737.

—I have just set down Sir *Samuel Garth* at the Opera. He bid me tell you, that every body is pleas'd with your Translation, but a few at *Button*'s; and that Sir *Richard Steele* told him, that Mr. *Addison* said *Tickel*'s translation was the best that ever was in any language. He treated me with extream civility, and out of kindness gave me a squeeze by the Sore finger.—I am inform'd that at *Button*'s your character is made very free with as to morals, &c. and Mr. *A[ddison]* says, that your translation and *Tickel*'s are both very well done, but that the latter has more of *Homer*.

(f) Thomas Burnet, extract from a letter to George Duckett, co-author of *Homeride*, 7 August 1715, *The Letters of Thomas Burnet to George Duckett, 1712–1722*, ed. D. N. Smith (1914), p. 92.

And by Mr Addison's direction I have enclosed in the Trunk afore-said . . . Mr Tickel's Translation of the first Book of the Iliad, which I dare say you will approve of; to me it seems to have all the Beauty and Majesty which Homer's loose way of writing carryes with it: whilest Pope's, if you were extravagant enough to buy it, woud appear only like a smooth soft Poem, rather of Dryden's than Homer's Composing.

(g) Joseph Addison, extract from *The Freeholder*, no. 40, 7 May 1716, reprinted in *The Works of the Right Honourable Joseph Addison, Esq.*, ed. T. Tickell (1721), iv. 506–7.

When I consider my self as a *British* Free-holder, I am in a particular manner pleased with the labours of those who have improved our

language with the translation of old *Latin* and *Greek* Authors; and by
that means let us into the knowledge of what passed in the famous
governments of *Greece* and *Rome*. We have already most of their
historians in our own tongue: and what is still more for the honour
of our language, it has been taught to express with elegance the greatest
of their Poets in each nation. The illiterate among our countrymen,
may learn to judge from *Dryden's Virgil* of the most perfect epic
performance: and those parts of *Homer*, which have already been
published by Mr. *Pope*, give us reason to think that the *Iliad* will appear
in *English* with as little disadvantage to that immortal Poem.

(h) J. D. Breval (under the pseudonym of 'Joseph Gay'), extract from
The Confederates: A Farce (1717), pp. 32–3. During this farce, which
mocks Pope, Arbuthnot, and Gay for their collaboration in *Three
Hours After Marriage*, Pope turns on his publisher Lintot, who fears that
the failure of the play will lose him money. Published 30 March 1717.

> P[*ope*]. Ungrateful Man! *Fame's Temple*, call to mind,
> My *Forest*, *Rape*, and *Satires on Mankind*;
> Think how by These thou hast increas'd thy Store.
> L[*intot*]. Look on your Homer, there, behind the Door.
> Thou little dream'st what Crowds I daily see,
> That call for Tickell, and that spurn at Thee!
> Neglected there, your Prince of Poets lyes,
> By Dennis justly damn'd,[1] and kept for Pyes.
> Alas! his Outside I enrich in vain,
> And by the Gilding, Custom hope to gain:
> With some dull Fop, perhaps, the Book may pass,
> And help to make a Show in Case of Glass.
> But your fam'd Heroes, with their warlike Bands,
> Grace the same Shelf where Ogilby now stands,
> And rot on mine, or on Subscribers hands.
>   . . .
> You may with Curll your Quarrel now repent,
> Or else to him you might for Help have sent:
> But he with *Ballads* will debauch the Town,
> And cloak your small Remainder of Renown.
> Your *quondam* Vogue is now for ever lost;
> As sure as on my Sign *Two Keys* are *cross'd*.

[1] [See No. 30]

29. Theobald praises the *Iliad*

January 1717

Lewis Theobald (1688–1744), extract from *The Censor*, no. xxxiii
(5 January 1717:1717 ed., ii. 18-20). In view of Theobald's later
enmity toward Pope, this generous assessment of the *Iliad* is of
particular interest. It is ironical that the extract concludes with an
attack on Dennis. Prior to the extract, Theobald has been taking
ill-natured and carping critics to task.

In opposition to this Conduct, I promise the Publick to be as true an
Attendant upon Vertue, as a Spy upon Vice; to be more forward in
Praising, than Condemning the Works of my Contemporaries according to their intrinsick Merit. I cannot give them a better Specimen
of my Inclination, than by telling them that I have read with Pleasure
the new *Translation* of the first *eight* Books of *Homer*, and if I were to
commend the Author, I should do it in these excellent Lines of a Modern to Mr. *Dryden*:

> The Copy casts a fairer Light on all,
> And still out-shines the bright Original.

The Spirit of *Homer* breaths all through this Translation, and I am
in doubt whether I should most admire the Justness of the Original,
or the Force and Beauty of the Language, or the sounding Variety of
the Numbers; but when I find all these meet, it puts me in mind of
what the Poet says of one of his Heroes, that he *alone* raised and flung
with ease a weighty Stone that Two common Men could not lift from
the Ground; just so one single Person has performed in this Translation, what I once despaired to have seen done by the force even of
several masterly Hands. Let the Reader observe these two similitudes
of the Motion of the *Græcian* Army in the *Second* Book, and I am
sure he will be of my Opinion.

> The Sceptred Rulers lead; the following Host,
> Pour'd forth in Millions, darkness all the Coast,

As from some Rocky Cleft the Shepherd sees
Clustring in Heaps on Heaps the driving Bees,
Rolling, and blackning, Swarms succeeding Swarms,
With deeper Murmurs, and more hoarse Alarms,
Dusky they spread, a close-embodied Croud,
And o'er the Vale descends the living Cloud.

[ii. 109–16]

And soon after.—

Murm'ring they move, as when old *Ocean* roars,
And heaves huge Surges to the *trembling Shores*;
The groaning Banks are burst with bellowing Sound,
The Rocks remurmur, and the Deeps rebound.

[ii. 249–52]

I could with a great deal of Pleasure point out the particular Beauties of these Verses, which are not perhaps obvious to every Eye; but I have already said enough to call the Critick *Furius*[1] upon my Back, and therefore leave them to the private Judgment of every Reader.

---

[1] [I.e. John Dennis. Theobald abused Dennis persistently in *The Censor*, but had ceased hostilities by the time he praised the older critic in *Shakespeare Restored* (1726). Theobald did indeed call Dennis's wrath upon his back: see the next item]

30. 'Sir Tremendous Longinus' replies

February 1717

John Dennis, *Remarks upon Mr. Pope's Translation of Homer. With Two Letters Concerning Windsor Forest, and the Temple of Fame* (1717), *Critical Works*, ii. 122–5.

Dennis's *Remarks* were published 12–28 February. When he first jotted down his response to Pope's *Iliad* sometime between 20 September 1716 and 1 February 1717, Dennis had no thoughts of publication. However, Lewis Theobald's praise of Pope's translation which was coupled with an attack on the critic (5 January 1717, see No. 29), was closely followed by the portrait of Dennis as Sir Tremendous Longinus in *Three Hours After Marriage*, first performed 16–23 January. This twin affront to his dignity provoked Dennis into gathering together his notes on the *Iliad*, and his unpublished letters on *Windsor Forest* (see No. 16) and *The Temple of Fame*. For a fuller account of the background to the publication of the *Remarks*, see E. N. Hooker, 'Pope and Dennis', *English Literary History*, vii (1940), 188–98.

Only a small portion of Dennis's enraged cavilling is given here.

. . . to satisfie the Reader of [Pope's] Incapacity to Translate HOMER, or of writing any thing of his own that is barely tolerable, I shall lay before the Reader some Observations upon the late Translation of HOMER, upon *Windsor Forest*, *The Temple of Fame*, and *The Rape of the Lock*. We shall begin with the Translation of HOMER.

There is a notorious Ideot, one Hight *Whachum*,[1] who from an under-spur Leather to the Law, is become an under-strapper to the Play-House, who has lately burlesqu'd the *Metamorphoses* of OVID, by a vile Translation of him, and alter'd him so much from what he was, that the *Roman* treats of no Transformation half so strange as his own:

---

[1] [Lewis Theobald. His translation of Ovid's *Metamorphoses* was published in 1716]

This Fellow is concern'd in an impertinent Paper which is call'd the *Censor*. In the Third of which he is pleased to extol the late Translation of HOMER. *I know not which I should most admire*, says he, *the justness of the Original* (where I suppose he means, the Justness of the Original expressed in the Translation) *or the Force and Beauty of the Language, or the Sounding Variety of the Numbers*.[1] He may admire which of these he pleases. But the Truth of the Matter is, that there is in this Translation neither the Justness of the Original, even where the Original is just; nor any Beauty of Language, nor any Variety of Numbers. Instead of the Justness of the Original, there is in this Translation Absurdity and Extravagance. Instead of the beautiful Language of the Original, there is in the Translation Solecism and barbarous English.

Indeed it is impossible for any Translator, and much less for this, to express in a Translation the Poetical Language of HOMER. By the Advantage of the Language in which he wrote, he had several ways of rendering his Language Poetical, which a Translator can never have; as the frequent Use of compounded and decompounded Words; the Use of Words which were as it were at one and the same time both Grecian and Foreign; as being confin'd in their vulgar Use to some particular Part of *Greece*; as likewise the Use of Words which were purely Poetick, and which were seldom or never us'd in Prose; the contracting or lengthening the Words which he used, and the frequent transposing of Syllables; and, lastly, the altering the Terminations of Words, by means of the different Dialects. But a Translator of HOMER has but one way of rendering his Diction Poetical; and that is, the frequent Use of Figures, and above all Figures of Metaphors. And therefore, where-ever in the late Translation of HOMER, there is no Use of Figures, there we may justly conclude, that the Diction is Prosaick; though at the same time, the Diction of the Original, in that very Place, even without Figures, may be truly Poetical, for Reasons mention'd above. Now, in the late Translation of HOMER, there are, modestly speaking, Twenty Lines where there is no Figure, for One that is Figurative; and, consequently, there are Twenty Prosaick Lines, for One that is Poetical. Indeed, the late Translator of HOMER, by his want of Genius, and by his writing figuratively, where the *Grecian* has writ plainly, has often made his Diction the very Reverse of that of the Original: Where the Original is pure, the Translation is often

---

[1] [I.e. Lewis Theobald's comments on Pope's translation in No. 29 above. Theobald there characterizes Dennis under the name of 'Furius']

barbarous; often obscure, where the Original is clear and bright; often flat and vile, where the other is great and lofty; and often, too often, affected and unnatural, where the Original is simple and un-affected; as it is frequently stiff and awkward, where the Original is easie, graceful, and numerous. In short, the HOMER which LINTOTT prints, does not talk like HOMER, but like POPE, and is so far from expressing the Beauty of HOMER's Language, that he makes him speak *English* as awkwardly as other Foreigners do; and sometimes makes him talk as merrily as a Monsieur, who comes to live among us in his Old Age, and, with a great deal of Pains, acquires *English* enough to be laugh'd at. So that the little Gentleman who translated him, with a most comical and unparallel'd Assurance, has undertaken to trans-late HOMER from *Greek*, of which he does not know one Word, into *English*, which he understands almost as little. And from hence it pro-ceeds, that instead of making him *English*, he sometimes makes him *Irish*; and one would swear, that he had a Hill in *Tipperary*, for his *Parnassus*, and a Puddle in some Bog, for his *Hippocrene*.

But because it may be said, that this is only Talking, I will prove all this from the very Lines, which *Censor Whachum* has brought to show the Excellence of this Translation, which he will show, he says, from the Two Similitudes of the Motion of the *Grecian* Army, in the Second Book of the *Ilias*:

> The Scepter'd Rulers lead; the following Host,
> Pour'd forth in Millions, darkens all the Coast.
>
> [ii. 109–10][1]

Now, where is the Justness of the Original in these two Lines? Though HOMER is said to nod sometimes, yet 'tis hard if he snores so like a Sot, as to give the Lye to his own Calculation which he makes in this very Book, by which Calculation it appears, that the Army of the *Grecians* did not amount to above a Hundred Thousand in all. And if any one happens to answer this, That their Numbers are augmented by Poetical License; to that I reply, That no Poetical License ever extended to such an Augmentation of Numbers, as to make a Poet give the Lye to his own Calculations; or to make us believe, that Two and Three make Six. Never human Army yet consisted of Millions. No Place upon Earth can contain such Numbers congregated, but what at the same time will starve them. But let us proceed:

[1] [Altered in 1720 to read 'Pour'd forth by thousands']

As from some rocky Cleft the Shepherd sees,
Clust'ring in Heaps on Heaps, the driving Bees.
[ii. 111–12]

Now where is the Justness of the Original here again? For while the
Bees *drive*, they cannot possibly *cluster*.

Rolling and black'ning, Swarms succeeding Swarms,
With deeper Murmurs, and more hoarse Alarms.
[ii. 113–14]

Here again, there is nothing of the Justness of the Original; since
but One Swarm of Bees can come from One Cleft of a Rock.

Dusky they spread, a close embodied Crowd,
And o'er the Vale descends the living Cloud.
[ii. 115–16]

The first Line here presents us with a Contradiction in Terms; for
while the Bees are a *close embodied Crowd*, how can they possibly *spread*?
Besides, what does the Translator mean, by a *close embodied Crowd*?
What Tautology, what Fustian is this? As if every *Crowd* was not
close. And what does he mean by *embodied*? What Idea to the Mind
does that Word clearly and distinctly present? In short, *Crowd* is nothing but a Botch, and a meer Crambo[1] to *Cloud*. For who ever heard
of a Crowd of Bees? A Crowd of any thing implies Confusion; but it
appears by the following Lines of VIRGIL, that Bees when they swarm,
are under Command, and, by consequence, not without Order;
no more than the *Grecian* Army, when it *pour'd it self forth*, as Mr.
Censor Whachum says, in *Millions*.

At cum incerta volant cœloque examina ludunt,
Contemnuntq; favos, & frigida tecta relinquunt;
Instabiles animos ludo prohibebis inani.
Nec magnus prohibere labor: tu regibus alas
Eripe: no illis quisquam cunctantibus altum
Ire iter, aut castris audebit vellere signa.[2]

---

[1] [I.e. repetition, rhyme]
[2] [Virgil, *Georgics*, iv. 103–108: 'But when the swarms flit aimlessly and sport in the air,
scorning their cells, and leaving their hives chill, you must check their fickle spirit from
such idle play. No hard task it is to check them. Do you tear from the monarchs their
wings; while they tarry, no one will dare to go forth aloft, or pluck the standards from the
camps']

For the last Line of the foresaid Simile:

And o'er the Vale descends the living Cloud: [ii. 116]

There is neither Sense, nor *English* in it. To descend *to*, or *into*, to descend *on*, or *upon*, is *English*, but to descend *o'er*, is barbarous; as will appear plainly, by taking away the Contraction of the Preposition, and changing the Metaphor for the common Name: And then the Line will run thus:

A Swarm of Bees descends over the Vale.

What Sense is here? What clear Idea of any Thing? or of any particular local Motion? Where is this boasted Beauty of the Language? Where is the Justness of the Original? HOMER, indeed, does compare the Motion of the *Grecian* Army, to the Motion of a Swarm of Bees; but he does it with a beautiful Simplicity; nor does he use any such impertinent Metaphor, as *living Cloud*, which can serve for nothing but to distract the Mind of the Reader, and to divert it from the Idea which the Poet design'd to lay before it of the Motion of the *Grecian* Army. . . .

31. Lady Mary Wortley Montagu's praise

September 1717

Lady Mary Wortley Montagu, extract from a letter to Pope, 1 September 1717, *Corresp.*, i. 423.

I long much to tread upon English ground, that I may see you and Mr. Congreve, who render that ground *classick ground*; nor will you refuse our present Secretary[1] a part of that merit, whatever reasons you may have to be dissatisfied with him in other respects. You are the three happiest poets I ever heard of; one a secretary of state, the other en-

[1] [Addison, became one of the Secretaries of State on 16 April 1717]

joying leisure with dignity in two lucrative employments;[1] and you, tho' your religious profession is an obstacle to court promotion, and disqualifies you from filling civil employments, have found the *Philosophers stone*, since by making the Iliad pass through your poetical crucible into an English form without losing aught of its original beauty, you have drawn the golden current of Pactolus[2] to Twickenham. I call this finding the Philosophers stone, since you alone found out the secret, and nobody else has got into it. A[ddiso]n and T[ickel]l tried it, but their experiments failed; and they lost, if not their money, at least a certain portion of their fame in the trial—while you touched the mantle of the divine Bard, and imbibed his spirit. I hope we shall have the Odyssey soon from your happy hand, and I think I shall follow with singular pleasure the traveller Ulysses, who was an observer of men and manners, when he travels in your harmonious numbers.

[1] [Congreve held a number of minor government posts from 1695 onwards. They were not particularly 'lucrative', nor were they easy sinecures. Further, see J. C. Hodges, *William Congreve the Man* (New York, 1941)]

[2] [A small river in Asia Minor, once famous for the patricles of gold in its sands]

32. An eminent French scholar attacks Pope's view of Homer

1719

Mme Anne Dacier, extracts from 'Reflexions sur la premiere Partie de la Preface de M. Pope', *l'Iliade d'Homere* (2nd ed., Paris, 1719), iii, extra gathering at end. The translation given here, which is somewhat free, is that reprinted in *The Popiad* (1728), pp. 26–32 from 'T. Parnell's' translation published in 1724.

Anne Dacier (1654–1720) published her important prose translation of Homer in 1699. Her work was influential and widely known in France and England, and Pope made use of it for his own translation. With her husband André, Mme Dacier was an acknowledged classical authority of long standing. The 'Reflexions' were added to the second edition of her translation at the last moment. Although Mme Dacier's remarks are directed against Pope's opinions of Homer and not at the translation itself, they are of considerable interest for the light they throw on Pope's attempt to remake Homer in an Augustan image. They also testify to French interest in his version of Homer.

UPON the finishing of the *second Edition* of my Translation of HOMER, a particular friend sent me a Translation of part of Mr. *Pope*'s Preface to his Version of the ILIAD. As I do not understand *English*, I cannot form any Judgment of his Performance, tho' I have heard much of it. I am indeed willing to believe that the Praise[s] it has met with are not unmerited, because whatever Work is approved by the *English* Nation, cannot be bad; but yet I hope I may be permitted to judge of that part of the Preface which has been transmitted to me, and I here take the liberty of giving my Sentiments thereon. I must freely acknowledge, that Mr. POPE's *Invention* is very lively, tho' he seems to have been guilty of the same Fault into which he owns we are often precipitated by our *Invention*, when we depend too much upon the

Strength of it: *As Magnanimity, says he, may run up to Profusion and Extravagance, so may a great Invention to Redundancy or Wildness.*

This has been the very Case of Mr. *Pope* himself; nothing is more overstrained or more false than the Images in which his Fancy has represented HOMER; sometimes he tells us, that the ILIAD is a '*wild Paradise, where if we cannot see all the Beauties, as in an ordered Garden, it is only because the Number of them is infinitely greater*'. Sometimes he compares him to '*a copious Nursery, which contains the Seeds and first Productions of every kind*'; and, lastly, he represents him under the Notion of a '*mighty Tree, which rises from the most vigorous Seed, is improved with Industry, flourishes and produces the finest Fruit, but bears too many Branches, which might be lopped into Form, to give it a more regular Appearance*'.[1]

What! Is *Homer's* Poem then, according to Mr. *Pope*, a confused Heap of Beauties, without Order or Symmetry, a Plat[2] whereon nothing but Seeds, nor nothing perfect or formed is to be found; and a Production loaded with many unprofitable things, which ought to be retrenched, and which choak or disfigure those which deserve to be preserved?

The most inveterate Enemies to *Homer*, never said any thing more injurious, or more unjust, against that Poet.

As I have defended him, with pretty good Success, against the Cavils of so many ignorant Censors, who have condemned him because they did not understand him, I find my self again obliged to defend him against the Reproaches of one of greater Penetration, and may therefore do him more Injury in the Minds of unlearned Readers, tho' at the same time he pretends to have a great Veneration for him.

Mr. *Pope* will pardon me then if I here oppose these three Comparisons, which to me appear very false, and entirely contrary to what the greatest, antient, and modern Criticks ever thought.

To the Point then, the ILIAD is so far from being a wild Paradise, that it is the most regular Garden, and laid out with more Symmetry than any ever was. Monsieur *le Nostre*,[3] who was the first Man of the World in his Art, never observed in his Gardens a more perfect or more admirable Symmetry, than *Homer* has observed in his Poems. Every thing therein, is not only in the Place it ought to have, but every thing is made for the Place it hath. He presents you at first with that

---

[1] [For the quotations from Pope's Preface, see Twickenham, vii. 13, 3, 17 (shortened)]
[2] ['A small piece of ground'] [3] [André le Nôtre (1612–1700)] Gardiner to *Lewis XIV*. He laid out the Gardens of *Versailles, Marli*, &c.

which ought to be first seen, he places in the middle what ought to be in the middle, and what would improperly be at the Beginning or End, and he removes what ought to be at a greater Distance, to create the more agreeable Surprize; and, to use a Comparison drawn from Painting, he places that in the greatest Light which cannot be too visible, and sinks, in the Obscurity of the Shade, what does not require a full View: so that it may be said, that *Homer* is the Painter who best knew how to employ the Shades and Lights, and it was this wonderfully beauteous Order which *Horace* admired in his Poems, and on which he founded his Rules for the perfecting of the *Art* of *Poetry.*

The second Comparison is as unjust: How could Mr. *Pope* say, that one can only discover '*Seeds and first Productions of every kind in the* ILIAD'? Every Beauty is therein to so great a perfection, that the following Ages could add nothing to those of any kind; and the Antients have always proposed *Homer* as the most perfect Model in all kinds of Poetry.

The third Comparison is composed of the Errors of the two former; *Homer* had certain an incomparable Fertility of Invention, but his Fertility is always checked by that just Sense, which made him reject every superfluous thing which his vast Imagination could offer him, to retain only what was useful or necessary. Judgment guided the Hand of this admirable Gardiner, and was the Pruning-Hook he employ'd to lop off every useless Branch; he has done what *Horace* directs.

Inutilesque falce ramos amputans Feliciores inserit.[1]

Mr. *Pope* had done us a great Piece of Service, if he had pointed out the useless Branches that ought to be lopp'd from this Tree. The Symmetry which ought to be given to that wild Garden to render it more regular, and the Perfection which is wanting to the several Beauties, he says *Homer* has only sketched out; it would be very happy for the present Age, and glorious to *England*, to have produced so perfect a Critick.

Now I have defended *Homer*, I must also defend myself against a Criticism he has made upon a part of my Preface; where speaking of the Manners of *Homer*'s Heroes, so like those of the Patriarchs, I have said, '*I find these ancient Times so much the finer, as they the less resemble our Own.*'[2] Upon this Mr. *Pope* exclaims, '*Who can be so prejudiced in*

---

[1] [*Epod.* ii. 13–14: 'and cutting off useless branches with the pruning knife, engrafts more fruitful ones']

[2] [*L'Iliade d'Homère* (1711), i, p. xxv]

their favour, as to magnify their Felicity, when a Spirit of Revenge and Cruelty reigned through the World, when no Mercy was shewn but for the sake of Lucre when the greatest Princes were put to the Sword, and their Wives and Daughters made Slaves and Concubines?'[1] Mr. *Pope* sure mistook me!

When I said so, could I mean that the Manners of these heroical Times were perfect and without fault! Were they so in more happy Times! Were there no Tokens then of Cruelty or Revenge! Were there no Captives made! Were there no Kings put to the Sword! Were there no Concubines seen among them! And since the Christian Religion has taught a more perfect Morality, was there never a Spirit of Revenge and Cruelty seen amongst Christians! Do they not make no more Prisoners of War! and do not they redeem them! Was there never a Concubine, and something worse, seen among them! Did all these Vices, which Mr. *Pope* blames those antient Times for, hinder Nature from being then very plain, far from the Luxury, Pomp, and Effeminacy which have corrupted the following Ages! Are not these Manners of *Homer*'s Heroes very like those of the Patriarchs, and very unlike these of our Own Time! I might then say, that those Times and Manners seemed so much the more excellent to me, as they less resemble those of our own. Durst Mr. *Pope* himself prefer the Manners of the present Age to those of the antient Times! no, without doubt; for 6 Lines after he embraces my Opinion, which he had blamed: '*I find,*' says he, '*a Pleasure in observing the Simplicity of that Age, in opposition to the Pomp and Luxury of the following Ages.*'[2] One may then, according to his own Sense, prefer those Ages of natural Simplicity to these that are corrupted with Pomp and Luxury.

I own I did not expect to find my self attacked by Mr. *Pope,* in a Preface wherein I might have expected some small Token of Acknowledgement, or at least some slight Approbation; for having been so happy as to think on several Things in the way he himself does, especially on the Manners of the Antients, after I had said in my Preface, '*That Princes tended their Flocks, That Princesses drew Water at the Spring,*' and brought Examples to prove this from the Holy Scriptures, and the *Roman* History itself, I conclude with these words: '*I love to see Juno dressing herself without the Trinkets of a Toilet, or the Assistance of a Waiting-Woman; it is the same with the Heroes as with the Gods, one sees neither Footmen, nor Valets de Chambre, nor Guards about* ACHILLES,

---

[1] [Preface to *Iliad,* Twickenham, vii. 14]
[2] [*Ibid.*]

AGAMEMNON, &c. HERCULES *and* THESEUS *had none of these.*' Mr. POPE says the same thing, '*There is a Pleasure in beholding Monarchs without their Guards, Princes tending* their Flocks, and Princesses drawing Water *from the Springs*'.[1]

I am overjoyed to find that Mr. *Pope* is as much in love with the Simplicity of the antient Times as I am; It is a Token that he abhors the Pomp and Luxury of our own, and gives me Reason to hope, that a little Reflection will induce him to approve what I have said, and he has so justly condemned. . . .

[Mme Dacier takes up Pope's comments on Homer's invention of his fable, and interpretation of Aristotle. She concludes]

The Faults I blame him for, are so trivial, that they ought not to hinder the *English* Nation from expecting from this *new Poet* the great Advantages that are to be hoped for, from a *Reformer* of HOMER. So bright a Man will not confine himself to perfect only the *Art* of *Epick Poesy*, that would be a trifling Matter; No; he will perfect the *Art of Politicks*, much more valuable and more important than that of *Epick Poesy*. A Man capable to correct HOMER, will be able to form the Manners of Men; ALCIBIADES was of that Opinion, for a *Grammarian* having made his Brags before him, that he had in his Closet an HOMER corrected with his own Hand, *What! Friend*, said he, *art thou capable to correct* HOMER? *and dost thou waste thy time in teaching Children? why dost thou not apply thy self to form the Manners of Men?*

Of what infinite Consequence then, will Mr. POPE be to a State, since he can reform HOMER?

[1] This Preface of Madame *Dacier* was written long before Mr. *Pope* wrote his, and I think the Lady is very modest when he uses her own Words, to say that she was happy in having *thought* as he did; tho' it is plain that he borrowed this *Thought* from her. . . .

33. William Melmoth's opinion

1719

William Melmoth, extract from letter xi, 'To Euphronius', dated 10 October 1719, *Letters on Several Subjects. By the late Sir Thomas Fitzosborne, Bart* . . ., i (1748), 41-3, 46-50.

Melmoth (1710-99) was commissioner of bankrupts as well as an author. See also *Pope's Iliad: An Examination by William Melmoth*, ed. G. Cronin and P. A. Doyle (Washington, D.C., 1960), which reprints letters ix, lxiv, lxx, all concerned with the *Iliad*.

I HAVE often mentioned to you the pleasure I received from Mr. Pope's late translation of the Iliad: but my admiration of that inimitable performance has encreased upon me, since you tempted me to compare the copy with the original. To say of this noble work, that it is the best which ever appeared of the kind, would be speaking in much lower terms that it deserves; the world perhaps scarce ever before saw a truly poetical translation: for, as Denham observes,

> Such is our pride, our folly, or our fate,
> That few, but those who cannot write, translate.[1]

But Mr. Pope seems in most places to have been inspired with the same sublime spirit that animates his original; as he often takes fire from a single hint in his author, and blazes out even with a stronger and brighter flame of poetry. Thus the character of Thersites, as it stands in the English Iliad, is heighten'd, I think, with more masterly strokes of satyr than appear in the Greek; as many of those similies in Homer, which would appear, perhaps, to a modern eye too naked and un-ornamented, are painted by Pope in all the beautiful drapery of the most graceful metaphor. With what propriety of figure, for instance, has he raised the following comparison:

[Quotes in Greek, *Iliad*, iii. 10-14: 'Even as when the South Wind

[1] ['To Sir Richard Fanshaw upon his Translation of *Pastor Fido*', ll. 1-2]

sheddeth a mist over the peaks of a mountain, a mist that the shepherd
loveth not, but that to the robber is better than night, and a man can
see only so far as he casteth a stone; even in such wise rose the dense
dust-cloud from beneath their feet as they went.']

> Thus from his flaggy wings when Eurus sheds
> A night of vapours round the mountain-heads,
> Swift gliding mists the dusky fields invade;
> To thieves more grateful than the midnight shade:
> While scarce the swains their feeding flocks survey,
> Lost and confus'd amidst the thicken'd day:
> So wrapt in gath'ring dust the Græcian train,
> A moving cloud, swept on and hid the plain.   [iii. 15–22]

WHEN Mars, being wounded by Diomed, flies back to heaven,
Homer compares him in his passage to a dark cloud raised by summer
heats, and driven by the wind.

[Quotes in Greek, *Iliad*, v. 864–5: 'Even as a black darkness appeareth
from the clouds when after heat a blustering wind ariseth.']

The inimitable translator improves this image by throwing in some
circumstances, which, though not in the original, are exactly in the
spirit of Homer:

> As vapours, blown by Auster's sultry breath,
> Pregnant with plagues, and shedding seeds of death,
> Beneath the rage of burning Sirius rise,
> Choak the parch'd earth, and blacken all the skies;
> In such a cloud the god, from combat driv'n,
> High o'er the dusty whirlwind scales the heav'n.
>
> > [v. 1058–63]

[Melmoth compares two further passages, and then remarks]

THERE is no antient author more likely to betray an injudicious interpreter into meannesses than Homer; as it requires the utmost skill and
address to preserve that venerable air of simplicity which is one of
the characteristical marks of that poet, without sinking the expression
or the sentiment into contempt. . . .

BUT among many other passages of this sort I observ'd one in the
same book, which rais'd my curiosity to examine in what manner

Mr. Pope had conducted it. Juno, in a general council of the gods, thus accosts Jupiter:

[Quotes in Greek, *Iliad*, iv. 25–8]

which is as much as if she had said in plain English, 'Why surely, Jupiter, you won't be so cruel as to render ineffectual all my expence of labour and sweat. Have I not tired every horse in my stable in order to raise forces to ruin Priam and his family?' It requires the most delicate touches imaginable, to raise such a sentiment as this into any tolerable degree of dignity. But a skilful artist knows how to embellish the most ordinary subject, and what would be low and spiritless from a less masterly pencil, becomes pleasing and graceful when work'd up by Mr. Pope's:

> Shall then, O tyrant of th' ethereal plain,[1]
> My schemes, my labours, and my hopes be vain?
> Have I for this shook Ilion with alarms,
> Assembled nations, set two worlds in arms?
> To spread the war I flew from shore to shore,
> Th'immortal coursers scarce the labour bore.   [iv. 34–40]

BUT to shew you that I am not so enthusiastic an admirer of this glorious performance, as to be blind to its imperfections; I will venture to point out a passage or two (amongst others which might be mentioned) wherein Mr. Pope's usual judgment seems to have failed him:

WHEN Iris is sent to inform Helen that Paris and Menelaus are going to decide the fate of both nations by single combat, and were actually upon the point of engaging; Homer describes her as hastily throwing her veil over her face and flying to the Scaean gate, from whence she might have a full view of the field of battle:

[Quotes in Greek, *Iliad*, iii. 141–3, 145: 'And straightway she veiled herself with shining linen, and went forth from her chamber, letting fall round tears, not alone, for with her followed two handmaids as well . . . and with speed they came to the place where were the Scæan gates.']

NOTHING could possibly be more interesting to Helen than the circumstances in which she is here represented: it was necessary therefore to exhibit her, as Homer we see has, with much eagerness and

[1] [Pope has 'Reign!']

impetuosity in her motion. But what can be more calm and quiet than
the attitude wherein the Helen of Mr. Pope appears:

> O'er her fair face a snowy veil she threw,
> And softly sighing from the loom *withdrew*
> Her handmaids —— —— *wait*
> Her *silent* footsteps to the Scæan gate. [iii. 187–90]

THOSE expressions of speed and impetuosity which occur so often in
the original lines, viz. [142–3] would have been sufficient, one should
have imagined, to have guarded a translator from falling into an
Impropriety of this kind.

A ROMAN CATHOLICK VERSION
OF THE FIRST PSALM

30 June 1716

34. Blackmore on Pope's profane obscenity

1717

Sir Richard Blackmore, extract from *Essays upon Several Subjects*, ii (1717), 270. Blackmore's book was published on 26 March 1717.

Blackmore (d. 1729) was a physician, moralizer, and an inveterate composer of epics. He became a central butt in the *Bathos*. In this passage Blackmore turns from an attack on immoral writers for a concluding blast at Pope.

I cannot but here take notice, that one of these Champions of Vice is the reputed Author of a detestable Paper, that has lately been handed about in Manuscript, and now appears in Print, in which the godless Author has burlesqu'd the *First Psalm* of *David* in so obscene and profane a manner, that perhaps no Age ever saw such an insolent Affront offer'd to the establish'd Religion of their Country, and this, good Heaven! with Impunity. A sad Demonstration this, of the low Ebb to which the *British* Vertue is reduc'd in these degenerate Times.

35. Matthew Prior's and James Delacour's praise

1719, 1730

(a) Matthew Prior, *Alma*, ii. 287–304, *Literary Works of Matthew Prior*, ed. H. B. Wright and M. Spears (1959), i. 492–3. Prior's poem was first published in *Poems on Several Occasions* (1718), published 17 March 1719. Lord Bathurst told Warton that Pope was not pleased with this compliment, *An Essay on the Genius and Writings of Pope*, i (3rd ed., 1772), 316 note.

> O ABELARD, ill-fated Youth,
> Thy Tale will justify the Truth:
> But well I weet, thy cruel Wrong
> Adorns a nobler Poet's Song.
> *Dan* POPE for thy Misfortune griev'd,
> With kind Concern, and Skill has weav'd
> A silken Web; and ne'er shall fade
> It's Colors: gently has He laid
> The Mantle o'er thy sad Distress:
> And VENUS shall the Texture bless.
> He o'er the weeping Nun has drawn,
> Such artful Folds of Sacred Lawn,
> That LOVE with equal Grief and Pride,
> Shall see the Crime, He strives to hide:
> And softly drawing back the Veil,
> The God shall to his Vot'ries tell
> Each conscious Tear, each blushing Grace,
> That deck'd Dear ELOISA's Face.

(b) James Delacour, preface to *Abelard to Eloisa, In Answer to Mr. Pope's fine Piece of Eloisa to Abelard* (Dublin, 1730), sig. A2–3.

I Doubt not in the least, but some will think it absurd to write a Preface to so small a Piece as this Letter [i.e., his poem] shews it self to be: I confess they may be so far in the right; But, however, I must make my self understood so as to avoid the Censures that may be otherwise thrown upon me for writing it. In the first Place, it was not Publish'd with a Design to rival any thing of this Nature that went before it: Every Person that has read Mr. *Pope's* justly admired Piece, are convinced that it has Beauties scarce to be imitated, much less transcended. 'Tis built upon a Story undoubtedly true, the Circumstances happ'ning in the twelfth Century and deliver'd down to us by Authors of reputed Veracity. All that have heard them join in Pity to deplore so moving a Relation. *Abelard* and *Eloisa* by all Accounts were two of the most distinguish'd Persons in the Age they liv'd in for natural and refin'd Parts, early they tasted the forbidden Fruit and as early suffer'd for it. He was pitch'd upon by her Uncle who was an Abbot in *France* to be her Præceptor in Philosophy; by which means this unlucky Passion first took its rise, that was to cost them so many Tears afterwards. The Liberties of an unconfin'd Conversation serv'd only to blow it higher: Two of the most beautiful Persons in that Age could not behold each other long with the Eyes of Insensibility; They lov'd and indulg'd their mutual Wishes, and one Evening when all they thought was safe, all private, all secure, the Abbot who had suspected them a good while before, bounc'd into the Room and seiz'd them in the very Fact. O who can describe the Surprize in each of their Faces, *Eloisa* was hurried away that Instant from his Sight, never to behold her more but in a Convent; and the unhappy *Abelard* was soon deprived forcibly of the Means of ever tasting those Joys again, by the hands of Ruffians. Thus did those faithful Lovers retire from the Vanities of a treacherous World, they went to a separate Convent and consecrated the remainder of their Days to Religion. Long after this a letter falling by chance into *Eloisa's* Hands, that was writ by *Abelard* to some of his Friends in which he gives them an Account of his unheard of Calamities and Afflictions. This awaken'd all her Tenderness and occasion'd those celebrated Letters which Mr. *Pope* and all the World will say, do give the most lively Description of the Struggles of Nature, Virtue and Passion. They died after this and were buried in the Monastery called the *Paraclete*, in the same Tomb or in Monuments adjoining.

I have read Mr. *Pope*'s Letter, and do think it impossible for Futurity to produce in our Language any thing softer in its kind than that celebrated Epistle. The many gloomy Horrors, and mournful Images work'd up here and there, and soften'd with his all-tender Expressions, make it a Master-piece for succeeding Ages. As I read him with the Pleasure of an Admirer, so I hope I have not wanted to care to imitate him. If I fall, I greatly fall, my Ambition leading me to imitate one of the finest Pieces of the kind now extant; Nay, if I have my leave to say so, I think it even excels Mr. Prior's *Henry* to *Emma*,[1] which did charm the finest Tastes Abroad and at Home. How I have study'd Mr. *Pope*'s Stile, I leave to the Ladies, who are much the properest Judges in those Affairs, and for whom it was chiefly design'd—If I'm so happy as to be approv'd of by them, Let the rest of the World Censure as they Please, I shall remain still their humble Servant,

—— J—— D——.

[1] [But see G. Tillotson, Twickenham, ii. 413–14]

ELEGY TO THE MEMORY OF AN UNFORTUNATE LADY

3 June 1717

36. Blacklock is 'thrown into Agitation'

c. 1742

Thomas Blacklock, conversation with David Hume *c.* 1742, reported in a letter of 15 October 1754, from Hume to Rev. Joseph Spence, *Anecdotes*, ed. S. W. Singer (1820), p. 448.

Hume was writing to Spence on behalf of Blacklock (1721–91), the self-educated blind bard of Dumfries.

I soon found [Blacklock] to possess a *very delicate Taste, along with a passionate Love of Learning. . . . I repeated to him Mr. Pope's Elegy to the Memory of an Unfortunate Lady*, which I happen'd to have by heart: And though I be a very bad Reciter, I saw it affected him extremely. His eyes, indeed, the great Index of the Mind, cou'd express no Passion: *but his whole Body was thrown into Agitation*: That Poem was equally qualified, to touch the Delicacy of his Taste, and the Tenderness of his Feelings.

EPITAPH ON JOHN HEWET AND SARAH DREW IN THE CHURCH-YARD AT STANTON HARCOURT

20–23 September 1718

---

37. Reactions of Atterbury and Lady Mary Wortley Montagu

1718

(a) Francis Atterbury (1662–1732), Bishop of Rochester, extracts from a letter to Pope, 12 September 1718, *Corresp.*, i. 502–4. Pope sent Atterbury a twelve-line version of the *Epitaph* on 3 September for his 'opinion both as to the doctrine and to the poetry', and followed his advice by omitting a couplet before it was carved on a memorial tablet placed on the outside wall of the church.

I like the Lines well: they are Yours, and they are Good, & on both accounts, very welcome to me. You know my Opinion, That Poetry without a Moral is a Body without a Soul. Let the Lines be never so finely turn'd, if they do not point at some Useful Truth, if there be no degree of Instruction at the bottom of them, they can give no true delight to a Reasonable mind; they are *versus inopes rerum, nugæque, canoræ*;[1] and as such they may tinkle prettily in the Ear, but will never reach the Heart, or leave a durable Impression behind them. No body that reads your Verses, will blame you on this account for they are all over Morality, from the beginning to the End of them. And it pleases me the better, because I fancy it drawn from Horace's Fountain, for I cannot help thinking, that his *Si fractus illabatur Orbis—Impavidum ferient ruinæ*[2] was, whether you attended to it or no, the Original, from

---

[1] [Horace, *Ars Poetica*, l. 322: 'verses void of thought, and sonorous trifles']
[2] [*Odes*, III. iii. 7–8: 'Were the vault of heaven to break and fall upon him, its ruins would smite him undismayed']

144

whence your two last Verses were Copy'd. I wish, you had prepar'd the way for the latter of them, as he has done, for the Idea given us by *fractus illabatur Orbis*, is strong enough to support that which follows, *Impavidum ferient ruinæ*, whereas you *melt the Ball* at once, without giving us any warning, and are led, on the sudden, from a particular Accident to the General Conflagration; & That too is to be effected by a *Flash*, a word, me thinks, not equal to the work on which you have employ'd it. Pardon this freedom! but my Old Master, Roscommon, has an Expression, which I always look'd upon as very happy and Significant (He that[1] *proportion'd wonders* can disclose) without that just Proportion, nothing is truly admirable! Will you forgive me, if I add, that *melting the Ball*, without that Preparation of the Reader I mention'd, is too apt to lead us into the Image of a Snow Ball. Waller, I am per-swaded, for the sake of the Fs and Bs, of which he was remarkably fond, would have rather chosen to say, and face the Flash, that Burns the Ball. I am far from proposing this, as an Improvement. I do not think it such: or if I did, yet I would not offer it; for, where the Images themselves are not well suited, 'tis in vain to alter a particular Expression.

I know not, Whither I am going in this Tract of Criticism, to which I have been long a Stranger. But since I am in for it, Pergite Pierides[2]—

Virtue unmov'd should you not rather say *Goodness*, than repeat the word, Virtue, which you had us'd three Lines before? So you had *Call*, also: but that Repetition is graceful; the Verb being chang'd into a Substantive, and becoming by that means a new word which echoes to the former and yet differs from it. *Aliudque et idem nascitur*,[3] says he, who says every thing better than anyone but Virgil.

Your Second Stanza is full of good Sense shortly express'd. But, me-thinks, there is some Obscurity in it *quo vitio minime teneri soles*, as Suetonius says of Horace.[4] For, when God calls the Virtuous to his Grace, tho' he be alike just, whether he calls him soon or late, yet it should not be said, that he is alike merciful, whether he kills or saves him: for, if he saves him, the very Supposition of his being call'd to the Grave, is destroy'd. Nor am I perfectly satisfy'd with that Phrase (when God calls Virtue to the Grave): tho' if the Connexion of it with

---

[1] [I.e., 'He that proportion'd Wonders can disclose, / At once his Fancy and his Judg-ment shows.' Actually, the couplet comes from a poem by Waller prefixed to Roscom-mon's translation of Horace's *Art of Poetry* (1717)]

[2] [Virgil, *Eclogues*, vi. 13: 'Proceed, Pierian maids!']

[3] [Horace, *Carm. Saec.*, ll. 10-11: 'And thou art reborn another and the same']

[4] [*Life of Horace*: 'which was by no means one of his faults']

the 4th Line were exact in point of Sense, the Expression it self would not shock me.

In the first Stanza I must take the Liberty to Object against *so faithful*, and *so pure*, because they are *so near* to one another, and yet belong to different Sentences. Nor can I approve that confusion of Ideas, which seems to be in the two last Lines. Elijah indeed was *snatch'd* up in a Chariot of Fire:[1] but pure Victims, consum'd *by* fire from heaven, cannot be said to be snatch'd up *in* it. Has the word Celestial, in the 4th Line any force? If Heaven snatches them in fire, that fire must needs be Celestial, i.e. heavenly. . . .

I say nothing to you about Rhime, because 'tis a Subject upon which I have so much to say. Why should you forego an Advantage; which you enjoy in perfection? and own that way of writing not to be the best in which you write better than any Man? I am not so unreasonable as to expect it. But I know I have the Testimony of your Poetical Conscience on my side, tho' you are wise enough not to own so unpopular and unproffitable a Truth.

(b) Lady Mary Wortley Montagu, extract from letter to Pope, ?1 November 1718, *Corresp.*, i. 523.

I must applaud your good nature in supposing that your pastoral lovers, (vulgarly called Haymakers) would have lived in everlasting joy and harmony, if the lightning had not interrupted their scheme of happiness. I see no reason to imagine that *John Hughes* and *Sarah Drew* were either wise or more virtuous than their neighbours. That a well-set man of twenty-five should have a fancy to marry a brown woman of eighteen, is nothing marvellous; and I cannot help thinking that had they married, their lives would have passed in the common track with their fellow-parishioners. His endeavouring to shield her from a storm was a natural action, and what he would have certainly done for his horse, if he had been in the same situation. Neither am I of opinion that their sudden death was a reward of their mutual virtue. You know the Jews were reprov'd for thinking a village destroyed by fire, more wicked than those that had escaped the thunder. Time and chance happen to all men.

---

[1] [Atterbury is here objecting to the following couplet: 'Their Souls on Wings of Lightning fly / So soard Eliah to the Sky.' Pope omitted them from the memorial tablet as a result of Atterbury's remarks]

38. Concanen praises Pope with Eusden

1722

Matthew Concanen, extract from 'A Letter to a Critick, In Vindication of the Modern Poets', *Poems upon Several Occasions* (1722), p. 51.

This passage includes Concanen's undiscriminating praise of Eusden. Having put Pope on a critical parity with this poet, it is not surprising that Concanen later attacked Pope, and in return found himself in *The Dunciad* (A), ii. 130.

 Great and Unmatch'd is Laurel'd *EUSDEN*'s Praise,
At once to merit, and adorn the Bays;
Like some smooth Riv'let flows his charming Strain,
Which neither Rocks disturb, nor Floods distain.
Such Depth and Clearness in his Verses meet,
Strong as the Stream, and as its Murmurs sweet.

 With pleasing Notes the Woods and Valleys ring,
If *POPE*'s harmonious Hand but touch the String;
His gentle Numbers charm the ravish'd Plains,
While still Attention holds the wond'ring Swains.
As when the Birds of ev'ry tuneful Kind,
Within the Limits of a Grove confin'd;
Their artless Musick warble thro' the Sprays,
And in Divine Confusion mix their Lays:
The Note still chang'd, our raptur'd Sense confounds,
With mingling Melody, and blending Sounds;

While none its single Excellence can boast,
But in the gen'ral Harmony is lost.
Such are his Works, and such his ev'ry Song,
Alike all easy, and alike all strong.

39. Bolingbroke gives advice

1724

Henry St John, Viscount Bolingbroke, extract from letter to Pope, 18 February 1724, *Corresp.*, ii. 219–20.

. . . you must not look on your translations of Homer as the great Work of your Life. You owe a great deal more to your self, to your Country, to the present Age, and to Posterity: Prelude with translations if you please, but after translating what was writ three Thousand Years ago, it is incombent upon you that you write, because you are able to Write, what will deserve to be translated three Thousand years hence into Languages as yet perhaps unform'd. I hear all your Objections at this distance. What write for Fame in a living Language which changes every year, and which is hardly known beyond the bounds of our Island, continue to Write, and you'll contribute to fix it. Claudian, nay Lucan who was so much elder, had not certainly the Diction of Virgil; but if Virgil had not Writ, both these, and Silius Italicus and several others, who came between them, or after them, would have writ worse; and we should find the Latin tongue degenerate in the course of so many Centurys much more than it improv'd in that short space between the Age of Lucilius or of Ennius, and that of the Mantuan (the very contrary of which is the Truth). You have said I am sure to your self at least, *tentanda via est quâ me quoque possim tollere humo*,[1] and if you

[1] [*Georgics*, iii. 8–9: 'I must essay a path whereby I, too, may rise from earth and fly victorious on the lips of men'. The quotation is completed at the end of the sentence]

add that you have succeeded you are not in the wrong, but there remains half a Verse and half your task behind—*Victorque virum volitare
per ora*. This perhaps you despair of atchieving, and it is that despair I
would recover you from. Virgil indeed wrote when the Roman Arms
had carry'd the Roman Language from the Euphrates to the Western
Ocean, and from the Deserts of Lybia to the Danube and the Rhine: but
your friend Homer wrote for a parcel of little States who compos'd in
his days a Nation much inferior every way to what our Nation is in
yours. Recall to your mind the image of Ancient Greece which Thuci-
dides gives in the Introduction to his History, and which may be form'd
out of Herodotus, Pausanias, Strabo, Plutarch &c. You will soon agree
that your Theatre is vastly more considerable than that of Hesiod and
Homer, and you will conceive much more reasonable hopes than they
could entertain of immortality. Luxury & Learning made the Greeks
famous in process of time, and brought their Language into use, as well
as their Vices, even among their Conquerors, for Greek like Christianity has spread by Persecution, and Latin like Mahometanism by Victory.
The French and the Italians have more lessons of Luxury to give than
we, but we have been these several Years their Masters in Learning.
Methinks we should improve this advantage. The Philosophers of the
Continent learn English, and the Mathematicians might have been
under the same necessity if Sir Isaac Newton had pleased.[1] But there are
few Philosophers and Mathematicians any where. A Language which is
design'd to spread, must recommend it self by Poetry, by Eloquence, by
History. I believe England has produced as much Genius first as any
Country. Why then is our Poetry so little in request among Strangers?
several Reasons may be given, and this certainly as the most considerable, that we have not one Original great Work of that kind wrote near
enough to perfection to pique the Curiosity of other Nations, as the
Epick Poetry of the Italians, and the Dramatick Poetry of the French
pique ours. Eloquence and History are God knows, at the lowest ebb
imaginable among us. The different Stiles are not fix'd, the Bar and the
Pulpit have no Standard, and our Historys are Gazettes ill digested, &
worse writ. The case is far otherwise in France and in Italy. Eloquence
has been extreamly cultivated in both Countrys, and I know not
whether the Italians have not equall'd the Greeks and the Romans in
writing History. Guicciardine[2] seems to me superior to Thusidides on a
Subject still more complicated than that of the Peloponesian war, and

---

[1] [I.e., if the *Principia* had been in English rather than Latin]
[2] [Francesco Guicciardini (1483–1540), Italian historian]

perhaps the vastness of the undertaking is the principal advantage which Livy has over Davila.[1] In short excellent original writings can alone recommend a Language, and contribute to the spreading of it. No man will learn English to read Homer or Virgil. Whilst you translate therefore you neglect to propagate the English Tongue; and whilst you do so, you neglect to extend your own reputation, for depend upon it your writings will live as long and go as far as the Language, longer or further they cannot.

40. Young urges Pope to satire

1725

Dr Edward Young, extract from *The Universal Passion*, Satire i (1725), pp. 2-3.

Young (1683-1765), the author of *Night Thoughts* (1742), was pursuing a literary career at this point in his life. He entered the church in 1728, but continued to write. The rather automatic praise of Pope given here shows how far his pre-eminence was established, though it may also indicate that Young was half-hearted (see No. 28c): by 1759, when he published his *Conjectures on Original Composition* (No. 112), Young had turned against Pope's neoclassicism.

> Shall Poesy, like Law, turn wrong to right,
> And Dedications wash an *Æthiop* white,
> Set up each senseless wretch for Nature's boast,
> On whom Praise shines as Trophies on a Post?
> Shall Funeral Eloquence her Colours spread,
> And scatter Roses on the Wealthy Dead?

[1] [Enrico Caterino Davila (1576-1631), Italian historian]

Shall Authors smile on these Illustrious Days,
And Satyrize with nothing—but their Praise?
    Why slumbers *Pope*, who leads the tuneful Train,
Nor hears that Virtue, which He loves, complain?
Donne, Dorset, Dryden, Rochester, are dead,
And Guilt's chief Foe in *Addison* is fled;
Congreve, who, crown'd with Lawrels, fairly won,
Sits smiling at the Goal, while Others run,
He will not Write; and (more provoking still!)
Ye Gods! He will not write, and *Maevius* will.

41. Praise from a young admirer

1727

Walter Harte, extract from 'To Mr. Pope', *Poems on Several
Occasions* (1727), pp. 99–101. Further on Harte, see No. 59 and
headnote.

To move the springs of nature as we please,
To think with spirit, but to write with ease:
With living words to warm the conscious heart,
Or please the soul with nicer charms of art,
For this the *Grecian* soar'd in *Epic* strains,
And softer *Maro* left the *Mantuan* plains:
Melodious *Spenser* felt the lover's fire,
And awful *Milton* strung his heav'nly lyre.

    'Tis yours, like these, with curious toil to trace
The pow'rs of language, harmony, and grace,
How nature's self with living lustre shines;
How judgment strengthens, and how art refines;

How to grow bold with conscious sense of fame,
And force a pleasure which we dare not blame:
To charm us more thro' negligence than pains,
And give ev'n life and action to the strains:
Led by some law, whose pow'rful impulse guides
Each happy stroke, and in the soul presides:
Some fairer image of perfection, giv'n
T'inspire mankind, itself deriv'd from heav'n.

   O ever worthy, ever crown'd with praise;
Blest in thy life, and blest in all thy lays!
Add that the *Sisters* ev'ry thought refine:
Or ev'n thy life be faultless as thy line;
Yet envy still with fiercer rage pursues,
Obscures the virtue, and defames the muse.
A soul like thine, in pains, in grief resign'd,
Views with vain scorn the malice of mankind:
Not critics, but their planets prove unjust:
And are they blam'd who sin because they must?

   Yet sure not so must all peruse thy lays;
I cannot rival—and yet dare to praise.
A thousand charms at once my thoughts engage,
Sappho's soft sweetness, *Pindar*'s warmer rage,
Statius' free vigour, *Virgil*'s studious care,
And *Homer*'s force, and *Ovid*'s easier air.

42. Voltaire on Pope

1726, 1726–9

(a) Voltaire, extract from letter to N. C. Thieriot, 26 October 1726, *Voltaire's Correspondence*, ed. T. Besterman (Geneva, 1953–65), ii. 36:

J intend to send you two or three poems of Mr Pope. the best poet in England, and at present in the world. J hope you are acquainted enough with the English tongue, to be sensible of all the charms of his works. For my part j look on his poem call'd the essay on criticism as superior to the art of poetry of Horace; and his rape of the lock, la boucle de cheveux, (that is a comical one) is in my opinion above the lutrin of Despreaux. J never saw so amiable an imagination, so gentle graces, so great varyety, so much wit, and so refind knowledge of the world, as in this little performance.

(b) Voltaire, extract from Letter 22, *Letters concerning the English Nation* (1733), pp. 215–16, the English version of *Lettres philosophiques*, which were written between 10 June 1726 and March 1729; for the comments on *An Essay on Man* which Voltaire added to the *Lettres* in 1756 see No. 109:

'Twill be much easier for you to form an Idea of Mr. *Pope's* Works. He is in my Opinion the most elegant, the most correct Poet; and at the same Time the most harmonious (a Circumstance which redounds very much to the Honour of [his] Muse) that *England* ever gave Birth to. He has mellow'd the harsh sounds of the *English* Trumpet to the soft Accents of the Flute. His Compositions may be easily translated, because they are vastly clear and perspicuous; besides, most of his Subjects are general, and relative to all Nations.

43. An American admirer

1727, 1728

Mather Byles, extracts from letters to Pope, *Corresp.*, ii. 450–1, 494–5.

This, like No. 67, is a record of American interest in Pope. Byles writes from Boston, where his son was to become the librarian of Harvard College, 1755–7. For further letters and information, see A. Warren, *PMLA*, xlviii (1933), 68–9.

(a) Extract from letter to Pope, 7 October 1727:

Sir,—You are doubtless wondring at the Novelty of an Epistle from the remote Shores where this dates its Origin; as well as from so obscure a Hand as that which subscribes it. But what Corner of the Earth so secret, as not to have heard the Fame of Mr. POPE? Or who so retired as not to be acquainted with his admirable Compositions or so stupid as not to be ravished with them.

Fame after a Man is dead, has been by some ingenious Writers, compared to an Applause in some distant Region. If this be a just Similitude, you may take the pleasure of an admired Name in *America*, and of spreading a Transport over the Face of a New World: By which you may, in some measure, imagine the Renown in which your Name will flourish many Ages to come, and anticipate a Thousand Years of Futurity. . . .

How often have I been sooth'd and charmed with the ever-blooming Landscapes of your *Windsor-Forest*? And how does my very Soul melt away, at the soft Complaints of the languishing *Eloisa*? How frequently has the *Rape of the Lock* commanded the various passions of my Mind: Provoked Laughter; breathed a Tranquility; or inspired a Transport? And how have I been raised, and born away by the resistless Fire of the *Iliad*, as it gl[ow]s in your immortal Translation?

(b) Extract from letter to Pope, 18 May 1728:

I have already been charmed with most of your happy Compositions, but have not yet seen them all. Those I have seen are the following. In o[u]r Colledge[1] Library, at *Cambridge* (a Town about three miles from *Boston*) we have your Translation of the *Iliad* in 12mo and your Poems in a large Folio: In which is the only picture I have seen of you in a modern Dress,[2] tho your smaller pictures in a poetical one are frequent, and most of o[u]r Genteel Rooms are embellished with your large mezzotinto.[3] For my own Library, your *Iliad* glitters in a distinguished Box, and close by, your two Volumes of Miscellanies:[4] Besides what of your poetry is in the Sixth Volume of *Drydens* Miscellany; and of your prose in the *Tatler, Spectator,* and *Guardian,* which I would gladly know how, more infallibly, to distinguish. I have also borrowed and read the three first Volumes of your *Odyssey,* but could never learn that the Two last are yet in my Country. And tho' I have given orders to several of o[u]r Booksellers to send over for the whole lot compleat, they have not yet arrived.[5]

The polite and learned Part of my Country-men, agree with me, to look upon such exalted Genius's as Mr. *Pope,* o' tother Side the inconceivable Breadth of Ocean, in the same Light, in which you behold the admired Classicks. We read you with Transport, and talk of you with Wonder. We look upon your Letter as you would upon the original parchment of *Homer.* We pay you a deference & veneration belonging to a Race of Superior Beings and you appear to our Imaginations, like so many Deities in Human Shape. But when we vote you all people of the Elyzium. we please our selves to fancy how much Mr. *Pope* appears the Musæus of the shining Company

> *Musæum ante omnes: medium nam plurima turba*
> *Hunc habet, atque humeris exstantem suscipit altis.*[6]

---

[1] [I.e., Harvard College]
[2] [The folding portrait in *Poems* (1717)]
[3] [Engraved by I. Smith from a Kneller portrait in 1717]
[4] [Lintot's *Miscellaneous Poems,* 1712 or 1720]
[5] [Pope sent a set as a gift]
[6] [*Aeneid,* vi. 667–8: 'Musaeus before all; for he is centre of the vast throng that gazes up to him, as with shoulders high he towers aloft']

44. Dennis reacts to the news of *The Dunciad*

May 1728

John Dennis (?), extract from a letter to the *Daily Journal*, 11 May 1728,[1] *Critical Works*, ii. 416–17. Hooker considers that the letter was written by Dennis 'or by someone who knew his work and imitated his manner' (ed. cit., ii. 526).

As [Pope] has been constantly meditating Mischief, he has, like his *African* and *Asiatick* Relations the Jackanapes's and Quidnunchi's,[2] been always mimicking every Body and every Thing: But in his mimical Essays he always *sinks* as far below those whom he endeavours to counterfeit, as the Actions of a Monkey fall short of those of a Man.

In his Rhapsody of *Windsor Forest*, which was impudently writ in Emulation of the *Cooper's-Hill* of Sir *John Denham*, one of the most beautiful and most artful Poems that we have in *English Rhime*, *A. P—E sinks* as far below Sir *John Denham*, as the Bottom of *Windsor Forest* is below the Summit of *Cooper's-Hill*.

In the *Ode* which the same *Pantomimical Creature* wrote upon St. *Cæcilia*'s Day, an Ode which was vainly and foolishly writ in Emulation of Mr. *Dryden*'s *Feast of Alexander*, he has not the least Shadow of any of Mr. *Dryden*'s great Qualities, neither of his Art, his Variety, his Passion, his Enthusiasm, or his Harmony. The very Numbers in Mr. *Dryden*'s incomparable Ode, are themselves incomparable, and are always adapted and adjusted by that great Poet to his Passion and his Enthusiasm.

Tho' I have not for several Years read *Chaucer*'s *Temple of Fame*, yet I am well enough acquainted with his Character, to know that he has too much Genius, and too much good Sense to have committed many

---

[1] [*The Dunciad* was published on 18 May, but news of its composition was abroad before its appearance]

[2] [From the Latin meaning 'what now?' Hence a term for an inquisitive person, a gossip]

Absurdities; whereas the *Temple of Fame*, writ by the *Pantomimical A. P—E*, is one long Chain of Blunders and Boggisms, and one continued Absurdity.

All the World knows how very much he falls short of *Ambrose Philips* in *Pastorals*; but in the *Drama*, he is *below* even *Tom Durfey*. The *Marriage-Hater match'd*, and the *Boarding-School*, tho' but indifferent Performances, are yet ten times better Dramatical Pieces than the whimsical *What d'ye call it*.

And yet this little turbulent Creature has endeavoured to decry and calumniate every Author who has excelled him, and shone a superior Region to him, moved partly by his natural Envy and Malice, (the Deformity of his *Mind* answering to that of his *Body*) and partly by that Ignorance and Stupidity which make a Dog howl at the Moon.

Yet notwithstanding his Ignorance and his Stupidity, this *Animal-culum* of an Author, is, forsooth! at this very Juncture, writing the *Progress of Dulness*. Yes! the Author of *Windsor Forest*, of the *Temple of Fame*, of the *What d'ye call it*; nay, the Author even of the *Profund*, is writing the *Progress of Dulness*! A most vain and impertinent Enterprize! For they who have read his several Pieces which we mentioned above, have read the *Progress of Dulness*; a Progress that began in *Windsor Forest*, and ended in the *Profund*; as the short Progress of the *Devil's Hogs* ended in the *Depth of the Sea*.

45. Concanen turns against Pope

August 1728

Matthew Concanen, extracts from A Supplement to the Profound. Containing Several Examples, very proper to Illustrate the Rules laid down in a late Treatise, called the Art of Sinking in Poetry. Extracted from the Poetical Works of the ingenious Authors of that accurate Piece, and published for the Use of their Admirers *(1728), pp. 4–6, 12–15, 28–9. As the title suggests, Concanen, who had been among those attacked in the* Bathos, *created his own version from the poetry of Swift and Pope. Four of the sections are quoted here: an extract from the Preface will be found as No. 51. Pope's own copy (B.M. C. 116. b. 2[4]) has a few of his comments, which are given as footnotes here.* A Supplement *was published on 16 August 1728.*

3d. The *EXPLETIVE.*

The Beauty of this Style, according to our Authors, consists chiefly in the Choice of the Epithets. I don't very well conceive any material Difference between it, and an Ornament of Speech, call'd *Tautology.* You won't be offended, if what I throw at present under this Head, should happen to be Examples of both; if any other should hereafter occur to me, you may expect them, when I shall more particularly treat of the Figures.

The Authors are forced to coin Examples of this, as appears by their quoting no Authors Names to the Verses they produce? How much better is the following than any of the Lines they give us?

> —*With* both *his* Hands *he* clung,
> *And stuck* adherent, *and* suspended hung.
>
> 5th Odyssey [545–6: Pope]

That is he stuck *sticking*, and hung *hanging*. The *Homer* of the *Bathos*, as those Gentlemen call him, is excell'd here, as will appear to you from a Comparison between the foregoing and a Line of his *Alfred*, perhaps the most profound in all his Works.

The stagnant *Air* unventilated *stood.*
[*Alfred: an Epick Poem* (1723), Book vi, p. 205]

The following will serve very well, not only for the present Purpose; but as an Example of the *Tautology,* the *Macrology* and *Pleonasm,* and several others.

—*The purple Hand of Death*
Clos'd his dim Eyes, and Fate suppress'd his Breath.

5th *Iliad* [108–9]

Most admirable! Profund indeed! *Fate kills* a Man, whom *Death* had *dispatch'd* before: perhaps it may be objected, that the Thought seems borrowed from *Falstaff's* killing *Piercy,* whom the Prince had before put to Death [*1 Henry IV*, V. iv. 77–128]; but this is no Fault: Mr. *P.* has not publish'd *Shakespeare* for nothing. This is the Advantage of reading much.

In the former Example, *Fate* play'd a Trick upon *Death*; in the following, Death comes up with him.

For he no more must draw his Country's Breath,
Already snatch'd by Fate, *and the black* Doom *of* Death.

3d *Odyssey* [298–9: Pope]

Notwithstanding the Tautology of this be apparent enough, yet I am afraid the Abuse of another Figure is the most profund Part of it: To be *snatch'd by a Doom,* is a hard Case; but to be snatch'd by a *black* Doom, is really lamentable.

Spent and *o'erpower'd* he *barely* breathes, *at most.*   16th *Iliad* [136]

Here's Expletive and Tautology in Perfection, the *English* of it is, the Man was out of Breath; but it would not be true Profund, if he was not first *spent,* then *o'erpower'd,* then breath'd *barely,* then breath'd *at most*: This Verse shews the Use of Rhime to the Profund: If the Gingle of the preceding Line had not absolutely demanded it, perhaps Posterity had been depriv'd of those elegant Expletives, *at most.* . . .

6. The *A-la-mode STYLE.*

Fine, as the Authors call it, by being *New*; is, when a Poet puts down for pretty Conceits, Things which have no Foundation in Truth or Nature; but expects the Gingle of Verse shall carry them safely through the Observations of gentle Readers. For Example,

Heav'n is feasting on the World's green End.   *Iliad* xxiii [255]

The *World's End* is comical, but the *World's green End*, is highly pleasant and proper.[1]

> *So when the Nightingale to Rest removes,*
> *The Thrush may chant to the forsaken Groves;*
> *But charm'd to Silence, listens while she Sings,*
> And all th' Aerial Audience clap their Wings.[2]
>
> > Pope's *Past.* [i. 13–16]

The Agreement between the Thrush and Nightingale, to sing by turns, is an ingenious Thought. The *clapping of Wings, by way of Applause*, is borrowed from the Play-house, and therefore very fit for Pastoral; but the best Conceit of all, is, that the poor Birds should *clap their Wings* at the Voice of the Nightingale, whose Time of singing is, when all the rest are asleep.

The Poet, in the above Lines, supposes all the Aerial Audience silent, when the Nightingale sings; in the following, wherein he describes the Morning, he makes the Linnet and Nightingale sing together, at an Hour when 'tis generally thought the latter is asleep.

> *Why sit we mute, when* early Linnets *sing,*
> *When* warbling Philomel *salutes the Spring.*
>
> > Pope's *Past.* [i. 25–6]

Not to mention the Propriety of making an *English* Clown call a well-known Bird by a classical Name.[3]

In the two following Instances, the Poet plays pretty Tricks with the Word *Ivy*. The first is a dedicatory Couplet.

> *Accept, O Garth, the Muse's early Lays,*
> *That adds this Wreath of* Ivy *to thy Bays.*
>
> > Pope's *Past.* [ii. 9–10]

Here *Ivy* is made the Patron's Crown.

> *Immortal* Vida! *on whose honour'd Brow,*
> *The Poets Bays, and Criticks* Ivy *grow.*
>
> > *Essay on Crit.* [ll. 705–6]

---

[1] ['Milton': Pope's MS. note. The reference is to *Comus*, l. 1014. 'The World's End' was a resort of ill-repute in Chelsea]

[2] ['Dryden': Pope's MS. note. The reference is to *Verses to Her Highness the Duchess of York*, ll. 57–8]

[3] ['Spenser & Ph[?ilips]': Pope's MS. note]

Here it becomes the Criticks; in both equally New and Bold; the Ancients always gave Ivy to the Poets, as may appear from numberless Places in the Classicks; nor was it ever apply'd to Patrons or Criticks, in Contradistinction to Poets, by any but this ingenious Author.

> There died the best of Passions, Love and Fame.
> Eloisa to Abel. [l. 40]

Exceedingly A-la-mode! Fame a *Passion*, good! *The best of Passions*, better. Both *Love* and *Fame* the *best of Passions*, best of all! This is the Way to be pathetick, surprizing, admirable and unintelligible, which last is the *best* and safest of Qualities in a Poet of this Stamp. . . .

7. The *PRURIENT*.

In which is included the *Finical*; for Examples of the meer Finical, I must refer you to several Lines cited under the foregoing Heads; for the *Prurient* and *Finical* together, take the Description of Castration in *Eloisa*'s Epistle to *Abelard*.

> Cut from the Root, *my perish'd Joys I see*,
> And Love's warm Tide *for ever stop'd in thee*.[1]

The Miscellany so often quoted, affords the following Examples, and abundance more of the gross, rank, prurient Style.

> *Women tho' not sans Leacherie*,
> *Ne swinken but with Secrecie*.

> *The Duck sore tickleth his* Erse Roote.

> *Bette is to pine on Coals and Chalke*,
> *Than trust on Mon whose* Yerde *can talke*.[2]

> *Maids turn Bottles, call aloud for Corks*.

. . . .

> Rape of the Lock [iv. 54]

The *ANTITHESIS* or *See-Saw*.

Whereby Contraries and Oppositions (say our Authors) *are ballanced in*

---

[1] [This couplet was omitted from the final version, but is to be found in the editions published 1717–20. See Twickenham, ii. note to l. 258]
[2] ['Imitation of Chaucer' (1727 version), ll. 1–2, 18, 25–6]

such a Way, as to cause a Reader to remain suspended between them, to his exceeding Delight and Recreation. I have no great Opinion of the Use of this Figure to the *Profund*, and therefore shall present you with only one Instance of it; but, as the Fable says, *That one is a Lyon.*

> —*Though all Things differ, all agree.*
>
> > *Windsor Forest* [l. 16]

Besides the Seven before mentioned, *we may rank under the Article of Confusing,* a Figure call'd,

> The *Compound* or *Mixture of Figures.*

Which (according to our Authors) *raises so many Images, as to give you no Image at all. But its principal Beauty is, when it gives an Idea just opposite to what it seem'd meant to describe. Thus an ingenious Artist painting the* Spring, *talks of a* Snow *of Blossoms, and thereby raises an unexpected Picture of* Winter. *Of this sort are the following;*

> *Swift as a* Flood of Fire, *when Storms arise,*
> Floats *the wide Field, and* blazes *to the Skies.*
>
> > *Iliad,* ii. [948–9]

What a noble Confusion is here? First, it's a *Flood,* then it's a *Fire,* thirdly, it *floats,* and, lastly,[1] it *blazes.*
Behold another in almost the same Terms.

> —*The Winds with rising Flames conspire*
> *To whelm some City under* Waves *of Fire.*
>
> > *Iliad,* xvii. [825–6]

I dare appeal to the meanest Capacity in Behalf of the Profundity of this last; surely the *Snow of Blossoms* are rather inferior to the *Waves of Fire.*

> Buoy'd *by some inward Force, he seems to* Swim,
> *And feels a* Pinion *lifting every Limb.*
>
> > *Iliad,* xix. [418–19] and repeated xxiii. [1039–40]

This is very extraordinary, *swimming* and *flying* at the same time; 'tis what even no flying Fish ever performed before.

---

[1] [Pope's MS. note alters this to read: '. . . then it's a *Fire,* therefore first it *floats,* and, then, *lastly,* it *blazes'*]

46. Savage and Atterbury on Pope's superiority

1729

(a) Richard Savage, extract from *The Wanderer: A Vision* (1729), *The Poetical Works of Richard Savage*, ed. C. Tracy (1962), pp. 107–8 (ll. 369–78). The poem was advertised on 18 January 1729.

> O POPE!—Since Envy is decreed by Fate,
> Since she pursues alone the Wise, and Great;
> In one small, emblematic Landscape see,
> How vast a Distance 'twixt thy Foe, and Thee!
> *Truth* from an Eminence surveys our Scene,
> (A Hill, where all is clear, and all serene.)
> Rude, earth-bred Storms o'er meaner Valleys blow,
> And wand'ring Mists roll, black'ning, far below;
> Dark, and debas'd, like them, is *Envy's* Aim,
> And clear, and eminent, like Truth, thy Fame.

(b) Francis Atterbury, Bishop of Rochester, extract from a letter to Pope, 20 November 1729, *Corresp.*, iii. 76–7.

You outdo Others, on all occasions: my hope, and my opinion is, that on Moral Subjects, and in drawing Characters, you will outdo your self. Your mind is as yet unbroken by Age, and ill Accidents; your Knowledge and Judgment are at the height: use them in writing somewhat, that may teach the present and future times, and, if not gain equally the Applause of both, may yet raise the Envy of the one, and secure the Admiration of the other. Remember, Virgil dy'd at 52, and Horace at 58; and, as bad as both their Constitutions were, Yours is yet more delicate and tender. Employ not your precious Moments, and great Talents, on little Men, and little things: but choose a Subject every way worthy of you; and handle it, as you can, in a manner which no body else can equal, or imitate.

ODYSSEY

23 April 1725–June 1726

47. 'Homerides' on Pope's sharp practice

July 1725

'Homerides', extract from a letter printed in *The London Journal*, 17 July 1725; the text is that given by George Sherburn in *The Early Career of Alexander Pope* (1734), pp. 262–4.

Much of the immediate response to the translation was concerned with Pope's devious and, many thought, dishonest, use of his collaborators, Broome and Fenton.

And yet, I fear there is a Practice of this sort coming into Fashion, of more mischievous Consequence than any of the former; which is that of an eminent Poet's taking in *Subscriptions* for any Work, for the sake of *Lucre*, and getting it done by *Hackney-Hands* for the sake of *Idleness*, and at length publishing it in his *own Name*.

In short, what gave occasion to these Reflections, is the late Translation of *Homer's Odyssey*, which was published by Subscription, and proposed to be done by the Translator of the *Iliad*; but it is confidently reported, that other Persons have had the chief Hand in it, and that They do not pretend to deny it themselves. I own, that, upon perusal of some Part of it, I had a Jealousy of this Nature; and I was strengthened in my Suspicions, upon comparing the *Patents* which are prefixed to both these Works. In that before the *Iliad*, it is recited that
—*Whereas our trusty and well-beloved* Bernard Lintot, *of our City of* London, *Bookseller, hath, by his Petition, humbly represented unto us, that he is now preparing for the Press a Translation of the* Iliad *of* Homer, *by Mr.* Alexander Pope, *Gent.* &c.

In the other it runs thus,

Whereas Bernard Lintot, *of our* City of London, Bookseller, *hath, by his Petition, humbly represented unto us, that he is now printing a Translation,* UNDERTAKEN *by our* trusty *and* well-beloved Alexander Pope, Esquire, *of the* Odyssey *of* Homer, *&c.*

Methinks the Word *Undertaken*, in the latter, savours strongly of *Jesuitical* Prevarication, and very much confirms these Suspicions. However, it is in the Power of that ingenious Gentleman to do himself Justice, by publicly declaring, that he has *bonâ fide* translated it all himself; in which case I will as publicly acknowledge, that I was mistaken in my Surmises as to this Particular, whatever I may think of the Performance it self. But if he does not think fit to do this, I must take the Liberty, as an Enemy to all Imposition, to advertise the Publick not to look upon him as the *Translator*, but only the *Publisher*; or, as it is expressed in his Patent, the *Undertaker* of this Translation.

We have frequently heard of celebrated Poets, who have published their light unfinished Pieces, under some subordinate Name; in which Case the Publick is agreeably deceived: But I thought the natural Pride of a Good Author would not suffer him, upon any Account, to father the Works of one less famous than himself; and for that Reason, I thought we were safe from any such Imposition: But if once *Avarice* gets the better of *Pride* in this Point, we may live to see the most eminent Writers keep half a Dozen Journeymen a-piece, and vend their hireling Labours, as *How* did his *Knives*, by putting his own Name upon them all.

I shall not say any thing concerning the Persons who are supposed to be our *Poetical Undertaker*'s Deputies in this Affair, because were they as able to translate *Homer* as even their *Taskmaster* himself, yet to have one or more Authors obtruded upon us, without our Knowledge or Consent, under the Name and Character of another to whom we have subscribed, is *Quackery* and *C[atho]licism* in the greatest Perfection.

I have a great veneration for this admired Poet, and also for his ingenious Bookseller; but I hope they will not always expect to impose *extravagant Prices* upon us, for *bad Paper, old Types,* and *Journey work Poetry.*

I am SIR, | Your humble Servant, | HOMERIDES.

48. Defoe defends Pope's business ethics

July 1725

Daniel Defoe, 'On Pope's Translation of Homer', *Applebee's Original Weekly Journal*, 31 July 1725. Defoe signed his ironic defence of Pope's collaborative enterprise as 'Ante-Pope'.

Sir, I Suppose, among the rest of our Friends, you have not been ignorant of the Clamour which has been made upon a certain Author, for publishing his Translation, or Version, of your old Friend *Homer* under his own Name, when it seems he has not been, nay, some have had the hardiness to say, *could not have been* the real Operator.

I must confess, I cannot come into all the resentments of the learned World upon that Subject, and I am not without my Reasons for my Opinion, as I suppose they have shewn their Reasons for theirs.

Writing you know, Mr. *Applebee*, is become a very considerable Branch of the English Commerce; Composing, Inventing, Translating, Versifying, &c., are the several Manufactures which supply this Commercing: The Booksellers are the Master Manufacturers or Employers; the several Writers, Authors, Copyers, Sub-Writers, and all other Operators with Pen and Ink, are the Workmen employed by the said Master Manufacture[r]s, in the forming, dressing, and finishing the said Manufactures; as the Combers, Spinners, Weavers, Fullers, Dressers, &c., are in our Cloathing Manufactures, by the Master Clothiers, &c.

If a Clothier employs a Master Workman to weave him so many Pieces of Cloth, and agrees with him for so much Money, the Weaver brings them home finish'd, and puts his own Mark on them, and this Weaver, being known to be a good Workman, the Master Clothier recommends the Cloths to his Customers, as the Work and Weaving of such a known and eminent Weaver; at the same time, this Clothier knows very well that the said Weaver could not be able to weave them all himself; perhaps also he knows some of them are of a much meaner Workmanship than that Weaver us'd to Work, yet the Weaver and the Clothier conniving together, they all carry the same Mark; nay, sometimes the Weaver brings a better Workman than himself into the Loom, but having an Opportunity to get his Work cheaper he takes him in; and thus, a Medley of Goods are put off together, all under the Mark, and in the Name of the Master Weaver.

Now upon the whole, pray, Mr. *Applebee*, who is the greatest Cheat in this Affair, the Clothier or the Manufacturer, the Master Employer, or the Weaver? not but that they may be both R[ogue]s Mr. *Applebee*, but who is most concern'd in the Fraud, seeing it is the Master Clothier who puts the Goods off in the Weaver's Name, tho' he knows there are 'Prentices, and Scoundrels for the sake of a low Price, employ'd in the making them.

As to Writing, Mr. *Applebee*, Do we expect that every Man that publishes a Book, and sets his Name to it, should *Bona fide*, be the Author *of it all* himself? Do we not know how several Booksellers of Note at this Time, keep Authors of different Fame employ'd, some at one Price, some at another, to form the same Pieces of Work; and have not several Authors, who are particular for being Volumnious, their several Journeymen that work for them, some in one Jail, some in another, some in one fluxing House, some in another; nay, has not the Right Reverend Author himself, who made this very complaint, his Deputy Journalist, and his supply of Operators, as Occasion requires, tho' the Labourers receive their Esteem from his own illustrious Character, and are all called his Own?

Did not the late celebrated *Tatlers* pass, even to the end of the Work, for the Labours of the worthy Editor Sir *Dick St*[*eele*]? And did it not come out at last, *when he could conceal it no longer*, that he had abundance of *Aid de plumes* under him? and might we not give the same Account of several laborious Tracts, which the World to this Day honours the Names of Authors for, who had the least share in the Labour?

But to carry this Complaint higher, a Merry Fellow of my Acquaintance assures me, that our Cousin *Homer* himself was guilty of the same *Plagiarism*. Cousin *Homer* you must note was an old blind Ballad Singer at *Athens*, and went about the Country there, and at other Places in *Greece*, singing his Ballads from Door to Door, only with this difference, that the Ballads he sung were generally of his own Making: Hence I suppose it was, that one of the same Profession here in *London*, who, tho' blind too, made his own Ballads, was so universally called *Old Homer*: But, says my Friend, this *Homer*, in process of Time, when he had gotten some Fame, and perhaps more Money than Poets ought to be trusted with, grew Lazy and Knavish, and got one *Andronicus* a

Spartan, and one Dr. S——l, a Philosopher of *Athens*, both pretty good Poets, but less eminent than himself, to make his Songs for him, which, they being poor and starving, did for him for a small matter, and so the Poet never did much himself, only publish'd and sold his Ballads still, in his own Name, as if they had been his own, and by that, got great Subscriptions, and a high Price for them.

Now, Mr. *Applebee*, if my Friend be in the right, was not Cousin *Homer* a Knave, for imposing thus upon the *Grecian* World? *In a Word*, it seems to me that Old *Homer*, was a mere Mr. P[ope], and Mr. P[ope], in that Particular, a meer *Homer*, so that there's ne'er a Barrel the better Herring, except the *Master Manufacturer*, who, like a Bawd to a W[hore], knew the Fraud, and imposed it upon his Customers, and so has been worse than both of them.

Your Servant,
Ante-Pope.

49. Joseph Spence on the *Odyssey*

June 1726

Rev. Joseph Spence, extracts from *An Essay on Pope's Odyssey: in which Some particular Beauties and Blemishes of that Work are consider'd . . .*, part i (1726). The first volume of Spence's work appeared early in June 1726, fourteen months after the publication of books i–xiv of the *Odyssey*. A second part was published in 1727 (see next item), after the completion of the *Odyssey*.

Joseph Spence (1699–1768) is mainly remembered for his invaluable but posthumous *Anecdotes*, which provide one of the crucial sources for Pope's biography. In the eighteenth century Spence was a respected critic, whose weighty *Polymetis; or An Enquiry concerning the Agreement between the Works of the Roman Poets and the Remains of the Antient Artists* (1747) remained a standard work despite Lessing's attack upon it in the *Laokoön*. The

Essay was Spence's first published work, written when he was a young Fellow of New College, Oxford.

After the publication in 1726 of the first part of Spence's *Essay*, Pope quickly took the initiative in making the anonymous writer's acquaintance. Prior to the appearance of the second part, Pope himself went over Spence's manuscript (see Twickenham, x. 594–605), and also exercised his interest when the young critic gained the Professorship of Poetry at Oxford in 1728 (see Spence, *Anecdotes*, i, pp. xxiv–vii).

The *Essay* is written in dialogue form—the 'old *Platonick* way, which *Cicero* brought over from *Greece*' in Spence's words—as it had been developed by Fontenelle, Dryden, and Addison. Bouhours's *La manière de bien penser* (1687, translated 1705) also affected Spence's handling of the form. It is important to note that Spence was not aware when writing the *Essay* which books of the *Odyssey* had been translated by his assistants. Consequently, Spence makes no distinction between books iii, v, vii, ix, x, xiii–xv, xvii, xxi, xxii, xxiv, translated by Pope, and books i, iv, xix, and xx, translated by Fenton, and books ii, vi, viii, xi, xii, xvi, xviii, and xxiii translated by Broome. Like Johnson he thought the translation a uniform work. For the nature of Pope's collaboration, and for the way in which he revised the work of Fenton and Broome, see the authoritative discussion in Twickenham, vii, pp. cxciii–ccii.

Most of the first evening's dialogue between the two friends, Antiphaus and Philypsus, is reprinted here, along with selections from the other four dialogues. Spence's notes and references have been retained, though line numbers are silently normalized to refer to the first line of each quotation. A second edition of the *Essay* was published in 1737, and contains several changes, mostly stylistic (thus, 'the translator' is frequently substituted for 'Mr *Pope*'); these changes are only recorded if they throw light on Spence's meaning, or if they seem to represent a modification of his views. Further, see Introduction, pp. 14–15.

EVENING the FIRST.

Antiphaus manag'd his Affairs so as to get this Winter sooner than usual to the Country-seat of his Friend *Philypsus*. It is there that he passes his time, when ever he can clear himself from the hurry of Business, in a retirement every way agreeable; and in a full enjoyment of those Pleasures, which attend on a particular Friendship, in an open and improving Conversation. The Conversation there does not run in the present polite way of *saying and saying nothing*; when alone, they usually fall into some Points of Learning; and as both of them are particularly fond of Poetry, their Disputes turn more frequently on that Subject, than any other. Indeed their differing in Sentiment can scarce be call'd *Disputes*; for whenever their Thoughts do not meet, each of them shews a diffidence in his own Opinion, and a willingness to submit to the Judgment of his Friend.

It is by this means that they fall into each others Sentiments, more than cou'd well be expected from Men of so different a Turn. The enlarged Genius of *Philypsus* always led him to dwell upon the most beautiful Parts of a Poem with the greatest Pleasure; while *Antiphaus*, who has a very clear Head, and has given much into a strict way of thinking, is taken most with just Descriptions, and plain natural Ideas: The one was so possest with the Pleasure which he felt from fine Thoughts and warm Expressions, that He did not take a full Satisfaction in low Beauty, and simple Representations of Nature; the other, on the contrary, had such an aversion to *glitterings* and *elevation*, that he was distasted at any the least appearance of either. If the latter was prejudiced[1] for the Ancients, from the Purity and Justness, which we find in most of their Works; *Philypsus* had his *foible* too, and was sometimes caught by the Flourish and Colouring of the Moderns. In a word, if *Philypsus* wou'd sometimes contemn a Point as low and mean, tho' in reality proper enough, and naturally express'd; *Antiphaus*, in his turn, might happen now and then to blame a Passage which requir'd a good degree of Ornament, as being too glaring and artificial.

Among several other Topicks, one Evening, they happen'd to fall into a discourse on Mr. *Pope*'s new Translation of the *Odyssey*. As they both found Beauties in that Piece agreeable to their particular Tastes, they had read it over with a great deal of Pleasure: however *Philypsus* was the Person who admired it the most. There are some Lines, says he to *Antiphaus* (pointing to the *Odyssey* which lay before them) there are some Favourites of mine in that Poem, which you must not look upon with your usual severity: Prithee *Antiphaus*, be more sensible to the Flame and Spirit of a Writer, who is evidently Our present *Laureate in Genius*, and the most enliven'd Translator of the Age.

[1] *prejudiced*] *too much prejudiced* 1737.

I will very readily allow what you say of that Great Man, return'd *Antiphaus*; and shall always pay a deference to your more lively taste of the Fine and Sublime in Poetry; but you must give me leave to dissent from you in some Particulars: if I do not agree with your Sentiments, in relation to several Lines and Passages of that Translation, 'tis perhaps because I fall so much short of you, in your *inward sense* of the high and elevated Beauties of Language.

As I cannot imagine that to be the reason, says *Philypsus*, I beg to hear those Particulars you talk'd of; I am perswaded, several of the Passages, which I have observ'd you to be less taken with in reading the Translation, will upon a closer view appear to be really Beauties; to tell you the truth, I long to make a Convert of you; and beg you wou'd be full and large in communicating whatever Remarks you have made on this Performance. The Evenings are long; we have sufficient time upon our Hands; and I know not how we can pass it away more agreeably.

Antiphaus paus'd for some time, and seem'd to be taken up in recollecting his Thoughts on this Point: at last taking a Tablet out of his Pocket, Since you desire it (says he) I will shew you what Observations I made as I went over the Work; they are the Thoughts which struck me *en passant*,[1] and many of them will perhaps appear little and trifling.

You will allow me, I believe, in the first place, That Lines very good in themselves, may be bad when consider'd as a Translation. The aim of a Translator is to give us the *Spirit* of the Original; and where the Original is just, the very *manner* is to be observ'd. By the Manner, I would not intend the express words, or the meer turn of a Period; but that the Imitation ought to be easy, simple, and unadorn'd, wherever the first Writer uses either of those Styles with Judgment. You are well acquainted with that plain humble manner of *Homer*, which is more particularly kept up by him in the *Odyssey*: And as much as I admire several parts in this Translation, I cannot but think there are places in it, which differ from the Manner of *Homer*, without sufficient reason for a Change. The Poet, in several parts of that Work, seems to me to have let fall some Lines that are forc'd; some of too much flourish, and ornament; and a few, even swelling, and unnatural; where the Original is with good reason plain, and natural, and unadorn'd.

Where we admire the Simplicity of *Homer* with Justice, we cannot avoid blaming the want of it in his Translator. Mr. *Pope* intimates in one

[1] *en passant*] *at first sight* 1737.

of his Notes,[1] *That* no Reproach has ever fall'n upon *Homer*, in relation to his sinking too Low, or being too Familiar; That as to these Particulars he preserves an Universal Justness: and that there is not any one place in his Poem, which can be justly censur'd upon this account. If so, a Translator of *Homer* has no occasion for raising any thing, beyond what it is in the Original; If he follows his Master it is sufficient: All additional Flourish and Glitterings, where we should meet with the plain and the familiar, are at best so many beautiful Excrescencies.

There is one Case, which seems more particularly to lead Mr. *Pope* into a glaring Stile: 'tis almost ever to be found in his Descriptions of *Day*, of *Light*, and of the *Morning*. 'Tis true, these are subjects which in themselves may require some brightness in the language; but there is a great difference between giving one Light, and dazling ones Eyes. Beside the conformity to the Original, there is another certain and easy way of judging, whether the Brightning in these or any other Points, be proper or not: that Light, we may be sure, falls in a wrong manner, or an undue proportion, which does not make the thing more visible.

There are of these Descriptions, *Philypsus*, which seem both to refine too much upon the Original, and to err according to this Rule. Did you ever observe those lines on one of the most agreeable Images in the World, The break of Day? they are in the beginning of the third Book: If you will give me leave, I will read them to you.

> The *sacred* Sun, above the Waters rais'd,
> Thro' Heaven's *eternal, brazen Portals blaz'd*;
> And wide o'er Earth diffus'd his *chearing* Ray,
> To Gods and Men, to *give the golden Day.*

> [Book iii. i–4: Pope]

Several of these Expressions seemed to me at first sight to take from the Nature and Simplicity of the Description; and when I turn'd to the Greek, I found those very Expressions to have no Foundation there. 'Tis the same Case in the following Lines:

> Soon as the Morn, in *orient Purple drest*,
> *Unbarr'd the Portal* of the roseate East *&c.*[2]

> —When the Morning-Star with early Ray
> *Flam'd in the front of Heaven*, &c.—[3]

[1] Book xiv. i. [The second edition reads, 'It is intimated in one of the notes', since Spence had found that Pope was not himself the author of the notes]

[2] Book iv. 411 [Fenton]; Homer, iv. 306.

[3] Book xiii. 112 [Pope]; Homer, xiii. 93.

You will find these Short Sketches in *Homer* to be much more simple and natural: I leave it to your Judgment, whether they appear better with these Colourings, or not. To add one Instance more of the same thing. Is it more proper for *Circe* to tell *Ulysses*, That he should stay that Night with her, and *set sail the next Morning*? or to hear her giving him leave, to

> Spread his broad Sails, and *plough the liquid way*,
> Soon as the Morn *unveils her Saffron Ray*.[1]

I must own, says *Philypsus*, this would have been more fit for the Description of a Voyage, than for a Speech: in a Place too, where we only find Orders given for setting Sail at such a time.

To me, proceeded *Antiphaus*, Mr. *Pope* seems to Beautify too much[2] in several other Points, beside those Topicks we have been talking of: as where he calls the Nobles of *Phœacia*, *A radiant Band* of *Noblemen*;[3] and where he introduces *Helen* with a *Gale of rich Perfume breathing before her*.[4] If *Homer* mentions *Cups of solid Gold*; in Mr. *Pope*,

> The Gold gives *lustre* to the *purple* Draught:[5]

> And in the *dazling* Goblet *laughs* the Wine.[6]

You cannot but observe, by the way, that the Original here is designed to signify the *real* intrinsick Value; while only the *outside* and more glittering Circumstances are what the *English* dwells upon entirely: but to go on. ——The Horns of a Bullock are in this new Language, *Budding Honours*;[7] and those of a Ram (if I am not much mistaken) *translucent Crescents*.[8] *Pallas* is well known to have had *Blue Eyes* given her by the Ancients; now it is

> Celestial Azure brightning in her Eyes.[9]

---

[1] Book xii. 35 [Broome]; Homer, xii. 24. [Spence quotes inaccurately. The couplet reads: 'And when the morn unveils her safron ray, / Spread your broad sails, and plow the liquid way.']

[2] *Mr. Pope . . . much*] *there seems to be too much of this Spirit of Beautifying* 1737.

[3] Book vi. 306 [Broome]; Homer, vi. 257.

[4] Book iv. 158 [Fenton]; Homer, iv. 121.

[5] Book i. 188 [Fenton]; Homer, i. 142.

[6] Book iii. 601 [Pope]; Homer, iii. 472.

[7] Book iii. 493 [Pope]; Homer, iii. 384.

[8] Book iv. 107 [Fenton]; Homer, iv. 85. [In fact the line reads, 'And two fair crescents of translucent horn'.]

[9] Book i. 408 [Fenton]; Homer, i. 314.

This heightning of things, by a severe Critick might be thought blameable; and indeed whenever it interferes, where the Passions ought to be touch'd, it certainly is so in an higher degree. The Reader is delighted when, after a melancholly Scene, he sees *Penelope* reviv'd by a Message from the Gods; and secretly enjoying the Satisfaction of her Soul: but what Passion, what Idea has he, when instead of this he is told of her *Hearts dilating and glowing with florid Joy?*[1]——Paint to him that unhappy Princess in her Distress, retiring *silently*, and crying herself to Sleep; only shew the Circumstances, and the Reader must be moved: Does her Behaviour and her Sufferings strike him so forcibly, when he finds it embellish'd into

——*Echoing Grief, and Silver-streaming Eyes?*[2]

But however these Passages may seem to be weaken'd by the finery and luxuriance of the Language, this certainly is not so much the fault of *Pope*, as of the Age: We give much into an airy way: If a Verse runs off smooth, 'tis no matter for depth or[3] clearness; and as the Ancients valued Thoughts more than Sound, we seem to be taken with Sounds more than Thought. To speak out, we are got into an idle manner of Versifying; and if Mr. *Pope* sometimes falls into it, we are not so much to blame him for those Particulars, as to wonder, that he does not do it more frequently, in so general a debauch of Taste among us.

Hold (interrupted *Philypsus*) if You go on at this rate, You will seem only to be got into the old Cant of running down our own Times: I do not believe, but that I cou'd name some Poet among us, to answer any of those who flourish'd in the *Augustan* Age. As to the present Point, we rarely hear of any such thing as *Translation* among them: In *Satyr*, we have the great Names of *Rochester*, *Dryden*, and *Oldham*: (not to mention the new kind of Satyr, introduc'd among us by *Butler*.[4]) In *Critical Poems*, there are (You know) two or three very good, beside that incomparable Piece by Mr. *Pope*, all to weigh against poor *Horace*. As for *miscellaneous* Subjects; think of *Cowley*, *Pope*,[5] *Waller* and *Pryor*, to mention no more of them. In the *Epick*, *Milton* may dispute the Laurel with either *Virgil*, or *Homer*; and in *Dramatick* Pieces, of either kind, we have Writers that indisputably exceed any of the Ancients.

[1] Book iv. 1096 [Fenton]; Homer, iv. 840.
[2] Book i. 462, 464 [Fenton]; Homer, i. 363.
[3] or] *and* 1737.
[4] Butler.]~; *or that by which Dr. Garth got so much reputation.* 1737.
[5] Cowley, Pope,] Mr. Pope *again, and of* Cowley 1737.

Antiphaus was not inclin'd to enter into a dispute of this nature. I was only speaking, says he, of our present Taste in Poetry, and the prevailing manner of those writers who are now upon the Stage. As to this, *Philypsus*, give me leave to say, that the language of our Writers, and the practice of the World, is much infected with the *Finesse*.[1] I think 'tis Mr. *Locke observes, that the humours of a People, may be learnt from their usage of words.* This symptom of the disease is very strong in the present Case: thus to say that a verse is *bien tourné* is the highest commendation among the French Criticks: in general, the *Beau Monde* is the only name now, for what was call'd by a very different one formerly;[2] as a *fine* Scholar, *polite* Literature, and the *Belles Lettres* are the leading expressions, when we would speak of Learning in the best sense. And I appeal to you, who are so well acquainted with all our Poets, whether their practise, in particular, does not fall more and more into the *Finesses*,[3] we have been complaining of. We may partly judge of this from some Lines in the Best of them, the Writer whose Works lye before us: I was just going to give you a few more instances of it, from the *Odyssey*.

Is there any Figure so much abus'd by the Moderns, as what they call the *Antithesis*? they run it into a down right playing upon Words. *Cowley*'s Poetry cou'd not *live* without it; *Dryden* uses it almost perpetually, in his Translation of *Virgil*; and was ridicul'd. You know, on that head by the late Duke of *Buckingham*.[4] I have observ'd with pleasure, that Mr. *Pope*, in his Translation, very much avoids this little beauty, which the other affected so excessively; yet I have a place before me, where one of this kind has slipt from his Pen: It runs thus. (He is speaking of a Stranger's Arrival at the Court of *Penelope*, disorder'd so much by the riot of the Suitors.)

> —When, to taste her hospitable board,
> Some Guest arrives, with rumours of her Lord;
> And these *indulge their want*, and *those their woe*;
> And *here the tears, and there the goblets flow.*[5]

Pardon me, says *Philypsus*, there you do not seem to do the Translator Justice; the Figure is countenanc'd by *Homer* himself: You see here is an *Antithesis* in the Original.

---

[1] *the* Finesse] *a Desire of appearing Smart and Pretty* 1737.
[2] *in . . . formerly*] *om.* 1737.
[3] Finesses] *Prettinesses* 1737.
[4] [See *The Rehearsal*, IV. ii]
[5] Book xiv. 413 [Pope]; Homer, xiv. 376.

That (answer'd *Antiphaus*) seems rather to be a Contrast, to set the riot of the Suitors in a stronger light: But call it what you please, it is only single there, whereas you see it multiplied, and worn to Rags in the Translation. This over-doing a Point is observable in many other Cases, as much as in the former; and in some, is carried on to a degree which borders upon the *Forc'd*, and *Unnatural*.

Telemachus, bursting into Tears at the Name of his Father, endeavours to hide his Sorrow from *Menelaus*, who was then talking with him. *Homer* says only, that *Menelaus observ'd him*; which words Mr. *Pope* draws out into this Couplet:

> The Conscious Monarch pierc'd the coy disguise,
> And view'd his filial love with vast surprize.[1]

For an humble natural Description of a Tripod (or Caldron) set upon the Fire, I wou'd recommend you to the following lines:

> The Flames *climb* round it with a *fierce embrace*;
> The fuming Waters *bubble o'er the Blaze*.[2]

But above all, in my Opinion, are these on a Person tired and quite spent:

> —*Lost in lassitude lay all the Man*,
> Depriv'd of Voice, of Motion, and of Breath;
> *The Soul scarce waking, in the Arms of Death*.[3]

Or these:

> Ye Gods! since this *worn frame refection knew*,
> What scenes have I survey'd of dreadful view?[4]

Wou'd you Imagine, that all which countenances this in the Original, is a Passage in *Ulysses*'s Speech after his Shipwreck, in which he intimates, *That he had not bath'd for a considerable time*?

I find it so, (says *Philypsus*) and own the Lines to be somewhat forc'd and unnatural; indeed those you have repeated seem generally to draw too near to that Character. But I cannot conceive by what means they sound so harsh to me at present: when I read the Piece, there was scarce a Line of them which gave me any offence.—Yes; it must be by your tearing them from the Body of the work, that they now seem not so

[1] Book iv. 153 [Fenton]; Homer, iv. 116.
[2] Book viii. 473 [Broome]; Homer, viii. 437.
[3] Book v. 585 [Pope]; Homer, v. 450.
[4] Book vi. 261 [Broome]; Homer, vi. 220.

agreeable. Really, *Antiphaus*, this is not fair usage of an Author; You rob them of their Order and Connection; and 'tis thence that they perfectly lose the Beauty, which they had in the Whole.

Very true, reply'd *Antiphaus*; the warmth of Reading, the thread of the Story, and a general tunableness in the Verse, will carry a Man on strangely; and may sometimes cheat him into a false Pleasure. But then it is for this very reason, that I shou'd think, the justest method of forming a judgment on Particulars is, to consider them apart. However, let us try it for once in a more entire Passage, than any of the former. Let me see; The place I have dipt upon, is where *Minerva* tells *Ulysses* that she will transform him into the figure of an Old Man; that he may view the posture of his Affairs unsuspected and unknown: The Lines in *Homer* may be thus read into English.

Odyssey, xiii. 397–403.

I will make you (says that Goddess to the Hero) entirely unknown to all Men; the beauty and smoothness of your Skin shall be taken away, your Limbs bent, and the Hair of your Head turn'd grey. I will then fling a Garb over you that shall make you frightful and odious to those that see you. All that flame and life in your Eyes shall be lost; I will so far deform them that you shall look contemptible to all the Suitors, to your own *Penelope*, and to your Son, whom You left yet an Infant in your Palace.

You know that Mr. *Pope*, in comparing some Passages in the Prophesies of *Isaiah* with the famous Eclogue of *Virgil*,[1] turns the latter into Prose; If we follow that Example in the present case, his Translation of these Lines runs thus:

Odyssey, xiii. 453–65.

If fits thee at present, to wear a dark disguise, and walk secret, unknown to the Eyes of Mortals: For this my Hand shall wither every Beauty, and every elegance of Form and Face, *Spread* a bark of Wrinkles *over thy smooth Skin,* turn the auburn honours of thy Head *hoar, disfigure with coarse attire every Limb, and extinguish all the Fire in thy Eyes; add all the decays of Life, and all the wants of it, estrange thee from thy Own, thy Son and thy Wife;* every sight shall turn from the loath'd object, and the blind suitors *scorn their destruction.*

Give me leave to go out of my way a little, to try the same Experiment on a single Passage from the *Iliad*, which is flourish'd, and set off in

---

[1] [See Pope's Advertisement to the *Messiah*, Twickenham, i. 111]

an extraordinary manner. It is in the [Twentieth] Book, where we have a poetical account of a fine Breed of Horses; The Original runs thus:

Iliad, xx. 221–5.

Three Thousand Mares graz'd these Meads, with their young Foals running by them; *Boreas* was enamour'd of them as they fed there, and turning himself into the shape of a fine black Horse, accomplish'd his desires: Of this breed, were twelve of the Colts.

Mr. *Pope*'s Translation, (only allowing equivalent Expressions to blind the Rhimes) runs thus:

Iliad, xx. 262–70.

His spacious pastures bred three Thousand Mares, and three Thousand *Foals fed beside* their Mothers: *Boreas enamour'd of the* sprightly train, *conceal'd his* God-head in the Locks of Hair *that flow'd over his Shoulders; he* neigh'd *to his* Loves with dissembled Voice, *and* cours'd the dapple Beauties *o'er the Meadow: Twelve others of* unrival'd sort *sprung hence,* swift as their Mother *Mares* and Father *Wind*.

This, if over-wrought, is the more blameable, because the matter is carried very far even in the Original, and so is the less capable of being stretch'd any farther. Mr. *Pope*, in his note upon the Place observes, *That Homer has the happiness of making the least Circumstance considerable; and that the plainest matter shines in his dress of Poetry.* It is true, it shines sufficiently in that. Some brightning is necessary in Poetry: but an excess of it, *Philypsus*, may dazle, or may blind our Eyes; it can never assist, or delight them.

By comparing these Passages, You will see that which I intend; the difference of Manner in the Ancient and Modern Poetry: In the latter we find Expressions added, which seem to be added for beauties, and which in reality perhaps only turn the Plainness and Strength of the Original, into the *Fine* and the *Artificial*.

Upon *Philypsus*'s acknowledging that he thought the Point too much labour'd, and the Translation unequal; Yes, says *Antiphaus*, the Translator himself seems to be sensible of it in the present Case; for soon after, when the former Passage is repeated in the Original,[1] he gives an entirely new Turn to it; And I believe, upon hearing the Lines, you will be of opinion that (excepting a word or two) it is render'd with a better grace and with more Justice, than we find in the former.

[1] Book xiii. 430 [Pope].

She spake, then touch'd him with her powerful Wand:
The Skin shrunk up, and wither'd at her Hand:
A swift Old-Age o'er all his Members spread,
A sudden Frost was sprinkled on his Head.
Nor longer in the heavy Eye-ball shin'd
The glance Divine, forth beaming from the Mind;
His Robe which Spots indelible besmear,
In Rags dishonest flutters with the Air.[1]

Mr. *Pope* without question is happy in a great share of Judgment, as
well as Vivacity and Spirit in Writing: but it is next to impossible, in so
long a Translation, especially as it is in *Rhime*, not to give sometimes
into Sound and Ornament; when to crown all, the Vogue of the World
goes so strong for both. Do not ask, whether I should desire to see
both of them banisht out of Poetry; far from it: Expressive Sounds are
of use in the most natural, and Variety in the management of them, is
necessary to keep up Attention in the Reader: That, and Ornament, is
what sets Poetry above Prose. All I wou'd say is this, that Sound is not
sufficient where we might expect Sense; and that in *humble* Passages, in
natural Descriptions, or in moving most of the *Passions*, additional
ornaments are so many blemishes. Dressing up the expressiveness of
Homer, in such fineries, is much the same as if one shou'd throw a very
gay modern dress over the *Hercules* of *Farnese*, or any of the most Nervous Statues of the Ancients.

But You will allow Ornament, where the subject will bear it, and
where the Original leads the Way.

In a translation (answer'd *Antiphaus*) it is proper perhaps, only in the
latter Case; but allowing it in both, it shou'd never be over-wrought in
either. Too much Finery is always Affectation: and I wish our Writers
at present were not so generally given *to elevate and surprize, and all that,*
as Mr. *Bayes* calls it.[2]

The running into this excess so much, is what has unsinew'd our
Poetry. 'Tis with Poetry, as it is in Buildings; the being vastly Studious
of Ornament does not only take away from the Strength of the Work,
but is a sure token of a vitiated taste in the Designer.

You are always blaming the Modern Refinements, says *Philypsus*;
but will you not allow that this taste of the Age is a sufficient justification at least of Mr. *Pope*, in those cases where he complies with it?—We
must *write* so as to please the World, and *speak* so as to be most easily
understood: Custom will often wear away the propriety of things of

---

[1] Book xiii. 496 [Pope].   [2] [See *The Rehearsal*, I. i]

this Nature; and as for the propriety of language, that depends upon it entirely. I allow, to use your own thought, that a profusion of Lace and Embroidery wou'd be a disguise upon an Old Hero; but they are so far from being improper, that they are becoming on the Heroes of our Age.—

They may become the Heroes of our Age (replied *Antiphaus* smiling) perhaps on a far different account: there is another Character now wove into and blended with that of a Soldier, to which these things are very agreeable: How many are there of these Heroes, as you call them, whose Courage reaches no farther than their Sword-knot, and whose Conduct is taken up wholly in their Dress? But consider a Man barely as a Soldier; think of him in the midst of some warm Action, and these little Ideas of him will disappear: Then it is *that* posture, *that* pressing on the foe, *that* grasping of his Sword, *that* fierceness in his Eyes, *that* serenity and *that* eagerness on his countenance, which strike us wholly, and take up all our attention. Yes, *Philypsus*, if you view a real modern Hero in a true light, those fineries do not sit[1] well upon him: and I think, I never saw any thing more truly ridiculous, than the Piece we were laughing at the other Day, in your Picture-Gallery.—Good Heaven! The Duke of *Marlborough* in the heat of an Engagement, with a full-bottom'd Wigg, very carefully spread over his Shoulders!

But to return to the present taste in Poetry.—If this Corruption of the Age cou'd excuse a Writer for what he composes now, must it be carried down as far as *Homer*'s Days? must his Heroes love, and talk, and fight *a-la-mode*? must his strong, sententious lines, be set to the new polite airs of *Handel* and *Bononcini*[2]? Yet, were what you wou'd alledge of any force, it wou'd carry the matter thus far; and the whole *Iliad* and *Odyssey* ought to be enervated down to the present taste. No, whatever may be allow'd to any of the proper genuine productions of this Age, it ought not to make an inrode upon all others: let *Homer*'s *energy* and *pathos* be violated as little as is possible; Nature ought to rule in his Works, and those of the Antients: as ornament, and surprize, and elevation, have in their turn the Empire of the Modern World.

You see I begin to shew the old heat, that this subject (I think) always betrays me into.—I beg pardon, *Philypsus*; and will attend more to what I am about for the future.—I shou'd have given you some in-

---

[1] *sit*] 1737; *set* 1726.

[2] [G. V. Bononcini (1672?–1750?), the Italian composer, was Handel's great rival between 1720 and 1731]

stances of this *Elevation* from the translation before us. *A-propos*, What a glaring description of a Sword have we in the Eighth *Odyssey*?

> —Whose blade of Brass *displays*
> *A ruddy gleam*; whose hilt *a Silver blaze*;
> Whose ivory sheath *inwrought* with *curious pride*,
> Adds *graceful terror to the wearer's side*.[1]

Homer says, that *Hermione* was *as beautiful as Venus*: this is low and humble in comparison of Mr. *Pope*'s *Hermione*,

> On whom *a radiant Pomp of Graces* wait,
> Resembling *Venus* in *attractive state*.[2]

Where a prodigy is sent to the *Ithacensians* in Council, *Homer* says that *they were struck at the sight of it, and revolv'd in their Minds what it might presage to them*: this Mr. *Pope* renders after the following manner,

> The wondring rivals gaze with cares opprest,
> And chilling horrors freeze in every Breast.[3]

How mean is it, and how much like prose, to tell us, that *Penelope heard the mirth of the Suitors*? to elevate this sufficiently, You must say

> *The shrilling Airs the vaulted Roof rebounds,*
> *Reflecting to the Queen the Silver Sounds.*[4]

This false way of *animating* Poetry, as no doubt many will be pleas'd to call it, grows particularly prejudicial and absurd in any case, where the *Passions* are to be rais'd in the Reader, or describ'd in the Persons of the Poem. Where we wou'd move Pity, in particular, nothing is *more odious than a shew of Eloquence*.[5] Nature has provided a Sympathy in our Souls; She has put a biass into our Temper, that inclines us forcibly to Compassion; and we shou'd leave her to her own work in such points, without any of the impertinent assistances of Art[6]. . . . [pp. 1–25]

---

[1] Book viii. 438 [Broome]; Homer, viii. 403.
[2] Book iv. 19 [Fenton]; Homer, iv. 14.
[3] Book ii. 183 [Broome]; Homer, ii. 156.
[4] Book i. 425 [Fenton]; Homer, i. 328.
[5] Odi reum cui esse diserto vacet (Quintilian, *Institutio Oratorio* XI. i. 50). [Spence shortens and adapts the Latin]
[6] Quidquid meris adjicietur adfectibus, omnes eorum diluet vires, et miserationem securitate laxabit (Quintilian, *Institutio Oratorio*, XI. i. 52). ['Will not all embellishment of pure emotion merely impair its force and dispel compassion by such a display of apparent unconcern?']

Metaphor, says *Philypsus*, is certainly the most universal enlivener of Poetry. At the same time that it adds to the dignity of Verse, it gives it an agreeable variety; together with a power of Painting out all its Images, in the boldest and strongest manner in the World. 'Tis this which animates those objects, which must otherwise be still and un-affecting: it flings every thing into Motion, Life, and Action: By this the Arrow is *eager* and on the Wing, by this the Sword *thirsts* for Blood, and the Spear *rages* in the Hands of the Warriour. *Metaphor* raises each subject out of the heavy narrative way: it creates new Beings; it represents the passions of Men, and even meer *Names*, as animated and imbodied; and shews them in the posture and attitudes of Agents. Thus when the Battles are going to join, You see *Rage stalk* amidst the Combatants; pointing with one *Hand* to the Enemy, and in the other, shaking the *Torch of War*. By this, the Valleys and Moun-tains *rejoice*, when *Peace* once more *spreads* her downy Wings, and *Plenty* descends from Heaven upon the *happy* climate. 'Tis *Metaphor* which makes the Woods and Caves *answer* to the voice of the Poet, and the murmuring Stream *compassionate* his complaints: 'Tis this which makes the *Nile know Cæsar*; and *the Sea*, its present *Monarch*.

If Mr. *Pope* manages this powerful Figure frequently to the best advantage, sometimes he happens not to be so happy in the use of it. The force of *Metaphor* is to make things strong, clear, and sensible: any confusion destroys the very end of it; and yet a little inaccuracy may occasion gross errors in this way. Sometimes what is just with the *Figurative*, may disagree with the *Proper*: sometimes again, an idea which might stand with the *proper* expression, will be inconsistent with the *figurative*. A misapplication either way is very obvious, and yet it gives a jar to the Ideas, and makes the sense of a line to be perplexed and in confusion.

It sounds but oddly to talk of a Person, and of his Picture, without any manner of distinction: To say, that *the piece, drawn by Sir Godfrey Kneller for Mr. Pope, is an excellent Poet and Writes with the greatest Comman dimaginable*; Or, that *Mr. Pope is a very good piece, and his face very well colour'd, tho' he is but just recover'd from a fit of Sickness*; either of them wou'd carry a mixt incoherent sense with them: This I take to be partly the Case in the following Lines,[1]

> Now from my *fond embrace* by Tempests torn,
> Our other *Column of the State* is born;

[1] Book iv. 962 [Fenton]; Homer, iv. 727.

Nor took a *kind adieu.*—
They *sweep* Neptunes smooth *Face.*[1]

Declining, with his *sloping Wheels*
Down *sunk* the *Sun.*—[2]

To say *the God of Light was driving his Car, down the Steep of Heaven* (as Mr. *Pope* somewhere expresses it) is metaphorical; To say *the Sun is setting*, is proper: but shou'd one say, *The Sun is setting with sloping Wheels*, This would be neither Metaphorical, nor Proper; nor cou'd it raise any thing in the Mind, but a confusion of Ideas.

Again:

As some lone Mountain's monstrous growth he stood,
Crown'd with rough thickets and a nodding wood.[3]

Again:

Hear me, Oh *Neptune!* thou whose *Arms* are *hurl'd*
From Shore to Shore, and *gird* the solid World.[4]

I think, *Neptune* has the luck of it; for 'tis the same Deity, that in another place makes just such a Figure, as I have seen him in some *Mortlock-Hangings:*

The raging Monarch shook his *azure Head,*
And thus in secret to his Soul he said, &c.[5]

This said, his *Sea-green Steeds* divide the Foam.[6]

Such confusions of the *Metaphor* and the *Proper* have a great resemblance to that absurdity (of mixing *Fable* and *Reality* together) which appears so grosly in Mr. *Dryden's Hind and Panther*; and which was the very thing, that provoked Lord *Halifax* to ridicule that Piece, with such infinite[7] humour and good sense. The Noble Author's Words on that

---

[1] Book ix. 209 [Pope]; Homer, ix. 180.
[2] Book ii. 436 [Broome]; Homer, ii. 388.
[3] Book ix. 223 [Pope]; Homer, ix. 192. [This example is dropped in the second edition]
[4] Book ix. 617 [Pope]; Homer, ix. 528.
[5] Book v. 365 [Pope]; Homer, v. 285. ['Mortlock-Hangings' are Mortlake tapestries]
[6] Book v. 486 [Pope]; Homer, v. 380.
[7] *such infinite*] *so much* 1737

subject, may give a Side-light to what I mean in the present Case. Speaking of the Ancient [1] Fabulists,

They wrote (says he) in Signs, and spoke in Parables: all their Fables carry a double meaning: The Story is one and entire; The Characters the same throughout; not broken, or chang'd, and always conformable to the nature of the Creatures they introduce. They never tell you that *the Dog*, which *snapt* at a shadow, lost his *Troop of Horse*; that wou'd be unintelligible.—This is his (*Dryden's*) new way of telling a Story, and confounding the *Moral* and the *Fable* together.

After instancing from the *Hind and Panther*, he goes on thus.

What relation has the *Hind* to our *Saviour?* or what notion have we of a *Panther's Bible?* if you say, he means the *Church*, how does the *Church feed on Lawns, or range in the Forest?* Let it be always a Church, or always the Cloven-footed Beast, for we cannot bear his shifting the Scene every Line. [2]

I had almost forgot to tell You, that upon consulting the Original there was no *Metaphor* at all to be found, for either of the Lines, I last repeated from the *Odyssey*. We have now *Metaphors* perpetually; the Translator is vastly fond of them. I need not say that an Excess this way is very blameable; You know the Criticks speak against it in a high strain, and one of them goes so far as to say, that this *Figure, when frequent, obscures the Piece, and fatigues the Reader; when continual, 'tis no longer a Poem, 'tis all Allegory and Enigma.* [3]

As a false Mixture of the proper and the figurative confuses the sense; The joining *Metaphors* together, which do not agree, makes it still more dark and perplexed. These are like (what they call) *Medley-Pieces*; a huddled kind of Pictures, which shew a Variety of Objects, flung together without any order or design: As that in the beginning of *Horace's Art of Poetry*, they join the Limbs of one Creature to the Body of another; and confuse all the properties and circumstances of an Action.

If the Poet be not very careful he may by these means tye not only things improper, but even contrarieties, together. Do not the following

---

[1] *Speaking ... Ancient*] *I think the Book is behind you. If you will be so good as to reach it down, I'll just read that Passage in their Preface to you, where they are speaking of this odd Mixture. O, here it is. It begins with mentioning the antient* 1737.

[2] Preface to *The Hind and the Panther Transvers'd* (1687). [*Literary Works of Matthew Prior*, ed. H. B. Wright and M. K. Spears (1959), i. 35–36]

[3] Frequens (*Metaphoræ usus*) et obscurat et tæ dio complet: continuus vero in allegorias et ænigmata exit (Quintilian, *Institutio Oratorio*, VIII. vi. 14).

Lines border on this? to me the *Metaphors* in them seem to be improperly united.

> From *Elatreus*'s strong Arm the *Discus* flies,
> And *Sings with unmatch'd Force* along the Skies:
> And *Laodame whirls High*, with dreadful sway,
> *The Gloves of Death.*—[1]

At the same Time, nothing can be more *Proper* and *Narrative* than the Original in that place. *Again:*

> From his Eyes *pour'd down the tender Dew.*[2]

> But *Anticlus* unable to controul,
> Spoke *loud* the *languish* of his yearning Soul.[3]

In these the Action is described in words, that import a *violence*; while the Act to be express'd, is plainly something *still* and *gentle*.

Nothing is more known in relation to the *Metaphor*, than that rule of Cicero's; *That it shou'd be so modest, as to seem to have been handed into the place of the proper Word, not to have forced its Way thither: it shou'd fall into it in a free, voluntary manner.*[4] Otherwise it will make the sense dark and intricate; and that absolutely destroys all the use of it: for as *Metaphor* shou'd be the *greatest Light and Ornament of Language, Obscurity is the most absurd thing, and the most to be avoided in Metaphor.*[5] . . .

[pp. 29–35].

EVENING the SECOND

[In the next evening's dialogue, Philypsus defends Pope by pointing to his 'beauties', arguing that in many places he 'improves' upon Homer. Here he shows the ability of Pope's verse to enact passion, and then replies to Antiphaus's earlier attack upon the diction of the translation:]

. . . There is one Speech more of those I mention'd at first, which I cannot forbear repeating to you; tho' I am sensible, that I have been too long upon this Head already. It is that of *Circe* to *Ulysses*, in the tenth *Odyssey*:[6]

---

[1] Book viii. 137 [Broome]; Homer, viii. 130.
[2] Book xi. 486 [Broome]; Homer, xi. 390.
[3] Book iv. 387 [Fenton]; Homer, iv. 286.
[4] Verecunda esse debet Translatio, ut deducta esse in alienum locum, non iruisse; atque ut precario, non vi venisse videatur (Cicero, *De Oratore*, III. xli. 165).
[5] Est hoc magnum ornamentum orationis, in quo obscuritas fugienda est (*ibid.*, 167).
[6] Book x. 380 [Pope]; Homer, x. 330.

Then wav'd the wand, and then the word was given:
Hence to thy fellows! (dreadful she began)
Go, be a Beast!—I heard and yet was Man.
Then sudden whirling like a waving Flame
My beamy faulchion, I assault the Dame:
Struck with unusual fear, she trembling cries,
She faints, she falls; she lifts her weeping eyes.
What are thou? say! from whence, from whom you came?
O more than human! tell thy race, thy name.
Amazing strength these poisons to sustain!
Not mortal thou, nor mortal is thy Brain.
Or art thou he? the Man to come (foretold
By *Hermes* powerful with the Wand of Gold)
The Man from *Troy*, who wander'd Ocean round,
The Man, for Wisdom's various Arts renown'd:
Ulysses?—Oh? thy threatning fury cease.—

What starts? what terror, and amazement? What passionate breaks are there in these lines? How solemn is the beginning? how emphatical the account of the action? and how lively the surprize and confusion of the Inchantress, upon finding the inefficacy of her Charms? Nature here appears in every Word that she says; if the Disappointment is great and shocking, the lines too are all impetuous and abrupt: if the passions strong and various, the Expressions in the Translation are instant and pressing, and the stile often chang'd: How great and swift is the Alteration, from an imperious cruel Tyrant, to a poor weak helpless Woman? And how is it equal'd by that judicious shifting of the scene in this piece? There the change is as sudden and immediate; and nothing can be greater than the fall from the haughtiness of *Go, be a Beast!* to the meanness of the line, just after,

She faints, she falls; she lifts her weeping Eyes.

You cannot but observe farther, my *Antiphaus*, that the lines in this description, are every where improv'd with those Figures, which the Ancient *Criticks* have always look'd upon as the most proper to express an hurry of Passion. The *Transposition,* the *Omission* of Words, the pressing use of *Exclaiming* and *Interrogation,* and the general *Inconnection* which runs through it, are all apply'd in the most natural and poetical Manner. There is a Note of the Translator on a Passage not long before this, which gives us in one view several excellent Observations of this kind, and which no doubt he had in his Eye here; for the rules of it are exactly follow'd in the present case. This Poet is the best Commentator on himself; give me leave therefore just to look back for his Note on the Speech of *Eurylocus*; that you may see how exactly those Observations tally with his performance here, in every particular Article.

We have here (says he) a very lively picture of a Person in a great fright:— the very manner of speaking, represents the disorder of the speaker; he is in too great an Emotion to introduce his Speech by any Preface, he breaks at once into it, without preparation, as if he could not soon enough deliver his thoughts.[1]

–*Again*: There is nothing[2] which gives more life to a Discourse, than the taking away the Connections and Conjunctions; when the discourse is not bound together and embarass'd, it walks and slides along of it self. *Periods* thus cut off, and yet pronounc'd with Precipitation, are signs of a lively Sorrow; which at the same time hinders, yet forces him to speak.

–*Again* (in a like case): He speaks short, and in broken and interrupted Periods, which excellently represent the agony of his thoughts.—Afterwards we see he breaks out into Interrogations, which, as *Longinus* observes,[3] give great motion, strength, and action to Discourse. If the Poet had proceeded simply, the Expression had not been equal to the occasion; but by these short Questions, he gives strength to it, and shews the disorder of the speaker, by the sudden starts and vehemence of the Periods.

All these animated Figures, all those Arts of expressing the Passions, are beautifully wove into this single piece of Poetry: But there is one peculiar Excellence in it yet behind, which I admire beyond all the rest. It is a power almost unknown even to Poetry before, and the Criticks have not as yet found out any Name for it. The extraordinary Beauty I mean, is that *Insight* which the Poet gives his Readers into *Circe*'s *Mind*: We look into her Soul, and see the Ideas pass there in Train. At first she is ignorant, then dubious, and at last discovers gradually in her Thoughts the Character, and very Name of the Heroe. *Circe*, skill'd as she was in all the arts of Magick, is limited in her Knowledge and Discovery of things: and in the present Discovery of the Person of *Ulysses*, her Mind acts with Tumult and Rapidity, but at the same time with a series and gradual Collection of Truths, at first unknown. Every one may perceive the Tumult, and the *successive Enlightnings* of her Mind. We are led into a full View of the shifting of her thoughts; and behold the various openings of them in her Soul.

[1] Book x. 295 note. [Spence has taken only a small part of Pope's long note.]
[2] Longinus, *De Sublimitate*, xix. 2.
[3] Longinus, *De Sublimitate*, xix. 2.

What are thou? say! from whence, from whom you came.
Or art thou He? *the Man to come* foretold—
The Man, from Troy?——
The Man, for *wisdom's* various arts renown'd,
Ulysses?——

I never read any thing which sets the actings of another's Mind so distinctly to the view. *Circe's* very Thoughts are made visible to us; they are set full in our Eyes; and we see the different degrees, as it were of Light, breaking in upon her Soul.—'Tis a most charming piece of Poetry! and upon turning it every way, and considering all its several perfections, I believe one might venture to pronounce it, the most finisht Piece, the most *compleat Beauty* in the whole Translation.

These are the productions of a Sublime Genius, and speak an uncommon Spirit, together with a firm extensive Judgment, and an exact Sense of things. But you *Antiphaus* chiefly complain of this Writer for his Refinements and Elevation: there is too much of the *Enflure* (as the *French* call it) in his Works; and you cannot bear with such a profusion of Glitter and Embroidery in the Language. [pp. 55–60]

[Pope's pictorial imagination]

It wou'd be endless to repeat every thing of this Nature; There are a Thousand sketches of it in the *Odyssey*. 'Tis sufficient at present to observe, that Mr. *Pope* generally gives them to us in very lively Colours; and excells almost every where in the *Pathetick*.

'Tis certain (says *Antiphaus*) that he has an excellent Hand; his Images, which you have set before me, are as strong as any of the Works of the Pencil.

They are so, answered *Philypsus*; and, on that account, you will Pardon me for borrowing so many Metaphors from Painting in this Case; 'Tis unavoidable. The designs of Painting and Poetry are so united, that to me the Poet and the Painter seem scarcely to differ in any thing, except the *Mean* they make use of, to arrive at one and the same end. Both are to express Nature: but the Materials of the one are Words, and Sound; of the other, Figure and Colours. *Poetry* can paint more particularly, more largely, and with greater coherence: *Painting* is the more concise, and emphatical. If *This* may excell in shewing one View distinctly, *That* can shew several in succession, without any manner of Confusion. Any figure in *Painting* is confin'd to one Attitude; but *Poetry* can give as great a variety of Motion and Postures, as the reality it self. What seems a Paradox of Art in either, is their power of expressing two *opposite Passions* in the same face. Of this sort (among a Multitude of like instances) is the Mother of *Lewis* the Thirteenth, in the Gallery of *Luxembourg*;[1] and every Piece in that fine Episode, which concludes the sixth *Iliad*. In that *Picture*, the Queens Face strongly expresses the Pain and Anguish of her Condition, mix'd with a regard toward her Son, full of the greatest Pleasure and Complacence. In the *Poem* we have the greater variety, and each piece is perfectly just and finish'd. *Hector* shews a fierceness for the War, and a tenderness that inclines him to stay for a last interview; little *Astyanax* has a Fondness and a Terror in his Eyes, at the sight of his Father; while *Andromache*'s Face is all soften'd into a tender Smile; and at the same time, wet with the Tears, that fall for her *Hector*. [pp. 75–6]

[In the following passage, Philypsus points to Pope's use of allusion in his endeavours to 'improve' Homer]

Mr. *Pope* has a very great happiness in *Transferring Beauties*. He often guides his Translation of *Homer* by some fine thought, or good expression in any other eminent writer; and this has been the occasion of several improvements in that work.

Have you never observ'd how he introduces the Elegance of *Virgil*, into the Majesty of *Homer*? There are two speeches of *Circe*,[2] which have much of the air of that of *Proetus*, in the fourth *Georgick*; and that of the *Sybill*'s in the sixth *Æneid*. The speech of *Tiresias*[3] is improv'd, from another of the *Sybill*; so also is the Prophetical speech, in the second *Odyssey*.[4]

There are several Imitations (in a shorter compass) of natural Images, and the like, introduc'd into *Homer* from the same treasury: Thus the following Lines

> Down-sunk the Heavy beast.[5]

> *Læstrigonia*'s gates arise distinct in air.[6]

> ——The [*Siren*] shores like mists arise.[7]

> And all above is Sky and Ocean all around, &c.[8]

---

[1] [Rubens painted twenty-four pictures celebrating the life of Maria de Medici, Queen of France, and mother of Louis XIII. They are now in the Louvre]
[2] Book x. 387ff. [Pope]. [Spence refers to only one speech in his footnote]
[3] Book xi. 130ff. [Broome]; *Aeneid*, vi. 87ff.   [4] ll. 203ff.
[5] Book xiv. 572 [Pope].   [6] Book x. 93 [Pope]; *Aeneid*, iii. 206.
[7] Book xii. 201 [Broome].   [8] Book xii. 474 [Broome]; *Aeneid*, iii. 193.

Although the Translator adds these fine strokes from other Hands, they are brought in so naturally, that they seem to spring out of *Homer*'s sentiment: And if an Instance or two shou'd be found among them which may vary a little from the Original, it is only to add some apposite Thought, that is not only finer, but at the same time perfectly agreeable to the Subject. In such cases a Translator may demand the greater liberty of enlarging: as a *Flattering Resemblance* is always allow'd to Painters. I like that very ingenious Friend of yours, who calls the *French* Translation of *Tacitus, La belle Infidelle*: That piece, you know, tho' not very precise and constant to its Author, is the more beautiful, and the more engaging.

However, 'tis seldom that Mr. *Pope* varies much in these additional Beauties; his Translation is generally faithful, even where it improves upon *Homer*: And he keeps the chief mark steadily in his Eye, tho' at the same Time it admits the side glances of Light, from other objects. Thus you will scarce ever find him deviating from his Author in such cases: tho' this manner of improving him by imitation from others is vastly frequent; and often so plain, that one may trace it thro' whole scenes together: In particular, I cou'd almost be positive that Mr. *Pope* read over the *Eclogues* of *Virgil*, before he set about that Part of the Story, which lies between *Ulysses* and *Eumæus*; and indeed I should be apt to conjecture that he usually read those Pastorals, before he sat down to any rural Scene in this Piece:[1] If I am mistaken in this, 'tis the resemblance of their beauties, which has deceiv'd me.

Sometimes we find the *Diction* beautified by such Resemblances, or the Sentiment improv'd from other hands. From the *Sacred Writings* frequently;[2] from parallel places in *Homer* himself:[3] From *Ovid, Seneca, Horace, &c.*[4] among the Ancients; And from *Dryden, Addison, Milton*, and several others of the most celebrated Moderns.[5] In his *Speeches*, we meet with improvements from the Examples and Rules of

[1] [Passages] from Virgil; Books xiv. 76 [Pope], v. 96 [Pope]. See also Book ii. 26 [Broome] (*Aeneid*, iii. 627), Books ii. 55 [Broome], iii. 126 [Pope], iv. 509 [Fenton], vi. 197 [Broome], x. 569 [Pope], xi. 433, 434 [Broome], etc.

[2] [Passages from] *Scripture*; Books i. 483 [Fenton], iii. 424, 451 [Pope], iv. 145, 438 [Fenton], v. 288 [Pope], vi. 235 [Broome], x. 591 [Pope], xi. 239 [Broome], xiv. 109 [Pope]. And frequently in other places.

[3] [Passages from] *Iliad*; Book xi. 415 [Broome] (*Iliad*, vi. 41), etc.

[4] [Passages from] *Ovid*; Books iv. 808 [Fenton], x. 282 [Pope], xiii. 193 [Pope], xiv. 224 [Pope]: *Seneca*; Book v. 573 [Pope]: *Horace*; Books x. 556, 557 [Pope], xiv. 519 [Pope].

[5] [Passages from] *Dryden*; Books v. 80 [Pope], xi. 531 [Broome], etc.: *Addison*; Books iv. 371 [Fenton], xi. 684 [Broome]: *Milton*; Book xi. 725 [Broome]. And frequently in other places.

the Orators of old; and many, from our own Dramatick pieces. It wou'd not be difficult, for a Man of a good Taste, to discern the Air sometimes of *Dryden*, sometimes of *Shakespear*,[1] and at others of *Otway*, among the speeches in the *Odyssey*. I shall only point out to you those of *Agamemnon*, which are so very pathetick, in the Eleventh Book:[2] You will easily see that they have a new manner, which exceedingly resembles the hand of the most moving of all our Tragick Writers, since *Shakespear*.

Antiphaus, upon consulting the passages, immediately perceiv'd the spirit of *Otway* in them; He then desired *Philypsus* to direct him to the other imitations he had mention'd: at first he did not think they deserv'd so much commendation; but when he came to Compare the original Lines from the *Odyssey*, with those of Mr. *Pope*, he was convinc'd of their beauty: It delighted him to see, what Foundation the Original gave for such a turn, and yet how new that turn was in the Translation; he found almost in every one of them some addition for the better, and scarce in any a deviation from the sense of *Homer*: It was *Homer*'s sense, but the Expression of it was improv'd.

I thank you, (says he turning to *Philypsus*) I thank you for this clearer view you have given me of the beauties of this Translation: beside these last, how many things have you repeated to me that are extremely just, pure, close, and *emphatical*? how many perfectly true, and *natural*? how many handsomly beautified, and *enliven'd*? what *Pictures* of Things? what *Descriptions* of Actions? and what beautiful Expressions, both of the *thoughts*, and of the *passions* of the soul? in a word, what *improvements*, in some strokes, upon the greatest Genius of the World?

Yes, added *Philypsus*, upon the greatest Genius of the World, assisted by the native use of the most Noble, and most Poetical of all Languages. Then were we to consider the inconveniences on the other side; the general difficulties of Translation, and the difficulty of this in particular: How hard is it for a Poet to keep up his spirit and flame in another's Work? and how natural to flag in representing Thoughts not our own? To maintain the vigour of Language and the poetick warmth thorough so long a work, and to express the Soul of *Homer*, what a Genius does it require? what Spirit wou'd not sink under so large an undertaking? Yet does Mr. *Pope* hitherto sustain his Character in an handsome equal manner: and we may safely promise ourselves the same of the remaining part of this work: As he enter'd upon this stage with the greatest

---

[1] [Passages from] *Shakespear*; Books ix. 420 [Pope], x. 410 [Pope], etc.
[2] See Books xi. 531, 537-44 [Broome].

expectations of all Men, I doubt not but he will leave it with an Universal *Plaudite*.

But however great and handsome his performance is in the whole, I own with you that it has its faults, the common marks of Humanity: Yes, my *Antiphaus*, you convinc'd me the former Evening, that it is unavoidable for the greatest Genius not to fail sometimes.

For my part (says *Antiphaus*,) I shall make no Apologies for the freedoms with which I then us'd this excellent writer: Any thing of that kind might look odd to you from one, whose constant Sentiment you know to be this; *that* the kindest way of commending a writer is to find fault with him now and then, at proper intervals.   [pp. 94–99]

EVENING the THIRD

[Antiphaus on rhyme and sound effects in Pope's verse]

The constant returns of Rhime unavoidably unnerve a Poem: The Age is in Love with this Weakness; and Mr. *Pope*, in indulging their humour has[1] taken much from the strength of his Genius: had he been less obliging to the taste of his Readers, his performance might have been more sinewy, and more compleat. This ought certainly to be taken into the account: and wherever the Translation falls short of the force and nervousness of *Homer*, we ought constantly to ask our selves this question; Whether *Homer* himself cou'd have carried it farther, had he wrote (as Mr. *Pope* does) in *English*, and in *Rhime*?

'Tis true, all this may be said of his Translation of the *Iliad*; but if that Piece exceed this of the *Odyssey*, it is very natural upon other Accounts that it shou'd do so. *Homer* exceeds himself in that Poem.—Great Actions strike the Soul with rapidity; while all the things that relate to lower Life, are less vigorous and affecting:—The description of Warriors and moral Precepts have a very different effect, on the writers themselves; those assist the Poetical flame, while these fling the Mind into a more sedentary Posture. 'Tis natural almost for People to sleep at Sermons: But a Battle rouzes and animates the Spectators, as well as those who are engaged in it. Thus there must be less spirit in the Writer, as well as less attentiveness in the Reader of the *Odyssey*: and a Translation of it, even from one and the same Hand, cou'd not fairly be expected to equal a Translation of the *Iliad*. The Reader and the Poet have both of them the disadvantage of a cooler and more unactive Subject: A *Poet* (as Age always is) vastly talkative; A *Fable* laid in-

---

[1] *has*] has perhaps 1737.

finitely lower; and a *Diction*, almost perpetual in moral Sentences and Reflections, give a pattern very different from *Homer*, in all his vigour, describing the Passion of *Achilles*; and sounding out the Wars of the *Greeks*, with an air the most martial and animated, that can be imagined.

Here *Antiphaus* rose up from his seat, and as *Philypsus* perceiv'd that he had finish'd; I was unwilling to interrupt you (says he) otherwise I shou'd have observ'd on a verse or two, which you repeated, as rough, and of a bad turn. What were those Lines of *the Rocks*, which you mention'd just now?

—Of the Rocks? (says *Antiphaus*) let me see—Oh, I remember them;

> No Bird of air, no Dove of swiftest wing
> Shuns the dire rocks: in vain she cuts the skies,
> The dire rocks meet and crush her as she flies.[1]

The same says *Philypsus*: these and that other verse,

> Rich Tapestry, stiff with inwoven gold,[2]

sound indeed rough; but to me their roughness, is their beauty: the turn of them seems design'd; and their manner to be expressive of their sense.

If that be the Case, I beg pardon, says *Antiphaus*: Were I the greatest enemy in the World to meer harmony, and the stated returns and gingle of syllables; I shou'd be one of the first among the admirers of *Sound*, whenever it is made serviceable to nature and true sense.

That is the Art (says *Philypsus*) and the Mastery, for which I particularly admire Mr. *Pope*: It is he who took up that great Rule of *the Sounds being a comment on the Sense*, and enforc'd it beyond any of the Criticks who went before him. To this Writer we chiefly owe the revival of the nobler art of Numbers; and the method of signifying motions, and actions, and all that vast variety of our own passions by *Sounds*. In his incomparable *Essay on Criticism*, this Writer has given us the best Advises, and interwove the most beautiful Examples into them, in a manner that will always be admired. The first *Stanza*, in his *Ode* on St. *Cæcilia's Day*, is the fullest Piece of this kind perhaps extant in any Language: 'tis it self a perfect Confort. In the Translations of *Homer* we find him very frequent, and very just, in the same manner of Expressing things: I call it so; and cou'd almost be perswaded to think it a

[1] [Book xii. 78: Broome]   [2] [Book iv. 206: Fenton]

better way of Expressing, than in the common way of *Words*. These
have a Sense affixt to them by Custom; while the other speaks by the
Ideas of things; That is a flowing, variable help; this is the Voice of
Nature, and a sort of *Universal* Poetical *Language*.

Mr. *Pope* affords us infinite Examples of this Beauty in his Translation
of the *Odyssey*; it wou'd be endless to repeat them all, or to admire them
as they deserve. But amidst all this variety, there is a single Point,
which I have observ'd more than any of the rest: Whenever the Poet is
speaking of the watry Element, or any thing belonging to it, his
management of Sounds is particularly frequent and beautiful.

Tho' it might not be much observ'd at the first view, I know no
place where a greater variety of things are express'd this way, than in
the Twelfth *Odyssey*; 'Tis where *Ulysses* is giving an account of his
setting sail from the Island of *Circe*:[1]

> —We rush'd into the Main;
> Then bending to the stroke, their oars they drew
> To their broad breasts, and swift the galley flew.
> Up sprung a brisker breeze: with freshning gales
> The friendly Goddess stretch'd the swelling sails;
> We drop our oars: at ease the pilot guides;
> The vessel light along the level glides.
> Then rising sad and slow, with pensive look,
> Thus to the melancholly train I spoke.

The objects shift perpetually in these Lines; and yet there is not a
single period or pause in them, the sound and turn of which does not
agree perfectly with the sentiment: I do not intend to enlarge much
upon them; but had it been wrote in the Days of *Dionysius Halicar-
nassæus*, I doubt not but he wou'd have given us a Dissertation, on a
passage which so variously expresses that Art, of which he was
particularly fond.

That is the Critick, I think, says *Antiphaus*, who first observ'd this
Beauty in the noted Description of *Sisyphus* his Stone?[2]

Yes, answer'd *Philypsus*; and every one knows how perfectly well the
excellence of that Passage is preserv'd in Mr. *Pope*'s Translation.[3]

Words give us the bare Ideas of things; but words, thus managed,

[1] Book xii. 181 [Broome].
[2] Περὶ συνθέσεως ὀνομάτων, p. 29. Ed. *R. Steph.* [presumably the edition printed by R. Stephani, 1546–7].
[3] Book xi. 735 [Broome].

impress them very strongly and sensibly upon the mind: Do you not perceive the Storm rising *When the wild Winds whistle o'er the main?*[1] and are you not in the midst of it when *East, West together roar, and South and North roll mountains to the Shore?*[2] Then are we hurried o'er the Deep, and see all the *rocks* and dangers of it:

> Dire *Scylla* there a scene of Horror forms,
> And here *Charybdis* fills the sea with storms;
> When the tide rushes from her rumbling caves
> The rough rock roars; tumultuous boil the waves;
> They toss: they foam.——[3]

The next moment if the Poet pleases (like the *Dæmon* he speaks of) He can make all as gentle and serene, as it was before rough and boistrous.

> Sunk were at once the winds: the air above
> And waves below, at once forgot to move:
> Some *Dæmon* calm'd the air, and smooth'd the deep,
> Hush'd the loud winds, and charm'd the waves to sleep.[4]

Did you ever see a more perfect Calm? Yet smooth and hush'd as these Lines are, you may easily perceive a difference between the description of a still Sea, and the easy beautiful current of a River.

> Smooth flows the gentle stream with wanton pride,
> And in soft mazes rolls a silver tide.[5]

How happy is the hand of the Poet, and what a Command has he of Nature, to make the numbers of his verse speak his Sentiments; Thus to paint even sounds; and to draw by Measures, what does not come under the power of the Pencil? In this Writer, Sir *John Denham*'s Wish is effected: His Lines always flow as his Subject;

> Tho' deep, yet clear; tho' gentle, yet not dull:
> Strong, without rage; without o'erflowing full.[6]

I thank you (says *Antiphaus* bowing) I thank you, my dear *Philypsus*, for this unexpected view of one of the greatest Beauties in Poetry. I cou'd willingly stay to hear you farther on this Head, and am perfectly angry with the Night for wearing away so fast.

---

[1] Book xii. 379 [Broome].   [2] Book v. 379 [Pope].
[3] Book xii. 280 [Broome].   [4] Book xii. 202 [Broome].
[5] Book xi. 285 [Broome].   [6] [*Cooper's Hill*, ll. 191–2]

I hope we shall soon find an opportunity of resuming the Subject (answer'd *Philypsus*) I need not tell you how agreeable it is to me, even to be convinc'd of my Errors by *Antiphaus*; and I'm satisfy'd that you take a delight in any occasion of admiring Mr. *Pope*. I beg you would tell me *Antiphaus*; do you not approve of him in some points, more than you have formerly?

I do not know how it is, (says *Antiphaus*) but I seem to be both more pleas'd, and more displeas'd with him, than I was before this enquiry: his Excellencies, from the light in which you have set them, strike me more agreeably than ever; but then this looking so closely into his Defects has made those too the more gross and visible.

However (concluded *Philypsus*) you will still acknowledge with me, *That his faults are the faults of a Man, but his beauties are the beauties of an Angel.*—You don't seem to like the word: it may sound perhaps too high; but I mean only of a *Great and Uncommon Genius.* [pp. 148–56]

50. Further remarks by Joseph Spence

August 1727

Rev. Joseph Spence, extracts from *An Essay on Pope's Odyssey* . . ., part ii (1727). First published August 1727.

Pope went over the second volume in manuscript. For his comments on the manuscript (now in the Osborn Collection at Yale), see Twickenham, x. 594–605.

Only a small part of the second volume is given here since it continues, rather repetitiously, the kind of criticism established by Spence's comments on books i–xiv. Further, see Introduction pp. 14–15 and headnote to preceding item.

EVENING the FOURTH

[Antiphaus moves into a further discussion of Pope's versification and diction]

As for my part, after a Research of some care thro' the whole Translation, I find no reason at all to alter my Opinion, That the Beauties of it are far more numerous, and far more considerable, than its Blemishes: even taking all those things for *real* Blemishes, which we may only *imagine* to be such.

If the fashionable Choice of *Verse* be justly blameable; it may as justly be said that no one moves with more freedom in his Fetters. In particular Lines, there may be some farther disagreeable *Likenesses* of Sound; but the *Variety* of Numbers in general is great and handsome: What Smoothness and Harmony do we find thro' the course of the Poem; and how seldom are they interrupted either by the *Littleness*, or the *Vastness* of the Words? by the *Openness* of the Vowels, the *Clashing* of Consonants, or any other Roughnesses whatever: Not to mention against these, that *Significance* of Sound, which is more frequent, and more happily practis'd by Mr. *Pope*, in particular, than by any other of the Modern Poets.

As to the *Diction*; not only the Poem but our Language itself is enrich'd by it. Where it is once Mean, it is in many instances Great, Noble, and Solemn. Where a Simplicity beyond our Taste is to be preserv'd, we may expect some Flatnesses: And it may be to these perhaps we owe that Justness and Purity, which in so many places makes us imagine, that we are conversing with Persons of those First Ages of the World, in all their Plainness and Honesty of Behaviour. At other times the Narration is rais'd, and the Images strengthen'd by a figurative way of speaking, tho' no doubt, in some cases, to excess: but these Excesses may well be pass'd over, when we consider, that they proceed from Liberties, which are highly useful in rendering the Stile the more various and poetical; so far, as frequently to improve upon *Homer* himself.

Above all, is that *flame* and *spirit* difus'd thro' the whole Poem; and oftentimes so well kept up, as to make us forget, that we are reading a Translation. When we are engag'd in the Piece, do not the *great* and *generous* Sentiments we meet with perpetually, make a few Thoughts, which have something *cold* or *little* in them, appear inconsiderable upon the first Comparison? What *Eclaircisements*[1] have we, and how little *Obscurity*? What a number of natural Thoughts, Images, and Descriptions might be produc'd, to over-ballance such Lines in it, as may seem to be Affected, or too Artificial?

Thus which ever way we turn ourselves, whether we consider the *Poetical Spirit*, the *Language*, or the *Versification*; in each of them the Beauties far exceed the Defects. It is with this Notion we ought to proceed in our Enquiries: we must carry this Thought all along with us. Let us remember *Philypsus*, That all human Excellence stands merely on Comparison: that no one is without Faults, and that very few arrive in any tolerable degree towards Perfection: That Mr. *Pope* does not only appear among the Few, but that his Superiority is every way visible: If we compare his Compositions in general with those of our other Poets, the Disproportion is as great, as when we compare the Blemishes of his own Poetry, with the Beauties which every where abound in it.

Some of these we are now to consider; and we may enter on this View with the greater Pleasure, as we have the advantage of Mr *Pope*'s own Observations in several Points, both as to those things, in which he met with the greatest difficulty; and the Methods he has taken of raising his Language, and improving the Versification.

[1] Eclaircisements] *Openings* 1737.

One of the greatest Sources of raising, as well as enlarging the Poetical Language, is by inventing New Words, or importing old Ones from a foreign Soil. Words, when they are us'd vulgarly, grow mean: Like other Fashions, when their use is once got among the Populace, they soon begin to be rejected by the politer Part of the World. This it is (as the *Gentlemen* of *Port Royal* very justly observe[1]) which necessitates the introducing of New Words into every Language; it occasions a continual Decay, and demands continual Supplies. Thus whoever has a Felicity this way, is a Benefactor to the Publick: he adds so much to the Bank; and gives his Assistance in supporting the present Credit of Language among us.

It wou'd be equally trifling and laborious, to give all the particular Instances of this Version's enriching our Language. It is every where visible; there is no reading a Book in the *Odyssey*, without observing it frequently. You will almost constantly find his new Words to be apt, easy, and poetical. Sometimes he introduces the Expressions, and even the *Peculiarities* of other Languages into our own: These, when unforc'd, please us very particularly, by the Variety, and Novelty, they bring along with them. We admire the Stranger in our Habit; and are extremely taken to see him look as free and easy as if he were a Native, and had been always truly English.

The Poet has the same Art and Delicacy in *Connecting* two Words into one, a thing much more difficult than *Inventing*:[2] The Union is proper and insensible; there is no Knot, where they are ingrafted: in short, they may be said rather to grow into one another, than to be brought together by Art. I do not say, that this hits so naturally in all the Instances; there may be some Words less tractable, or less harmonious than others:[3] But in general we may affirm, that as his Translation is wrought off from a Language, which in this Respect greatly exceeds all that ever were; So the Imitations of it, this way, are unusually Beautiful and Harmonious.

To deviate from the strict Rules which Grammarians wou'd impose on Words, either single, or as they stand in their relations to one another, gives an agreeable uncommon Air to Language; but in the very Notion of it carries something of difficulty, and niceness along with it. Mr. *Pope* seems to have thought it the safest way in such Cases

[1] *Art de bien Parler.* Part I. Chap. 4. Sect. 5.

[2] Thus: *Mellifluous, attemper'd; ever-shady, ill-perswading, serpent-mazes,* and several others in this Translation.

[3] Thus perhaps: *Sea-girt, end-long, love-dittied, woman-state,* &c. in the same.

to follow or resemble those Deviations, which have been already Authoriz'd by some Masterly hand: and where he strikes more boldly into any new Freedom, he is generally careful of giving things such an Openness, that they may neither perplex the Sense, nor embarrass the Period.

A thing more useful and agreeable than either of these, is to turn the stream of Words out of their common Channel.—There is a good deal of Stiffness, which yet attends our Language, from the stated order of Words in such a repeated Succession: and tho' we are much freer than our Neighbours the *French* in this particular, I shou'd be glad to see our Poets, at least, go yet farther towards the Liberties of the old *Greeks* and *Romans*. Mr. *Pope* has some strokes toward this: he is sometimes bold in varying the expected range of Words, to give his Sentences a new and agreeable air: he transposes their order, often by his own Judgment, and often in imitation of some of our best Poets, who have succeeded in it before.

I wou'd not have a certain Grammarian, or two, over-hear me commending these Liberties so freely: it wou'd certainly cost one a Dispute. You know the Men: they are as strict in the Punctilio's of Words, as some formal People are in the little Points of Behaviour. I warrant you, your Neighbour, The Doctor, wou'd stand as strictly upon the *Nominative Case's going before the Verb*, as *Wicquefort* wou'd for the Precedence of an Embassador:[1] 'Tis certain he can settle all the Rules of Place from undeniable Authorities; disposes of the Upper-hand with perfect Oeconomy; and, upon the whole, would make an Excellent *Master of the Ceremonies* among Words and Syllables.

However, with this Gentleman's leave, there are several just *Liberties* which may be allow'd for varying the Poetical Stile:[2] and many Aids, proper to enliven and elevate it in the more noble Parts of a Poem.

Among the latter, Mr. *Pope* has made very good use of Antiquated Words; and no less of Expressions borrow'd from our Translation of the Sacred Writings. The Language of Scripture, as it is receiv'd from the first with a certain religious Awe, will still retain something venerable, and august: it may therefore be of signal Service in giving to the

---

[1] [Abraham van Wiquefort, *L'Ambassadeur et ses Fonctions* (1681, etc.)]

[2] Plurimæ sint locutiones *apud Poetas usitatissimæ*, & in primis *elegantes*, quæ scriptis Prosaicis usurpatæ etiam Grammaticæ leges violant. See *Trapp*'s Præl[ectiones] Poet[icae (2nd ed., 1722),] Page 49, &c. to Page 53. [The translation, *Lectures on Poetry* (1745), gives a rather truncated version: 'the Poets use many Phrases, even with the greatest Elegance, which a Prose Writer could not, without the Imputation of false *Latin*. . . .' (p. 37)]

Heroick Muse that Majesty, which so well becomes the Sublime Air she ought to assume. 'Tis much the same in the revival of old Words: Antiquity always carries a sort of Solemnity with it, in its very Rough-nesses and Decays: The *Rustick* strikes the Mind, as strongly, as any thing in Architecture; and Ruins themselves have often something awful and majestick in them.

I wou'd not willingly interrupt you (says *Philypsus*) but the humour of heaping superannuated Words in some late Poems, is too provoking to be pass'd by. How have our *Miltonick* Writers, in particular, prostituted them on all occasions: in what an undistinguishing manner do they labour to draw into their Works, any word which their great Master has adopted into his *Paradise Lost?—Erst, Nathless, Behests, Welkin,* and a Thousand other Expressions of equal beauty and agree-ableness of Sound, are repeated ten times in every Sheet of theirs: in short, these Gentlemen have made me quite sick of People's going two Hundred Years backward for their Language; and furnishing out half their Poems from the Vocabularies annex'd to *Spencer* and *Chaucer.*

As for some of those Writers (reply'd *Antiphaus* calmly) You have reason to be angry with them; but if we may reject any thing meerly for the *abuse* of it, there is nothing of the greatest *use*, that we may not fairly reject. *Virgil* made particular use of this method in his Poems, and was admired by his Countrymen on that account:[1] What is your Opinion of our *Milton*? Are you displeas'd with the antiquated Words in his Writings? No, *Philypsus*, I know your Taste too well to imagine any thing of that nature. And even of those, that have follow'd his Example, there is one or two who make good use of them. This we see in *Philips's* pieces; not to mention the new Poem[2] we were reading the other Day: the Author of which, beside several other Beauties, is by no means unhappy in his Management of this sort of Words. I agree with you, the *Abuse* of them is frequent, and much to be condemn'd: If perpetual, they run into a meer Barbarism; and indeed where-ever they are thrust in, without any other reason except their being Ancient, they give a Roughness and Disorder, instead of the proper Solemnity: But when they are plac'd here and there with Judgment, they support the

---

[1] Cum sint [autem] verba Propria, ficta, translata; Propriis dignitatem dat *Antiquitas: eo ornamento* Virgilius *unice est usus.* Quintillian, *Institutiones,* VIII. iii. 24. ['Words are *proper, newly-coined* or *metaphorical.* In the case of proper words there is a special dignity conferred by antiquity . . . this is a form of ornament of which Virgil has made unique use.'] *Again,* IX. iii. 14.

[2] *WINTER*: by Mr *Thompson.* [*Winter,* the first part of Thomson's *Seasons,* was pub-lished in 1726]

greatness of our Ideas, and reflect a venerableness on the subject. Were the Old Oaks, that are left standing in the Gardens of *Blenheim*, more numerous, that Design might have too much of the Forest in it: but as they are, they serve to communicate the nobler air of Antiquity to the things about them; and appear in a Majesty of Years, equal to the Grandeur of the Place.

I wou'd desire you to commend the insertion of Solemn Words, only as they are proper to the Places in which they are us'd. We see by Mr. *Pope*'s Observations on this Head, that he understands the Benefit of them perfectly well; as his Works shew that he practises up to his own Rules; and scarce ever inserts either the Words of former Centuries, or the Language of Scripture, but where the Subject demands a solemn and venerable Turn.

As these are the chief Methods of *ennobling* the Poetick Stile; so the chief to *enliven* it, is the free and various use of *Epithets*. No one thing is of greater service to the Poets for distinguishing their Language from Prose. This has occasion'd that large and unrestrain'd use of them,[1] so much beyond what we find in Oratory: And tho' *Homer* is more bold and frequent in this, than any of the Poets who have wrote since; I know not any of the *Ancient* Criticks who have ever blam'd him on that account. 'Tis partly from his uncommon liberties this way, that Mr. *Pope* looks upon his Epithets,[2] as one of the *Distinguishing Marks* of that Poet. In *Homer* they have on several accounts a peculiar air: and this Translation not only preserves their proper beauties, but shews many Methods of improving upon them. Sometimes the Old are set in a stronger light, and sometimes New ones added with a peculiar grace: Sometimes several are applied to the same thing,[3] without that strictness of connexion, which wou'd flatten the energy of them;[4] and where the poverty of our Language will not convey their full Sense in the Conciseness of the Original, they are enlarged upon in the Translation, and laid more open to our view.

[1] Eo (*Epitheto*) poetæ & frequentius & liberius utuntur: Namque illis satis est convenire [*id*] verbo, cui apponitur; & ita *Dentes albos*, & *Humida Vina*, in his non reprehend[emus]. Quintilian, *Institutiones*, VIII. vi. 40. ['Poets employ epithets with special frequency and freedom, since for them it is sufficient that the epithet should fit the word to which it is applied: consequently we shall not blame them when they speak of "white teeth" or "liquid wine"']
[2] Preface to *Iliad* [Twickenham, vii. 9ff.].
[3] Huge, horrid, vast! (Book v. 227 [Pope]); Homer, v. 175.
[4] Τὸ τοιοῦτο, κυρτὰ φαληριόωντα, τῇ ἐξαιρέσει τοῦ συνδέσμου μεγαλειότερον ἀπέβη ['A phrase like "arching, crested with foam" (*Iliad*, xiii. 799) is stronger for the removal of connexions']. Demetrius of Phalerum.

Epithets, *Philypsus*, like Pictures in Miniature, are often entire descriptions in one Word. This may be either from their own significance, or by their immediate connexion with some known object. We see the thing, when the Poet only mentions the *Nodding Crest* of an Hero; and form a larger Idea of *Jove* from the single Epithet of *Cloud-compelling*, than we might find in a description more diffuse. It was chiefly from[1] *two Poetical Epithets*, that *Phidias* design'd the countenance of his *Olympian Jupiter*; as, in Reverse, we often see the Person in his Epithet, from our being acquainted with some Statue, or Picture, to which it refers: Thus when *Apollo* is call'd the *Archer-God*, it recalls to our memory the representations we have so often seen of that Deity: the compleat Figure is rais'd up in the Mind, by touching upon that single circumstance.

'Tis by the same means, that one single Epithet gives us the Idea of any Object, which has been common and familiar to us. Meadows, Fields, Woods, Rivers, and the Sea itself, are often imag'd by one well-chosen word. Thus in that beautiful Description of *Calypso*'s Bower,[2] you see the Groves *of living green*; the Alders *ever quivering*; the *nodding* Cypress, and its high Branches, *waving* with the Storm: 'Tis by Epithets that the ancient Poets paint their *Elysian Groves*; and the Modern, their *Windsor-Forests*.

Where our Language will not admit of this conciseness, we find the Image preserv'd by a Description more full and diffusive; thus,

> —The Morning Sun encreasing bright
> O'er Heavens pure Azure spread the growing light.[3]

I shou'd think that the Opening of the Sense in a larger Compass may often be approv'd, even where we are not driven to it by the poverty of our Language. *Homer* himself, who has the advantage of single Words so much stronger and more significant, often chuses to draw out his Sentiments, into several Lines: and sometimes the very same Sentiment, which upon other Occasions he has express'd in one word only.[4] May not the same Liberty be allow'd to his Translators? Is it not a fine Enlargement for Instance, where *Homer* is speaking of *Penelope's Veil* with the Epithet of *Pellucid* only, to say that the Transparent Veil

---

[1] See Mr. *Pope*'s Note on *Iliad*, i. 683.
[2] Book v. 80 [Pope].
[3] Book ix. 63 [Pope]; Homer, ix. 56.
[4] Νώροψ ['flashing, bright'] which is beautifully expressed by *Horace* in three words (*nimium lubricus aspici*) is enlarged by *Homer* himself, on a fit occasion, into three lines: Compare *Iliad*, iv. 16 with xiii. 340.

Her beauty seems and only seems to shade.[1]

Tho' these imaging and descriptive Epithets are the more Beautiful, those which add Strength and Emphasis are by no means to be contemn'd. This way they are of great Service in all *Satire*; and particularly in that Abusiveness, which *Homer* is not over nice in bestowing upon, his Gods: they appear well in the Ridicule of the Suitors; and are strong and vehement in any *Arrogant Character*, particularly in all Contemners of the Gods. I shall give you only one instance of the latter; from *Polypheme*'s Answer to *Ulysses*:[2]

> Fools that you are! (the monster made reply,
> His inward fury blazing at his eye)
> Or strangers distant far from our abodes,
> To bid me reverence or regard the Gods.
> Know, that we Cyclops are a race above
> Those *air-bred people*, and their *goat-nurs'd Jove*.

You must have observ'd (*Philypsus*) several other Methods of using Epithets poetically. I need not mention the peculiar fitness and strength, which they may acquire, from the *occasions* on which they are us'd, or the *Light* they are set in:[3] That *Substantives* are sometimes us'd as *Epithets*,[4] and sometimes *Epithets* as *Substantives*:[5] Sometimes the *Metaphor* is convey'd this way with a good Grace;[6] and at others, two *Thwarting Ideas* are mixt together in a very agreeable manner. Mr. *Addison* is the first I know of, that observ'd upon these, and gave them their Name, and of this kind is the *Vegetable Venom* in the fourth *Odyssey*,[7] which answers his Instance of *Aurum Frondens* from *Virgil*.[8]

I know not whether I perfectly apprehend you, or not (interpos'd *Philypsus*): Do You not mean that particular sort of Metaphor, when some strange *quality* in a thing, is turn'd into an *Epithet*, and directly applied to it?—Either that; or else some strange Circumstance applied in the same manner: in both 'tis the Novelty and the Surprize, that please us—I take you, says *Philypsus*; and believe I now see a farther

[1] Book xviii. 250 [Broome]; Homer, xviii. 209. Λιπαρά ['smooth, shining'].
[2] Book ix. 330 [Pope, who has 'savage' not 'monster']; Homer, ix. 276.
[3] Book xxiii. 217–18 [Broome] compared with verse 227–8.
[4] Book i. 389 [Fenton]; Homer, i. 299.
[5] Book xix. 110 [Fenton]; Homer, xix. 91.
[6] Book x. 291 [Pope].
[7] Book iv. 320 [Fenton]; Homer, iv. 230.
[8] Addison's *Miscellaneous Works*, ed. T. Tickell (1726), i. 245. [One of Addison's notes to his translation of Ovid, *Metamorphoses*, Book iii.]

Reason, why a very natural Passage (in another Poem by Mr. *Pope*) has always been so agreeable to me. 'Tis where he speaks of the odd Appearance of things from their inversion in a River: I think I can repeat it:

> Oft in the Stream—The musing Shepherd spies
> The head-long Mountains and the downward Skies,
> The watry Landskip of the pendant Woods,
> And absent trees that tremble in the floods;
> In the clear azure Gleam the Flocks are seen,
> And floating Forests paint the Waves with green.[1]

These are of the kind I mean, says *Antiphaus*; they are bold, but they are natural: Indeed with due caution, greater Contrarieties than these may be join'd, under some particular Circumstance, to justify so unexpected an Union. Thus all Epithets, which contradict the general Sense of the Thing, but agree with the particular Occasion; Thus is *Grief* call'd *pleasing*; there are *Kindnesses* which are *terrible*:[2] And in many cases *Death* and even *Disgrace* may be *desirable*. Instances of this kind, are very frequent, especially among our modern Poets. There are many in this Translation:[3] in particular, 'tis this which gives a new Air to that gay Speech of *Mercury* in the Eighth Book.[4]   [pp. 6–22]

[Philypsus and Antiphaus have been talking about the beauty of 'breaks' in Homer, in which 'Passions break out in short violent Flashes'. Their discussion moves to Pope, and Philypsus speaks]

There is yet another sort of Breaks, *Antiphaus*, which proceed not from the Artifice of the Writer, but the Passion he feels upon some great or unexpected Calamity. There might be Instances of this given from the Poem before us: but we must go to another Piece of Mr. *Pope*'s for the finest that ever I met with in my Life. 'Tis in the Charming *Ode* on *Musick*, where he is speaking of that great Master of it, *Orpheus*:

> See wild as the winds o'er the mountains he flies,
> Hark *Hæmus* resounds with the *Bacchinals* cries!
> —Ah, see! he dies.[5]

---

[1] *Windsor Forest*, l. 211. [Pope has, 'Oft in her Glass . . .']

[2] As when *Cyclops*, in the height of his good nature, promises *Ulysses*, that he shall be the last he will devour, Book ix. 436 [Pope].

[3] Books i. 449 [Fenton], xv. 435 [Pope], *otherwise* xii. 52 [Broome], xviii. 284 [ibid.], etc.

[4] l. 380 [Broome].

[5] ll. 110–13. [Pope has 'Desarts' not 'mountains']

Those Passions, which break off our Language in this manner, and confine it to short catches and starts; when they are wrought up to the highest pitch, or croud in many of them together upon the Mind, are best exprest by *Silence*. Such Silences as these ... are the voice of Nature. 'Tis true in the common Method of speaking, there are only a few particular Organs concern'd: but in stronger Emotions, in the Violence of any Passion, the whole Body may be *talkative*. Every Look, and Turn, and Motion is significant; and each Nerve can have its own share in making up (what our *Shakespear* calls) *A kind of Excellent Dumb Discourse*.

To be more plain: Our Passions are often too strong to be express'd immediately by words; they often choak up the passage for them: and yet at the same time they are most apparent. The more any one is a stranger to art and disguises, the more he is moved on these Occasions: these Silences are the pure effects of Nature; and the Descriptions of them are the most natural, as well as the most beautiful Passages in the whole Poem.   [pp. 44-5]

51. Concanen on Pope as translator

1728

Matthew Concanen, extract from the preface to *A Supplement to the Profound* ... (1728), pp. v–vi. For another extract from this piece, see No. 45. It was advertised as published on 16 August 1728.

Let it not be objected, that the Translator of *Homer* is not accountable for the Meannesses of his Work, which perhaps says a Friend,[1] are owing to the Original: It is demonstrable to all Readers of the *Greek*, that this Poet has stuck so little to the Original, as to give Occasion to have his Knowledge of it call'd in Question; and he and his Admirers

---

[1] [Joseph Spence in his *Essay*, ii. 146ff.?]

seem to lay the whole Stress of his Merit upon the *fine Verses* of the Translation, not upon the Truth or Exactness of it.[1] This, therefore, as far as it concerns that Work, is a Criticism to the meer *English* Readers, who seem to be his best Friends: The *Literati*, are generally agreed about the Merit of the Translator: This is to display his Talents as a Poet; to the great Surprize, I foresee, of some, the Satisfaction of others, and the Displeasure of a few obstinate Bigots, who, having first liked odd Things, without Reasons, are resolved never to dislike them for any.

[1] [In his own copy of this pamphlet (British Museum, C. 116. b. 2[4]) Pope wrote in the margin, 'Yet this remark[er]'s observatio[ns] proceed almost all fr[om] his own ignorance of yᵉ Greek']

18 May 1728

Criticism of *The Dunciad* followed its first appearance on 18 May 1728, a secondary burst was occasioned by *The Dunciad Variorum* on 10 April 1729, and a final flood marked the appearance of the final versions in 1742 and 1743. These responses have been kept in their chronological order (Nos 55–60, 90–5).

---

52. A 'Club' of dunce retorts

May 1728

W.A., letter dated 29 May 1728, published in *Mist's Weekly Journal*, 8 June 1728. Pope believed this piece to have been written by 'some or other of the Club of Theobald, Dennis, Moore, Concanen, Cooke'. E. N. Hooker denies that Dennis had any part in the letter (*Critical Works*, ii. 516–17). It censures Pope strongly, but even so has some room for praise.

Sir,

The DUNCIAD being now a prevailing Amusement, I hope, you will postpone one Lecture in Politicks for the sake of such *sublime Heroicks*. . . .

The Preface to the Poem declares the Author to be the Friend and Advocate of Mr. *P[ope]*; his profess'd Design is to scourge that Gentleman's Enemies, and his great Complaint, that of all that ingenious Person's Admirers, *modestly computed* within these *three Kingdoms*, to be *One hundred thousand*, not *one* has appear'd in Defence of his Character, which has long been the Subject of general Satire, and suffer'd unusual Insults.

Now I think this Complaint must prejudice the most indifferent

Reader against Mr. P[ope], that having so prodigious an Interest with the Publick, he had not one Advocate amongst an hundred thousand Admirers; a Misfortune which in common Reason he can only owe to the worst Cause, and most palpable Injustice.

I am therefore of Opinion, the Preface to the *Dunciad* is a Satire on Mr. P[ope], infinitely more *severe* than any that has yet appear'd.

I am likewise heartily sorry that so great a Genius, and so worthy a Gentleman, amongst his numerous Friends, should find so little Service, and wish, for his Sake, the *mean Creature* who writ the *Dunciad*, had never undertook a Cause which he knew not how to defend, but at the Expence of common Sense, and common Humanity; nay, of Mr. P[ope]'s own Character also.

Yet, I must confess, nothing better could have been expected from such a Hand as the Person to whom this Work is ascrib'd, and to whom it can only belong: The Publick were convinc'd immediately, by infallible Evidence, from what Quarter it came; and even the Gentleman's own Party acknowledge the Truth.

The Author is allow'd to be a perfect Master of an easy and elegant Versification; In all his Works we find the most happy Turns, and natural Similies, wonderfully short and thick sown; nor is he less distinguish'd by an uncommon Contempt of all Men less wealthy than himself. Hence he is at all Times possess'd with the most over-bearing Insolence, as if neither Wit, or Worth, or common Sense, can belong to the Man without Riches.

This Gentleman, in his Rise, was strongly supported by a noble Genius, deservedly honour'd with the Name of *Maro*.[1] He rais'd this Author from an humble Obscurity, obtain'd him the Acquaintance and Friendship of the whole Body of our Nobility, and transferr'd his powerful Interests with those great Men, to this *rising Bard*, who frequently levy'd by that Means, unusual Contributions on the Publick.

It happen'd, a Translation done by this Hand,[2] was not, in all Respects, conformable to the fine Taste, and exact Judgment of his Friend; and, what was worse, the *tenacious* Gentleman would not be convinc'd a more perfect Piece was possible. *Maro*, to confute him, employ'd a younger Muse [Tickell] in an Undertaking of this Kind, which he supervis'd himself. When a Specimen of this was produc'd, the World allow'd it much more correct than our Author, closer translated, and yet retaining all the Beauties and Graces he could boast.[3]

Thus confuted by the Judgment of Mankind, he thought fit to yield,

---

[1] [Addison]   [2] [Pope's *Iliad*]   [3] [See Nos 27–32]

not without Reluctancy; but there was Friendship to preserve, and Profit in View; he therefore continu'd his Assiduity to his generous Benefactor, making Speeches in his Praise, and Poems to his Fame, as a certain *Dissertation upon Medals* can testify; where the most glowing Love, and uncommon Esteem, are expressed in Honour to *Maro*.[1]

But no sooner was his Body lifeless, and that Genius fled, which was the Boast and Glory of the *British* Nation, but the *Author* whose Works are now in Question, reviving his Resentments, at the Expence of all Gratitude and Decency, libelled the Memory of his departed Friend, traduc'd him in a sharp Invective; and, what was still more heinous, he made the Scandal publick.[2]

The Point of the Satire was not only wrong applied, but most unnaturally and unjust; it reproach'd a Person for the Exercise of his own private Judgment, and abus'd him for not being severe, or ill-natur'd, to the Party he could not approve.

And what shew'd the ungenerous Disposition of the Author more than all, he work'd up the Satire with the most inhuman unmanly Reflections on Persons distress'd by involuntary Evils, charging it on them as *criminal*, that they were *poor* and *unbefriended*; a Fate that has often befel the bravest and the worthiest Men; a Fate which *Dryden*, *Butler*, and *Cowley*, could not escape; which even the *great* HOMER suffer'd, to whose immortal Work he owes so much Wealth himself, and which had possibly been his own Lot, had not better Stars decreed him *Maro*, the Friend whom he thus abus'd.

After this, he *undertook* a Translation [*Odyssey*], the Sequel of that Work which occasion'd this Contention; and having secur'd the Success by a numerous Subscription, he employ'd some *Underlings* to perform what, according to his Proposal, should come from his own Hands.

And now we must explain the Occasion of the DUNCIAD. An eminent *Bibliopole* [Lintot], well known for his *thriving Genius*, was desirous to publish a correct Edition of a fam'd *British* Poet [Shakespeare], and applied to this Gentleman as the ablest Hand, in his Opinion, that could do him Justice. Our Author, being thus applied to, nam'd a Sum, which he thought a reasonable Premium; and, on that Consideration, undertook the Work. The Bookseller immediately propos'd it by Subscription, and rais'd some Thousands of Pounds for the same; I believe the Gentleman did not share in the Profits of this extravagant Subscription,

[1] [See 'To Mr Addison, Occasioned by his Dialogue on Medals', written 1713, published 1720]

[2] [The 'Atticus' portrait (*Epistle to Dr. Arbuthnot*, ll. 193-214) was published in 1722 without Pope's knowledge].

yet this is no Excuse for publishing the Author with so many Errors, and is no Satisfaction to the Subscribers for that vast Price they paid for a bad Edition.

As the World resented the Imposition, and were angry with the Man who had given the Sanction of his Name to such an Abuse, a different Hand [Theobald] thought he had sufficient Right to restore the Original Text, which, without invading any Property the Editors could claim, he perform'd to the Satisfaction of the Publick, and obtain'd a kind Reception, tho' unassisted by any Subscription.

Our ingenious Author, on this Occasion, thought fit to exert his uncommon Ill-nature; and having collected all the *Rubbish* of twenty Years,[1] the best Part whereof was none of his own, he inserted the famous Satire I have mentioned, with some Lines expung'd, and others added, to express his Indignation at the Man who had supplied his Defects without his Reward, and faithfully perform'd what himself undertook, and ought to have discharged.

The Reproach our Author made use of in this Case, was, that his opponent *Rival* had no Genius; a rare Objection, I confess, when his own exalted Self, with all his great Abilities, never discharg'd the Labour which gain'd his *Opponent* such Credit!

And it being impracticable to expose any Errors in that Work, he was extravagantly witty on some earlier Productions of his Antagonist; a poor Shift in Truth, and very little to the Purpose! the Question to the Publick was, Who had done most Justice to *Shakespear*? or, in other Words, Who understood him best? and such ungenerous Reprisals did more Mischief than Service to our Author's Reputation.

At this Time likewise, many Bickerings and Skirmishes happen'd; a barbarous unnatural Civil War being commenced between *our Author*, and the *minor Poets*, some complain'd of Characters abus'd, and others of Collections plunder'd; which latter was unprecedented Cruelty; for the Gentleman might have scorn'd to rob *those* Persons he had libell'd for their *Poverty*; nor was it any *Honour* to defraud those of their Works whom he had decry'd as *Dunces*.

At length he published the DUNCIAD to abuse all his Friends, and scourge all his Enemies. The sublime Poet *Maurus*,[2] and his *Arthurs*, were introduced to adorn the Work, and save the Expence of Invention. Poor *Namby Pamby* [Philips] likewise was aspersed, because he had written much better *Pastorals* than himself: And his *Persian Tales* were *censur'd* in the next Place, because they were translated for *thirty Pence* a

---

[1] [I.e., the 'Last Volume', *Miscellanies* (1727)]   [2] [Blackmore]

Piece:—a Crime indeed, that deserves a Reproach; for it is not the Virtue of all Men to deal in *Five Guinea* Subscriptions!

But the Hero of his Farce, was the Man who had incurr'd his eternal Vengeance, by doing Justice to poor *Shakespeare*: Over him, and all the Brethren of the Quill, he triumph'd in heroick Rage; tho' I cannot but think he might have spar'd *C[i]bb[e]r*, for having shewn less Mercy to *Shakespeare* than he himself.

He took an uncommon Delight in burlesquing the Dramatick Pieces of his Enemy [Cibber], and was unmerciful in his Usage to abundance of Poets and Poems; but his own *Plays* and *Farces* would have adorned the *Dunciad* much more gracefully, for he had neither Genius for Tragedy or Comedy; and when he had laid aside his inimitable Jingle of Rhimes, he wanted Spirit, Taste, and Sense, as much as any Man whatever.

The Model of his Poem seems copied from *Mack-Fleckno*, and the *Dispensary*; but is as different from *Dryden*, if compared with that pointed Satyr, as it is below the admir'd and elegant Reflections, which are the Beauties of *Garth*. The smooth Numbers of the *Dunciad* are all that recommend it, nor has it any other Merit.

It is, thro' the Whole, a Merciless Satire on Poverty, the Hunger, the Necessity and Distress of particular Men; the Miseries which should move a just and tender Compassion, are there turn'd into Ridicule. *Supperless Bards, Books unpawn'd, unpaid Taylors*, &c. are the choice Flowers of our Poet. You have not one Moral to guide the Pursuits of Virtue, nor one Instruction of useful Science. He reproaches his Enemies as poor and dull; and to prove them *poor*, he asserts they are *dull*; and to prove them *dull*, he asserts they are *poor*. Such Stuff as this, and no other, is the Tenor of his Argument; and the most of his Reflections are shocking and dishonourable to human Nature.

Nor has he preserved *common Decency* in his Poem; *O[rdu]re* and *U[rin]e*, and such like Figures, are plentifully interspers'd with equal Variety and Absurdity.

Whereas in every Poem there ought to be a *Moral*, a Lesson of Instruction that runs thro' all the Scenes, and animates the whole Story. *Dryden* and *Garth* are as fruitful of *just Reflection* as of *fine Images*; nor have they any *poetical Grace*, but what adorns and illustrates a *moral Sentiment*.

And, in every Satyr, no Action should be censur'd, burlesqu'd, or ridicul'd, but what is in the Nature of Things essentially wrong. *Juvenal, Persius*, and the noblest Wits of the *Latin* Poets, always stigmatiz'd Avarice and Ostentation; and thought the Contempt of Poverty, or Cruelty shewn to Misery, the most crying Evils of their Times.

'Tis the Glory of a refin'd Understanding, and inseparable from it, to inspire generous Virtues, and benevolent Qualities. An honest Mind will love and esteem a Man of Worth, tho' he be poor or deform'd: The want of Fortune in one Man, or the decripid Person of another, are no Reflections upon their Genius, or Understandings, yet the Author of the *Dunciad* has libelled a Person for his *rueful Length of Face*.[1] In short, such Reproaches are so mean, it does them too much Honour to expose them.

Our Author, therefore, is justly the Contempt of Mankind: With all the *Eclat* of a great Genius, he has not one just Pretension to it: He thinks of nothing so much as his own Possessions, and despises nothing so much as Poverty. In this View he compares himself, and his Enemies; his own *Subscriptions* on one Side, and their *Necessities* on the other.

I might pursue him farther with a great deal of Justice, but, I hope, I have done him sufficient Service. And am, Sir,

Gray's-Inn,   Your humble Servant,
May 29. 1728.

                                                        W.A.

[1] [*The Dunciad* (B), ii. 142]

53. *The Dunciad* a misuse of Pope's genius

27 June 1728

Anonymous, extracts from *An Essay on the Dunciad: An Heroick Poem* (1728), pp. 8–11, 17–23, 26–7. This is another piece in response to the first appearance of *The Dunciad*. It was published on 27 June, and Pope later attributed it to Theobald.

Since Mr. POPE has obtain'd such an universal Name over all *England*, and the neighbouring States, so that even Foreigners, as it is very rightly observ'd, have translated him into their own Language; is it consistent with Reason, that he should debase himself so much, as to vent his Scandal upon those very Men, who, for the most part, are his Admirers, and so run the risk of losing that vast Reputation, which he has so firmly rooted into the Hearts of all the World?

I must own, the Author, whoever he is, has aim'd at something of an Imitation of Mr. POPE's way of Writing, which is only peculiar to himself: I can't say quite throughout, but here and there you may trace some Glimmerings of his Fancy, and some Structure of his Verse. . . .

The Author . . . has endeavoured to imitate Mr. POPE's Way of writing, as you may observe in this Verse, where

> *Keen, hollow Winds howl though the bleak Recess.*
>
> [1728, i. 19]

This I must own is a very good Imitation, and represents the Image; but yet one may easily discern the Bristol-Stone from the Diamond. . . .

The Author describing the Race betwixt C[ur]ll and L[into]tt, has these Lines.

> *Full in the middle way there stood a Lake*
> *Which C[ur]ll's Corrinna chanc'd that morn to make;*
> *Here fortun'd C[ur]ll to slide.—* [1728, ii. 53–7]

Which I think is a very good Imitation of *Virgil*, where speaking of the Race betwixt *Nisus* and *Eurylus*, and the rest, he says as follows:

> ——*levi cum sanguine Nisus,*
> *Labitur infelix; cæsis ut forte juvencis,*
> *Fusus humum, viridesque super madefacerat herbas.*
>
> [*Aeneid*, v. 328–30]

The only Difference between the *Roman* Racer and the *English*, was that the one slipp'd down in Bull's Blood, the other in a Sir-Reverence: but however, C[ur]ll had the Proverb on his Side, *sh[itte]n Luck's good Luck*, for he stunk along, you see afterwards, and won the Race. But I must needs own that such a Fall would vex a Gentleman, you know, and set him to Prayers immediately; but, poor Man, he had not much Time to make a long Prayer; I think it isn't above three or four Lines: and I fancy there's very few who would ever have thought of any Prayers in such a nasty Condition as he was, except himself; for you must know he's a very religious, chaste, good Man; and very likely, if he had not said that Prayer, he'd have never won the Race.

> *To move, to raise, to ravish every Heart*
> *With* Shakespear's *Nature, or with* Johnson's *Art,*
> *Let others aim*——
>
> [1728, ii. 203–5]

These last Lines are another very good Imitation of Mr. POPE's excellent Prologue to the Tragedy of *Cato*.

The DIVING, I fancy, is a Game which no body could ever think of, but the Author of the DUNCIAD; however, it is work'd up admirably well, and comes very near the Spirit of Mr. POPE: especially in those Lines where he describes E[usde]n rising up again, which are as follow:

> *Sudden a Burst of Thunder shook the Flood:*
> *Lo!* E[usde]n *rose, tremendous all in Mud!*
> *Shaking the Horrors of his sable Brows,*
> *And each ferocious Feature grim with Ooze.*
> *Greater he looks, and more than Mortal stares,*
> *That thus the Wonders of the Deep declares.*
>
> [1728, ii. 287–92]

Then comes the gentler Exercise to lull all the Senses asleep by a magick Art, which, as the Author very well observes, the *Cambridge* Sophs are best at; not to mention the three pert *Templars*, that came not at all inferior to the former in their Talents and Taste.

——*And in one lazy Tone*
Thro' the long, heavy, painful Page, drawl on.

And then again:

At every Line they stretch, they yawn, they doze.

[1728, ii. 341–2, 344]

This very well imitates the slow Drowsiness in which they proceed: It is impossible for any one, who has a poetical Ear, to read these Lines, without perceiving the Heaviness that lags in the Verse, to imitate the Action which it describes.

The Simile of the Pines is very just, and adapted well to the Subject. There's another too, which I forgot to mention in its place, which is that of the Dabchick waddling thro' the Copse; 'tis in the Race between C[ur]ll and L[into]tt.

As when a Dab-chick waddles thro' the Copse,
On Legs and Wings, and flies, and wades, and hops.

[1728, ii. 47–8]

And all was hush'd, as Folly's self lay dead.

[1728, ii. 372]

In Imitation of that line in *Dryden's Ind[ian] Emp[eror*, III, ii. 1]

All things are hush'd, as Nature's self lay dead.

Ascend this Hill, whose cloudy Point, &c.

[1728, iii. 59]

I suppose the Author, when he wrote this, had his Eye upon that Place in *Milton*, where the Angel takes *Adam* upon an high Mountain, and shews him all the Country round, and tells him of things that shall come to pass hereafter.

From the strong Fate of Drams if thou get free,
Another Durfey ✱✱✱ *shall sing in thee.*

[1728, iii. 131–2]

This is another very good Imitation of that admir'd Passage in the 6th Book of *Virgil*, where speaking of young *Marcellus*, the Poet thus delivers himself in the Words of *Anchises*:

Heu! miserande Puer! si qua fata aspera rumpas,
Tu MARCELLUS *eris.*

.   .   .   .   .   .

This POEM, in my Opinion, looks as if it was wrote with a great deal of Malice and Envy: it seems as if the Author was afraid others should rise above him, and so he endeavours to blast their Characters. . . .

. . . I can't possibly reconcile my self to the Belief of Mr. POPE's being the Author of this Poem. I wish some abler Person than my self, would be at the Trouble of examining this Poem somewhat stricter than I have, and then let him give out his Opinion: for I would not have it ever be said, that Mr. POPE, who is the Honour of our *English* Nation, was the Author of such a notorious Libel.

54. Swift on *The Dunciad*'s Obscurity

July 1728

Jonathan Swift, extract from a letter to Pope, 16 July 1728, *Corresp.*, ii. 504–5.

Swift was staying at Market Hill, near Armagh, with Sir Arthur Acheson.

I have often run over the *Dunciad* in an Irish edition. . . . The notes I could wish to be very large, in what relates to the persons concern'd; for I have long observ'd that twenty miles from London no body understands hints, initial letters, or town-facts and passages; and in a few years not even those who live in London. I would have the names of those scriblers printed indexically at the beginning or end of the Poem, with an account of their works, for the reader to refer to. I would have all the Parodies (as they are call'd) referred to the author they imitate—When I began this long paper, I thought I should have fill'd it with setting down the several passages I had marked in the edition I had, but I find it unnecessary, so many of them falling under the same rule. After twenty times reading the whole, I never in my opinion saw so much good satire, or more good sense, in so many lines. How it passes in Dublin I know not yet; but I am sure it will be a great disadvantage to the poem, that the persons and facts will not be understood, till the explanation comes out, and a very full one. I imagine it is not to be published till towards winter, when folks begin to gather in town. Again I insist, you must have your Asterisks fill'd up with some real names of real Dunces.

THE DUNCIAD VARIORUM

10 April 1729

The publication of *The Dunciad* with a few alterations and the addition of the footnotes and Scriblerian apparatus, provoked a fresh surge of interest and anger.

---

55. Objections to Pope's obscenity and character assassination

May 1729

Anonymous, extract from *Pope Alexander's Supremacy and Infallibility examin'd* (1729), pp. 11–13. Published 13 May 1729. Pope attributed this pamphlet to John Dennis and George Duckett, but E. N. Hooker and D. N. Smith have denied that either were concerned in its production. The passage given here occurs in 'A Letter to a Noble Lord: Occasion'd by the late Publication of the *Dunciad Variorum*' signed 'Will. Flogg' and dated 5 April 1729: its author calls *The Dunciad* a 'mishapen Lump of Malice and Ill-nature' and a 'Master-piece of Scandal' (p. 14).

You will not, I am sure, expect that I should enter into an Examination of the Poetical Merit of [*The Dunciad*]; that would subject me to a Task, for which I am wholly unfit; I mean, the reading it a second Time. But I am well inform'd, that the Reception which the first Edition met with from the Town, shewed that the Performance was thought as mean as the Design. In my cursory View of it, tho' I met with some Lines here and there Poetical enough, yet I thought the Generality of them very Prosaick, the whole Tale loose and unconnected, the Transitions unnatural, the Parodies on the most admir'd Passages of the Ancients, were not only too frequent, but likewise too faintly and poorly wrought up, either to strike or delight the Reader; and besides, the Nastiness of the *Games*, and of all the Imagery in the Poem, the very Language often sunk into downright Ribaldry, as when a *Gentlewomans Breasts* are stiled her *Fore-Buttocks* or her *Cow-like Udders* [ii. 156]. Upon the whole, I judg'd this *Dunciad* to be below all Criticism, both as to its Stile and Versification.

Indeed, the Morality of it, as well as of the Notes of *Scriblerus* and *Variorum*, may deserve a much stricter Scrutiny. Felons in the Condemn'd Hold at *Newgate*, who have no Characters to forfeit, and but little Enjoyment of Life to lose, may venture to attack the Reputations of other Men, without Fear or Shame; but, unless under those Circumstances, none but a Madman could be tempted to do it. How shall I astonish your Lordship then, when I assure you, that no desperate Raver, but a poor Reptile; who, as he is the most helpless, is likewise the most timid Creature living, has acted this Part. He is become a voluntary Prisoner to his own House, rather than not enjoy the pitiful Pleasure of aspersing with Impunity, Persons, all of them better Members of the Community than himself, and many of them of a much higher Rank in Life than he must ever pretend to; who can only derive a *Mock Title*, not from his Ancestors, but his Shoulders. In his first Edition he had traduc'd certain Characters, for which every one has always had the utmost Veneration, and thinks now, by leaving out the Names of some, and falsly filling up the Blanks of others, as well as by absconding for a Time, to escape the Stripes that ought to be the just Reward of such Writings. How monstrous therefore has it been, to insinuate, that they have reach'd a Presence, where *Good Nature*, *Truth*, and *Humanity* only can be graciously receiv'd or encourag'd; the Reverse whereof are the *Characteristicks* of the *Dunciad*?

I am sensible that the Retailers in Scandal have always endeavour'd to pass upon the World by the laudable Appellation of Satyrists, and would take Shelter under the great Names of *Horace*, *Juvenal*, and *Boileau*. Not considering, that these Precedents will never be to their Purpose; those generous Correctors of Vice, never attack'd Persons, but Errors, nor ever expos'd the private Character, but the publick Appearance of Men, at the same Time taking especial Care to pay the strictest Regard to Truth, even while the Scourge was in their Hands; and therefore, *Boileau*, in his own Vindication, speaking of *Chapelain*, who was a bad Poet, says,

En blamant ses ecrits, ai je d'un Style Affreux
Distillé sur sa Vie un Venin Dangereux.[1]

I must likewise inform this half-learned Tribe, that the *Codrus* of *Juvenal*, which these abusive Writers so often quote for their Justification, was no real Person, but a Name design'd in general to signify any bad Poet.

True and just Satyr will always have its Weight; Scandal will always be condemn'd: The one is beneficial to Society, the other is detrimental to it. Whensoever a Man has taken upon himself the Profession of any Art of Science, by Writing, or otherwise, he has certainly submitted his Talents therein to the Judgment of the World. A Writer therefore, who in that Art or Science, consistent with good Manners, exposes the Defects of his Fellow Writer, be it by Ridicule or Argument, is guilty of nothing that is blameable, but rather does a Praise-worthy Action, by endeavouring to rectify the Judgments of Men, and prevent Pretenders to Science from imposing on the Publick. The censuring an Author then, only as such, is what every Man has a Right to do, from the Moment he appears in Print, *Hanc Veniam petimusq; Damusq; vicissim.*[2] But under this Pretext to attack his private Reputation, as a Member of Society, must be the Result of the same villainous Principles, as would lead a Man to be guilty of Robbery or Murder, had he Courage enough for the Road. The Civil Magistrate alone has a Right to enquire into Mens Personal Characters, and if they deserve it, to expose and punish them: And it seems but just, that this Authority should be vested solely in him, since no one else can, with any Certainty, be inform'd of what passes in private Life.

The Predecessors of the Writer of the *Dunciad*, the elaborate Authors of *Grubstreet*, have frequently transgress'd this equitable Rule, and finding too general a Propensity towards enquiring into the Blemishes of (otherwise) Great Characters, have sometimes been pretty liberal of their Personal Reflections, in order to render their several *Dunciads* the more Saleable: Yet these Men had at least so much Decency, as to do this under feign'd Names, or by pointing at Persons only by their initial Letters, which were lyable to various Readings. Thus, whilst the Obscurity of their Scandal screen'd them from Punishment, their very Proceeding was a tacit Confession of the Guilt of such Invectives. But it

---

[1] [*Satire*, ix. 209-10: 'In censuring his writings, have I used a hideous style to exude a dangerous poison onto his life?']

[2] [Horace, *Ars Poetica*, l. 11: 'this licence we [poets] claim, and in our turn we grant the like']

was doubtless reserv'd for the *Modest* Author of the *Dunciad* to invent the *Ne plus ultra* of Scandal, by calling Men, every Way his Superiors, *Rogues, Blockheads, Drunkards,* and *Liars,* in Print, with their Names at length, whilst he suppresses his own, that he may be exempt from the Fear of a very low Punishment, but to which his Ears seem to be legally intitled.

56. Dennis on *The Dunciad*

July 1729

John Dennis, extract from *Remarks upon Several Passages in the Preliminaries to the Dunciad* . . . (1729), *Critical Works,* ii. 358–62. Dennis's pamphlet was published on 7 July 1729. After the publication of *The Dunciad* (1728) Pope believed (mistakenly) that Dennis had a hand in the letter to *Mist's Weekly Journal,* published 8 June 1728 (No. 52). His response was to attack Dennis in the 'Testimonies of Authors' and in the notes of *The Dunciad Variorum.* Dennis's attempt at self-defence, of which only a brief portion is given here, was his last assault on Pope and his last piece of literary criticism. He survived, suffering from age and poverty, until 6 January 1734.

I hope [my arguments] will convince his Patrons and his Admirers, who have purchas'd Scurrility and Nonsense at so dear a Rate, that nothing is more easy than to give foul Language, but that 'tis Ten times more excusable in Me than it is in Him; first, because *læsit prior* [he attacked first], I only retort the Language he gave; secondly, because in the Remarks which I formerly made upon the several Things he has publish'd, I have given such Reasons, why this Language is his Due, as have convinc'd every sensible impartial Reader, that there is not in any of those Trifles the least Degree of that Solidity, that Morality, and that good Sense, which are the Principles and Fountain of all good Writing in Poetry: I shall pursue the same Method in the Animadversions, which from time to time I shall send you upon the brutal *Dunciad*; and before I have done with this first Preliminary, I shall take one Occasion from it, to convince the Reader, that this bouncing Bully of *Parnassus*, is nothing but a false Brave, a mere bragging pretending Empirick, and utterly ignorant of the first Rudiments of an Art which he has more than Twenty Years professed, and in which he has nothing but Impudence and Ignorance, and Falshood to support him.

In order to shew this, let us see the Account[1] that *P[ope]* himself gives of his *Dunciad*. *It is stil'd*, says he, *Heroick, as being doubly so, not only with respect to its Nature, which according to the best Rules of the Antients, and strictest Ideas of the Moderns, is critically such; but also with regard to the heroical Disposition, and high Courage of the Writer, who dar'd to stir up such a formidable, irritable, and implacable Race of Mortals.*

Thus *P[ope]* all at once makes himself the Hero of his wonderful Rhapsody, and stiles his Folly, his Impudence, his Insolence, and his want of Capacity to discern and to distinguish, high Courage; for want of which Capacity, he must be told, that a Bully is of all Mortals, the most Foolish, the most Impudent, and the most Insolent, but at the same time Cowardly. And here, Sir, give me leave to observe what the scandalous Chronicle reports, That as soon as the Rhapsody was publish'd, *P[ope]* never dar'd to appear without a tall *Irishman* attending him, who is so inseparable from him, that one would swear that he owes his Wit as well as his Courage to him.

But there is now a Necessity for going back a little: *The Dunciad*, says *P[ope]*, *is stiled Heroick with respect to its Nature, which, according to the best Rules of the Antients, and strictest Ideas of the Moderns, is critically such.* Here then let us see what the Proposition of every Epick Poem, whether Serious and Real, or Mock and Ridiculous, ought to be; and then whether *P[ope]*'s Proposition is agreeable to it.

The Proposition of an Epick Poem, says Bossu, *is that first Part of the Poem, in which the Author proposes briefly, and in general, what he designs to say in the Body of his Work; in which there are two Things to be considered, the one is what the Poet proposes, and the other is the Manner of his proposing it.*

The Proposition, continues he, *ought to contain the Matter of the Poem only; that is to say, the Action of it, and the Persons who execute that Action, whether those Persons are Divine or Human: We find all that in the* Iliad, *in the* Odysses, *and in the* Æneid.

[1] [The 'Account' is part of the preface to the 'imperfect' editions of the 1728 *Dunciad*]

The Action that Homer *proposes to sing in the* Iliad, *is the Revenge that* Achilles *takes for the Affront that is offered him; that of the* Odysses *is the Return of* Ulysses *to Ithaca; and that of the* Æneid, *is the Empire of* Troy *transferr'd by* Æneas *to Italy.*

We ought not to suffer ourselves to be surprized by the Expression of Homer *in the Beginning of his* Iliad, *where he says that he sings the pernicious Wrath of* Achilles, *nor believe that he proposes that Wrath as the Subject of his Poem: At that rate he could not relate an Action to his Reader, but a Passion; We ought not to stop there, since he himself has not stopp'd there. He tells us, that he sings the Wrath which caus'd the* Greeks *to suffer such mighty Losses, and was the Death of so many Heroes. He proposes then an Action, and not a simple Passion for the Matter of his Poem; and that Action is, as we said before, the Revenge that* Achilles *takes for the Affront that is offered him.*

Thus in the other two Poems, they propose at first a Man; but the Propositions stop not there; they add, that Ulysses *suffered very much in his Endeavour to return into his Country, or that the Design of* Æneas's *Voyage was to establish himself in* Italy. *Both the one and the other, then, of the two Poets proposes to sing an Action.*[1]

But so much for serious and real Epick or Heroick Poems. Let us now come to the Mock and the Comick ones, and we shall find, that this Poem, by changing its Nature, does not change its Manner. *Boileau*, who was one of the greatest of the *French* Poets, and one of the most judicious of their Criticks, calls his *Lutrin, Poeme Heroique*, an Heroical or Epick Poem; and yet in the Proposition to this Poem, which was designed purely for Pleasantry, he proposes to sing an Action, as appears by the Proposition itself.

> *Je Chante les combats, et ce Prelat terrible,*
> *Qui par ses longs Travaux et sa Force invincible,*
> *Dans un illustre Eglise exerçant son grand cœur*
> *Fit placer a la fin un Lutrin dans le Chœur.*
> *C'est en vain que le Chantre appuié d'un vain Titre,*
> *Deux fois l'en fit oter par les mains du Chapitre;*
> *De Prelat sur le Banc de son Rival altier*
> *Deux fois le rapportant l'en couvrit tout entier.*[2]

Which in *English* Prose is thus,

I sing the Combats, and that terrible Prelate, who, by his long Labours, and his invincible Courage, causing his great Soul to be seen by his Actions, in an illustrious

---

[1] [*Traité du pöeme epique*, III. iii (Paris, 1693), pp. 190–91]   [2] [*Le Lutrin*, ll. 1–8]

Church, caused at length a stately Pulpit to be erected in the Choir. In vain did the Chanter, supported by an empty Title, twice cause it to be taken down by the Hands of the Chapter; and twice did the Prelate, causing it to be carried back again, fix it before the Seat of his proud Rival, and covering him, and hiding him from the Congregation, mortify him severely.

Thus *Boileau*, in the Proposition to a mock Epick, or Heroick Poem, proposes to sing an Action; and accordingly entertains the Reader with it. . . . [1]

Now let us take a short View of *P[ope]*'s Proposition to his *Dunciad;* and after that you will easily judge *how far 'tis Heroick with respect to its Nature, and how far it is critically such, according to the best Rules of the Antients, and strictest Ideas of the Moderns.*

> *Books, and the Man, I sing, the first who brings*
> *The Smithfield Muses to the Ears of Kings.*

Let us divest it of its Jingle, since Rhyme is of no use to the Nonsense of such Prose as this, but to render it more ridiculous, and more unintelligible.

I sing Books, and I sing the Man, the first Man, who carries the Muses of Smithfield to the Ear of Kings.

Thus *P[ope]* sings Books, and not an Action; and the Author who pretends in an Epick Poem to sing Books instead of singing an Action, is only qualified to sing Ballads. And as Nature has begun to qualify him for that melodious Vocation, by giving him that Face, that Shape, and that Stature; so if Fortune would but finish what Nature has begun, he would be a Nonpareillo in that Employment. As he has for several Months last past, been bringing down a wooden Tempest upon his Carcass, if one Eye and one Leg should suffer severely by the Storm, which may very well happen, do not you think, Sir, that his rare Figure would proclaim him the Prince of Ballad Singers, as, by justly deposing you, he has made himself the King of Dunces?

P[ope] is so far from singing an Action, that there is no such Thing as Action in his whimsical Rhapsody, unless what proceeds from Dulness, that is, from Privation; a very pretty Principle of Action, and very worthy of *P[ope]*'s Invention! The Thing is divided into Three Books. In the First, instead of Action there is Description and Declamation. In the Third, instead of Action we have nothing but a feverish Dream. The Second is made up of Nastiness, Obscenity, and Absurdity; and is so far

[1] [Dennis has a paragraph here to show that Butler's *Hudibras* also 'sings' an 'action']

from being Part of an Action, that it runs counter to the Design of the whole Thing, if there could be any Design in it; for Vigour of Action can never proceed from Dulness, though it may from Madness. The Hero of the Piece does nothing at all, and never speaks but once, unless it be half a Line in the Third Book. In the First Book, indeed, he offers to burn his Works, but is hinder'd by the Goddess: Now those Works are either Good or Bad; if they are Good, they render him incapable of being King of the Dunces; if they are Bad, the Offer to burn them shews his Judgment, and Judgment must be always contrary to Dulness, otherwise P[ope] would be the brightest Creature that ever God made.

Whether an Epick Poem, is grave or mock Epick, the Action must have Probability in all its Parts: Both antient and modern Cricicks agree in this.

Ficta voluptatis causâ sint proxima veris,[1]

says *Horace*; *Let every Thing that is invented to give the Reader Pleasure, be attended with Probability*: Nay, *Boileau* makes Probability more necessary than Truth itself, as several of the Antients and Moderns have likewise done.

Jamais au spectateur n'offrez rien d'incroyable,
Le vrai peut quelque fois n'etre pas vraisemblable.
Une merveille absurde est pour moy sans appas,
L'esprit n'est point emu de ce qu'il ne croit pas.[2]

Never offer any thing that is incredible either to the Reader or the Spectator. Truth sometimes may not have Probability. That which is absurd, at the same Time that 'tis wonderful, has no Charms for me. The Soul is never mov'd with that which it does not believe.

And the Reason that he gives for this is very solid, *viz.* Truth may sometimes have the Appearance of a Lye, but Probability has always the Appearance of Truth. And this mock Probability, *Butler* in his *Hudibras*, and *Boileau* in his *Lutrin*, have preserved inviolably. But what Probability is there in P[ope]'s Rhapsody? What Probability in the Games which take up a third Part of the Piece? Is it not monstrous to imagine any Thing like that in the Master Street of a populous City; a Street eternally crowded with Carriages, Carts, Coaches, Chairs, and Men passing in the greatest Hurry about Private and Publick Affairs? What Prob-

---

[1] [Horace, *Ars Poetica*, l. 338: 'Fictions meant to please should be close to the real.']
[2] [Boileau, *Art poétique*, iii. 47–50]

ability in that noble Invention of *Fleet Ditch*, which, besides its Extrava-
gancy, and its Stupidity, shews the nasty Soul of the Author?

> *Immodest Words admit of no Defence,*
> *For want of Decency, is want of Sense.*

For all that is said there, must be excessively shocking to all Men of
common Sense, as shewing want of Respect to the Reader, as much as
to the Authors mentioned there. Every Man of good Breeding, as well
as good Sense, must be mov'd with Indignation,

> *At bawling Infamy, with Language base.*[1]
>
> Dryden.

57. *The Dunciad* beneath Pope's dignity

August 1729

Francis Atterbury, Bishop of Rochester, extract from a letter to
his son-in-law, William Morice, 3–14 August, *The Epistolary
Correspondence . . . of . . . Francis Atterbury, D.D.*, ed. J. Nichol
(1783–7), iv. 136–8.

I find many are of my sentiment with regard to the Dunciad, and think
the writer has engaged himself in a very improper and troublesome
scuffle, not worthy of his pen at all, which was designed for greater
purposes. Nor can all the good poetry in those three cantos make
amends for the trouble and teasing they will occasion to him. Tell him
so, directly, in my name; and tell him, that what I say proceeds from
tender regard I have for every thing that concerns him. I find by
Mist,[2] that Pope will be pursued with all the little spite of which that set

---

[1] [Wentworth Dillon, Earl of Roscommon, *Essay on Translated Verse* (1684), ll. 113–14]
[2] [That is, the attacks on Pope in *Mist's Weekly Journal*. For an example see No. 52]

of poor creatures is capable;—and that they will endeavour to hurt him chiefly upon the head of good-nature and probity; allowing him all kind of advantages in poetry.

58. Jacob supports Dennis

December 1729

Giles Jacob, extract from a letter to John Dennis, 18 December 1729, printed in *The Mirrour: or, Letters Satyrical, Panegyrical, Serious, and Humorous, on the Present Times*. . . . (1733), pp. 7–9. For Jacob's earlier praise of Pope, see No. 6a.

. . . SINCE the famous Mr. *Pope*'s malevolent Treatment of other Persons arises from his Vanity, I'll endeavour to lay open and discover to him and his Readers what it is he has to be vain of. As to his Person, there can be nothing seen there in the most flattering Mirror to highten his Self-Opinion, but, on the contrary, to humble and mortify him: So that it is from his Mind alone, whence this Source of Vanity essentially springs; and as his Body is so very unpromising a Figure, his Mind should be rare and excellent indeed to lift him to that Pitch of Pride which he hath lately so eminently display'd.

Now I am come to the Mind of this Poet, or rather his Productions which shew it. Is there in his *Windsor Forest, Temple of Fame, Rape of the Lock, Essay on Criticism*, or any of his other Poems, on a strict Examination, the least Appearance of that—

Mens Divinior atque Os—Magna Sonaturum[1]

described by *Horace*, and which *Spenser, Milton, Cowley, Dryden, Prior*, and some others of our famous Countrymen, have, in great Measure, come up to? Or is there any Thing appears in the Poetry of Mr. *Pope*,

[1] [*Sat.*, I. iv. 43–4: 'soul divine and tongue of noble utterance']

but either the most trifling Imitation of celebrated Poets; or smooth
flowing Words and jingling Rhime, adapted to the Ear only? Or, in
short, is there in his Poems any Thing but sinnewless Versification, and
sonorous Nonsense? If this be the Truth of the Case, that he hath not
the Sublimity of a great Writer; pray what hath he to boast of? I fear
little else but his Impudence!

AND I know of no Instance of his *Mens Divinior, &c.* unless he has
luckily hit upon it in the following Lines in Book the Second of his
Dunciad:

> *As oil'd with magick Juices for the Course,*
> *Renew'd by Ordure's sympathetick Force,*
> *Vig'rous he rises, from th'Effluvia strong*
> *Imbibes new Life, and scours and stinks along.*
>
> [*The Dunciad* (A): ii. 95–8][1]

These inimitable Verses on one of his Booksellers in the filthy Race after
John Gay and divers other Authors, are a sufficient Example and Testimony of the Sublimity of this Poet's Genius, his Fire, and his Judgment.

IF Mr. *Pope* has nothing that is excellent in his Qualifications, but
hath an evident Deficiency of good Sense and Judgment, he must
inevitably submit to the glorious Character which he so liberally
confers on others. For that Poet, be his Numbers ever so flowing, who
shews an Impotency of Sense in every Thing he does, can certainly, at
best, be no other than a bright Son of his Goddess of Dulness: And in
his Defence of himself, and his *Notes* to his *Dunciad*, he is so intollerably
dull that he is writing to Children, or his Readers must infallibly take
him for a Child.

ALL this and more you have prov'd upon *Pope* in your excellent
Remarks [upon . . . the Dunciad],[2] in which you have likewise, with the
utmost Justice, defended your Reputation against the extraordinary
Efforts of his impotent Malice. As for my self, notwithstanding the
Abuse of me by this Poet, I doubt not but it will be confess'd that my
Writings in their Way are more useful and beneficial to the World,
and of consequence more likely to last longer, than the idle nonsensical
Poems and maim'd Translations of Mr. *Alexander Pope*: And if so, I
shall stand justified in the Opinion of all Men of Sense.

[1] [Jacob has transposed the first two lines]
[2] [See No. 56 above]

59. Walter Harte defends Pope's satire

1731

Walter Harte, extracts from *An Essay on Satire, Particularly on the Dunciad* (1730), pp. 5–23, 37. Reprinted Augustan Reprint Society, no. 132 (Los Angeles, 1968), ed. T. B. Gilmore. The poem was actually published 7–14 January 1731.

Harte (1709–74), who was only twenty-one, had already published his *Poems on Several Occasions* (1727), which Pope himself had corrected (*Corresp.*, ii. 430n.). He was a friend of the Rev. Joseph Spence, who had praised Pope's *Odyssey* (Nos 49–50). Harte's *Essay* is an important statement of a neoclassical theory of satire sympathetic to Pope's practice (see Introduction, p. 6). It begins with an account of the history and development of satire, and culminates in a defence of *The Dunciad*. For a further piece by Harte, see No. 41.

> T'Exalt the Soul, or make the Heart sincere,
> To arm our Lives with honesty severe,
> To shake the wretch beyond the reach of Law,
> Deter the young, and touch the bold with awe,
> To raise the fal'n, to hear the sufferer's cries,
> And sanctify the virtues of the wise,
> Old Satire rose from Probity of mind,
> The noblest Ethicks to reform mankind.
>   As *Cynthia*'s Orb excels the gems of night:
> So *Epic Satire* shines distinctly bright.
> Here *Genius* lives, and strength in every part,
> And lights and shades, and fancy fix'd by art.
> A second beauty in its nature lies,
> It gives not *Things*, but *Beings* to our eyes,
> *Life*, *Substance*, *Spirit* animate the whole;
> *Fiction* and *Fable* are the Sense and Soul.

The *common Dulness* of mankind, array'd
In pomp, here lives and breathes, a *wond'rous Maid:*
The Poet decks her with each unknown Grace,
Clears her dull brain, and brightens her dark face:
See! Father *Chaos* o'er his First-born nods,
And Mother *Night*, in Majesty of Gods!
See *Querno's* Throne, by hands Pontific rise,
And a *Fool's Pandæmonium* strike our Eyes![1]
Ev'n what on C[url]l the Publick bounteous pours,
Is sublimated here to *Golden show'rs*.

   A *Dunciad* or a *Lutrin* is compleat,
And *one* in action; ludicrously great.
Each wheel rolls round in due degrees of force;
E'en *Episodes* are *needful*, or *of course:*
Of course, when things are virtually begun
E'er the first ends, the Father and the Son:
Or else so *needful*, and exactly grac'd,
That nothing is *ill-suited*, or *ill-plac'd*.

   True Epic's a vast World, and this a small;
One has its *proper* beauties, and one *all*.
Like *Cynthia*, one in *thirty days* appears,
Like *Saturn* one, rolls round in *thirty years*.
There opens a wide Tract, a length of Floods,
A height of Mountains, and a waste of Woods:
Here but one Spot; nor Leaf, nor Green depart
From Rules, e'en Nature seems the Child of Art.
As *Unities* in Epick works appear,
So must they shine in full distinction here.
Ev'n the warm *Iliad* moves with slower separate pow'rs:
That forty days demands, This forty hours.

   Each other Satire humbler arts has known,
Content with meaner Beauties, tho' its own:
Enough for that, if rugged in its course
The Verse but rolls with Vehemence and Force;
Or nicely pointed in th'*Horatian* way
Wounds keen, like *Syrens* mischievously gay.

---

[1] [For Pope's treatment of Querno, see *The Dunciad* (A), ii. 9–12 and the Appendix, 'Of the Poet Laureate' (Twickenham, v. 412ff.), which first appeared in *The Grub-Street Journal*, 19 November 1730, though it was not added to *The Dunciad* until 1743]

Here, All has *Wit*, yet must that Wit be *strong*,
Beyond the Turns of *Epigram*, or *Song*.
The *Thought* must rise exactly from the vice,
Sudden, yet *finish'd*, *clear*, and yet *concise*.
One Harmony must *first* with *last* unite;
As all true Paintings have their *Place* and *Light*.
Transitions must be *quick*, and yet *design'd*,
Not made to fill, but just retain the mind:
And *Similies*, like meteors of the night,
Just give one flash of momentary Light.
　　As thinking makes the Soul, low things exprest
In high-rais'd terms, define a *Dunciad* best.
Books and the Man demands as much, or more,
Than *He* who *wander'd to the Latian shore*:
For here (eternal Grief to *Duns*'s soul,
And *B[lackmore]*'s thin Ghost!) the *Part* contains the *Whole*:
Since in Mock-Epic none succeeds but he
Who tastes the Whole of Epic Poesy.
　　The *Moral* must be clear and understood;
But finer still, if negatively good:
Blaspheming *Capaneus* obliquely shows
T'adore those Gods *Æneas* fears and knows.
A *Fool*'s the *Heroe*; but the *Poet*'s end
Is, to be *candid, modest*, and a *Friend*.
　　Let *Classic Learning* sanctify each Part,
Not only show your Reading, but your Art.
　　The charms of *Parody*, like those of Wit,
If well *contrasted*, never fail to hit;
One half in light, and one in darkness drest,
(For contraries oppos'd still shine the best.)
When a cold Page half breaks the Writer's heart,
By this it warms, and brightens into Art.
When Rhet'ric glitters with too pompous pride,
By this, like *Circe*, 'tis un-deify'd.
So *Berecynthia*,[1] while her off-spring vye
In homage to the Mother of the sky,
(Deck'd in rich robes, of trees, and plants, and flow'rs,
And crown'd illustrious with an hundred tow'rs)
O'er all *Parnassus* casts her eyes at once,

---

[1] [Cf. *The Dunciad* (A), iii. 123–30]

And sees an hundred Sons—*and each a Dunce.*
   The *Language* next: from hence new pleasure springs:
For *Styles* are dignify'd, as well as *Things.*
Tho' Sense subsists, distinct from phrase or sound,
Yet *Gravity* conveys a surer wound.
The chymic secret which your pains wou'd find,
Breaks out, unsought for, in *Cervantes*' mind;
And *Quixot's* wildness, like that King's of old,
Turns all he touches, into *Pomp* and *Gold.*
Yet in this Pomp discretion must be had;
Tho' *grave*, not *stiff*; tho' *whimsical*, not *mad*:
In Works like these if *Fustian* might appear,
Mock-Epics, *Blackmore*, would not cost thee dear.
   We grant, that *Butler* ravishes the Heart,
As *Shakespear* soar'd beyond the reach of Art;
(For Nature form'd those Poets without Rules,
To fill the world with *imitating Fools.*)
What *Burlesque* could, was by that Genius done;
Yet faults it has, impossible to shun:
Th'unchanging strain for want of grandeur cloys,
And gives too oft the horse-laugh mirth of Boys:
The short-legg'd verse, and double-gingling Sound,
So quick surprize us, that our heads run round:
Yet in this Work peculiar Life presides,
And *Wit*, for all the world to glean besides.
   Here pause, my Muse, too daring and too young!
Nor rashly aim at Precepts yet unsung.
Can Man the Master of the *Dunciad* teach?
And these new Bays what others hope to reach?
'Twere better judg'd, to study and explain
Each ancient Grace he copies not in vain;
To trace thee, Satire, to thy utmost Spring,
Thy Form, thy Changes, and thy Authors sing.
   All Nations with this Liberty dispense,
And bid us shock the Man that shocks Good Sense.
   Great *Homer* first the Mimic Sketch design'd
What grasp'd not *Homer's* comprehensive mind?
By him who *Virtue* prais'd, was *Folly* curst,
And who *Achilles* sung, drew *Dunce the First.*[1]

[1] Margites.

233

[Harte continues with his history of satire written in Greek, Latin, Italian, and French (pp. 14–19), before turning to an account of English satire]

> In *Albion* then, with equal lustre bright,
> Great *Dryden* rose, and steer'd by Nature's light.
> Two glimmering Orbs he just observ'd from far,
> The Ocean wide, and dubious either Star,
> *Donne* teem'd with Wit, but all was maim'd and bruis'd,
> The period endless, and the sense confus'd:
> *Oldham* rush'd on, impetuous and sublime,
> But lame in Language, Harmony, and Rhyme;
> These (with new graces) vig'rous Nature join'd
> In one, and center'd 'em in *Dryden*'s mind.
> How full thy verse? Thy meaning how severe?
> How dark thy theme? yet made exactly clear.
> Not mortal is thy accent, nor thy rage,
> Yet mercy softens, or contracts each Page.
> Dread Bard! instruct us to revere thy rules,
> And hate like thee, all Rebels, and all Fools.

[Harte goes on to praise Garth, and to flatter Pope as an 'Instructor', a patron, and a friend]

> O *Pope*! . . .
> Thou taught'st old Satire nobler fruits to bear,
> And check'd her Licence with a moral Care:
> Thou gav'st the Thought new beauties not its own,
> And touch'd the Verse with Graces yet unknown.
> Each lawless branch thy level eye survey'd,
> And still corrected Nature as she stray'd:
> Warm'd *Boileau*'s Sense with *Britain*'s genuine Fire,
> And added Softness to *Tassone*'s Lyre.
> Yet mark the hideous nonsense of the age,
> And thou thy self the subject of its rage.

> .   .   .   .   .

> If *Pope* but writes, the Devil *Legion* raves,
> And meagre Critics mutter in their caves:
> (Such Critics of necessity consume
> All Wit, as Hangmen ravish'd Maids at *Rome*.)

Names he a Scribler? all the world's in arms,
Augusta, Granta, Rhedecyna swarms:
The guilty reader fancies what he fears,
And every *Midas* trembles for his ears.   [pp. 5–23]

.   .   .   .   .

. . . *Pope* restrain'd his awful hand,
Wept o'er poor *Niniveh*, and her dull band,
'Till Fools like Weeds rose up, and choak'd the Land.
Long, long he slumber'd e'er th'avenging hour;
For dubious Mercy half o'er-rul'd his pow'r:
'Till the wing'd bolt [i.e. *The Dunciad*], red-hissing from above
Pierc'd Millions thro'—For such the Wrath of *Jove*.
Hell, Chaos, Darkness, tremble at the sound,
And prostrate Fools bestrow the vast Profound. . . .

[p. 37]

60. Fielding on Pope's achievement

1739

Henry Fielding, extract from *The Champion*, 27 November 1739,
The Champion, 2nd ed. (1743), i. 34.

. . . *Pope* (whose Works will be coeval with the Language in which
they are writ) hath condescended to transmit to Posterity many
Heroical Persons, who, without his kind Assistance would have never
been known to have dared to lift their Pens against the greatest Poet of
his Time.

GENERAL REACTIONS

1730–44

---

61. Richardson assesses Pope

c. 1730–4

Samuel Richardson, extract from a letter to Aaron Hill, undated, but written before 25 April 1743, Victoria & Albert Museum, Forster Collection, XIII. iii. f. 12. Richardson describes the cause of his broken relationship with Nathaniel Hooke (d. 1763), translator, historian, and friend of Pope. Richardson printed Hooke's translation of 'Chevalier' Ramsay's *Cyrus* (1730), and the exchange appears to have taken place between that date and 1734.

... But happening in Conversation to prefer some Things in the Cooper's Hill to some in Windsor Forest; and Dryden's Alexander's Feast to the Ode on St Cæcilia, and even taking the Liberty (and no great Glory to the Person present I thought) to think Mr. Theobald would give a better Edition of Shakespear than Mr. Pope, who I presumed to think undervalued his Genius in stooping to the Drudgery of being an Editor; I offended the Gentleman, and have Reason to think, inconsiderable as I am, Mr. Pope too, tho' I never had the Honour to be known to the latter personally. ...

62. Pope as Augustan poet

1730

George Lyttelton, later Baron Lyttelton, *An Epistle to Mr. Pope, From a Young Gentleman at Rome* (1730). The poem bears the date 7 May, and was published on 30 June. Like many critics, Lyttelton (1709–73) thought satire a waste of Pope's genius. More important here (and the probable reason for the poem's inclusion among the Recommendatory Poems prefixed to later editions of Pope's *Works*) is its thoroughgoing expression of the Augustan myth, seeing in eighteenth-century England a recrudescence of the political and literary virtues of classical Rome at its apogee, with Pope as its Virgil.

Immortal Bard! for whom each Muse has wove,
The fairest Garlands of th'*Aonian* Grove,
O born, our drooping Genius to restore,
When ADDISON and CONGREVE are no more;
After so many Stars extinct in Night,
The darken'd Age's last remaining Light!
To Thee from *Latian* Realms this Verse is writ,
Inspir'd by Memory of ancient Wit,
For now no more these Climes their influence boast,
Fall'n is their Glory, and their Virtue lost:
From Tyrants and from Priests the Muses fly,
Daughters of *Reason* and of *Liberty*.
Nor *Baiæ* now, nor *Umbria*'s Plain they love,
Nor on the Banks of *Nar*, or *Mincio* rove,
To *Thames*'s flow'ry Borders they retire,
And kindle in thy Breast the *Roman* Fire:
So in the Shades, where cheer'd with Summer-rays,
Melodious Linnets warbled sprightly Lays;
Soon as the faded falling Leaves complain
Of gloomy Winter's inauspicious Reign,

No tuneful Voice is heard of Joy or Love,
But mournful Silence saddens all the Grove.

    Unhappy *Italy!* whose alter'd State
Has felt the worst Severity of Fate:
Not that Barbarian Hands her *Rods*[1] have broke,
And bow'd her haughty Neck beneath thy Yoke;
Not that her Palaces to Earth are thrown,
Her Cities desert, and her Fields unsown;
But that her ancient Spirit is decay'd,
That sacred Wisdom from her Bounds is fled,
That there the Source of Science flows no more,
Whence its rich Streams supply'd the World before.

    Illustrious Names! that once in *Latium* shin'd,
Born to instruct and to command Mankind;
Chiefs, by whose Virtue mighty ROME was rais'd,
And Poets, who those Chiefs sublimely prais'd;
Oft I the Traces you have left explore,
Visit your Ashes, and your Urns adore;
Oft kiss, with Lips devout, some mould'ring Stone,
With Ivy's venerable Shade o'ergrown;
Those hallow'd Ruins better pleas'd to see,
Than all the Pomp of modern Luxury.

    As late on VIRGIL's Tomb fresh Flow'rs I strow'd,
While with th'inspiring Muse my Bosom glow'd,
Crown'd with unfading Bays, my ravish'd Eyes
Beheld the Poet's awful Form arise;
'Stranger, he said, whose pious Hand has paid
Those grateful Rites to my attentive Shade,
When thou shalt breathe thy happy native Air,
To POPE this Message from his Master bear:

    'Great Bard! whose Numbers I my self inspire,
To whom I gave my own harmonious Lyre,
If mounted high upon the Throne of Wit,
Near Me and HOMER thou aspire to sit;

---

[1] *Fasces* [i.e., Roman lictor's rod, a symbol of authority]

No more let meaner Satire taint thy Bays,
And strain the Glory of thy nobler Lays;
In all the flow'ry Paths of *Pindus* stray,
But shun that thorny, that unpleasing Way:
Why wou'd'st thou force thy Genius from its End?
Form'd to Delight, why striv'st thou to offend?
When every soft, engaging Muse is thine,
Why court the least attractive of the Nine?

  'Of Thee more worthy were the Task to raise
A lasting Column to thy country's Praise;
To sing the Land, which now alone can boast
That LIBERTY unhappy ROME has lost;
Where SCIENCE in the Arms of PEACE is laid,
And plants her Palm beneath the Olive's Shade;
Where Honours on distinguish'd Merit wait;
And Virtue is no more a Foe to State.

  'Such was the Theme for which my Lyre I strung,
Such was the People whose Exploits I sung;
Brave, yet refin'd, for Arms and Arts renown'd,
With different Bays by *Mars* and *Phoebus* crown'd,
Dauntless Opposers of Tyrannick Sway,
But pleas'd a mild AUGUSTUS to obey.'

  If these Commands submissive thou receive,
Immortal and unblam'd thy Name shall live;
Envy to black *Cocytus* shall retire,
And howl with Furies in tormenting Fire:
Remotest Times shall consecrate thy Lays,
And join the PATRIOT's to the POET's Praise.

63. Pope compared to Boileau

Summer 1733

'Chevalier' Andrew Michael Ramsay, conversation with Rev. Joseph Spence in the summer of 1733, *Anecdotes*, i. 223. Ramsay, the son of a Scottish baker, 'rose to become intimate with statesmen, theologians, philosophers, and even with the royalty of two courts' (*ibid.*, i. 441). His remarkably successful career as an expatriate in France was based upon his Jacobite sympathies, his close relationship with Fénelon, and upon his literary abilities. This conversation took place during a visit to England to promote the English version of his highly regarded romance, *The Travels of Cyrus*.

At some time in the same period, Ramsay made a somewhat similar statement of his opinion of Pope: '[Ramsay] said the same preferring Mr. Pope to Boileau that Dr. C[occhi] did: Boileau wanted that great poetic genius. He copied the ancients, but his copies are so good that he has made them his own' (*ibid.*, i. 475).

Pope and Boileau are certainly the two best poets of all the moderns. They both write extremely well, but I should prefer Pope to Boileau because he excels in what is most material in the character of a poet. Boileau writes more correctly and better than Pope, but Pope thinks more nobly and has much more of the true spirit of poetry than Boileau.

RAMSAY *1733*

This had the more weight with one because Dr. Cocchi[1] and some other good judges that I met with, both in France and Italy, agreed exactly in the same sentiments throughout, though they might express themselves in other words.

SPENCE

[1] [Dr Antonio Cocchi was a Florentine medical man, and something of a polymath. He was appointed as the Grand Duke's antiquary, in charge of all the galleries in Florence, and was 'a particular friend' of Spence's]

64. Pope's manly satire

June 1733

Anonymous, extracts from *The Satirist: In Imitation of The Fourth Satire of Horace* (1733), pp. 5, 15. This piece was advertised on 7 June 1733. Unlike most defenders of Pope, the author not only admits that individuals *are* hit by his satire, but claims this as its proper function. 'Awful *Johnson*', Wycherley's 'strong' scenes, and '*Congreve*'s pointed Wit', are set up as patterns of satirists who,

> Aw'd by no Fear, expecting no Reward,
> Lash'd the rich Villain, or the courtly Lord.   (p. 3)

Few but run o'er [Pope's] manly Page,
Trembling they know some Vice of Folly shewn,
Half dead with Fear, they dread it is their own;
For general Satire will all Vices fit,
And ev'ry Fool or Knave will think he's hit.

.   .   .   .   .

But *Pope* you say with Pleasure flings his Darts,
And each so touch'd it wounds a thousand Hearts:
They fly promiscuous at the Good or Ill,
At War with All, he cares not whom they kill.
    Whence, Sir, your Knowledge to the Man unknown?
That true your Charge what injur'd Friend will own,
Who with him quaffs the Heart-revealing Bowl,
Judge of his Life and Partner of his Soul?
Cou'd such a Man by *Mordaunt*[1] be approv'd,
By *Burlington* admir'd, by *Bathurst* lov'd?

---

[1] [Charles, third Earl of Peterborough]

65. The Poet finish'd in prose

June 1735

Anonymous, extracts from *The Poet finish'd in Prose. Being a Dialogue Concerning Mr. Pope and his Writings* (1735). Published 24–6 June 1735.

This piece is cast in the form of a dialogue between A., a gentleman from the country who dislikes Pope's recent work, and B., a representative of the fashionable taste of the town who defends Pope.

B. Well, Sir, but pray tell me how you lik'd Mr. *Pope's* two Epistles I sent you. I hope they pleas'd you.
A. I could have found some Entertainment in 'em indeed, if I had not lov'd Mr. *Pope* on the Account of his former Writings. But as I esteem the Man, I could not help being mortify'd at his late Works. I always us'd to look upon him as the best Poet we have had since *Dryden*, for indeed he has written some very good Things. But oh!

Quantum mutatus ab illo![1]

B. Hey day! I doubt your Head's a little turn'd. All the World agrees that his last Writings excell his former as much as can be imagin'd.
A. And do you think so?
B. Yes, indeed, I do.
A. Then in that Point you must give me leave to dissent from you.
B. I shall be glad however to know your Reasons for it.
A. . . . With all my Heart. First then I blame that affected Obscurity which runs thro' most of his late Works. The Essays on *Man*, otherwise most excellent Performances, are not free from it. That on *False Taste*, and that on the *Use of Riches* are full of it. And, in general, you meet with a great deal of it in all these Poems which are call'd his *Æthick Epistles*. Now I look upon this to be a capital Fault in writing; for 'tis inverting the Use of Language, which is design'd to convey your Ideas

---

[1] ['How much changed from what he was!']

in the clearest and most obvious manner to those you converse with, or write to. Why therefore an Author shou'd affect to deliver his Sentiments with all the Ænigmatical Obscurity of an Oracle, I can't conceive, especially since it gives no one additional Grace to justify it. . . .

[pp. 10–11]

A. . . . 'tis his Reproach to have made *Homer* as *witty* and as *triffling* as *Ovid*. Instead of keeping up that noble and majestick Grandeur of the best of Poets, *Pope* plays the *Buffoon*, and tickles your Ears with a *Witticism* or a *Conceit*. He is a *Cup-Bearer*, like Vulcan, that can't give you *Nectar* but he must make you *laugh*. *Homer* presents us with solid, substantial Food; Viands appropriate to such Heroes as his own: Then comes *Pope*, and by a whimsical kind of poetical Chymistry, converts it into a *Whip-Syllabub*, fit only for the nicer Palates of the *Ladies* and *Beaux*. . . .

But I should not be glad to be too far provok'd, lest it should oblige me to collect the *Blunders* of his *Translation*; for really the *Jingle* of *Homer* in *Rhyme* makes my Head ache. But if I should bear to read him over once again, I would engage to point out some thousand Passages, where he has either ignorantly, or maliciously, misrepresented his Author; and to shew, that as to the *Versification*, Mr. *Pope* is vastly superior to either *Chapman* or *Hobbes*; but as to the *Sense*, inferior to both. [p. 37]

B. Surely he has touch'd the Passions finely in his *Eloisa*?
A. 'Tis indeed soft and tender enough; and nothing can exceed the *Language* and the *Versification*. I believe Mr. *Pope* could put *Cook upon Littleton* into *Rhyme*; or if he would translate the *Records* in the *Tower*, he could make 'em *witty*. But those Heroic Sentiments, that Force of Imagination, that Fire and Impetuosity, which the *Greeks* admir'd in *A[e]schylus*, *Sophocles*, and *Eurypides*; the *French* in *Corneille* and *Racine*; and we in *Shakespear*, is what I never expect to see in any of Mr. *Pope*'s Writings.' [p. 43]

66. Ordure from Grub Street

November 1735

Anonymous poem, *The Prompter*, no. cvii (18 November 1735).

EPIGRAM the Second.
OF *Merit Deserted.*

1.

P——E, who, *oft, overflows,* both with *Wit,* and with *Spleen,*
Felt the Want of a *Dung-Cart,* to keep himself *Clean:*
So, He furnish'd a *Priest,* with a *Carriage,* ding, dong:
And, made him his *Drayman,* to drive it along.

2.

Then, as oft as the *Muse's Satirical Itch,*
For the Poet's *Discharge,* lent his *Vengeance* a Switch;
Hey-gee-ho was the Word—'Take it, *Parson,* away'—
And, the *reverenc'd Excrement* loaded the *Dray.*

3.

Sir Gravity, charm'd with the *Call,* for his *Freight,*
Betwixt *Load,* and *Load,* found it tedious, to *wait:*
And *Himself* having *Nothing,* to keep up the Trade,
Told his Master, with Tears, *how his Custom decay'd,*
'*What* is *Once,* in two *Months?*—Now t'would make the Wheels *creak,*
Wou'd *You find wherewithal,* to load *once a Week!*'

4.

'*Stand aloof,*' answer'd P——e, 'Such a Trade as *You* drive,
May be *needful:*—but, welcome to no Man alive.
Tho' I love to *dress light,* I'm too *neat,* in my *Cloaths,*
To let a Tom T——d-man, *live under my Nose.*'
                    Desunt Cætera.

244

67. An epistle from South Carolina

1737

Thomas Dale, extract from *An Epistle to Alexander Pope, Esq;
From South Carolina* (1737), pp. 5–8. A. Warren in an article, 'To
Mr. Pope: Epistles from America', *PMLA*, xlviii (1933), 63–7, says
that this pamphlet is listed in the *Gentleman's Magazine* for August
1731. I have been unable to find such an entry, and therefore adopt
the date, 1737, from the title page of the British Museum copy.

From warmer Lands, ally'd to latest Fame,
In gracious CAROLINE's immortal Name;
Part of that Sylvan World *Columbus* found,
Where GEORGE should be rever'd, and YOU renown'd;
Hear Heav'n-taught Bard! and hearing spare the Lyre,
Your real Worth, your real Wrongs, inspire.
  Tho' radiant Graces sparkle thro' your Line,
With darting Beauty, and with Flame divine;
Where magic Verse, in all her Splendor crown'd,
Combines the Nerves of Sense, and Charms of Sound;
Tho' *Britain* boast her Iliad all Divine,
Worthy the *Græcian* Genius—worthy Thine;
Tho' rising Art and smiling Nature view
Their Powers increas'd, their Charms improv'd in You;
Yet wou'd I check the Raptures You infuse;
And with such Worth to warm an equal Muse.
  But when lean Envy darts her hissing Tongue,
And cank'rous Malice barks in Virtue's Wrong:
I check no more the low, yet gen'rous Lay,
But with glad Pride my righteous Wrath obey.
Merit aspers'd his Homage doubled finds,
Who glows with Fires unknown to little Minds.
  O if one Breast of all the clam'rous Throng,
E'er felt indeed the sacred Fire of Song,

Say for what hidden Crime, or open Shame,
Has Heaven incens'd resum'd the blissful Flame?
The genuine Muse the noblest Pleasure loves,
And, slowly blaming, joyfully approves:
But Envy, by each Charm with Torture smit,
Is scorch'd with ev'ry vital Beam of Wit.
Your Goodness could not wish an equal Pain,
To things you pity—things below Disdain:
Themselves, their Being, but for thee forgot;
We own a *Mœvius*, when a *Maro* wrote.
Mean time, as if whene'er a Genius rose
To prove his Title, he must thank his Foes;
Must gain against the Storm, and spurn the Tide,
Nor think his Worth admitted, till deny'd;
The Poetaster's Wit, the Critick's Toil,
Attest the Glory which they strive to foil;
As *Rome*, with her compleatest Triumphs, gave
Amidst a shouting World, a railing Slave.

68. Isaac Watts and the Countess of Hertford on Pope's later work

1738, 1739

(a) Dr Isaac Watts (1674–1748), extract from letter to Countess or Hertford, 15 June 1738, H. S. Hughes, 'More Popeana: Items from an Unpublished Correspondence', *PMLA*, xliv (1929), 1095–6. For a further comment, see No. 70.

I thank your La:^p for the enclosed Hymn.[1] It answers your character of it perfectly, & strikes my heart w:^th devout & agreeable sentir ments.

[1] [The Countess had sent Watts a copy of John Dalton's *Epistle to a Young Nobleman*. Dalton, the adaptor of *Comus*, was her son's tutor]

Would not Mr Pope, that bright Genius & that supreme Poet, more happily entertain & improve Mankind, could he be persuaded to turn his pen to such sort of Lyric Odes, than by all his satyrick imitations of Horace? Can you think, Madam, that if that ancient Roman Writer had been as obscure in his Satyrs, & so hard to be understood as his Imitator is, his sense would have been known at fifteen hundred years distance? Has not y^e *Epistle to a young Nobleman from his Preceptor* at least four times the Beauties in it that any of those late Imitations can boast of?

(b) Frances Thynne (*c.* 1699–1745), Countess of Hertford, extract from letter to Isaac Watts, 8 August 1738, in Thomas Gibbons, *Memoirs of the Rev. Isaac Watts* (1780), pp. 386–7.

I think every body must wish a muse like *Mr. Pope*'s were more inclined to exert itself on divine and goodnatured subjets; but I am afraid *Satire* is his highest talent, for I think his *Universal Prayer* is by no means equal to some of his other works; and I think his tenth stanza an instance how blind the wisest men may be to the errors of their own hearts; for he certainly did not mean to imprecate such a proportion of vengeance on himself, as he is too apt to load those with whom he dislikes; nor would he wish to have his own failings exposed to the eye of the world with all the invective and ridicule, with which he publishes those of his fellow-creatures.

(c) The same, extract from letter to Henrietta Louisa Jeffreys, Countess of Pomfret, 20 May 1739, H. S. Hughes, *op. cit.*, p. 1094n.

I feel not only a justifiable Pride but an inexhaustible fund of entertainment from all you write; I cannot say the same of a new Volume of Poems, which Mr Pope has thought fit to publish, there is in it his Sober Advice, his Epistle to Augustus, & in short several things that he had sold singly before; there is also an Epitaph upon the late duke of Buckingham, & two or three Epigrams; as a sample I send you one which is prefac'd with the pompous Title Engraved on the Collar of a Dog, which I gave his Royal Highness

> I am his Highness Dog at Kew
> Pray tell me S^r whose Dog are you.

does it not remind you of one of a more ancient date, which I believe is repeated in all the Nurserys in England

Bow wow wow wow
Whose dog art thou &c

I do not inferr from hence that Mr Pope finds himself returning into Child-hood & therefore imitates this Venerable Author, in order to Shine amongst the innocent inhabitants of the Apartments, where his Works are the most in Vogue; but I suppose it is to show that he has the same Alacrity in sinking to the Bathos, as of soaring to the Summit of Parnassus.

69. A tribute to Pope's greatness

1739

Henry Brooke, extract from a letter to Pope, November 1739, *Corresp.*, iv. 198–200. Shortly before this letter was written, Brooke (1703–83), the Irish author, had been living near Twickenham. Pope had helped him revise his *Universal Passion* (1735), but when speaking to Spence in June 1739, Pope remarked, 'They are quite destroying our language (speaking of Brooke's *Universal Beauty* and the buskin style)', *Anecdotes*, i. 169.

I remember Mr. Spence and I had a dispute about you one day in the park; he asserted you were the greatest poet that the world ever produced, but I differed from him in that respect; I told him to the purpose, that Virgil gave me equal pleasure, Homer equal warmth, Shakespeare greater rapture, and Milton more astonishment, so ungrateful was I to refuse you your due praise, when it was not unknown to me that I got friends and reputation by your saying things of me which no one would have thought I merited, had not you said them.

But I spoke without book at the time; I had not then entered into the spirit of your works, and I believe there are few who have. Far be it from my intention, and farther be it from the power of any man to compliment you; I only speak the ruder parts of my sincerity, and am little concerned how I fail in point of ceremony, since I shall never fail in my good intentions towards you.

Any one of your original writings is indisputably a more finished and perfect piece than has been wrote by any other man; there is one great and consistent genius evident through the whole of your works, but that genius seems smaller by being divided, by being looked upon only in parts, and that deception makes greatly against you; you are truly but one man through many volumes, and yet the eye can attend you but in one single view; each distinct performance is as the performance of a separate author, and no one being large enough to contain you in your full dimensions, though perfectly drawn, you appear too much in miniature; your genius is like your sense; one is too crowded for a common eye, and the other for a common reader. Shall I dare to say that I am heartily angry at it, and that I wish all the profits of Homer were sunk in the sea, provided you had never improved him, but spent your time in excelling him his own way. Is it yet too late?

I should not have presumed to express myself thus far if it had not come in my way, as I was going to speak to you upon a matter that is much nearer and dearer to me than even your fame. I have often heard it insinuated, that you had too much wit to be a man of religion, and too refined a taste to be that trifling thing called a Christian; those who spoke this, perhaps, intended it to your praise, but to me it was a cloud that intercepted the brightness of your character; I am amazed whence this could proceed, and now I feel that they little knew you. I had not read your Messiah, your Ode of the dying Christian to his Soul, and your Letters to that great and good man the Bishop of Rochester, till very lately, and that at a time when sickness indisposing me for light thoughts, gave me a true and affecting relish for them, and I am sure it is as impossible for any other than a Christian to write them, as it is for the best Christian to read and not be made better by them.

I wish you had wrote more upon divine subjects, or that you would go on to make your ethics perfect, as I am confident you would rather improve a single man to his advantage, than entertain thousands to your own fame.

70. Isaac Watts on Pope

1731

Dr Isaac Watts, extracts from *The Improvement of the Mind* . . . (1741), pp. 357–8 (XX. xxxvi. 3).

Watts (1674–1748) was the Nonconformist theologian and hymn writer. For other comments by Watts, see No. 68a.

PERHAPS there has hardly been a Writer in any Nation, and I may dare to affirm, there is none in ours, has a richer and happier Talent of painting to the Life, or has ever discover'd such a large and inexhausted Variety of Description as the celebrated Mr. *Pope*. If you read his Translation of *Homer's Iliad* you will find almost all the Terms or Phrases in our Tongue that are needful to express anything that is grand or magnificent: But if you peruse his *Odyssee*, which descends much more into common Life, there is scarce any usual[1] subject of Discourse or Thought, or any ordinary Occurrence which he has not cultivated and dress'd in the most proper Language; and yet still he has ennobled and enliven'd even the lower Subjects with the brightest and most agreeable Ornaments.

I SHOULD add here also, that if the same Author had more frequently employ'd his Pen on Divine Themes, his short Poem on the *Messiah*, and some Part of his Letters between *Abelard and Eloisa*, with that Ode on the *dying Christian*, &c. sufficiently assure us that his Pen would have honourably imitated some of the tender Scenes of penitential Sorrow, as well as the sublimer Odes of the *Hebrew* Psalmist, and perhaps discover'd to us in a better manner than any other Translation has done,[2] how great a Poet sat upon the Throne of *Israel*.

[1] *usual*] 1741; *useful* later edd.
[2] [Watts himself had published a translation of *The Psalms of David* (1719)]

71. Satire a betrayal of Pope's genius

1742

Lord Hervey, extract from *A Letter to Mr. C—b—r* . . . (1742), pp. 11–14. Published 19–21 August, and occasioned by *A Letter from Mr. Cibber to Mr. Pope* (No. 91). For another extract from Hervey's pamphlet, see No. 85.

John Hervey, Baron Hervey of Ickworth (1696–1743), was involved in other pamphlet attacks on Pope, and helped Lady Mary Wortley Montagu with her *Verses Address'd to the Imitator of Horace* (No. 77). In 1720 Hervey married Pope's friend, Mary Lepel. He did not enter politics seriously until 1729, when he rejected efforts to enlist him for the opposition benches and threw in his lot with Walpole. In 1730 he was appointed Vice-Chamberlain, and quickly became the Queen's confidant as well as being Walpole's most trusted agent in the palace. Pope attacked him on a number of occasions and after his death put him in *The Dunciad* (B, i. 298).

Mr. *Pope* was certainly once so good a Versificator, that his Predecessor Mr. *Dryden*, and his Cotemporary Mr. *Prior* excepted, I think the Harmony of his Numbers equal to any body's; and when other People thought for him (that is, when he was a Translator) he had all the Merit that a Man can have in the Execution of a Task where Genius is not necessary, and to which no Man of true Genius can, or will submit. Nor will the finest Versification, the most flowing Numbers, the best chosen and best sorted Words, without any other Merit, make a fine Poem, any more than the best chosen and best made Apparel will make a fine Woman; the one will ornament and heighten Sense, as the other will decorate and become Beauty; but tho' each can aid, neither can create; and as Genius and Beauty are Gifts, not Arts, so the most perfect Versificator, without one of these Gifts, will no more from the mechanic Part of Poetry come out a Poet, than the genteelest dress'd Woman without the other will appear handsome.

But even this Merit of Versification (the single one he ever possess'd in Poetry) and which at best is nothing more than the Shoemaker to good Sense by helping it to run well, Mr. *Pope* in his late Epistles, and what he calls Satires, has either from Age and Rust entirely lost, or from an Affectation of the *sermo pedestris* '[prosaic style'] chosen to abdicate. Which puts me in mind of a former silly Friend and old Acquaintance of yours, poor Mrs. *Booth*,[1] who hating to do what she did tolerably well, and loving to do what she did intolerably ill, always chose to act and be hiss'd, rather than to dance and be applauded; and by an ill-understood Pursuit of Fame, thus equally lost the Admirers she coveted, by what she *did* and *did not* do; 'till she upon the Stage, and *Pope* in the Press, might say from *the Liturgy, We have left undone those things which we ought to have done, and we have done those things which we ought not have done, and there is no Judgment in us.*

[1] [The wife of Barton Booth the actor. She began her career as a dancer]

72. Sawney and Colley

1742

Anonymous, extracts from *Sawney and Colley, A Poetical Dialogue: Occasioned by A Late Letter from The Laureat of St. James's, To the Homer of Twickenham* . . . (1742). Published after 31 August 1742. As the title suggests, this pamphlet was occasioned by Cibber's *Letter* (No. 91). The poem describes Pope's reactions on seeing Cibber's description of his supposed adventures on the Mount of Love, and then makes Pope pay a visit to the Laureate. *Sawney and Colley* attacks both men, and gives a comprehensive statement of the usual charges against Pope. It also adds a new feature, mockery of Pope's relations with his mother. The poem is reprinted, along with two further attacks on Pope, by W. Powell Jones, Augustan Reprint Society, no. 83 (Los Angeles, 1960).

ONE Morning, in his *Twickenham* Grott,
As *Little* SAWNEY sat a-squat;
His throbbing Head on[1] Palm reclin'd,
And Rancour brooding in his Mind,
Unknowing whom to blacken next,
So thread-bare he had worn his Text;
Had stung so oft, his Sting was gone,
And now commenc'd a harmless Drone:
When strait dire Sounds his Heart appall'd,
Whilst thus a Villain-Hawker bawl'd
—'Here's a New-Letter, *Cibber*'s Letter!
To *Pope*:—Hark! fly, and bring it,[2] *Setter!*'

[1] SAWNEY who is subject to a perpetual *Throbbing* at Head, as well as Heart, generally sits in this Posture.

[2] A notorious poetical Pander, or Jack-call, to SAWNEY, which provides *Savage* Provender for that *roaring Lyon, who goeth about seeking whom he may devour.* [A reference to Richard Savage, who was suspected by the Dunces of supplying Pope with ammunition against them]

Quoth SAWNEY—Quick he run it o'er,
As Spendthrifts do their long-stood Score;
Dreading to see the whole Amount,
Well knowing they can ne'er account.
But when to the TOM-TIT he came,
An instant Tempest shook his Frame;
Cold Horrors thrill'd through ev'ry Vein,
Rage rent his fretful Soul in twain;
His *aking* Head began to swim,
A Numbness crept o'er ev'ry Limb;
His trembling Fingers dropt the Pen,
Nay, he be-paw'd himself—and then,
Wiping, in fierce tho' sh—ten Mien,
With COLLEY's Sheets, his *Bumkin* clean,
He Silence burst—'O! To my Shame,
Thou hast not lost thy cruel Aim!
This is the very *Knell*—Damnation!
Of my departed Reputation.
'Sdeath, that TOM-TIT! 'twill never down—
My Chariot, *John*—drive on to Town:
Oh, I'll that babbling Villain rattle!
Drive quick, I say,—what crawling Cattle!
Not COLLEY's *Pegasus* is duller—
I might as well have took a *Skuller*.'
　　At length he light at COLLEY's Door,
And rapp'd for Entrance—but, before,
Lugg'd out, and shook his *pigmy Oar*.
　　COLLEY sat snug in Elbow-Chair,
Wrapt round with philosophic Air;
Gnawing his Thumbs, in room of *Thinking*,
And his salubrious *Scarb'rough*[1] drinking;
Before him much *Waste*-Paper lay,
Embrioes of many an unborn *Play*;
Doom'd never to behold the Light,
Secure to die on the *first* Night;
For why, the *Yahooes* of the Pit
Would always *piss* out COLLEY's Wit:
To save it from which gross Abuse,
He turn'd it to a fitter Use;

[1] [Spa water from Scarborough]

A daily Sacrifice, supine,
At *Cloacina*'s candid Shrine. . . .

[An attack follows on Cibber's notorious daughter, Charlotte Charke, and his dissolute son, Theobald. Cibber asks them to leave when Pope knocks]

They went—P[OP]E enter'd—COLLEY rose,
And, plying with *Rappee*[1] his Nose—
'—Hah, old Acquaintance, this is kind!
Come, there's no Enmity I find;
True *Gladiators* ne'er complain,
Since he that's *cut* shares half the Gain
Nor Boxers, tho' they *weep* at Nose,
Shed Tears, when Silver salves the Blows:
So, Thee and I may make a Pother,
And closely press, in *Print*, each other;
The more we rail, the more bespatter,
'Twill make our *Pamphlets* sell the better;
Write *Satire*, then, for *Daily*-bread;
By G[o]d, you'll not by *Prayer*[2] be fed.
Do you *Dunce* me, I'll *Tom-Tit* you—'
SAWNEY. Heavens! Villain! what dost say thou'lt do?
Dare but to mutter that again,
I swear by *Stix*, or worse, my *Pen*,
The keenest Vengeance thou shalt feel—
COLLEY. Ah, SAWNEY, I am ribb'd with Steel:
COLLEY's impenetrable still!—
SAWNEY. 'Tis well, you'll see me draw my *Quill*.
COLLEY. Oh! Sir, I've seen your *Quill* before,
So did your *Lord*, and eke your *Whore*;
But 'twas so *very, very small*,
I trust, it holds but little *Gall*.
SAWNEY. On that String yet,—d'ye know me, Elf?
COLLEY. Um—better than you know yourself.
I know you first, Sir, by your *Make*—
Dear SAWNEY, don't my Words Mistake,

[1] [A coarse kind of snuff]
[2] Alluding to a wretched Deistical Comment on the *Lord's-Prayer*, call'd *The Universal-Prayer*.

A Hillock on the Breast, or *Back*,
Admits, I own, of no Attack;
Unless, when hung out as a *Blind*
To hide within a *hump-back'd* Mind.

   I know Thee, next, a *Waspish* Thing,
Whose Bus'ness is to *buzz* and sting;
Replete with Malice, Spleen, and Spite,
I know that thou can'st *Libels* write;
From sacred Throne to Stage profane
Each spotless Character can'st stain.
But thus thy *Satire*'s guiltless grown,
Who slanders *all* Men, slanders *none*;
As impotent in *Spite* as *Love*,
Contempt alone by each you move.
   Tho' lives a *Traytor* in the Land,
He claims thy *Panegyric* Hand:
Plac'd on a Column of thy Verse,
Aloft he stands, and shews his A[r]se:
For why, so *God-like* is his Mein,
His *Back-parts* only must be seen. . . .
A little longer silent sit,
I han't quite done *your* Picture yet:
SAWNEY. Thine's Sign-post Dawbing—
COLLEY. 'Faith that's true,
It would not else resemble you.

   But, to proceed—you next apply
Your Mind to Heath'nish '*Losophy*:
You, and your *God-A'mighty*,[1] club
Your uncreating Pates, and dub
Poor mortal MAN *a Thing of Nought*,[2]
Just what the *pamper'd Gander* thought,
And bravely prove, in *Reason's Spite*,
That Right is *wrong*, and Wrong is *right*;
That the same Things both *good* and *evil*,
And *pound* together *God* and *Devil*.

  [1] A certain *noble Wit* [Bolingbroke] deified by SAWNEY in his *Essay on Man*, and in Concert with whom that Poem was written, containing the most incomprehensible System of Ph[i]losophy that was ever broach'd.
  [2] Vide *Essay on Man*.

Then *Women* felt your righteous Fury,
Hung all at once without a Jury;
And pierc'd with more *hard Words*, than P[A]GE[1]
E'er gave to Felons in his Rage:
For, *ev'ry Woman*, you are sure,
Is, in her *Heart*, a *very Whore*;[2]

'Troth, TIT-TE, I'll allow this much,
You ne'er knew *Woman* but was *such.*
For who, except a venal *Punkey*,
That car'd not whether Man or *Monkey*,
But set to Sale her *Titillation*,
For Bread, not carnal Recreation,
Would suffer Thee, *small* Friend, to come
Within ten Foot of her *Fore-bum?*

But, SAWNEY, if thy Maxim's true!
Let's see how well 'twill fit on you:
What think'st thou, then, of thy own *Mammy*,
'Bout whom thou talk'st, and talk'st so?[3]—Damn ye?
She had the *like at Heart*, no doubt;
If so, *'Gad, split me!* it would out;
No Woman ever wish'd *that same*,
But got, by Hook or Crook, her Aim:
So, SAWNEY, Thou'rt, perhaps, the Spawn,
Not of thy good Old *Name-sake* gone,
But of some *Serpent*-JESUIT,
Or other petulant TOM-TIT.

SAWNEY. Villain! profane my Mother's Name!
Hark, Sir, but touch her spotless Fame,
Thou'lt find a *Trigger* I can draw—
COLLEY. No Wrath, my *tiny Man of Straw:*
I've of your Mother said no more,
Than you had said of *mine* before.

---

[1] [A notorious judge: see *Imitations of Horace, Sat.* II. i. 82]

[2] *Vide* his *Characters of Women* [l. 216].

[3] *Vide* his *Letters, &c.* where he is perpetually TRUMPETTING forth his *filial Piety* to his *Mamma*, and the many Virtues and Excellencies of that good old Lady, whilst at the same Time he runs riot on all the rest of her Sex, for which *Crimen lasa Pulchritudinis*, or *High Treason*, against the *Fair*, no apter Punishment, we deem, could be inflicted, than that he should have his *Bumkin* scourged to the Bone, by a Committee of MATRONS chosen for that Purpose.

And wherefore, Child, this Cruelty
On all the Sex?—Um—I guess why.
SAWNEY, I know thy *ruling Passion*
Is *Love of Women*; but the Fashion
Of that *warpt* Carcase, and sad Grace,
Which hangs upon thy *Wezel* Face,
Could only cold Contempt procure,
And 'gainst thee barr'd the *fringed* Door:
Hence all thy Libels on the *Fair*,
Born not of *Hatred*, but *Despair*;
So *spiteful Imps* the Heav'n prophane,
Which they can never hope to gain.
SAWNEY. For that, Sir, I'll appeal to B[LOUNT][1]
COLLEY. *C[unt]*'s dumb, or I'd be judg'd by *C[unt]*
In whose good Graces thou hast ne'er been,
Since that *drole* Hour I caught thee therein,
And by the *Heels* my Hero pluck—
Hiatus Magnus * * * * * * * * *

. . . .

Ye mortified Mortals all,
Who since have ru'd the poisonous Gall,
Distill'd from his Satyric Pen,
Forgive my saving of him *then*:
I meant it well for HOMER's Sake,
But oft lament my dire Mistake.
Could HOMER from Elysium steal
O! how he'd curse both Hands and Heel.

    Much Thanks to *France*, but *none* to *Greece*,
A *patch'd*, *vamp'd*, old, *reviv'd*, new *Piece*,[2]
Translation from DACIER's *Translation*,
A HOMER of his *own* Creation
Is SAWNEY's Version—SAWNEY. Stroler, how!
My HOMER all Men will allow—
COLLEY. Yes, that 'tis Metre on *all-four*,
A purling Riv'let void of Oar;

---

[1] The Reader will find, in the Collection of SAWNEY's *Letters*, several written by him to one Mrs. B[LOUN]T.
[2] [See *Dunciad* (A), i. 237-8]

Not the strong Stream the *Grecian* flows,
Whose Depth with Golden Bullion glows:
In short, poor HOMER, in thy Wit,
Is dwindled to a mere TOM-TIT.
SAWNEY. Buffoon!—COLLEY. Ay,—yet I would not
    change
My Mirth for thy corroding Mange.
I laugh, am laugh'd at, Sir, 'tis true;
Your curse all Men, and *all Men* you.
    Remember, Child, remember TASTE![1]
There mark thy best good Friend disgrac'd:
He, at whose Table thou wer't fed,
Lampoon'd for *filling Thee with Bread*;
He, who was ne'er *thy* Friend design'd,
Because he's one to *all Mankind*.
    SAWNEY. I, Sycophant! call no Man *Friend*,
For any *mercenary* End;
Nor own one such whom Folly stains,
However great might be the Gains.
Fair Virtue, and her Friend are mine,[2]
COLLEY. Yes!—*virtuous* B[o]L[ING]B[RO]KE is thine:
He, SAWNEY, just as much as you,
Abhors the Thoughts of *private* View;
Inspired with a diviner Flame,
The *Publick* is his godlike Aim,
Whose Welfare he had still at Heart,
For whom he acted *many* a Part,
Was *In*, was *Out*, *did* and *undid*,
And brought *to light* the Things were *hid*;
Conducted *War* as none *durst* do,
And made *amazing* Treaties[3] too.
Then, as he held all *K[ing]s* were *Curses*,
Instead of their dear Country's *Nurses*,

---

[1] *Vide*, the Character of TIMON in SAWNEY's *Epistle upon* TASTE, wherein he has cruelly and scurri[l]ously treated a noble *Duke* of the Realm, who is as eminent for *Generosity* and *Phylantbropy*, as this *Bard* is for the *contrary*, and who never gave Occasion for one *Satyrical* Reflection, but that of his being a *Friend* to SAWNEY.

[2] Alluding to a Line upon Himself, in one of his Satires from HORACE, *To Virtue only and her Friends a Friend* [*Imit. Horace, Sat.* II. i. 121].

[3] The Treaty of UTRETCH, amongst other great Atchievements, was the Work of this glorious Patriot's Hand.

Whenever call'd into their *Aid*,
He surely *each* of them *betray'd*.

Such are thy Friends, their Virtues *such*—
SAWNEY. Blasphemer! how, my *Idol* touch!
I'll tell thee, Knave! 'tis Slander all,
A *Stygian* Picture drawn in Gall.
That *Genius* is all-wise, all-good,
Sprung, sure, from *more* than mortal Blood,
Thrice better than the best of Men—
COLLEY. Why, so are *you*, believe your Pen;
But, mark your *Actions* and your *Heart*,
You should be *flogg'd* at Vice's Cart.
What! no one *mercenary* View!
Has MACKBETH *murder'd Mem'ry*[1] too,
As you did *Shakespear?*[2] O, for Shame!
To TONSON *Hackney* out your Name!
As Beggars to a *barren* Friend,
For sake of *Snacks*, their *Bantlings* lend!
Promote an infamous *Deception*,
Meanly to *steal* a vast *Subscription*:
Then give us nothing for the same,
Save, in the Title, your *sweet Name!*
Tho' this is small to what you can,
TONSON's *an honourable Man!*
But with the *Wizard*, C[URL]L, to *juggle*,
And, *Hocus Pocus*, help him *smuggle*
Thy *Correspondence*[3] with thy Betters,
Theirs, extemp're, Thine studied LETTERS,

[1] It is said in SHAKESPEAR's *Mackbeth*,
————*Mackbeth has murder'd Sleep.*

[2] SAWNEY took in an immense Subscription, for a new and, as he set, forth, more correct Edition of *Shakespear*; but it appear'd, upon its Publication, that the Chief he had done in it was giving the *Publisher* Liberty to prefix his Name in the Title-page; and that, where he attempted any thing farther, his Subscribers found *nothing*, like the *Fool* in the Play, but what *was to their Loss*.

[3] The current Report, concerning this extraordinary Transaction, is as follows:— Mr. C[URL]L, the noted Mr. C[URL]L! some Years since published two or three Volumes of *private Letters* between SAWNEY and his Friends; whereupon the latter made a great Outcry at the Insolence and Injustice of the Thing, yea, went so far as to apply to a certain Lord, some of whose *Letters* were in the Collection, to complain of it in the House of Peers, as a Breach of their Privilege.—In the Interim SAWNEY published a more corre[ct] Edition of the said Letters, in his own Name, (staying, by the by, till C[URL]L's Edition was quite sold off) which he professes to have done, purely out of Vindication of himself and his Friends. Upon the Whole, it was universally deem'd, that the first Appearance of these

Cloath'd in a stiff, pedantic Dress,
Each Line corrected for the Press;
Intending thus to let us see
They're but, at best, a *Foil* to *Thee!*
Fye, SAWNEY, fye!—but that's not all,
In Publick 'gainst the Deed you bawl;
You C[URL]L, and C[URL]L you Villain, call.
So *Lawyers*, leagu'd to *fleece* a Freehold,
Be-Rogue each other *thick* and *threefold*:
Nay, more, to rivet the Deceit,
Thy *Lord* must consecrate the Cheat;
An insult on the House of P[ee]rs,
For which you ought to've *lost your Ears*,
Then thou and C[URL]L,[1] A'kin by Trade,
Had been *par nob'le Fratrum* made.
SAWNEY. 'Sdeath! Sir, d'ye couple C[URL]L with me?
COLLEY. Odso, your Pardon——let me see——
Oh, no, Friend C[URL]L, I wrong you there,
You vow you never lost an Ear:
And, tho' oft pillory'd, have still,
Both your *Auriculars* at will.

Thus, 'Squire, I've pointed out a few
Of those rare Virtues which *indue*
Your dear-beloved Friends and you
And many an Instance more could lug in,
Which you imagin'd to lie snug in
You clubb'd in that damn'd *Farce* Obscene,[2]

[1] SAWNEY and C[URL]L are said to be *A'kin* by Trade, on Account of the former's having lately turned *Bookseller* to himself, selling all his own Pieces, by Means of a *Publisher*, without giving his Bookseller any Share in them; and likewise practising, in all respects, the lowest Craft of the Trade such as different Editions in various Forms, with perpetual Additions and improvements, so as to render but the *last* worth nothing; and, by that Means, fooling many People into buying them several times over.

[2] A Play, called *Three Hours after Marriage* (1717), abounding with *Ribaldry* and *Obscenity*, written by SAWNEY in Conjunction with some of his Friends, and damn'd by the Town; in which were introduced two Lovers in the Shape of a *Crocodile* and a *Mummy*. Vide CIBBER's *Letter*.

Letters was owing to SAWNEY's own Contrivance, he having just *Modesty* and human *Prudence* enough to conclude, that it would draw down upon him an Accusation of most unparalelled Vanity as well as Treachery to be publickly known in it. [For an account of the tangled history of the publication of Pope's letters, see G. Sherburn's Introduction to *Corresp.*]

Which first 'gainst COLLEY whet your Spleen,
And, for the Joke, still daily hum-me
On Messieurs *Crocodile* and *Mummy*.
Twas you made DAVID[1] talk low *Smut*,
And sober HORACE[2] sent to *rut*.

  Now fairly view this Portrait, Elf!
And swear, if can'st,'tis not Thyself.
Then, prithee, why still most severe
On Vices to thyself most dear?
SAWNEY, repent thee of this Evil—
SAWNEY. 'Sblews, learn Repentance from the Dev[i]l!
Thou Owl, Bat, Vultur, Dragon, Boar,
Both Son and Father of a Whore!—
Rage! Vengeance!—O!—I can no more—
—Here SAWNEY sunk into the Chair,
When COLLEY, judging to a Hair,
Perceiving that he did not winch,[3]
(But first he took a sober *Pinch*)
Some *Assa-fœtida* minister'd,
By Vulgar Quacks y'clipt, *White Dog's T[ur]d*.
Then, *Teague-like*, laid him on his Back,
And dosing him with GEOR[GE]'s *Sack*,
It made him *puke*, and brought him back:

  Struck, by his strong Convultions, weak,
Long SAWNEY *yawn'd, but could not speak*.[4]
At length he sputters, foams, and stares,
And, crawling, as he could, down Stairs,
To COLLEY, speechless, left the Field,
In Par'lous Wrath to *Twit'nam* wheel'd,
And, ʃ[a]rt[in]g all the Way he went,
Ten thousand Curses *backward* sent.

---

[1] Alluding to an infamous, obscene Parody on the *first Psalm*, affirmed to be written by the *pious* SAWNEY.

[2] —To another Performance of the same delicate and virtuous Bard, titled *Sober Advice to the young Fellows about Town*.—This was in Imitation of one of HORACE's *Satires*, which, tho' the *least Modes* of any that Heathen Writer produced, was, however, so much over done in the *haut Gout* by our seemingly Religious *Reformer*, that HORACE may justly claim the Epithet of *Sober* on the Comparison. SAWNEY, upon the first Publication of that Piece, as absolutely denied it's being his, as he had done the *Psalm* before; but has suffered it since to be inserted in his Works.

[3] [I.e., 'flinch']   [4] A Parody on a Line of his in the *New Dunciad*.

'ETHICK EPISTLES'
(an abandoned project)

1729–36

An Essay on Man, the *Moral Essays*, and other poems were to have formed part of this grandiose structure: further, see p. 18 above.

---

73. Bolingbroke and Swift comment

1734, 1736

(a) Henry St John, Viscount Bolingbroke, extract from letter to Swift, 27 June–6 July 1734, *The Correspondence of Jonathan Swift*, ed. Sir H. Williams (1963), iv. 242.

I am glad you approve his moral essays.[1] they will do more good than the sermons and writings of some who had a mind to find great fault with them, and if the doctrines taught, hinted att, and implyed in them, and the trains of consequences deducible from these doctrines were to be disputed in prose, I think he would have no reason to apprehend either the free-thinkers on the one hand, or the narrow Dogmatists on the other. Some very few things may be expressed a little hardly, but none are I believe, unintelligible.

(b) Jonathan Swift, extract from letter to Pope, 2 December 1736, *ibid.*, iv. 547.

. . . I had reason to expect from some of your Letters that we were to hope for more Epistles of Morality, and I assure you, my Acquaintance resents that they have not Seen my name at the head of one. The Subjects of Such Epistles are more usefull to the Publick, by your manner of

---

1 [The 'Ethick Epistles' were referred to under various titles]

handling them than any of all your Writings, and although in so profligate a world as ours they may possibly not much mend our manners, yet Posterity will enjoy the Benefit whenever a Court happens to have the least relish for Virtue and Religion.

MORAL ESSAYS IV:
EPISTLE TO BURLINGTON, OF TASTE

14 December 1731

Pope's satire on 'Timon's Villa' (ll. 99–168) was widely attacked at the time as a satire on Lord Chandos's seat at Cannons, and became an important example of Pope's malevolence and supposed ingratitude. The charge seems to have been fabricated by Welsted, in order to divert Pope's satire from its real object, Sir Robert Walpole's country house at Houghton. Further, see Introduction, p. 19, and the two following items.

---

74. Chandos exculpates Pope

1731

James Brydges, Duke of Chandos, extract from letter to Pope, 21 December 1731, *Corresp.*, iii. 262–3.

Sir—I am much troubled to find by your favour of the 22d you are under any uneasiness, at the application the Town has made of Timon's Character, in your Epistle to the Earl of Burlington. For my own part I have recieved so many instances of the will they bear me, that I am as little surprized as I am affected with this further proof of it; It would indeed be a real concern to me did I beleive One of your Judgment had designedly given grounds for their imbibing an Opinion, so disadvantageous of me. But as your obliging Letter, is sufficient to free me from this apprehension, I can with great indifference bear the insults they bestow, and not find myself hurt by 'em: nor have I reason to be much disturb'd, when I consider how many better persons are the daily objects of their unjust censures.

75. Welsted on Pope's 'Libel'

1732

Leonard Welsted, extract from *Of Dulness and Scandal. Occasion'd by the Character of Lord Timon, in Mr. Pope's Epistle to the Earl of Burlington* (1732), pp. 5–end. Originally published on 3 January 1732.

> See, POLLIO [Chandos] falls a Victim to the Rage,
> Which Goodness could not charm, nor Friendship swage;
>
> . . . .
>
>   INGLORIOUS Rhimer! low licentious Slave!
> Who blasts the Beauteous, and belies the Brave:
> In scurril Verse who robs, and dull Essays,
> Nymphs of their charms, and Heroes of their Praise:
> All Laws for Pique or Caprice will forego;
> The friend of CATILINE, and TULLY's foe!
>   OH! born to blacken every virtuous Name;
> To pass, like Blightings, o'er the Blooms of Fame;
> The Venom of thy baneful Quill to shed
> Alike on living Merit, and the dead!
> Sure, that fam'd MACHIAVIL, what time he drew
> The Soul's dark Workings in the crooked Few;
> The rancour'd Spirit, and malignant Will,
> By *Instinct* base, by *Nature* shap'd to ill,
> An unborn Demon was inspir'd to see,
> And in his Rapture prophesied of thee.
>   ORDAIN'D a hated Name by Guilt to raise;
> To bless with Libel, and to curse with Praise!
> A softling Head! that spleeny Whims devour;
> With Will to Satyr, while deny'd the Power!
> A Soul corrupt! that hireling Praise suborns!
> That hates for Genius, and for Virtue scorns!
> A Coxcomb's Talents, with a Pedant's Art!

A Bigot's Fury in an Atheist's Heart!
Lewd without Lust, and without Wit profane!
Outrageous, and afraid! contemn'd, and vain!
   IMMUR'D, whilst young, in Convents hadst thou been,
VICTORIA[1] still with Rapture we had seen:
But now our Wishes by the Fates are crost;
We've gain'd a THERSITE, and an HELEN lost:
The envious Planet has deceiv'd our Hope;
We've lost a ST. LEGER,[2] and gain'd a POPE.
   A little MONK thou wert by Nature made!
Wert fashion'd for the *Jesuit's* Gossip Trade!
A lean Church-pandar, to procure, or lie!
A Pimp at Altars, or in Courts a Spy!
   The Verse, that Blockheads dawb, shall swift decay,
And JERVASE'[3] Fame in Fustian fade away:
Forgot the self-applauding Strain shall be;
Though own'd by WALSH, or palm'd on WYCHERLEY:
While Time, nor Fate, this faithful *Sketch* erase,
Which shews thy mind, as REISBANK's bust thy face.
   'Yet *thou proceed;*'[4] impeach with stedfast Hate
What-e'er is God-like, and what-e'er is Great:
Debase, in low Burlesque, the Song divine,
And level DAVID's deathless Muse[5] to thine:
Be Bawdry, still, thy ribald Canto's theme:
Traduce for Satyr, and for Wit blaspheme:
Each chast Idea of thy Mind review;
Make CUPIDS squirt, and gaping TRITONS spew:[6]
All STERNHOLD's Spirit in thy verse Restore,
And be what BASS and HEYWOOD were before.[7]

---

  [1] [I.e., a victorious Britain]
  [2] [Possibly a reference to St Leger, mutilated and martyred in 678, and therefore a hit at Pope's supposed impotence. See D. Fineman, 'The Case of the Lady "Killed by Alexander Pope"', *Modern Language Quarterly*, xii (1957), 137–49]
  [3] [Charles Jervas (1675–1739), painter, was a friend of Pope. The charge that Pope forged Wycherley's complimentary verses (No. 8) was an old one. Rysbrack made several busts of Pope]
  [4] [*Moral Essays*, IV. 191]
  [5] ['A Roman Catholick Version of the First Psalm']
  [6] [*Moral Essays*, IV. 111, 154]
  [7] [Parody of *ibid.*, ll. 193–4. The references are to Thomas Sternhold's doggerel versions of the psalms, to (possibly) William Basse, the Spenserian, and either to John Heywood, the sixteenth-century court poet, or Thomas Heywood, the Elizabethan dramatist]

MORAL ESSAYS III: TO ALLEN LORD BATHURST, OF THE USE OF RICHES

15 January 1733

---

76. Swift on obscurity

1733

Jonathan Swift, extract from a letter to Pope, [January] 1733, *Corresp.*, iii. 343. Written from Dublin.

Your poem on the Use of Riches hath been just printed here,[1] and we have no objection but the obscurity of several passages by our ignorance in facts and persons, which make us lose abundance of the Satyr. Had the printer given me notice, I would have honestly printed the names at length, where I happened to know them; and writ explanatory notes, which however would have been but few, for my long absence hath made me ignorant of what passes out of the scene where I am.

---

[1] [The poem appeared in London about 15 January. This Dublin edition may have come at the tail-end of the month]

77. Lady Mary Wortley Montagu replies in kind

March 1733

Lady Mary Wortley Montagu, *Verses Address'd to the Imitator of the First Satire of the Second Book of Horace. By a Lady* (1733). Pope's couplet on Sappho (ll. 83–4)—

> From furious Sappho scarce a milder fate,
> P——x'd by her love, or libell'd by her hate.

—was aimed at Lady Mary, with whom Pope had earlier been on intimate terms (see No. 31). By 1728 relations between them were at an end, and Pope (mistakenly) considered that she had a hand in one or two attacks upon him. When Lady Mary persuaded the Earl of Peterborough to ask Pope if she was indeed intended by Sappho, Pope's reply was to claim that the couplet was general satire, and referred with greater aptness to women writers like Mrs Centlivre, Mrs Haywood, Mrs Manley or Aphra Behn. Undeterred, Lady Mary wrote the *Verses*, with the help of Lord Hervey, and promptly published them. The cuts at Pope are bitter and angry, but they are also shrewd. The poem is perhaps the best written of the many vicious attacks upon Pope's personality and physique. It was published 9 March 1733. There was a reissue, a piracy, and at least two further editions in 1733.

IN two large Columns, on thy motly Page,
Where *Roman* Wit is striped with *English* Rage;

Where Ribaldry to Satire makes pretence,
And modern Scandal rolls with ancient Sense:
Whilst on one side we see how *Horace* thought;
And on the other, how he never wrote:
Who can believe, who views the bad and good,
That the dull Cop[y]ist better understood
That *Spirit*, he pretends to imitate,
Than heretofore that *Greek* he did translate?

    Thine is just such an Image of *his* Pen,
As thou thy self art of the Sons of Men:
Where our own Species in Burlesque we trace,
A Sign-post Likeness of the noble Race;
That is at once Resemblance and Disgrace.

    Horace can laugh, is delicate, is clear;
You, only coarsely rail, or darkly sneer:
His Style is elegant, his Diction pure,
Whilst none thy crabbed Numbers can endure;
Hard as thy Heart, and as thy Birth obscure.

    If *He* has Thorns, they all on Roses grow;
Thine like rude Thistles, and mean Brambles show;
With this Exception, that tho' rank the Soil,
Weeds, as they are, they seem produc'd by Toil.

    Satire shou'd, like a polish'd Razor keen,
Wound with a Touch, that's scarcely felt or seen.
Thine is an Oyster-Knife, that hacks and hews;
The Rage, but not the Talent of Abuse;
And is in *Hate*, what *Love* is in the Stews.
'Tis the gross *Lust* of Hate, that still annoys,
Without Distinction, as gross Love enjoys:
Neither to Folly, nor to Vice confin'd;
The Object of thy Spleen is Human Kind:
It preys on all, who yield, or who resist;
To Thee 'tis Provocation to exist.

    But if thou see'st a great and gen'rous Heart,[1]
Thy Bow is doubly bent to force a Dart.
Nor only Justice vainly we demand,
But even Benefits can't rein thy Hand:
To this or that alike in vain we trust,
Nor find Thee less Ungrateful than Unjust.

[1] *See* TASTE, *an Epistle* [i.e. *Epistle to Burlington*].

Not even Youth and Beauty can controul
The universal Rancour of thy Soul;
Charms that might soften Superstition's Rage,
Might humble Pride, or thaw the Ice of Age——
But how should'st thou by Beauty's Force be mov'd,
No more for loving made, than to be lov'd?
It was the Equity of right'ous Heav'n,
That such a Soul to such a Form was giv'n;
And shews the Uniformity of Fate,
That one so odious, should be born to hate.

    When God created Thee, one would believe,
He'd said the same, as *to the Snake of Eve*;
To Human Race Antipathy declare,
'Twixt them and thee be everlasting War.
But, Oh! the Sequel of the Sentence dread,
And whilst you *bruise their Heel, beware your Head.*

    Nor think thy Weakness shall be thy Defence;
The Female-Scold's Protection in Offence.
Sure 'tis as fair to beat who cannot fight,
As 'tis to libel those who cannot write.
And if thou drawst thy Pen to aid the Law,
Others a Cudgel, or a Rod, may draw.

    If none with Vengeance yet thy Crimes pursue,
Or give thy manifold Affronts their due;
If Limbs unbroken, Skin without a Stain,
Unwhipt, unblanketed, unkick'd, unslain;
That wretched little Carcase you retain:
The Reason is, not, that the World wants Eyes;
But thou'rt so mean, they see, and they despise.
When fretful *Porcupines*, with rancorous Will,
From mounted Backs shoot forth a harmless Quill,
Cool the Spectators stand; and all the while,
Upon the angry little Monster smile:
Thus 'tis with thee:—whilst impotently safe,
You strike unwounding, we unhurt can laugh.
Who but must laugh, this Bully when he sees,
A little Insect shiv'ring at a Breeze.[1]
One over-match'd by ev'ry Blast of Wind,
Insulting and provoking all Mankind.

[1] [An adaptation of the *Epistle to Burlington*, ll. 107–8

Is this the *Thing* to keep Mankind in awe,
To make those tremble who escape the Law?[1]
Is this the *Ridicule* to live so long,
The *deathless Satire*, and *immortal Song?*
No; like thy self-blown Praise, thy Scandal flies,
And, as we're told of Wasps, it stings and dies.

If none then yet return th'intended Blow;
You all your Safety, to you Dulness owe:
But whilst that Armour thy poor Corps defends,
'Twill make thy Readers few, as are thy Friends;
Those, who thy Nature loath'd, yet lov'd thy Art,
Who lik'd thy Head, and yet abhor'd thy Heart;
Chose thee, to read, but never to converse,
And scorn'd in Prose, him whom they priz'd in Verse.
Even they shall now their partial Error see,
Shall shun thy Writing like thy Company;
And to thy Books shall ope their Eyes no more,
Than to thy Person they wou'd do their Door.

Nor thou the Justice of the World disown,
That leaves Thee thus an Out-cast, and alone;
For tho' in Law, to murder be to kill,
In Equity the Murder's in the Will:
Then whilst with Coward Hand you stab a Name,
And try at least t'assassinate our Fame;
Like the first bold Assassin's be thy Lot,
Ne'er be thy Guilt forgiven, or forgot;
But as thou hate'st, be hated by Mankind,
And with the Emblem of thy crooked Mind,
Mark'd on thy Back, like *Cain*, by God's own Hand;
Wander like him, accursed through the Land.

[1] [An adaptation of *Imitations of Horace, Sat.* II. i. 79]

78. Satire as Pope's vice

March 1733

Anonymous, extract from *An Epistle to the Little Satyrist of Twickenham* (1733), pp. 5–10. This letter of advice to Pope, which was published 30 March 1733, takes the common position that the move to satire betrayed Pope's early genius.

> You were your Country's Pride and Pleasure born,
> Excell'd when e'en your Life was in its Morn,
> And young the Gift of Numbers was to you,
> Which still encreas'd with Age and as you grew,
> 'Till to Perfection you at last arriv'd,
> Which none have e'er excell'd that ever liv'd;
> But let me ask with what you are endu'd?
> A Pow'r, that as you use it's bad or good;
> Because for Poetry your Taste is nice,
> D'ye think that you are free from ev'ry Vice?
>
> There's nothing moves a Man's Compassion more,
> Than Man reduc'd who had been Great before;
> For you I feel that gen'rous Passion mov'd,
> So hated now, who once was so belov'd.
>
> Who'ere unprejudic'd Opinion gives,
> Will own, you are excell'd by none that lives.
> Whence shou'd this universal Scorn abound,
> But from the Scandal that you scatter round?
> By Name uninjur'd to detract in Satire,
> I own gives shrewd Suspicion of ill Nature.
>
> There's few at Home, if candidly they'd look,
> But wou'd find something worthy of Rebuke.
> *Satire your Weapon;*[1] if you will attack,
> Be careful that the Scandal don't fly back;

[1] [*Imitations of Horace, Sat.* II. i. 69]

For, as the Boy that shoots the hast'ning Ball,
Thoughtless, against th' impenetrable Wall,
In painful Anguish the Rebound may rue;
In tainting Reputations, so may you.

You wear it only in a Land of Hectors,
Thieves, Super-Cargoes, Sharpers, and Directors:[1]
Then how cou'd *Timon* tingle in your Rhyme,
Who no one ever charg'd with any Crime;
Your Benefactor too, who all Men know
Is Virtue's strictest Friend, and Vice's Foe;
A Pattern to the Great, to all a Friend,
Who all Men love, and All, but You, commend.
A kind Compassion prompts me to conclude,
That *Timon's* Study you had never view'd;[2]
Not LOCK, nor MILTON, nor *a modern Book*,
Has Truth your Tongue, or Sight your Eyes forsook?
And English'd *Homer* there you might have found,
Not b' *Aldus* printed, nor *du Suëil* bound,
Which cost, a I have heard, *Five Hundred Pound.*

What can the Motive be that eggs you on?
If Pride, won't Panegyrick fill a Song;
But Pride's a Passion of so ill Effect,
That Virtue ne'er can see but will correct.

If 'tis in Search of Happiness you'r bent,
Why don't you seek it in a calm Content;
'Tis there, and only there it will be found,
Altho' you search the Universe around:
But as the Sun's obscur'd by gloomy Clouds,
So Passions hide it from the tainted Crowds.
Ambition hurries Kings in Arms to roam,
Whilst Reason whispers, they've enough at Home.
The Miser's rich, and yet, for want of more,
He starves, 'cause he himself imagines poor.
The Mind that's ting'd with Envy, soon or late,
Is tempted to detract the Good and Great:

[1] [*Imitations of Horace, Sat.* II. i. 79]
[2] *See,* The Taste [i.e., *Epistle to Burlington,* ll. 99ff.]

And he, where Malice guides the yielding Mind,
Wou'd ruin and undo all human Kind.
Malice and Hatred are of one Degree,
And join to terminate Society.
The angry Man's unguarded in his Deeds,
And, causeless, often wounds his Friend, or bleeds.
Malice and Anger do Revenge compose,
And blindly wou'd destroy both Friends and Foes.
To these add Pride, for she too needs must fall,
That haughty Dame's the Mother of 'em all.
Upon these Passions I have more enlarg'd,
Because with these you are so loudly charg'd;
Wou'd I cou'd vouch you absolutely free;
But Virtue raises few to that Degree.

On th' imitated Satire 'twill suffice,
To send you my Opinion and Advice.
Abstract the Vice from Virtue it contains,
And judge ye by the Virtue that remains.

First, let Ambition be th' impartial Theme,
What Share that Vice may in the Satire claim;
The Virtuous are what others wou'd be thought,
What few Men are, but all Men know they ought.
To Virtue only, and her Friends, a Friend;[1]
But him so bless'd, to hear, it wou'd offend.
For when that Virtue is indeed possess'd,
It is in Silence, and the Owner's bless'd.

If thou'rt ambitious to be thought a Poet,
Write Panegyrick, and the World will know it.

The next, in Turn, will Avarice remain;
And 't has been urg'd, you write for odious Gain,
And know that nothing but the rankest Satire
Will sell, the Town's so poison'd with ill Nature.
From this sad Crime, pray Heav'n you may be free,
For what's so vile as Scandal for a Fee?

---

[1] [*Imitations of Horace, Sat.* II. i. 121]

The envious Man can Virtue ne'er behold,
But with Distaste and Spleen that cannot hold:
Old *Æsop* tells us of a Toad that swell'd,
And burst with Envy, 'cause he was excell'd;
So you, th' impartial World contemptuous cry,
At your Superiours swell, and burst, and die.

Malicious you're accounted, 'cause a Rage,
They say, appears unjust in ev'ry Page;
Tho' some first prove the Subject of your Spite,
The World conceives you hate 'em all alike.

To Anger prone you've own'd yourself before;
But touch me, and no Minister so sore:[1]
'Tis natural, the Proverb does evince,
The Horse that's gaul'd when touch'd will surely wince.
Be always careful that your Anger be
From Pride, from Malice, and Ill-Nature free;
From them Men fancy was the *Dunciad* born,
A Mixture of Ill-Nature, Spleen, and Scorn.

From whence shou'd all these Passions flow but Pride?
And that I must accuse you of and chide.
You say, *impartially your Muse intends
Fair to expose yourself, your Foes, and Friends.*[2]
And Leaf by Leaf your Writings I have turn'd
To find the Page wherein your Faults are mourn'd
Still self-blown Praise presents itself to View,
As if Vice *heard ye, trembled,* and withdrew.

'*With Eyes that pry not, Tongue that ne'er repeats,
Fond to spread Friendships, but to cover Heats,
To help who wants, to forward who excell,
This all who know me, know, who love me, tell.*'[3]

Thus vainly your Opinion you belye,
Lay Claim to Virtue, and your Vice deny.
For he that's good shou'd start at ev'ry Wind,
Of Vice be conscious, to his Virtue blind;

---

[1] [*Imitations of Horace, Sat.* II. i. 76]
[2] [*Imitations of Horace, Sat.* II. i. 57–8]
[3] [*Ibid.,* ll. 135–8]

Not think that *all the Din the World can keep*
Rolls o'er his Grotto and but sooths his Sleep:[1]
For he so lost will live, in endless Fame,
An everlasting Monument of Shame;
For if such horrid Spots as these appear,
How does it prove *the Medium must be clear?*[2]

[1] [*Ibid.*, ll. 123–4]   [2] [*Ibid.*, l. 56]

79. Pope describes the poem's reception

1733

Pope, extract from letter to John Caryll, 8 March 1733, *Corresp.*, iii. 354.

Since *An Essay on Man* was published anonymously, Pope was able to write to Caryll keeping up the pretence.

The town is now very full of a new poem intitled *an Essay on Man*, attributed, I think with reason, to a divine. It has merit in my opinion but not so much as they give it; at least it is incorrect and has some inaccuracies in the expressions; one or two of an unhappy kind, for they may cause the author's sense to be turned, contrary to what I think his intention a little unorthodoxically. Nothing is so plain as that he quits his proper subject, *this present world*, to insert his belief of *a future state* and yet there is an *If* instead of a *Since* that would overthrow his meaning and at the end he uses the Words *God*, the *Soul* of the *World*, which at first glance may be taken for heathenism, while his whole paragraph proves him quite Christian in his system, from *Man* up to *Seraphim*. I want to know your opinion of it after twice or thrice reading. I give you my thoughts very candidly of it, tho' I find there is a sort of faction to set up the author and his piece in opposition to me and my little things, which I confess are not of so much importance as to the subject, but I hope they conduce to morality in their way, which way is at least more generally to be understood and the seasoning of satire renders it more palatable to the generality.

80. Initial reactions

(a) Leonard Welsted, extract from a letter to Pope printed among the 'Testimonies of Authors' prefixed to *The Dunciad* (1743), *Corresp.*, iii. 355–6. Pope commented, 'Mr. LEONARD WELSTED thus wrote to the unknown author, on the first publication of the said Essay [on Man].' Welsted's letter dates from 12 March 1733. His praise would have been tempered had he known the author (see Nos 4, 75).

I must own, after the reception which the vilest and most immoral ribaldry hath lately met with, I was surprised to see what I had long despaired, a performance deserving the name of a poet. Such, Sir, is your work. It is, indeed, above all commendation, and ought to have been published in an age and country more worthy of it. If my testimony be of weight any where, you are sure to have it in the amplest manner, *&c. &c. &c.*

(b) Dr Alured Clarke, extract from a letter to Mrs Charlotte Clayton (later Lady Sundon), 10 April 1733, *Memoirs of Viscountess Sundon*, ed. Mrs Thomson (1847), ii. 195. Pope was later to satirize Clarke; see *Epilogue to the Satires*, ii. 194, and Spence, *Anecdotes*, i. 148.

. . . I fancied for some time after I had read [the first epistle of *An Essay on Man*], that the poet had enabled me to be a perfect hero in affliction, if it had come soon in my way to be put to the trial. I hope the author (when he is known) will be found to be a *very good* man, or else his scholars—that is, his readers—must be very much mortified. I think, upon the whole, it is the most extraordinary performance I have met with; and if the man and his work are of a piece, I wish he may meet with as good a friend as Vespasian, the Roman Emperor, was said to be, who, though otherwise very penurious, gave annual pensions of 800*l.* per annum to good orators and poets, and not above half as much to a ragged lord. I have seen the Second Essay, which in many places is too hard to be understood; and taken altogether, is, I think, not comparable to the first, though it has many beauties. But I did not intend to say a word of books, and do not know how I got into the feast.

(c) A.Z., extract from *The Gentleman's Magazine*, iv (February 1734), 96.

The short Extracts we have made from the *Essay on Man* . . . have not only caused those Epistles to be order'd into the Country . . . but have also been the Occasion of a Letter from the North, sign'd *A.Z.* which we received with more Pleasure, as it is chiefly in Praise of that excellent Poem, which, says the Letter Writer,

Comprizes the most Nervous Reasonning in the Advancement of profound natural Truths. In a Word, the Nobleness of the Subject is preferable in the Opinion of the Judicious, to every Thing extant; for, tho' several other Pieces may claim just Admiration, yet their Subjects are light and trifling if compared with this, which when read with deliberate Attention, at once enlarges the Understanding, convinces the Judgment, and touches the Heart.—The four Epistles contain but 1174 single Lines, and the Price is four Shillings: So that if we consider the small Quantity of the Matter, 'tis the dearest; but if again the Dignity of the Subject, 'tis the cheapest, as it is the sublimest Piece of Poetry in its Kind.—But, Mr. *Urban*, I'm afraid your selecting here and there a Passage may seem a Disadvantage to the Great Genius the Author; for in Truth the whole Composition is all over Beauty.

(d) I.C., poem, *ibid*., p. 97.

To the Unknown AUTHOR of the ESSAY ON MAN.

> To praise thy judgment or commend thy strain,
> In this were all superfluous or vain.
> Hail, then, instructing bard (whoe'er thou art)
> That opens thus our eyes and clears our heart!
> Few such arise in this licentious age:
> Some rack their wit t'abuse the sacred page;
> Others will write, but to debase mankind,
> And strive, below the brute, to sink his mind;
> Whilst you, in your ESSAY, enforce the whole
> That's good to man, for body, and for soul.

(e) Robert Dodsley, extract from *An Epistle to Mr. Pope, Occasion'd by his Essay on Man* (1734), pp. 4–5. Dodsley's poem appeared in November 1734.

> So when at first I view'd thy wond'rous Plan,
> Leading thro' all the winding Maze of Man;
> Bewilder'd, weak, unable to pursue,
> My Pride would fain have laid the Fault on You.
> This false, That ill-exprest, this Thought not good;
> And all was wrong which I mis-understood.
> But reading more attentive, soon I found,
> The Diction nervous, and the Doctrine sound.
> Saw Man, a Part of that stupendous Whole,
> *Whose Body Nature is, and God the Soul.*[1]
> Saw in the Scale of Things his middle State,
> And all his Powers adapted just to That.
> Saw Reason, Passion, Weakness, how of use,
> How all to Good, to Happiness conduce.
> Saw my own Weakness, thy superior Power,
> And still the more I read, admire the more.

(f) Jonathan Swift, extract from a letter to Pope, 1 November 1734, *The Correspondence of Jonathan Swift*, ed. Sir H. Williams (1963), iv. 263.

Surely I never doubted about your Essay on Man, & I would lay any odds, that I would never fayl to discover you in six lines, unless you had a mind to write below or beside your self on purpose. I confess I did never imagine you were so deep in Morals, or that so many new & excellent Rules could be produced so advantageously & agreably in that Science from any one head. I confess in some few places I was forced to read twice; I believe I told you before what the Duke of D[orset] said to me on that occasion. How a Judge[2] here who knows you, told the D[uke] that on the first reading those Essays, he was much pleased, but found some lines a little dark; On the second most of them cleared up, & his pleasure increased; On the third he had no doubt remained, & then he admired the whole.

---

[1] [See *An Essay on Man*, i. 167–8]
[2] [Possibly John Wainwright, Baron of the Irish Exchequer]

81. Pope's orthodoxy queried

1736

Mr Bridges, extract from the Preface to *Divine Wisdom and Providence; An Essay Occasion'd by the Essay on Man* (2nd ed., 1736), pp. ii–iii. Bridges's poem was first published about 31 March 1736, and is one of the few pieces which had doubts, even though minor ones, about the orthodoxy of *An Essay on Man* prior to Crousaz's *Examen*.

Mr. POPE . . . lays down this Principle, as the general Foundation of his reasoning, that God, when he intended to make the Universe was guided by his infinite Wisdom to form the best (or wisest) System that was possible; that in such a System there must necessarily be a Fulness or Coherence, or regular Gradations and Subordinations of Things to one another, from the highest to the lowest; and that in Consequence of such a Fulness, and such Gradations, it was necessary there should be such a Creature as Man.

It would not be very difficult, if it was necessary, to shew the Precariousness, at least, of this Principle of Mr. POPE's, if he had only the *Imperfections*, and not the *Evils* of our Beings to account for. But how will it follow, from infinite Wisdom forming the best (or wisest) System, that Evil should any where, or in any Degree, be admitted into such a System? It is no true Wisdom in Man to be the Author and Contriver of what is bad, much less is it such in God, the adorable Fountain of all Good, and all Perfection.

If Evils proceeded from the original Intention and Appointment of the Deity, they must either argue a Defect of *Goodness*, or of *Wisdom* in him. If it was in his Power, so to have contrived the System of the World, as to have prevented these Evils; his *not* preventing them argues a Defect of his *Goodness*: If he could not have made Things without these Imperfections and Disorders, his *thus* making them argues a Defect of his Wisdom. But will any one say, or can any one reasonably think, that, in God, there is the least Defect of either of these Perfections?

To say that *partial Evil is universal Good*; or, with my Ld S[*haftes-bur*]*y*, that nothing is *absolutely* ill, if it is *any where* good in *any other*, or in the *universal* System is saying nothing to the Disproof of the real Existence of Evil. Evil is still Evil, tho' it be made conducive to the general Good of the *whole*, and tho' *few*, in respect of the whole, be Sufferers by it. It is true God can bring *Good* out of *Evil*, but he cannot be said to be the Cause of Evil for the Sake of Good. It is one Thing to say, that God can produce Good out of the Evil he has *permitted*, and another to say, he was the Cause of Evil, in order to make it subservient to a greater Good, which he could not effect without it.

It would be much more for the Honour of the divine Perfections to suppose, that his Works, when they first came out of his Hands, were much more pure and perfect, than we now see them; and if we can find any Cause of their Depravation, it would surely inspire us with more amiable Ideas of our great and good Creator to think that Order, Beauty and Happiness proceeded from him; and that Disorder, Deformity and Evil are derived from another Source: Not from any evil Principle, as some have thought, counterworking the Designs of a good Principle, but from the Abuse of moral Liberty in the Creatures, which was the Occasion both of their own personal Disorders, and the Disorders observable in the present Frame and Constitution of Nature.

But tho' there are many Disorders in the natural World, it is far from being so disordered as not very plainly to appear the Work of an intelligent and wise Being. There are still infinite Beauties in it to engage our Admiration of its great Author. The humane Body is a System of Matter, formed with admirable Art and Contrivance; and yet to how many Diseases and Disorders is it obnoxious! But do we conclude from these Diseases and Disorders, that there is no Art and Contrivance in the Formation and Structure of it? Apply but this Observation to Nature, and you will no more be offended with her Irregularities, than with the Diseases of your own Bodies. You will draw no other Conclusion from one than the other, but will find Matter enough, for Wonder in both to make you reverence and adore that Being, who in great Wisdom has made all Things; many incontestable Evidences of which are still visible amidst all the Deformities and Disorders occasioned by Sin.

But it may be questioned, that, if there is the Appearance of so much Evil in the World, how come we to know that the Maker of the World was not the immediate Cause of all the Evil that is in it? The Answer to which is this; That we know it from a due Consideration of the present State of our own Minds; the Impressions that are still left there, concerning Goodness, Justice, and other moral Excellencies, giving us a very just Notion of the divine Perfections, and being a convincing and strong Evidence, that there are such Perfections in the divine Nature. Besides, the Conclusion drawn from the Weakness of our Reason, and the Strength and Prevalency of our Passions, that we are in a disordered, lapsed Condition, being just and rational in itself, as well as assented to by many of the greatest Heathen Philosophers, it is very obvious to infer that all the Evils and Disorders of the natural World can be no other than the Consequences of the Depravity and Corruption of the moral.

I am far from charging Mr. POPE with writing with any Design against Christianity; but if he builds upon such Principles as appear to others entirely destructive of the Foundation of the Christian System, he must excuse them if they shew their Dislike of such Principles, and endeavour that such Writings as his may not be made an ill Use of, to the Prejudice of that Religion, for which they have the most awful Regard and Veneration. Had another Writer of less Reputation and Influence in the World, advanced the same Notions it would have been less material to have taken any Notice of him; but Mr. POPE is too considerable to be neglected in such a Case; as he is the first Man one would desire to have engaged in a good Cause, and the last one would chuse to maintain a bad one. I am persuaded, that in what I oppose him, his Intention was truely commendable, and that he thought it for the Honour of God to vindicate his Proceedings in the Manner he has done. I desire no more than that he will think as candidly of this Opposition; and as for the Reasonableness of either his Hypothesis or mine, that must be left to our Readers, to whom I should be glad to be able to give the same Poetical Entertainment that he has done; but I am so far from pretending any Competition with him this Way, that I profess myself to be in the first Rank of his Admirers, and instead of expecting the Reader to approve the following Poem, I shall esteem it a sufficient Favour from him, if he will be so indulgent as to excuse its many Imperfections.

82. Abbé du Resnel's opinion

1736

Abbé J. F. du Resnel, extracts from 'Discours préliminaire du tra-ducteur', *Les principes de la morale et du gout. En deux poëmes traduits de l'Anglois* (Paris, 1736). Dr Johnson's translation is given here from *A Commentary On Mr. Pope's Principles of Morality . . . By Mons. Crousaz* (1742, a re-issue of 1739 ed.), pp. 300–11, 316–17, 325–6.

Du Resnel had published a translation of *An Essay on Criticism* in 1730. The 1736 volume reprints this, along with his translation of the *Essay on Man*, prefaced by the 'Discours préliminaire'.

THE Taste of the present Age seems to be confined to Romances, Stories and Novels, nor does the polite Part of the World appear sensible of any other Merit either in Men or Books, than the Quality of diverting; a Quality so much in Esteem, that Authors are afraid of professing any thing beyond it, and think Excuses and Vindications necessary when they attempt to profit or instruct. It required therefore no small Degree of Courage to present the Public at one Time with two Performances, of which the first is filled with profound Truths and severe Morality, entirely opposite to those trifling and licentious Systems which some Authors of late Times labour to support, and the other contains Principles of Criticism, and Precepts of Taste wholly irreconcileable with that which is daily encroaching upon us, insensibly getting Possession both of our Authors and Readers.

I published, in 1730, a poetical Translation of Mr. *Pope's Essay on Criticism*, a Production which had done him more Honour than any other, and the only Piece, except the *Essay on Man*, which he has published without being attacked by the Criticks of his own Country.[1]

---

[1] The Essay on Criticism was animadverted upon by Mr. *Dennis*, with great Fury and Malice, and has been denied by others, who could not but allow its Excellence, to be Mr. *Pope*'s; but not to have heard of these Censures and Calumnies is very pardonable in a Foreigner, since there are perhaps not many, even of our own Countrymen, better acquainted with them. [Johnson]

I have now in my Hand about twenty Pamphlets written against the great Poet, without the least Regard to *Decency*, and with all the Virulence that Envy of superior Abilities can produce in a narrow Mind; yet even in these the Essay on Criticism is never mentioned, but with Commendations, and the same Respect which is paid in *France* to *Boileau*'s Art of Poetry.

The only Reason for which this Poem can be properly termed an Essay is, that the Author has not formed his Plan with all the Regularity of Method which it might have admitted; but this Omission must be allowed to be more pardonable in him than in *Aristotle* and *Horace*, because a compleat Treatise is not promised. Such a Piece well deserved, in my Opinion, to be translated into our Language; and the favourable Reception which my Version has found, encourages me to believe, that I have not wholly miscarried in my Attempt, and that my Performance is, in some measure, what I intended.

But as the Faculties of the Understanding constitute no more than half of the Man, and, if not associated with Rectitude of Mind, have often no other Effect than that of making him more abject and despicable; I thought it not improper to add to the *Essay on Criticism* the *Essay on Man*, another of Mr. *Pope*'s Productions, which is regarded by the *English* as one of the most beautiful Poems in their Language; being, by the Persuasions of many Persons, whose Virtue and Capacity gave them a Claim to Respect and Distinction, prevailed upon to engage in a second Task of the same Kind, however laborious and unpleasing, in hopes that these two Poems published together, might contribute at the same Time to rectify the Taste and the Inclinations, to improve the Genius, and reform the Conduct of great Numbers, who want either Leisure or Learning to go regularly through the Studies of Morality and polite Literature.

From the *Essay on Man* the Reader will learn to know the Tendency of his own Genius, to comprehend the endless Diversity that is to be found in the Minds of Men, and to remark the original Causes of our Errors and false Opinions; he will there be shewn the Sources from which he must draw Precepts for forming his Judgment, and will learn what are the true and valuable Beauties of a Writer of Genius, what Caution a Reader is to use, that he may not confound Excellencies with Faults, and what are the Qualities that constitute not only a good Critick, but a good Author.

In the *Essay on Man* he will meet with all that Metaphysics teach, with any great Degree of Certainty, relating to the Knowledge of ourselves, and all the necessary Rules which Morality lays down for the Practice of our Duty to God and Man.

Poetry and Methaphysics, say the Authors of *The Memoirs of Trevoux*,[1] are generally considered as two Kinds of Writing inconsistent with each other; nor is that Opinion without some Foundation in Experience. The Extasies and Flights of the Poet, and the Nicety and cool Argumentation of the abstracted Reasoner, are not easily united. This Conjunction has not been attempted by many Writers; and of those few that have endeavoured it, yet fewer have succeeded. To form such a Design, and execute it in such a Manner, as to attain the Applause of all true Judges, was an Honour reserved in these later Ages for Mr. *Pope*.

He begins with an Examination of the Nature of Man, according to the Light of unassisted Reason, and shews, in the *first Epistle*, that Reason represents Man as created to inhabit this World; and that from this Notion of his State considered together with our Ideas of the Wisdom and Goodness of the supreme Being, we may conclude, that he has all the Perfections suitable to his present State, and to the Relation which he bears both to his Fellow-Creatures here, and to the other Parts of the Universe; that as we do not see this Relation in its whole Extent, we cannot discover what Degree of Wisdom God has exerted in the Formation of the human Species; but we know in the general, that Man is a finite Being, and therefore cannot reasonably be surprised at the Weakness and Imperfection both of his Mind and Body.

In the *second* he discovers, that the Goodness and Wisdom of God are conspicuous even in those Miseries and Infirmities which are so numerous in our present Condition, and which are sometimes useful and advantageous; that the Passions are good in themselves, and that by using them well or ill, we produce as well private as publick Happiness or Calamities. That the Notion embraced by Man, *that all is made for him*, is the original of his Mistakes, and of his unreasonable Complaints against Providence, it being certain that He is made for the Whole, not the Whole for Him.

The *third Epistle* teaches Man, that it is vain to endeavour after an Happiness unconnected with that of others; and that he neither can nor ought to be happy, but as he contributes to the reciprocal Communication of Happiness established between all the different Parts of

---

[1] *June* 1736. [Further, see R. W. Rogers, 'Critiques of the *Essay on Man* in France and Germany 1736–1755', *English Literary History*, xv (1948), 176–93]

the Universe, which is the great Object of the Creator's Regard. This Disposition for Happiness can be produced only by Virtue, and therefore as Men improve in Virtue, they advance in Felicity.

But the Author does not confine himself to inspire his Readers with that Justice, Benevolence, and Rectitude of Mind which constitutes an honest Man, but raises their Thoughts, by a just Gradation from natural and moral Virtues, to the Perfection which mere Nature cannot attain. Though Christianity presupposes moral Honesty, there is nevertheless a great Distance from one to the other; Faith only can bring to Perfection those Virtues which Reason can only sketch out: He therefore shews, in the *fourth Epistle*, that whoever would attain to the utmost Happiness which his present Condition admits, and assure himself of eternal Felicity in a future State, must elevate his Mind, above the Doctrines of mere Reason, apply himself to the Precepts of Religion, and found his Happiness upon a steady Faith, an unshaken Hope, and a glowing Charity.

This is a short View of the general Plan of the Poem, which has no other Tendency than to inflame us with an ardent Love both of God and Man, to raise in us an exalted Idea of the great Creator, and enforce an implicit Submission to his Will. I am therefore surprised that some Readers of this Translation, after having owned, that in some Places they could not understand it, should pretend to discover in it a lurking Poison, and charge it with the Absurdities of *Spinosa*'s System. An Accusation so ill-grounded does not deserve that any Time should be spent in confuting it, as it has obtained Credit only among very few, and these either unable to form a true Judgment of the Question, or misled by a Desire to discover in Mr. *Pope* those Notions which they have themselves unhappily adopted. I shall therefore forbear to engage in so needless a Controversy, and refer it to the *Journal des Scavans*,[1] the *Memoires de Trevoux*,[2] and the *Observations upon modern Writings*, Vol. IV. Letter 47. The Character of Mr. *Pope* is a sufficient Vindication, and ought to secure his Work from such odious Suspicions. He has always openly professed the Catholick Religion, in which he was born and educated, in a Country where so much is lost by dissenting from the established Religion, that every Man who adheres to any other Communion, gives a sufficient Testimony of his Sincerity. Those Enemies which his Merit has raised in his own Country, are so far from doubting his Principles, that they reproach him with them in their Libels, and pretend, however ridiculously, that his Popery affects his

[1] *April 1736.*   [2] *June 1736.*

Compositions, and deprives them of that daring Freedom of Thought which they regard as the very Soul of Poetry.

Strict Justice however requires, that in reading the following Poem, we never suffer ourselves to forget the Title, and that we always remember that we are not promised a compleat Body or System, but a mere *Essay*, and that this is only *the general Map of Man*.[1]

It was not his Design to give us a Collection of all that might be said on so extensive a Subject, but only to lay down the general Principles upon which Morality is founded. It is always to be remembred that he writes not in the Character of a Divine, but of a Philosopher, a Philosopher professing Christianity, who, by making the proper Use of the Light of Reason, disposes the Mind to admit the brighter Illuminations of Faith, and ends at the very Point at which the Divine is to begin.

I therefore cannot but flatter myself that I have done some Service to the Publick, by translating this Work, which is of a particular Kind, too short to frighten away Indolence by its Bulk, and yet large enough to instruct and improve, written with too much Truth and Judgment to shock the Reader with unheard of Singularities, and yet so disposed and contrived as to recommend the most common Maxims and known Truths, by an Air of Novelty, too much embellished to appear tedious or jejune, and yet so just and solid as to engage the Attention rather by the Strength of Argument, and Importance of Precept, than by the Glare of Expression, and Variety of Images. *It is with Poetry*, says Mr. *de Fenelon, as with Architecture, the necessary Parts must be made ornamental, but every Ornament which serves no other Purpose than that of Embellishment is to be rejected as superfluous*.[2] This Precept Mr. *Pope* seems always to have had before him; he was determined to write in Verse rather than Prose only by the Desire of expressing himself with greater Closeness; and it is well known that Precepts written in Verse have this farther Advantage, that they strike with more Force upon the Mind, and fix themselves more deeply in the Memory.

Lord *Roscommon* in his Essay upon translated Poetry, affirms, that to succeed in a Translation, we must single out some Writer whose Taste and Sentiments resemble our own.

—*Chuse an Author as you chuse a Friend,*
United by this sympathetic Bond,
You grow familiar, intimate and fond,

[1] *Vide* Pref.
[2] *Lettre à l'Académie Françoise* [*sur l'éloquence, la poesie, l'histoire, Œuvres*, ed. M. Villemain (Paris, 1829), ii. 196].

Your Thoughts, your Words, your Stiles, your Tastes agree,
No longer his Interpreter, but he.[1]

Gladly should I persuade myself that my Choice of this Work was produced, by the Similitude of my own Sentiments to those of my Author; but who would dare to attempt a Translation of him, if such a Resemblance was necessary to his Success?

That Poetry can only be translated into Verse, is agreed, I think, by all the Learned, except Madam *Dacier*, whose Interest in the Question makes her Judgment of no great Weight; and Experience, without Authority, is a sufficient Proof of the Justness of that Opinion, which I shall the less labour to support here, because a Man of the first Character, who has shewn the present Generation, what those learned Magistrates were that appeared in the Time of the Revival of Learning, has in a Work lately published,[2] proved both by unanswerable Arguments, and by his own Example, that nothing but Poetry can give any Representation of the Genius and Manner of a Poet. As this is true of Poetry in general, it is in my Opinion more eminently true of the *English* Poetry. The Writers of that Nation make Use, even in Prose, of such daring Sentiments, and strong Expressions, as our Poetry scarcely ventures to admit, or is able to copy, without losing some Part of their Force. How then shall we, without grasping all the Advantages, and taking all the Liberties which Verse is allowed, be able to give any Idea of their *Poetry*, which rises very far above the Prose even of that Language.

The *English* is allowed, by all who understand it, to be the most concise Language in the World; and this Quality it is in which the Writers of that Country place its Beauty, and for which they prefer it to the *French*, a Language which Lord *Roscommon*, who is acknowledged to have held the first Rank among their Criticks, allows to be copious, florid, pleasing to the Ear, and to have more Softness than the *English*; but defies us to produce a single Instance of equal Strength, Closeness and Energy. A Thought, says he, which we comprehend in a single Line, diffused by a *French* Author, would glitter through whole Pages.[3]

---

[1] [*Critical Essays of the Seventeenth Century*, ed. J. E. Spingarn (1908), ii. 300. In the fourth line, 'Tastes' should read 'souls']

[2] President *Bouhier*'s poetical Translation of *Petronius* on the Civil War.

[3] I know not what Edition of *Roscommon* has fallen into the Hands of Mr. *Du Resnel*, or whence it proceeds, that the Quotation which he has subjoined in his Margin, differs from those Copies which I have seen. The Passage, as he has published it, is this:

In reading this Production of Mr. *Pope*, it is not easy to forbear thinking that he had the Honour of the *English* Brevity in View, which he has preserved so tenaciously, that some have accused him of cramping his Stile, by crouding it too closely. I know not indeed any Writer either of the former or later Ages that can enter into Competition with him, for the Prize of Conciseness, or has said so much in so few Words; but then it must be owned that he sometimes presumes too much upon the Penetration of his Readers, for which Reason some Passages in these Epistles resemble the first rough Draughts of a great Master; they are struck out with a Strength and Spirit that charm the Judicious, but escape the Observation of common Eyes. Those Touches which the Critic looks upon with Admiration, appear rude and artless to the Unskilful, who are inclined to imagine that there are not really in those Sketches the Beauties which more knowing Spectators discover and applaud. If in these Poems there appear some Expressions that may be cut off, either as Superfluities or Repetitions, there is not, even in those considered by themselves, a single Word unnecessary. There is a Distinction to be made between exact Closeness of Expression, which our Critics will not deny the *English*, and exact Regularity of Thought, which they will not so easily allow them.

This Brevity was, in my Opinion, to be most successfully imitated by a close Stile, not weakened by scrupulous Regard to Connection, or a rigid Adherence to the Niceties of Construction. I would not willingly have made Use in my Version of any other Liberties than such as the Author himself must have taken, had he attempted a *French* Translation of his own Work; but I was, by the unanimous Opinion of all those whom I have consulted on this Occasion, and among them of several *Englishmen* compleatly skilled in both Languages, obliged to follow a different Method. The *French* are not satisfied with Sentiments, however beautiful, unless they are methodically disposed. Method

---

> *'Tis copious, florid, pleasing to your Ear,*
> *With Softness, more, perhaps, than ours can bear.*
> *But who did ever in* French *Authors, &c.*

Which in all the Editions that I have read, stands thus:

> *'Tis courtly, florid, and abounds in Words*
> *Of softer Sound than ours perhaps affords.*

How much more poetical and correct this Reading is, requires no Proof, nor is the Difference only in Elegance but in Truth. The genuine reading only admits that the *French* Language is *courtly*, a Quality which cannot be denied to a Speech consisting wholly of Hyperbole: The Passage, as cited by *Du Resnel*, asserts it to be copious, an Excellence for which even their own Writers have never ventured to commend it. [Johnson]

being the Characteristic that distinguishes our Performances from those of our Neighbours, and almost the only Excellence which they agree to allow us. That Mr. *Pope* did not think himself confined to a regular Plan in writing his Essay on Criticism I have already observed. I have therefore, by a necessary Compliance with our Taste, divided it into five Cantos; nor have I only in this Particular deviated from the Original, but have changed the Place of some Sentiments, which seemed too far distant from each other, and have connected some Passages which appeared independent of the main Work.

The Essay on Man is in Reality more methodically drawn up, tho' the Order of its Parts is not very easily discovered by those who are accustomed to the exact Regularity of our Treatises in Prose. But every one knows that Poetry could not admit of Divisions, Definitions, Proofs, Objections, and Solutions, without losing its Spirit, languishing into Prose, and being entirely deprived of that Freedom and Wildness that constitute its Character. But tho' a Poet may, without Censure, pass from one Thought to another, without leading the Reader through a regular Transition, yet he is to take Care that his Thoughts have, tho' not a verbal, an intellectual Connection, and that they follow one another in such a Train as corresponds with the natural Order of Things. And therefore whenever Mr. *Pope* appeared to have neglected to follow this Rule, I have chosen to conform to the Taste of our Nation, without regarding whether Strangers will call it Weakness or Accuracy, or being at all solicitous about the Censure usually thrown upon us, that we are Babes that cannot take a single Step without being led. But it was not in my Power to reduce these Poems to such a Method as a *Frenchman* expects, without forsaking the Province of a Translator, and modelling them afresh; it is, however, not so much the Manner in which the *English* range their Notions that has made several considerable Alterations necessary, as that in which they form them.

Whatever is foreign, says *Aristotle*, raises Admiration, and whatever raises Admiration gives Pleasure; a Remark, which, tho' perhaps generally true, is not applicable to us, who are accused of endeavouring by a national Prejudice, which we call the Love of Elegance, to reduce every Thing to our own Notions; and certain it is, that a foreign Air is so far from a Recommendation to our Favour, that we are strongly pre-possessed to its Disadvantage. As in this Particular we resign our-selves up rather to Inclination than to Reason, these Impressions can only be effaced by Time and Custom; Reformers, that proceed but slowly, and act generally in a Manner that we ourselves scarcely perceive.

Since the last Peace we have begun to be more acquainted with the *English*, and most who desire to be thought either Men of Taste or Learning, think themselves obliged to study their Language. We are now no longer Strangers to the great Writers of that Nation, from whom some of our Authors, if they could be suspected of understanding them, might be reasonably imagined to have learned the Use of some very extraordinary Words, as well as the Art of distinguishing between the several Passions and Inclinations of the Mind, where scarcely any Difference is to be found, and the Practice of expressing these Subtilties in a metaphysical Cant, not more intelligible than that of the Schools. But this Kind of Conformity is of too late a Commencement to prove that we are naturally disposed to a Simularity of Notions; and it is Matter of Wonder that these two Nations, so near to each other by Situation, should be so remote in their Tastes and Ideas. We approach more nearly to the *Italians*, tho' neither they, nor the *English*, are without something in their Writings which appears to us extremely odd and singular; but their Singularities or Oddnesses are different; and this Difference it may not be improper to explain, that the Reader may have a more adequate Conception of the *English* Writers.

The *Italian*, transported by his Fire, and Vigour of Imagination, flies off, if I may use that Term, in Spirit, and presents us with the Quintessence of his Genius. The *Englishman* dives into himself, and draws all his Conceptions from the Depth of his own Breast. The *Italian* only pleases us by his Ingenuity, the *Englishman* only strikes us by his Solidity. . . .

[Du Resnel continues to compare the English and Italian genius, then the English and French. He notes]

. . . Mr. *Pope*, in his *Essay on Criticism*, uses this Comparison:

> So modern 'Pothecaries taught the Art,
> By Doctors Bills, to play the Doctor's Part;
> Bold in the Practice of mistaken Rules,
> Prescribe, apply, and call their Masters Fools.   [ll. 108–11]

This Image with which the *English* are pleased, shocks every *Frenchman* to whom I have mentioned it. It may be remarked that the Word *Apothecary* is the same, except the Termination, in both Languages, and therefore no Reason can be given why it may not be used in both with equal Dignity or Propriety; or why certain unpleasing Ideas annexed in common Conception to that Profession, may not as well be revived by the Mention of it, in one Country as another. We can therefore only ascribe this Difference to the opposite Character of the two Nations, of which one regards every Thing that is of Use in common Life, as indifferent at least, if not elevated, provided it have nothing contrary to our natural Ideas; and the other habitually considers every Phrase appropriated to those Actions or Employments which do not belong to Persons of high Rank, as low and despicable.

[Du Resnel develops the question of the relativity of taste. He defends his translation of Pope, and concludes]

. . . With regard to my Stile, I suppose it is not necessary to inform the Reader, that he is not to expect here the Pomp and Elevation of the Epic Language, or of those Poems of which the Diction is adapted to marvellous Events, and great Actions. Instruction, not Imagery, is the Business of the didactic Writer, and the Excellencies of his Stile are Simplicity, Accuracy, and Perspicuity. The Poets of this Class, if they can claim that Title, apply to the Reason, not the Imagination, and are therefore not at Liberty to give full Play to the Efforts of Genius. So generally has this Truth been allowed, that *Horace* has, by many Critics,[1] been affirmed to have descended in his Epistles from the natural Sublimity of his Stile to make his Precepts more efficacious, and to shew that his Instructions were founded on Truth, and needed not the Assistance of sounding Syllables, or Magnificence of Language.

There are, however, some Elegancies and Ornaments which didactic Poetry may properly admit, tho' its Province is always rather that of instructing than entertaining; and even Mr. *Pope*, tho' he teaches with more Politeness, Insinuation and Address, than his Predecessors, is nevertheless a Teacher, and has consequently something disgusting in his Manner. He endeavours not to dissipate the Attention by Variety, but to contract it to a single Point. To impress his Precepts with more Force, he sometimes traces back his own Reasonings, and returns to his first Principles.

For the Relief of his Readers he sometimes roves into Digressions, but there are few who are willing to be fatigued for the sake of knowing the Satisfaction of Repose. Satire contributes much to the Pleasure of this kind of Performances, but the Strokes which are to be found here,

---

[1] [Du Resnel has a note: 'Voyez les jugemens des Sçavans, par M. Baillet à l'Article d'Horace.']

will not much gratify the Malignity of corrupt Hearts, because they are for the most Part general, or, if ever pointed at particular Persons, directed at such as are not known in our Country. Whoever therefore will be his Pupil here, must attend only from principles of Reason, a Kind of Attention, which even Philosophers can rarely support without some Struggles and Reluctance.

These Poems are therefore by no Means accommodated to those who read, rather to lull themselves in Tranquillity and Indolence, than to enlarge their Views and fortify their Minds. But those who penetrate farther, who are not afraid of the Labour of Reflection, and whose Judgments are too solid to applaud a Book which does not require more than a single reading, will find here no disagreeable Employment.

Should any Man attempt to run over the Maxims of *Rochefoucault* with equal Rapidity as a Novel or a History, he would harass himself without Advantage, and would find only a Croud of Maxims that would burthen the Mind, without enriching it, unless he allowed himself Time to dwell upon them, and to apply them to his own Ideas and Experience.

To make the Translation of the *Essay on Criticism* more compleat, and more useful to young Readers desirous of forming a Taste, and qualifying themselves to judge upon solid and extensive Principles, not only of Poetry, but of all the polite Arts, I have subjoined to some particular Passages, either my own Observations, or Remarks extracted from Authors ancient or modern of greater Authority, in which some of Mr. *Pope*'s Sentiments are more fully explained. . . .

83. Crousaz attacks *An Essay on Man*

1737

J. P. de Crousaz, extract from *Examen de l'essai de M. Pope sur l'homme* (1737). The translation given here is that by Elizabeth Carter, *An Examination of Mr Pope's Essay on Man. Translated from the French of M. Crousaz* (1739).

Crousaz (1663–1748) was a Protestant professor at Lausanne who vigorously opposed Bayle and Leibniz. His conviction that Pope's *Essay on Man* was 'Spinozist', which he expressed at length in the *Examen* and later in his *Commentaire* (1738), provided the centre for the long and bitter debate over the poem's religious tendencies. Further, see Introduction, pp. 20–2. The passage given here is only a fragment of his long and heavy-handed analysis. Elizabeth Carter's translation was completed by November 1738, but not published until 1739. The footnotes are Dr. Johnson's.

PREFACE

I DO not remember that ever I experienc'd the Power of Poetry so strongly as in Mr. *Pope's Essay*. What Author is there who is not lost in a Translation? And what Poet who is not misrepresented in Prose? If any are to be excepted, Mr. *Pope* is one of the first. We find in him one of the most judicious Remarks in *Horace* exactly verify'd.

IT is not enough to constitute a Poem, that the Verses be composed of certain Words in Number and Measure, if, when you displace them, the Expressions are reduced to mere Prose. But change the Situation and Order of these Words as much as you please, there will always remain a certain noble and sublime Air, that still retains the Rapture of Poetry. [*Sermones*, I. iv. 56ff.]

THE Justice which I have now done Mr. *Pope* is agreeable to the public Voice. This goes so far, that I have seen several of his Readers admire him, like the rest, tho' they did not understand him, and indeed were very far from understanding him. I am pleased with thinking that a few Lines from his Pen have had Credit enough to reconcile the Vulgar to the Notion of a Plurality of Worlds, which a great many Persons, even now, refuse to admit. However, this is a Notion that our Age has great Reason to congratulate itself upon; it seems to me to be of very great Use to raise our Admiration of the incomprehensible Infinity of our Creator. . . .   [pp. i–ii]

AN EXAMINATION OF MR POPE'S ESSAY ON MAN

. . . To write as a Philosopher we must conform ourselves to this Method, or one like it; whereas, a Poet is the Master of his Subject, and in this Quality he disposes it as he thinks proper. The Philosopher takes a Pride in giving Instruction, in resolving Difficulties, and dissipating Doubts and Obscurities. But the Poet, without any Intention to deceive, aims to surprize, to agitate, and wholly to engage his Reader. Mr. *Pope*'s Essay in particular seems to me an Imitation of the Epic Poem. *Homer* begins his with the *Wrath* of *Achilles*, and in his Progress finds means to recur to the Original of the *Trojan War*. Mr. *Pope* begins his *Essay on Man*, by attacking his Pride; and his Enthusiasm inflaming his Aversion and Contempt of this Vice, he cannot suffer any thing which has the least Tendency to it, even in the Chiefs of the Universe. After having fall'n severely upon their Ambition, he gives himself the utmost Liberty, and his Reader too grants it him, with regard to Man in general. He begins with promising a good deal; and his Reader allur'd thereby, takes heart to follow him thro' all his bold Career. He makes him hope for Diversion, v. 15. but 'tis an innocent one.——

Laugh where we must,—

This we are obliged to him for. Afterwards he gains our Esteem by adding—

—be candid where we can.

And at last we respectfully give ourselves up to his Guidance, when he finishes the Period in Terms so becoming a Man of Sense——

But vindicate the Ways of God to Man. v. 16.

He is to speak of the rest *en passant:* But this is the End, we expect, he will never lose Sight of.

AFTER an Invitation to Rapture and Wit, which we should find it difficult to refuse, Mr. *Pope* enters upon his Subject, and gives us reason to hope that he will at once treat of God and Man.[1] This Plan is a very judicious one. What Benefit would the Knowledge of ourselves afford us, if we remain ignorant of our Creator? I know nothing of myself, if I know not from whence I came. It is with great Propriety too that he adds, 'Tis ours to seek God in that World wherein he has placed us.[2] This Notion is exactly agreeable to that of those sage Divines who put a Distinction between searching what God is in himself, and what he is with respect to us, that is to say, those Relations he has been pleased to enter into with Man. The Light of Revelation is entirely conformable to this Plan, and it instructs us chiefly in that which God judges proper to be with regard to us.

THO' Mr. *Pope* asks, v. 19.

> *Of Man what see we but his Station here?*

he had said a little before, v. 3, 4.

> —— *Life can little more supply*
> *Than just to look about us and to die.*

This is, indeed, very little, and should seem hardly worth the Trouble of composing a Book.

BUT I hope, Sir, you have not forgot a Remark which I almost begun with; it is, that the Poet is Master of his Subject. Writers of this Sort have long been granted a Power of chusing what they think fit to say, and disposing it in what Order they please. Mr. *Pope* makes it appear at first Sight, that his Design is to humble Man: This is an End he always keeps in view, and certainly nothing is more *little*, or more contemptible than Man, if this be all his Lot. To finish a Course so short, so laborious, so perplex'd and dark, is not worth the being born for.

IN order to support the Right he assumes to look upon Man with so much Contempt, he bears him down with Questions. After having led

---

[1] *Mr. Pope's Words are:*

> Say first of God above, and Man below,
> What can we *reason*, but from what we *know?*

ESSAY *on* MAN, *Epist.* I. *v.* 17, 18.
[Johnson]

[2] *Mr. Crousaz has this Distich in view:*

> Thro' Worlds unnumber'd tho' the God be known,
> 'Tis ours to trace him only in our own.

v. 22.
[Johnson]

him thro' the Immensities of Space and innumerable Worlds that fill the Extent of the Universe, after having imitated a Flight of *Homer*, and spoken of the *great Chain*,

> —— *which draws all to agree,*
> *And drawn supports* ——   Verse 33.

he does not give him Time to recover breath, but asks him, with an insulting Air,

> *Presumptuous Man! the Reason would'st thou find*
> *Why form'd so weak, so little, and so blind;*
> *First, if thou canst, the harder Reason guess,*
> *Why form'd no weaker, blinder, and no less?*
> *Ask of thy Mother Earth, why Oaks were made*
> *Taller or stronger than the Weeds they shade?*
> *Or ask of yonder argent Fields above,*
> *Why* Jove's *Satellites are less than* Jove?   Verse 35, &c.

IT is an easy Matter to perplex a Man after having stupified him with so many and such great Objects, which he has been forced to run through in so rapid a Manner; and I am persuaded, that the major Part of Mr. *Pope*'s Readers will find themselves reduced to Silence, and will think that Way the most eligible. However,[1] we have no need to enquire of the azure Plains in order to be inform'd by them how it comes to pass that the Satellites of *Jupiter* are less than the great Planet to whose Uses they are assign'd; it was not necessary for *him* to have them larger, and the Bigness of our Moon is sufficient for *us*. Oaks are much larger than the Shrubs that grow at their Feet, and their Fruits are of a different Use from that of those Shrubs. *Animals* stand in Need of this Abundance, and the Timber of Oak is of great Service to *us* in our Edifices and Ships. Mr. *Pope* (I repeat it) has not undertook to give

---

[1] See the subsequent Verses.
> *Respecting* Man *whatever wrong we call,*
> *May, must be right, as relative to* All.
> *In human Works, though labour'd on with Pain,*
> *A thousand Movements scarce one Purpose gain;*
> *In God's, one single can its End produce,*
> *Yet serves to second too some other Use.*
> *So Man, who here seems principal alone,*
> *Perhaps acts second to some Sphere unknown,*
> *Touches some Wheel, or verges to some Goal;*
> *'Tis but a Part we see, and not a Whole.*   Ep. I. ver. 51, &c.

us a compleat System of human Nature. His Intention was not to extricate us from our Ignorance, but to mortify our Pride. And lest we should be mistaken here, and bound his Ideas of *Man* too much, he insinuates from the Beginning, that *Man* comprehends much more than he designs to mention. v. 6, 7.

> *A might Maze, but not without a Plan;*
> *A Wild where Weeds and Flowers promiscuous shoot.*

HE hints by this at the Contradictions which are found to be included in Man. Several Authors have discoursed very wisely and judiciously upon our Excellencies and Defects, and 'tis incontestable, that we are obliged by our Duty to the Necessity of studying ourselves either in one or other of these Lights.

A MAN who can be satisfied to be ignorant of the Value of those Talents which God has given him, does not elevate his Mind in Thanksgiving, but passes his Life in a voluntary and criminal Ingratitude. On the other hand, a Man who does not make a proper Animadversion upon his Weakness, may easily presume too much on his Strength, and not be circumspect enough in his Study of himself and other Objects. But Mr. *Pope* has not entered into an Engagement of exhausting his Subject. He was not obliged to it, he confin'd himself to a Poem in which unfolds only *Part* of *Man*.

WHEN a young Tree leans on one Side, and by that means forms a disagreeable Figure, we are not content to set it upright, but bend it rather more than it ought on the opposite Side. This is a vulgar, but a just Comparison. Mr. *Pope*, that he may the more effectually compass his End, does not scruple to make use of exaggerated Expressions. Verse 35, &c.

> —— *The Reason would'st thou find,*
> *Why form'd so weak, so little, and so blind?*

WE are very far from being nothing but Weakness; for, with regard to the Body, Man has invented Machines, by the Means of which he can lift and transport Burdens too heavy for the strongest Animal; and as to the Mind, to what a Length have Discoveries already been carried, and how large a Way is opened for those who are willing to use their Endeavours to extend them farther!

THE Terms, *little* and *great*, are relative Terms; this is so true, that we are at the same time both very great and very little: Nor is this peculiar to us; there are no Objects but what are at the same Time infinitely great and infinitely little. As to that Blindness which Mr. *Pope* imputes to us, the Expression is strong, but metaphorical. We are not born blind, nay, have the immediate Use of our Eyes. With regard to our Understanding, 'tis true, we are born in Ignorance, but we are born likewise with an Ability of extricating ourselves from it. It is in our Power to produce in ourselves a Knowledge capable of enlightning us; we are born very imperfect, but with the rich and invaluable Present of being able ourselves to work out our own Perfection.

I WILL add too (but by the way) that the Question why we are form'd so weak, so little, and so blind, may be interpreted in an ill Sense; for 'tis to ourselves that we ought to impute our Errors.[1] A Philosopher, who knew more than Mr. *Pope*, than I, and many other Men, after having well consider'd it, stands fast to this Truth, That *God made Man upright, but they have sought out many Inventions*, that is to say, they have reason'd wrong, they have sought out those Reasonings, and been pleased with them.

FROM all this I conclude, that Mr. *Pope*'s Poem ought not to discourage us. If Mr. *Pope* should be asked, how it comes to pass that he, so weak, so little, so blind a Poet, could presume to bring *Homer* back again to Life, and make him a Native of *England*, worthy the Admiration, not only of the Age wherein he lived, but of all Posterity? All who are acquainted with Mr. *Pope*, and I among them, though I have not that Honour, would be extremely offended at such a Question.

MR. *Pope* seems to run the Hazard of an Answer to the Questions he has raised, and even proposes one with a Confidence which looks very unlike a Genius that believes itself to be *little*, *weak*, and *blind*.

> *Then, in the Scale of Life and Sense, 'tis plain,*
> *There must be some where such a Rank as Man.* v. 48.

THIS Consequence, which he asserts to be so evident, he draws from Mr. *Leibnitz*'s System, which is, that *the infinite Wisdom of the Creator must of all possible Systems have preferred the Best, and that in which every Thing should be compleat.*

---

[1] Mr. *Pope* in this Place considers Man only in his *natural* State, and does not speak of his *moral* Defects. Nor does he at all dissent from *Solomon*, in describing Man as weak, and little, and blind; for so he certainly is, when compared with Beings of a superior Rank, and yet may be very perfect in his own. For (as Mr. *Crousaz* observ'd of *great* and *little*) Perfection is a relative Term, and varies its Signification according as it is differently apply'd. [Johnson]

PERHAPS, Sir, you are acquainted with this System only in general, and in a superficial Manner. I will, therefore, first give you a true Idea of it as briefly as possible, and then consider it as delivered by Mr. *Pope*, whom I would not willingly injure, by laying Opinions to his Charge, which perhaps he is very far from entertaining.

MR. *Leibnitz* agrees, that God created the World, and that he is a Being quite distinct from his Work; in this he differs from *Spinosa*, who seems to have confounded the Cause with its Effect.

GOD, that is to say, the Eternal Being, is such, that it implies a Contradiction for him not to be; Infinite in Power, infinite in Knowledge, he comprehends in himself the Ideas of every Thing he has Power to give Being to. An Infinity of Worlds presents itself to his Mind, but among the Ideas of these innumerable Worlds, there appeared one which, upon the whole, presented a Work more perfect than all the others; and God, infinitely wise and infinitely perfect, was determined, not by constraint, or against his Will, but with a full and perfect Approbation, to prefer to all the rest the System which at present exists, and of which we ourselves make a Part: The all-perfect Nature of God did not suffer him to chuse any other.

These are the Notions of those who defend this System; there is something specious and sublime in it, and very proper to deceive.

LET us examine what is built on these Principles. In order that the Universe might be infallibly such as God its Creator had conceiv'd it, every Thing which it comprehends must subsist by Necessity, and every Thing that is doing in it necessarily and infallibly come to pass.

FOR this end the World is an immense and universal Machine, composed of an infinite number of Machines all depending one upon another; their Springs are framed with so much Accuracy and Force, that not one of them fails of playing its Part; and all Events which succeed one another, are the inevitable Consequences of the first Impulse that set them in Motion.

AMONG these Machines, which hold their Existence from the Eternal Creator, we are acquainted with two Sorts; the one merely Corporeal, the other capable of Thoughts, Sentiments, Desires, &c. and to these we have given the name of Spirits, or Intellectual Substances.

MAN is composed of these two Substances; but, say these Gentlemen, this Truth has great need of Explanation, and People have been hitherto very grossly deceived in it.

A BODY is incapable of producing any Thing whatever upon a Soul; it can cause neither Ideas, Sentiments, nor Volitions to be raised in it:

The Soul for its Part has no greater Power over the Body, and is equally incapable either of inclining or restraining its own. What then is Man? According to these Gentlemen, he is this:

As soon as one of these Machines which we call the human Body is, by the Effect of an innumerable Succession of Combinations, all inevitable, and necessarily join'd to one another, arrived to a certain Degree of Activity and Bigness; at the same Time, and by the Effect of another Succession of Combinations equally necessary and inevitable, a Thinking Being perceives Ideas, Sentiments, Volitions, exactly corresponding to the different Conditions of this Body; and among these Manners of Thinking, there is one of them which governs and reigns universally: It is the Imagination of this Soul, which persuades itself that it receives Impressions from its Body, and makes it act conformably to its Will. *Mere Imaginations*, say they, *perpetual Illusions!*

[pp. 5–19]

. . . LET us carry the System further, for we must bear Mr. *Pope* company. Every Thing which we see, comes to pass by an inevitable Consequence of the first Impulse, which was impress'd on the universal Machine, and on all the Parts that compose it. One says, that there is no God, and looks upon the Imagination of one as extravagant. *Spinosa* admits one, but who as effectually destroys all Religion, as the *Atheist* does. Mr. *Leibnitz* too has formed an Idea of one after his Manner, which, in the general opinion of Mankind, no less overturns Religion. It would require whole Volumes to give but a tolerable Idea of the Pagan Divinities and their Worship. I tremble, and am not able to express the Consequences of this System with regard to *Moses* and the Prophets, to *Jesus Christ* and his Apostles, and to *Mahomet* and his Followers. The Universe would have been a Work too imperfect, and too unworthy the Choice of its Author, if there had been but so much as one of these Imaginations wanting. It is the same with regard to Crimes: Since there have been Parricides, it was essential to the Perfection of the Universe that there should be such; it was necessary that there should be Poisoners, Assassins, perjur'd Villains, Traitors, Cheats of all Kinds; it was necessary there should be unnatural Conjunctions; in a word, not one of those Horrors should be wanting, which are the Reproach of Human Nature. It was necessary there should be Inquisitors to exercise without Mercy, all the horrid Cruelties on good People, whose Crime consisted in so great a Veneration for what they believed true, as not to abjure it: All that we have been saying, and an infinite number of Events of this Nature, would have for their first invincible and inevitable Cause, the Eternal Being, the Principle of all.

THE *Athenians* had no Law against Assassins, and those who poison their Parents, because this was a Case that never entered into their Mind, and was believed impossible. But how imperfect was the Universe then! There were no Parricides, and Circumstances had not yet given an Opportunity for them to *play*.

A WOMAN is determined to cause her Husband to be assassinated; the Fear of Death makes her resolve to affirm the Negative, in spite of the sharpest Torments; at last she yields, and loses her Life in the Shame, and Punishment, which by such horrible Torments she had sought to avoid. She was handsome and well shap'd, she had Wit, a tender Heart, and Sprightliness; the Sight of her drew Tears from the Eyes even of those Persons who were shock'd at her Crime. But if the *Leibnitzian* System be adopted, in what will the Fault of this unfortunate Creature be made to consist? Such is the immutable Nature of the Eternal Being, that it was not possible but that this Woman, so handsome, so genteel, must run into all that she acted, at the Time destined and appointed for this Event, its Origin, and its Consequences; all this was a Result of the inevitable Construction of the Universe, and of the first impulse impressed on it.

I HAVE been assured, that in *Scotland* a Minister assassinated his Son without hating him, and without showing by any other Sign that his Reason was disorder'd. We may call the Dispositions, which were the Cause of it, a *cold Madness*; being brought before the Judges, he confess'd with great Tranquillity to them, that the *Fact was* an horrid one. *Why then did you do it? Alas!* answer'd he, *how could I avoid it? The Event proves that I had not this Power, the Moment and Manner of my Son's death were inevitably appointed.* He was not yet initiated into Mr. *Leibnitz*'s System, else he would have added, If my Machine had not played in this Manner, the whole Universe would have been in disorder; the further Cohesion of its Parts, one single Piece failing, is quite interrupted, and the rest can no longer keep on its Progress.[1]

---

[1] I suppose the following Lines are alluded to; perhaps the Remarker strains them a little too much.

> —*In the full Creation leave a Void,*
> *Where, one Step broken, the great Scale's destroy'd:*
> *From Nature's Chain whatever Link you strike,*
> *Tenth, or ten thousandth, breaks the Chain alike.*

Mr. *Pope*'s ESSAY on MAN, Epist. I. v. 235.
[Johnson

THIS, Sir, is an Idea of the System; when 'tis comprized in an Epitome, one Part is hid, and all the Horror of it is not suffered to be seen. I design to enlarge it, and from thence examine this Idea in all its Particulars; but this shall be in another Work. I imagine you are impatient to ask me, whether I believe that Mr. *Pope* has actually adopted this System?[1] I answer you, that I refuse to believe this, till I am forced to it by more Proofs than I find of it in his Book: For after all, ought a Reader to take the Liberty of making a celebrated Author guilty of a Contradiction?

> *Laugh where we must, be candid where we can;*
> *But vindicate the Ways of God to Man.*   Ver. 15.

THIS is the great End that Mr. *Pope* in express Terms takes upon himself. Shall we dare affirm that, after this magnificent Promise, he all on a sudden mistakes, and instead of justifying the Ways of God, justifies Man, who has it not in his Power to avoid any one thing of all he does, so that the Creator alone stands charged with all the Horrors and Confusions that make the Reproach of Human Nature?

ANOTHER palpable Contradiction; WHATEVER IS, IS RIGHT, says he, at the End of his first Book. At the Sight of King *Charles* the First's losing his Head on a Scaffold, he ought to have said, THIS IS RIGHT. At the Sight of the Judges who condemn'd him, he must have said too THIS IS RIGHT. On seeing some of those very Judges taken and condemned for having done what was acknowledged to be RIGHT, he must have cried out, DOUBLY RIGHT. When his dear Friend, Lord *Bolingbroke*, was disgraced, the System required that he should say, THIS IS RIGHT. But Mr. *Pope* himself makes this Prediction:

> *When Heroes, Statesmen, Kings in Dust repose,*
> *Whose Sons shall blush their Fathers were thy Foes,*
>   Epist. IV. Verse 74.

What should they blush at? At that which is right? They could not blush at any Thing else, for

WHATEVER IS, IS RIGHT.

---

[1] See Mr. *Pope's Universal Prayer*, the third Stanza.

> *Yet left me in this dark Estate,*
> *To know the Good from Ill;*
> *And binding* Nature *fast in* Fate,
> *Left Conscience free and Will.*

You will ask me too, Sir, perhaps with more Impatience, How it comes to pass that Mr. *Pope* fix'd on this Episode? I answer, that it is quite useful to his End; his great Design is to humble Man, and what can be more mortifying for Man than a System full of Horror, invented, colour'd, dress'd up, and publish'd by a Man who knew how to acquire a great Reputation. 'Tis on this Occasion that one may ask,

O *human Soul, weak, bounded, and blind*, who dost not know thyself, how darest thou undertake to sound the Depths of the Divine Nature? How darest thou rely so confidently on thy weak Understanding, as not to dread the terrible Consequences which flow so naturally and inevitably from thy daring Principles?

Is it permitted to a Man to believe that he is well enough assured of the Depths of Divine Knowledge, and has an Idea of it just enough to conclude from thence, that it was not possible for this infinite Intelligence to form different Plans of the Universe, every one of which, upon the whole, should be as perfect, and as worthy of the Choice of its divine Author as the rest?

HE alone is the absolutely perfect Infinite; it is impossible that what is produced from nothing can have a Perfection equal to his; and among Beings whose Perfection does not reach to an infinite Degree, why may there not be some equal to one another? Even if one should be easy enough to agree to this strange Paradox, that *two finite Beings distinct from one another, but entirely equal, should be but one and the same Being*; of two different Things, why might not one have as much Perfection as the other? To deny that the Divine Power extends to such a Production, seems to me one of the most daring Pieces of Temerity.

GOD stands in need of nothing. The perfect Infinite is self-sufficient. Can one dare to think that he was not enough satisfied with himself, till after he had exercised his Power in the Production of Creatures? Without them he is THE ETERNAL, THE INFINITE, THE PERFECT, THE BLESSED GOD; 'tis by a Choice of his Goodness, entirely free, that he was determined to create, rather than not to create.

[pp. 24–33]

84. Dr Warburton replies to Crousaz

1738

William Warburton, *A Vindication of Mr. Pope's Essay on Man, from the Misrepresentations of M^r De Crousaz . . . In Six* [i.e. seven] *Letters* ([1740] 2nd ed., 1740), pp. 1-2, 17-28.

Warburton's six letters, of which the second is given here in its entirety, first appeared in the *Works of the Learned*, iv (December 1738), 425ff., and v (January–April 1739), 56ff., 89ff., 159ff., 330ff. This material was reworked for Warburton's *Critical and Philosophical Commentary on Mr. Pope's Essay on Man* published in 1742. The quotations from Crousaz are not from Elizabeth Carter's translation (No. 83), and seem to come direct from the French.

Pope was deeply grateful for Warburton's intervention on his behalf. Further, see Introduction, pp. 21-2.

LETTER I.

WHEN a great Genius, whose Writings have afforded the World much Pleasure and Instruction, happens to be enviously attack'd and wrongfully accused, it is natural to think, that a Sense of Gratitude due from Readers so agreeably entertain'd, or a Sense of that Honour resulting to our Country from such a Writer, should raise a general Indignation. But every Day's Experience shews us the very contrary. Some take a malignant Satisfaction in the Attack; others a foolish Pleasure in a literary Conflict; and the greater Part look on with an absolute Indifference.

M^r *De Crousaz's* Remarks on Mr. *Pope's Essay on Man*, as he saw it thro' the Medium of a *French* Translation, have just fallen into my Hands. As those Remarks appear to me very groundless and unjust, I thought so much due to Truth, as to vindicate our Countryman from his Censure.

I shall therefore in the first place give the Reader a fair and just Idea of the *Reasoning* of that Epistle, so egregiously misrepresented; in which I shall not consider it as a *Poem*, (for it stands not in need of the Licence of such kind of Works to defend it,) but as a *System of Philosophy*; and content myself with a plain Representation of the Sobriety, Force, and Connection of that Reasoning. . . .

LETTER II.

HAVING shewn what Mr. *Pope*'s System really is, I come now to shew what it is *not*; namely, what Mr *Crousaz* has the Injustice, or the Folly, to represent it. He begins with saying, that 'Mr. *Pope* seems to him quite throughout his System to embrace the *pre-established Harmony* of the celebrated *Leibnitz*, which, in his Opinion, establishes a Fatality destructive of all Religion and Morality.'—That the *pre-established Harmony* of *Leibnitz* terminates in Fate, I readily allow; but that Mr. *Pope* has espoused that impious Whimsy, is an utter Chimæra. The *pre-established Harmony* was built upon, and is an outrageous Extension of, a Conception of *Plato*'s; who combating the atheistical Objections about the Origin of Evil, employs this Argument in Defence of Providence. That amongst an infinite Number of possible Worlds in God's Idea, this which he hath created, and brought into being, with a Mixture of Evil, is the *best*. But if the *best*, then Evil consequently is *partial*, comparatively small, and *tends* to the greater Perfection of the *whole*.— This Notion was espoused and illustrated by Lord *Shaftesbury*, and since by Mr. *Pope*. But neither was *Plato* a fatalist, nor is there any Fatalism in the Argument. As to the Truth of the Notion, that is another Question; and how far it clears up the very difficult controversy about the Origin of Evil, that is still *another*. That it is a full Solution of the Difficulties about the Origin of Evil, I cannot think, for Reasons too long to be given in this Place. Perhaps we shall never have a full Solution here. However, what may justify Mr. *Pope* in embracing this *Platonic* Notion, is, that it has been received by the most celebrated and orthodox *Fathers* and *Divines* of the ancient and modern Church.

This Doctrine, we own, was taken up by *Leibnitz*; but it was to ingraft upon it a most pernicious Fatalism. *Plato* said, God *chose* the best: *Leibnitz* said, he *could not but* chuse the best. *Plato* supposed Freedom in God, to chuse one of two Things equally good: *Leibnitz* contended that the Supposition was absurd; but however, admitting the Case, God could *not* chuse one of two Things equally good. Thus it appears the first contended for *Freedom*; and that the latter, notwithstanding the most artful Disguises in his *Theodice* [1710], was a rank *Fatalist*.

Now we see, that from the Principle of *Plato*, as well as that of *Leibnitz*, this grand Consequence follows, THAT WHATEVER IS, IS RIGHT; because every thing in this World, even Evil itself, tends to the greater Perfection of the *whole*. This Mr. *Pope* employs as a *Principle* throughout a Poem, intended to humble the Pride of Man, who would impiously make God accountable for his Creation. What then does common Sense teach us to understand by *whatever is, is right*? Did the Poet mean *right* with regard to Man, or *right* with regard to God? *Right* with regard to itself, or *right* with regard to its ultimate Tendency? Surely *with regard to God*: For he tells us, his Design is

> To vindicate the Ways of God to Man.

Surely with regard to its ultimate Tendency: For he tell us again,

> All Partial Ill is universal Good.

Yet M^r *De Crousaz* preposterously takes it the other way; and so perversely interpreted, it is no Wonder that he, and his wise Friends, should find the Poem full of Contradictions.

In a Word then, I say, the Principle Mr. *Pope* goes upon is *Plato*'s, and every thing he says is agreeable to the system of *Freedom*, and utterly inconsistent with that of *Fate*: Yet M^r *De Crousaz* persists in his Charge: And the first Proof he produces is the following Passage:

> As much that End a constant Course requires
> Of Showers and Sunshine, as of Man's Desires;
> As much eternal Springs and cloudless Skies,
> As Men for ever temp'rate, calm and wise.   [i. 151–4]

On which the Examiner thus remarks. —— 'A continual Spring and a Heaven without Clouds would be fatal to the Earth and its Inhabitants; but can we regard it as a Misfortune that Men are always sage, calm and temperate? I am quite in the dark as to this Comparison.'—Let us see if we can enlighten him. The Argument stands thus.—Presumptious Man complains of Moral Evil; Mr. *Pope* informs and checks him thus: This Evil, says he, that you complain of, tends to universal Good; for as Clouds, and Rain, and Tempest, are necessary to preserve Health and Plenty in this sublunary World, so the Evils that spring from disorder'd Passions are necessary.—To what? Not to Man's Happiness here, but to the Perfection of the Universe in general. Again,

If Plagues or Earthquakes break not Heav'n's Design,
Why then a *Borgia* or a *Cataline*?   [i. 155–6]

On which the Examiner —— 'These Lines have no Sense but on the
System of *Leibnitz*, which confounds Morals with Physics; and in
which, all that we call Pleasures, Grief, Contentment, Inquietude,
Wisdom, Virtue, Truth, Error, Vices, Crimes, Abominations, are the
inevitable Consequences of a fatal Chain of Things as ancient as the
World. But this is it which renders the System so horrible, as to make
all honest Men shudder at it. It is, indeed, sufficient to humble human
Nature, to reflect that this was invented by a Man, and that others have
adopted it.' —— This is, indeed, very tragical; but we have shewn
above, that it has its Sense on the *Platonic* not the *Leibnitzian* System;
and besides, that the Context confines us to that Sense.

What hath misled the Examiner is, his supposing that the Comparison
is between the Effects of *two Things in this sublunary World*; when not
only the *Elegancy*, but the *Justness of it* consists in its being between the
Effects of a Thing in the *Universe at large*, and the familiar and known
Effects of one in *this sublunary World*. For what is the *Position* inforc'd
in these Lines but this, *that partial Evil tends to the Good of the whole.
How* does the Poet inforce it? Why, if you will believe the Examiner,
by illustrating the Effects of partial moral Evil in a particular System,
by that of partial natural Evil in the same System, and so leaves his
Position in the Lurch; but we must never believe the great Poet could
talk so idly. Does not every one see, that the Way of proving his Point
was by illustrating the Effect of partial moral Evil in the *Universe*, by
partial natural Evil in a *particular System*? And will any one say this was
not his Meaning? Whether partial moral Evil tends to the Good of the
Universe, being a *Question* which, by reason of our Ignorance of many
Parts of that Universe, we cannot decide, but from known Effects; the
Rules of Logick require that it be proved by Analogy, *i.e.* by comparing
it to a Thing certain; and it is a Thing certain, that partial natural Evil
tends to the Good of our particular System. Who then will any
longer doubt that this is the true Meaning of this famous Comparison?
And if so, it stands clear of M^r *De Crousaz*'s Objection, and of *Leibnitz*'s
Fatalism.

The Poet, indeed, might have been more explicit in this place, for
the Sake of common Readers; but he studied *Conciseness*, as he himself
tells us in his Preface, where he gives the Reason of his Method; and
this the Examiner should, in Equity, have considered; for not only the

Genius and *Design* of an Author, but his *Method* likewise should be brought into Account, if we would make a true Estimate of his Performance.

The next Passage the Examiner attacks is the following:

> Better for us, perhaps, it might appear,
> Were there all Harmony, all Virtue here;
> That never Air or Ocean felt the Wind;
> That never Passion discompos'd the Mind;
> But all subsists by elemental Strife,
> *And Passions are the Elements of Life.*   [i. 165–70]

Here the Examiner upbraids Mr. *Pope* for degrading himself so far as to write to the gross Prejudices of the People.

In the corporeal Nature (says he) there is no Piece of Matter that is perfectly simple; all are composed of small Particles, called elementary; a Fermentation proceeds from their Mixture, sometimes weak, and sometimes strong, which still farther attenuates these Particles; and thus agitated and divided, they serve for the Nourishment and Growth of organic Bodies; to this Growth it is we give the Name of Life. But what have the Passions in common with these Particles? Do their Mixture and Fermentation serve for the Nourishment of that Substance which thinks, and do they constitute the Life of that Substance?

—Thus M^r *De Crousaz*, who, as before he could not see the *Nature* of the Comparison, so here, by a more deplorable Blindness, could not see that there was *any* Comparison *at all*, but which yet is so visible, that it only wants repeating to be sensible of it. 'You, says Mr. *Pope*, perhaps may think it would be better, that neither Air or Ocean was vexed with Tempests, nor that the Mind was ever discomposed by Passion; but consider, that as in the one Case our material system subsists by the Strife of its elementary Particles, so in the Intellectual, the Passions of the Mind are, as it were, the Elements of *human Life, i.e.* Actions.' All here is clear, solid, and well-reasoned. What must we say then to our Examiner's wild Talk of *the Mixture and Fermentation of elementary Particles of Matter for the Nourishment of that Substance that thinks, and of its constituting in Life of that Substance.* I call it the Examiner's, for you see it is not Mr. *Pope*'s; and he ought to be loaded with it, because it may be questioned whether it was a *Simple Blunder,* he urging it in so invidious a Manner, as to insinuate that Mr. *Pope* might probably hold the *Materiality of the Soul.* However, if it was a mere

Mistake, it was a pleasant one, and arose from the Ambiguity of the Word *Life*, which in the *English* Tongue, as *la vie* in *French*, signifies both *Existence* and *human Action*, and is always to have its Sense determined by the Context.

But now we come to the most terrible Passage of all:

> All are but Parts of one stupendous Whole,
> Whose Body Nature is, and God the Soul.
> That chang'd thro' all, &c. [i. 267ff.]

On which our Examiner—*A Spinozist* (says he) *would express himself in this Manner*. I believe he would, and so would St. *Paul* too, writing on the same Subject, namely, the Omnipresence of God in his Providence, and in his Substance. *In him we live and move, and have our Being*; i.e. we are *Parts* of him, *his Offspring*, as the *Greek* Poet, a *Pantheist*, quoted by the Apostle, observes: And the Reason is, because both profess to believe the Omnipresence of God. But would *Spinoza*, as Mr *Pope* does, call God *the great directing Mind of all*, who has intentionally created a perfect Universe?[1] Or would Mr. *Pope*, like *Spinoza*, say there is but one universal Substance in the Universe, and that blind too? We know *Spinoza* would not say the first; and we ought not to think Mr. *Pope* would say the latter, because he says the direct contrary throughout the Poem. But it is *this* latter only that is *Spinozism*.

But admitting, for Argument's sake, that there is an Ambiguity in these Expressions, so great, that a *Spinozist* might employ them to express his own particular Principles; (and such a thing might well be, without any Reflection on Mr. *Pope*'s Religion, or Exactness as a Writer, because the *Spinozists*, in order to hide the Impiety of their Principle, are used to express the *Omnipresence* of God in Terms that any religious Theist might employ.) In this Case, I say, how are we to judge of Mr. *Pope*'s Meaning? Surely by the whole Tenor of his Argument. Now take the Words in the Sense of the *Spinozists*, and the Poet labours, in the Conclusion of his Epistle, to overthrow all he has been advancing throughout the Body of it: For *Spinozism* is the Destruction of an Universe, where every Thing tends, by a foreseen Contrivance in all its Parts, to the Perfection of the *Whole*. But suppose him to employ

---

[1] For that is the Meaning of,

> All Nature is but Art unknown to thee,
> All Chance, Direction which thou canst not see. [i. 289–90]

the Passage in the Sense of St. *Paul, that we and all Creatures live, and move, and have our Being in God,* and then it will be the most logical Conclusion from all that had preceded. For the Poet having, as we say, labour'd throughout his Epistle, to prove that every Thing in the Universe tends, by a foreseen Contrivance, and a present Direction of all its Parts, to the Perfection of the *Whole*; it might be objected that such a Disposition of Things implying in God a painful, operose and inconceivable Extent of Providence, it could not be thought that such Care extended to the Whole, but was confined to the more noble Parts of the Creation. This gross Conception of the First Cause the Poet exposes, by shewing that God is equally and intimately present to every Particle of Matter, to every Sort of Substance, and in every Instant of Being, in these charming Lines:

> All are but Parts of one stupendous Whole,
> Whose Body Nature is, and God the Soul;
> That chang'd thro' all, and yet in all the same,
> Great in the Earth, as in th' ætherial Frame,
> Warms in the Sun, refreshes in the Breeze,
> Glows in the Stars, and blossoms in the Trees,
> Lives thro' all Life, extends thro' all Extent,
> Spreads undivided, operates unspent,
> Breathes in our Soul, informs our mortal Part,
> As full, as perfect, in a Hair as Heart;
> As full, as perfect, in vile Man that mourns,
> As the rapt Seraph that adores and burns:
> To him no high, no low, no great, no small,
> He fills, he bounds, connects, and equals all.   [i. 267–80]

How exactly true this is, may be seen by *the Inquiry into the Nature of the human Soul,* a Work that has entirely demolished the whole System of *Spinoza,* where the excellent Author has shewn the Necessity of the *immediate influence of God,* in every Moment of Time, to keep Matter from falling into its original Nothing.

The Examiner goes on: 'Mr. *Pope* has Reason to call this Whole a *stupendous Whole*; nothing being more paradoxical and incredible, if we take his Description literally.' I will add, nor nothing more so than St. *Paul's, in him we live, and move, and have our Being,* if taken literally. I have met with one who took it so, and from thence fell into a monstrous Opinion, *that* SPACE *was* GOD.

But the Examiner pursues Mr. *Pope* to the very End, and cavils even at the following Lines, which might have set him right about the Sense of the foregoing.

> All Nature is but Art unknown to thee,
> All Chance, Direction which thou can'st not see;
> All Discord Harmony not understood,
> *All partial Evil universal Good*;
> And spight of Pride, in erring Reason's Spight,
> One Truth is clear, *Whatever is, is* RIGHT.   [i. 289–94]

How unaccountable is his Perverseness! Mr. *Pope*, in this very Poem, has himself thus explained *Whatever is, is right*.

> Respecting Man, whatever wrong we call,
> May, must be right, as relative to *all*.
> —So Man, who here seems Principal alone,
> Perhaps acts Second to some Sphere unknown,
> Touches some Wheel, or verges to some Gole;
> 'Tis but a Part we see, and not a Whole.   [i. 51–60]

But without any regard to the Evidence of this Illustration, Mr *Crousaz* thus exclaims: 'See Mr. *Pope*'s general Conclusion, *all that is, is right*. So that at the Sight of *Charles* the First losing his Head on the Scaffold, Mr. *Pope* must have said, *this is right*; at the Sight too of his Judges condemning him, he must have said, *this is right*; at the Sight of some of these Judges, taken and condemned for the Action which he had owned to be right, he must have cried out *this is doubly right*.'—Never was any thing more amazing than that the Absurdities arising from the sense in which the Examiner takes Mr. *Pope*'s grand Principle, *whatever is, is right*, should not have shewn him that he had mistaken the Meaning; for could any one in his senses employ a Proposition in a Sense from whence such evident Absurdities immediately arise? I had observed before, that this Proposition of Mr. *Pope*'s, *that whatever is, is right*, is a Consequence of this Principle, that *partial Evil tends to universal Good*. This shews us the only Sense in which the Proposition can be understood, namely, that WHATEVER IS, IS RIGHT, WITH REGARD TO THE DISPOSITION OF GOD, AND TO ITS ULTIMATE TENDENCY. Now is this any Encouragement to Vice? Or does it take off from the Crime of him who commits it, that God providentially produces Good out of Evil? Had Mr. *Pope* abruptly said in his Conclusion, *the Result of all is, that whatever is, is right*, M^r *De Crousaz* had even then been inexcusable for putting so absurd a Sense upon the *Words*, when he might have seen that it was a Conclusion from the general Principle above-mentioned; and therefore must necessarily have another Meaning: But what must we think of him? when the Poet, to prevent Mistakes, had delivered in this very place, the *Principle* itself, and this *Proposition* as the Consequence of it:

> All Discord Harmony not understood;
> *All partial Evil universal Good*;
> And spight of Pride, in erring Reason's Spight,
> One Truth is clear, *Whatever is, is right.* [i. 291–4]

I cannot see how he could have told his Reader plainer, that *this* was the Consequence of *that* Principle, unless he had wrote THEREFORE, in great Church Letters.

In Conclusion, if it were of such Men as these that Mr. *Pope* speaks, when he expresses his Contempt for Modern Philosophers, he might well say,

> Yes, I despise the Man to Books confin'd,
> Who from his Study rails at human Kind,
> Tho' what he learns he speaks, and may advance
> Some general Maxims, or be right by Chance.
>
> [*Epistle to Cobham*, ll. 1–4]
>
> I am, Sir, &c.

85. 'A Hodge-Podge Mess of Philosophy'

1742

Lord Hervey, extract from *A Letter to Mr. C——b——r* ...
(1742), pp. 14–16. Published 19–21 August 1742. For a further
extract from this pamphlet, see No. 71.

Another Proof of Mr. *Pope*'s Want of *Judgment*, as well as *Invention*,
and that he himself understands *the best* of his late Writings no more
than his Readers can understand *the worst*, is his *Essay upon Man*;
in which, resolving to turn *Philosopher*, he has, in order to fit himself
for the Execution of that Task, read every speculative Book upon the
Subject he treats; and whenever a Passage happen'd to strike him in
any of these different Authors, writing upon different Principles, tho'
on the same Subject, and consequently maintaining different Opinions,
and exhibiting different Sentiments, he has put them into most *harmonious Verse*, I confess, but such *discordant Sense*, that he has jumbled
together my Ld *Shaftsbury*, *Montagne*, Lord *Herbert*, *Mandeville*, and
fifty & *cæteras*; till from these fine uniform Originals drawing only
some incongruous Scraps, his whole Work is nothing but a Heap of
poetical Contradictions, and a jarring Series of Doctrines, Principles,
Opinions and Sentiments, diametrically opposite to each other; making
together just such an *Olio, Hodge-Podge Mess of Philosophy*, as one of
Cloe's best Dinners would make of *Food*, if you took his four Courses,
and his hundred and fifty well-dress'd, well-tasted Dishes, and mix'd
them all up together in one great Cauldron, with all their different
Seasonings and Sauces; and thinking there could never be too many,
or too much of good Things, seized the Butler's Charge, and the
Confectioner's Art, the Furniture of the Side-board, and all the Ingredients of the Desert, and threw them into the Bargain amongst the
rest; and then christen'd the whole, *An Essay upon Cookery and good
Eating*.

EPITAPH ON MR. GAY IN WESTMINSTER ABBEY

June/July 1733

86. Swift's criticisms

1733

Jonathan Swift, extract from letter to Pope [30 March 1733], *The Correspondence of Jonathan Swift*, ed. Sir H. Williams (1963), iv. 133.

There are three versions of the epitaph (see Twickenham, vi. 349–52). Pope accepted most of Swift's suggestions. For Dr Johnson's criticism of the poem, see pp. 418–19 below.

I have not seen in so few lines more good sence, or more proper to the Subject. Yet I will tell you my remarks and submit them. The whole is intended for an Apostrophe to the dead person, which however doth not appear till the eighth line, Therefore as I checkt a little at the article *the* twice used in the second line, I imagined it might be changed into *thy* and then the Apostrophe will appear at first, and be clearer to common readers. My Lord Orrery your great admirer saith the word *mixed* suits not so properly the Heroes bust, as the dust of Kings. Perhaps My Lord may be too exact, yet you may please to consider it. The beginning of the last Line, *striking their aking bosoms.*[1] Those last two participles come so near, and sounding so like, I could wish [them] altered, if it might be easily done. The Scripture expression upon our Saviour's death is that the People *smote their breasts*. You will pardon me, for since I have left off writing, I am sunk into a Critick. Some Gentlemen here, object against the expression in the second line, *A*

---

[1] [Swift again attacked this phrase on 1 May, *Correspondence, ed. cit.*, iv. 153]

Child's Simplicity. Not against the propriety but in complyance with the vulgar, who cannot distinguish *Simplicity* & Folly. And it is argued that your Epitaph quite contrary to your other writings, will have a hundred vulgar Readers, for one who is otherwise, I confess, I lay little weight upon this, although some friends of very good understanding, and who have great honor for you, mentioned it to me.

28 December 1734

87. Thomas Bentley satirizes Pope

1735

Thomas Bentley, extracts from *A Letter to Mr. Pope, Occasion'd by Sober Advice from Horace, &c.* (1735), pp. 3-5, 9-18. Published 1-4 March 1735.

Thomas (1693?-1742) was the nephew of Richard Bentley, and a classical scholar like his uncle. The immediate cause for the pamphlet lay in Pope's far from sober and often gross parodies of Richard Bentley's annotations. His nephew's reply considers *An Essay on Man*, the 'Ethic Epistles', and the *Imitations of Horace*, as well as *Sober Advice*. Further on Thomas Bentley, see Twickenham, v. 305-6, 492. Pope's original enmity towards Richard Bentley is traditionally ascribed to a remark, made in his hearing, that the *Iliad* translation 'is not Homer, it is Spondanus' (Joseph Warton, *An Essay on the Genius and Writings of Pope*, ii [1782], 296). However, Bentley had taken the side of the Ancients in the Phalaris controversy, and this together with his unwieldy erudition, made him, in Pope's eyes, a major example of 'False Learning'.

SIR,
I HAVE not met with any body yet, that disputed in the least your being the Author of *Sober Advice from* HORACE, *as delivered in his second Sermon*; nor any body that did not wonder you would publish such a piece. You deny it; and, they say, that's all the Satisfaction one ought to expect. But see now what you have done: You have given us

319

An Imitation of the first Satire of the Second Book of HORACE, mighty pretty; of the *second Satire*, not so well; intending, I guess, to go through the whole; for they not only divert the Town, but, I hear, bring you each of them a round Sum of Money. Deuce take the Author of the *Sermon of Sober Advice*, say I, for anticipating you. He has not acted the part of that *zealous and affectionate Admirer* he professes himself. Here has he published a most obscene thing, worse than any *Bacchanalian* Song made for a Bawdy-house, and gravely told the World, that 'tis *in the Manner of Mr.* POPE. And in his Address to you he says, he can't doubt but you will patronize an Imitation so much in your own Manner, and whose Birth he *can truly say* is owing to you. If you are not the *Author* therefore, you are the *Cause* of it, and on that score not free from Blame. For it was you that first struck into this new way of Writing. An admirable Expedient, and worthy of your Sagacity, *to get upon the Back of* HORACE, that you may abuse every body you don't like, with Impunity! But this Imitator did not know himself, nor you. You are a *Rasor*, he a *Wedge*. You please and ravish every where without Affectation; he blasphemes, and talks Bawdy. You make a man's Blood crawl upon his Back, even whilst you are describing and tearing to pieces one of the finest Gentlemen and politest Scholars in the Kingdom [Richard Bentley]. Your Imitator thinks there's *Wit* in calling HORACE's *Sermones, Sermons*;[1] in naming *Reverend Doctor*, and *Doctor in Divinity*; in putting *Bentley* to Notes that wou'd be pointless and stupid, but that they are swoln with *rigid C[unn]i, & caudæ turgent* [cunts, and rising pricks], To see a Man of Dr. *Bentley's* Age and Dignity and incomparable Learning, writing *Bougre* and *Foutre* Remarks, how delicious it must needs be!

Your *Admirer*, out of his *singular* and *inward Respect* for you, keeps closer to his Master POPE, than his Master HORACE. For whereas HORACE satirizes one *Avidienus*, and calls him *Dog*, you have found a Wife for him 1800 Years after; call her *Bitch*, and then sputter out against her all the *Pus atque venenum* ['gall and poison'] collected in your Breast; even so our *sober Adviser* finding *Fufidius* in HORACE, turns him into *Fufidia*, and then persecutes the poor imaginary Woman with most *horrid* and *brutal Ribaldry*, for which there's not the least Foundation in the Original. He was afraid, as much as you, of dwindling into a sorry Translator. He might indeed as well have said he was *imitating the Prophet* ISAIAH. This same *Fufidia*, he says,

---

[1] As *delivered* in his second *Sermon. Delivered* too very smart! *Vid. Title Page.*

—— *thirsts and hungers only at one End.* [l. 24]

But we have just before one *Rufa*, that is

—*at either End a Common Shoar.* [l. 29]

For *Rufa*, hang her, she's a nasty *Bitch*; what, both *above* and *below*? Now *Fufidia*, because she *hungers and thirsts only at one End*, she shall be *filled*; as you'll find it written in *another Sermon* besides FLACCUS's.

After all, it may be useful to have some Women complaisant with the *lower Labia*, and some with the *upper*; for as our Imitator tells us,

> *Different Taste in diff'rent Men prevails,*
> *And one is fir'd by* Heads, *and one by* Tails. [ll. 35–6]

The very next Lines to a Verse of yours; a delicate one indeed, and worthy to be had in everlasting Remembrance,

> *Spreads her Fore-buttocks to the Navel bare.*[1]

a verse too you seem to be fond of; for I had read it in the *Miscell-* [*anies*] and *Dunciad* before it came here. . . .

Your Essays on Man, or Ethic Epistles, are much read and commended. Yet I have met with very knowing People, that think you are not equal to the Undertaking. There's an Exuberance of Wit and good Language; and several Parts of them are *good*, but not the *whole*. There are Starts and Flights of Poetry very fine, but you *prove* nothing. You are often obscure, twice or thrice unintelligible. You make false Judgments of Things, and reason wrong from *Premisses*. When we fancy we are going to learn some valuable thing, you fly off, and leave us in a Smoak. Let any man tell me, when he has read one, or all the Epistles, whether he is either wiser or better for't. If he answers, YES, he is *acuter* than I am. There are four Lines in the second Ethick Epistle, Ver. 31. generally admired and repeated.

> *Superior Beings, when of late they saw*
> *A mortal Man unfold all Nature's Law,*
> *Admir'd such Wisdom in an earthly Shape,*
> *And shew'd a* NEWTON *as we shew an* Ape.
> [*An Essay on Man*, ii. 31–4]

---

[1] [Line 34. It occurred in the 1728 versions of *The Dunciad*, but was omitted from the *Variorum*. See notes to *The Dunciad* (A), ii. 152 in the Twickenham edition]

Now I think the Sentiment here is not just. For how are we to take it? Are you *mocking* those same *superior Beings*, for regarding NEWTON in no better a light than we do a *Baboon*? Or are you *satirizing* the Philosopher for presuming to pry into *them*? 'Tis plain, that an Ape is ugly and ridiculous (a *Manteger*[1] more so) because she is like a Man both in Shape and Manners. *Simia*, in TULLY, *turpissima bestia, quam similis nobis!*[2] So that if the Gods shew NEWTON, as we shew an *Ape*, they must think him the most absurd, ridiculous, ugly thing that ever came amongst them; and as they made Monkeys here below for us to laugh at, they must be glad they have got NEWTON in Heaven above, to laugh at themselves.

I will write down twenty Verses together from the End of your Fourth *Ethic Epistle*; not only because I have a mind to make two or three Remarks upon them, but because there appears in them such a Sharpness of Wit, and Vigour of Spirit, as one seldom or never meets with. I can truly say, that I have more Pleasure in reading or transcribing some of your Writings, than in hearing FARINELLI.[3]

[Quotes *An Essay on Man*, iv. 373–90, in praise of Bolingbroke]

It was thought strange, I assure you, that you would celebrate in immortal Verse Lord BOLINGBROKE; and pitch upon him for your *Genius*, your *Guide*, and your *Friend*. Are you then really content to go down to Posterity with that Gentleman in the same *Bottom*, or a little *Bark attendant*? Can you think the Christian Religion true (you say you *believe* and *go to Prayers*) and not fear being *damned* with him also, not, as *Cromwel*, to *everlasting Fame*, but to *everlasting Torments*?

> *To fall with Dignity, with Temper rise.*   [*ibid.*, l. 378]

Did he *rise with Temper*, when he drove furiously out of the Kingdom the Duke of MARLBOROUGH? Or did he *fall with Dignity*, when he fled from Justice himself, and joined the PRETENDER?

> *When Statesmen, Heroes, Kings, in Dust repose,*
> *Whose Sons shall blush their Fathers were thy Foes.*[4]
>
> [*ibid.*, ll. 387–8]

[1] ['Some kind of baboon' (18th cent.)]
[2] [*De natura deorum*, i. 97: 'How like us is that ugly brute, the ape!' Cicero quotes from Ennius. Bentley confuses the word order]
[3] [Stage name of Carlo Broschi (1705–82), Italian singer, who supported the anti-Handel faction in London, 1734–7]
[4] These two Verses are added by the Author of the *Ethic Epistles*, to the last Edition [*Works* (1735), octavo, vol. ii. Griffiths, 388]: Which Edition, they say, costs a Guinea,

Never blush! till our Liberties are *gone,* Popery *come*; which, some say, is stalking towards us *grandi gradu* ['with large steps']. Keep it out, I beseech you, O King, Lords, and Commons!

You say to Lord BOLINGBROKE, Ver. 261.

> *Condemn'd in Business, or in Arts to drudge,*
> *Without a Second, or without a Judge.*
> *Truths would you teach, or save a sinking Land?*
> *All fear, none aid you, and few understand.*
>
> [*ibid.,* ll. 263–6]

Save a sinking Land! Shocking Words, and almost treasonable! He *save the Nation!* It was never *sunk* lower than when he was at the *Helm.* But who *fears,* or does not *understand* him?

> *Painful Preheminence! your self to view*
> *Above Life's Weakness, and its Comforts too.*
>
> [*ibid.,* ll. 267–8]

I should have thought this strange stuff, if I had met with it in Prose. But the *Inspired* can say nothing but what is right. What is it, *to be above Life's Weakness and its Comforts too?* It is above my Comprehension.

You make a great ado with your *Virtue only,*[1] and your *Uni æquus virtuti atque ejus amicis.*[2] VIRTUE ONLY in Capitals is one of the Marks to know you by. Is BOLINGBROKE one of your *Virtutis Amici?* Pray, let us know then what you mean by *Virtue.* Is it *Graian* or *Roman?* Or do you mean *Evangelical Graces?* Is it *Charity,* that *suffereth long, and is kind, that vaunteth not itself, nor is puffed up?* Is it *Humility, Love of Enemies, &c?* He has nothing of them: You have but little your self. I have sometimes thought, that you put *Virtue* for *Self,* and that *Virtue only* is *Self only*; and that *Uni æquus virtuti atque ejus amicis* ['just only to virtue and to virtue's friends'], means only, *Uni mihi æquus, & mihi amicis* ['just to myself and to my friends'];[2]

> *To my self only and my Friends a Friend.*

Your *Γνῶθι σεαυτὸν* ['know thyself'] is the Motto you had best keep to. There are some Particularities in your Writings, that one would

---

[1] [*An Essay on Man,* iii. 212, iv. 397.]
[2] [Horace, *Sat.* II. i. 121]

---

though there are but about twelve hundred Lines in all the four Epistles; the Length of One Book of *Virgil.*

almost suspect you *affected*; and yet they are *Coxcombs*, you say, that think they know you by your Turn and Manner. Why not? Readers in all Ages have pretended to discover a good Writer by that single Criterion. You are always *smooth* and *concise*; one of the *Veneres scribendi* ['graces of literature'] hard to gain. There are several Moles, perhaps unseen by yourself, in your Verses, that fix them yours. Good Judges are sure, whether you *deny* or *own*. Besides, you have few or no Rivals in Poetry. What is good must come from POPE. No body else can, or no body else will *write*. I have heard too, that when you are going to print any thing, you not only carry it in Manuscript to your best judging Friends for their Approbation, which is right; but also when 'tis out, you run about Town to catch People's Sentiments, and

> *To be treated and flatter'd and tickled with Scandal,*
> *From Dammyblood B——t to Lick-spittle M——*

From the highest to the lowest of Mortals; from BURL[INGTO]N *Master-builder* to CH[ESELD]EN the *Stone-cutter.*[1] An Imitation, both in Verse and Prose, of those Lines of yours in the Epistle to Dr. ARBUTHNOT:

> *Yet ne'r one Sprig of Laurel grac'd these Ribalds,*
> *From slashing* B[ENT]LEY *down to piddling* T[IBA]LDS.

[ll. 163-4]

You are a *Ribald* your self (if I know what the Word means) for such *lewd* and *licentious* talking. From Verse 146 to Verse 209, above Threescore Lines, of this Epistle was printed before, twice or thrice, I think, in the Volumes of the *Miscellanies.*[2] 'Tis called there, *the Fragment of a Satire*;[3] and instead of *From slashing* B[ENT]LEY, 'tis *From sanguine* SEW[ALL] Who this SEW[ALL] is, I don't know;[4] but why must BENTLEY come *slashing*, and take his Place?

You are grown very angry, it seems, at Dr. BENTLEY of late. Is it because he said (*to your Face*, I have been told) that your HOMER was *miserable Stuff*? That it might be called, HOMER *modernised*, or something *to that effect*; but that there were very little or no *Vestiges* at all of the

[1] [William Cheselden (1688–1752), a friend of Pope's, and famous as a surgeon for his removal of gall-stones]
[2] [Bentley exaggerates somewhat; see Twickenham, vi. 283]
[3] The Epistle to Dr. ARBUTHNOT is improperly called an *Epistle*. 'Tis a *Satire* throughout. HORACE made a Difference. His Epistles to his polite Friends are not stuffed with Bills of Complaint and cruel Descriptions, like Mr. POPE's.
[4] ['*Sew—*' is the 1727 reading; George Sewall (d. 1726) was a hack writer, and added a seventh volume of the non-dramatic writings to Pope's edition of Shakespeare]

old Grecian. Dr. BENTLEY said right. Hundreds have said the same *behind your Back.* For HOMER *translated, first* in English, *secondly* in Rhyme, *thirdly,* not from the Original, but, *fourthly,* from a *French Translation,* and that in *Prose,* by a *Woman* too,[1] how the Devil should it be *Homer?* As for the *Greek* Language, every body that *knows* it and has compared your Version with the Original, as I have done in many Places, must *know* too that you *know* nothing of it. I my self am satisfied, but don't expect to make any body else believe so, that you can but barely construe *Latin.* Were I to allow that you can give the true Sense of a Page in *Livy* or *Tacitus* at sight, It would be too much. You have not that compass of human Learning, always thought necessary to a true Poet. Nor have you so much Philosophy and Knowledge of human Nature, as you fancy you have. Let me advise you as a Friend (for a Friend I am, and adore your very Foot-steps as a polite Writer) don't hurt your self by your own Writings; have it always before your Eyes, That no Man is demolished but by himself.

This *Sermon* has done you more Mischief than all the *Dunciad* People together: Or rather, *they* have done you none, *this* a great deal. Whether your's or not, is not the Point now. Every body in Talk is *sure* you are. Every body, except a few *Provoked,* would rejoice to be convinced of the contrary. I have heard Friends as well as Foes say, it was a *shameful* thing, 'twas *villainous*; that the Author deserved the Pillory: That to *forge* a *Note* under Dr. BENTLEY's *Hand,* and then set his *Name* to it, was of the same nature with Sir P. STRANGER's Crime, and ought to be expiated by the loss of Ears. What CHARTRES would not have done to get less than 500 Pounds, that you are *thought* to have done to get perhaps 40 or 50. Your Friends are quite mute; Enemies talk on. The old *Et dici potuisse, & non potuisse refelli,*[2] sticks as close to you as an invenomed Shirt. I have been told, that the great Critic himself, who did not read the *Sermon,* till he heard *something* about his Son and you, said after, *'Tis an impudent Dog; but I talked against his* HOMER, *and the portentous Cub never forgives.*

I won't conceal what I have heard said of your *Imitations.* That if any body has a mind to taste HORACE, they need only read *them.* A Cart-load of Commentaries will signify nothing without 'em. There's more Wit in 'em, than in HORACE's Original *Sermones.* That you was born to improve and raise and refine every thing you touch.

[1] [Anne Dacier, *Iliade d'Homère* (Paris, 1699)]
[2] [Ovid, *Metamorphoses,* i. 758; 'It's a disgrace that such slanderous accusations could have been made, and could not be refuted.']

You are pulled to pieces for more Imitations. You sold those already published for 40 or 50 Pounds each. *Fifty Pounds* for 150, or 200 Lines! The third Satire of the second Book comes next, and has twice as many Verses as any of the others. You intend to have an hundred Pounds for that. If you have JUVENAL in your view after HORACE, his Sixth Satire will be worth 150 Pounds. It will come *a propos* just before the second Book of Ethic Epistles, *Of the Use of Things*;[1] in the second of which you promise to treat of *the particular Characters of Women*. Is the *Epistle* to a Lady, *Of the Characters of Women*, all we are to expect? I wonder you would set your Name to such a Piece of poor unmeaning *Galimatias*,[2] patch'd up out of the Third Volume of *Miscellanies*? *Silvia, a Fragment*, and *Verses to Mrs. M. B. &c.* make a great part of it.[3] How dare you impose upon the Public at this rate? 'Tis *sly*, if not *dishonest*. 'Tis a sign of an *avaritious* Temper, and shews want of *Invention*. You have sold them already *three* or *four* times. They are coming out again in *Quarto* and *Folio*. Δίς κράμβη Θάνατος, *Crambe* [cabbage][4] *twice served* was *Death* amongst the *Greeks*. The Proverb

---

[1] What *Things*? *Quære* whether *C[u]nnorum* [of cunts], or *Condonorum*? *God's good Things*, or *Man's good Things*? See p. 6. of *Sober Advice*.

    '*Tis in thy self, and not in* God's good Thing [l. 103].

HORACE has it,

    Tuo vitio, rerumne labores?
    ['whether your trouble is due to your own faults
    or to circumstances']

In the same Page he tells us, That not *one*, but *divers* Duchesses are poxed. He ought to have excepted *nominatim* his Angel M[ONTAG]UE [see l. 166].

Can there be a more odd Sight, that to see this Sermoniser, Mr. POPE, or his Admirer, no matter which, come forth all naked and bloody, with his *Testes & Cauda salax* [testicles and lecherous tail] in his Hands? *Et pugillares defert in balnea raucus testiculos*, JUVEN[AL, xi. 156: 'And the loud-voiced fellow conveys his organs to the bath-house where they may be touched']. What an *Erection* of Wit, what a *Tentigo*[lecherousness] of Parts in his Notes! How he triumphs, and dashes his Sp[erm?] about him! Keep off, O ye Duchesses and Ladies of Quality; for he is just entered into the deep Meaning of *Permingere*[to urinate] and *Permolere*[to grind up]. Nay, he would not let BENTLEY have the Credit of this glorious Note: 'Tis entirely his own. You will see presently how delighted he is to have *got hold of* that savoury Word *Cunnum*: He dresses it in *Capitals*; tells us, 'tis in *English*, *Thing*. Then again in his Note, (hey, jingo!) *Thing* signifies in *Latin*, *Cunnus*. Filthy Satyr! didst thou fear, lest somebody, not well versed in *the Use of Things*, should imagine, that *C[unnus]* stood for a *P[rick]*? A Note in the Manner of Mr. POPE's Admirer!

[2] ['Confused language, meaningless talk, nonsense']

[3] [For the details of Pope's 'patching up', see Twickenham, III. ii. 53–4, 69–70, vi. 287, 244–7]

[4] [Bentley provides the translation. Compare Juvenal, 'occidit miseros crambe repetita magistros' .'Crambe' (cabbage) also puns on 'crambo', a child's rhyming game, hence meaning 'repetition', 'mere rhyme']

would be more apposite indeed, if your Verses were *bad*. *Good* as they are, they become *Crambe*, by being recocted and obtruded over and over again. But *Virtue only* cures all things.

Your *Ethic Epistles* cost you much more Pains and Study than your *Imitations*; and yet you won't get so much by them. Not so many have a Relish for abstracted Reasoning and Metaphysics. I compute, that if you go on, you will clear near a Thousand Pounds. Now your *Ape* the *Sober Adviser* despises Money. He only took about Fifty Guineas of B[ore]m[a]n for this *Sermon* of HORACE, though he knew it would sell so prodigiously. 'Tis certain he might have had an Hundred. For when it was whisper'd amongst the Booksellers, That the thing was damn'd scurrilous and brutally bawdy——That Bishops and Arch-bishops[1] were maul'd in it—— That there was *C[unni]* and *Testes & Cauda salax* ['testicles and lecherous tail'] and *f*—— in every other Line—— That the Notes were more bawdy, if possible, than the Text; and, to crown all, the *Reverend* RICHARD BENTLEY *Doctor in Divinity his Name* put to 'em; they were all quite mad to have it.

I will just mention one Thing more, that appears to me perfectly *Ridicule*; and shews what a strange pitch of Conceitedness you are come to. You have put for a Motto before your *Epistle to Doctor* ARBUTHNOT, the Words of TULLY, spoken by one *Great* SCIPIO to *Another*.[2] These you apply to your self in a most awkward manner, for no reason, that I can see, but because you found *Ipsa Virtus* [Virtue itself] amongst them. AFRICANUS, one of the greatest Men that ever existed, would not have said them of *himself*. 'Tis very amazing, to see a little Creature, scarce four Foot high,[3] whose very Sight makes one laugh, strutting

The Story of my Lord of L[ondo]n and a noted Dean [ll. 39–44], with the Reason why the said Lord taxes another Spiritual Lord with Adultery, will be further enucleated in an Epistle to be publish'd with all convenient Speed, *Of the Principles and Use of Ecclesiastical Polity.*

[2] [*De re publica*, VI. xxiii: 'you will no longer attend to the gossip of the vulgar herd or put your trust in human rewards for your exploits. Virtue herself, by her own charms, should lead you to true glory. Let what others say of you be their own concern, whatever it is, they will say it in any case.']

[3] HORACE was still shorter; a mere Dwarf, if we may take his own Word for't:

——*longos imitaris, ab imo*
Ad summum totus moduli bipedalis.   HOR. Sat. 2, 4. Ver. 308.
['you try to ape big men, though from top to toe
your full height is but two feet']

Our *English* Bard may truly say, that he is *less ridiculous* than the *Roman* was:
——*ridiculus minus illa* ['less ridiculous than he'],   Ver. 311.

unless the *Roman* Foot was longer than the *British*; a Point I shall leave to be discussed by those dull Rogues the Critics and Commentators.

and swelling like the Frog in HORACE, and demanding the Adoration of all Mankind, because *it* can make fine Verses. This is *sume superbiam* [the height of pride] with a vengeance. Enough for you, sure, to be called as HORACE was by AUGUSTUS, *Pu[r]issimum penem, the purest Wag-prick*; and *Lepidissimum homuncionem, the cleverest parted little Fellow in the World*.[1]

[1] [Reported by Suetonius, *De poetis*, xxiv. 35]

AN EPISTLE FROM MR. POPE TO DR. ARBUTHNOT

2 January 1735

---

88. Three opinions

1734–42

(a) Elizabeth Rowe, extract from letter to Lady Hertford, dating from 1734–5, H. S. Hughes, 'More Popeana: Items from an Unpublished Correspondence', *PMLA*, xliv (1929), 1093. Elizabeth Rowe (1674–1737) was a minor poetess.

I am glad y^r La^{sp} is disgruntled with Mr. Pope's treatment of Mr. Addison [ll. 193–214] . . . the whole seems writ with a Mallice more than human it has something infernal in it 'tis surprising that a man can divest himself of the tender sentiments of nature so far as deliberately to give Anguish and Confusion to Beings of his own kind. Slander and Invective is an Injury never to be repair'd, & by consequence is an unpardonable sin.

(b) Lady Mary Wortley Montagu, letter to Dr Arbuthnot, 3 January 1735, *Corresp.*, iii. 448–9.

Sir,—I have perus'd the last Lampoon of your ingenious Friend, & am not supriz'd you did not find me out under the name of Sapho [ll. 101, 369], because there is nothing I ever heard in our Characters or circumstances to make a parallel, but as the Town (except you who know better) generally suppose Pope means me whenever he mentions that name, I cannot help taking Notice of the terrible malice he bears against the Lady signify'd by that name, which appears to be irritated by supposing her writer of the verses to the Imitator of Horace, now I can assure him they were wrote (without my knowledge) by a Gentleman of great merit, whom I very much esteem, who he will

329

never guess, & who, if he did know he durst not attack;[1] but I own the design was so well meant, & so excellently executed that I cannot be sorry they were written; I wish you would advise poor Pope to turn to some more honest livelihood than libelling, I know he will alledge in his excuse, that he must write to eat, & he is now grown sensible that nobody will buy his verses, except their curiosity is piqued to it, by what is said of their Acquaintance, but I think this method of Gain so exceeding vile that it admits of no excuse at all. Can any thing be more detestable than his abusing poor Moor scarce cold in his Grave,[2] when it is plain he kept back his Poem while he liv'd for fear he should beat him for it? this is shocking to me tho' of a man I never spoke to, & hardly knew by sight, but I am seriously concern'd at the worse scandal he has heap'd on Mr Congreve who was my Friend, & whom I am oblig'd to Justify because I can do it on my own knowledge, & which is yet farther bring wittness of it, from those who were then often with me, that he was so far from loveing Popes Rhyme, both that & his Conversation were perpetual jokes to him, exceeding despicable in his Opinion, & he has often made us laugh in talking of them being particularly pleasant on that subject.[3] as to Pope's being born of Honest Parents I verily believe it, & will add one praise to his mothers Character that (tho' I only knew her very old) she allways appear'd to me to have much better sense than himselfe. I desire Sir as a favour that you would shew this Letter to Pope & you will very much oblige Sir your humble Servant M W Montagu.

(c) Colley Cibber, extract from *A Letter from Mr. Cibber to Mr. Pope* (1742), p. 41. For further extracts from this pamphlet, see No. 91.

However, to shew I am not blind to your Merit, I own your Epistle to Dr. *Arbuthnot* (though I there find myself contemptibly spoken of) gives me more Delight in the whole, than any one Poem of the kind I ever read. The only Prejudice or wrong Bias of Judgment, I am afraid I may be guilty of is, when I cannot help thinking, that your Wit is remarkably bare and barren, whenever it would fall foul upon *Cibber*, than upon any other Person or Occasion whatsoever: I therefore could wish the Reader may have sometimes considered those Passages, that if I do you Injustice, he may as justly condemn me for it.

[1] [The *Verses* (No. 77) were written by Lady Mary with the help of Lord Hervey]

[2] [Line 385. James Moore Smythe had died the preceding October. Smythe's *One Epistle to Mr. Pope* (1735) provided Pope with reason to attack him]

[3] [Probably an exaggeration of Congreve's opinion]

EPILOGUE TO THE SATIRES: DIALOGUE II

18 July 1738

89. Opinions of Aaron Hill and Swift

1738

(a) Aaron Hill, extract from letter to Pope, 31 July 1738, *Corresp.*, iv. 112.

Stor'd with beauties, as every thing must be, that you write, for the public, shall I dare to confess, that I did not use to consider your works, of *this* vein, as those, from which you were surest of the love and admiration of posterity; but I find, in this, satire, something inexpressibly daring and generous. It carries the acrimony of *Juvenal*, with the *Horatian* air of ease and serenity. It reaches *heights* the most elevated, without seeming to design any *soaring*. It is raised and familiar at once. It opposes just *praise* to just *censure*, and, thereby, doubles the *power* of either. It places the *Poet* in a light for which *nature* and *reason* designed him; and attones all the pitiful *sins* of the *trade*, for, to a *trade*, and a *vile* one, poetry is irrecoverably sunk, in this kingdom. What a pity, that our rottenness begins at the *core*! and is a corruption, not of *persons* alone, but of *things*! One would, else, strongly hope, from a ridicule so sharp, and so morally pointed, that wicked men might be laughed into something, like penitence. But, alas! they are only bit by *Tarantula's*, who can be cured by the power of *musick*.—Not even the harp of *Apollo* had a charm to expel *vipers*, that have crept into the *entrails*.

Go on, however, to make *war*, with a courage, that reproaches a *nation's*; and live (would you *could*) just as long as 'till the *virtues*, your spirit would propagate, become as general, as the esteem of your genius!

(b) Jonathan Swift, extract from letter to Pope and Bolingbroke, 8 August 1738, *The Correspondence of Jonathan Swift*, ed. Sir H. Williams (1963), v. 119–20. Swift is writing from Dublin.

. . . I take your second Dialogue that you lately sent me, to equal almost any thing you ever writ; although I live so much out of the world, that I am ignorant of the facts and persons, which I presume are very well known from Temple-bar to St. James's; (I mean the Court exclusive.)[1]

---

[1] [Swift voiced the same opinion to John Barber on 8 August, *ibid.*, p. 117]

THE NEW DUNCIAD: AS IT WAS FOUND IN THE YEAR 1741

20 March 1742

This version of the poem includes book iv for the first time. Theobald, however, remains the hero.

---

90. The reaction of Shenstone and Grey

March–April 1742

(a) William Shenstone (1714–63), extract from letter to Rev. William Jago, [March 1742], *The Letters of William Shenstone*, ed. Majorie Williams (Oxford, 1939), p. 44:

The Dunciad is, doubtless, Mr. Pope's dotage, Τὰ Διὸς ἐνύπνια ['the dreams of Zeus']; flat in the whole, and including, with several tolerable lines, a *number* of weak, obscure, and even punning ones.

(b) Thomas Gray (1716–71), extract from letter to Gilbert West, *c.* 1 April 1742, *The Correspondence of Thomas Gray*, ed. Paget Toynbee and Leonard Whibley (1935), i. 189:

As to the Dunciad, it is greatly admired: the Genii of Operas and Schools [iv. 45ff.], with their attendants, the pleas of the Virtuosos and Florists [iv. 347ff.], and the yawn of dulness in the end [iv. 650ff.], are as fine as anything he has written. The Metaphysician's part [iv. 239ff.] is to me the worst; and here and there a few ill-expressed lines, and some hardly intelligible.

91. Cibber's story of Pope on the 'Mount of Love'

July 1742

Colley Cibber, extracts from *A Letter from Mr. Cibber to Mr. Pope, Inquiring into the Motives that might induce him in his Satyrical Works, to be so frequently fond of Mr. Cibber's Name* (1742), pp. 8–12, 44–50.

Cibber was deliberately incited by Pope in the early months of 1742, and his attack appeared 24–30 July, with the claim that it was only published at the insistence of friends. Cibber became the hero of *The Dunciad* in the following year. Further, see Introduction, p. 22. The notorious account of the young Earl of Warwick's attempted bawdy-house trick on Pope appeared in Cibber's *Letter* for the first time. For a further extract see No. 88c.

. . . I will now, Sir, have the last Word with you: For let the Odds of your Wit be never so great, or its Pen Dipt in whatever Venom it may, while I am conscious you can say nothing truly of me, that ought to put an honest Man to the Blush, what, in God's Name, can I have to fear from you? As to the Reputation of my Attempts, in Poetry, that has taken its Ply long ago, and can now no more be lessened by your coldest Contempt, than it can be raised by your warmest Commendation. . . . Every Man's Work must and will always speak *For*, or *Against* itself, whilst it has a remaining Reader in the World. All I shall say then as to that Point, is, that I wrote more to be Fed, than be Famous, and since my writings still give me a Dinner, do you rhyme me out of my Stomach if you can. And I own myself so contented as a Dunce, that I would not have even your merited Fame in Poetry, if it were to be attended with half that fretful Solicitude you seem to have lain under to maintain it; of which the laborious Rout you make about it, in those Loads of Prose Rubbish, wherewith you have almost smother'd your *Dunciad*, is so sore a Proof: And though I grant it a better Poem of its kind, than ever was writ; yet when I read it, with those vain-glorious encumbrances of Notes, and Remarks, upon almost every Line of it, I find myself in the uneasy Condition I was once in at an Opera, where sitting with a silent Desire to hear a favourite Air, by a famous Performer, a Coxcombly Connoisseur, at my Elbow, was so fond of shewing his own Taste, that by his continual Remarks, and prating in Praise of every Grace and Cadence, my Attention and Pleasure in the Song was quite lost and confounded.

It is also amazing, that you, who have writ with such masterly Spirit, upon the *Ruling Passion* [Moral Essays I: *Epistle to Cobham* ll. 174ff.], should be so blind a Slave to your own, as not to have seen, how far a low Avarice of Praise might prejudice, or debase that valuable Character, which your Works, without your own commendatory Notes upon them, might have maintained. . . . For what have you gain'd by [*The Dunciad*]? a mighty Matter! a Victory over a parcel of poor Wretches, that were not able to hurt or resist you, so weak, it was almost Cowardice to conquer them; or if they actually *did* hurt you, how much weaker have you shown yourself in so openly owning it? Besides, your Conduct seems hardly reconcileable to your own Opinion: For after you have lash'd them (in your Epistle to Dr. *Arbuthnot*, ver. 84) you excuse the Cruelty of it in the following Line.

> ——*Take it for a Rule,*
> *No Creature smarts so little as a Fool.*

Now if this be true, to what purpose did you correct them? For wise Men, without your taking such Pains to tell them, knew what they were before. And that publick-spirited Pretence of your only chastising them, *in terrorem* to others of the same malicious Disposition, I doubt is but too thin a Disguise of the many restless Hours they have given you. If your Revenge upon them was necessary, we must own you have amply enjoy'd it: But to make that Revenge the chief Motive of writing your *Dunciad*, seems to me a Weakness, that an Author of your Abilities should rather have chosen to conceal. A Man might as well triumph for his having kill'd so many Flies that offended him. Could you have let them alone, by this time, poor souls, they had been all peaceably buried in Oblivion! But the very Lines, you have so sharply pointed to destroy them, will now remain but so many of their Epitaphs, to transmit their Names to Posterity: Which probably too they think a more eligible Fate than that of being totally forgotten.

[pp. 8–12]

[Pope on the 'Mount of Love']

. . . In excusing the Freedom of your Satyr, you urge that it galls no body, because no body minds it enough to be mended by it. This is your Plea——

> *Whom have I hurt! has Poet yet, or Peer,*
> *Lost the arch'd Eye-brow, or Parnassian Sneer?*
> *And has not* Colley *too his Lord, and Whore?* &c.
> [*Epistle to Dr. Arbuthnot*, ll. 95–7]

If I thought the Christian Name of *Colley* could belong to any other Man than myself, I would insist upon my Right of not supposing you meant this last Line to Me; because it is equally applicable to five thousand other People: But as your Good-will to me is a little too well known, to pass it as imaginable that you could intend it for any one else, I am afraid I must abide it.

Well then! *Colley has his Lord and Whore!* Now suppose, Sir, upon the same Occasion, that *Colley* as happily inspired as Mr. *Pope*, had turned the same Verse upon *Him*, and with only the Name changed had made it run thus—

> *And has not* Sawney *too his Lord and Whore?*

Would not the Satyr have been equally just? Or would any sober Reader have seen more in the Line, than a wide mouthful of Ill-Manners? Or would my professing myself a Satyrist give me a Title to wipe my foul Pen upon the Face of every Man I did not like? Or would my Impudence be less Impudence in Verse than in Prose? or in private Company? What ought I to expect less, than that you would knock me down for it? unless the happy Weakness of my Person might be my Protection? Why then may I not insist that *Colley* or *Sawney* in the Verse would make no Difference in the Satyr! Now let us examine how far there would be Truth in it. . . .

. . . as Mr. *Pope* has so particularly picked me out of the Number to make an Example of: Why may I not take the same Liberty, and even single him out for another to keep me in Countenance? He must excuse me, then, if in what I am going to relate, I am reduced to make bold with a little private Conversation: But as he has shewn no Mercy to *Colley*, why should so unprovok'd an Aggressor expect any for himself? And if Truth hurts him, I can't help it. He may remember, then (or if he won't I will) when *Button*'s Coffee-house was in vogue, and so long ago, as when he had not translated above two or three Books of *Homer*; there was a late young Nobleman (as much his *Lord* as mine)[1] who had a good deal of wicked Humour, and who, though he was fond of having Wits in his Company, was not so restrained by his Conscience, but that he lov'd to laugh at any merry Mischief he could do them: This noble Wag, I say, in his usual *Gayetè de Cœur*, with another Gentleman still in Being, one Evening slily seduced the celebrated Mr. *Pope* as a Wit, and myself as a Laugher, to a certain House of Carnal Recreation, near the *Hay-Market*; where his Lordship's Frolick propos'd was to slip his little *Homer*, as he call'd him, at a Girl of the Game, that he might see what sort of Figure a Man of his Size, Sobriety, and Vigour (in Verse) would make, when the frail Fit of Love had got into him; in which he so far succeeded, that the smirking Damsel, who serv'd us with Tea, happen'd to have Charms sufficient to tempt the little-tiny Manhood of Mr. *Pope* into the next Room with her: at which you may imagine, his Lordship was in as much Joy, at what might happen within, as our small Friend could probably be in Possession of it: But I (forgive me all ye mortified Mortals whom his fell Satyr has since fallen upon) observing he had staid as long as without hazard of his Health he might, I,

Prick'd to it by foolish Honesty and Love,

As *Shakespear* says,[2] without Ceremony, threw open the Door upon him, where I found this little hasty Hero, like a terrible *Tom Tit*, pertly perching upon the Mount of Love! But such was my Surprize, that I fairly laid hold of his Heels, and actually drew him down safe and sound from his Danger. My Lord, who staid tittering without, in hopes the sweet Mischief he came for would have been compleated, upon my giving an Account of the Action within, began to curse, and call me an hundred silly Puppies, for my impertinently spoiling the Sport; to which with great Gravity I reply'd; pray, my Lord, consider what I have done was, in regard to the Honour of our Nation! For would you have had so glorious a Work as that of making *Homer* speak elegant *English*, cut short by laying up our little Gentleman of a Malady, which his thin Body might never have been cured of? No, my Lord! *Homer* would have been too serious a Sacrifice to our Evening Merriment. Now as his *Homer* has since been so happily compleated, who can say, that the World may not have been obliged to the kindly Care of *Colley* that so great a Work ever came to Perfection?

[1] [I.e., the young Earl of Warwick]   [2] [*Othello*, III. iii. 146]

337

And now again, gentle Reader, let it be judged, whether the *Lord* and the *Whore* above-mention'd might not, with equal Justice, have been apply'd to sober *Sawney* the Satyrist, as to *Colley* the Criminal?

Though I confess Recrimination to be but a poor Defence for one's own Faults; yet when the Guilty are Accusers, it seems but just, to make use of any Truth, that may invalidate their Evidence; I therefore hope, whatever the serious Reader may think amiss in this Story, will be excused, by my being to hardly driven to tell it.

I could wish too, it might be observed, that whatever Faults I find with the Morals of Mr. *Pope*, I charge none to his Poetical Capacity, but chiefly to his *Ruling Passion*, which is so much his Master, that we must allow, his inimitable verse is generally warmest, where his too fond Indulgence of that Passion inspires it. How much brighter still might that Genius shine, could it be equally inspired by Good-Nature!

[pp. 44–50]

92. Fielding champions Pope

August 1742

Henry Fielding, 31 August 1742, *The Champion*, quoted by W. Powell Jones, *Sawney and Colley (1742) and Other Pope Pamphlets*, Augustan Reprint Society, no. 83 (Los Angeles, 1960), pp. iv–v. Fielding's commonsensical and energetic reply was directed at the scurrilous attacks on Pope which had followed the publication of Cibber's *Letter* in March. As Powell Jones points out, these attacks had centred on Pope's deformity. Fielding's article appeared on the same day as *Sawney and Colley* (No. 72), and must have been welcome to Pope.

These gentlemen[1] have a strong inclination to be wittily ill-natured, but what is great baulk to them, they want abilities. And what is worst of all, is, that Mr. Pope should be the unfortunate gentleman against whom their satire is chiefly levelled. I think those who pretend to be public Champions ought, for their own honour, to enter the lists fairly. They should give the world as plain an instance that Mr. Pope is malicious (since that is what they accuse him of) as he has given them that they are ridiculous. If satire is accomodated to general characters, when an individual resents it, it is only letting the world know, that he is the only person guilty, and if he rails against the poet as malicious, it is with great injustice. For if a person takes all the follies of mankind upon himself voluntarily, why should he call that imputation unjust or malicious which he verifies in his own character? Or why should he accuse him of spleen who is so human as to pity his condition, and so good-natured as to laugh him into a reformation?

[1] [I.e. those who had attacked Pope, such as Ned Ward in *The Cudgel, Or, a Crab-tree Lecture*, and the author of *Blast upon Blast*, etc.]

93. Richardson on *The Dunciad* (1742)

1743

Samuel Richardson, extract from a letter to George Cheyne, 21 January 1743, *Selected Letters of Samuel Richardson*, ed. J. Carroll (1964), pp. 56–7.

I send the Dean of Coleraine in French,[1] and the first Volume in English, by Mr. Leake's Parcel: And when the continuation of this *everlasting* Work of exposing *transitory* Dunces is published, I will take Care of that also.

Methinks, Sir, Mr. Pope might employ his Time, and his admirable Genius better than in exposing Insects of a Day: For if these Authors would live longer, they should not be put down as Dunces: As long, especially, as the World, like the Theatre, has its Pit, Boxes, and Upper-Gallery. A Quarles and a Bunyan may be of greater Use to the Multitude who cannot taste, or edify by, the Superlative than Mr. Pope's writings. Are all Men born to Taste?—No. If they were, what Punishment would be too severe for those petty Writers who were to mislead it? But neither are the Works of all even fine Writers, to be compared to those of the two I have named, in their Morality and Piety. Some of the Pieces of Pope, of Swift, & other eminent Authors, of the Poetical Tribe especially, ought to be called in, and burnt by the Hands of the common Hangman, were there to have been none other Writers permitted but them.

The Greek Homer did a worthy because a grateful Thing, when he immortalized his benevolent Tanner, by making him tan the Seven Bulls Hides, that lined the shield of Ajax:[2] But the English Homer, tho' very kind, (partially so, I doubt, sometimes) to his Friends, has no Mercy on those whom he inrolls in the contrary List: Having, as I

---

[1] [I.e., Prévost's *Le Doyen de Killerine*]
[2] [Pope's notes to the *Iliad* tell the story of Tychius, whom Homer was said to have put into the *Iliad* as the maker of Ajax's shield in return for hospitality he had offered the poet, Book vii. 269]

have often thought no opinion of the Lesson, that teaches us *to give the Devil his Due.*

After all, Mr. Pope is (even in his Dunciad methinks) much more worthily employ'd than Domitian was; since it is nobler to immortalize Flies than to destroy them. But, were he to fall upon the Design you once mentioned to me in one of your Letters, of translating the Psalms of David, and applying the Profits to some charitable Use (to the Use of your general Hospital, suppose?) how much more noble a Work would that be, than any he has been employ'd in? Since it wd. put admirable Sense and admirable Poetry into the Mouths of Millions, who would praise their God in his Version, who gave him Talents which adorn and distinguish him above all his Cotemporaries.

THE DUNCIAD IN FOUR BOOKS

19 October 1743

This was the final version of *The Dunciad*, in which Colley Cibber replaced Theobald as the hero.

---

94. 'Orator' Henley on *The Dunciad* (1743)

1743

John Henley, extracts from *Why How now, Gossip Pope? Or, The Sweet Singing-Bird of Parnassus taken out of its pretty Cage to be roasted. . . . Exposing the Malice Wickedness and Vanity of his aspersions on J. H[enley] in That Monument of his own Misery and Spleen, the Dunciad* (1743), pp. 10–13, 16. Published on 3 March 1743. This edition, the only one available to the editor, has on the title page 'Printed in 1736', though the references to Crousaz suggest a later date. 'Orator' Henley (1692–1756), a minor eccentric, and an engagingly megalomaniac polymath rather in intention than ability, set up his 'Oratory' in '*Newport*-Market, Butcher-Row'. According to Pope 'he preach'd on the Sundays Theological matters, and on the Wednesdays upon all other Sciences' (note to *The Dunciad* (A), iii. 195, Twickenham, v. 173). Henley's account, biased as it probably is, nevertheless suggests the very large and wide-ranging audience commanded by Pope, and the support he received from the 'polite' (and foppish) part of the Town. Henley's running battle with Pope was carried on by sermons at his Oratory, by newspaper advertisements (1728–44), and in his *Hyp-Doctor*, rather than through the medium of pamphlets.

I intended to animadvert regularly on your Facts, your Reasonings from them, and your Amplifications on both; but I have found myself reduc'd to the last, which have neither Facts nor Reasonings for the

Foundation of them: A Poet is privileg'd to lay on his Dawbing, or cast his Dirt, as he pleases, and it is sufficient to settle or unsettle a Character, if it be describ'd, whether it be the real Person or a *Creature of the Bard's Fancy*, that never existed but in the *World of the Moon*, *Fairy Land*, or *Utopia*: The World loves *Romance*, and Mr. POPE can hit that just Taste at the Expense of any Man's or Family's Reputation, with the Art of a Pick-Pocket, the Address of a Juggler, and the Principles of *Jonathan Wild*, in which MacHeath was an Hero to him: He *cruizes* of the good Names of Men, is a *Buccaneer* in *Satire*, a *Guarda Costa* in *Wit*, thinks all *lawfull Prize* that he lays hold on, and places his Heaven, all the Enjoyment of his Being in private Vanity and publick Mischief. On his Way of Thinking, on the Foot of his Practice, any Person who is conscious, or imagines he has an Ascendant, or an Advantage over another by his Strength or Deceit, may over-power any, plunder and kill him: This point pursued in the Manner of the *Dunciad*, would introduce universal Confusion; as Mr. POPE, by the Conceit of his Talents, Wit, Numbers, Popularity, and Diction, thinks himself entitled to destroy and blast the credit of every or any Person, right or wrong, so all others on the like Imagination of superior Force or Skill, might *murder*, *hack*, and *maul* as they pleased, and what *He objects of corrupt Ministers*, is thoroughly ridiculous, since, on the Basis of his Thoughts and Conduct, *Immorality* is *Virtue*, and the most fortunate and bold Wickedness is the most Divine Rectitude.

This, Sir, is no *Dunciad* on *you*, it is *your self*, your Works make it self-evident.

Your Description of me might, in the Articles that compose it, be equally apply'd to any *Publick Orator*, *Speaker*, *Preacher*, *Barrister at Law*, or to any Person who converses, or reads in Conversation on Arts and Sciences, on Divinity, or any subject you intimate: Characters of Ridicule of this Kind might be and are made by *a Recipe*, and a *common Place* of Calumny. . . .

Take a Quantity of *Meanness*, and *Nonsense*, *Impudence*, and *Affectation*, *Absurdity*, and *Inconsistence*, *Preacher* and *Zany*, *Stage* and *Pulpit*, *Ægypt* and *Monkey-Gods*, *Priestly Stalls* and *Butchers*, *Meek Modern Faith* and *Toland*, *Tindal*, and *Woolston*,[1] a Pound or two of *this*, and Ounces and Drams of *one and the other*, without a *Scruple* of *Honesty* in the Poet, the *Dunciad* is perfect, and the Portrait is immortal. . . .

You tell the World, that I was for putting Questions and *none would dispute with me* [i.e., at his Oratory]: Professors of most Parts of

---

[1] [Henley refers to Pope's attack on him, *The Dunciad* (A), iii. 191–208]

Literature, many Clergymen, Students from both the Universities, Poets, Counsellors, Physicians, Dissenters of all Sorts, *Romish* Priests, *Carmelites, Jesuits, Dominicans, Benedictines,* Gentlemen of all Ranks, ingenious Artists, have maintain'd publick Disputations there, very frequently: Your Works have been undertaken to be defended there, and come off very ill; those who have written for you against Mr. *Crouzas* (the Scheme of whose Work preexisted in our Disputations, the Date in the Register of them may be compar'd) as Mr. *Warburton,* &c. have been very unsuccessful: your Discourse on *Pastoral, your Pastorals, your* Notion of *Poetical Probability* in the Translation of *Homer,* your *Ethical* Epistles, your Character of *me* in your *Dunciad,* have been disputed upon distinctly, and wofully vindicated; your Admirers have shown in their Arguments for you, what Reason you have to triumph in their Admiration: *Pretty Beaux* have been rude and mobb'd, and lively *Petit-Maitres* have drawn their terrible Blades for you, in want of Sense: *Whites,* the *Bedford, Tom's, Nando's, George's,* and the *Crown* &c. have pour'd forth their well-dress'd Auxiliaries, Lace, Bag, Sword, Toupee and Snuff-Box, all the *Rival Modes,* in support of Mr. POPE's Right to be esteem'd the first of the Age: but their Apologies have been *murder'd, hack'd and maul'd,* even *butcher'd* in the *Priestly Stall,* and your exemplary Wit hung up in *Effigy,* as only fit for a *Scare-Crow,* like *your self.* . . .

Your *whole Piece* [*The Dunciad*] is only refining on the low Jests of *Porters* and *Fish-Women, as you live by the Water-side* [in Twickenham]; or dressing the *insolent Scurrility* of *Link-Boys* and *Hackney-Coachmen* in something (not much) genteeler Language; *they* talk of *Monkey-Nonsense, Pots* and *Pipes, hacking and mauling, neither said nor sung, impudent, brazen, and blushing thro' a thick Skin,* just in the sublime Dialect of the famous Mr. POPE:[1] The *Dunciad* was compil'd from the *Stairs* between the *Temple* and *Twickenham,* out of the Jokes crack'd and stolen there: *Footmen* and *Chairmen* every Day practice more elegant Conversation, and would be asham'd of the stale weather-beaten Drollery.

As a *Poet, your Similes are like nothing,* your *Turns* in the *Hyperbole,* your *Satire-Fiction,* your *Diction Common-Place* as well as *your Scandal;* a *Pinchbeck's Machine* with Chimes might excell it *in native Bronze,* your *Characters* will *fit any Body,* and may be *retorted* with a *truer Grace on your self,* as a moderate Versifier might prove by one Experiment on your Lines against me: I was once poetically addicted, and had I *perserver'd in the Sin,* or had I been inspir'd with *your Muses,* a fan-

[1] [*The Dunciad,* ref. cit.]

tastical *Imagination*, a *very vain Head*, and a *consummately evil Heart*, as you are incomparably possess'd with a Legion of such Sort of Dæmons, could by this Time have surpassed you; but universal Learning, and more generous Principles and Habits, have naturally made me the Object of a meritorious Aversion in Knaves and Coxcombs, and [it] fatigue[s] me longer to dwell on YOU, the most Illustrious Ornament of that renowned Fraternity, that ever has been, is, or will be, *per Sæcula Sæculorum, Amen.*

95. Richardson on *The Dunciad* (1744)

1744

Samuel Richardson, extract from letter to Aaron Hill, 19 January 1744, *Selected Letters*, ed. cit., p. 60.

I have bought Mr. Pope over so often, and his Dunciad so lately before his last new-vampt one, that I am tir'd of the Extravagance; and wonder every Body else is not. Especially, as now by this, he confesses that his Abuse of his first hero, was for Abuse-sake, having no better Object for his Abuse. I admire Mr. Pope's Genius, and his Versification: But forgive me, Sir, to say, I am scandaliz'd for human Nature, and such Talents, sunk so low. Has he no Invention, Sir, to be better employ'd about? No Talents for worthier Subjects?—Must all be personal Satire, or Imitations of others Temples of Fame, Alexander's Feasts, Coopers Hills, MacFlecknoe's? Yet his Essay on Man convinces one he can stand upon his own Legs. But what must then be the strength of that Vanity and of that Ill-nature that can sink such Talents in a Dunciad, and its Scriblerus-Prolegomena-Stuff?

96. An Elegy by a friend

1744

Anonymous, *An Elegy on Mr. Pope. Humbly Inscribed to Henry St. John, Lord Bolingbroke. By a Friend* (1744). *An Elegy* was published on 5 June 1744: Pope had died only a few days before, during the evening of 30 May. Several elegies and effusions were occasioned by Pope's death; this is one of the more dignified.

I can't forbear—not Tears alone shall flow,
But Words, uncull'd by Art, shall tell my Woe;
No Muse I call to lend her lofty Wings;
'Tis Truth that dictates, and 'tis Love that sings;
Soft Elegy the strong sublime disdains;
Its Style is gentle, humble are its Strains;
In low Simplicity its Grief express'd,
Like the true Mourner in plain Habit dress'd.
   THE brightest Ornament of ALBION gone,
Of the poetick World th'illustrious Sun,
Forbid to shine by rigid Fate's Decree,
Sorrowing I sing; for, POPE, I sing of thee.
   WHEN common Wits, like common Mortals die,
The Grief how limited how low the Sigh!
But when the first distinguish'd Genius falls,
That Loss for universal Mourning calls!
Sorrow it claims, where'er bright Sense appears,
And puts BRITANNIA and the World in Tears.
   What mortal Man, his Grandeur e'er so high,
Could e'er so honour'd, so lamented die?
Not the good Monarch, to his Subjects dear
For true parental Tenderness and Care;

Not *He*, when once he pours his latest Breath,
Is wept with Tears more gen'ral at his Death:
Not GEORGE returning to his native sky,
From these sad Scenes shall with more Glory fly,
Than POPE who in his loftier Sphere did sit
Sov'reign of POETRY, and Prince of WIT,
Whose Fame wide Earth's remotest Corners heard,
And own'd and lov'd th' inimitable Bard.

   THE raptur'd Bard is one, 'tis justly said,
Whom Nature forms, whom Art alone ne'er made;
His Vein with true poetick Vigour fir'd,
Which smiling *Phœbus* at his Birth inspir'd,
Judgment and Art may check and guide its Course,
But the bold Flight is rais'd by Nature's Force.
Such was POPE's Genius, for all feel and own
The vivid Fire was Nature's gen'rous Boon;
Yet the rich Store, by prudent Art refin'd,
Though not so strong, with purer Lustre shin'd.
Fancy's just Flights correctly skill'd to know,
His Muse ne'er soar'd too high, nor sunk too low;
But to each Theme its full Demand allow'd,
On each its proper Ornaments bestow'd.
His Genius thus its just Perfection gain'd;
Its Vigour thus, and thus its Charms maintain'd.

   To Reason's cooler Use the *Youth* scarce came,
But quick rush'd out the Poet's livelier Flame;
Not to full Glory by Degrees it goes,
But all at once in high Perfection rose;
Thus our first Parent knew no growing Years,
But at his first Formation *Man* appears.
In POPE's first Draughts such manly Beauties live,
Not mellowing Age could more Perfection give.
His Verse so strong, so pure his Numbers flow,
The Laurel soon adorns his honour'd Brow.
Soon as his Lyre was tun'd and touch'd the Ear,
Dryden's Admirers start aside to hear;
For not by *Dryden*'s Voice, nor *Waller*'s Tongue,
Such Harmony of melting Sounds was sung.

   The living Wits no rival Praise could claim,
Great *Prior* sunk beneath his tow'ring Fame.

Garth, *Swift*, and *Congreve*, at his stronger Blaze,
Shrunk in their Spheres, and shone with fainter Rays.
His Fame, so high by *Cato*'s Strains that rose,
For its chief Lustre now relies on Prose;
While *Pope*'s, tho' on the Muses' Basis plac'd,
Owns no one's *Prose* with brighter Beauties grac'd;
None, whose just Periods boast a finer Strain,
None, where more Elegance and Spirit reign.

The ancient Criticks spread before his View,
Lights that refin'd his Judgment thence he drew;
'Twas there the Sources of true Wit he trac'd,
There saw the Reasons of just Style and Taste;
Reasons by clearest Evidence declar'd,
Why pleas'd the Reader, pleasing why the Bard;
There saw the Rules the great *Longinus* taught
Both of Sublimity of Words and Thought;
The Rules, which *Dionysius*' Labours teach
To range our Words, and modulate our Speech.
How smooth, how nervous all our Diction flows,
When by true verbal Structure we compose!
But, Words misplac'd, which form'd just Strength and Tone,
How lost their Grandeur, how their Musick gone!
In POPE how amicably both conspire,
The Critick's Judgment, and the Poet's Fire!
On both POPE built his never-dying Fame;
He wrote with Coolness, and he thought with Flame.

In him so sweetly BRITAIN's Language flows,
We wonder how each pure Refinement rose.
To harmonize so well our ruder Speech,
What other Art, or other Ear could teach?
Had his but been the *Latian* living Tongue,
Not MARO's Muse had more harmonious sung;
Or had but MARO breath'd on *Britain*'s shore,
MARO had charm'd like POPE, not charm'd us more.

Of Nature's Scenes in all their Beauties dress'd
So strong th' Ideas on his Soul impress'd;
That our pleas'd Minds his just Descriptions fire,
Equal to what th' Originals inspire.
Whate'er he paints and sings, we see and hear,
Just as if Nature charm'd our Eye, or Ear;

As if we saw the living Meadow grow;
As if we heard the murm'ring Riv'let flow.
Pleasing or terrible, whate'er the Song,
'Tis sweet as Nature, or as Nature strong.
With equal Force he makes the Torrent pour;
With equal Sound he makes the Thunder roar;
With equal Fury makes the Tempest tear;
With equal Horror makes the Lightnings glare.
   With equal Art and Judgment too we find
He paints the Passions of the human Mind;
The human Mind, with corresponding Frame
As Nature's self as various, and the same;
For there the gentle lull the peaceful Soul,
There the rough Passions shake it, and controul;
Those the soft Air, and sweet refreshing Breeze;
These the rough Tempests, or the raging Seas.
To all, with justest Thought and happiest Art,
Could POPE th' exact Resemblances impart;
Their proper Features all describe so true,
No truer, e'er the finest Pencil drew;
Not Sculpture's Art could e'er so strong design,
As POPE's expressive Page, and nervous Line.
   But tho' so fine his Thought, so pure his Style
O'er his Descriptions all the Graces smile;
Tho' when, and where he pleas'd, t' enrich the Show,
His copious Hand the choicest Flow'rs could strow;
Tho' Musick's mighty Pow'r he knew so well,
As softest Notes to sweeten, loudest swell;
Tho' form'd th' Imagination to delight
With all, the richest Genius e'er could write:
A nobler End in Poetry he views,
Than just to please, and barely to amuse;
To more exalted Purposes must shine,
Heav'n's Inspiration, and the Flame divine.
This then our Poet's Province, this his Art,
T' awake fair Virtue, and instruct the Heart.
The glorious Aim of the great *Ethic Scheme*,
To vindicate the Ways of Heav'ns SUPREME;
To prove, howe'er Pride boasts her erring Light,
All He permits, and all He acts is right.

That Charity's the universal Law;
Sole Principle that Man to Heav'n can draw.
That *Faith*, and *Law*, and *Morals*, all began,
All end, in LOVE of GOD, and LOVE of MAN.

Part II

Later Criticism

1745–82

97. An early biographer's assessment

1745

William Ayre, extracts from *Memoirs of the Life and Writings of Alexander Pope, Esq.* . . . . (1745), 2 vols.

Ayre's biography was announced in January 1745, seven months after Pope's death, and echoes the admiration common at this time. The author of *Remarks on Squire Ayre's Memoirs* (1745) claimed that 'William Ayre' was a cover for Curll (pp. 6–8), but this seems unlikely: see G. Sherburn, *The Early Career of Alexander Pope* (1934), p. 4.

[*An Essay on Man*, 'The Universal Prayer']

It would be difficult to pick out any Lines in all the four Essays on Man, which do not greatly excel the same Number of Lines wrote by any other *English* Poet, supposing them to be Rhimes; for he alone has the Manner of keeping up the greatest Harmony in his Verses, without spinning his Thoughts to Threads, it being scarcely possible to render the same Thoughts again in so Words, even in Prose.

The *Universal Prayer*, except a doubtful Word or two, is one continued Confession of Benevolence and Humility, and might become the Mouth of a dying Saint: It shews, that speculative Divinity pleased him less than practical; that his Words were not artfully contrived to teach his Heart what it ought to be, but arose from it, and do more Honour to his Memory than all his other Works, great and sublime as they are, put together.   [i, p. xii]

[*Eloisa to Abelard*]

There is a Spirit of Tenderness and a Delicacy of Sentiments runs all through the Letter; but the prodigious Conflict, the War within, the Difficulty of making Love give up to religious Vows, and Impossibility of forgetting a first real Passion, shine above all the rest.   [i. 71]

[*Pastorals*]

Either [Pope's or Philips's pastorals] may serve for future Poets to imitate, who purpose to excel in this *Sicilian*, or *Arcadian* Pastoral Stile: Many Friends has this Manner of Writing, its Softness stealing thro' the Ear; most young Minds are strongly affected with it, it warms the very Hearts of all who are touch'd with the fine Passion of Love, and infuses a disinterested and noble Spirit into the Soul: It banishes from the Breast every Thing mean and contemptible, and places in the Stead, a generous Beneficence and Benevolence, so that the Mind becomes perfectly serene and humane.   [ii. 145–6]

[*The Dunciad*, Book iv (1743)]

Mr. *Pope* has been in this Piece equal to himself. Some there are, who at this Crisis, when the *publick Dulness* of ten Years past was come under *Inquiry*, were in great Expectations of meeting with a *political Satire*; but the ingenious Author has given the World only a Satire on *Modern Life*, and the Conduct of it in general; from the *School* to the *University*, from the *University* to *Travel*, from *Travel* into the various Branches of *Dulness*; in which *false Wits* and Men of *false Taste*, *false Philosophers*, and Men of *false Religion*, exercise their Faculties. The Poet has not particulariz'd many Follies of the fair Sex; however, he has not paid them any Compliment, as he has made the Sovereign of *Dulness* a Female, coming in all the Majesty of a Goddess, to destroy *Science* and *Learning*: But then he has given to the Sex some of the greatest Excellencies human Nature is capable of possessing. The Description of *Science*, *Wit*, &c. Captives at the Footstool of *Dulness*, is a Picture so full of Imagery, that every Figure as much presents itself to your View, as if drawn by the Pencil of *Le Brun*.

[Quotes *The Dunciad* (B), iv. 21–44]

. . . . . .

Though *Satire*, in its Name carries a common Idea of Censure, not to say Spleen or Ill-nature; yet *Horace*, the best Satirist, in most Mens Opinions, took an Opportunity, amidst his Ridicule of Folly and Vice, to introduce a Contrast, and set up Merit and Virtue in Opposition to them: The intervening Light of those were strong enough for the Shade of the other. Our *English Horace* pursues this Method: Affected Learning, Want of publick Spirit, &c. are deservedly expos'd; yet *Wynd-*

ham and *Talbot, Friend, Alsop* and *Murray*, receive all the Oblations due
to Men of refin'd Taste, Learning and Merit.   [ii. 231–4]

. . . The Speech of the Governor to *Dulness*, in Recommendation of his
Charge, is a just Censure on modern Education; I shall quote only that
Part, which describes his foreign Tour:

> Intrepid then o'er Seas and Lands he flew,
> *Europe* he saw, and *Europe* saw him too.
> There all *thy* Gifts and Graces we display,
> *Thou*, only *thou*, directing all our Way,
> To where the *Seine*, obsequious as she runs,
> Pours at great *Bourbon*'s Feet her silken Sons:
> Or *Tyber*, now no longer *Roman*, rolls,
> Vain of *Italian* Arts, *Italian* Souls;
> To Isles of Fragrance, lilly-silver'd Vales,
> Diffusing Languor in the panting Gales;
> To Lands of singing or of dancing Slaves,
> Love-whisp'ring Woods, and lute-resounding Waves.
> But chief her[1] Shrine where naked *Venus* keeps,
> And *Cupids* ride the Lion of the Deeps.
> Led by my Hand, he saunter'd *Europe* round,
> And gather'd every Vice on Christian Ground;
> Saw every Court, heard every King declare
> His royal Sense of Op'ras and the Fair.
> The Stews and Palace equally explor'd,
> Intrigu'd with Glory, and with Spirit whor'd.
> > [*The Dunciad* (B), iv. 293–315]

This is, to the Shame of our young Gentry be it spoke, too just a
Description of their beginning and finishing their Travels; we have,
however, some Exceptions, and some young Noblemen who have
done an Honour to their Country *abroad*; and by acquiring a Knowledge of Men, of Commerce, of the Interests and Tempers of foreign
Courts, with the different Policies of different Nations, will be of
Service to their Country at *home*. Lord *Halifax* in the House of Peers,
and several Gentlemen in the Commons, are illustrious Examples for
the young *British* Gentry: These have greatly serv'd their Country in
the Senate, at a Time of Life when most others employ theirs in
Pleasure and Libertinism.   [ii. 237–8]

[1] Venice, *whose Arms are a flying Lyon.*

[*An Essay on Man*]

In these last Lines of this Epistle have been notic'd several great Beauties.
  1. The first and chief is a Grandeur and Sublimity of Conception:

> Come then, my Friend! my Genius come along,
> Of Master of the Poet, and the Song!
> And while the Muse now stoops, and now ascends,
> To Man's low Passions, or their glorious Ends.
>
>   [iv. 373–6]

  2. The Second, that pathetick Enthusiasm, which at the same Time melts and enflames:

> Teach me, like thee, in various Nature wise,
> To fall with Dignity, with Temper rise,
> Form'd by thy Converse, happily to steer
> From grave to gay, from lively to severe,
> Correct with Spirit, eloquent with Ease,
> Intent to reason, or polite to please.   [iv. 377–82]

  3. A certain elegant Formation and Ordinance of Figures:

> O! while along the Stream of Time, thy Name,
> Expanded flies, and gathers all its Fame,
> Say, shall my little Bark attendant fail,
> Pursue the Triumph and partake the Gale?   [iv. 383–6]

  4. A splendid Diction.

> When Statesmen, Heroes, Kings, in Dust repose,
> Whose Sons shall blush their Fathers were thy Foes,
> Shall then this Verse to future Age pretend
> Thou wert my Guide, Philosopher, and Friend?
> That, urg'd by thee, I turn'd the tuneful Art,
> From Sounds to Things, from Fancy to the Heart;
> For Wit's false Mirror held up Nature's Light;
>
>   [iv. 387–93]

And Fifthly, which includes in itself all the rest, a Weight and Dignity in the Composition:

> Shew'd erring Pride, whatever is, is right;
> That Reason, Passion, answer one great Aim;

> That true Self-love and Social are the same;
> That Virtue only makes our Bliss below;
> And all our Knowledge is ourselves to know?
>
> [iv. 394–8]

These last five Lines are a Summary of the Whole: But whether Reason and Passion answer one great End or no, or whether Self-love and Social be the same, or whether there be any other Happiness than Virtue, or whether we know any Thing but ourselves; If WHATEVER IS, IS RIGHT, (which is Mr. *Pope's* first last and main Argument) it is of no Importance; because, if we were capable of other science besides that of Man, or could find out some Happiness that was not in Virtue, or find a social Passion in our Minds not selfish, or distinguish our Reason to have different Aims from our Passions, we are still just where we were; for there yet remains unconquer'd the undeniable Sentence, WHATEVER IS, IS RIGHT.

Such was Mr. *Pope's* Philosophy, and such his fine Poetry, which, as it never had, perhaps never will have any Equal in our Language.

> [ii. 372–4]

98. Gray on Pope and virtue

1746

Thomas Gray, extract from a letter to Horace Walpole, 3 February 1746, *Horace Walpole's Correspondence*, ed. W. S. Lewis, *et al.* (New Haven, 1937–   ), xiv. 2–3.

I can say no more for Mr. Pope. . . . It is natural to wish the finest writer, one of them, we ever had should be an honest man. It is for the interest even of that virtue whose friend he professed himself, and whose beauties he sung, that he should not be found a dirty animal.[1] But

[1] [A reference to the posthumous publication in 1746 of Pope's lines on 'Atossa', accompanied by an accusation that he accepted a bribe from the Duchess of Marlborough to suppress the lines]

however this is Mr. Warburton's business,[1] not mine, who may scribble his pen to the stumps and all in vain, if these facts are so. It is not from what he told me about himself,[2] that I thought well of him, but from a humanity and goodness of heart, ay, and greatness of mind, that runs through his private correspondence, not less apparent than are a thousand little vanities and weaknesses mixed with those good qualities, for nobody ever took him for a philosopher.

99. Johnson on 'Sound and Sense'

1751

Dr Samuel Johnson, extract from the *Rambler*, no. 92, 2 February 1751 (1753 ed., i. 549–50).

Johnson's essay argues for the necessity of criticism's *analysing* aural effects in poetry. Lord Kames and George Campbell took up Johnson's point in greater detail (Nos 117, 124), and Johnson makes some further remarks in his *Life of Pope* (pp. 495–6). After examining examples from Homer and Virgil, *Rambler* no. 92 turns to Pope's verse.

FROM *Vida*,[3] Mr. *Pope* seems to have transplanted this Flower [the imitation of action in sound]; which is the Growth of happier Climates, into a Soil less adapted to its Nature, and less favourable to its Increase.

> Soft is the Strain when *Zephyr* gently blows,
> And the smooth Stream in smoother Numbers flows;

[1] [I.e., his edition of Pope]

[2] [It is not known when Gray met Pope, though it may have been through the offices of the Rev. Joseph Spence]

[3] *Vida*, Mr.] 1751; *the Italian gardens* 1752. [Marco Girolamo Vida (c. 1489–1566) was an Italian scholar and poet.]

But when loud Billows lash the sounding Shore,
The hoarse rough Verse should like the Torrent roar.
When *Ajax* strives, some Rock's vast Weight to throw,
The Line too labours, and the Words move slow;
Not so when swift *Camilla* scours the Plain,
Flies o'er th'unbending Corn, and skims along the Main.

[*An Essay on Criticism*, ll. 366–73]

FROM these Lines, laboured with great Attention, and celebrated by a rival Wit,[1] may be judged what can be expected from the most diligent Endeavours after this Imagery of Sound. The Verse intended to represent the whisper of the Vernal Breeze, must surely be confessed, not much to excel in Softness or Volubility; and the smooth Stream, runs with a perpetual Clash of jarring Consonants. The Noise and Turbulence of the Torrent is, indeed, distinctly imaged; for it requires very little Skill to make our Language rough. But in the Lines, which mention the Effort of *Ajax*, there is no particular Heaviness[2] or Delay. The Swiftness of *Camilla* is rather contrasted than exemplified. Why the Verse should be lengthened to express Speed, will not easily be discovered. In the Dactyls used for that Purpose by the Ancients, two short Syllables were pronounced with such Rapidity, as to be equal only to one long; they, therefore, naturally exhibit the Act of passing though a long Space in a short Time. But the *Alexandrine*, by its Pause in the midst, is a tardy and stately Measure; and the Word *unbending*, one of the most sluggish and slow which our Language affords, cannot much accelerate its Motion.

[1] [Addison; see No. 11]
[2] *Heaviness*] 1751; *Heaviness, obstruction*, 1752.

100. Warburton as editorial commentator

1751

Dr William Warburton, extracts from his commentary in *The Works of Alexander Pope Esq. In Nine Volumes Complete.... Together with the Commentary and Notes of Mr. Warburton* ([1751] 2nd ed., 1760). On the commentary, see Introduction, p. 23.

[*An Essay on Criticism*]

The poem is in one book, but divided into three principal parts or members. The first (to ver. 201.) gives rules for the *Study in the Art of Criticism*: the second (from thence to ver. 560.) exposes the *Causes of wrong Judgment*; and the third (from thence to the end) marks out the *Morals of the Critic*.

In order to a right conception of this poem, it will be necessary to observe, that tho' it be intitled simply *An Essay on Criticism*, yet several of the precepts relate equally to the good *writing* as well as to the true *judging* of a poem. This is so far from violating the *Unity* of the subject, that it preserves and completes it: or from disordering the regularity of the *Form*, that it adds beauty to it, as will appear by the following considerations: 1. It was impossible to give a full and exact idea of the Art of *Poetical Criticism*, without considering at the same time the *Art of Poetry*; so far as Poetry is an *Art*. These therefore being closely connected in nature, the author has, with much judgment, interwoven the precepts of each reciprocally thro' his whole poem. 2. As the rules of the ancient Critics were taken from Poets who copied nature, this is another reason why every Poet should be a Critic: Therefore, as the subject is *poetical Criticism*, it is frequently addressed to the *critical Poet*. And 3dly, the Art of Criticism is as properly, and much more usefully exercised in *writing* than in *judging*.

But readers have been misled by the modesty of the *Title*, which only promises an Art of *Criticism*, to expect little, where they will find a great deal; a treatise, and that no incomplete one, of the Art both of *Criticism* and *Poetry*. This, and the not attending to the considerations offered above, was what, perhaps, misled a very candid writer, after having given the ESSAY ON CRITICISM all the praises on the side of genius and poetry which his true taste could not refuse it, to say, that *the observations follow one another like those in* Horace's Art of Poetry, *without that methodical regularity which would have been requisite in a prose writer.* Spec. N° 235 [No. 11]. I do not see how *method* can hurt any one grace of Poetry; or what prerogative there is in Verse to dispense with *regularity.* The remark is false in every part of it. Mr. Pope's *Essay on Criticism*, the Reader will soon see, is a regular piece: And a very learned Critic has lately shewn, that *Horace* had the same attention to method in his *Art of Poetry*. See *Mr.* Hurd's *Comment on the Epistle to the Pisos* [Introduction to Hurd's edition, Q. *Horatii Flacci. Ars Poetica* (1748)].

VER. 1. *'Tis hard to say*, etc.] The Poem opens (from ver. 1 to 9.) with shewing the use and seasonableness of the subject. Its *use*, from the greater mischief in wrong Criticism than in ill Poetry; this only tiring, that misleading the reader: Its *seasonableness*, from the growing number of bad Critics, which now vastly exceeds that of bad Poets.

VER. 9.] *'Tis with our Judgments, etc.*] The author having shewn us the expediency of his subject, the Art of *Criticism*, inquires next (from ver. 8 to 15) into the proper *Qualities* of a *true Critic:* and observes first, that JUDGMENT alone, is not sufficient to constitute this character, because *Judgment*, like the *artificial measures of Time*, goes different, and yet each relies upon his own. The reasoning is conclusive; and the similitude extremely just. For *Judgment*, when it goes alone, is generally regulated, or at least much influenced, by custom, fashion, and habit; and never certain and constant but when founded upon TASTE: which is the same in the *Critic*, as GENIUS in the *Poet:* both are derived from Heaven, and like the Sun, the *natural measure of Time*, always constant and equable.

Nor need we wonder that Judgment alone, will not make a Critic in poetry, when we see that it will not make a Poet. And on examination we shall find, that *Genius* and *Taste* are but one and the same faculty, differently exerting itself under different names, in the two professions of *Poetry* and *Criticism*. For the Art of Poetry consists in *selecting*, out of all those images which present themselves to the fancy, such of them as are truly beautiful. And the Art of Criticism in discerning, and fully relishing what it finds so selected. 'Tis an exertion of the same faculty of the mind in both cases, and by almost the same operation. The main difference is, that in the POET, this faculty is eminently joined to a *bright imagination*, and *extensive comprehension*, which provide stores for the selection, and can form that selection, by proportioned parts, into a regular whole: In the CRITIC, to a *solid judgment* and *accurate discernment*, which penetrate into the causes of an excellence, and so, can display that excellence in all its variety of lights. Longinus had *taste* in an eminent degree; therefore, this quality, which all true Critics have in common, our Author makes his distinguishing character,

> Thee, bold Longinus! all the Nine inspire,
> And bless their Critic with a Poet's fire.

i.e. with *taste* or *genius*. . . .   [i. 151–3]

['The Universal Prayer']

It may be proper to observe, that some passages in the preceding *Essay* [*on Man*], having been unjustly suspected of a tendency towards Fate and *Naturalism*, the Author composed this Prayer as the sum of all; to shew that his system was founded in *free-will*, and terminated in piety: that the First Cause was as well the Lord and Governor of the Universe as the Creator of it; and that, by submission to his will, (the great principle inforced throughout the *Essay*) was not meant suffering ourselves to be carried along by a blind determination, but resting in a religious acquiescence, and confidence full of *Hope* and Immortality. To give all this the greater weight, the Poet chose for his model the LORD's PRAYER, which, of all others, best deserves the title prefixed to his Paraphrase.

> *If I am right, thy grace impart,—*
> *If I am wrong, O teach my heart.*

As the *imparting of grace*, on the Christian system, is a stronger exertion of the Divine Power than the natural illumination of the heart, one would expect that *right* and *wrong* should change places; more aid being required to *restore* men to right, than to *keep* them in it. But as it was the Poet's purpose to insinuate that Revelation was the *right*, nothing could better express his purpose, than making the *right* secured by the guards of *grace*.   [iii. 205–7]

[*Moral Essays II: To a Lady*]

Of the Characters of WOMEN.] There is nothing in Mr. Pope's works more highly finished, or written with greater spirit, than this Epistle: Yet its success was in no proportion to the pains he took in composing it, or the effort of genius displayed in adorning it. Something he chanced to drop in a short advertisement prefixed to it, on its first publication, may perhaps account for the small attention the Public gave to it. He said, that *no one Character in it was drawn from the Life*. They believed him on his word; and expressed little curiosity about a satire in which there was nothing personal.

VER. I. *Nothing so true, &c.*] The reader, perhaps, may be disappointed to find that this *epistle*, which proposes the same subject with the preceding, is conducted on very different rules of composition; for instead of being disposed in the same logical method, and filled with the like philosophical remarks, it is wholly taken up in drawing a great variety of capital characters: But if he would reflect, that the *two Sexes* make but *one Species*, and consequently, that the characters of both must be studied and explained on the same principles, he would see, that when the Poet had done this in the preceding epistle, his business here was, not to repeat what he had already delivered, but only to verify and illustrate his doctrine, by every *view* of that perplexity of Nature, which *his* philosophy only can explain. If the reader therefore will but be at the pains to study these characters with any degree of attention, as they are drawn with a force of wit, sublimity, and true poetry never hitherto equalled, one important particular (for which the Poet has artfully prepared him by the introduction) will very forcibly strike his observation; and that is, that all the great strokes in the several characters of *Women* are not only infinitely perplexed and discordant, like those in *Men*, but absolutely inconsistent, and in a much higher degree contradictory. As strange as this may appear, yet he will see that the Poet has all the while strictly followed Nature, whose ways, we find by the former epistle, are not a little mysterious; and a mystery this might have remained, had not our Author explained it at Ver. 207, where he shuts up his *characters* with this philosophical reflection:

> In Men, we *various ruling Passions* find;
> In Women, *two* almost divide the kind;
> Those, only fix'd, they first or last obey,
> The love of Pleasure, and the love of Sway.

If this account be true, we see the perpetual necessity (which is not the case in *Men*) that *Women* lie under of *disguising* their *ruling Passion*. Now the variety of arts employed to this purpose, must needs draw them into infinite contradictions, even in those *actions* from whence their general and obvious character is denominated: To verify this observation, let the reader examine all the characters here drawn, and try whether, with this key, he cannot discover that all their contradictions arise from a desire to *hide the ruling Passion*.

But this is not the worst. The Poet afterwards (from Ver. 218 to 249.) takes notice of another mischief arising from this necessity of hiding their ruling Passions; which is, that generally the end of each is defeated, even there where they are most violently pursued: For the necessity of hiding them inducing an habitual dissipation of mind, Reason, whose office it is to regulate the *ruling Passion*, loses all its force and direction; and these unhappy victims to their principles, though with their attention *still fixed* upon them, are ever prosecuting the means destructive of their end; and thus become ridiculous in youth, and miserable in old age.

Let me not omit to observe the great beauty of the conclusion: It is an encomium on an *imaginary* Lady, to whom the epistle is addressed; and artfully turns upon the fact which makes the subject of the epistle, *the contradiction of a Woman's character*; in which contradiction, he shews, all the lustre even of the best character consists:

> And yet, believe me, good as well as ill,
> Woman's at best a *contradiction* still, &c.

> [iii. 249–51]

[Imitations of Horace: Sat. II. i]

WHOEVER expects a *Paraphrase* of Horace, or a faithful Copy of his genius, or manner of writing, in these IMITATIONS, will be much disappointed. Our Author uses the Roman Poet for little more than his canvas: And if the old design or colouring chance to suit his purpose, it is well: if not, he employs his own, without scruple or ceremony. Hence it is, he is so frequently serious when Horace is in jest; and at ease where Horace is disturbed. In a word, he regulates his movements no further on his Original, than was necessary for his concurrence, in promoting their common plan of *Reformation of manners*.

Had it been his purpose merely to paraphrase an ancient Satirist, he had hardly made choice of Horace; with whom, as a Poet, he held little in common, besides a comprehensive knowledge of life and manners, and a certain *curious felicity* of expression, which consists in using the simplest language with dignity, and the most ornamented, with ease. For the rest, his harmony and strength of numbers, his force and splendor of colouring, his gravity and sublime of sentiment, would have rather led him to another model. Nor was his temper less unlike that of Horace, than his talents. What Horace would only smile at, Mr. Pope would treat with the grave severity of Persius: And what Mr. Pope would strike with the caustic lightening of Juvenal, Horace would content himself with turning into ridicule.

If it be asked then, why he took any body at all to *imitate*, he has informed us in his *Advertisement*. To which we may add, that this sort of Imitations, which are of the nature of *Parodies*, throws reflected grace and splendor on original wit. Besides, he deemed it more modest to give the name of Imitations to his Satires, than, like Despreaux, to give the name of Satires to Imitations. [iv. 53]

[*Imitations of Horace: The Second and Fourth Satires of Dr. John Donne Versifyed*]

THE *manly Wit* of Donne, which was the character of his genius, suited best with *Satire*; and in this he excelled, though he wrote but little; six short poems being all we find amongst his writings of this sort. Mr. Pope has embellished two of them with his wit and harmony. He called it *versifying* them, because indeed the lines have nothing more of numbers than their being composed of a certain quantity of syllables. This is the more to be admired, because, as appears by his other poems, and especially from that fine fragment, called the *Progress of the Soul*, his Verse did not want harmony. But, I suppose, he took the *sermoni propiora* of Horace too seriously. . . . [iv. 241]

101. Catherine Talbot on Pope

1751

Catherine Talbot (1721–70), extract from a letter to Elizabeth Carter, 16 August 1751, *A Series of Letters between Mrs Elizabeth Carter and Miss Catherine Talbot. . . .* (1809), ii. 46–7.

Our present after-supper author is Mr. Pope, in Mr. Warburton's edition. Is it because one's strongest partialities, when in any point deceived, turn to the strongest prejudice of dislike, that I read those admirable poems and letters with a considerable mixture of pain and indignation? At some uncharitable moments one can scarce help looking upon all those eloquent expressions of benevolence and affection as too much parade, while one sees them overbalanced by such bitterness and cutting severity. I wish I knew the history of Patty [Blount]. Till I do I cannot read the Letters of friendship to her father with any satisfaction. I am afraid you will be angry with me for all this, but while every reading makes me more admire his genius, every one makes me more doubt his heart. One thing I am extremely offended at in his poems, and of which I never took so much notice before, his frequent quotations of Scripture phrases in much too ludicrous a way.

102. Cowper on Pope's Homer

c. 1753–7

William Cowper, extract from letter to Clotworthy Rowley, 21 February 1788, *A Selection from Cowper's Letters*, ed. E. V. Lucas (1911), p. 326. Here Cowper describes his attitude in the years 1753–7 to Pope's translation of the *Iliad*. In 1788 Cowper was translating the *Iliad* himself, and had cause to recall his poor opinion of Pope's work. See also his letter to Rev. John Newton, 10 December 1785, *op. cit.*, pp. 226–7.

Not much less than thirty years since, Alston and I read Homer through together. We compared Pope with his original all the way. The result was a discovery, that there is hardly the thing in the world of which Pope was so entirely destitute, as a taste for Homer. . . . I remembered how we had been disgusted; how often we had sought the simplicity and majesty of Homer in his English representative, and had found instead of them, puerile conceits, extravagant metaphors, and the tinsel of modern embellishment in every possible position. Neither did I forget how often we were on the point of burning Pope['s translation]. . . .

103. French praise for the *Pastorals*

1753

—— de Lustrac, extract from 'Avertissement', *Les Pastorales d'Alexandre Pope....* (Paris, 1753), sig. aiv-v. The translation was registered on 13 April 1753.

Among Pope's various works there are none which merit more esteem than his pastorals. They are regarded in England as a masterpiece of their genre, and this approval will not be contradicted in France, particularly by those who claim that our best eclogues cannot even be called by this name. It seems surprising, the French having so strongly shown their taste for the pastoral genius by the reception they gave to the *Aminta* and to *Pastor Fido* (although we have no satisfactory translation of it), that no-one has thought[1] up to now of putting into their hands works of the same kind, works if not as tender or with as lively expression, are at least simpler, more natural, more regular, and equally refined.

Pope's *Pastorals* form a complete work bearing the names of the four seasons which are depicted there with boundless art, beneath the appearance of the most agreeable natural simplicity. They are preceded by a discourse on pastoral poetry, which seems to be far above anything that we have on this subject.

Joined to this work is the poem on Windsor Forest, which ought to be put alongside Pope's *Pastorals*. It contains the description of a rural visit, and is adorned with all the graces of pastoral. It is a model for beautiful poetry which will always raise admiration in all good judges.

[1] The Eclogues that Madame de Montegut [1709–52] has made in imitation of Pope's *Pastorals*, and which one has seen in the *Recueils de l'Académie des Jeux Florales*, of which she was mistress, are the only known work in which anyone has attempted to give us some idea of these *Pastorals*.

104. A mid-century comparison of Pope and Dryden

February 1753

Robert Shiels, extract from his account of Pope in Theophilus Cibber's *Lives of the Poets of Great-Britain and Ireland* . . . (1753), v. 247–52.

Shiels (d. 1753), a Scotsman, was one of Johnson's amanuenses for the *Dictionary*. Although the *Lives of the Poets of Great-Britain and Ireland* was published under Cibber's name, Johnson claimed that Cibber had merely lent his name to Shiels's work for a ten-guinea fee. Cibber, however, did a considerable part of the work. On the whole Shiels is an admirer of Pope, though his account of the versification is an odd mixture of unquestioning admiration with the suggestion that its sound is monotonous. Curiously, Shiels does not allow Dryden's *MacFlecknoe* to be mock-heroic. Johnson took up Shiels's comparison of Dryden and Pope in his *Life of Pope* (pp. 489–91).

This great man [Pope] is allowed to have been one of the first rank among the poets of our nation, and to acknowledge the superiority of none but Shakespear, Milton, and Dryden. With the two former, it is unnatural to compare him, as their province in writing is so very different. Pope has never attempted the drama, nor published an Epic Poem, in which these two distinguished genius's have so wonderfully succeeded. Though Pope's genius was great, it was yet of so different a cast from Shakespear's, and Milton's, that no comparison can be justly formed. But if this may be said of the former two, it will by no means hold with respect to the latter, for between him and Dryden, there is a great similarity of writing, and a very striking coincidence of genius. It will not perhaps be unpleasing to our readers, if we pursue this comparison, and endeavour to discover to whom the superiority is justly to be attributed, and to which of them poetry owes the highest obligations.

When Dryden came into the world, he found poetry in a very imperfect state; its numbers were unpolished; its cadences rough, and there was nothing of harmony or mellifluence to give it a graceful of flow. In this harsh, unmusical situation, Dryden found it (for the refinements of Waller were but puerile and unsubstantial) he polished the rough diamond, he taught it to shine, and connected beauty, elegance, and strength, in all his poetical compositions. Though Dryden thus polished our English numbers, and thus harmonized versification, it cannot be said, that he carried his art to perfection. Much was yet left undone; his lines with all their smoothness were often rambling, and expletives were frequently introduced to compleat his measures. It was apparent therefore that an additional harmony might still be given to our numbers, and that cadences were yet capable of a more musical modulation. To effect this purpose Mr. Pope arose, who with an ear elegantly delicate, and the advantage of the finest genius, so harmonized the English numbers, as to make them compleatly musical. His numbers are likewise so minutely correct, that it would be difficult to conceive how any of his lines can be altered to advantage. He has created a kind of mechanical versification; every line is alike; and though they are sweetly musical, they want diversity, for he has not studied so great a variety of pauses, and where the accents may be laid gracefully. The structure of his verse is the best, and a line of his is more musical than any other line can be made, by placing the accents elsewhere; but we are not quite certain, whether the ear is not apt to be soon cloy'd with this uniformity of elegance, this sameness of harmony. It must be acknowledged however, that he has much improved upon Dryden in the article of versification, and in that part of poetry is greatly his superior. But though this must be acknowledged, perhaps it will not necessarily follow that his genius was therefore superior.

The grand characteristic of a poet is his invention, the surest distinction of a great genius. In Mr. Pope, nothing is so truly original as his Rape of the Lock, nor discovers so much invention. In this kind of mock-heroic, he is without a rival in our language, for Dryden has written nothing of the kind. His other work which discovers invention, fine designing, and admirable execution, is his Dunciad; which, tho' built on Dryden's Mac Flecknoe, is yet so much superior, that in satiric writing, the Palm must justly be yielded to him. In Mr. Dryden's Absalom and Achitophel, there are indeed the most poignant strokes of satire, and characters drawn with the most masterly touches; but this poem with all its excellencies is much inferior to the Dunciad, though Dryden had advantages which Mr. Pope had not; for Dryden's characters are men of great eminence and figure in the state, while Pope has to expose men of obscure birth and unimportant lives only distinguished from the herd of mankind, by a glimmering of genius, which rendered the greatest part of them more emphatically contemptible. Pope's was the hardest task, and he has executed it with the greatest success. As Mr. Dryden must undoubtedly have yielded to Pope in satyric writing, it is incumbent on the partizans of Dryden to name another species of composition, in which the former excells so as to throw the ballance again upon the side of Dryden. This species is the Lyric, in which the warmest votaries of Pope must certainly acknowledge, that he is much inferior; as an irresistable proof of this we need only compare Mr. Dryden's Ode on St. Cecilia's Day, with Mr. Pope's; in which the disparity is so apparent, that we know not if the most finished of Pope's compositions has discovered such a variety and command of numbers.

It hath been generally acknowledged, that the Lyric is a more excellent kind of writing than the Satiric; and consequently he who excells in the most excellent species, must undoubtedly be esteemed the greatest poet.——Mr. Pope has very happily succeeded in many of his occasional pieces, such as Eloisa to Abelard, his Elegy on an unfortunate young Lady, and a variety of other performances deservedly celebrated. To these may be opposed Mr. Dryden's Fables, which though written in a very advanced age, are yet the most perfect of his works. In these Fables there is perhaps a greater variety than in Pope's occasional pieces: Many of them indeed are translations, but such as are original shew a great extent of invention, and a large compass of genius.

There are not in Pope's works such poignant discoveries of wit, or such a general knowledge of the humours and characters of men, as in the Prologues and Epilogues of Dryden, which are the best records of the whims and capricious oddities of the times in which they are written.

When these two great genius's are considered in the light of translators, it will indeed be difficult to determine into whose scale the ballance should be thrown: That Mr. Pope had a more arduous province in doing justice to Homer, than Dryden with regard to Virgil is certainly true; as Homer is a more various and diffuse poet than Virgil; and it is likewise true, that Pope has even exceeded Dryden in the execution, and none will deny, that Pope's Homer's Iliad, is a finer poem than Dryden's Æneis of Virgil: Making a proper allowance for the disproportion of the original authors. But then a candid critic should reflect, that as Dryden was prior in the great attempt of rendering Virgil into English; so did he perform the task under many disadvantages, which Pope, by a happier situation in life, was enabled to avoid; and could not but improve upon Dryden's errors, though the authors translated were not the same: And it is much to be doubted, if Dryden were to translate the Æneid now, with that attention which the correctness of the present age would force upon him, whether the preference would be due to Pope's Homer.

But supposing it to be yielded (as it certainly must) that the latter bard was the greatest translator; we are now to throw into Mr. Dryden's scale all his dramatic works; which though not the most excellent of his writings, yet as nothing of Mr. Pope's can be opposed to them, they have an undoubted right to turn the ballance greatly in favour of Mr. Dryden.——When the two poets are considered as critics, the comparison will very imperfectly hold. Dryden's Dedications and Prefaces, besides that they are more numerous, and are the best models for courtly panegyric, shew that he understood poetry as an art, beyond any man that ever lived. And he explained this art so well, that he taught his antagonists to turn the tables against himself; for he so illuminated the mind by his clear and perspicuous reasoning, that dullness itself became capable of discerning; and when at any time his performances fell short of his own ideas of excellence; his enemies tried him by rules of his own establishing; and though they owed to him the ability of judging, they seldom had candour enough to spare him.

Perhaps it may be true that Pope's works are read with more appetite, as there is a greater evenness and correctness in them; but in perusing the works of Dryden the mind will take a wider range, and be more fraught with poetical ideas: We admire Dryden as the greater genius, and Pope as the most pleasing versifier.

105. Warton on Pope's borrowings

1753

Joseph Warton, *The Adventurer*, no. 63, 12 June 1753, 2nd ed. (1754), ii. 227–35. See Introduction, p. 24.

Pereant, qui ante nos nostra dixerunt!
DONATUS apud JEROM.[1]

Perish those! who have said our good things before us.

THE number of original writers, of writers who discover any traces of native thought, or veins of new expression, is found to be extremely small in every branch of literature. Few possess ability or courage to think for themselves, to trust to their own powers, to rely on their own stock; and, therefore, the generality creep tamely and cautiously in the track of their predecessors. The quintessence of the largest libraries might be reduced to the compass of a few volumes, if all useless repetitions and acknowledged truths were to be omitted in this process of critical chemistry. A learned Frenchman informs us, that he intended to compile a treatise . . . 'concerning things that had been said but ONCE,' which certainly would have been contained in a very small pamphlet.

IT happens unfortunately in poetry, which principally claims the merit of novelty and invention, that this want of originality arises frequently, not from a barrenness and timidity of genius, but from invincible necessity and the nature of things. The works of those who profess an art whose essence is imitation, must needs be stamped with a close resemblance to each other; since the objects material or animate, extraneous or internal, which they all imitate, lie equally open to the observation of all, and are perfectly similar. Descriptions, therefore, that are faithful and just, must be uniform and alike: the first copier may be, perhaps, entitled to the praise of priority; but a succeeding one ought not certainly to be condemned for plagiarism.

[1] [Cited by Jerome in his *Commentarias in Ecclesiasticen*, I. 9/10 (*S. Hieronymi presbyteri opera*, I. i, Corpus Christiana Latina Series, lxxii. 257) from Donatus, *Comm. in Terent. Eun.*]

I AM inclined to think, that notwithstanding the manifold alterations diffused in modern times over the face of nature, by the invention of arts and manufactures, by the extent of commerce, by the improvements in philosophy and mathematics, by the manner of fortifying and fighting, by the important discovery of both the Indies, and above all by the total change of religion; yet an epic or dramatic writer, though surrounded with such a multitude of novelties, would find it difficult or impossible to be totally original, and essentially different from HOMER and SOPHOCLES. The causes that excite and the operations that exemplify the greater passions, will always have an exact coincidence, though perhaps a little diversified by climate or custom: every exasperated hero must rage like ACHILLES, and every afflicted widow mourn like ANDRO-MACHE: an abandoned ARMIDA will make use of DIDO's execrations; and a Jew will nearly resemble a Grecian, when placed almost in the same situation; that is, the IÖAS of RACINE in his incomparable ATHALIA, will be very like the IÖN of EURIPIDES.

BOILEAU observes, that a new and extraordinary thought is by no means a thought which no person ever conceived before, or could possibly conceive; on the contrary, it is such a thought as must have occurred to every man in the like case, and have been one of the first in any person's mind upon the same occasion: and it is a maxim of POPE, that whatever is very good sense, must have been common sense in all times.

BUT if from the foregoing reflections it may appear difficult, to distinguish imitation and plagiarism from necessary resemblance and unavoidable analogy, yet the following passages of POPE, which, because they have never been taken notice of, may possibly entertain curious and critical readers, seem evidently to be borrowed, though they are improved.

THE dying CHRISTIAN addresses his soul with a fine spirit of poetical enthusiasm:

> Vital spark of heavenly flame!
> Quit, O quit this mortal frame!
> Trembling, hoping, ling'ring, flying,
> O! the pain, the bliss of dying!—
> Hark; they whisper—Angels say,
> Sister spirit, come away! [ll. 1–8]

I was surprized to find this animated passage closely copied from one of the vile Pindaric writers in the time of Charles the second:

When on my sick bed I languish,
Full of sorrow, full of anguish,
Fainting, gasping, trembling, crying,
Panting, groaning, speechless, dying!—
Methinks I hear some gentle spirit say,
Be not fearful, come away!   FLATMAN.[1]

PALINGENIUS and CHARRON furnished him with the two following thoughts in the Essay on Man:

Superior beings, when of late they saw
A mortal man unfold all nature's law;
Admir'd such wisdom in an earthly shape,
And shew'd a NEWTON, as we shew an ape.

POPE. [*An Essay on Man*, ii. 31-4]

Utque movet nobis imitatrix simia risum,
Sic nos cœlicolis, quoties cervice superba
Ventosi gradimur——[2]

And again,

Simia cœlicolûm, risusque jocusque deorum est
Tunc homo, quum temerè ingenio confidit, & audet
Abdita naturæ scrutari, arcanaque divûm.   PALINGENIUS.[3]

While man exclaims, 'see all things for my use!'
'See man for mine!' replies a pamper'd goose.

POPE. [*An Essay on Man*, iii. 44-5]

'Man scruples not to say, that he enjoyeth the heavens and the elements; as if all had been made, and still move, only for him. In this sense a gosling may say as much, and perhaps with more truth and justness.'
CHARRON.[4]

THAT he hath borrowed not only sentiments but even expressions from WOLLASTON and PASCAL cannot be doubted, if we consider two more passages:

[1] [T. Flatman, 'A Thought of Death', ll. 1-4, 12-13]
[2] [Palingenius, *Zodiacus Vitae*, v. 26-8: Barnabe Googe translates, 'And as the Ape that counterfets, to us doth laughter move, / So we likewise doe cause and move the Saintes to laugh above / As oft as stately steps we tread with looke of proud disdaine']
[3] [Palingenius, *op. cit.*, vi. 182-4: 'An ape and iesting stock is man to God in skye, / As oft as he doth trust his wit to much, presuming hye, / Dare searche the things of nature hid his secrets for to speake.']
[4] [P. Charron, *Of Wisdom*, tr. H. Stanhope, 3rd ed. (1729), I. xl]

When the loose mountain trembles from on high,
Shall gravitation cease if you go by?
Or some old temple nodding to its fall,
For Chartres' head reserve the hanging wall?

POPE. [An Essay on Man, iii. 127–30]

'If a good man be passing by an infirm building, just in the article of falling; can it be expected, that GOD should suspend the force of gravitation till he is gone by, in order to his deliverance?'

WOLLASTON.[1]

Chaos of thought and passion all confus'd,
Still by himself abus'd, or disabus'd;
Created half to rise, and half to fall,
Great lord of all things, yet a prey to all;
Sole judge of truth, in endless error hurl'd,
The glory, jest, and riddle of the world.

POPE. [An Essay on Man, ii. 13–18]

'What a chimera then is man! what a confused chaos! what a subject of contradiction! a professed judge of all things, and yet a feeble worm of the earth! the great depositary and guardian of truth, and yet a mere huddle of uncertainty! the glory and the scandal of the universe!'

PASCAL.[2]

THE witty allusion to the punishment of avarice, in the Epistle on Riches,

Damn'd to the mines, an equal fate betides
The slave that digs it, and the slave that hides;

[ll. 111–12]

is plainly taken from 'The causes of the decay of Christian piety,'[3] where that excellent and neglected writer says, 'It has always been held the severest treatment of slaves and malefactors,' *damnare ad metalla*, 'to force them to dig in the mines: now this is the covetous man's lot, from which he is never to expect a release.' COWLEY also has used the same allusion. The celebrated reflection with which CHARTRES's epitaph,[4] in the same epistle, concludes, is the property of BRUYERE.

---

[1] [William Wollaston, *The Religion of Nature Delineated*, 7th ed. (1750), pp. 178–9]

[2] [*Thoughts on Religion, and Other Curious Subjects*, tr. B. Kennett, 3rd ed. (1731), p. 162]

[3] [By Richard Allestree, published 1667]

[4] [Chartres's epitaph is in fact by Dr Arbuthnot. Pope gives it as a note, *Moral Essays*, iii. 20]

To rock the cradle of reposing age,
> *[Epistle to Dr. Arbuthnot*, l. 409]

is a tender and elegant image of filial piety, for which POPE is indebted to MONTAGNE, who wishes, in one of his essays, to find a son-in-law that may 'kindly cherish his old age, and rock it asleep.' And the character of HELLUO the glutton, introduced to exemplify the force and continuance of the ruling passion, who in the agonies of death exclaimed,

—— Then bring the JOWL!
> *[Moral Essays I: To Cobham*, l. 237]

is taken from that tale in FONTAINE, which ends,

> —— *Puis qui'il faut que je meure*
> *Sans faire tant de facon,*
> *Qu'on m'apporte tout à l'heure*
> *Le reste de mon poisson.*[1]

THE conclusion of the epitaph on GAY, where he observes that his honour consists not in being entombed among kings and heroes,

> But that the worthy and the good may say,
> Striking their pensive bosoms—Here lies GAY;
> > [ll. 11–12]

is adopted from an old latin elegy on the death of prince HENRY.

IN several parts of his writings, POPE seems to have formed himself on the model of BOILEAU; as might appear, from a large deduction of particular passages, almost literally translated, from that nervous and sensible satyrist.

> —— Happily to steer
> From grave to gay, from lively to severe.
> > POPE. [*An Essay on Man*, iv. 379–80]

> —— *D'une voix legere*
> *Passer du grave au doux, du plaisant au severe!*   BOILEAU.[2]

Pride, malice, folly, against DRYDEN rose,
In various shaps of parsons, critics, beaus.
> POPE. [*An Essay on Criticism*, ll. 458–9]

---

[1] [*Contes et Novelles en Vers* (Amsterdam, 1685), ii. 96: 'Since I must die without making a fuss, let them bring me the rest of my fish right on the hour.' Further, see F. W. Bateson's note, Twickenham, III. ii]

[2] [*Art poétique*, i. 75–6: 'with a light style to pass from grave to gentle, from the pleasing to the severe.' See also Twickenham, III. i. 165n.]

L'ignorance, & l'erreur a ses naissantes pieces,
En habits de marquis, en robbes de comtesses,
Venoient pour diffamer son chef-d-œuvre noveau.

BOILEAU.[1]

While I am transcribing these similarities, I feel great uneasiness, lest I should be accused of vainly and impotently endeavouring to cast clouds over the reputation of this exalted and truly original genius, 'whose memory,' to use an expression of BEN JONSON, 'I do honour, on this side idolatry, as much as any;' and lest the reader should be cloyed and disgusted with a cluster of quotations: it happens, however, fortunately, that each passage I have produced, contains some important moral truth, or conveys some pleasing image to the mind.

CRITICS seem agreed in giving greater latitude to the imitation of the ancients, than of later writers. To enrich a composition with the sentiments and images of Greece and Rome, is ever esteemed, not only lawful, but meritorious. We adorn our writings with their ideas, with as little scruple, as our houses with their statues. And POUSSIN is not accused of plagiarism, for having painted AGRIPPINA covering her face with both her hands at the death of GERMANICUS; though TIMANTHES had represented AGAMEMNON closely veiled at the sacrifice of his daughter, judiciously leaving the spectator to guess at a sorrow inexpressible, and that mocked the power of the pencil.[2]

---

[1] [*Épître*, vii. 23-5. Boileau's lines are on Molière: 'Ignorance and error at his new-born pieces, in the clothes of a marquis, the robes of countesses, have deformed his new chef d'œuvre.']

[2] [Timanthes, a Greek painter of the fourth century B.C. His most celebrated work was a picture of the sacrifice of Iphigenia, in which despairing of picturing Agamemnon's grief, Timanthes presented him veiling his face. A painting of this subject found at Pompeii is thought to be a copy. Poussin's 'Death of Germanicus' is now in the Minneapolis Institute of Arts. It was one of his most popular works in the eighteenth century. Agrippina has only one hand over her face.]

106. Warton's *Essay*, volume i

1756

Joseph Warton, extracts from *An Essay on the Writings and Genius of Pope*, i (1756). The first volume appeared in March or April.

Warton made revisions to his text over the five subsequent editions of 1762, 1772, and 1782. Twenty-six years later he published the second volume of his work. For an account of the history of the editions, see W. D. MacClintock, *Joseph Warton's Essay on Pope: A History of Five Editions* (Chapel Hill, 1933). The text of the first volume is taken from the first edition. Major revisions and additions made over the years are given in the footnotes, since these give a valuable account of Warton's changing opinions. Some notes, more concerned with literary history than Pope, have been omitted. Extracts from volume ii are given as No. 128.

Warton's dedicatory letter to Edward Young is of particular interest since his *Essay*, and Young's own *Conjectures on Original Composition* (1759) given here as No. 112, are important statements of new critical standards (see Introduction, pp. 24–6). Dr Johnson's immediate response to Warton's views is given as No. 107.

TO THE REVEREND
DR YOUNG,

RECTOR of WELWYN
IN HERTFORDSHIRE.

DEAR SIR,
PERMIT me to break into your retirement, the residence of virtue and literature, and to trouble you with a few reflections on the merits and real character of an admired author, and on other collateral subjects, that will naturally arise.[1] No love of singularity, no affectation of paradoxical opinions, gave rise to the following work. I revere the memory of POPE, I respect and honour his abilities; but I do not think

[1] *arise.*] ~ *in the course of such an inquiry.* 1762–82.

379

him at the head of his profession. In other words, in that species of poetry wherein POPE excelled, he is superior to all mankind: and I only say, that this species of poetry is not the most excellent one of the art.[1] We do not, it should seem, sufficiently attend to the difference there is, betwixt a MAN OF WIT, a MAN OF SENSE, and a TRUE POET. Donne and Swift, were undoubtedly men of wit, and men of sense: but what traces have they left of PURE POETRY?[2] Fontenelle and La Motte are entitled to the former character; but what can they urge to gain the latter? Which of these characters is the most valuable and useful, is entirely out of the question: all I plead for, is, to have their several provinces kept distinct from each other; and to impress on the reader, that a clear head, and acute understanding are not sufficient, alone, to make a POET; that the most solid observations on human life, expressed with the utmost elegance and brevity, are MORALITY, and not POETRY; that the EPISTLES of Boileau in RHYME, are no more poetical, than the CHARACTERS of Bruyere in PROSE; and that it is a creative and glowing IMAGINATION, 'acer spiritus ac vis',[3] and that alone, that can stamp a writer with this exalted and very uncommon character, which so few possess, and of which so few can properly judge.

FOR one person, who can adequately relish, and enjoy, a work of imagination, twenty are to be found who can taste and judge of, observations on familiar life, and the manners of the age. The satires of Ariosto, are more read than the Orlando Furioso, or even Dante. Are there so many cordial admirers of Spenser and Milton, as of Hudibras? —If we strike out of the number of these supposed admirers, those who appear such out of fashion, and not of feeling. Swift's rhapsody on poetry is far more popular, than Akenside's noble ode to Lord Huntingdon. The EPISTLES on the Characters of men and women, and your sprightly satires, my good friend, are more frequently perused, and quoted, than L'Allegro and Il Penseroso of Milton. Had you written only these satires,[4] you would indeed have gained the title of a man of wit, and a man of sense; but, I am confident, would not insist on being denominated a POET, MERELY on their account.

NON SATIS EST PURIS VERSUM PERSCRIBERE VERBIS.[5]

---

[1] art.] new paragraph here, 1762–82.

[2] POETRY?] 1762–82 add: *It is remarkable, that Dryden says of Donne; He was the greatest wit, tho' not the greatest poet of this nation.* [See *Essays of John Dryden*, ed. W. P. Ker (1900), ii. 102]

[3] ['The fire and force of inspiration', Horace, *Sermones*, I. iv. 46]

[4] [Young's *Universal Passion* (1725–8)]

[5] [Horace, *Sermones*, I. iv. 54: 'It is not enough to write out a line of simple words']

IT is amazing this matter should ever have been mistaken, when Horace has taken particular and repeated pains, to settle and adjust the opinion in question. He has more than once disclaimed all right and title to the name of POET, on the score of his ethic and satiric pieces.

——NEQUE ENIM CONCLUDERE VERSUM
DIXERIS ESSE SATIS——[1]

are lines, often repeated, but whose meaning is not extended and weighed as it ought to be. Nothing can be more judicious than the method he prescribes, of trying whether any composition be essentially poetical or not; which is, to drop entirely the measures and numbers, and transpose and invert the order of the words: and in this unadorned manner to peruse the passage.[2] If there be really in it a true poetical spirit, all your inversions and transpositions will not disguise and extinguish it; but it will retain its lustre, like a diamond, unset, and thrown back into the rubbish of the mine. Let us make a little experiment on the following well-known lines;

Yes, you despise the man that is confined to books, who rails at human kind from his study; tho' what he learns, he speaks; and may perhaps advance some general maxims, or may be right by chance. The coxcomb bird, so grave and so talkative, that cries whore, knave, and cuckold, from his cage, tho' he rightly call many a passenger, you hold him no philosopher. And yet, such is the fate of all extremes, men may be read too much, as well as books. We grow more partial, for the sake of the observer, to observations which we ourselves make; less, so, to written wisdom, because another's. Maxims are drawn from notions, and those from guess.[3]

What shall we say of this passage?—Why, that it is most excellent sense, but just as poetical as the 'Qui fit Mæcenas' of the author who recommends this method of trial. Take any[4] ten lines of the Iliad, Paradise Lost, or even of the Georgics of Virgil, and see whether by any process of critical chymistry, you can lower and reduce them to the tameness of prose. You will find that they will appear like Ulysses in his disguise of rags, still a hero, tho' lodged in the cottage of the herdsman Eumæus.

THE Sublime and the Pathetic are the two chief nerves of all genuine poesy. What is there very sublime or very Pathetic[5] in POPE? In his works there is indeed, 'nihil inane, nihil arcessitum;—puro tamen fonti quam magno flumini propior;' as the excellent Quintilian remarks of

[1] [*Ibid.*, I. iv. 40: 'For you would not call it enough to round off a verse']
[2] [See Horace, *Sermones*, I. iv. 56ff.; also Sidney's *Defense of Poesy* (1595)]
[3] [*Moral Essays* I, *Epistle to Cobham*, ll. 1–14]   [4] *any*] *om.* 1762–82.
[5] *very . . . Pathetic*] *transcendently Sublime or Poetic* 1762–82.

Lysias.[1] And because I am perhaps ashamed or afraid[2] to speak out in plain English, I will adopt the following passage of Voltaire, which, in my opinion, as exactly characterizes POPE, as it does his model Boileau, for whom it was originally designed. 'INCAPABLE PEUTETRE DU SUBLIME QUI ELEVE L' AME, ET DU SENTIMENT QUI L' ATTENDRIT, MAIS FAIT POUR ECLAIRER CEUX A QUI LA NATURE ACCORDA L' UN ET L' AUTRE, LABORIEUX, SEVERE, PRECIS, PUR, HARMONIEUX, IL DEVINT, ENFIN, LE POETE DE LA RAISON.'[3]

OUR English poets may, I think, be disposed in four different classes and degrees. In the first class, I would place, first, our only three sublime and pathetic poets; SPENSER, SHAKESPEARE, MILTON; and then, at proper intervals, OTWAY and LEE.[4] In the second class should be placed, such as possessed the true poetical genius, in a more moderate degree, but had noble talents for moral and ethical[5] poesy. At the head of these are DRYDEN, DONNE, DENHAM, COWLEY, CONGREVE.[6] In the third class may be placed, men of wit, of elegant taste, and some fancy[7] in describing familiar life.[8] Here may be numbered, PRIOR, WALLER, PARNELL, SWIFT, FENTON.[9] In the fourth class, the mere versifiers, however smooth and mellifluous some of them may be thought, should be ranked. Such as PITT, SANDYS, FAIRFAX, BROOME, BUCKINGHAM, LANSDOWN.[10] In which of these classes POPE deserves to be placed, the following work is intended to determine.

> I am DEAR SIR,
> Your affectionate
> And faithful servant.
> [i, pp. iii–xii]

[1] [*Institutio Oratorio*, X. i. 78: 'Nothing irrelevant or far-fetched. None the less I would compare him to a clear stream rather than a mighty river']

[2] *ashamed or afraid*] *unwilling* 1762–82.

[3] ['Incapable, perhaps, of the sublime which lifts up the soul, and of the feeling which softens it, but made to enlighten those upon whom nature bestowed the one and the other, hard-working, stern, precise, pure, harmonious, he becomes, finally, the poet of reason', *Discours à sa réception à l'Académie française, prononcée le lundi 9 Mai 1746* (*Oeuvres* [1748], xlvii. 12)]

[4] *; and . . . LEE.*] om. 1762–82.

[5] *moral and ethical*] *moral, ethical, and panegyrical* 1762–82.

[6] DRYDEN . . . CONGREVE.] DRYDEN, PRIOR, ADDISON, COWLEY, WALLER, GARTH, FENTON, GAY, DENHAM, PARNELL 1762–82.

[7] *some fancy*] *lively fancy* 1762–82.

[8] *life.*] *life, though not the higher scenes of poetry.* 1762–82.

[9] PRIOR . . . FENTON.] BUTLER, SWIFT, ROCHESTER, DONNE, DORSET, OLDHAM. 1762–82.

[10] LANSDOWN.] ~ . *This enumeration is not intended as a complete catalogue, but only to mark out briefly the different species of our celebrated writers.* 1762; . . . *catalogue of writers, and in their proper order,* . . . 1772–82.

[*Pastorals*]

PRINCES and Authors are seldom spoken of, during their lives, with justice and impartiality. Admiration and envy, their constant attendants, like two unskilful artists, are apt to overcharge their pieces with too great a quantity of light or of shade; and are disqualified happily to hit upon that middle colour, that mixture of error and excellence, which alone renders every representation of man just and natural. This perhaps may be one reason, among others, why we have never yet seen a fair and candid criticism on the character and merits of our last great poet, Mr. POPE. I have therefore thought, that it would be no unpleasing amusement, or uninstructive employment to examine at large, without blind panegyric, or petulant invective, the writings of this English Classic, in the order in which they are arranged in the elegant edition of Mr. Warburton. As I shall neither censure nor commend, without alleging the reason on which my opinion is founded, I shall be entirely unmoved at the imputation of malignity, or the clamours of popular prejudice.

IT is something[1] strange, that in the pastorals of a young poet there should not be found a single rural image that is new: but this I am afraid is the case in the PASTORALS before us. The ideas of Theocritus, Virgil, and Spenser, are indeed here exhibited in language equally mellifluous and pure; but the descriptions and sentiments are trite and common. That the design of pastoral poesy is, to represent the undisturbed felicity of the golden age, is an empty notion, which, though supported by a Rapin and a Fontenelle,[2] I think, all rational critics have agreed to exstirpate and explode. But I do not remember, that even these last-mentioned[3] critics have remarked the circumstance that gave origin to the opinion that any golden age was intended. Theocritus, the father and the model of this enchanting species of composition, lived and wrote in Sicily. The climate of Sicily was delicious, and the face of the country various, and beautiful: it's vallies and it's precipices, it's grottos and cascades were SWEETLY INTERCHANGED, and it's fruits and flowers[4] were lavish and luscious. The poet described what he saw and felt: and had no need to have recourse to those artificial assemblages of pleasing

---

[1] *something*] *somewhat* 1762–82.

[2] *Fontenelle*] 1782 adds a footnote on Fontenelle's attempts to 'depreciate the ancients'. [See *Idylliums of Theocritus with Rapin's Discourse of Pastorals* (1684) and Fontenelle's *Poésies pastorales* (Paris, 1688)]

[3] *last-mentioned*] ∼, *or any* 1762–82.

[4] *fruits and flowers*] *flowers and fruits* 1762–82.

objects, which are not to be found in nature. The figs and the honey which he assigns as a reward to a victorious shepherd were in themselves exquisite, and are therefore assigned with great propriety:[1] and the beauties of that luxurious landschape so richly and circumstantially delineated in the close of the seventh idyllium, where all things smelt of summer and smelt of autumn,

[Quotes in Greek, *Idyll*. i. 143: 'All nature smelt of the opulent summertime, smelt of the season of fruit']

were present and real. Succeeding writers supposing these beauties too great and abundant to be real, referred them to the fictitious and imaginary scenes of a golden age.

A MIXTURE of British and Grecian ideas may justly be deemed a blemish in the PASTORALS of POPE: and propriety is certainly violated, when he couples Pactolus with Thames, and Windsor with Hybla. Complaints of IMMODERATE heat, and wishes to be conveyed to cooling caverns, when uttered by the inhabitants of Greece, have a decorum and consistency, which they totally lose in the character of a British shepherd: and Theocritus, during the ardors of Sirius, must have heard the murmurings of a brook, and the whispers of a pine,[2] with more home-felt pleasure, than Pope could possibly experience upon the same occasion.[3] We can never completely relish, or adequately understand any author, especially any Ancient, except we constantly keep in our eye his climate, his country, and his age. POPE himself informs us, in a note, that he judiciously omitted the following verse,

And list'ning wolves grow milder as they hear[4]

on account of the absurdity, which Spenser overlooked, of introducing wolves into England. But on this principle, which is certainly a just one, may it not be asked, why he should speak, the scene lying in Windsor-Forest, of the SULTRY SIRIUS, of the GRATEFUL CLUSTERS *of grapes*, of a *pipe of reeds*, the antique fistula, of *thanking Ceres for a plentiful harvest*, of *the sacrifice of lambs*,[5] with many other instances that might be adduced to this purpose. That POPE however was sensible of the importance of adapting images to the scene of action, is obvious from the following example of his judgment; for in translating,

[1] *Idyllium*, i. 146.
[2] *Ibid.*, i. 1.
[3] *Pastorals*, iv. 1.
[4] *Pastorals*, ii. [79 note]
[5] *Pastorals*, ii. 21, iii. 74, ii. 43, 66, iv. 81.

Audiit EUROTAS, jussitque ediscere LAUROS[1]

he has dextrously dropt the *laurels* appropriated to Eurotas, as he is speaking of the river Thames, and has rendered it,

> THAMES heard the numbers, as he flow'd along,
> And bade his *willows* learn the moving song.[2]

IN the passages which POPE has imitated from Theocritus, and from his Latin translator Virgil, he has merited but little applause. It may not be unentertaining to see how coldly and unpoetically POPE has copied the subsequent appeal to the nymphs on the death of Daphnis, in comparison of Milton on LYCIDAS, one of his juvenile[3] pieces.

[Quotes in Greek, *Idyll*. i. 66: 'Where were ye, nymphs, where were ye, when Daphnis was wasting? In the fair vales of Penius or of Pindus? for surely you kept not the mighty stream of Anapus, nor the peak of Etna, nor the sacred rill of Acis']

> Where stray, ye muses, in what lawn or grove,
> While your Alexis pines in hopeless love?
> In those fair fields where sacred Isis glides,
> Or else where Cam his winding vales divides.[4]

> Where were ye, nymphs, when the remorseless deep
> Clos'd o'er the head of your lov'd Lycidas?
> For neither were ye playing on the steep
> Where your old bards, the famous Druids, lie;
> Nor on the shaggy top of Mona high,
> Nor yet where Deva spreads her wizard stream.[5]

THE mention of places remarkably romantic, the supposed habitation of Druids, bards, and wizards, is far more pleasing to the imagination, than the obvious introduction of Cam and Isis, as seats of the Muses.

A SHEPHERD in Theocritus wishes with much tenderness and elegance, both which must suffer in a literal translation, 'Would I could become a murmuring bee, fly into your grotto, and be permitted to creep among the leaves of ivy and fern that compose the chaplet which adorns your head.'[6]

---

[1] Virgil, *Eclogue* vi. 83. ['Eurotas listened and bade his laurels learn']
[2] *Pastorals*, iv. 14.   [3] *juvenile*] *most exquisite* 1762–82.
[4] *Pastorals*, ii. 23.   [5] Milton, *Lycidas*, l. 50.
[6] [*Idyll*. iii. 12–14: 'would I might become yon buzzing bee, and come into thy cave through the ivy and fern that hides thee' (A. S. F. Gow)].

Pope has thus altered this image,

> Oh! were I made by some transforming pow'r,
> The captive bird that sings within thy bow'r!
> Then might my voice thy list'ning ears employ;
> And I, those kisses he receives, enjoy.[1]

On three accounts the former image is preferable to the latter: for the pastoral wildness, the delicacy, and the uncommonness of the thought. I cannot forbear adding, that the riddle of the *Royal Oak*, in the first Pastoral, invented in imitation of the Virgilian ænigmas in the third eclogue, savours of pun, and puerile conceit.

> Say, Daphnis, say in what glad soil appears
> A wondrous tree, that sacred monarchs bears?[2]

With what propriety could the tree, whose shade protected the king, be said to be prolific of princes?

THAT POPE had not equalled Theocritus, will indeed appear less surprising, if we reflect, that no original writer ever remained so un-rivalled by succeeding copyists, as this Sicilian master.

IF it should be objected, that the barrenness of invention imputed to POPE from a view of his PASTORALS, is equally imputable to the Buco-lics of Virgil, it may be answered, that whatever may be determined of the rest, yet the first and last Eclogues of Virgil are indisputable proofs of true genius, and power of fancy. The influence of war on the tran-quillity of rural life,[3] rendered the subject of the first new, and interest-ing: its composition is truly dramatic; and the characters of its two shepherds are well supported, and happily contrasted: and the last has expressively painted the changeful resolutions, the wild wishes, the passionate and abrupt exclamations, of a disappointed and despairing lover.

UPON the whole, the principal merit of the PASTORALS of POPE con-sists, in their correct and musical versification; musical, to a degree of which rhyme could hardly be thought capable: and in giving the first specimen of that harmony in English verse, which is now become indispensably necessary; and which has so forcibly and universally influenced the publick ear, as to have rendered every moderate rhymer

---

[1] [*Pastorals*, ii. 45.]   [2] *Pastorals*, i. 85.

[3] I have been lately highly entertained with the accidental perusal of FIVE PASTORALS, written on this plan, descriptive of the calamities supposed to have been felt by the shep-herds of Germany during the last war: They abound in many new circumstances of pas-toral distress, and many tender images. I cannot learn the name of the author. [Omitted 1762–82]

melodious. POPE lengthened the abruptness of Waller, and at the same time contracted the exuberance of Dryden.   [pp. 1–10]

[Windsor Forest]

DESCRIPTIVE Poetry was by no means the shining talent of POPE. This assertion may be manifested by the few images introduced into the poem [Windsor Forest] before us, which are not equally applicable to any place whatsoever. Rural beauty in general, and not the peculiar beauties of the forest of Windsor, are here described. Nor are the sports of setting, shooting, and fishing, included between the ninety-third and one hundred and forty-sixth verses, to which the reader is referred, at all more appropriated. The stag-chase, that immediately follows, although some of the lines are incomparably good,[1] is not so full, so animated, and so circumstantiated, as that of Somerville. . . .[2] [p. 20]

IT is one of the greatest and most pleasing arts of descriptive poetry, to introduce moral sentences and instructions in an oblique and indirect manner, in places where one naturally expects only painting and amusement. We have virtue, as POPE remarks,[3] put upon us by surprize, and are pleased to find a thing where we should never have looked to meet with it. I must do a noble[4] English poet the justice to observe, that it is this particular art that is the very distinguishing excellence of COOPER'S-HILL; throughout which, the descriptions of places, and images raised by the poet, are still tending to some hint, or leading into some reflection, upon moral life, or political institution; much in the same manner as the real sight of such scenes and prospects is apt to give the mind a composed turn, and incline it to thoughts and contemplations that have a relation to the object. This is the great charm of the incomparable ELEGY written in a Country Church-Yard. Having mentioned the rustic monuments and simple epitaphs of the swains, the amiable poet falls into a very natural reflection:

> For who, to dumb forgetfulness a prey,
> This pleasing anxious being e'er resign'd,
> Left the warm precincts of the chearful day,
> Nor cast one longing lingring look behind?   [ll. 85–8]

---

[1] See particularly, ver. 151.
[2] [William Somervile (1672–1745), *The Chace* (1735)]
[3] [*Iliad*, xvi. 465 note]
[4] *noble*] pleasing 1782.

OF this art Mr. POPE has exhibited some specimens in the poem we are examining, but not so many as might be expected from a mind so strongly inclined to a moral way of writing. After speaking of hunting the hare, he immediately subjoins, much in the spirit of Denham,

> Beasts urg'd by us their fellow beasts pursue,
> And learn of man each other to undo.[1]   [ll. 123-4]

Where he is describing the tyrannies formerly exercised in this kingdom,

> Cities laid waste, they storm'd the dens and caves,

He instantly adds, with an indignation becoming a true lover of liberty, as such he was,[2]

> For wiser brutes were backward to be slaves. . . .
>   [ll. 49-50]

A PATHETIC reflection, properly introduced into a descriptive poem, will have greater force and beauty, and more deeply interest a reader, than a moral one. When POPE therefore has described a pheasant shot, he breaks out into a very masterly exclamation;

> Ah! what avail his glossy varying dyes,
> His purple crest, and scarlet-circled eyes,
> The vivid green his shining plumes unfold,
> His painted wings, and breast that flames with gold.
>   [ll. 115-18]

where this[3] exquisite picture heightens the distress, and powerfully excites the commiseration of the reader.

[Warton goes on to discuss *Georgics*, iii. 525ff.]

OF English poets, perhaps, none have excelled the ingenious Mr. Dyer in this oblique instruction, into which he frequently steals imperceptibly, in his little descriptive poem entitled GRONGAR HILL, where he disposes every object so as it may give occasion for some observation on human life. Denham himself is not superiour to this neglected author[4] in this particular. . . .

---

[1] [1782 adds a footnote: *But a critic of taste has objected to me the use of the word* undo: *and of the word* backward *in a subsequent line*.]

[2] *as such he was*] omitted 1762-82.

[3] *where this*] THIS 1762-82.

[4] *this neglected author*] Mr. Dyer 1762-82.

THE unexpected insertion of such reflections, imparts to us the same pleasure that we feel, when in wandering through a wilderness or grove, we suddenly behold in the turning of the walk, a statue of some VIRTUE or MUSE. [i. 30–6]

[An Essay on Criticism]

WE are now arrived at a poem of that species, for which our author's genius was particularly turned, the DIDACTIC and the MORAL; it is therefore, as might be expected, a master-piece in its kind. I have been sometimes inclined to think, that the praises Addison has bestowed on it,[1] were a little partial and invidious. 'The observations, says he, follow one another, like those in Horace's Art of Poetry, without that methodical regularity which would have been requisite in a prose writer.' It is however certain, that the poem before us is by no means destitute of a just integrity, and a lucid order: each of the precepts and remarks naturally introduce the succeeding ones, so as to form an entire whole. The ingenious Mr.[2] Hurd, hath also usefully shewn,[3] that Horace observed a strict method, and unity of design, in his epistle to the Pisones, and that altho the connexions are delicately fine and almost imperceptible, like the secret hinges of a well-wrought box, yet they artfully and closely unite each part together, and give coherence, uniformity, and beauty to the work. The Spectator adds; 'The observations in this essay are *some* of them *uncommon*;' there is, I fear, a small mixture of ill-nature in these words; for this ESSAY tho' on a beaten subject, abounds in many new remarks, and original rules, as well as in many happy and beautiful illustrations, and applications of the old ones. We are indeed amazed to find such a knowledge of the world, such a maturity of judgment, and such a penetration into human nature, as are here displayed, in so very young a writer as was POPE, when he produced this ESSAY; for he was not twenty years old. Correctness and a just taste, are usually not attained but by long practice and experience in any art; but a clear head, and strong sense were the characteristical qualities of our author, and every man soonest displays his radical excellencies. . . . [pp. 100–2]

---

[1] [*The Spectator*, No. 253 (see No. 11)]

[2] *Mr.*] Dr. 1782.

[3] *usefully shewn*] *endeavoured to shew* 1782. [The reference is to Hurd's edition of the *Ars Poetica* (1748), Introduction]

[The Simile of the Alps]

[Warton quotes *An Essay on Criticism*, ll. 225–32, which compare progress in learning to a traveller crossing the Alps. He comments]

THIS comparison is frequently mentioned, as an instance of the strength of fancy. The images however appear too general and indistinct, and the last line conveys no new idea to the mind. . . .

[Warton goes on to cite an irrelevant description of the Alps from Shaftesbury. For Johnson's reply to Warton, see pp. 410, 494–5 below].

[pp. 141–2]

['Correctness' insufficient]

51. Such late was WALSH, the muse's judge and friend.

[*An Essay on Criticism*, l. 729]

IF POPE has here given too magnificent an e[u]logy to Walsh, it must be pardonably[1] attributed to friendship, rather than to judgment. Walsh was in general a flimzy and frigid writer. The Rambler calls his works PAGES OF INANITY. His three letters to POPE, however, are well written. His remarks on the nature of pastoral poetry, on borrowing from the ancients, and against florid conceits, are worthy perusal.[2] POPE owed much to Walsh: it was he who gave him a very important piece of advice, in his early youth; for he used to tell our author, that there was one way still left open for him, by which he might excell any of his predecessors, which was, by CORRECTNESS; that though indeed we had several great poets, we as yet could boast of none that were perfectly CORRECT; and that therefore, he advised him to make this quality his particular study.

CORRECTNESS is a vague term, frequently used without meaning and precision. It is perpetually the nauseous cant of the French critics, and of their advocates and pupils, that the English writers are generally INCORRECT. If CORRECTNESS implies an absence of petty faults, this perhaps may be granted. If it means, that, because their tragedians have avoided the irregularities of Shakespeare, and have observed a juster œconomy in their fables, therefore the Athalia, for instance, is preferable to Lear, the notion is groundless and absurd. The Henriade is

---

[1] *pardonably*] *omitted* 1762–82.
[2] [*Corresp.*, i. 18, 20–3]

free from any very gross faults; but who will dare to rank it with the
Paradise Lost?[1]   [pp. 20–2]

[The Rape of the Lock]

IF the Moderns have excelled the Ancients in any species of writing, it
seems to be in satire: and, particularly in that kind of satire, which is
conveyed in the form of the epopee,[2] a pleasing vehicle of satire never[3]
used by the ancients.[4] As the poet disappears in this way of writing, and
does not deliver the intended censure in his own proper person, the
satire becomes more delicate, because more oblique. Add to this, that a
tale or story more strongly engages and interests the reader, than a
series of precepts of reproofs, or even of characters themselves, however lively and natural. An heroi-comic poem may therefore be justly
esteemed the most excellent kind of satire. . . . [Warton goes on to
discuss the 'heroic-comic' poems of Tassoni, Boileau, and Garth.]

THE RAPE OF THE LOCK, now before us, is the fourth, and most excellent of the heroi-comic poems. The subject was a quarrel occasioned by
a little piece of gallantry of Lord Petre, who, in a party of pleasure
found means to cut off a favourite lock of Mrs. Arabella Fermour's hair.
POPE was desired to write it, in order to put an end to the quarrel it
produced, by Mr. Caryl. . . . [The poem] was so universally applauded,
that, in the next year our poet enriched it with the machinery of the
sylphs, and extended it to five cantos; when it was printed with a letter
to Mrs. Fermour, far superior to any of Voiture. The insertion of the

[1] *The Henriade . . . Lost?*] *Tho' the Henriade should be allowed to be free from any very gross
absurdities; yet who will dare to rank it with the Paradise Lost?* 1782. ['Henriade' is given a
footnote in 1762–82, which begins with an anecdote about Voltaire, and then proceeds:]
. . . *Voltaire has dropt a remark in the last edition of his Essay on Epic Poetry, which is not
indeed very favourable to the taste of his countrymen, but is perfectly true and just, and which he
seems to have forgotten in some of his late assertions:*

'*It must be owned, that it is more difficult for a Frenchman to succeed in epic poetry, than for any
other person; but neither the constraint of rhyme, nor the dryness of our language is the cause of this
difficulty. Shall I venture to name the cause? It is, because of all polished nations, ours is the
least poetic. The works in verse, which are most in vogue in France, are pieces for the Theatre. These
pieces must be written in a style that approaches to that of conversation. Despreaux [i.e. Boileau]
has treated only* Didactic *subjects, which require simplicity. It is well known, that exactness and
elgance constitute the chief merit of his verses and those of Racine; and when Despreaux attempted
a sublime ode, he was no longer Despreaux. These examples have accustomed the French to too
uniform a march——.*'

[2] [I.e., epic]

[3] *never*] *seldom, if ever* 1762–82.

[4] *ancients.*] ~ ; *for we know so little of the Margites of Homer, that it cannot be produced as an
example.* 1762–82.

machinery of the sylphs in proper places, without the least appearance of it's being aukwardly stitched in, is one of the happiest efforts of judgment and art. He took the idea of these invisible beings, so proper to be employed in a poem of this nature, from a little french book entitled, Le Comte de Gabalis. . . .

. . . On a diligent perusal of this book, I cannot find that POPE has borrowed any particular circumstances relating to these spirits, but merely the general idea of their existence.

THESE machines are vastly superior to the allegorical personages of Boileau and Garth; not only on account of their novelty, but for the exquisite poetry, and oblique satire, which they have given the poet an opportunity to display. The business and petty concerns of a fine lady, receive an air of importance from the notion of their being perpetually overlooked and conducted, by the interposition of celestial agents.

IT is judicious to open the poem, by introducing the Guardian Sylph, warning Belinda against some secret impending danger. The account which Ariel[1] gives of the nature, office, and employment of these inhabitants of air, is finely fancied: into which several strokes of satire are thrown with great delicacy and address.

> Think what an equipage thou hast in air,
> And view with scorn two pages and a chair.   [i. 44–5]

The transformation of women of different tempers into different kinds of spirits, cannot be too much applauded.

> The sprites of fiery Termagants, in flame
> Mount up, and take a salamander's name.
> Soft yielding minds to water glide away,
> And sip with Nymphs, their elemental tea.
> The graver Prude sinks downward to a gnome,
> In search of mischief still on earth to roam.
> The light Coquettes in sylphs aloft repair,
> And sport and flutter in the fields of air.[2]   [i. 59–66]

The description of the[3] toilette, which succeeds, is judiciously given in such magnificent turns, as dignify the offices performed at it. Belinda dressing is painted in as pompous a manner, as Achilles arming. The canto ends with a circumstance, artfully contrived to keep this beautiful

---

[1] *The Rape of the Lock*, i. 27–114.
[2] [Warton gives a translation of these lines into Latin.]
[3] *The Rape of the Lock*, i. 121.

machinery in the readers eye: for after the poet has said, that the fair heroine

> Repairs her smiles, awakens ev'ry grace,
> And calls forth all the wonders of her face,   [i. 141–2]

He immediately subjoins,

> The busy sylphs surround their darling care,
> These set the head, and those divide the hair:
> Some fold the sleeve, whilst others plait the gown,
> And Betty's prais'd for labours not her own.   [i. 145–8]

THE mention of the LOCK,[1] on which the poem turns, is rightly reserved to the second canto. The sacrifice of the baron to implore success to his undertaking, is another instance of our poet's judgement, in heightening the subject.[2] The succeeding scene of sailing upon the Thames is most gay and *riant*; and impresses the most pleasing pictures upon the imagination. Here too the machinery is again introduced with much propriety.

. . . [Warton goes on to analyse Shakespeare's use of fairies in *A Midsummer Night's Dream*.]

If it should be thought, that Shakespeare has the merit of being the first who assigned proper employments to imaginary persons, in the foregoing lines,[3] yet it must be granted, that by the addition of the most delicate satire to the most lively fancy, POPE, in the following passage, has excelled anything in Shakespeare, or in any other author,

[quotes *The Rape of the Lock*, ii. 91–100, giving 'rough' for 'rude' in l. 93]

THE seeming importance given to every part of female dress, each of which is committed to the care and protection of a different sylph, with all the solemnity of a general appointing the several posts in his army, renders the following passage admirable, on account of it's politeness, poignancy, and poetry.

> Haste then ye spirits, to your charge repair;
> The fluttering fan be Zephyretta's care;

[1] *Ibid.*, ii. 20.
[2] *Ibid.*, ii. 37.
[3] [*A Midsummer Night's Dream*, III. i. 166–75]

The drops to thee, Brillante we consign;
And, Momentilla, let the watch be thine;
Do thou, Crispissa, tend the fav'rite lock;
Ariel himself shall be the guard of Shock.[1]

The celebrated raillery of Addison on the hoop-petticoat [*Tatler*, no. 116], has nothing equal to the following circumstance; which marks the difficulty of guarding a part of dress of such high consequence.

To fifty chosen sylphs, of special note,
We trust th'important charge the PETTICOAT:
Oft have we known that sevenfold fence to fail,
Though stiff with hoops, and arm'd with ribs of whale;
Form a strong line about the silver bound,
And guard the wide circumference around.   [ii. 117]

RIDET HOC, INQUAM, VENUS IPSA; RIDENT
SIMPLICES NYMPHÆ, FERUS ET CUPIDO.[2]

OUR poet still rises in the delicacy of his satire, where he employs, with the utmost judgment and elegance, all the implements and furniture of the toilette, as instruments of punishment to those spirits, who shall be careless of their charge: of punishment such as sylphs alone could undergo. Each of the delinquents,

Shall feel sharp vengeance soon o'ertake his sins,
Be stop'd in vials, or transfix'd with pins;
Or plung'd in lakes of bitter washes lie;
Or wedg'd whole ages in a bodkin's eye;
Gums and pomatums shall his flight restrain,
While clog'd he beats his silver wings in vain;
Or alum-styptics with contracting pow'r,
Shrink his thin essence like a rivell'd flow'r,
Or, as Ixion fix'd, the wretch shall feel
The giddy motion of the whirling mill;
In fumes of burning chocolate shall glow,
And tremble at the sea that froths below.   [ii. 123]

If Virgil has merited such perpetual commendation for exalting his bees, by the majesty and magnificence of his diction, does not POPE

---

[1] *The Rape of the Lock*, ii. 111.
[2] [Horace, *Carmina*, II. viii. 13–14: 'All this but makes sport for Venus (upon my word, it does!) and for the artless Nymphs, and cruel Cupid.']

deserve equal praises, for the pomp and lustre of his language, on so trivial a subject?

THE same mastery of language, appears in the lively and elegant description of the game at Ombre; which is certainly imitated from the Scacchia of Vida,[1] and as certainly equal to it, if not superiour. Both of them have elevated and enlivened their subjects, by such similes as the epic poets use; but as chess is a play of a far higher order than Ombre, POPE had a more difficult task than Vida, to raise this his inferior subject, into equal dignity and gracefulness. Here again our poet artfully introduces his machinery:

> Soon as she spreads her hand, th'aërial guard
> Descend, and sit on each important card;
> First Ariel perch'd upon a mattadore.   [iii. 31]

The majesty with which the kings of spades and clubs, and the knaves of diamonds and clubs, are spoken of, is very amusing to the imagination: and the whole game is conducted with great art and judgment. I question whether Hoyle[2] could have played it better than Belinda. It is finely contrived that she should be victorious; as it occasions a change of fortune in the dreadful loss she was speedily to undergo, and gives occasion to the poet to introduce a moral reflection from Virgil, which adds to the pleasantry of the story. In one of the passages where POPE has copied Vida, he has lost the propriety of the original, which arises from the different colours of the *men*, at chess.

> Thus, when dispers'd a routed army runs, &c.   [iii. 81]

> Non aliter, campis legio se buxea utrinque
> Composuit, duplici digestis ordine turmis,
> Adversisque ambæ fulsere coloribus alæ;
> Quam Gallorum acies, Alpino frigore lactea
> Corpora, si tendant albis prælia signis,
> Auroræ populos contra, et Phaetonte perustos
> Infano Æthiopas, et nigri Memnonis alas.[3]

---

[1] [On Pope's early knowledge of Vida, see Twickenham, ii. 106, 204 note. Pope included the *Scacchia Ludus* in his *Selecta Poemata Italorum* (1704).]

[2] [Edmond Hoyle (1672–1769), famous for his formulation of the rules of whist]

[3] Vidæ Scacchia Ludus, Ver. 74, &c. [G. Vida, *Sacchia Ludus: or, the Game of Chess . . . translated into English by Mr. Erskine* (1736), pp. 29–31: 'Not otherwise the Legions were dispos'd, / In both the Camps of double Lines compos'd, / The various Mixture of the black and white, / Alternately delights the ravish'd sight. / As if the *Gallians* fair with *Alpium* Frosts / Should thro' the Icy Mountains lead their Hosts / 'Gainst *Æthiopians* or *Memnon*'s Race, / Turn'd black with Heat since *Phaeton*'s Disgrace.']

To this scene succeeds the tea-table. It is doubtless, as hard to make a coffee-pot shine in poetry as a plough: yet POPE has succeeded in giving elegance to so familiar an object, as well as Virgil. The guardian spirits are again active, and importantly employed;

>   Strait round the fair her airy band;
>   Some, as she sipp'd, the fuming liquor fann'd.   [iii. 113]

Then follows an instance of assiduity, fancied with great delicacy,

>   Some o'er her lap their careful plumes display'd,
>   Trembling, and conscious of the rich brocade.
>   [iii. 115–16]

But nothing can excell the behaviour of the sylphs, and their wakeful sollicitude for their charge, when the danger grows more imminent, and the catastrophe approaches.

>   Swift to the lock a thousand sprites repair.[1]   [iii. 135]

The methods by which they endeavoured to preserve her from the intended mischief, are such only as could be executed by a sylph; and have therefore an admirable propriety, as well as the utmost elegance.

>   A thousand wings by turns blow back the hair;
>   And thrice they TWITCH'D the diamond in her ear,
>   Thrice she look'd back, and thrice the foe drew near.
>   [iii. 136–8]

Still farther to heighten the piece, and to preserve the characters of his machines to the last, just when the fatal forfex[2] was spread,

>   Ev'n then, before the fatal engine clos'd,
>   A wretched sylph too fondly interpos'd;
>   Fate urg'd the sheers, and cut the sylph in twain,
>   (But airy substance soon unites again.) ——
>   [iii. 149–51]

Which last line is an admirable parody on that passage of Milton, which, perhaps oddly enough, describes Satan wounded:

---

[1] *repair*] 1782 adds a footnote on Mme de Sevigné.

[2] Observe the many periphrasis's, and uncommon appellations, POPE has used for *Scissars*, which would sound too vulgar,—'Fatal Engine,'—'Forfex,'—'Sheers,'—'Meeting-Points,' etc.

The griding sword, with discontinuous wound,
Pass'd through him; but th'etherial substance clos'd
Not long divisible. — — — — —

[*Paradise Lost*, vi. 329–31]

The parodies are some of the most exquisite parts of this poem. That
which follows from the 'Dum juga montis aper,' of Virgil,[1] contains
some of the most artful strokes of satire, and the most poignant ridicule
imaginable.

> While fish in streams, or birds delight in air,
> Or in a coach and six the British fair,
> As long as Atalantis shall be read,
> Or the small pillow grace a lady's bed,
> While visits shall be paid on solemn days,
> When numerous wax-lights in bright order blaze,
> While nymphs take treats, or assignations give,
> So long my honour, name and praise, shall live.

[iii. 163–70]

The introduction of frequent parodies on serious and solemn passages of
Homer and Virgil, give much life and spirit to heroi-comic poetry. 'Tu
dors, Prelat? tu dors?' in Boileau,[2] is the Εὔδεις, ᾽Ατρέος υἱὲ ['Son of
Atreus are you asleep'] of Homer, and is full of humour. The wife of
the barber, talks in the language of Dido in her expostulations to her
Æneas, at the beginning of the second canto of the Lutrin.[3] POPE'S
parodies of the speech of Sarpedon in Homer, canto v. verse 9, and of
the description of Achilles's scepter, canto iv. verse 133, and the[4]
description of the scales of Jupiter from Homer, Virgil, and Milton,
canto v. verse 72, are judiciously introduced in their several places, are
perhaps superiour to those Boileau or Garth have used, and are worked
up with peculiar pleasantry. The mind of the reader is engaged by
novelty, when it so unexpectedly finds a thought or object it had been
accustomed to survey in another form, suddenly arrayed in a ridiculous
garb. A mixture of comic and ridiculous images, with serious and
important ones, is[5] also, no small beauty to this species of poetry. As in

---

1 [Virgil, *Eclogues*, vi. 76ff. Warburton had made the comparison, but for other parallels
see Twickenham, ii. 180–1]
2 [*Le Lutrin*, i. 73ff., which parodies *The Iliad*, ii. 23]
3 [*Le Lutrin*, ii. 12ff.]
4 *and the*] *together with the* 1762–82: the references are footnoted in 1762–82.
5 *is*] *adds* 1782.

the following passages, where real and imaginary distresses are coupled together.

> Not youthful kings in battle seiz'd alive,
> Not scornful virgins who their charms survive,
> Not ardent lovers robb'd of all their bliss,
> Not ancient ladies when refus'd a kiss,
> Not tyrants fierce that unrepenting die,   [iv. 3–7]

Nay, to carry the climax still higher,

> Not Cynthia when her manteau's pinn'd awry,
> E'er felt such rage, resentment and despair.   [iv. 8–9]

This is much superiour to a similar passage in the Dispensary, which POPE might have had in his eye;

> At this the victors own such ecstasies,
> As Memphian priests if their Osiris sneeze;
> Or champions with Olympic clangor fir'd,
> Or simp'ring prudes with spritely Nantz inspir'd,
> Or Sultans rais'd from dungeons to a crown,
> Or fasting zealots when the sermon's done.[1]

These objects have no reference to Garth's subject, as almost all of POPE's have, in the passage in question, where some female foible is glanced at. In this same canto, the cave of SPLEEN, the pictures of her attendants, ILL-NATURE and AFFECTATION, the effects of the vapour that hung over her palace, the imaginary diseases she occasions, the speech[2] of Umbriel, a gnome, to this malignant deity, the vial of female sorrows, the speech of Thalestris to aggravate the misfortune, the breaking the vial with its direful effects, and the speech of the disconsolate Belinda; all these circumstances are poetically imagined, and are far superiour to any of Boileau and Garth. . . .

[1] [Canto v. The passage is not in the first edition, but is in the twelfth (Dublin, 1730), p. 53]

[2] Especially when he adjures the goddess by an account of his services, Cant. iv. Ver. 72.

> If e'er with airy horns I planted heads,
> Or rumpled petticoats, or tumbled beds,
> Or caus'd suspicion when no soul was rude,
> Or discompos'd the head-dress of a prude,
> Or e'er to costive lapdog gave disease—
> Hear me, and touch Belinda with chagrin,
> That single act gives half the world the spleen.

Nothing can equal this beautiful panegyric, but the satirical touches that go before.

UPON the whole, I hope it will not be thought an exaggerated panegyric to say, that the RAPE OF THE LOCK, is the BEST SATIRE extant; that it
contains the truest and liveliest picture of modern life; and that the
subject is of a more elegant nature, as well as more artfully conducted,
than that of any other heroi-comic poem. POPE here appears in the light
of a man of gallantry, and of a thorough knowledge of the world;
and indeed, he had nothing, in his carriage and deportment, of that
affected singularity, which has induced some men of genius to
despise, and depart from, the established rules of politeness and civil
life. . . .

OUR nation can boast also, of having produced one or two more
poems of the burlesque kind, that are excellent; particularly the
SPLENDID SHILLING, that admirable copy of the solemn irony of
Cervantes; who is the father and unrivalled model of the true mock-
heroic: and the MUSCIPULA, written with the purity of Virgil, whom
the author so perfectly understood, and with the pleasantry of Lucian:
to which I cannot forbear adding, the SCRIBLERIAD of Mr. Cambridge.[1]

IF some of the most candid among the French critics begin to
acknowledge, that they have produced nothing in point of SUBLIMITY
and MAJESTY equal to the Paradise Lost, we may also venture to affirm,
that in point of DELICACY, ELEGANCE, and fine-turned RAILLERY, on
which they have so much valued themselves, they have produced
nothing equal to the RAPE OF THE LOCK. It is in this composition, POPE
principally appears a POET; in which he has displayed more imagination
than in all his other works taken together. It should however be remembered, that he was not the FIRST former and creator of those beautiful machines, the sylphs; on which his claim to imagination is chiefly
founded. He found them existing ready to his hand; but has, indeed,
employed them with singular judgment and artifice.   [pp. 205–48]

---

[1] This learned and ingenious writer hath made a new remark, in his preface, worth
examination and attention. He says, that in first reading the *four* celebrated mock heroic
poems, he perceived they had all some radical defect. That at last he found by a diligent
perusal of Don Quixote, that *Propriety* was the fundamental excellence of that Work. That
all the *Marvellous* was reconcileable to *Probability*, as the author led his hero into *that* species
of absurdity only, which it was *natural* for an imagination heated with the continual reading
of books of chivalry to fall into. That the want of attention to this was the fundamental
error of those poems. For with what PROPRIETY do *Churchmen, Physicians, Beaux,* and
Belles, or *Booksellers,* in the Lutrin, Dispensary, Rape of the Lock, and Dunciad, address
themselves to heathen Gods, offer sacrifices, consult oracles, or talk the language of Homer,
and of the heroes of antiquity? [After *Mr. Cambridge* 1762–82 add: , *the* MACHINÆ GESTICU-
LANTES *of Addison, the* HOBBINOL *of Somerville, and the* TRIVIA *of Gay*]

[*Elegy to the Memory of an Unfortunate Lady*]

THE ELEGY *to the Memory of an Unfortunate Lady*, which is next to be spoken of, as it came from the heart, is very tender and pathetic; more so, I think, than any other copy of verses of our author. . . .

THIS ELEGY opens with a striking abruptness, and a strong image; the poet fancies he beholds suddenly the phantom of his murdered friend;

> What beck'ning ghost along, the moonlight shade,
> Invites my step, and points to yonder glade?
> 'Tis she!—but why that bleeding bosom gor'd,
> Why dimly gleams the visionary sword? [ll. 1–4]

This question alarms the reader; and puts one in mind of that lively and affecting image in the prophecy of Isaiah, so vigorously conceived, that it places the object full in one's eyes. 'Who is this that cometh from Edom? With dyed garments from Bofra?'[1] Akenside has begun one of his odes in the like manner;

> O fly! 'tis dire SUSPICION's mein;
> And meditating plagues unseen,
>   The sorc'ress hither bends!
> Behold her torch in gall imbru'd;
> Behold, her garments drop with blood
>   Of lovers and of friends![2]

The execrations on the cruelties of this lady's relations, which had driven her to this deplorable extremity, are very spirited and forcible; especially where the poet says emphatically,

> Thus, if eternal justice rules the ball,
> Thus shall your wives, and thus your children fall.
> [ll. 35–6]

He describes afterwards the desolation of this family, by the following lively circumstance and prosopopœia:

> There passengers shall stand, and pointing say,
> (While the long funerals blacken all the way)
> Lo! these were they, whose souls the furies steel'd,
> And curst with hearts unknowing how to yield! . . .
> So perish all, whose breast ne'er learn'd to glow
> For others good, or melt at others woe. [ll. 39–46]

[1] [Isaiah,] lxiii. 1.
[2] ['Ode III. Against Suspicion', *Odes on Several Subjects* (1745), p. 15]

The incident of her dying in a country remote from her relations and acquaintance, is touched with great tenderness, and introduced with propriety, to aggravate and heighten her lamentable fate;

> No friend's complaint, no kind domestic tear,[1]
> Pleas'd thy pale ghost, or grac'd thy mournful bier;
> By foreign hands thy dying eyes were clos'd,
> By foreign hands thy decent limbs compos'd,
> By foreign hands thy humble grave adorn'd,
> By strangers honour'd, and by strangers mourn'd!
>
> [ll. 49–54]

The force of the repetition of the significant epithet *foreign*, need not be pointed out to any reader of sensibility. The right[2] of sepulture of which she was deprived, from the manner of her death, is glanced at with great delicacy; nay, and a very poetical use is made of it.

> What though no sacred earth allow thee room,
> Nor hallow'd dirge be mutter'd o'er thy tomb?
> Yet shall thy grave with rising flowers be drest,
> And the green turf lie lightly on thy breast;
> There shall the morn her earliest tears bestow,
> There the first roses of the year shall blow.   [ll. 61–6]

IF this ELEGY be so excellent, it may be ascribed to this cause; that the occasion of it was real; for it is certainly an indisputable maxim, 'That nature is more powerful than fancy; that we can always feel more than we can imagine; and that the most artful fiction must give way to truth'.   [pp. 249–53]

[*Eloisa to Abelard*]

BUT of all stories, ancient or modern, there is not perhaps a more proper one to furnish out an elegiac epistle, than that of ELOISA and ABELARD. Their distresses were of a most SINGULAR and PECULIAR kind; and their names sufficiently known, but not grown trite or common, by too frequent usage. POPE was a most excellent IMPROVER, if no great original INVENTOR; for as we have seen what an elegant superstructure he has raised on the little dialogues of the Comte de Gabalis, so shall we perceive, in the sequel of this Section, how finely he has worked up the

---

[1] Something like that pathetic stroke in the Philoctetes of Sophocles, who, among other heavy circumstances of distress, is said not to have near him, any ξύντροφον ὄμμ' ['familiar face']. Ver. 171.—Not to be translated!

[2] *right*] 1762–82; *rite* 1756.

hints of distress, that are scattered up and down in Abelard's and Eloisa's Letters. . . . [Warton goes on to give an account of the story's sources: in the course of his critique, he compares Pope's poem with the Latin only (but cf. G. Tillotson, Twickenham, ii. 279–80).]

I now propose to pass through the EPISTLE,[1] in order to give the reader a view of the various turns and tumults of passion, and the different sentiments with which Eloisa is agitated: and at the same time, to point out what passages are borrowed, and how much improved, from the original Letters.[2] From this analysis, her struggles and conflicts, between duty and pleasure, between penitance and passion, will more amply and strikingly appear.

SHE begins with declaring, how the peacefulness of her situation has been disturbed, by a letter of her lover accidentally falling into her hands; this exordium is beautiful, being worked up with an awakening solemnity: she looks about her, and breaks out at once.

> In these deep solitudes and awful cells,[3]
> Where heavenly-pensive CONTEMPLATION dwells,
> And ever-musing MELANCHOLY reigns;
> What means this tumult in a vestals veins?
> Why rove my thoughts beyond this lost retreat?
> Why feels my heart it's long-forgotten heat?   [ll. 1–6]

She then resolves neither to mention nor to write the name of Abelard; but suddenly adds, in a dramatic manner,

> —the name appears
> Already written—wash it out, my tears!   [ll. 14–15]

She then addresses herself to the convent, where she was confined, in fine imagery:

> Relentless walls! whose darksom round contains
> Repentant sighs, and voluntary pains:
> Ye rugged rocks![4] which holy knees have worn;
> Ye grots and caverns shagg'd with horrid thorn!

[1] 1774–82 *add a footnote: The compliment which Prior paid our author on this* EPISTLE, *is at once full of elegance and very lively imagery. He addresses it to Abelard, and says that,* POPE *has wove* [quotes *Alma,* No. 35(a) above].

[2] [Warton's footnotes provide a running comparison, which has been omitted here]

[3] 'If I was ordered to find out the most happy, and the most miserable man in the World, I would look for them in a cloister;' said a man of penetration.

[4] This, and several other circumstances, in the scenery view of the monastery, which denotes antiquity, may perhaps be a little blamed, on account of their impropriety, when introduced into a place so lately founded as the Paraclete: but are so well imagined, and highly painted, that they demand excuse.

> Shrines where their vigils pale-ey'd virgins keep,
> And pitying saints, whose statues learn to weep!
> Tho' cold like you, unmov'd, and silent grown,
> I have not yet forgot my self to stone.[1]   [ll. 17–24]

[Warton discusses ll. 25–98, comparing them with the Latin sources]

Next [Eloisa] describes their unparalleled happiness in the full and free enjoyment of their loves; but all at once stops short, and exclaims[2] with eagerness, as if she at that instant saw the dreadful scene alluded to,

> Alas how chang'd! what sudden horrors rise!
> A naked Lover bound and bleeding lies!
> Where, where was Eloise? her voice, her hand,
> Her poynard, had oppos'd the dire command.
> Barbarian stay! *that* bloody stroke restrain;
> The crime was common, common be the pain.[3]
>   [ll. 99–104]

One knows not which most to applaud, the lively imagery, the pathetic, or the artful decency, with which this tra[n]saction is delicately hinted at, in these most excellent lines: which are the genuine voice of nature and passion, and place the object intended to be imprest on the reader full in his sight.

SHE next reminds Abelard of the solemnity of her taking the veil, from verse one hundred and [seven], to an hundred and eighteen,[4] which are highly beautiful, particularly these circumstances attending the rite—

> As with *cold* lips I kiss'd the sacred veil,
> The shrines all *trembled*, and the lamps *grew pale*!
>   [ll. 111–12: Warton's italics]

---

[1] 'Forget myself to marble' is an expression of Milton, as is also 'Caverns shagg'd with horrid thorn', and the epithets 'pale-ey'd, and twilight', are *first* used in the smaller poems of Milton, which POPE had just perhaps been reading.

[2] *exclaims*] 1762–82; *reclaims* 1756.

[3] It was difficult to speak of this catastrophe that befel Abelard with any dignity and grace: our poet however has done it. I know not where castration is a chief cause of distress, in any other poem, except in a very extraordinary one of Catullus, where Atys, struck with madness by Berecynthia, in a fit of enthusiasm, inflicts this punishment on himself. After which he laments his condition in very pathetic strains. . . . [*grace . . . it* is expanded in 1782 to read: grace: *in which there is still something* indelicate, *notwithstanding all the dexterity and management of our poet, in speaking of so untoward a circumstance*].

[4] *eighteen*] 1782; *eighty four* 1756–72.

These two circumstances are fancied with equal force and propriety: and this supposed prognostic of the uneasiness she would undergo in the monastic life, is very affecting. But her passion intruded itself even in the midst of this awful act of devotion; the strength of which she represents by this particular,

> Yet then, to those dread altars as I drew,
> Not on the *Cross* my eyes were fix'd, but *You*.
>
> [ll. 115–16: Warton's italics]

Here she gives her fondness leave to expatiate into many luscious[1] ideas;

> Still on that breast enamour'd let me lie,
> Still drink delicious poison from thy eye,
> Pant on thy lip, and to thy heart be prest;   [ll. 121–3]

And then follows a line exquisitely passionate, and worthy the *sensibility* of Sappho or of Eloisa,

> Give all thou *canst*—and let me dream the *rest*.
>
> [l. 124: Warton's italics]

[Warton continues his analysis of ll. 125–41]

No part of this poem, or indeed of any of POPE's productions is so truly poetical, and contains such strong painting, as the passage to which we are now arrived;—The description of the convent, where POPE's religion certainly aided his fancy. It is impossible to read it without being struck with a pensive pleasure, and a sacred awe, at the solemnity of the scene; so picturesque are the epithets.

> In these *lone* walls (their day's eternal bound)
> These *moss-grown* domes with *spiry* turrets crown'd,
> Where *awful* arches make a noon-day night,
> And the *dim* windows shed a *solemn* night;
> Thy eyes diffus'd a reconciling ray.
>
> [ll. 141–5: Warton's italics]

All the circumstances that can amuse and sooth the mind of a solitary, are next enumerated in this expressive manner: and the reader that shall be disgusted at the length of the quotation, one might pronounce, has no taste, either for painting or poetry:

---

[1] *luscious*] *amorous* 1762–82.

The darksome pines that o'er yon rocks reclin'd
Wave high, and murmur to the hollow wind,
The wand'ring streams that shine between the hills,
The grots that echo to the tinckling rills,
The dying gales that pant upon the trees,
The lakes that quiver to the curling breeze;
No more these scenes my meditation aid,
Or lull to rest the visionary mind.   [ll. 155–62]

The effect and influence, of MELANCHOLY who is beautifully personi-
fied, on every object that occurs, and on every part of the convent,
cannot be too much applauded, or too often read, as it is founded on
nature and experience. That temper of mind casts a gloom on all things.

But o'er the twilight groves and dusky caves,
Long-sounding iles, and intermingled graves,
Black MELANCHOLY sits, and round her throws
A death-like silence, and a dread repose;
Her gloomy presence saddens all the scene,
Shades every flower, and darkens every green,
Deepens the murmur of the falling floods,
And breathes a browner horror on the woods.   [ll. 163–70]

The figurative expressions, *throws* and *breathes*, and *browner horror*, are
I verily believe the[1] strongest and boldest in the English language. The
IMAGE of the Goddess MELANCHOLLY sitting over the convent, and as it
were expanding her dreadful wings over its whole circuit, and diffusing
her gloom all around it, is truely sublime, and strongly conceived. . . .

[Warton continues his analysis of ll. 170–240]

She proceeds to recount a dream; in which I was always heavily
disappointed, because the imagined distress is such, as might attend the
dream of any person whatever.[2]

Methinks we wand'ring go
Thro' dreary wastes, and weep each other's woe,
Where round some mouldring tow'r pale ivy creeps,
And low-brow'd rocks hang nodding o'er the deeps;
Sudden you mount, you beckon from the skies,
Clouds interpose, &c.   [ll. 241–6]

[1] *the*] *some of the* 1772–82.
[2] It is partly from Dido's dream.

These are, indisputably, picturesque lines; but what I[1] want is a VISION of some such appropriated, and peculiar distress, as could be incident to none but Eloisa; and which should be drawn from, and have reference to, her single story. What distinguishes Homer and Shakespear from all other poets, is, that they do not give their readers GENERAL ideas: every image is the particular and unalienable property of the person who uses it; it is suited to no other; it is made for him or her alone. . . .

[Warton continues his analysis of ll. 246–94]

The scene she paints is awful: she represents herself lying on a tomb, and thinking she heard some spirit calling to her in every low wind—

> Here as I watch'd the dying lamps around,
> From yonder shrine I heard a hollow sound,[2]
> Come, sister, come, (it said, or seem'd to say)
> The place is here, sad sister, come away!
> Once like thyself I trembled, wept and pray'd,[3]
> Love's victim then, but now a sainted maid.   [ll. 307–12]

This scene would make a fine subject for the pencil; and is worthy a capital painter. He might place Eloisa in the long *ile* [*sic*] of a great Gothic church; a lamp should hang over her head, whose dim and dismal ray should only afford light enough to make darkness visible. She herself should be presented in the *instant*, when she first hears this aërial voice, and in the attitude of *starting round* with astonishment and fear. . . .

[after further discussion, Warton concludes his assessment]

ELOISA, at the conclusion of the EPISTLE to which we are now arrived, is judiciously represented as gradually settling into a tranquillity of mind, and seemingly reconciled to her fate. She can bear to speak of their being buried together, without violent emotions. Two lovers are introduced as visiting their celebrated tombs, and the behaviour of these strangers is finely imagined;[4]

---

[1] *I*] *we* 1772–82.

[2] Virgil may however have given the hint.—*Hinc exaudiri voces, & verba vocantis visa viri*—[*Aeneid*] iv. 460–1. ['Thence (Dido) heard, it seemed, sound and speech of her husband calling.']

[3] It is well contrived, that this invisible speaker should be a person that has been under the very same kind of misfortunes with Eloisa.

[4] *imagined;*] 1772–82 quote ll. 347–52 here, and add a sentence before picking up the lines above: *The poet adds, still farther, what impressions a view of their sepulchre would make even on a spectator less interested than these two lovers; and how it would affect his mind, even in the midst of the most solemn acts of religion;*

From the full quire when loud Hosannas rise,
And swell the pomp of *dreadful* sacrifice,
Amid that scene, if some relenting eye,
Glance on the stone where our cold relics lie,
Devotion's self shall steal a thought from heav'n,
One human tear shall drop—and be forgiv'n!   [ll. 353–8]

With this line, in my opinion,[1] the poem should have ended, for the eight additional ones,[2] concerning some poet, that haply might arise to sing their misfortunes, are languid and flat, and diminish the pathos of the foregoing sentiments. They might stand for the conclusion of almost any story.[3]

THIS EPISTLE, is, on the whole, one of the most highly finish'd, and certainly the most interesting, of the pieces of our author; and, together with the ELEGY to the Memory of an Unfortunate Lady, is the only instance of the Pathetic POPE has given us. I think one may venture to remark, that the reputation of POPE, as a poet, among posterity, will be principally owing to his WINDSOR-FOREST, his RAPE OF THE LOCK, and his ELOISA TO ABELARD; whilst the facts and characters alluded to and exposed, in his later writings, will be forgotten and unknown, and their poignancy and propriety little relished. For WIT and SATIRE are transitory and perishable, but NATURE and PASSION are eternal.

[pp. 298–334]

---

[1] *in my opinion] at first it appears 1762–82.*

[2] *ones,] verses, 1762–82, which also quote ll. 359–66.*

[3] *story.] 1762–82, with minor differences, add: ~ , were we not informed, that they were added by the Poet in allusion to his own case, and the state of his own mind. For I am well-informed, that what determined him in the choice of the subject of this epistle, was the retreat of that lady into a nunnery, whose death he had lately so pathetically lamented, in a foregoing Elegy, and for whom he had conceived a violent passion. She was first beloved by a nobleman *, an intimate friend of POPE, and, on his deserting her, retired into France; when, before she had made her last vows in the convent to which she had retreated, she put an end to her unfortunate life. The recollection of this circumstance will add a beauty and pathos to many passages in the poem, and will confirm the doctrine delivered above concerning the choice of subject [namely, that it should be founded on fact].*

* *The duke of Buckingham—Sheffield.*

107. Johnson reviews Warton

before 15 May 1756

Dr Samuel Johnson, from *Literary Magazine, or Universal Review*, i (1756), 35–8. The first issue of the magazine is undated; the second is dated 15 May.

Johnson's *Life* reworks some of the material in this review.

THIS is a very curious and entertaining miscellany of critical remarks and literary history. Though the book promises nothing but observations on the writings of *Pope*, yet no opportunity is neglected of introducing the character of any other writer, or the mention of any performance or event in which learning is interested. From *Pope*, however, he always takes his hint, and to *Pope* he returns again from his digressions. The facts which he mentions, though they are seldom anecdotes in a rigorous sense, are often such as are very little known, and such as will delight more readers than naked criticism.

As he examines the works of this great poet in an order nearly chronological, he necessarily begins with his pastorals,[1] which considered as representations of any kind of life, he very justly censures; for there is in them a mixture of *Grecian* and *English*, of ancient and modern, images. *Windsor* is coupled with *Hybla*, and *Thames* with *Pactolus*. He then compares some passages which *Pope* has imitated or translated with the imitation or version, and gives the preference to the originals, perhaps not always upon convincing arguments.

Theocritus makes his lover wish to be a bee, that he might creep among the leaves that form the chaplet of his mistress. *Pope*'s enamoured swain longs to be made the captive bird that sings in his fair one's bower, that she might listen to his songs, and reward them with her kisses. The critick prefers the image of *Theocritus* as more wild, more delicate, and more uncommon.

It is natural for a lover to wish that he might be any thing that could come near to his lady. But we more naturally desire to be that which she

[1] [See Warton, pp. 383–7 above]

fondles and caresses, than that which she would avoid, at least would neglect. The superiour delicacy of *Theocritus* I cannot discover, nor can indeed find, that either in the one or the other image there is any want of delicacy. Which of the two images was less common in the time of the poet who used it, for on that consideration the merit of novelty depends, I think it is now out of any critick's power to decide.

He remarks, I am afraid with too much justice, that there is not a single new thought in the pastorals, and with equal reason declares, that their chief beauty consists in their *correct and musical versification, which has so influenced the* English *ear, as to render every moderate rhymer harmonious.*[1]

In his examination of the *Messiah,* he justly observes some deviations from the inspired author, which weaken the imagery, and dispirit the expression.

On *Windsor-forest,* he declares,[2] I think without proof, that descriptive poetry was by no means the excellence of *Pope;* he draws this inference from the few images introduced in this poem, which would not equally belong to any other place. He must inquire whether *Windsor-forest* has in reality any thing peculiar.

The *Stag-chace is not, he says, so full, so animated, and so circumstantiated as Somerville's.* Barely to say, that one performance is not so good as another, is to criticise with little exactness. But *Pope* has directed that we should *in every work regard the author's end.* The *Stag-chace* is the main subject of *Somerville,* and might therefore be properly dilated into all its circumstances; in *Pope* it is only incidental, and was to be despatched in a few lines.

He makes a just observation, 'that the description of the external beauties of nature is usually the first effect of a young genius, before he hath studied nature and passions. Some of *Milton*'s most early as well as most exquisite pieces are his *Lycidas, l'Allegro,* and *Il Penseroso,* if we may except his ode on the nativity of CHRIST, which is indeed prior in order of time, and in which a penetrating critic might have observed the seeds of that boundless imagination, which was one day to produce the *Paradise Lost.*'

Mentioning *Thomson* and other descriptive poets, he remarks, that writers fail in their copies for want of acquaintance with originals, and justly ridicules those who think they can form just ideas of valleys, mountains, and rivers, in a garret of the *Strand.* For this reason I cannot

---

[1] [Warton, pp. 386–7 above]
[2] [Warton, pp. 387–9 above]

regret with this author,[1] that *Pope* laid aside his design of writing *American* pastorals; for as he must have painted scenes which he never saw, and manners which he never knew, his performance, though it might have been a pleasing amusement of fancy, would have exhibited no representation of nature or of life. . . .

He comes next to the *Essay on Criticism*,[2] the stupendous performance of a youth not yet twenty years old, and after having detailed the felicities of condition, to which he imagines *Pope* to have owed his wonderful prematurity of mind, he tells us that he is well informed, this essay was first written in prose. . . . [a piece of information whose truth Johnson doubts, with justification.]

He proceeds on examining passage after passage of this essay; but we must pass over all these criticisms to which we have not something to add or object, or where this author does not differ from the general voice of mankind. We cannot agree with him in his censure of the comparison of a student advancing in science with a traveller passing the *Alps*, which is, perhaps, the best simile in our language; that in which the most exact resemblance is traced between things in appearance totally unrelated to each other.[3] That the *last line conveys* no new IDEA is not true, it makes particular what was before general. Whether the description which he adds from another author be, as he says, more *full and striking*, than that of *Pope*, is not to be inquired. *Pope's* description is relative, and can admit no greater length than is usually allowed to a simile, nor any other particulars than such as form the correspondence.

Unvaried rhymes, says this writer, *highly disgust readers of a good ear*.[4] It is surely not the ear, but the mind that is offended; the fault rising from the use of common rhymes, is that by reading the past line the second may be guessed, and half the composition loses the grace of novelty. . . .

[Johnson discusses Warton's comments on the Alexandrine and the revival of learning]

The *Rape of the Lock* was always regarded by *Pope* as the highest production of his genius. On occasion of this work the history of the comic heroic is given, and we are told, that it descended from *Tassoni* to *Boileau*, from *Boileau* to *Garth*, and from *Garth* to *Pope*. *Garth* is mentioned perhaps with too much honour; but all are confessed to be

---

[1] [Warton, *Essay*, i (1756), p. 11]
[2] [Warton, pp. 389–91 above]
[3] [Johnson expands this discussion in the *Life*, pp. 494–5 below]
[4] [Warton, p. 15]

inferior to *Pope*.[1] There is in his remarks on this work no discovery of any latent beauty, nor any thing subtle or striking; he is indeed commonly right, but has discussed no difficult question. . . .

[Johnson summarizes Warton's circling progress through the other early poems up to *Eloisa to Abelard*]

. . . the epistle of *Eloisa* to *Abelard* . . . may be regarded as one of the works on which the reputation of *Pope* will stand in future times.

The critic[2] pursues *Eloisa* through all the changes of passion, produces the passages of her letters to which any allusion is made, and intersperses many agreeable particulars and incidental relations. There is not much profundity of criticism, because the beauties are sentiments of nature, which the learned and the ignorant feel alike. It is justly remarked by him, that the wish of *Eloisa* for the happy passage of *Abelard* into the other world, is formed according to the ideas of mystic devotion.

These are the pieces examined in this volume; whether the remaining part of the work will be one volume or more, perhaps the writer himself cannot yet inform us.[3] This piece is, however, a complete work, so far as it goes, and the writer is of opinion that he has dispatched the chief part of his task: for he ventures to remark, that the reputation of *Pope* as a poet, among posterity, will be principally founded on his *Windsor-Forest*, *Rape of the Lock*, and *Eloisa to Abelard*, while the facts and characters alluded to in his late writings will be forgotten and unknown, and their poignancy and propriety little relished; for wit and satire are transitory and perishable, but nature and passion are eternal. . . .

[Johnson here gives an outline of Pope's early life as reported by Warton]

In this extract [i.e., review] it was thought convenient to dwell chiefly upon such observations as relate immediately to *Pope*, without deviating with the author into incidental inquiries. We intend to kindle, not to extinguish, curiosity, by this slight sketch of a work abounding with curious quotations and pleasing disquisitions. He must be much acquainted with literary history both of remote and late times, who does not find in this essay many things which he did not know before; and if there be any too learned to be instructed in facts or opinions, he may yet properly read this book as a just specimen of literary moderation.

[1] [Warton, p. 398 above]   [2] [Warton, pp. 401–7 above]
[3] [The second volume was published in 1782. See No. 128]

108. Johnson on Pope's Epitaphs

1756

Dr Samuel Johnson, extracts from 'A Dissertation on the Epitaphs of Pope', *The Universal Visiter*, May (1756), 205-15, 217-19. Appended (with minor changes) to the *Life of Pope*, Johnson's 'Dissertation' is a notable instance of his powers of practical criticism.

EVERY art is best taught by example. Nothing contributes more to the cultivation of propriety than remarks on the works of those who have most excelled. I shall therefore endeavour, at this *visit*, to entertain the young students in poetry, with an examination of Pope's *Epitaphs*:

To define an *epitaph* is useless; every one knows that it is an inscription on a tomb. An *epitaph*, therefore, implies no particular character of writing, but may be composed in verse or prose. It is indeed commonly panegyrical, because we are seldom distinguished with a stone but by our friends; but it has no rule to restrain or modify it, except this, that it ought not to be longer than common beholders may be expected to have leisure and patience to peruse.

I.

On CHARLES Earl of DORSET, in the Church of Wythyham in Sussex.

> *DORSET*, the grace of courts, the muses pride,
> Patron of arts, and judge of nature, dy'd.
> The scourge of pride, tho' sanctify'd or great,
> Of fops in learning, and of knaves in state;
> Yet soft his nature, tho' severe his lay,
> His anger moral, and his wisdom gay.
> Blest satyrist! who touch'd the mean so true,
> As show'd, vice had his hate and pity too.
> Blest courtier! who could king and country please,
> Yet sacred keep his friendship, and his Ease.

> Blest peer! his great forefathers ev'ry grace
> Reflecting, and reflected on his race;
> Where other *Buckhursts*, or *Dorsets* shine,
> And patriots still, or poets, deck the line.

The first distich of this *epitaph* contains a kind of information which few would want, that the man for whom the tomb was erected 'died.' There are indeed some qualities worthy of praise ascribed to the dead, but none that were likely to exempt him from the lot of man, or incline us much to wonder that he should die. What is meant by *judge of nature*, is not easy to say. Nature is not the object of human judgement, for it is vain to judge where we cannot alter. If by nature is meant, what is commonly called *nature* by the critics, a just representation of things really existing, and actions really performed, nature cannot be properly opposed to *art*; nature being, in this sense, only the best effect of *art*.

> *The scourge of pride—*

Of this couplet the second line is not, what is intended, an illustration of the former. Pride in the great is indeed well enough connected with knaves in state, though *knaves* is a word rather too ludicrous and light; but the mention of *sanctified* pride will not lead the thoughts to *fops in learning*, but rather to some species of tyranny or oppression, something more gloomy and more formidable than foppery.

> *Yet soft his nature—*

This is a high compliment, but was not first bestowed on *Dorset* by *Pope*. The next verse is extremely beautiful.

> *Blest satyrist—*

In this distich is another line of which Pope was not the author.[1] I do not mean to blame these imitations with much harshness; in long performances they are scarcely to be avoided, and in slender[2] they may be indulged, because the train of the composition may naturally involve them, or the scantiness of the subject allow little choice. However, what is borrowed is not to be enjoyed as our own, and it is the business of critical justice to give every bird of the muses his proper feather.

> *Blest courtier—*

Whether a courtier can properly be commended for keeping his *ease*

---

[1] [Cf. Rochester's line on Dorset: 'The best-good man, with the worst-natured Muse']
[2] *slender*] *Universal Visiter; shorter* Life of Pope.

sacred may perhaps be disputable. To please king and country, without sacrificing friendship to any change of times, was a very uncommon instance of prudence or felicity, and deserved to be kept separate from so poor a commendation as care of his ease. I wish our poets would attend a little more accurately to the use of the word *sacred*, which surely should never be applied in a serious composition but where some reference may be made to a higher being, or where some duty is exacted or implied. A man may keep his friendship *sacred*, because promises of friendships are very awful ties; but methinks he cannot, but in a burlesque sense, be said to keep his ease *sacred*.

> *Blest peer—*

The blessing ascribed to the *peer* has no connection with his peerage; they might happen to any other man, whose ancestors were remembered, or whose posterity were likely to be regarded.

I know not whether this *epitaph* be worthy either of the writer, or of the man entombed.

II.

On Sir WILLIAM TRUMBUL,[1] *One of the Principal Secretaries of State to King* William III. *who having resigned his Place, died in his retirement at* Easthampsted *in* Berkshire, 1716.

> A pleasing form, a firm, yet cautious mind,
> Sincere, tho' prudent; constant, yet resign'd;
> Honour unchang'd, a principle profest,
> Fix'd to one side, but mod'rate to the rest:
> An honest courtier, yet a patriot too,
> Just to his prince, and to his country true.
> Fill'd with the sense of age, the fire of youth,
> A scorn of wrangling, yet a zeal for truth;
> A gen'rous faith, from superstition free;
> A love to peace, and hate of tyranny;
> Such this man was; who now, from earth remov'd,
> At length enjoys that liberty he lov'd.

In this *epitaph*, as in many others, there appears, at the first view, a fault which I think scarcely any beauty can compensate. The name is omitted. The end of an *epitaph* is to convey some account of the dead,

---

[1] [I.e., Sir William Trumbull, an early friend and encourager of Pope. Pope took the first six lines of this epitaph from one he had written on John Caryll (d. 1711)]

and to what purpose is any thing told of him whose name is concealed? An *epitaph*, and a history, of a nameless hero, are equally absurd, since the virtues and qualities so recounted in either, are scattered at the mercy of fortune to be appropriated by guess. The name, it is true, may be read upon the stone, but what obligation has it to the poet, whose verses wander over the earth, and leave their subject behind them, and who is forced, like an unskilful painter, to make his purpose known by adventitious help?

This *epitaph* is wholly without elevation, and contains nothing striking or particular; but the poet is not to be blamed for the defects of his subject. He said perhaps the best that could be said. There are however some defects which were not made necessary by the character in which he was employed. There is no opposition between an *honest courtier* and a *patriot*, for an *honest courtier* cannot but be a *patriot*.

It was unsuitable to the nicety required in short compositions, to close his verse with the word *too*; every rhyme should be a word of emphasis, nor can this rule be safely neglected, except where the length of the poem makes slight inaccuracies excusable, or allows room for beauties sufficient to over-power the effects of petty faults.

At the beginning of the seventh line the word *filled* is weak and prosaic, having no particular adaptation to any of the words that follow it.

The thought in the last line is impertinent, having no connexion with the foregoing character, nor with the condition of the man described. Had the *epitaph* been written on the poor conspirator[1] who died lately in prison, after a confinement of more than forty years, without any crime proved against him, the sentiment had been just and pathetical; but why should *Trumbul* be congratulated upon his liberty, who had never known restraint? . . .

VI.

On Mrs. CORBET, *who died of a Cancer in her Breast.*

> Here rests a woman, good without pretence,
> Blest with plain reason, and with sober sense;
> No conquests she, but o'er herself desir'd,
> No arts essay'd, but not to be admir'd.

[1] [Major John Bernardi, who died in Newgate in 1736 'where he had been a state prisoner 40 years, for a conspiracy against King William III' (*The Gentleman's Magazine*, vi (1736), 553]

> Passion and pride were to her soul unknown,
> Convinc'd that virtue only is our own.
> So unaffected, so compos'd a mind,
> So firm, yet soft, so strong, yet so refin'd,
> Heav'n as its purest gold, by tortures try'd,
> The saint sustain'd it, but the woman dy'd.

I have always considered this as the most valuable of all *Pope's epitaphs*; the subject of it is a character not discriminated by any shining or eminent peculiarities; yet that which really makes, though not the splendor, the felicity of life, and that which every wise man will choose for his final and lasting companion in the languor of age, in the quiet of privacy, when he departs weary and disgusted from the ostentatious, the volatile, and the vain. Of such a character, which the dull overlook, and the gay despise, it was fit that the value should be made known, and the dignity established. Domestick virtue, as it is exerted without great occasions, or conspicuous consequences, in an even unnoted tenor, required the genius of *Pope* to display it in such a manner as might attract regard, and enforce reverence. Who can forbear to lament that this amiable woman has no name in the verses?

If the particular lines of this inscription be examined it will appear less faulty than the rest. There is scarce one line taken from common places, unless it be that in which *only virtue* is said to be *our own*. I once heard a lady[1] of great beauty and elegance[2] object to the fourth line, that it contained an unnatural and incredible panegyrick. Of this let the ladies judge.

VII.

On the Monument of the Hon. ROBERT DIGBY, *and of his Sister* MARY, *erected by their Father the Lord* DIGBY, *in the Church of* Sherborne *in* Dorsetshire, 1727.

> Go! fair example of untainted youth,
> Of modest wisdom, and pacifick truth:
> Compos'd in suff'rings, and in joy sedate,
> Good without noise, without pretension great.

---

[1] [Miss Molly Aston according to Mrs Piozzi, *Johnsonian Miscellanies*, ed. G. B. Hill (1897), i. 258]

[2] *elegance*] *Universal Visiter; excellence* Life of Pope.

Just of thy word, in ev'ry thought sincere,
Who knew no wish but what the world might hear:
Of softest manners, unaffected mind,
Lover of peace, and friend of human kind:
Go, live! for heav'n's eternal year is thine,
Go, and exalt thy mortal to divine.
    And thou, blest maid! attendant on his doom,
Pensive hast follow'd to the silent tomb,
Steer'd the same course to the same quiet shore,
Not parted long, and now to part no more!
Go, then, where only bliss sincere is known!
Go, where to love and to enjoy are one!
    Yet take these tears, mortality's relief,
And till we share your joys, forgive our grief:
These little rites, a stone, a verse receive,
'Tis all a father, all a friend can give!

This *epitaph* contains of the brother, only a general indiscriminate character, and of the sister tells nothing, but that she died. The difficulty in writing *epitaphs* is to give a particular and appropriate praise. This, however, is not always to be performed, whatever be the diligence or ability of the writer; for the greater part of mankind *have no character at all*, have little that distinguishes them from others equally good or bad, and therefore nothing can be said of them which may not be applied with equal propriety to a thousand more. It is indeed no great panegyrick, that there is inclosed in this tomb one who was born in one year, and died in another; yet many useful and amiable lives have been spent which yet leave little materials for any other memorial. These are however not the proper subjects of poetry; and whenever friendship, or any other motive, obliges a poet to write on such subjects, he must be forgiven if he sometimes wanders in generalities, and utters the same praises over different tombs.

The scantiness of human praises can scarcely be made more apparent than by remarking how often *Pope* has, in the few *epitaphs* which he composed, found it necessary to borrow from himself. The fourteen *epitaphs*, which he has written comprise about an hundred and forty lines, in which there are more repetitions than will easily be found in all the rest of his works. In the eight lines which make the character of *Digby*, there is scarce any thought, or word, which may not be found in the other *epitaphs*.

417

The ninth line, which is far the strongest and most elegant, is borrowed.[1] The conclusion is the same with that on *Harcourt*, but is here more elegant and better connected.

XI.

On Mr. GAY.
In Westminster-Abbey, 1732.[2]

Of manners gentle, of affections mild;
In wit, a man; simplicity, a child:
With native humour temp'ring virtuous rage,
Form'd to delight at once and lash the age:
Above temptation, in a low estate,
And uncorrupted, even among the great:
A safe companion, and an easy friend,
Unblam'd thro' life, lamented in thy end.
These are thy honours! not that here thy bust
Is mix'd with heroes, or with kings thy dust;
But that the worthy and the good shall say,
Striking their pensive bosoms—*Here lies GAY.*

As *Gay* was the favourite of our author, this *epitaph* was probably written with an uncommon degree of attention yet it is not more successfully executed than the rest, for it does not always happen that the success of a poet is proportionate to his labour. The same observation may be extended to all works of imagination, which are often influenced by causes wholly out of the performer's power, by hints of which he perceives not the origin, by sudden elevations of mind which he cannot produce in himself, and which sometimes rise when he expects them least.

The two parts of the first line are only echoes of each other, *gentle manners* and *mild affections*, if they mean anything, must mean the same.

That *Gay* was a *man in wit* is a very frigid commendation; to have the wit of a man is not much for a poet. The *wit of man* and the *simplicity of a child*, make a poor and vulgar contrast, and raise no ideas of excellence, either intellectual or moral.

In the next couplet *rage* is less properly introduced after the mention

---

[1] *borrowed.] Universal Visiter; ~ from Dryden.* ['To the Pious Memory of Mrs. Anne Killigrew', ll. 14–15] Life of Pope.
[2] [For Swift's comments on an early draft of this epitaph, see No. 86]

of *mildness* and *gentleness*, which are made the constituents of his character, for a man so *mild* and *gentle* to *temper* his *rage* was not difficult.

The next line is unharmonious in its sound, and mean in its conception, the opposition is obvious, and the word *lash* used absolutely, and without any modification, is gross and improper.

To be *above temptation* in poverty, and *free from corruption among the great*, is indeed such a peculiarity as deserved notice. But to be a *safe companion* is praise merely negative, arising not from the possession of virtue, but the absence of vice, and that one of the most odious.

As little can be added to his character by asserting that he was *lamented in his end*. Every man that dies is, at least by the writer of his *epitaph*, supposed to be lamented, and therefore this general lamentation does no honour to *Gay*.

The first eight lines have no grammar, the adjectives are without any substantive, and the epithets without a subject.

The thought in the last line, that *Gay* is buried in the bosoms of the *worthy* and the *good*, who are distinguished only to lengthen the line, is so dark that few understand it; and so harsh, when it is explained, that still fewer approve. . . .

XIII.

On EDMUND *Duke of* BUCKINGHAM, *who died in the* 19th *Year of his Age*,
1735.

> If modest youth, with cool reflection crown'd,
> And ev'ry opening virtue blooming round,
> Could save a parent's justest pride from fate,
> Or add one patriot to a sinking state;
> This weeping marble had not ask'd thy tear,
> Or sadly told, how many hopes lie here!
> The living virtue now had shone approv'd,
> The senate heard him, and his country lov'd.
> Yet softer honours, and less noisy fame
> Attend the shade of gentle *Buckingham*:
> In whom a race, for courage fam'd and art,
> Ends in the milder merit of the heart;
> And chiefs or sages long to Britain giv'n,
> Pays the last tribute of a saint to heav'n.

This *epitaph* Mr. *Warburton* prefers to the rest, but I know not for what reason. To *crown* with *reflection* is surely a mode of speech approaching to nonsense. *Opening virtues blooming round,* is something like tautology; the six following lines are poor and prosaic. *Art* is in another couplet used for *arts,* that a rhyme may be had to *heart.* The six last lines are the best, but not excellent.

The rest of his sepulchral performances hardly deserve the notice of criticism. The contemptible *Dialogue* between HE and SHE should have been suppressed for the author's sake.[1]

In his last *epitaph* on himself, in which he attempts to be jocular upon one of the few things that make wise men serious, he confounds the living man with the dead:

> *Under this stone, or under this sill,*
> *Or under this turf, &c.*[2]

When a man is once buried the question, under what he is buried, is easily decided. He forgot that though he wrote the *epitaph* in a state of uncertainty, yet it could not be laid over him till his grave was made. Such is the folly of wit when it is ill employed.

---

[1] ['Epitaph for Dr. Francis Atterbury, Bishop of Rochester, who died in exile at Paris, in 1732']
[2] ['Epitaph on Himself']

109. Voltaire on Pope as *philosophe*

1756

Voltaire, extract translated from passage added to Lettre 22, *Lettres Philosophiques* in 1756. The text is given in *Lettres Philosophiques*, ed. F. A. Taylor (1943), pp. 141–2.

Pope's *Essay on Man* seems to me the most beautiful didactic poem and the most usefull and sublime that has ever been written in any language. It is true that its roots are found entirely in Lord Shaftesbury's *Characteristics*: and I do not know why Mr. Pope gives sole credit to Mr. Bolingbroke, without saying a word of the celebrated Shaftesbury, the disciple of Locke.

As everything which is maintained by metaphysics has been thought at all times and by all people who cultivate their minds, this system depends much upon that of Leibniz, who claims that of all possible worlds God must have chosen the best, and that, in this best of worlds, it is certainly necessary that the irregularities of our globe and the stupidities of its inhabitants should have their place. It also resembles Plato's idea, that in the Great Chain of Being, our earth, our body, our soul, are amongst the number of necessary links. But neither Leibniz or Pope admits the alterations which Plato imagined to have overtaken these links, these souls, and our bodies: Plato spoke as a poet in barely intelligible prose; and Pope speaks as a 'philosophe' in admirable verse. He says that since the beginning everything has been what it ought to have been, and as it is.

I have been flattered, I confess, to see that he agrees with me in one thing that I said several years ago. 'You are astonished that God has made Man so limited, so ignorant, and so unhappy. Does it not astonish you that He did not make man more limited, more ignorant, and more unhappy?' When a Frenchman and an Englishman think the same thing, they must be right.

110. Richardson on Pope's lack of genius

1757

Samuel Richardson, extract from a letter to Dr Edward Young, dating from 1757, *Selected Letters of Samuel Richardson*, ed. J. Carroll (1964), pp. 333–4.

Richardson's letter comments on a manuscript version of Young's *Conjectures on Original Composition* (1759), part of which is reproduced as No. 112. The page reference is to Young's manuscript: the published text of the *Conjectures* retains no sign of the praise of Pope which provoked Richardson's disagreement.

P. 19—Pope's, sir, I venture to say, was not the genius to *lift our souls to Heaven*, had it soared ever so freely, since it soared not in the Christian beam; but there is an eagle, whose eyes pierce through the shades of midnight, that does indeed *transport* us, and the apotheosis is your's. Whether this may suggest any softening or any improvement to the passage, must be submitted to you, but, surely, an *heroic* poem ought not to be mentioned in these terms, which so exactly belong to a *divine* one. The Author of one wishes to have his name swim down the stream of time on the wreck of Bolingbroke; the other dedicates his early muse to *Him who gave him Voice*, and consequently *his work is remote from all imitation*. Should there not be here some distinction of *imitators of other authors*, and imitation of nature, in which respect poetry is called one of the imitative arts? The tame imitator of other poets is a copier of portraits, the true genius a noble painter of originals, to whom nature delights to sit in every variety of attitude.

Indeed, sir, I cannot imagine that Pope would have shone in blank verse; and do you really think he had invention enough to make him a great poet? Did he not want the assistance of rhyme, of jingle? What originality is there in the works for which he is most famed? Shall I say, that I wish you would be pleased to reconsider all you say of the creative power of Pope? There is a hasty scratch through some of the lines in this page; excuse it, sir, and let me beg of you to alter, particularly, the same paragraphs, lest you should be thought to degrade, by a too minute allusion, the awful wonders of creation. Suppose, sir, when you ask, What does the name of poet mean? you answer after some such manner as this—'*It means a maker*, and, consequently, *his work is something original, quite his own.* It is not the laboured improvement of a modern cultivator bestowed on a soil already fertile, and refining on a plan already formed; but the touch of Armida's wand, that calls forth blooming spring out of the shapeless waste, and presents in a moment objects new and various, which his genius only could have formed in that peculiar manner, and his taste only arranged with that peculiar grace. These two enchanting gifts of taste and genius were *possessed by Shakespeare in a surprising degree, in both dramas,*' &c.

111. Critical clichés of 1759

W. H. Dilworth, extracts from *The Life of Alexander Pope, Esq; With a View of his Writings* . . . (1759). This hack biography may have been, as George Sherburn suggests, an attempt to benefit by the interest created by the publication of Warton's *Essay* three years earlier. Although Dilworth attempted to replace what he called the 'farrago' of Ayre's *Memoirs* (see No. 97), *The Life of Alexander Pope, Esq* is shapeless and carelessly strung together; into the bargain, it uses passages from the earlier book without bothering to acknowledge the source.

[Early poems]

His *Pastorals* having been previously perused and approved by the above mentioned lords and gentlemen, and others of the best poets and critics, were published. Their uncommon elegance of style, and smoothness of versification, joined to the youth of their author, made them to be universally admired, and put in competition with the best productions of that kind in the English language. They were by many preferred to those of Mr. Ambrose Philips, author of *The Distrest Mother*, which led their partisans to support them in opposition to Mr. Pope's. . . .

ALTHO', by all candid critics the poems in question of both must be allowed to be pastoral, yet Steele[1] inclined to refuse that apellation to those of Mr. Pope, which he politely evasive called too elevated, saying, they savoured too much of the golden age. He asserted, that Mr Philips was nearer the standard of Nature, having been careful to imitate Spenser in some places; and that, where requisite, he was capable of elevating his style.   [pp. 12–13]

. . . Mr. Pope . . . appeared . . . from time to time in elegant performances, particularly the *Messiah*, a sacred poem in imitation of Virgil's *Pollio*, which it far exceeds, being enriched with the rapturous imagery and expressions of the prophet Isaiah.

SOON after appeared that masterly and unequalled piece of landskip poetry, called *Windsor Forest*, in which all rural beauties appear with advantage, thro' a perspicuous elegance of stile, couched in the most easy and most flowing numbers, varyingly appropriated to the different subjects that are delineated.

AGAINST all cavillers, who have maliciously endeavoured to prove, that Mr. Pope had no invention, fancy, or imagination, and that all his merit consisted in being a correct plagiarist, *The Rape of the Lock* may be quoted. It abounds with fancy and fine humour, and is the foremost of heroi-comic poems.

THIS truly elegant piece in five cantos was wrote to expose the little unguarded follies of the fair sex. The passages are fabulous, and the machinery raised on the foundation of the Rosicrucian doctrine of spirits, according to which the four elements are supposed to be inhabited, the air by sylphs, the earth by gnomes, the water by nymphs, and the fire by salamanders.

THIS celebrated poem, that has run thro' such a number of editions, has more true humour and good natured mirth in it, than any other extant, either in the ancient or modern languages.   [pp. 19–20]

MR. Pope was by this time got so far into favour and reputation with the town, that he needed no other recommendation than his own merit; and he began (as he was justly entitled) to assume the name of a critic, and to give rules to others in his *Essay on Criticism*, which abounds with wit, beautiful turns, variety of metaphors, and masterly observations on poetry and criticism. It is the best work of the kind that has appeared among the ancients or moderns.   [p. 27]

[1] [A reference to Pope's anonymous *Guardian* no. 40; see No. 9]

MR. POPE wrote a most excellent letter in verse from Eloisa to Abelard. . . . It may be asserted, that it is not in the power of our language to go beyond this poem in tenderness and harmony. The only production of even our author that can be put in competition with it, is the piece so justly admired for its beauties, called *Verses to the Memory of an unfortunate Young Lady*. [pp. 31–3]

[*The Dunciad*]

THE *Dunciad* was an interrupted work, which he wrote from time to time, and has made it the most complete piece of poetical castigation in our language. He had indeed ample matter, having a numerous body of dunces to take cognizance of. Some who did not absolutely deserve that appellation, he has rapped over the knuckles.

THIS poem, as was observed above, is dedicated to the humorous and satyrical Dr. Swift, who called it Mr. Pope's master-piece. The rewe beg to differ in opinion with that great man, tho' at the same time we allow the *Dunciad* to be the most excellent piece in its kind that we have, or perhaps any other nation is possessed of.

SWIFT's preference may be accounted for from his own fondness for satyr, at which he was a master-hand, and from a personal resentment to many of the scriblers therein exposed. Altho' it be written in the spirit of Dryden's *Macfleckno*, it is more comprehensive; the latter poem having but one object, whereas the *Dunciad* has many. . . . [pp. 77–8]

[*Moral Essays*]

IT is now time to speak of the *Ethic Epistles*, which are to bad men, what the *Dunciad* is to bad poets; and as in the latter, so in the former, he does not intirely spare the ladies. It would have been highly erroneous in our great moral censor to neglect being of service to that desireable and most lovely part of human society.

BESIDES, their natural tendency to vanity must have been too much encouraged, on finding themselves let pass free of all censure, and seeing the other sex so mauled.

THE first *Ethic Epistle*, which is on the knowledge and character of men, our poet addressed to lord Cobham, who honoured him with his friendship, finding him so thorough a hearted Englishman, which was an additional merit to his excellence as a poet.

IT was remarkable of Mr. Pope that he never appeared so fond of any foreigners (whatever might be their religion) as he was of his own countrymen. He was a strenuous discourager, so far as in him lay, of Italian operas.

BESIDES, he was a warm promoter of English sense, and of all valuable productions in his native language, which he deemed superior to all the modern, and consequently the nearest to the Latin and Greek tongues, for energic prose, and harmonious versification.

HE had so sanguine, so truly patriot an attachment to the manufactures of Old England, that when in compliance with fashion he was necessitated to use things of foreign produce, or manufactures, his national expression was—'Pardon me, my country, I offend but seldom.'

[pp. 94–5]

112. Young on Pope's lack of originality

1759

Dr Edward Young, extracts from *Conjectures on Original Composition* (1759), pp. 20–2, 56–60, 65–9, 71, 96–9.

The text is based on the 2nd ed. of 1759. For other earlier examples of Young's opinion of Pope, see Nos 28c, 40. For Richardson's comments on an early text of that part of the *Conjectures* concerned with Pope, see No. 110.

Must we then, you say, not imitate antient authors? Imitate them, by all means; but imitate aright. He that imitates the divine *Iliad*, does not imitate *Homer*; but he who takes the same method, which *Homer* took, for arriving at a capacity of accomplishing a work so great. Tread in his steps to the sole Fountain of Immortality; drink where he drank, at the true *Helicon*, that is, at the breast of Nature: Imitate; but imitate not the *Composition*, but the *Man*. For may not this Paradox pass into a Maxim? *viz.* 'The less we copy the renowned Antients, we shall resemble them the more.'

But possibly you may reply, that you must either imitate *Homer*, or depart from Nature. Not so: For suppose You was to change place, in time, with *Homer*; then, if you write naturally, you might as well charge *Homer* with an imitation of You. Can you be said to imitate *Homer* for writing *so*, as you would have written, if *Homer* had never been? As far as a regard to Nature, and sound Sense, will permit a Departure from your great Predecessors; so far, ambitiously, depart from them; the farther from them in *Similitude*, the nearer are you to them in *Excellence*; you rise by it into an *Original*; become a noble Collateral, not an humble Descendant from them. . . .

Such meanness of mind, such prostration of our own powers,[1] proceeds from too great admiration of others. Admiration has, generally, a degree of two very bad ingredients in it; of Ignorance, and of Fear; and does mischief in Composition, and in Life. Proud as the world is, there is more superiority in it *given*, than *assumed*: And its Grandees of all kinds owe more of their elevation to the Littleness of others minds, than to the Greatness of their own. Were not prostrate spirits their voluntary pedestals, the figure they make among mankind would not stand so high. *Imitators* and *Translators* are somewhat of the pedestal-kind, and sometimes rather raise their *Original*'s reputation, by showing him to be by them inimitable, than their own. *Homer* has been translated into most languages; *Ælian* tells us, that the *Indians*, (hopeful tutors!) have taught him to speak their tongue. What expect we from them? Not *Homer*'s *Achilles*, but something, which, like *Patroclus*, assumes his name, and, at its peril, appears in his stead; nor expect we *Homer*'s *Ulysses*, gloriously bursting out of his cloud into royal grandeur, but an *Ulysses* under disguise, and a beggar to the last. Such is that inimitable father of poetry, and Oracle of all the wise, whom *Lycurgus* transcribed; and for an annual publick recital of whose works *Solon* enacted a law; that it is much to be feared, that his so numerous translations are but as the publish'd testimonials of so many nations, and ages, that this author so divine is untranslated still.

But here,

> *Cynthius aurem*
> *Vellit,*—

VIRG[IL][2]

and demands justice for his favourite, and ours. Great things he has done; but he might have done greater. What a fall is it from *Homer*'s

---

[1] [I.e., the imitation of classical writers to the exclusion of originality]

[2] [*Ecl.* vi. 3: 'Cynthius (i.e. Apollo) plucked my ear.']

numbers, free as air, lofty and harmonious as the spheres, into childish shackles, and tinkling sounds! But, in his fall, he is still great—

> Nor appears
> Less than Archangel ruin'd, and the excess
> Of glory obscur'd.—
>
> <div align="right">MILT[ON <i>Paradise Lost</i>, i. 592–4]</div>

Had *Milton* never wrote, *Pope* had been less to blame: But when in *Milton*'s Genius, *Homer*, as it were, personally rose to forbid *Britons* doing him that ignoble wrong; it is less pardonable, by that *effeminate* decoration, to put *Achilles* in petticoats a second time: How much nobler had it been, if his numbers had rolled on in full flow, through the various modulations of *masculine* melody, into those grandeurs of solemn sound, which are indispensably demanded by the native dignity of Heroick song? How much nobler, if he had resisted the temptation of that *Gothic* Dæmon, which modern Poesy tasting, became mortal? O how unlike the deathless, divine harmony of three great names (how justly join'd!), of *Milton, Greece,* and *Rome*? His Verse, but for this little speck of mortality, in its extreme parts, as his Hero had in his Heel; like him, had been invulnerable, and immortal. But, unfortunately, *that* was undipt in *Helicon*; as *this*, in *Styx*. Harmony as well as Eloquence is essential to poesy; and a murder of his Musick is putting half *Homer* to death. *Blank* is a term of diminution; what we mean by blank verse, is, verse unfallen, uncurst; verse reclaim'd, reinthron'd in the true *language of the Gods*; who never thunder'd, nor suffer'd their *Homer* to thunder, in Rhime; and therefore, I beg you, my Friend, to crown it with some nobler term; nor let the greatness of the thing lie under the defamation of such a name.

But supposing *Pope*'s *Iliad* to have been perfect in its kind; yet it is a *Translation* still; which differs as much from an *Original*, as the moon from the sun. . . .

[Young goes on to attack Swift]

Would not his friend *Pope* have succeeded better in an *original* attempt? Talents untried are talents unknown. All that I know, is, that, contrary to these sentiments, he was not only an avowed professor of Imitation, but a zealous recommender of it also. Nor could he recommend any thing better, except Emulation, to those who write. One of these all writers must call to their aid; but aids they are of unequal repute. Imitation is inferiority confessed; Emulation is superiority contested, or denied; Imitation is servile, Emulation generous; That fetters, This fires; That may give a name; This, a name immortal: This made *Athens* to succeeding ages the rule of taste, and the standard of perfection. Her men of Genius struck fire against each other; and kindled, by conflict, into glories no time shall extinguish. We thank *Eschylus* for *Sophocles*; and *Parrhasius* for *Zeuxis*; *Emulation*, for both. That bids us fly the general fault of *Imitators*; bids us not be struck with the loud report of former fame, as with a Knell, which damps the spirits; but, as with a Trumpet, which inspires ardour to rival the renown'd. Emulation exhorts us, instead of learning our discipline for ever, like raw troops, under antient leaders in composition, to put those laurel'd veterans in some hazard of losing their superior posts in glory.

Such is Emulation's high-spirited advice, such her immortalizing call. *Pope* would not hear, pre-engaged with Imitation, which blessed him with all her charms. He chose rather, with his namesake of *Greece*, to triumph in the old world, than to look out for a new. His taste partook the error of his Religion; it denied not worship to Saints and Angels; that is, to writers, who, canonized for ages, have received their apotheosis from established and universal fame. True Poesy, like true Religion, abhors idolatry; and though it honours the memory of the exemplary, and takes them willingly (yet cautiously) as guides in the way to glory; real, though unexampled, excellence is its only aim; nor looks it for any inspiration less than divine.

Though *Pope's* noble muse may boast her illustrious descent from *Homer, Virgil, Horace*, yet is an *Original* author more nobly born.[1] As *Tacitus* says of *Curtius Rufus*, an *Original* author is born of himself, is his own progenitor, and will probably propagate a numerous offspring of Imitators, to eternize his glory; while mule-like Imitators die without issue. Therefore, though we stand much obliged for his giving us an *Homer*, yet had he doubled our obligation, by giving us—a *Pope*. Had he a strong Imagination, and the true Sublime? That granted, we might have had two *Homers* instead of one, if longer had been his life; for I heard the dying swan talk over an Epic plan a few weeks before his decease. . . .

. . . *Originals* shine, like comets; have no peer in their path; are rival'd by none, and the gaze of all: All other compositions (if they shine at all) shine in clusters; like the stars in the galaxy; where, like bad

---

[1] [For Samuel Richardson's comment upon Young's first version of his account of Pope in the *Conjectures*, see No. 110]

neighbours, all suffer from all; each particular being diminished, and almost lost in the throng. . . .

. . . [Addison] has a more refined, decent, judicious, and extensive Genius, than *Pope*, or *Swift*. To distinguish this triumvirate from each other, and, like *Newton*, to discover the different colours in these genuine and meridian rays of literary light, *Swift* is a singular wit, *Pope* a correct poet, *Addison* a great author. *Swift* looked on Wit as the *Jus divinum* [divine right] to dominion and sway in the world; and considered as usurpation, all power that was lodged in persons of less sparkling understandings. This inclined him to tyranny in wit; *Pope* was somewhat of his opinion, but was for softening tyranny into lawful monarchy; yet were there some acts of severity in his reign; *Addison*'s crown was elective, he reigned by the public voice:

> . . . *Volentes*
> *Per populos dat jura, viamque affectat Olympo.*
>
> VIRG[IL] [1]

But as good books are the medicine of the mind, if we should dethrone these authors, and consider them, not in their royal, but their medicinal capacity, might it not then be said, that *Addison* prescribed a wholesome and pleasant regimen, which was universally relished, and did much good; that *Pope* preferred a purgative of satire, which, tho' wholesome, was too painful in its operation; and that *Swift* insisted on a large dose of ipecacuanha,[2] which, tho' readily swallowed from the fame of the physician, yet, if the patient had any delicacy of taste, he threw up the remedy, instead of the disease?

Addison wrote little in Verse, much in sweet, elegant, *Virgilian*, Prose; so let me call it, since *Longinus* calls *Herodotus* most *Homeric*, and *Thucydides* is said to have formed his style on *Pindar*. *Addison*'s compositions are built with the finest materials, in the taste of the antients, and (to speak his own language) on truly *Classic ground*; And tho' they are the delight of the present age, yet am I persuaded that they will receive more justice from posterity. . . .

---

[1] [*Georgics*, iv. 562: 'gave [a victor's] laws unto willing nations, and essayed the path to Heaven.' Virgil is speaking of Octavian's victory at Actium, 31 BC]

[2] [Root of a South American shrub used as an emetic and purge]

113. Algarotti on Pope

1759

Conte Francesco Algarotti (1712–64), extract translated from letter to Agostino Paradisi, 4 October 1759, *Opere del Conte Algarotti*, 'Edizione novissima' (Venice, 1792), x. 10–13.

Your criticism of Pope is very fair. He is guilty of excess of blood as he himself states when speaking of authors who have too much wit:

> For works may have more wit, than does 'em good,
> As bodies perish thro' excess of blood.
>
> [*An Essay on Criticism*, ll. 303–4]

He does not give his reader enough time, does not allow him a pause but piles up thought upon thought, image upon image. His poems, for the most part those written in his youth, resemble those buildings on which all the framework is carved, none of which stands out from the rest thereby affording the viewer's eye some rest. And antithesis, a very beautiful figure in itself when it arises from the subject and is used in moderation, on occasions instils not a little satiety when employed by him.

Of his youthful work one must needs, however, make an exception of *The Rape of the Lock*. Such defects are not present in this charming work. It is vivified by wit and not burdened by it; it is a well-nourished body and not may I say a plethoric one. The gods who set the 'machinery' in motion in this poem are so suited to their subject that the poet's fantasy transports the reader to a world in which all proportions are geometrically observed, just as in Gulliver's by his friend Swift.

It seems that the very English language has become plainer, sweeter, more harmonious, and that the subject imparts quality and colour to it. It is by far superior both in inspiration and in every other respect to that other pleasant poem by his other friend Gay entitled *The Fan*. Even the French who are renowned for their good taste have no work to equal this and it must appear almost as strange that the most gallant poem there is should be born amongst the English as it is that arquebus powder [i.e. gunpowder] should be the invention of a monk.

When he was advanced in years Pope was purged of his youthful defects:

> You grow correct that once with rapture writ[1]

he makes himself say in one of his last works. It was therefore not altogether by chance that he found some consolation in this in Horace, his imitations of whom are so beautiful that these alone would suffice to qualify him as the greatest versifier, if not the greatest poet, England has produced.

In his imitations he has, on occasion, even improved on the original.

> Urit enim fulgore suo, qui praegravat artes
> Infra se positas; extinctus amabitur idem[2]

is a passage in which, because of its expression, I have never found Horace's customary refinement. The words 'urere' and 'praegravare' kick each other; there is no continuity of image; the heterogeneity of the metaphors offends by being superfluous. Pope has imitated it continuing the same figure with charm:

> Sure fate of all beneath whose rising ray
> Each star of meaner merit fades away!
> Oppress'd we feel the beam directly beat,
> Those suns of glory please not till they set.

He himself experienced a similar destiny, criticised, torn to shreds by malevolents. . . .

---

[1] [*Epilogue to the Satires*, I. 3]

[2] [*Ep.*, II. i. 12-13 (ll. 19-22 in Pope): 'For a man scorches with his own brilliance who outweighs merits lowlier than his own, yet he, too, will win affection, when his light is quenched']

114. Johnson on Pope and 'easy poetry'

October 1759

Dr Samuel Johnson, extract from *The Idler*, no. 77, 6 October 1759, *Works of Samuel Johnson*, vol. ii. ed. W. J. Bate, *et al.* (New Haven, 1963), pp. 239–41.

Easy poetry is universally admired, but I know not whether any rule has yet been fixed, by which it may be decided when poetry can properly be called easy; Horace has told us that it is such as 'every reader hopes to equal, but after long labour finds unattainable'.[1] This is a very loose description, in which only the effect is noted; the qualities which produce this effect remain to be investigated.

Easy poetry is that in which natural thoughts are expressed without violence to the language. The discriminating character of ease consists principally in the diction, for all true poetry requires that the sentiments be natural. Language suffers violence by harsh or daring figures, by transposition, by unusual acceptations of words, and by any licence, which would be avoided by a writer of prose. Where any artifice appears in the construction of the verse, that verse is no longer easy. Any epithet which can be ejected without diminution of the sense, any curious iteration of the same word, and all unusual, tho' not ungrammatical structure of speech, destroy the grace of easy poetry.

The first lines of Pope's *Iliad* afford examples of many licences which an easy writer must decline.

> Achilles' *wrath*, to Greece the *direful spring*
> Of woes unnumber'd, *heav'nly* Goddess sing,
> The wrath which *hurl'd* to Pluto's *gloomy reign*
> The souls of *mighty* chiefs untimely slain.

In the first couplet the language is distorted by inversions, clogged with superfluities, and clouded by a harsh metaphor; and in the second

---

[1] [*Ars Poetica*, ll. 240–2]

there are two words used in an uncommon sense, and two epithets inserted only to lengthen the line; all these practices may in a long work easily be pardoned, but they always produce some degree of obscurity and ruggedness.

Easy poetry has been so long excluded by ambition of ornament, and luxuriance of imagery, that its nature seems now to be forgotten. Affectation, however opposite to ease, is sometimes mistaken for it, and those who aspire to gentle elegance, collect female phrases and fashionable barbarisms, and imagine that style to be easy which custom has made familiar. Such was the idea of the poet[1] who wrote the following verses to a 'Countess Cutting Paper.'

> Pallas grew *vap'rish once and odd*,
>   She would not *do the least right thing*
> Either for Goddess or for God,
>   Nor work, nor play, nor paint, nor sing.
>
> Jove frown'd and 'Use (he cry'd) those eyes
>   So skillful, and those hands so taper;
> Do something exquisite and wise'—
>   She bow'd, obey'd him, and cut paper.
>
> This vexing him who gave her birth,
>   Thought by all heav'n a *burning shame*,
> *What does she next*, but bids on earth
>   Her Burlington do just the same?
>
> Pallas, you give yourself *strange airs*;
>   But sure you'll find it hard to spoil
> The sense and taste, of one that bears
>   The name of Savile and of Boyle.[2]
>
> Alas! one bad example shown,
>   How quickly all the sex pursue!
> See, madam! see, the arts o'erthrown
>   Between John Overton[3] and *you*.

---

[1] [Pope, 'On the Countess of Burlington Cutting Paper']
[2] [The Countess's maiden and married names]
[3] [A printseller, especially of mezzotints]

It is the prerogative of easy poetry to be understood as long as the language lasts; but modes of speech, which owe their prevalence only to modish folly, or to the eminence of those that use them, die away with their inventors, and their meaning, in a few years, is no longer known. . . .

115. Pope and Boileau in conversation

1760

Lord George Lyttelton, extract from 'Dialogue XIV. Boileau–Pope', *Dialogues of the Dead* (1760), pp. 112–17. Baron Lyttelton (1709–73), who had been a good friend of Pope, wrote this piece in middle age. The tradition of the Dialogue of the Dead was a commonplace one: for Lyttelton's effusive verse letter written as a young man to Pope, see No. 62.

BOILEAU.

MR. Pope, you have done me great Honour. I am told, that you made me your Model in Poetry, and walked on Parnassus in the same Paths which I had trod.

POPE.

We both followed Horace: but in our manner of Imitation, and in the turn of our natural Genius, there was I believe a great deal of Resemblance, which I am proud that others observe. Our Tempers too were the same in many respects. They were both very warm with the Love of good Morals, true Wit, and sound Learning, and fond of the Glory of our being their Champions. But they were too irritable, and too easily hurt by Offences, even from the lowest of Men. We turned the keen Edge of our Wit against those whom it was more a Shame to contend with than an Honour to vanquish. Yet our Muse was not

435

always severe and ill-humoured. She could smile on our Friends, and understood how to praise as well as to blame.

BOILEAU.

It would perhaps have been better if in some instances we had neither praised nor blamed so much. But in Panegyric and Satire Moderation is thought to be flat and insipid.

POPE.

Moderation is a cold *unpoetical* Virtue. Mere Historical Truth should be written in Prose. And therefore I think you did very well to burn your *History of Louis le Grand*, and trust his fame, and your own, to your Poems.

BOILEAU.

When those Poems were written he was the Idol of the French Nation as much as mine. If You and I had not known how to speak to the Passions, as well as to the sober Sense of Mankind, we should not have been the favourite Authors of the French and the English, nor have acquired that kind of despotic Authority in the Empire of Wit, which we both held as long as we lived.

POPE.

The Praise which My Friends had from me was *unbought*. In *this*, at least, I may boast a Superiority over the *pensioned Boileau*.

BOILEAU.

A *Pension* in France was an honourable Distinction. Had you been a Frenchman you would have sought it; had I been an Englishman I should have declined it. If our Merit in other respects be the same, *this* will not make a great Difference in it.

POPE.

It is not for me to draw a Comparison between our Works. But, if I may believe the best Critics with whom I have talked, my *Rape of the Lock* is not inferior to your *Lutrin*; and my *Art of Criticism* may well be compared with your *Art of Poetry*: my *Ethic Epistles* are thought at least to be equal to your's, and my *Satires* much better.

BOILEAU.

Hold, Mr. Pope—If there really is such a Sympathy in our Natures as
you have supposed, there may be reason to fear, that, if we go on comparing our Works, we shall not part in good Friendship.

POPE.

No, no:—the mild Air of the Elysian Fields has softened my temper,
as I presume it has your's. But in truth our reputations are nearly on a
Level. We both of us carried the Beauty of our *Diction*, and the Harmony of our *Numbers*, to the highest Perfection that our Languages
would admit. Our Poems were laboured and polished to the utmost
degree of Correctness, yet without losing their Fire, or the pleasing
Appearance of Freedom and Ease. The Spirit of the Ancients seemed to
animate all of them; and we both borrowed much from those excellent
Masters; though You perhaps more than I: but our Imitations had still
an Original Air.

BOILEAU.

I will confess, Sir, (to shew you that the Elysian Climate has had its
proper effects upon me) I will fairly confess, without any ill humour,
that in your *Temple of Fame*, your *Windsor Forest*, your *Eloisa to
Abelard*, and some other Pieces you wrote in your Youth, there is more
Imagination, more Sweetness, more Fire of Poetry, than in any of
mine. I will also allow, that you hit the *Manner* of Horace, and *the sly
Delicacy* of his Wit more exactly than I, or than any other Man who has
writ since his time.

POPE.

What do you think of my *Homer*?

BOILEAU.

Your *Homer* is the most spirited, the most poetical, the most elegant,
the most pleasing Translation, that ever was made of any ancient Poem;
tho' not so much in the *manner* of the Original, or so exact to the Sense
in all Places, as might be desired. But when I consider the Years you
spent in this Work, and how many fine original Poems you might with
less difficulty have produced in that time, I can't but regret that you
should have employed your Talents in a way, wherein their full
Energy could not be seen. A great Poet, tied down to a tedious Translation, is *a Columbus chained to an Oar*. What new Regions of Fancy might

you have explored, if you could have freely expanded your Sails, and
steered your own Course, under the conduct of your own Genius!—
But I am still more angry with you for your Edition of Shakespear.
The Work of an *Editor* was below you, and your mind was unfit for the
Drudgery of it. Would any body think of employing a Raphael to
clean an old Picture?

116. An Edinburgh professor's view

c. 1762

Hugh Blair (1718–1800), extract from *Lectures on Rhetoric and Belles
Lettres* (1783), ed. H. H. Harding (Carbondale and Edwardsville,
Ill., 1965), ii. 368–70. Harding notes that Blair's lectures, which
were highly successful when he gave them in Edinburgh, were
substantially complete by 1762, and that they probably received
only minor revision prior to their publication twenty years later
(*ibid.*, p. xi).

Didactic Epistles, of which I now speak, seldom admit of much elevation. They are commonly intended as observations on Authors, or on
Life and Characters; in delivering which, the Poet does not purpose to
compose a formal treatise, or to confine himself strictly to regular
method; but gives scope to his genius on some particular theme, which,
at the time, has prompted him to write. In all Didactic Poetry of this
kind, it is an important rule 'quicquid precipies, esto brevis.'[1] Much of
the grace, both of Satirical and Epistolary Writing, consists in a spirited
conciseness. This gives to such composition an edge and a liveliness,
which strike the fancy, and keep attention awake. Much of their merit
depends also on just and happy representations of characters. As they
are not supported by those high beauties of descriptive and poetical

[1] [Horace, *Ars Poetica*, l. 335; 'let whatever you teach be brief']

438

language which adorn other compositions, we expect, in return, to be entertained with lively paintings of men and manners, which are always pleasing; and in these, a certain sprightliness and turn of wit finds its proper place. The higher species of Poetry seldom admit it; but here it is seasonable and beautiful.

IN all these respects, Mr. Pope's Ethical Epistles deserve to be mentioned with signal honour, as a model, next to perfect, of this kind of Poetry. Here, perhaps, the strength of his genius appeared. In the more sublime parts of Poetry, he is not so distinguished. In the enthusiasm, the fire, the force and copiousness of poetic genius, Dryden, though a much less correct Writer, appears to have been superior to him. One can scarce think that he was capable of Epic or Tragic Poetry; but within a certain limited region, he has been outdone by no Poet. His translation of the Iliad will remain a lasting monument to his honour, as the most elegant and highly finished translation, that, perhaps, ever was given of any poetical work. That he was not incapable of tender Poetry, appears from the epistle of Eloisa to Abelard, and from the verses to the memory of an Unfortunate Lady, which are almost his only sentimental productions; and which indeed are excellent in their kind. But the qualities for which he is chiefly distinguished are, judgment and wit, with a concise and happy expression, and a melodious ficaversition. Few Poets ever had more wit, and at the same time more judgment, to direct the proper employment of that wit. This renders his Rape of the Lock the greatest master-piece that perhaps was ever composed, in the gay and sprightly Style; and in his serious works, such as his Essay on Man, and his Ethic Epistles, his wit just discovers itself as much, as to give a proper seasoning to grave reflexions. His imitations of Horace are so peculiarly happy, that one is at a loss, whether most to admire the original or the copy; and they are among the few imitations extant, that have all the grace and ease of an original. His paintings of characters are natural and lively in a high degree; and never was any Writer so happy in that concise spirited Style, which gives animation to Satyres and Epistles. We are never so sensible of the good effects of rhyme in English verse, as in reading these parts of his works. We see it adding to the Style, an elevation which otherwise it could not have possessed; while at the same time he manages it so artfully, that it never appears in the least to encumber him; but, on the contrary, serves to increase the liveliness of his manner. He tells us himself, that he could express moral observations more concisely, and therefore more forcibly, in rhyme, than he could do in prose.

117. Lord Kames on Pope

March 1762

Henry Home (1696–1782), Lord Kames, extracts from *Elements of Criticism* (1762), 7th ed. (1788), ii. 83–94.

The extract is from section iii of chapter xviii entitled 'Beauty of Language from a resemblance between Sound and Signification'. It takes up the relationship of sound and sense in poetry discussed by Addison and Johnson earlier (Nos 11, 99), and affected Johnson's return to the subject in his *Life*.

A Resemblance between the sound of certain words and their signification, is a beauty that has escaped no critical writer, and yet is not handled with accuracy by any of them. They have probably been of opinion, that a beauty so obvious to the feeling, requires no explanation. This is an error; and to avoid it, I shall give examples of the various resemblances between sound and signification, accompanied with an endeavour to explain why such resemblances are beautiful. I begin with examples where the resemblance between the sound and signification is the most entire; and next examples where the resemblance is less and less so.

There being frequently a strong resemblance of one sound to another, it will not be surprising to find an articulate sound resembling one that is not articulate: thus the sound of a bow-string is imitated by the words that express it:

> ——————————The string let fly,
> *Twang'd short and sharp*, like the shrill swallow's cry.
>
> Odyssey, xii. 448–9.

The sound of felling trees in a wood:

> Loud sounds the ax, redoubling strokes on strokes,
> On all sides round the forest hurls her oaks
> Headlong. Deep echoing groan the thickets brown,
> Then *rustling, crackling, crashing*, thunder down.
>
> Iliad, xxiii. 146.

But when loud surges lash the sounding shore,
The hoarse rough verse should like the torrent roar.
Pope's Essay on Criticism, l. 368.

Dire Scylla there a scene of horror forms,
And here Charybdis fills the deep with storms:
When the tide rushes from her rumbling caves,
The rough rock roars: tumultuous boil the waves.
[*Odyssey*, xii. 280.]

No person can be at a loss about the cause of this beauty: it is obviously that of imitation.

That there is any other natural resemblance of sound to signification, must not be taken for granted. There is no resemblance of sound to motion, nor of sound to sentiment. We are however apt to be deceived by artful pronunciation: the same passage may be pronounced in many different tones, elevated or humble, sweet or harsh, brisk or melancholy, so as to accord with the thought or sentiment: such concord must be distinguished from that concord between sound and sense, which is perceived in some expressions independent of artful pronunciation: the latter is the poet's work; the former must be attributed to the reader. Another thing contributes still more to the deceit; in language, sound and sense being intimately connected, the properties of the one are readily communicated to the other; for example, the quality of grandeur, of sweetness, or of melancholy, though belonging to the thought solely, is transferred to the words, which by that means resemble in appearance the thought that is expressed by them. I have great reason to recommend these observations to the reader, considering how inaccurately the present subject is handled by critics: not one of them distinguishes the natural resemblance of sound and signification, from the artificial resemblances now described; witness Vida in particular, who in a very long passage has given very few examples but what are of the latter kind.[1]

That there may be a resemblance of articulate sounds to some that are not articulate, is self-evident; and that in fact there exist such resemblances successfully employed by writers of genius, is clear from the foregoing examples, and from many others that might be given. But we may safely pronounce, that this natural resemblance can be carried no farther: the objects of the different senses, differ so widely from each other, as to exclude any resemblance; sound in particular, whether

---

[1] *Ars Poetica*, iii. 365–454.

articulate or inarticulate, resembles not in any degree taste, smell, nor motion; and as little can it resemble any internal sentiment, feeling or emotion. But must we then admit, that nothing but sound can be imitated by sound? Taking imitation in its proper sense, as importing a resemblance between two objects, the proposition must be admitted: and yet in many passages that are not descriptive of sound, every one must be sensible of a peculiar concord between the sound of the words and their meaning. As there can be no doubt of the fact, what remains is to inquire into its cause.

Resembling causes may produce effects that have no resemblance; and causes that have no resemblance may produce resembling effects. A magnificent building, for example, resembles not in any degree an heroic action; and yet the emotions they produce, are concordant, and bear a resemblance to each other. We are still more sensible of this resemblance in a song, when the music is properly adapted to the sentiment: there is no resemblance between thought and sound; but there is the strongest resemblance between the emotion raised by music tender and pathetic, and that raised by the complaint of an unsuccessful lover. Applying this observation to the present subject, it appears, that in some instances, the sound even of a single word makes an impression resembling that which is made by the thing it signifies: witness the word *running*, composed of two short syllables; and more remarkably the words *rapidity*, *impetuosity*, *precipitation*. Brutal manners produce in the spectator an emotion not unlike what is produced by a harsh and rough sound; and hence the beauty of the figurative expression *rugged* manners. Again, the word *little*, being pronounced with a very small aperture of the mouth, has a weak and faint sound, which makes an impression resembling that made by a diminutive object. This resemblance of effects is still more remarkable where a number of words are connected in a period: words pronounced in succession make often a strong impression; and when this impression happens to accord with that made by the sense, we are sensible of a complex emotion, peculiarly pleasant; one proceeding from the sentiment, and one from the melody or sound of the words. But the chief pleasure proceeds from having these two concordant emotions combined in perfect harmony, and carried on in the mind to a full close: Except in the single case where sound is described, all the examples given by critics of sense being imitated in sound, resolve into a resemblance of effects: emotions raised by sound and signification may have a resemblance; but sound itself cannot have a resemblance to any thing but sound.

Proceeding now to particulars, and beginning with those cases where the emotions have the strongest resemblance, I observe, first, That by a number of syllables in succession, an emotion is sometimes raised extremely similar to that raised by successive motion; which may be evident even to those who are defective in taste, from the following fact, that the term *movement* in all languages is equally applied to both. In this manner, successive motion, such as walking, running, galloping, can be imitated by a succession of long or short syllables, or by a due mixture of both. For example, slow motion may be justly imitated in a verse where long syllables prevail; especially when aided by a slow pronunciation.

> Illi inter sese magnâ vi brachia tollunt.[1]
>
> *Georgics* iv. 174.

On the other hand, swift motion is imitated by a succession of short syllables:

> Quadrupedante putrem sonitu quatit ungula campum.[2]

Again:

> Radit iter liquidum, celeres neque commovet alas.[3]

Thirdly, A line composed of monosyllables, makes an impression, by the frequency of its pauses, similar to what is made by laborious interrupted motion:

> With many a weary step, and many a groan,
> Up the high hill he heaves a huge round stone.
>
> *Odyssey*, xi. 735.

> First march the heavy mules securely slow;
> O'er hills, o'er dales, o'er craggs, o'er rocks they go.
>
> *Iliad*, xxiii. 140.

Fourthly, The impression made by rough sounds in succession, resembles that made by rough or tumultuous motion: on the other hand, the impression of smooth sounds resembles that of gentle motion. The following is an example of both.

---

[1] ['They lift their arms together with great force']
[2] [*Aeneid*, viii. 596: 'With clatter of hammering hooves they go galloping over the dry flats' (C. Day Lewis)]
[3] [*Aeneid*, v. 217: 'she skims her liquid way, and stirs not her swift pinions']

Two craggy rocks projecting to the main,
The roaring wind's tempestuous rage restrain;
Within, the waves in softer murmurs glide,
And ships secure without their haulsers ride.

Odyssey, xiii. 118.

Another example of the latter:

Soft is the strain when Zephyr gently blows,
And the smooth stream in smoother numbers flows.

Essay on Criticism, l. 366.

Fifthly, Prolonged motion is expressed in an Alexandrine line. The first example shall be of slow motion prolonged.

A needless Alexandrine ends the song;
That like a wounded snake, drags its slow length along,

Essay on Criticism, l. 356.

The next example is of forcible motion prolonged:

The waves behind impel the waves before,
Wide-rolling, foaming high, and tumbling to the shore.

Iliad, xiii. 1004.

The last shall be of rapid motion prolonged:

Not so when swift Camilla scours the plain,
Flies o'er th'unbending corn, and skims along the main.

Essay on Criticism, l. 372.

Again speaking of a rock torn from the brow of a mountain:

Still gath'ring force, it smokes, and urg'd amain,
Whirls, leaps, and thunders down, impetuous to the plain.

Iliad, xiii. 197.

Sixthly, a period consisting mostly of long syllables, that is, of syllables pronounced slow, produceth an emotion resembling faintly that which is produced by gravity and solemnity. Hence the beauty of the following verse:

Olli sedato respondit corde Latinus.[1]

It resembles equally an object that is insipid and uninteresting.

[1] [Virgil, *Aeneid*, xii. 18: 'To him Latinus with unruffled soul replied']

Tædet quotidianarum harum formarum.
                    Terence, Eunuchus, act 2. sc. 3.[1]

Seventhly, A slow succession of ideas is a circumstance that belongs
equally to settled melancholy, and to a period composed of poly-
syllables pronounced slow: and hence by similarity of emotions, the
latter is imitative of the former:

> In these deep solitudes, and awful cells,
> Where heav'nly pensive Contemplation dwells,
> And ever musing melancholy reigns.
>   *Pope, Eloisa to Abelard,* ll. 1–3.

Eighthly, A long syllable made short, or a short syllable made long,
raises, by the difficulty of pronouncing contrary to custom, a feeling
similar to that of hard labour:

> When Ajax strives some rock's *vast* weight to throw,
> The line too labours, and the words move slow.
>   *Essay on Criticism,* l. 370.

Ninthly, Harsh or rough words pronounced with difficulty, excite a
feeling similar to that which proceeds from the labour of thought to a
dull writer:

> Just writes to make his barrenness appear,
> And strains from hard-bound brains eight lines a-year.
>   *Pope's epistle to Dr. Arbuthnot,* l. 181.

I shall close with one example more, which of all makes the finest
figure. In the first section mention is made of a climax in sound; and in
the second, of a climax in sense. It belongs to the present subject to
observe, that when these coincide in the same passage, the concordance
of sound and sense is delightful: the reader is conscious not only of
pleasure from the two climaxes separately, but of an additional pleasure
from their concordance, and from finding the sense so justly imitated by
the sound. In this respect, no periods are more perfect than those borrowed from Cicero in the first section.

The concord between sense and sound is no less agreeable in what
may be termed an *anticlimax,* where the progress is from great to little;

---

[1] ['these everyday beauties are wearisome']

for this has the effect to make diminutive objects appear still more diminutive. Horace affords a striking example.

Parturient montes, nascetur ridiculus mus.[1]

The arrangement here is singularly artful: the first place is occupied by the verb, which is the capital word by its sense as well as sound: the close is reserved for the word that is the meanest in sense as well as in sound. And it must not be overlooked, that the resembling sounds of the two last syllables give a ludicrous air to the whole.

Reviewing the foregoing examples, it appears to me, contrary to expectation, that in passing from the strongest resemblances to those that are fainter, every step affords additional pleasure. Renewing the experiment again and again, I feel no wavering, but the greatest pleasure constantly from the faintest resemblances. And yet how can this be? for if the pleasure lie in imitation, must not the strongest re-semblance afford the greatest pleasure? From this vexing dilemma I am happily relieved, by reflecting on a doctrine established in the chapter of resemblance and contrast, that the pleasure of resemblance is the greatest, where it is least expected, and where the objects compared are in their capital circumstances widely different. Nor will this appear surprising, when we descend to familiar examples. It raiseth no degree of wonder to find the most perfect resemblance between two eggs of the same bird: it is more rare to find such resemblance between two human faces; and upon that account such an appearance raises some degree of wonder: but this emotion rises to a still greater height, when we find in a pebble, an agate, or other natural production, any resemblance to a tree or to any organized body. We cannot hesitate a moment, in applying these observations to the present subject: what occasion of wonder can it be to find one sound resembling another, where both are of the same kind? It is not so common to find a resemblance between an articulate sound and one not articulate; which accordingly affords some slight pleasure. But the pleasure swells greatly, when we employ sound to imitate things it resembles not otherwise than by the effects produced in the mind.

[1] [Horace, *Ars Poetica*, l. 139: 'Mountains will labour, to birth will come a ridiculous mouse']

118. Pope, Homer, and the nature of genius

1762

Arthur Murphy, extract from 'An Essay on the Life and Genius of Henry Fielding, Esq.', *The Works of Henry Fielding* (1762), i. 15–21.

Murphy (1727–1805), the Irish dramatist and actor, identifies himself firmly with the Augustan notion of genius. His defence of Pope is also a defence of Fielding. The analysis of the nature of originality he gives is part of the debate between neoclassicism and the views put forward by Warton and Young. Murphy's argument is intelligent and vigorous, and Johnson's remarks on the subject in his *Life of Pope* are indebted to this passage (see p. 27).

As this essay promises to treat of the genius, as well as the life of Henry Fielding, it may not be improper to pause here for an enquiry into his talents, though we are not arrived at that period of his life, when they displayed themselves in their full warmth and splendor. And here it is necessary to caution the reader not to confine his idea of what is intended by the word *genius* to any one single faculty of the mind; because it is observable that many mistakes have arisen, even among writers of penetrating judgment, and well versed in critical learning, by hastily attaching themselves to an imperfect notion of this term so common in literary dissertations. That invention is the first great leading talent of a poet has been a point long since determined, because it is principally owing to that faculty of the mind that he is able to create, and be as it were a MAKER, which is implied in his original title given to him by the consent of Greece. But surely there are many other powers of the mind as fully essential to constitute a fine poet, and therefore, in order to give the true character of any author's abilities, it should seem necessary to come to a right understanding of what is meant by GENIUS, and to analyse and arrange its several qualities. This once adjusted, it might prove no unpleasing task to examine what are the specific qualities of any poet in particular, to point out the talents of which he seems to have the freest command, or in the use of which he seems, as it were, to be left-handed. In this plain fair-dealing way the true and real value of an author will be easily ascertained; whereas in the more confined method of investigation, which establishes, at the outset, one giant-quality, and finding the object of the enquiry deficient in that, immediately proceeds to undervalue him in the whole, there seems to be danger of not trying his cause upon a full and equitable hearing. Thus, I think, a late celebrated poet is likely to suffer an unjust sentence from a gentleman, who has already obliged the public with the first volume of an Essay on his Life and Genius. The common assertion which has been in every half-critic's mouth, namely, that Mr. Pope had little invention, and therefore has but a bad claim to the name of poet, seems to be unguardedly adopted in the very beginning of that ingenious and entertaining work; and from that principle the conclusion will probably decide against our English Homer. From the elegant, and, in general, true spirit of criticism, which the Essayist on Mr. Pope's Life and writings is acknowledged to possess, it was reasonably to be expected that he would have taken a comprehensive view of what INVENTION is, and then examined how far the want of it can be charged upon his author. But in that point, does he not seem to think him defenceless, when he asserts that it is upon the merit of the Rape of the Lock that he will rank as a poet with posterity? The introduction of machinery into this beautiful poem, Mr. Wharton seems to think shews more invention than any other composition of the Twickenham bard; tho' even in this point he deals out to him the reputation of a MAKER with a sparing and a thrifty hand. As the book is near me, I will transcribe his words:

It is in this composition Pope principally appears a poet, in which he has displayed more imagination than in all his other works taken together: It should however be remembered that he was not the FIRST former and creator of those beautiful machines the Sylphs, on which his claim to imagination is chiefly founded. He found them existing ready to his hand, but has indeed employed them with singular judgment and artifice.[1]

But surely in the use made of the *Sylphs* and *Gnomes*, and the various employments assigned to those imaginary beings, the British author is as much a POET, as manifestly a MAKER, as the great father of the epic fable. Homer invented not the gods and goddesses which he has interwoven in his immortal Rhapsody. He took up the system of theology which he found received in Greece. 'He rose,' says Mr. Pope,

[1] [Warton, p. 399 above]

with the finest turn imaginable for poetry, and, designing to instruct mankind in the manner for which he was most adapted, made use of the ministry of the gods to give the highest air of veneration to his writings. Nor was it his business, when he undertook the province of a poet (not of a mere philosopher) to be the first who should discard that, which furnishes poetry with its most beautiful appearance. Whatever therefore he might think of his gods, he took them as he found them; he brought them into action according to the notions which were then entertained, and in such stories as were then believed.[1]

In the same manner, the author of the Rape of the Lock availed himself of the Rosicrucian system, as he found it set forth in a French book, called 'LE COMTE DE GABALIS,' and to those ideal beings he has given such a ministry, such interests, affections, and employments as carried with them sufficient poetical probability, and made a very beautiful machinery in his poem, enlarging the main action, and ennobling the trifles, which it celebrates; not to mention that the superintendency of those imaginary agents was as new in poetry, as the *Ministeria Deorum* in the Iliad or Odyssey. Perhaps, if the matter could be traced with accuracy, and a full knowledge of the state of learning, the various systems of theology, and all the doctrines, opinions, and fables, which existed in Homer's days, could be attained, we should find that the invention of the father of epic poetry, did not so much consist in creating new existencies, and striking out new ideas, as in making a poetic use of the fabulous deities which previously existed in the imaginations of mankind, and in forming new combinations of those ideas, which had been conceived before, but had never been arranged in those complexities into which his fancy was able to dispose them. . . .
. . . If Homer did not originally form and create those prodigious images which abound in his work; if he was not the MAKER of many of those fables, particularly the Descent into Hell, which mankind have so much admired, he at least found out the use and application of them; the combination of those ideas was his own; the scheme was his which assembled them all into that wonderful union; in other words, the general fable was Homer's, and it required no less a genius to give uniformity amidst such an exuberance of variety, intricacy and complication, with such a noble perspicuity, such a consent of parts so uniting, as the painters express it, into harmony, and rising gradually into such a wonderful whole, that, as Mr. Pope expresses it, *it shall always stand at the top of the sublime character, to be gazed at by readers with*

[1] [Not Pope's words, but Thomas Parnell's, 'Essay on the Life, Writings and Learning of Homer' prefixed to the *Iliad*, Twickenham, vii. 68]

*an admiration of its perfection, and by writers with a despair that it should
ever be emulated with success.*[1] There can be no manner of doubt but
Homer, from the fecundity of his own fancy, enriched his poetry with
many noble descriptions and beautiful episodes which had never presented themselves to any of his predecessors: but as the models of many
passages are still extant in the records of antiquity, it must be allowed
that he possessed two sorts of invention; one, primary and original,
which could associate images never before combined; the other,
secondary and subordinate, which could find out for those ideas, which
had been assembled before, a new place, a new order, and arrangement,
with new embellishments of the most harmonious and exalted language.
From this observation arises the true idea of INVENTION; and whether a
poet is hurried away into the description of a fictitious battle, or a
grand council of gods or men, or employs himself in giving poetic
colourings to a real system of *Mysteries*, (as Virgil has done in the sixth
Æneid) there is invention in both cases; and though the former may
astonish more, the latter will always have its rational admirers, and
from such a commentary as the Bishop of Gloucester's,[2] instead of losing
from its influence, will appear with a truer and more venerable sublime, than when it was considered as the mere visionary scheme of a
poetic imagination. Thus then we see the two provinces of INVENTION;
at one time it is employed in opening a new vein of thought; at another,
in placing ideas, that have been pre-occupied, in a new light, and lend-
ing them the advantages of novelty by the force of a sublimer diction,
or the turn of delicate composition. There is a poetic touch that changes
whatever it lights upon to gold; and surely he who calls forth from any
object in nature, or any image of the mind, appearances that have not
been observed before, is the INVENTOR, the MAKER of those additional
beauties. There is reason to believe, that of what we have called
PRIMARY, or ORIGINAL INVENTION, there has not been so much in any
one poet (not even excepting HOMER) as has been generally imagined;
and indeed, from the many fine descriptions in the Iliad and the Odyssey, which can fairly be proved to be copies, but the copies of a master-
poet, there seems room to think, that of the second sort he held a very
considerable portion. Nor should this remark be thought derogatory
from the high character of the bard, because it only tends to shew that
he availed himself of all the knowledge, religion, and mythology, that

[1] [Not Pope's words, but those of Thomas Parnell, 'Essay on the Life, Writings and
Learning of Homer' prefixed to the *Iliad*, Twickenham, vii. 80]
[2] [I.e., the commentary in Warburton's edition]

in his time were scattered over the different regions of Asia and Greece. What is here asserted concerning Homer, may also with truth be asserted of Mr. Pope. Determining to acquire the exalted character of a poet, he enriched his mind with all the knowledge that subsisted in his time; all that could be furnished by the valuable remains of antiquity, all the improvements in science which modern application has brought to light, the pure morality and sublime theology which revelation has delivered down to us, together with the various systems of philosophy, which speculative men have formed; and of all these he has made as noble an use as a fine imagination could suggest. The scheme of thought which introduces his acquired ideas into any of his poems, was surely his own; the VIRTUE and VENUS of ORDER, which he has given to them, was his own; the apt allusion which illustrates, the metaphor which raises his language into dignity, the general splendor of his diction, the harmony of his numbers, and in short, the poetic turn of his pieces, were all his own; and all these surely were the work of INVEN-TION. And as this INVENTION glows equally through all his poetry, it is not easy to conceive upon what principle it can be said, that upon the single strength of the Rape of the Lock he will rank as a poet with posterity. Can it be said that INVENTION solely consists in describing imaginary beings? or that where there is not what the critics call a Fable, that is to say, an unity of action, with all the various perplexities and incidents which retard or accelerate the progress of that action, together with a proper degree of marvellous machinery, INVENTION must be proscribed, and declared to have no hand in the work? Even in this way of reasoning, the DUNCIAD will be an everlasting instance of Mr. Pope's INVENTION, and will, perhaps, constitute him a poet in a degree superior to the *Rape of the Lock*, however exquisite it be in its kind. But these two pieces (if we except the latter part of the fourth Dunciad, which is in its subject important, and in its execution sublime) seem to be but the sportive exercise of the poet's fancy; or as he himself, talking of the *Batrachomyomachia*, has expressed it, they are 'a beautiful raillery, in which a great writer might delight to unbend himself; an instance of that agreeable trifling, which generally accompanies the character of a rich imagination; like a vein of *mercury* running mingled with a mine of *gold*.'[1] The Essay on Man will always stand at the *top of the sublime character*: a noble work indeed, where we find the thorny reasonings of philosophy blooming and shooting forth into all the flowers of poetry; *feret & rubus amomum!*[2] To give to a subject of this

[1] [Parnell, *ibid.*, vii. 527]   [2] [Virgil, Eclogue iii. 89: 'bear balm for him, ye thorns']

kind such beautiful embellishments, required, in Lord Shaftsbury's language, a *Muse-like apprehension*; and I cannot see why the treating of *essential truths* in a poetic manner should not be allowed as cogent an instance of INVENTION, as the ornamented display of an Egyptian theology. The Georgics would have gained Virgil the name of poet, though the *Æneid* had never been written; and Mr. Pope must ever be considered by posterity as a CHRISTIAN LUCRETIUS. It was perhaps harder to give a poetic air and grace to the following ideas, than to describe the imaginary beings of the *Rosicrucian* philosophy, or the fabulous deities of Greece.

> Say what the use, were finer optics given?
> T' inspect a mite, not comprehend the heaven!
> The touch, if tremblingly alive all o'er,
> To smart and agonize at ev'ry pore?
> Or, quick effluvia darting thro' the brain,
> Die of a rose in aromatic pain?
> If nature thunder'd in his op'ning ears,
> And stunn'd him with the musick of the spheres,
> How would he wish that heav'n had left him still
> The whisp'ring Zephir, and the purling rill?
>
> [*An Essay on Man*, i. 195–204]

An entire piece written in this true vein of poetry, requires as fine an imagination to give grace, elegance, and harmony to the composition, as any other subject whatever; and though fable, including various incidents, passions, and characters, be wanting, yet he who forms a plan such as the nature of his materials require, and in a barren field finds the most beautiful flowers to adorn his design, can never in reason be charged with a want of INVENTION. The three great primary branches of composition are finely united in the writings of Pope; the imagination is delighted, the passions are awakened, and reason receives conviction; there is poetry to charm, rhetoric to persuade, and argument to demonstrate: and perhaps if *Empedocles*, whom Aristotle pronounces a *phisiologist*, rather than a *poet*, had been thus excellent in the graces of stile, the great critic would have passed upon him a less severe sentence.

119. A French imitator of *The Dunciad*

1764

Charles Palissot de Montenoy, extract from 'Preface de l'Edition de
1764', *La Dunciade, poëme en dix chants* . . . ('A Londres' 1771), pp.
15–19.

Palissot (1713–1814), poet, dramatist, and critic, published the first
three books of his imitation of Pope in 1764. The 1771 edition
extended it to ten books.

It is well-known that the celebrated Pope has given England an immortal poem, known as the *Dunciad*. The model for this poem existed in no other nation. A singular mixture of bold, sometimes bizarre pictures, but always revealing the hand of the great master; all the riches of invention in a subject which appears sterile, the delicacy of raillery accompanied by a sustained gaiety, the piquant spice of witticisms, that of simplicity, often even the principles of the most delicate taste, come close to forming the character of this individual poem, of which we have no readable translation.

France, where gaiety was once so well received, naturally seems obliged to take possession of this poem, in which everything breathes sprightliness. But it is also necessary to admit that a certain earthiness (if one can risk this word) rules in this work, which must have discouraged anybody who might have intended to translate it. Its flashes of wit sometimes appear too affected, the pictures too overcharged, the jests too harsh, the metaphors too lavish. In fact, through an English licence, of which we would find more than one example among us today, the satire even strikes at morals. The government, which ought to be a stranger to all literary disputes and receive its fruits, has not had to buy the discretion of an author, who appears however to have been a little too occupied with revenging his own personal quarrels. Those are, doubtless, the reasons which have very rightly destroyed the idea of carrying over the beauties of the English poet into our language.

I intended, if it was possible, to grasp at the quality of this singular poem, without concealing the poet's ideas. I have tried to render the *Dunciad* in a form which would please in France, and to which, one judges, Pope would have subjected himself if he had written for us. It is thus that I had to imitate a work, nearly all whose beauties are purely local but whose overall idea is delightful. The disposition of the French poem [that is, Palissot's imitation], the supernatural, the fictions which are the soul of poetry, belong then solely to the new author.

The *Dunciad*, when it appeared in London, marked the date of a quite considerable revolution in literature; a revolution whose results still make themselves felt in England. We know how much the glory of nations is bound up with those of a small number of rare geniuses, who make them worthy of respect by their works. The names, today obscure, of Dennis, Ralph, Theobald, Norton [*sic*], Cibber, and Blackmore, having been delivered over in this poem to the ridicule they merit, the justice that was due to their celebrated adversaries was made prompter: the great men were consoled; the votes of the people, as yet divided, joined together. The names of Dryden, of Addison, of Swift, of Pope himself, were no more pronounced without respect, and genius was avenged.

One dares to believe that a work of this kind has become an even more indispensable necessity for Paris. 'There is no other way', said M. Voltaire, 'to make literature respectable, than to make those who outrage it tremble with fear. It is the last cause that Pope took up before dying. He made ridiculous for ever, in his *Dunciad*, all those who ought to be made ridiculous. They dared show themselves no more, they disappeared. The whole nation applauded him: for if, in the beginning, [the *Dunciad*'s] spitefulness gave a brief vogue to these cowardly enemies of Pope, Swift, and their friends, reason very soon took over. . . . The real talent of verse is as a weapon which must be used to avenge the human race.'

120. Pope, 'The Last English Muse'

1764, 1767

(a) Oliver Goldsmith, extract from *An History of England, in a Series of Letters from a Nobleman to his Son* (1764), *cited Collected Works of Oliver Goldsmith*, ed. A. Friedman (1966), v. 311n.

But of all who have added to the stock of English poetry, Pope, perhaps, deserves the first place. On him foreigners look as one of the most successful writers of his time; his versification is the most harmonious, and his correctness the most remarkable of all our poets. A noted cotemporary of his, calls the English the finest writers on moral topics, and Pope the noblest moral writer of all the English. Mr. Pope has somewhere named himself the last English Muse; and, indeed, since his time, we have seen scarce any production that can justly lay claim to immortality; he carried the language to its highest perfection; and those who have attempted still farther to improve it, instead of ornament, have only caught finery.

(b) Oliver Goldsmith, introductory remarks prefixed to Pope's poems printed in *The Beauties of English Poesy* (1767), *Collected Works of Oliver Goldsmith*, ed. cit., v. 319, 321–3. This volume was published on 6 April 1767.

The Rape of the Lock.

This seems to be Mr. Pope's most finished production, and is, perhaps, the most perfect in our language. It exhibits stronger powers of imagination, more harmony of numbers, and a greater knowledge of the world, than any other of this poet's works: and it is probable, if our country were called upon to shew a specimen of their genius to foreigners, this would be the work here fixed upon.

Eloisa to Abelard.

The harmony of numbers in this poem is very fine. It is rather drawn out to too tedious a length, altho' the passions vary with great judgement. It may be considered as superior to any thing in the epistolary way; and the many translations which have been made of it into the modern languages, are, in some measure, a proof of this.

Ode for Music
on
St. Cecilia's Day.

This ode has by many been thought equal to [Dryden's *Alexander's Feast*]. As it is a repetition of Dryden's manner, it is so far inferior to him. The whole hint of Orpheus, with many of the lines, have been taken from an obscure Ode upon Music, published in Tate's Miscellanies.[1]

Of
The Use of Riches.[2]

This poem, as Mr. Pope tells us himself, cost much attention and labour; and, from the easiness that appears in it, one would be apt to think as much.

[1] [Arthur Friedman identifies this as one Wilson's 'A Pindarique Ode upon Musick', *Poems by Several Hands*, ed. N. Tate (1685), pp. 400–1. The resemblances are not close]
[2] [Under this title Goldsmith prints *Moral Essays* III and IV]

121. Ruffhead replies to Warton

1769

Owen Ruffhead, extracts from *The Life of Alexander Pope, Esq. compiled from Original Manuscripts; with a Critical Essay* (1769).

Ruffhead's work was published between 1 January and May. It was intended to be the authoritative life of Pope, for Warburton, after long delaying his promised biography, had handed over all his materials to Ruffhead, a young lawyer. He died shortly after his book appeared. Since Ruffhead had Warburton's assistance, as well as facts gathered from Spence and from other first-hand accounts of Pope, a better book than finally emerged might have been expected. Ruffhead, a rather obtuse critic, took issue with Joseph Warton's *Essay*. Only a brief section is given here.

[*Pastorals*]

... I shall freely animadvert on the errors and inaccuracies of [Warton], and as candidly admit the justice of his censure, and the propriety of his corrections. In this critique, however, I shall pursue a different method from the author of the Essay: for before he enters into any examination of our poet's writings, he, in his dedication to Dr. Young, and in other places, more than hints his opinion of the nature and extent of our poet's genius. But I propose first to analyze Mr. POPE's writings, and from thence shall attempt to ascertain the nature and force of his genius: for as I should blush to mislead, so I equally scorn to prepossess the reader.

The *pastorals* are the first pieces which fall under the examination of our critic; and with respect to these, he observes in the very opening, 'that it is somewhat strange that in the pastorals of a young poet, there should not be found a single rural image that is new.' As the essayist, in the course of his criticisms, frequently objects a barrenness of invention to Mr. POPE, it is to be wished that he had previously defined what *invention* is, or at least what he intended by the use of that word. As he has omitted it however, an attempt will be made in its proper place, to ascertain the meaning of *invention*, the better to determine how far the want of it may be imputed to Mr. POPE.

At present it is sufficient to observe, that was it true as the critic objects, that there is not a single rural image in these pastorals that is new, it is no more than what our poet himself premises, with that candor and modesty which is ever attendant on genuine merit. For in his excellent discourse prefixed to these pastorals, he concludes with the following declaration. 'But after all, if they have any merit, it is to be attributed to some good old authors, whose works as I had leisure to study, so I hope I have not wanted care to imitate.' Notwithstanding this modest declaration, perhaps some passages may be justly deemed original.

It is observable that a pastoral is appropriated to each season of the year, and that the scene as well as the hour of the day, is artfully distinguished in each, which in some instances gives a peculiar beauty to the imagery; as in the following couplet describing the *summer* season: the scene is by a river side; and the time of the day, *noon*.

> Where dancing sun-beams on the waters play'd,
> And verdant Alders form'd a quiv'ring shade.   [ii. 3–4]

These lines are perfectly picturesque, nor are the following inferior.

> Soft as he mourn'd, the streams forgot to flow,
> The flocks around a dumb compassion show,
> The naiads wept in ev'ry watry bow'r,
> And Jove consented in a silent show'r.   [ii. 5–8]

Though it may be allowed that the new images in these pastorals are not frequent, yet in truth, it is too much to say, that they do not afford a single image that is new. Let any reader of sensibility attend to the following lines in the second pastoral, where the poet describes the charms of his mistress's voice.

> But would you sing and rival Orpheus' strain.
> The wond'ring forest soon should dance again,
> The moving mountains hear the pow'rful call,
> *And headlong streams hang list'ning in their fall.*   [ii. 81–4]

The last line surely presents a *new* image, and a bold one too.[1]

---

[1] Perhaps it will be thought that Mr. POPE had Milton's Masque in remembrance, wherein the latter speaks of Thyrsis,

> —whose artful strains have oft delay'd
> The huddling brook to hear his madrigal.   [*Comus*, l. 495]

The following couplet likewise from the fourth pastoral, describing the effects occasioned by the death of Daphne affords a new image, and the personification has a fine effect.

> The balmy *zephyrs*, silent since her death,
> Lament the ceasing of a sweeter breath.[1]　　[iv. 49–50]

The same may be said of the following beautiful couplet in this pastoral.

> No more the mounting larks, while Daphne sings,
> *Shall list'ning in mid-air suspend their wings.*　　[iv. 53–4]

The image of the birds listening with their wings suspended in mid-air, is striking; and I trust, new.[2]

Our critic having thus set out with denying our poet the merit of invention, he immediately makes a kind of digression in praise of Theocritus; whom he very frequently stiles the father and model of this enchanting kind of composition. Theocritus, he observes, derived many advantages from the climate in which he lived and wrote. 'The poet,' says he, 'described what he saw and felt, and had no need to have recourse to those artificial assemblages of pleasing objects, which are not to be found in nature. The figs and honey which he assigns[3] as a reward to a victorious shepherd, were in themselves exquisite, and are therefore assigned with great propriety.'[4]

---

[1] The four lines which precede these, are incomparably fine; but I know not whether they may not be considered as imitations of those beautiful pastoral images in Eve's speech to Adam; which are thus recapitulated:

> But neither breath of morn, when she ascends
> With charm of earliest birds, &c.　　[iv. 650–1]

[2] The two lines however which immediately follow,

> No more the birds shall imitate her lays,
> Or hush'd with wonder, hearken from the sprays,　　[iv. 655–6]

do but convey the same image, a little diversified.

[3] *Idyllium*, i. 146.

[4] [See pp. 383–4 below]

But this, compared to Mr. POPE's, is rather *narrative* than *descriptive*. Mr. POPE presents us with the *image* of *attention*, which is purely his own.

I cannot avoid taking notice of these beautifully plaintive lines in the same pastoral, which are not imitations of any writer I know of.

> Once I was skill'd in ev'ry plant that grew,
> And ev'ry herb that drinks the morning dew;
> Ah! wretched shepherd, what avails thy art
> To cure thy lambs, but not to heal thy heart.　　[ii. 31–4]

With due deference to our critic, however, these remarks do not appear to be well founded. The figs and honey of Sicily, however exquisite in themselves, were common to the inhabitants: and whoever is acquainted with the nature of the human appetites, will allow that things in general estimation, are not always valued because they are in themselves exquisite, but because they are scarce and rare. If they are common, they in some degree lose their value, and consequently any other reward, though less exquisite in itself, is most likely to become the object of desire. Any other premium than figs and honey, might therefore, in Sicily, have been assigned with greater propriety, and would have displayed more *invention* in the Sicilian bard.

A poet is not confined to his own country for images. He may range throughout the universe, and is not always, as Addison remarks, strictly bound by the laws of nature; much less restrained in his descriptions to the produce of particular climes. He may impregnate every soil with what seed best suits his purpose: he may make the spicy gales of Arabia, diffuse their fragrance over scentless and sterile wilds: he may bring the garden of the Hesperides from its native Africa, and make the golden fruit ripen in the most untoward clime. The following censure, therefore, will probably be thought too nice and captious. 'Complaints,' says he, 'of immoderate heat, and wishes to be conveyed to cooling caverns, when uttered by the inhabitants of Greece, have a decorum and consistency which they totally lose in the character of a British shepherd.'

That such causes of complaint will more frequently occur in the Grecian climate, is unquestionable; but is it necessary to make a complaint of this kind consistent, that every day should be a dog-day? The British shepherd might very consistently describe what he often felt, though not so frequently as the Grecian; and we have days in England, which might make even a Grecian faint.

He admits, however, that Mr. POPE was sensible of the importance of adapting images to the scene of action; which he instances in the translation of the following line:

Audit Eurotas, *jussitque ediscere lauros.*[1]

Here our poet, as the critic candidly observes, has dropped the *laurels* appropriated to Eurotas, as he is speaking of the river Thames; and has rendered it

[1] [Virgil, *Ecl.*, vi. 83: 'Eurotas listened, and bade the laurels learn by heart.']

Thames heard the numbers as he flow'd along,
And bade his *willows* learn the moving song.[1]   [iv. 13–14]

Our critic objects that 'a mixture of British and Grecian ideas, may be justly deemed a blemish in the PASTORALS of POPE: and propriety,' he adds, 'is certain to be violated when he *couples* Pactolus with the Thames,' &c. How far such a violation is to be imputed to our poet, let the lines from the mouth of the shepherd speak for themselves.

O'er golden sands let rich Pactolus flow,
And trees weep amber on the banks of Po;
Blest Thames'*s shores the brightest beauties yield*,[2]
Feed here, my lambs, I'll seek no distant field.   [i. 61–4]

What the critic means by *coupling* Pactolus with Thames, it is not easy to conjecture. They stand evidently *contradistinguished*: and surely the poet might draw a contrast from Greece, without being chargeable with a faulty *mixture* of British and Grecian ideas.

Ever partial to his favourite Sicilian, the critic prefers his imagery to Mr. POPE's in the following instance. 'A shepherd,' says he, 'in Theocritus, wishes with much tenderness and elegance, both which must suffer in a literal translation,—'Would I could become a murmuring bee, fly into your grotto, and be permitted to creep among the leaves of ivy and fern, that compose the chaplet which adorns your head.' POPE, he observes, has thus altered this image:

Oh! were I made by some transforming pow'r
The captive bird that sings within thy bow'r!
Then might my voice thy list'ning ears *employ*,
And I those kisses he receives, enjoy.   [ii. 45–8]

'On three accounts,' he concludes, 'the foregoing image is preferable

---

[1] The author of the Elements of Criticism, objects to this descriptive personification, as destitute of resemblance to any thing real. 'Admitting,' says he, 'that a river gently flowing, may be imagined a sensible being listening to a song; I cannot enter into the conceit of the river's ordering his laurels to learn the song: here all resemblance to any thing real is lost. This, however,' he concludes, 'is copied literally by one of our greatest poets' (Lord Kames, *Elements of Criticism* [7th ed., 1788], ii. 251).

It must indeed be confessed, that this fiction of the imagination, is, in the foregoing instance, used rather licentiously. But the critic is mistaken in saying, that our author has copied the original literally; since, as above observed, he has very judiciously changed the image, though he has given full scope to the fiction.

[2] The third line of this stanza, is very far from being smooth and harmonious. The genitive case hangs upon the tongue, and beside, occasions a very disagreeable hissing.

to the latter. For the pastoral wildness, delicacy, and uncommonness of the thought.'

It is somewhat strange that the critic should applaud the Greek image for the uncommonness of the thought: since it is the perfection of pastoral images to be simple and natural. The beauty of this kind of poetry, arises from a natural ease of thought, and smoothness of verse. Now nothing can be more simple and natural, and at the same time more plaintive and pathetic, than the image of Mr. POPE; nor can any thing be expressed with greater beauty, and harmony of numbers.[1]

A lover who wishes for a metamorphosis, for the sake of approaching more closely to his mistress, would undoubtedly wish to be transformed into something which might be the object of her caresses, and not into that from which she would shrink and retire.[2]

The image in Theocritus is strained and unnatural: that in POPE is natural and fervid.

The pleasure which the shepherd in Theocritus proposes from his transformation, of creeping among the leaves of ivy and fern which compose his mistress's chaplet, is cold and insipid, compared to the animated and glowing wish of POPE's shepherd, who longs to supplant his feathered rival; and dwell upon the enchanting lip of his favourite fair.

Impartial judgment must, nevertheless, in some degree, subscribe to the propriety of our critic's animadversion on the riddle of the Royal oak, in the first pastoral, which is in imitation of the Virgilian enigma; and, as he well observes, savours of pun and puerile conceit.

> Say, Daphnis, say, in what glad soil appears,
> A wond'rous tree that sacred monarchs bears?   [i. 85–6]

'With what propriety, the critic asks, could the tree whose shade protected the King, be said to be prolific of princes?' Here however, there does not seem to be the impropriety which the critic apprehends. For the tree, by preserving the royal line, may, not improperly, be said to be prolific of Princes. After all, if idle riddles be a rural amusement all the world over, there can be no great objection to their being introduced in pastoral scenes: and if reason would not justify the use of them without example, our bard could shelter himself under no authority more unexceptionable than that of Virgil.

---

[1] Perhaps, however, in point of strict propriety, the word *employ*, in the third line, is not happily chosen. To *employ*, is to call forth the exertion of some *active* faculty. But the ear in listening is *passive*: and if the rhyme would have admitted, the verb *engage* should seem most proper.

[2] [Ruffhead echoes Johnson, pp. 408–9 above]

Among these pastorals, the most conspicuous is the Messiah, a
sacred eclogue, in imitation of Virgil's Pollio.[1] This, the critic allows to
be superior to the Pollio: and indeed, if Mr. POPE had given no other
instance of the sublime, this alone would prove the sublimity of his
genius.[2] How solemn and awful is the following invocation!

> ——O Thou my voice inspire
> Who touch'd Isaiah's hallow'd lips with fire!   [ll. 5–6]

In what a bold exalted strain, does the poet break forth,

> Hark! a glad voice the lonely desart cheers;
> Prepare the way! a God, a God appears:
> A God, a God! the vocal hills reply,
> The rocks proclaim th' approaching Deity.
> Lo, earth receives him from the bending skies!
> Sink down, ye mountains, and, ye vallies, rise;
> With heads declin'd, ye cedars, homage pay:
> Be smooth, ye rocks; ye rapid floods, give way!
> The Saviour comes! by antient bards foretold:
> Hear him, ye deaf, and, all ye blind, behold.   [ll. 29–38]

Upon the whole, it is not too much to say of these pastorals, that
though they are *professedly* imitations of the antients; yet there are few
passages, which our poet has borrowed, without improving them; as
the reader may judge by comparing the imitations with the originals,
which are collected by the learned editor of his works [i.e. Warburton].

[pp. 30–41]

---

[1] It is but just to observe, that our critic has corrected a grammatical error in the *Messiah*,
where our poet should have said, The swain—

> *Shall* START amidst the thirsty wild to hear
> New falls of water murmuring in his ear.   [ll. 69–70]

[2] Sir Richard Steele, in one of his letters to our author, speaking of his eclogue, says,—
'I have turned to every verse and chapter, and think you have preserved the sublime
heavenly spirit throughout the whole.' [See No. 15]

122. Johnson reviews Ruffhead

1769

Dr Samuel Johnson, extract from review, *Gentleman's Magazine*,
xxxix (1769), 259–60.

For Johnson's authorship, see *Boswell's Life of Johnson*, ed. G. B.
Hill and L. F. Powell (1934–50), ii. 166n. Most of Johnson's review
is taken up with comments on the biographical side of Ruffhead's
book. In conclusion he turns to Ruffhead's attempted rebuttal of
Warton.

As to the genius of Pope, Mr Ruffhead, in order to place it in the first
class, has found himself obliged to lay down the following principle.

'The true distinguishing characteristic of poetry seems rather to
consist in the stile than in the matter; the essence of true poetry is
harmony.'

This principle being allowed, it will follow that he who writes the
best verses is the greatest poet; Pope incontestably wrote the best
English verses, therefore Pope is the greatest English poet.

The principle, however, may well be controverted, and if Mr Pope
cannot be proved to be a poet in matter as well as form, he must quit
the class in which this writer has placed him.

Pope, however, is perhaps pathetic and sublime, setting his numbers
aside, in as high degree as any poet, ancient or modern, will appear to be,
if their numbers are set aside; let the Messiah, the Epistle of Eloisa, the
Elegy to the Memory of an unfortunate Lady, and many other passages,
be set against the best that can be selected from other authors, and
perhaps they will lose nothing in the comparison. It may, indeed, be
said, that Pope has displayed his power to excel in the sublime and
pathetic, only occasionally; but, it might as well be objected to Milo's
strength, that he carried an ox but once, as to Pope's excellence in the
pathetic and sublime, that he did not always display it.

Mr Pope's invention in the Rape of the Lock, is allowed by all; he had therefore invention, which he might have exerted more frequently, if he had thought proper to chuse subjects that would have made it necessary or proper. It has been objected to Pope, that he did not invent the machinery of that Poem,[1] but it might as well be objected to Homer, that he did not invent the machinery of the Iliad: Homer found his machinery in the popular religion of his time, at least, the persons, in a state much fitter for his use, than Pope found his Sylphs and Gnomes, in the opinions of the Rosecrusians: the invention of both writers, appears in the use they have made of the imaginary beings, and Pope's invention thus tried, will, perhaps, appear to lose nothing in the comparison with Homer's, if they are both brought to this test.

Something of this Mr Ruffhead has suggested, and so far he has supported Pope's character.

123. Thomas Warton on *The Temple of Fame*

1774

Thomas Warton, *A History of English Poetry*, i. (1774), 396. Thomas Warton the younger (1728–90), was the brother of Joseph, and like him a minor poet. A scholar, and Professor of Poetry at Oxford, he was also an important early literary historian.

Pope has imitated this piece, with his usual elegance of diction and harmony of versification. But in the mean time, he has not only misrepresented the story, but marred the character of the poem. He has endeavoured to correct it's extravagancies, by new refinements and additions of another cast: but he did not consider, that extravagancies are essential to a poem of such a structure, and even constitute it's

[1] [By Warton, see p. 399 above. Johnson's defence of Pope's invention is based on Arthur Murphy's reply to Warton (No. 118)]

beauties. An attempt to unite order and exactness of imagery with a subject formed on principles so professedly romantic and anomalous, is like giving Corinthian pillars to a Gothic palace. When I read Pope's elegant imitation of this piece, I think I am walking among the modern monuments unsuitably placed in Westminster-abbey.

124. Sound and sense in Pope again

1776

George Campbell, extract from *The Philosophy of Rhetoric* (1776), ii. 237–41.

Campbell (1719–96), Scottish theologian and professor of divinity at Marischal College, is remembered chiefly for his reply to Hume in his *Dissertation on Miracles* (1763).

In a section entitled 'Words considered as sounds' (III. i. 3), Campbell turns to Pope to illustrate how 'Time and motion . . . is capable in some degree of being imitated by speech'.

BUT, in my opinion, Greek and Latin have here an advantage, at least in their heroic measure, over all modern tongues. Accordingly Homer and Virgil furnish us with some excellent specimens in this way. But that we may know what our own tongue and metre is capable of effecting, let us recur to our own poets, and first of all to the celebrated translator of the Grecian bard. I have made choice of him rather as he was perfectly sensible of this beauty in the original, which he copied, and endeavoured, as much as the materials he had to work upon would permit him, to exhibit it in his version. Let us take for an example the punishment of Sisyphus in the other world, a passage which had on this very account been much admired in Homer by all the critics both ancient and modern.

Up the high hill he heaves a huge round stone;
The huge round stone resulting with a bound,
Thunders impetuous down, and smoaks along the ground.[1]

[*Odyssey*, xi. 736–8: Broome]

It is remarkable that Homer (though greatly preferable to his translator in both) hath succeeded best in describing the fall of the stone, Pope, in relating how it was heaved up the hill. The success of the English poet here is not to be ascribed entirely to the length of the syllables, but partly to another cause, to be explained afterwards.

I OWN I do not approve the expedient which this admirable versifier hath used, of introducing an Alexandrine line for expressing rapidity. I entirely agree with Johnson,[2] that this kind of measure is rather stately than swift; yet our poet hath assigned this last quality as the reason of his choice. 'I was too sensible,' says he in the margin, 'of the beauty of this, not to endeavour to imitate it, though unsuccessfully. I have therefore thrown it into the swiftness of an Alexandrine, to make it of a more proportionable number of syllables with the Greek.' Ay, but to resemble in length is one thing, and to resemble in swiftness is another. The difference lies here: In Greek, an hexameter verse whereof all the feet save one are dactyls, though it hath several syllables more, is pronounced in the same time with an hexameter verse whereof all the feet

---

[1] In Greek thus,

―― λᾶαν ἄνω ὤθεσκε ποτὶ λόφον ――
αὖτις ἔπειτα πέδονδ' ἐκυλίνδετο λᾶας ἀναιδής.

In Latin verse, Vida, in his Art of Poetry, hath well exemplified this beauty, from his great master Virgil.

Ille autem membris, ac mole ignavius ingens
Incedit tardo molimine subsidendo.

[iii. 375–6: 'That, vast of size, his limbs huge, broad and strong, / Moves pond'rous, and scarce drags his bulk along', *Vida's Art of Poetry*, tr. Christopher Pitt (1725), p. 104] Here not only the frequency of the spondees, but the difficulty of forming the elisions; above all, the spondee in the fifth foot of the second line instead of a dactyl greatly retard the motion. For the contrary expression of speed,

Si se forte cava extulerit mala vipera terra,
Tolle moras, cape saxa manu, cape robora, pastor,
Ferte citi flammas, date tela, repellite pestem.

[iii. 421–3: 'And when the viper issues from the brake; / Be quick; with stones, and brands, and fire, attack / His rising crest, and drive the serpent back', *ibid.*, p. 107]
Here every thing concurs to accelerate the motion, the number of dactyls, no elision, no diphthong, no concurrence of consonants, unless where a long syllable is necessary, and even there the consonants of easy pronunciation.
[2] *Rambler*, no. 92 [see No. 99].

467

save one are spondees, and is therefore a just emblem of velocity; that is, of moving a great way in a short time. Whereas the Alexandrine line, as it consists of more syllables than the common English heroic, requires proportionably more time to the pronunciation. For this reason the same author, in another work, has, I think, with better success, made choice of this very measure, to exhibit slowness;

> A needless Alexandrine ends the song,
> That, like a wounded snake, drags its slow length along.
> [*An Essay on Criticism*, ll. 356–7]

It deserves our notice, that in this couplet he seems to give it as his opinion of the Alexandrine, that it is a dull and tardy measure. Yet, as if there were no end of his inconsistency on this subject, he introduceth a line of the same kind a little after in the same piece, to represent uncommon speed:

> Not so when swift Camilla scours the plain,
> Flies o'er th' unbending corn, and skims along the main.
> [*An Essay on Criticism*, ll. 372–3]

A most wonderful and peculiar felicity in this measure to be alike adapted to imitate the opposite qualities of swiftness and slowness. Such contradictions would almost tempt one to suspect, that this species of resemblance is imaginary altogether. Indeed, the fitness of the Alexandrine to express, in a certain degree, the last of these qualities, may be allowed, and is easily accounted for. But no one would ever have dreamt of its fitness for the first, who had not been misled by an erroneous conclusion from the effect of a very different measure, Greek and Latin hexameter. Yet Pope is not the only one of our poets who hath fallen into this error. Dryden had preceded him in it, and even gone much farther. Not satisfied with the Alexandrine, he hath chosen a line of fourteen syllables, for expressing uncommon celerity:

> Which urg'd, and labour'd, and forc'd up with pain,
> Recoils, and rowls impetuous down, and smoaks along the plain.[1]

Pope seems to have thought that in this instance, though the principle on which Dryden proceeded was good, he had exceeded all reasonable bounds in applying it; for it is this very line which he hath curtailed into an Alexandrine in the passage from the Odyssey already quoted. Indeed the impropriety here is not solely in the measure, but also in the diph-

[1] Translation, Lucretius, Book iii [ll. 210–11].

thongs *oi*, and *ow*, and *oa*, so frequently recurring, than which nothing, not even a collision of jarring consonants, is less fitted to express speed. The only word in the line that seems adapted to the poet's view, is the term *impetuous*, in which two short syllables being crowded into the time of one, have an effect similar to that produced by the dactyl in Greek and Latin.

125. Stockdale replies to Warton

1778

Percival Stockdale (1736–1811), extracts from *An Inquiry into the Nature, and Genuine Laws of Poetry; Including a particular Defence of the Writings, and Genius of Mr. Pope* (1778).

Stockdale's prefatory letter is dated 10 October 1777. *An Inquiry* is a belated reply to Warton's first volume, and is, as the Rev. John Walker remarked in 1835–6, 'A very unequal work' (Bodleian, 270. g. 472). Included here, for its curiosity, is Stockdale' closing invocation to Pope's ghost.

One would have thought that [Pope's] fame would have been permanent, and sacred; for he acquired it not by metaphysical subtleties, nor by deducing certain consequences from uncertain principles; but by addressing the common sense, the common perceptions, the common feelings; the strong, and the noble sentiments of mankind. Dr. Warton entitles his Book, 'An Essay on the Genius and Writings of Pope:'—a preposterous title which corresponds with the absurdity of the whole performance. For the genius of an Authour is discovered by his writings; the character of his writings is not inferred from his genius. Among his other scholastick dreams, he asserts, that to estimate the merit of any poet, we must divest his thoughts of measure, and rhyme, and read and weigh them in a prosaïc order; an assertion that shows how little He is acquainted with Poetry, either in judgement, or sentiment. True, and complete poetical excellence results, not only from extensive knowledge, and from a sentimental, vigorous, and ardent mind; but likewise from a delicate sagacity, and accuracy; or, in other words, from taste, and elegance. Dr Warton ought to have considered, that Poetry is *one*, and, by a long interval, *the first* of the fine arts; and therefore, that the fire of the poet, if he would reach his aim, if he would strike irresistably, and with all his force, must be modelled, and directed by deliberation, and choice. Hence, while He is heated with the warmth of inspiration, he is attentive to propriety, to order, and embellishment; not only to the most pertinent selection of words, but likewise to their position; to the strength, and harmony which are produced by their judicious, and fortunate arrangement. For these are indisputable and powerful constituents of Poetry. A particle may be so placed in a verse, that the sense of the Authour may be clear, and the idiom of our language may not be violated; yet even that particle, by a happy transposition, might acquire life, and energy, and give more animation, and lustre to the line. In the productions of the fine arts, nothing is indifferent; the minutest parts have their great importance and influence; they reflect proportion, and expression on the other parts, from which *they* likewise draw those advantages; and all the parts, as they are disposed, and compacted by the artist, form a striking whole. [pp. 4–8]

You ask what there is transcendently pathetick and sublime in Pope?[1] One would think the man had lost his senses. Many passages interspersed throughout his works; his filial Apostrophes to the age, and infirmities of an affectionate mother; his Elegy to the Memory of an unfortunate Lady; his Prologue to Cato; his Eloïsa to Abelard, are all transcendently pathetick. I believe it will be allowed that if any subject is, in it's nature, a ground-work for the pathetick, it is love: and I imagine it will be likewise granted that the Epistle from Eloïsa to Abelard, is the warmest, the most affecting, and admirable amorous Poem in the world. Now, pray, Sir, must not the soul of that writer have been peculiarly formed for the pathetick, who could inspire with all the force, and varieties of the passion, with it's ardour, and ecstacies; with it's anxieties, distresses, and excruciating torments, every verse of a poem which consists of almost four hundred lines? and after you had been conversant with that poem; after you had examined it's composi-

---

[1] [Warton, of course, had singled out for praise the same poems Stockdale goes on to cite]

tion; (shall I not pay you a compliment which you do not deserve, if I add) after you had felt it's fire?—and after you had quoted some of it's very striking parts; how could you have the absurdity, or the assurance to ask, what there is transcendently pathetick in Pope?

It may be objected by you, as it has been objected by other cavillers, that Mr. Pope, in this poem, is much indebted to Eloïsa's Letters, for sentiment, for description, and energy. I deny the charge. By far the greater part of his Epistle to Abelard; it's finest, and it's noblest passages, are totally the productions of his own genius. She gives Him, indeed, a few good hints; and as they are applied, enlarged, and embellished by the poet, they deserve not a stronger, and more extensive name. The stem of his generous, and luxurious thought, is, in two or three places, transplanted from the garden of Eloïsa: but on that stem Pope has ingrafted all it's beauty, and glory; it's diffusive, and romantick branches; the bright verdure of it's foliage; the orient hues, and aroma-tick fragrance of it's blossoms. His apposite use of a short combination of ideas which another Authour had formed; the augmentation, and lustre with which it was heightened, and adorned by Him, and the nervous, and genial strains that flowed entirely from his own source, prove that He never adopted any sentiment from a poverty of imagina-tion.   [pp. 69–73]

Dr. Warton asks, in the tenth page of his Dedication, *what there is transcendently sublime in Pope?*—An illiterate, and impertinent cox-comb; a French Abbé, ironically asked a gentleman, whom He heard profuse of encomium on a country which has been admired, and praised by a Montesquieu, and a Helvetius, *what there was remarkably great in England?* But I shall give a direct answer to the Doctor's question.

Pope's Universal Prayer is transcendently sublime. His Prologue to the Tragedy of Cato is transcendently sublime. So are many parts of his Essay on Man. In his Address to Lord Bolingbroke, at the conclusion of that excellent Poem, He displays, as Dr. Warburton justly observes, all the characteristicks, and ornaments which Longinus gives to the sub-lime, in a spirit, in a symmetry, and in a language, perhaps unequalled by man. Sir, a summer's day would elapse before we could read all that is transcendently sublime in Pope.

He was endowed with so feeling, so elegant, and ardent a soul; He was so eminently, so peculiarly qualified by nature to animate, and adorn any object which He intended to exhibit with all the graces, that if He had only favoured the world with his Translation of the Iliad, it would have ranked Him with our great, and celebrated poets. If we except the simplicity of the Greek bard; if we except the natural harmony, and energy of the Greek language; every reader who is truly learned; every manly scholar, whose mind is free from prejudice, and fraught with sentiment, must allow, that Pope, in general,[1] excells his original, in propriety, in beauty, and in fire. He *persued the path of the Mæonian Eagle*, with a vigorous wing, and with an undazzled eye. Emboldened by the flight of his daring *Master*, and emulous of his glory, He rose to heights, in the Æther of Parnassus, unexplored even by *Him*. In short, HE IMPROVED ON HOMER.

There perhaps never was a poet who softened, and mellowed such delicacy, and refinement, such dignity, and strength, with so liberal, and polite an ease as Pope. But such Poetry will not be admired by criticks of a vitiated, and insatiable taste. In a most happy selection of those ideas, and images which give a lively, and forcible pleasure to human nature; in their new, and beautiful connexion; in the spontaneous, but strong language of the heart, and passions, in which those ideas, and images are conveyed, *They* see nothing great; nothing above mediocrity. Their Gothick souls are only stimulated with the *transcendently* sublime; or, in other words, with the unnatural, the gigantick, and the incoherent. Are you ambitious of eulogium from such readers? If you can only astonish Them, They will immediately pronounce you sublime. In sentiment, give them all the extravagance, and madness of ill-imagined passion. In painting, let all your figures be grotesque; let all your colouring be Chinese. Give Them a huddle, and a crash of objects; the gardens of Sir William Chambers;—the very Advertisements of a Langford;[2]—the very Poetry of the Wartons.   [pp. 124–9]

An INVOCATION *to the* SHADE *of* POPE

As there have been more improbable Doctrines concerning the invisible world, than to suppose that Thou, O amiable, illustrious, and beautiful Shade, art not sometimes a witness to the language of a solitary, but active and sentimental mind;—that Thou sometimes whisperest virtue, and happiness to mortals;—deign to view this effort of my zeal for thy poetick fame (to which Thou are perhaps indifferent in thy present state) with a propitious eye. And if, with thy intuitive

---

[1] [A long footnote on praise and Homer is omitted here]

[2] [Sir William Chambers (1726–96), architect, supporter of the 'Chinese' style in gardening. Batty Langley (1696–1751) attempted to create a style based on medieval Gothic architecture]

penetration, Thou seest my want of power to do Thee justice, accept the gratitude, and ardour of my will.

Let me thank Thee for the consolation, for the pleasure, with which thy Muse hath alleviated, and brightened, my fluctuating, and adverse life. In my hours of poetical solitude (if, indeed, it is not pusillanimous to say that I was in solitude, while I conversed with *thy* moral, and mellifluous numbers) Thou hast made me impassive to the gloom of external objects; Thou hast made me independent of the gay companions of prosperity, and of the favour of the Great. While I caught strong inspiration from *Thee*, I have triumphed in my nature: I have felt, beyond a possibility of doubt, that I was superiour to accident, and to matter; that I was born to exist, and to be happy, in a better world.

May the benevolent, the platonick Virtue, who in *thy* strains, is so eloquent, and attractive, win me to the constant love of *Her*, and teach me to moderate my inferiour passions. Those obliquities, which, neither by my own endeavours, nor by thy influence, I shall be able to rectify, will be viewed, by Beings who are raised above all earthly ignorance, and envy, with an eye of generous compassion: and I hope they will be pardoned by OUR COMMON FATHER. May I never relinquish any good quality with which I am endowed! May I conquer the evils which yet await me;—may I retain my contempt of wealth, and grandeur, by the force, and splendour of poetical creation. For the colours of *thy* Muse are more glorious than oriental lustre; and as I know that I am above *low ambition, and the pride of Kings*, I would rather wish to possess *thy* abilities, than the power of a monarch.

When the last hour of my existence in *this* world approaches, may my parting soul be cheered with the celestial forms that charmed thy enraptured eye, and breathed serenity, and fragrance on thy evening-walks, along the banks of thy Thames, or in the groves of thy Windsor! May They bid langour smile, and smoothe the bed of death! For they have been my powerful auxiliaries, when I was assailed by objects more terrible than the grave. May they embolden me to anticipate life eternal; to maintain a strong, yet a humble hope, that I shall obtain that mercy, and happiness, which were denied me in *this* unequal state, from the FIRST GOOD, FIRST PERFECT, AND FIRST FAIR!   [pp. 181–7]

126. William Cowper on Pope

1780–1, 1782

(a) William Cowper, extract from *Table-Talk*, ll. 646–55, written in the winter of 1780 to 1781, *Poetical Works of William Cowper*, ed. J. Bruce, Aldine ed. (1870), i. 30–1.

> . . . POPE, as harmony itself exact,
> In verse well disciplined, complete, compact,
> Gave Virtue and Morality a grace,
> That, quite eclipsing Pleasure's painted face,
> Levied a tax of wonder and applause,
> E'en on the fools that trampled on their laws.
> But he (his musical finesse was such,
> So nice his ear, so delicate his touch)
> Made poetry a mere mechanic art,
> And every warbler has his tune by heart.

(b) *Ibid.*, extract from letter to Rev. William Unwin, 5 January 1782, *The Works of William Cowper*, ed. R. Southey (1836), iv. 168–9.

In the last Review, I mean in the last but one, I saw Johnson's critique upon Prior and Pope.[1] I am bound to acquiesce in his opinion of the latter, because it has always been my own. I could never agree with those who preferred him to Dryden; nor with others, (I have known such, and persons of taste and discernment too,) who could not allow him to be a poet at all. He was certainly a mechanical maker of verses, and in every line he ever wrote, we see indubitable marks of the most indefatigable industry and labour. Writers who find it necessary to make such strenuous and painful exertions, are generally as phlegmatic as they are correct; but Pope was, in this respect, exempted from the common lot of authors of that class. With the unwearied application of a plodding Flemish painter, who draws a shrimp with the most minute exactness, he had all the genius of one of the first masters. Never, I believe, were

[1] [I.e., *Monthly Review*, lxv. (November 1781), 335–62]

such talents and such drudgery united. But I admire Dryden most, who has succeeded by mere dint of genius, and in spite of a laziness and carelessness almost peculiar to himself. His faults are numberless, but so are his beauties. His faults are those of a great man, and his beauties are such, (at least sometimes,) as Pope, with all his touching and re-touching, could never equal. So far, therefore, I have no quarrel with Johnson.

127. Johnson on Pope

1781

Dr Samuel Johnson, extracts from the 'Life of Pope', *Lives of the most Eminent English Poets* (2nd ed., 1783), vol. iv. Johnson's account first appeared on 18 May 1781. The text given here is that of the second edition (1783), with a few variants from the first edition (1781) recorded at the foot of the page. On the *Life*, see Introduction, pp. 28–30.

[General]

He tells of himself, in his poems, that *he lisp'd in numbers*;[1] and used to say that he could not remember the time when he began to make verses. In the style of fiction it might have been said of him as of Pindar, that when he lay in his cradle, *the bees swarmed about his mouth*.

[p. 4]

He sometimes imitated the English poets, and professed to have written at fourteen his poem upon *Silence*, after Rochester's *Nothing*. He had now formed his versification, and in the smoothness of his numbers surpassed his original; but this is small part of his praise; he discovers such acquaintance with human life and public affairs, as is not easily conceived to have been attainable by a boy of fourteen in *Windsor Forest*.

[pp. 8–9]

[1] [*Epistle to Dr. Arbuthnot*, l. 128]

[*An Essay on Criticism*]

The same year [1709] [1] was written the *Essay on Criticism*; a work which displays such extent of comprehension, such nicety of distinction, such acquaintance with mankind, and such knowledge both of ancient and modern learning, as are not often attained by the maturest age and longest experience.

[Johnson goes on to describe Dennis's attack (No. 10). In the course of this he picks out Dennis's valid points]

. . . but [Dennis's] desire to do mischief is greater than his power. He has, however, justly criticized some passages, in these lines,

> There are whom heaven has bless'd with store of wit,
> Yet want as much again to manage it;
> For wit and judgement ever are at strife— [2]

it is apparent that *wit* has two meanings, and that what is wanted, though called *wit*, is truly judgment. So far Dennis is undoubtedly right; but, not content with argument, he will have a little mirth, and triumphs over the first couplet in terms too elegant to be forgotten. 'By the way, what rare numbers are here! Would not one swear that this youngster had espoused some antiquated Muse, who had sued out a divorce on account of impotence from some superannuated sinner [i.e. Wycherley]; and, having been p—xed by her former spouse, has got the gout in her decrepit age, which makes her hobble so damnably.' [3] This was the man who would reform a nation sinking into barbarity.

In another place Pope himself allowed that Dennis had detected one of those blunders which are called *bulls*. [4] The first edition had this line:

> What is this wit—
> Where wanted, scorn'd; and envied where acquir'd? [5]

---

[1] [Johnson's surety of the date of composition is not supported by the evidence; see Twickenham, i. 198–9]

[2] [*An Essay on Criticism*, ll. 80–3. Johnson gives the original text of 1711. In 1744 Pope altered the passage to, 'Some, to whom Heav'n in Wit has been profuse, / Want as much more to turn it to its use, / For *Wit* and *Judgment* often are at strife.' The changes do not entirely meet Dennis's point]

[3] [*Critical Works*, i. 404]

[4] ['Expression containing contradiction in terms.']

[5] [*An Essay on Criticism*, ll. 500–3. Pope revised the passage twice to meet the criticism; see Twickenham, i. 295. The final version reads, 'And still the more we *give*, the more *required*.']

'How,' says the critic, 'can wit be *scorn'd* where it is not? Is not this a figure frequently employed in Hibernian land? The person that wants this wit may indeed be scorned, but the scorn shews the honour which the contemner has for wit.'[1] Of this remark Pope made the proper use, by correcting the passage.

I have preserved, I think, all that is reasonable in Dennis's criticism. . . .

[pp. 14–18]

[*The Rape of the Lock*]

Not long after, he wrote the *Rape of the Lock*, the most airy, the most ingenious, and the most delightful of all his compositions, occasioned by a frolick of gallantry, rather too familiar, in which Lord Petre cut off a lock of Mrs. Arabella Fermor's hair. . . .

At its first appearance it was termed by Addison *merum sal* [pure wit]. Pope, however, saw that it was capable of improvement; and, having luckily contrived to borrow his machinery from the *Rosicrucians*, imparted the scheme with which his head was teeming to Addison, who told him that his work, as it stood, was *a delicious little thing*, and gave him no encouragement to retouch it. . . .

Addison's counsel was happily rejected. Pope foresaw the future efflorescence of imagery then budding in his mind, and resolved to spare no art, or industry of cultivation. The soft luxuriance of his fancy was already shooting, and all the gay varieties of diction were ready at his hand to colour and embellish it.

His attempt was justified by its success. The *Rape of the Lock* stands forward, in the classes of literature, as the most exquisite example of ludicrous poetry. Berkeley congratulated him upon the display of powers more truly poetical than he had shewn before;[2] with elegance of description and justness of precepts, he had now exhibited boundless fertility of invention.

He always considered the intermixture[3] of the machinery with the action as his most successful exertion of poetical art. He indeed could never afterwards produce any thing of such unexampled excellence. Those performances, which strike with wonder, are combinations of skilful genius with happy casualty; and it is not likely that any felicity, like the discovery of a new race of preternatural agents, should happen twice to the same man.

[1] [See below, p. 75]
[2] [See No. 18b]
[3] *intermixture*] 1783; *intertexture* 1781.

Of this poem the author was, I think, allowed to enjoy the praise for a long time without disturbance. Many years afterwards Dennis published some remarks[1] upon it, with very little force, and with no effect; for the opinion of the publick was already settled, and it was no longer at the mercy of criticism. [pp. 24–7]

[*Eloisa to Abelard*]

Of the Epistle from *Eloisa to Abelard*, I do not know the date. His first inclination to attempt a composition of that tender kind arose, as Mr. Savage told me, from his perusal of Prior's *Nut-brown Maid*. How much he has surpassed Prior's work it is not necessary to mention, when perhaps it may be said with justice, that he has excelled every composition of the same kind. The mixture of religious hope and resignation gives an elevation and dignity to disappointed love, which images merely natural cannot bestow. The gloom of a convent strikes the imagination with far greater force than the solitude of a grove.

[pp. 28–9]

[*Iliad*]

It [the translation of the *Iliad*] is certainly the noblest version of poetry which the world has ever seen; and its publication must therefore be considered as one of the great events in the annals of Learning.

[p. 45]

[*The Dunciad*]

The prevalence of this poem was gradual and slow: the plan, if not wholly new, was little understood by common readers. Many of the allusions required illustration; the names were often expressed only by the initial and final letters, and, if they had been printed at length, were such as few had known or recollected. The subject itself had nothing generally interesting; for whom did it concern to know that one or another scribbler was a dunce? If therefore it had been possible for those who were attacked to conceal their pain and their resentment, the *Dunciad* might have made its way very slowly in the world.

This, however, was not to be expected: every man is of importance to himself, and therefore, in his own opinion, to others; and, supposing the world already acquainted with all his pleasures and his pains, is perhaps the first to publish injuries or misfortunes which had never been

[1] [See No. 20]

known unless related by himself, and at which those that hear them will only laugh; for no man sympathises with the sorrows of vanity.

[p. 80]

[*An Essay on Man*]

. . . in 1733 was published the first part of the *Essay on Man*. There had been for some time a report that Pope was busy upon a System of Morality; but this design was not discovered in the new poem, which had a form and a title with which its readers were unacquainted. Its reception was not uniform; some thought it a very imperfect piece, though not without good lines. While the author was unknown, some, as will always happen, favoured him as an adventurer, and some censured him as an intruder; but all thought him above neglect;[1] the sale increased, and editions were multiplied.

The subsequent editions of the first Epistle exhibited two memorable corrections.[2] At first, the poet and his friend

> Expatiate freely o'er this scene of man,
> A mighty maze *of walks without a plan.*

For which he wrote afterwards

> A mighty maze, *but not without a plan*:

for, if there were no plan, it was in vain to describe or to trace the maze.

The other alteration was of these lines;

> And spite of pride, *and in thy reason's spite,*
> One truth is clear, whatever is, is right:

but having afterwards discovered, or been shewn, that the *truth* which subsisted *in spite of reason* could not be very *clear*, he substituted

> And spite of pride, *in erring reason's spite.*

To such oversights will the most vigorous mind be liable, when it is employed at once upon argument and poetry.

The second and third Epistles were published; and Pope was, I believe, more and more suspected of writing them; at last, in 1734, he avowed the fourth, and claimed the honour of a moral poet.

In the conclusion it is sufficiently acknowledged that the doctrine of the *Essay on Man* was received from Bolingbroke, who is said to have

---

[1] [See Nos 79–81]

[2] [*An Essay on Man*, i. 4–5, 293–4. The alterations were introduced in the second edition]

ridiculed Pope, among those who enjoyed his confidence, as having adopted and advanced principles of which he did not perceive the consequence, and as blindly propagating opinions contrary to his own. That those communications had been consolidated into a scheme regularly drawn, and delivered to Pope, from whom it returned only transformed from prose to verse, has been reported, but hardly can be true. The *Essay* plainly appears the fabrick of a poet: what Bolingbroke supplied could be only the first principles; the order, illustration, and embellishments must all be Pope's.[1]

These principles it is not my business to clear from obscurity, dogmatism, or falsehood; but they were not immediately examined; philosophy and poetry have not often the same readers; and the *Essay* abounded in splendid amplifications and sparkling sentences, which were read and admired with no great attention to their ultimate purpose; its flowers caught the eye, which did not see what the gay foliage concealed, and for a time flourished in the sunshine of universal approbation. So little was any evil tendency discovered, that, as innocence is unsuspicious, many read it for a manual of piety.

Its reputation soon invited a translator. It was first turned into French prose, and afterwards by Resnel into verse. Both translations fell into the hands of Crousaz, who first, when he had the version in prose, wrote a general censure, and afterwards reprinted Resnel's version with particular remarks upon every paragraph.[2]

Crousaz was a professor of Switzerland, eminent for his treatise of Logick and his *Examen de Pyrrhonisme*, and, however little known or regarded here,[3] was no mean antagonist. His mind was one of those in which philosophy and piety are happily united. He was accustomed to argument and disquisition, and perhaps was grown too desirous of detecting faults; but his intentions were always right, his opinions were solid, and his religion pure.

His incessant vigilance for the promotion of piety disposed him to look with distrust upon all metaphysical systems of Theology, and all schemes of virtue and happiness purely rational; and therefore it was not long before he was persuaded that the positions of Pope, as they terminated for the most part in natural religion, were intended to draw mankind away from revelation, and to represent the whole course of

[1] [Bolingbroke's influence of the *Essay on Man* is a vexed question. See Introduction, p. 21.]

[2] [For the introduction to Du Resnel's translation, see No. 82. Johnson translated (and annotated) Crousaz's *Commentaire*. Part of Crousaz's *Examen* is given as No. 83]

[3] *here*] 1783; *om.* 1781.

things as a necessary concatenation of indissoluble fatality; and it is undeniable that in many passages a religious eye may easily discover expressions not very favourable to morals, or to liberty.

About this time Warburton began to make his appearance in the first ranks of learning. He was a man of vigorous faculties, a mind fervid and vehement, supplied by incessant and unlimited enquiry, with wonderful extent and variety of knowledge, which yet had not oppressed his imagination, nor clouded his perspicacity. To every work he brought a memory full fraught, together with a fancy fertile of original combinations, and at once exerted the powers of the scholar, the reasoner, and the wit. But his knowledge was too multifarious to be always exact, and his pursuits were too eager to be always cautious. His abilities gave him an haughty confidence, which he disdained to conceal or mollify; and his impatience of opposition disposed him to treat his adversaries with such contemptuous superiority as made his readers commonly his enemies, and excited against the advocate[1] the wishes of some who favoured the cause. He seems to have adopted the Roman Emperor's determination, *oderint dum metuant*;[2] he used no allurements of gentle language, but wished to compel rather than persuade.

His style is copious without selection, and forcible without neatness; he took the words that presented themselves: his diction is coarse and impure, and his sentences are unmeasured.

He had, in the early part of his life, pleased himself with the notice of inferior wits, and corresponded with the enemies of Pope. A Letter was produced, when he had perhaps himself forgotten it, in which he tells *Concanen*, 'Dryden *I observe borrows for want of leasure, and* Pope *for want of genius*: Milton *out of pride, and* Addison *out of modesty*.'[3] And when Theobald published *Shakespeare*, in opposition to Pope, the best notes were supplied by Warburton.

But the time was now come when Warburton was to change his opinion, and Pope was to find a defender in him who had contributed so much to the exaltation of his rival.

The arrogance of Warburton excited against him every artifice of offence, and therefore it may be supposed that his union with Pope was

---

[1] *advocate*] 1783; *him* 1781.

[2] [Suetonius, *Caligula*, xxx: 'let them hate me, so that they but fear me'. Caligula uttered these words, taken from Accius, when a man other than the one he intended had been executed]

[3] [Printed in J. Nichols, *Illustrations of Literary History* (1817–58), ii. 195–6. *1781* paraphrases from memory, 'that *Milton* borrowed by affectation, *Dryden* by idleness, and *Pope* by necessity.']

censured as hypocritical inconstancy; but surely to think differently, at different times, of poetical merit, may be easily allowed. Such opinions are often admitted, and dismissed, without nice examination. Who is there that has not found reason for changing his mind about questions of greater importance?

Warburton, whatever was his motive, undertook without solicitation, to rescue Pope from the talons of Crousaz, by freeing him from the imputation of favouring fatality, or rejecting revelation; and from month to month continued a vindication of the *Essay on Man*, in the literary journal of that time called *The Republick of Letters*.[1]

Pope, who probably began to doubt the tendency of his own work, was glad that the positions, of which he perceived himself not to know the full meaning, could by any mode of interpretation be made to mean well. How much he was pleased with his gratuitous defender, the following Letter evidently shews:[2]

SIR,   March 24, 1743.

I have just received from Mr. R.[3] two more of your Letters. It is in the greatest hurry imaginable that I write this; but I cannot help thanking you in particular for your third Letter, which is so extremely clear, short, and full, that I think Mr. Crousaz ought never to have another answer, and deserved not so good an one. I can only say, you do him too much honour, and me too much right, so odd as the expression seems; for you have made my system as clear as I ought to have done, and could not. It is indeed the same system as mine, but illustrated with a ray of your own, as they say our natural body is the same still when it is glorified. I am sure I like it better than I did before, and so will every man else. I know I meant just what you explain; but I did not explain my own meaning so well as you. You understand me as well as I do myself; but you express me better than I could express myself. Pray accept the sincerest acknowledgements. I cannot but wish these Letters were put together in one Book,[4] and intend (with your leave) to procure a translation of part, at least, of all of them into French; but I shall not proceed a step without your consent and opinion, &c.

By this fond and eager acceptance of an exculpatory comment Pope testified that, whatever might be the seeming or real import of the

[1] [In fact Warburton's six letters first appeared in the *Works of the Learned* (see No. 84, headnote)]

[2] [*Corresp.*, iv. 171–2. The correct date is 11 April 1739]

[3] [Jacob Robinson, who published the *Works of the Learned*]

[4] [They were collected as *A Vindication of Mr. Pope's Essay on Man* (1740)]

principles which he had received from Bolingbroke, he had not intentionally attacked religion; and Bolingbroke, if he meant to make him
without his own consent an instrument of mischief, found him now
engaged with his eyes open on the side of truth.

It is known that Bolingbroke concealed from Pope his real opinions.
He once discovered them to Mr. Hooke, who related them again to
Pope, and was told by him that he must have mistaken the meaning of
what he heard; and Bolingbroke, when Pope's uneasiness incited him
to desire an explanation, declared that Hooke had misunderstood
him.

Bolingbroke hated Warburton, who had drawn his pupil from him;
and a little before Pope's death they had a dispute, from which they
parted with mutual aversion.

From this time Pope lived in the closest intimacy with his commentator, and amply rewarded his kindness and his zeal.[1] . . .

[pp. 98–108]

[Moral Essays, I–IV]

Beside the general system of morality supposed to be contained in the
Essay on Man, it was his intention to write distinct poems upon the
different duties or conditions of life; one of which is the Epistle to Lord
Bathurst (1733) on the Use of Riches, a piece on which he declared great
labour to have been bestowed.

Into this poem some incidents are historically thrown, and some
known characters are introduced, with others of which it is difficult to
say how far they are real or fictitious; but the praise of Kyrl, the Man of
Ross,[2] deserves particular examination, who, after a long and pompous
enumeration of his publick works and private charities, is said to have
diffused all those blessings from five hundred a year. Wonders are
willingly told, and willingly heard. The truth is, that Kyrl was a man of
known integrity, and active benevolence, by whose solicitation the
wealthy were persuaded to pay contributions to his charitable schemes;
this influence he obtained by an example of liberality exerted to the
utmost extent of his power, and was thus enabled to give more than he
had. This account Mr. Victor received from the minister of the place,
and I have preserved it, that the praise of a good man being made more
credible, may be more solid. Narrations of romantick and impracticable
virtue will be read with wonder, but that which is unattainable is

1 [Warburton was Pope's literary executor]
2 [Moral Essays III: Epistle to Bathurst, ll. 250–90]

recommended in vain; that good may be endeavoured, it must be shewn to be possible.

This is the only piece in which the author has given a hint of his religion, by ridiculing the ceremony of burning the pope, and by mentioning with some indignation the inscription on the Monument.

When this poem was first published, the dialogue, having no letters of direction, was perplexed and obscure. Pope seems to have written with no very distinct idea; for he calls that an *Epistle to Bathurst* in which Bathurst is introduced as speaking.[1]

He afterwards (1734) inscribed to Lord Cobham his *Characters of Men*, written with close attention to the operations of the mind and modifications of life. In this poem he has endeavoured to establish and exemplify his favourite theory of the *Ruling Passion*, by which he means an original direction of desire to some particular object, an innate affection which gives all action a determinate and invariable tendency, and operates upon the whole system of life, either openly, or more secretly by the intervention of some accidental or subordinate propension.

Of any passion, thus innate and irresistible, the existence may reasonably be doubted. Human characters are by no means constant; men change by change of place, of fortune, of acquaintance; he who is at one time a lover of pleasure, is at another a lover of money. Those indeed who attain any excellence, commonly spend life in one pursuit; for excellence is not often gained upon easier terms. But to the particular species of excellence men are directed, not by an ascendant planet or predominating humour, but by the first book which they read, some early conversation which they heard, or some accident which excited ardour and emulation.

It must be at least allowed that this *ruling Passion*, antecedent to reason and observation, must have an object independent on human contrivance; for there can be no natural desire of artificial good. No man therefore can be born, in the strict acceptation, a lover of money; for he may be born where money does not exist; nor can he be born, in a moral sense, a lover of his country; for society, politically regulated, is a state contradistinguished from a state of nature; and any attention to that coalition of interests which makes the happiness of a country, is possible only to those whom enquiry and reflection have enabled to comprehend it.

This doctrine is in itself pernicious as well as false: its tendency is to

[1] [But see F. W. Bateson, Twickenham, III. ii. 79–80]

produce the belief of a kind of moral predestination, or overruling principle which cannot be resisted; he that admits it is prepared to comply with every desire that caprice or opportunity shall excite, and to flatter himself that he submits only to the lawful dominion of Nature, in obeying the resistless authority of his *ruling Passion*.

Pope has formed his theory with so little skill, that, in the examples by which he illustrates and confirms it, he has confounded passions, appetites, and habits.

To the *Characters of Men* he added soon after, in an Epistle supposed to have been addressed to Martha Blount, but which the last edition has taken from her, the *Characters of Women*. This poem, which was laboured with great diligence, and, in the author's opinion with great success, was neglected at its first publication, as the commentator[1] supposes, because the publick was informed by an advertisement, that it contained *no Character drawn from the life*; an assertion which Pope probably did not expect or wish to have been believed, and which he soon gave his readers sufficient reason to distrust, by telling them in a note, that the work was imperfect, because part of his subject was *Vice too high* to be yet exposed.

The time however soon came in which it was safe to display the Dutchess of Marlborough under the name of *Atossa*, and her character was inserted with no great honour to the writer's gratitude.[2]

[pp. 110–15]

[Imitations of Horace]

He published from time to time (between 1730 and 1740) Imitations of different poems of Horace, generally with his name, and once as was suspected without it.[3] What he was upon moral principles ashamed to own, he ought to have suppressed. Of these pieces it is useless to settle the dates, as they had seldom much relation to the times, and perhaps had been long in his hands.

This mode of imitation, in which the ancients are familiarised, by adapting their sentiments to modern topicks, by making Horace say of Shakespeare what he originally said of Ennius,[4] and accommodating his satires on Pantolabus and Nomentanus to the flatterers and prodigals of our own time, was first practised in the reign of Charles the Second by

[1] [I.e. Warburton]
[2] [*Moral Essays II: To a Lady*, ll. 115–50]
[3] [*Sober Advice from Horace* (1734)]
[4] [Horace, *Ep.* II. i. 50–53; *Imitations of Horace, Ep.* II. i. 69–72]

Oldham and Rochester,[1] at least I remember no instances more ancient. It is a kind of middle composition between translation and original design, which pleases when the thoughts are unexpectedly applicable, and the parallels lucky. It seems to have been Pope's favourite amusement; for he has carried it further than any former poet.

He published likewise a revival, in smoother numbers, of Dr. Donne's Satires, which was recommended to him by the Duke of Shrewsbury and the Earl of Oxford. They made no great impression on the publick. Pope seems to have known their imbecillity, and therefore suppressed them while he was yet contending to rise in reputation, but ventured them when he thought their deficiencies more likely to be imputed to Donne than to himself.

The Epistle to Dr. Arbuthnot, which seems to be derived in its first design from Boileau's Address à son Esprit,[2] was published in January 1735, about a month before the death of him to whom it is inscribed. It is to be regretted that either honour or pleasure should have been missed by Arbuthnot; a man estimable for his learning, amiable for his life, and venerable for his piety.

Arbuthnot was a man of great comprehension, skilful in his profession, versed in the sciences, acquainted with ancient literature, and able to animate his mass of knowledge by a bright and active imagination; a scholar with great brilliancy of wit; a wit, who, in the crowd of life, retained and discovered a noble ardour of religious zeal.

In this poem Pope seems to reckon with the publick. He vindicates himself from censures; and with dignity, rather than arrogance, enforces his own claims to kindness and respect. [pp. 115–17]

[The Dunciad in Four Books]

But Pope's irascibility prevailed, and he resolved to tell the whole English world that he was at war with Cibber; and to shew that he thought him no common adversary, he prepared no common vengeance; he published a new edition of the Dunciad, in which he degraded Theobald from his painful pre-eminence, and enthroned Cibber in his stead. Unhappily the two heroes were of opposite characters, and Pope was unwilling to lose what he had already written; he has therefore depraved his poem by giving to Cibber the old books, the cold pedantry and sluggish pertinacity of Theobald.

[1] [Horace, Sat. II. i. 22. The poems referred to are Oldham's 'An Imitation of Horace' Sat. I. ix) and Rochester's 'Allusion to Horace']
[2] [I.e. Boileau's Épître à mes vers]

Pope was ignorant enough of his own interest, to make another change, and introduced Osborne contending for the prize among the booksellers.[1] Osborne was a man intirely destitute of shame, without sense of any disgrace but that of poverty. He told me, when he was doing that which raised Pope's resentment, that he should be put into the *Dunciad*; but he had the fate of *Cassandra*; I gave no credit to his prediction, till in time I saw it accomplished. The shafts of satire were directed equally in vain against Cibber and Osborne; being repelled by the impenetrable impudence of one, and deadened by the impassive dulness of the other. Pope confessed his own pain by his anger; but he gave no pain to those who had provoked him. He was able to hurt none but himself; by transferring the same ridicule from one to another, he destroyed its efficacy; for, by shewing that what he had said of one he was ready to say of another, he reduced himself to the insignificance of his own magpye, who from his cage calls cuckold at a venture.

[pp. 128–9]

[Critical Assessment of Pope and of his Individual Works]

Of his intellectual character, the constituent and fundamental principle was Good Sense, a prompt and intuitive perception of consonance and propriety. He saw immediately, of his own conceptions, what was to be chosen, and what to be rejected; and, in the works of others, what was to be shunned, and what to be copied.

But good sense alone is a sedate and quiescent quality, which manages its possessions well, but does not increase them; it collects few materials for its own operations, and preserves safety, but never gains supremacy. Pope had likewise genius; a mind active, ambitious, and adventurous, always investigating, always aspiring; in its widest searches still longing to go forward, in its highest flights still wishing to be higher; always imagining something greater than it knows, always endeavouring more than it can do.

To assist these powers, he is said to have had great strength and exactness of memory. That which he had heard or read was not easily lost; and he had before him not only what his own meditation suggested, but what he had found in other writers, that might be accommodated to his present purpose.

These benefits of nature he improved by incessant and unwearied diligence; he had recourse to every source of intelligence, and lost no opportunity of information; he consulted the living as well as the dead;

[1] [*The Dunciad* (B), ii. 167–78]

he read his compositions to his friends, and was never content with mediocrity when excellence could be attained. He considered poetry as the business of his life, and however he might seem to lament his occupation, he followed it with constancy; to make verses was his first labour, and to mend them was his last.

From his attention to poetry he was never diverted. If conversation offered any thing that could be improved, he committed it to paper; if a thought, or perhaps an expression more happy than was common, rose to his mind, he was careful to write it; an independent distich was preserved for an opportunity of insertion, and some little fragments have been found containing lines, or parts of lines, to be wrought upon at some other time.

He was one of those few whose labour is their pleasure: he was never elevated to negligence, nor wearied to impatience; he never passed a fault unamended by indifference, nor quitted it by despair. He laboured his works first to gain reputation, and afterwards to keep it.

Of composition there are different methods. Some employ at once memory and invention, and, with little intermediate use of the pen, form and polish large masses by continued meditation, and write their productions only when, in their own opinion, they have completed them. It is related of Virgil, that his custom was to pour out a great number of verses in the morning, and pass the day in retrenching exuberances and correcting inaccuracies. The method of Pope, as may be collected from his translation, was to write his first thoughts in his first words, and gradually to amplify, decorate, rectify, and refine them.

With such faculties, and such dispositions, he excelled every other writer in *poetical prudence*; he wrote in such a manner as might expose him to few hazards. He used almost always the same fabrick of verse; and, indeed, by those few essays which he made of any other, he did not enlarge his reputation. Of this uniformity the certain consequence was readiness and dexterity. By perpetual practice, language had in his mind a systematical arrangement; having always the same use for words, he had words so selected and combined as to be ready at his call. This increase of facility he confessed himself to have perceived in the progress of his translation.

But what was yet of more importance, his effusions were always voluntary, and his subjects chosen by himself. His independence secured him from drudging at a task, and labouring upon a barren topick: he never exchanged praise for money, nor opened a shop of condolence or congratulation. His poems, therefore, were scarce ever temporary. He suffered coronations and royal marriages to pass without a song, and derived no opportunities from recent events, nor any popularity from the accidental disposition of his readers. He was never reduced to the necessity of soliciting the sun to shine upon a birth-day, of calling the Graces and Virtues to a wedding, or of saying what multitudes have said before him. When he could produce nothing new, he was at liberty to be silent.

His publications were for the same reason never hasty. He is said to have sent nothing to the press till it had lain two years under his inspection: it is at least certain, that he ventured nothing without nice examination. He suffered the tumult of imagination to subside, and the novelties of invention to grow familiar. He knew that the mind is always enamoured of its own productions, and did not trust his first fondness. He consulted his friends, and listened with great willingness to criticism; and, what was of more importance, he consulted himself, and let nothing pass against his own judgement.

He professed to have learned his poetry from Dryden, whom, whenever an opportunity was presented, he praised through his whole life with unvaried liberality; and perhaps his character may receive some illustration if he be compared with his master.

Integrity of understanding and nicety of discernment were not allotted in a less proportion to Dryden than to Pope. The rectitude of Dryden's mind was sufficiently shewn by the dismission of his poetical prejudices, and the rejection of unnatural thoughts and rugged numbers. But Dryden never desired to apply all the judgement that he had. He wrote, and professed to write, merely for the people; and when he pleased others, he contented himself. He spent no time in struggles to rouse latent powers; he never attempted to make that better which was already good, nor often to mend what he must have known to be faulty. He wrote, as he tells us, with very little consideration; when occasion or necessity called upon him, he poured out what the present moment happened to supply, and, when once it had passed the press, ejected it from his mind; for when he had no pecuniary interest, he had no further solicitude.

Pope was not content to satisfy; he desired to excel, and therefore always endeavoured to do his best: he did not court the candour, but dared the judgement of his reader, and, expecting no indulgence from others, he shewed none to himself. He examined lines and words with minute and punctilious observation, and retouched every part with indefatigable diligence, till he had left nothing to be forgiven.

For this reason he kept his pieces very long in his hands, while he considered and reconsidered them. The only poems which can be supposed to have been written with such regard to the times as might hasten their publication, were the two satires of *Thirty-eight* [*Epilogue to the Satires*, i and ii]; of which Dodsley told me, that they were brought to him by the author, that they might be fairly copied. 'Almost every[1] line,' he said, 'was then written twice over; I gave him a clean transcript, which he sent some time afterwards to me for the press, with almost every line written twice over a second time.'

His declaration, that his care for his works ceased at their publication, was not strictly true. His parental attention never abandoned them; what he found amiss in the first edition, he silently corrected in those that followed. He appears to have revised the *Iliad*, and freed it from some of its imperfections; and the *Essay on Criticism* received many improvements after its first appearance. It will seldom be found that he altered without adding clearness, elegance, or vigour. Pope had perhaps the judgement of Dryden; but Dryden certainly wanted the diligence of Pope.

In acquired knowledge, the superiority must be allowed to Dryden, whose education was more scholastick, and who before he became an author had been allowed more time for study, with better means of information. His mind has a larger range, and he collects his images and illustrations from a more extensive circumference of science. Dryden knew more of man in his general nature, and Pope in his local manners. The notions of Dryden were formed by comprehensive speculation, and those of Pope by minute attention. There is more dignity in the knowledge of Dryden, and more certainty in that of Pope.

Poetry was not the sole praise of either; for both excelled likewise in prose; but Pope did not borrow his prose from his predecessor. The style of Dryden is capricious and varied, that of Pope is cautious and uniform; Dryden obeys the motions of his own mind, Pope constrains his mind to his own rules of composition. Dryden is sometimes vehement and rapid; Pope is always smooth, uniform, and gentle. Dryden's page is a natural field, rising into inequalities, and diversified by the varied exuberance of abundant vegetation; Pope's is a velvet lawn, shaven by the scythe, and levelled by the roller.

Of genius, that power which constitutes a poet; that quality without which judgement is cold and knowledge is inert; that energy which collects, combines, amplifies, and animates; the superiority must, with

[1] *Almost every*] 1783; *Every* 1781.

some hesitation, be allowed to Dryden. It is not to be inferred that of this poetical vigour Pope had only a little, because Dryden had more; for every other writer since Milton must give place to Pope; and even of Dryden it must be said that if he has brighter paragraphs, he has not better poems. Dryden's performances were always hasty, either excited by some external occasion, or extorted by domestick necessity; he composed without consideration, and published without correction. What his mind could supply at call, or gather in one excursion, was all that he sought, and all that he gave. The dilatory caution of Pope enabled him to condense his sentiments, to multiply his images, and to accumulate all that study might produce, or chance might supply. If the flights of Dryden therefore are higher, Pope continues longer on the wing. If of Dryden's fire the blaze is brighter, of Pope's the heat is more regular and constant. Dryden often surpasses expectation, and Pope never falls below it. Dryden is read with frequent astonishment, and Pope with perpetual delight.

This parallel will, I hope, when it is well considered, be found just; and if the reader should suspect me, as I suspect myself, of some partial fondness for the memory of Dryden, let him not too hastily condemn me; for meditation and enquiry may, perhaps, shew him the reasonableness of my determination.

THE Works of Pope are now to be distinctly examined, not so much with attention to slight faults or petty beauties, as to the *general character* and *effect* of each performance.

It seems natural for a young poet to initiate himself by Pastorals, which, not professing to imitate real life, require no experience, and, exhibiting only the simple operation of unmingled passions, admit no subtle reasoning or deep enquiry. Pope's *Pastorals* are not however composed but with close thought; they have reference to the times of the day, the seasons of the year, and the periods of human life. The last, that which turns the attention upon age and death, was the author's favourite. To tell of disappointment and misery, to thicken the darkness of futurity, and perplex the labyrinth of uncertainty, has been always a delicious employment of the poets. His preference was probably just. I wish, however, that his fondness had not overlooked a line in which the *Zephyrs* are made *to lament in silence*.

To charge these *Pastorals* with want of invention, is to require what never was intended.[1] The imitations are so ambitiously frequent, that

---

[1] [I.e. Warton's attack, see below pp. 383–7: for Johnson's immediate reaction to the *Essay*, see pp. 408–12. In conversation in 1769, however, 'Johnson said his *Pastorals* were

the writer evidently means rather to shew his literature than his wit. It is surely sufficient for an author of sixteen not only to be able to copy the poems of antiquity with judicious selection, but to have obtained sufficient power of language, and skill in metre, to exhibit a series of versification, which had in English poetry no precedent, nor has since had an imitation.

The design of *Windsor Forest* is evidently derived from *Cooper's Hill*, with some attention to Waller's poem on *The Park*; but Pope cannot be denied to excel his masters in variety and elegance, and the art of interchanging description, narrative, and morality. The objection made by Dennis is the want of plan, of a regular subordination of parts terminating in the principal and original design.[1] There is this want in most descriptive poems, because as the scenes, which they must exhibit successively, are all subsisting at the same time, the order in which they are shewn must by necessity be arbitrary, and more is not to be expected from the last part than from the first. The attention, therefore, which cannot be detained by suspense, must be excited by diversity, such as his poem offers to its reader.

But the desire of diversity may be too much indulged; the parts of *Windsor Forest* which deserve least praise are those which were added to enliven the stillness of the scene, the appearance of Father Thames, and the transformation of *Lodona*. Addison had in his *Campaign* derided the *Rivers* that *rise from their oozy beds* to tell stories of heroes,[2] and it is therefore strange that Pope should adopt a fiction not only unnatural but lately censured. The story of *Lodona* is told with sweetness; but a new metamorphosis is a ready and puerile expedient; nothing is easier than to tell how a flower was once a blooming virgin, or a rock an obdurate tyrant.

The *Temple of Fame* has, as Steele warmly declared, *a thousand beauties*.[3] Every part is splendid; there is great luxuriance of ornaments; the original vision of Chaucer was never denied to be much improved;[4] the allegory is very skilfully continued, the imagery is properly selected, and learnedly displayed: yet, with all this comprehension of excellence, as its scene is laid in remote ages, and its sentiments, if the concluding paragraph be excepted, have little relation to general manners or com-

---

[1] [See No. 16]

[2] [Addison, *The Campaign* (1705), p. 23]

[3] [Letter of 12 November 1712 to Pope, *Corresp.*, i. 152] [4] [But see No. 123]

---

poor things, though the versification was fine', *Boswell's Life of Johnson*, ed. G. B. Hill, rev. L. F. Powell (1934–40), ii. 84]

mon life, it never obtained much notice, but is turned silently over, and seldom quoted or mentioned with either praise or blame.

That the *Messiah* excels the *Pollio* is no great praise, if it be considered from what original the improvements are derived.

The *Verses on the unfortunate Lady* have drawn much attention by the illaudable singularity of treating suicide with respect; and they must be allowed to be written in some parts with vigorous animation, and in others with gentle tenderness; nor has Pope produced any poem in which the sense predominates more over the diction. But the tale is not skilfully told; it is not easy to discover the character of either the Lady or her Guardian. History relates that she was about to disparage herself by a marriage with an inferior; Pope praises her for the dignity of ambition, and yet condemns the unkle to detestation for his pride; the ambitious love of a niece may be opposed by the interest, malice, or envy of an unkle, but never by his pride. On such an occasion a poet may be allowed to be obscure, but inconsistency never can be right.

The *Ode for St. Cecilia's Day* was undertaken at the desire of Steele: in this the author is generally confessed to have miscarried, yet he has miscarried only as compared with Dryden; for he has far outgone other competitors. Dryden's plan is better chosen; history will always take stronger hold of the attention than fable: the passions excited by Dryden are the pleasures and pains of real life, the scene of Pope is laid in imaginary existence; Pope is read with calm acquiescence, Dryden with turbulent delight; Pope hangs upon the ear, and Dryden finds the passes of the mind.

Both the odes want the essential constituent of metrical compositions, the stated recurrence of settled numbers. It may be alleged that Pindar is said by Horace to have written *numeris lege solutis*:[1] but as no such lax performances have been transmitted to us, the meaning of that expression cannot be fixed; and perhaps the like return might properly be made to a modern Pindarist, as Mr. Cobb received from Bentley, who, when he found his criticisms upon a Greek Exercise, which Cobb had presented, refuted one after another by Pindar's authority, cried out at last, *Pindar was a bold fellow, but thou art an impudent one*.

If Pope's ode be particularly inspected, it will be found that the first stanza consists of sounds well chosen indeed, but only sounds.

The second consists of hyperbolical common-places, easily to be found, and perhaps without much difficulty to be as well expressed.

In the third, however, there are numbers, images, harmony, and

---

[1] [*Odes*, iv. 2. 11: 'measures freed from rule']

vigour, not unworthy the antagonist of Dryden. Had all been like this —but every part cannot be the best.

The next stanzas place and detain us in the dark and dismal regions of mythology, where neither hope nor fear, neither joy nor sorrow can be found: the poet however faithfully attends us; we have all that can be performed by elegance of diction, or sweetness of versification; but what can form avail without better matter?

The last stanza recurs again to common-places. The conclusion is too evidently modelled by that of Dryden; and it may be remarked that both end with the same fault, the comparison of each is literal on one side, and metaphorical on the other.

Poets do not always express their own thoughts; Pope, with all this labour in the praise of Musick, was ignorant of its principles, and insensible of its effects.

One of his greatest though of his earliest works is the *Essay on Criticism*, which, if he had written nothing else, would have placed him among the first criticks and the first poets, as it exhibits every mode of excellence that can embellish or dignify didactick composition, selection of matter, novelty of arrangement, justness of precept, splendour of illustration, and propriety of digression. I know not whether it be pleasing to consider that he produced this piece at twenty, and never afterwards excelled it: he that delights himself with observing that such powers may be so soon attained, cannot but grieve to think that life was ever after at a stand.

To mention the particular beauties of the Essay would be unprofitably tedious;[1] but I cannot forbear to observe, that the comparison of a student's progress in the sciences with the journey of a traveller in the Alps, is perhaps the best that English poetry can shew. A simile, to be perfect, must both illustrate and ennoble the subject; must shew it to the understanding in a clearer view, and display it to the fancy with greater dignity; but neither of these qualities may be sufficient to recommend it. In didactick poetry, of which the great purpose is instruction, a simile may be praised which illustrates, though it does not ennoble; in heroicks, that may be admitted which ennobles, though it does not illustrate. That it may be complete, it is required to exhibit, independently of its references, a pleasing image; for a simile is said to be a short episode. To this antiquity was so attentive, that circumstances were sometimes added, which, having no parallels, served only to fill

[1] [This paragraph develops remarks Johnson made when he reviewed Warton; see No. 107, and Warton, p. 390 above]

the imagination, and produced what Perrault ludicrously called *comparisons with a long tail*. In their similes the greatest writers have sometimes failed; the ship-race, compared with the chariot-race, is neither illustrated nor aggrandised; land and water make all the difference: when Apollo, running after Daphne, is likened to a greyhound chasing a hare, there is nothing gained; the ideas of pursuit and flight are too plain to be made plainer, and a god and the daughter of a god are not represented much to their advantage, by a hare and dog. The simile of the Alps has no useless parts, yet affords a striking picture by itself; it makes the foregoing position better understood, and enables it to take faster hold on the attention; it assists the apprehension, and elevates the fancy.

Let me likewise dwell a little on the celebrated paragraph, in which it is directed that *the sound should seem an echo to the sense*;[1] a precept which Pope is allowed to have observed beyond any other English poet.

This notion of representative metre, and the desire of discovering frequent adaptations of the sound to the sense, have produced, in my opinion, many wild conceits and imaginary beauties.[2] All that can furnish this representation are the sounds of the words considered singly, and the time in which they are pronounced. Every language has some words framed to exhibit the noises which they express, as *thump*, *rattle*, *growl*, *hiss*. These however are but few, and the poet cannot make them more, nor can they be of any use but when sound is to be mentioned. The time of pronunciation was in the dactylick measures of the learned languages capable of considerable variety; but that variety could be accommodated only to motion or duration, and different degrees of motion were perhaps expressed by verses rapid or slow, without much attention of the writer, when the image had full possession of his fancy; but our language having little flexibility, our verses can differ very little in their cadence. The fancied resemblances, I fear, arise sometimes merely from the ambiguity of words; there is supposed to be some relation between a *soft* line and a *soft* couch, or between *hard* syllables and *hard* fortune.

Motion, however, may be in some sort exemplified; and yet it may be suspected that even in such resemblances the mind often governs the ear, and the sounds are estimated by their meaning. One of the most successful attempts has been to describe the labour of Sisyphus:

---

[1] [*An Essay on Criticism*, l. 365]

[2] [An earlier version of most of what follows occurs as *Rambler*, nos 92, 94. For the first of these see No. 99 above. See also Nos 11, 13, 117, 124]

> With many a weary step, and many a groan,
> Up a high hill he heaves a huge round stone;
> The huge round stone, resulting with a bound,
> Thunders impetuous down, and smoaks along the ground.[1]

Who does not perceive the stone to move slowly upward, and roll violently back? But set the same numbers to another sense;

> While many a merry tale, and many a song,
> Chear'd the rough road, we wish'd the rough road long.
> The rough road then, returning in a round,
> Mock'd our impatient steps, for all was fairy ground.

We have now surely lost much of the delay, and much of the rapidity.

But to shew how little the greatest master of numbers can fix the principles of representative harmony, it will be sufficient to remark that the poet, who tells us, that

> When Ajax strives [some rock's vast weight to throw,
> The line too labours and] the words move slow:
> Not so when swift Camilla scours the plain,
> Flies o'er th' unbending corn, and skims along the main;
> [*An Essay on Criticism*, ll. 369–70]

when he had enjoyed for about thirty years the praise of Camilla's lightness of foot, tried another experiment upon *sound* and *time*, and produced this memorable triplet:

> Waller was smooth; but Dryden taught to join
> The varying verse, the full resounding line,
> The long majestick march, and energy divine.
> [*Imitations of Horace*, *Ep.* II. i. 267–9]

Here are the swiftness of the rapid race, and the march of slow-paced majesty, exhibited by the same poet in the same sequence of syllables, except that the exact prosodist will find the line of *swiftness* by one time longer than that of *tardiness*.

Beauties of this kind are commonly fancied; and when real, are technical and nugatory, not to be rejected, and not to be solicited.

To the praises which have been accumulated on *The Rape of the Lock* by readers of every class, from the critick to the waiting-maid, it is

[1] [These lines come from a book translated by Broome, though Pope said that he had 'loaded the second verse with monosyllables', *Odyssey*, xi. 736n., and had been discussed by George Campbell (No. 124)]

difficult to make any addition. Of that which is universally allowed to be the most attractive of all ludicrous compositions, let it rather be now enquired from what sources the power of pleasing is derived.

Dr. Warburton, who excelled in critical perspicacity, has remarked that the preternatural agents are very happily adapted to the purposes of the poem.[1] The heathen deities can no longer gain attention: we should have turned away from a contest between Venus and Diana. The employment of allegorical persons always excites conviction of its own absurdity; they may produce effects, but cannot conduct actions; when the phantom is put in motion, it dissolves; thus *Discord* may raise a mutiny, but *Discord* cannot conduct a march, nor besiege a town. Pope brought into view a new race of Beings, with powers and passions proportionate to their operation. The sylphs and gnomes act at the toilet and the tea-table, what more terrifick and more powerful phantoms perform on the stormy ocean, or the field of battle, they give their proper help, and do their proper mischief.

Pope is said, by an objector [Warton], not to have been the inventer of this petty nation; a charge which might with more justice have been brought against the author of the *Iliad*, who doubtless adopted the religious system of his country; for what is there but the names of his agents which Pope has not invented? Has he not assigned them characters and operations never heard of before? Has he not, at least, given them their first poetical existence? If this is not sufficient to denominate his work original, nothing original ever can be written. [Compare No. 118.]

In this work are exhibited, in a very high degree, the two most engaging powers of an author. New things are made familiar, and familiar things are made new. A race of aerial people, never heard of before, is presented to us in a manner so clear and easy, that the reader seeks for no further information, but immediately mingles with his new acquaintance, adopts their interests, and attends their pursuits, loves a sylph, and detests a gnome.

That familiar things are made new, every paragraph will prove. The subject of the poem is an event below the common incidents of common life; nothing real is introduced that is not seen so often as to be no longer regarded, yet the whole detail of a female-day is here brought before us invested with so much art of decoration, that, though nothing is disguised, every thing is striking, and we feel all the appetite of curiosity for that from which we have a thousand times turned fastidiously away.

[1] [See *The Works of Alexander Pope Esq* . . ., ed. W. Warburton (1751), i. 219–20]

The purpose of the Poet is, as he tells us, to laugh at *the little unguarded follies of the female sex.* It is therefore without justice that Dennis[1] charges the *Rape of the Lock* with the want of a moral, and for that reason sets it below the *Lutrin,* which exposes the pride and discord of the clergy. Perhaps neither Pope nor Boileau has made the world much better than he found it; but if they had both succeeded, it were easy to tell who would have deserved most from publick gratitude. The freaks, and humours, and spleen, and vanity of women, as they embroil families in discord, and fill houses with disquiet, do more to obstruct the happiness of life in a year than the ambition of the clergy in many centuries. It has been well observed, that the misery of man proceeds not from any single crush of overwhelming evil, but from small vexations continually repeated.

It is remarked by Dennis likewise, that the machinery is superfluous; that, by all the bustle of preternatural operation, the main event is neither hastened nor retarded. To this charge an efficacious answer is not easily made. The sylphs cannot be said to help or to oppose, and it must be allowed to imply some want of art, that their power has not been sufficiently intermingled with the action. Other parts may likewise be charged with want of connection; the game at *ombre* might be spared, but if the Lady had lost her hair while she was intent upon her cards, it might have been inferred that those who are too fond of play will be in danger of neglecting more important interests. Those perhaps are faults; but what are such faults to so much excellence!

The Epistle of *Eloise to Abelard* is one of the most happy productions of human wit: the subject is so judiciously chosen, that it would be difficult, in turning over the annals of the world, to find another which so many circumstances concur to recommend. We regularly interest ourselves most in the fortune of those who most deserve our notice. Abelard and Eloise were conspicuous in their days for eminence of merit. The heart naturally loves truth. The adventures and misfortunes of this illustrious pair are known from undisputed history. Their fate does not leave the mind in hopeless dejection; for they both found quiet and consolation in retirement and piety. So new and so affecting is their story, that it supersedes invention, and imagination ranges at full liberty without straggling into scenes of fable.

The story, thus skilfully adopted, has been diligently improved. Pope has left nothing behind him, which seems more the effect of studious perseverance and laborious revisal. Here is particularly observable the

[1] [See No. 20]

curiosa felicitas [careful happinesses], a fruitful soil, and careful cultivation. Here is no crudeness of sense, nor asperity of language.

The sources from which sentiments, which have so much vigour and efficacy, have been drawn are shewn to be the mystick writers by the learned author of the *Essay on the Life and Writings of Pope*;[1] a book which teaches how the brow of Criticism may be smoothed, and how she may be enabled, with all her severity, to attract and to delight.

The train of my disquisition has now conducted me to that poetical wonder, the translation of the *Iliad*; a performance which no age or nation can pretend to equal. To the Greeks translation was almost unknown; it was totally unknown to the inhabitants of Greece. They had no recourse to the Barbarians for poetical beauties, but sought for every thing in Homer, where, indeed, there is but little which they might not find.

The Italians have been very diligent translators; but I can hear of no version, unless perhaps Anguillara's *Ovid*[2] may be excepted, which is read with eagerness. The *Iliad* of Salvini[3] every reader may discover to be punctiliously exact; but it seems to be the work of a linguist skilfully pedantick, and his countrymen, the proper judges of its power to please, reject it with disgust.

Their predecessors the Romans have left some specimens of translation behind them, and that employment must have had some credit in which Tully and Germanicus engaged; but unless we suppose, what is perhaps true, that the plays of Terence were versions of Menander, nothing translated seems ever to have risen to high reputation. The French, in the meridian hour of their learning, were very laudably industrious to enrich their own language with the wisdom[4] of the ancients; but found themselves reduced, by whatever necessity, to turn the Greek and Roman poetry into prose. Whoever could read an author could translate him. From such rivals little can be feared.

The chief help of Pope in this arduous undertaking was drawn from the versions of Dryden. Virgil had borrowed much of his imagery from Homer, and part of the debt was now paid by his translator. Pope searched the pages of Dryden for happy combinations of heroick diction; but it will not be denied that he added much to what he found.

---

[1] [See above, pp. 401–7]
[2] [Giovanni Anguillara, *Le metamorfosi d'Ovidio* (Vinegia, 1584)]
[3] [Antonio Maria Salvini (1653–1729), *Iliade d'Omero* (1723)]
[4] *wisdom*] 1783; *learning* 1781

He cultivated our language with so much diligence and art, that he has left in his *Homer* a treasure of poetical elegances to posterity. His version may be said to have tuned the English tongue; for since its appearance no writer, however deficient in other powers, has wanted melody. Such a series of lines so elaborately corrected, and so sweetly modulated, took possession of the publick ear; the vulgar was enamoured of the poem, and the learned wondered at the translation.

But in the most general applause discordant voices will always be heard. It has been objected by some, who wish to be numbered among the sons of learning, that Pope's version of Homer is not Homerical; that it exhibits no resemblance of the original and characteristick manner of the Father of Poetry, as it wants his awful simplicity, his artless grandeur, his unaffected majesty. This cannot be totally denied; but it must be remembered that *necessitas quod cogit defendit* ['necessity defends what it compels'], that may be lawfully done which cannot be forborne. Time and place will always enforce regard. In estimating this translation, consideration must be had of the nature of our language, the form of our metre, and, above all, of the change which two thousand years have made in the modes of life and the habits of thought. Virgil wrote in a language of the same general fabrick with that of Homer, in verses of the same measure, and in an age nearer to Homer's time by eighteen hundred years; yet he found, even then, the state of the world so much altered, and the demand for elegance so much increased, that mere nature would be endured no longer; and perhaps, in the multitude of borrowed passages, very few can be shewn which he has not embellished.

There is a time when nations emerging from barbarity, and falling into regular subordination, gain leisure to grow wise, and feel the shame of ignorance and the craving pain of unsatisfied curiosity. To this hunger of the mind plain sense is grateful; that which fills the void removes uneasiness, and to be free from pain for a while is pleasure; but repletion generates fastidiousness; a saturated intellect soon becomes luxurious, and knowledge finds no willing reception till it is recommended by artificial diction. Thus it will be found, in the progress of learning, that in all nations the first writers are simple, and that every age improves in elegance. One refinement always makes way for another, and what was expedient to Virgil was necessary to Pope.

I suppose many readers of the English *Iliad*, when they have been touched with some unexpected beauty of the lighter kind, have tried to enjoy it in the original, where, alas! it was not to be found. Homer doubtless owes to his translator many *Ovidian* graces not exactly suitable to his character; but to have added can be no great crime, if nothing be taken away. Elegance is surely to be desired, if it be not gained at the expence of dignity. A hero would wish to be loved, as well as to be reverenced.

To a thousand cavils one answer is sufficient; the purpose of a writer is to be read, and the criticism which would destroy the power of pleasing must be blown aside. Pope wrote for his own age and his own nation: he knew that it was necessary to colour the images and point the sentiments of his author; he therefore made him graceful, but lost him some of his sublimity.

The copious notes with which the version is accompanied, and by which it is recommended to many readers, though they were undoubtedly written to swell the volumes, ought not to pass without praise: commentaries which attract the reader by the pleasure of perusal have not often appeared; the notes of others are read to clear difficulties, those of Pope to vary entertainment.

It has however been objected, with sufficient reason, that there is in the commentary too much of unseasonable levity and affected gaiety; that too many appeals are made to the Ladies, and the ease which is so carefully preserved is sometimes the ease of a trifler. Every art has its terms, and every kind of instruction its proper style; the gravity of common criticks may be tedious, but is less despicable than childish merriment.

Of the *Odyssey* nothing remains to be observed: the same general praise may be given to both translations, and a particular examination of either would require a large volume. The notes were written by Broome, who endeavoured not unsuccessfully to imitate his master.

Of the *Dunciad* the hint is confessedly taken from Dryden's *Mac Flecknoe*; but the plan is so enlarged and diversified as justly to claim the praise of an original, and affords perhaps the best specimen that has yet appeared of personal satire ludicrously pompous.

That the design was moral, whatever the author might tell either his readers or himself, I am not convinced. The first motive was the desire of revenging the contempt with which Theobald had treated his *Shakespeare*, and regaining the honour which he had lost, by crushing his opponent. Theobald was not of bulk enough to fill a poem, and therefore it was necessary to find other enemies with other names, at whose expence he might divert the publick.

In this design there was petulance and malignity enough; but I cannot think it very criminal.[1] An author places himself uncalled before the tribunal of Criticism, and solicits fame at the hazard of disgrace. Dulness or deformity are not culpable in themselves, but may be very justly reproached when they pretend to the honour of wit or the influence of beauty. If bad writers were to pass without reprehension what should restrain them? *impune diem consumpserit ingens Telephus;*[2] and upon bad writers only will censure have much effect. The satire which brought Theobald and Moore into contempt, dropped impotent from Bentley, like the javelin of Priam.[3]

All truth is valuable, and satirical criticism may be considered as useful when it rectifies error and improves judgement; he that refines the publick taste is a publick benefactor.

The beauties of this poem are well known; its chief fault is the grossness of its images. Pope and Swift had an unnatural delight in ideas physically impure, such as every other tongue utters with unwillingness, and of which every ear shrinks from the mention.

But even this fault, offensive as it is, may be forgiven for the excellence of other passages; such as the formation and dissolution of Moore, the account of the Traveller, the misfortune of the Florist, and the crouded thoughts and stately numbers which dignify the concluding paragraph [*The Dunciad* (B), ii. 35-50, 109-20, iv. 293-336, 403-36].

The alterations which have been made in the *Dunciad*, not always for the better, require that it should be published, as in the last collection, with all its variations.

The *Essay on Man* was a work of great labour and long consideration, but certainly not the happiest of Pope's performances. The subject is perhaps not very proper for poetry, and the poet was not sufficiently master of his subject; metaphysical morality was to him a new study, he was proud of his acquisitions, and, supposing himself master of great secrets, was in haste to teach what he had not learned. Thus he tells us, in the first Epistle, that from the nature of the Supreme Being may be deduced an order of beings such as mankind, because Infinite Excellence can do only what is best. He finds out that these beings must be

---

[1] [In 1778 Johnson remarked, 'he wrote his *Dunciad* for fame. That was his primary motive. . . . He delighted to vex [the Dunces], no doubt; but he had more delight in seeing how well he could vex them', *Boswell's Life of Johnson*, ed. G. B. Hill, rev. L. F. Powell (1934–50), ii. 334]

[2] [Juvenal, *Sat.* i. 4: 'no recompense for whole days wasted on prolix versions of Telephus' (Peter Green)]

[3] *Priam*] 1783; ~ *thrown at Neoptelemus* 1781.

somewhere, and[1] that *all the question is whether man be in a wrong place.*[2] Surely if, according to the poet's Leibnitzian reasoning, we may infer that man ought to be, only because he is, we may allow that his place is the right place, because he has it. Supreme Wisdom is not less infallible in disposing than in creating. But what is meant by *somewhere* and *place* and *wrong place*, it had been vain to ask Pope, who probably had never asked himself.

Having exalted himself into the chair of wisdom, he tells us much that every man knows, and much that he does not know himself; that we see but little, and that the order of the universe is beyond our comprehension;[3] an opinion not very uncommon; and that there is a chain of subordinate beings *from infinite to nothing,*[4] of which himself and his readers are equally ignorant. But he gives us one comfort, which, without his help, he supposes unattainable, in the position *that though we are fools, yet God is wise.*[5]

This Essay affords an egregious instance of the predominance of genius, the dazzling splendour of imagery, and the seductive powers of eloquence. Never were penury of knowledge and vulgarity of sentiment so happily disguised. The reader feels his mind full, though he learns nothing; and when he meets it in its new array, no longer knows the talk of his mother and his nurse. When these wonder-working sounds sink into sense, and the doctrine of the Essay, disrobed of its ornaments, is left to the powers of its naked excellence, what shall we discover? That we are, in comparison with our Creator, very weak and ignorant; that we do not uphold the chain of existence; and that we could not make one another with more skill than we are made.[6] We may learn yet more; that the arts of human life were copied from the instinctive operations of other animals; that if the world be made for man, it may be said that man was made for geese.[7] To these profound principles of natural knowledge are added some moral instructions equally new; that self-interest, well understood, will produce social concord; that men are mutual gainers by mutual benefits; that evil is sometimes balanced by good; that human advantages are unstable and fallacious, of uncertain duration, and doubtful effect; that our true honour is, not to have a great part, but to act it well; that virtue only is our own; and that happiness is always in our power.[8]

[1] *that . . . and*] 1783; *om.* 1781.   [2] [*An Essay on Man*, i. 43–50]
[3] [*Ibid.*, i. 51ff.]   [4] [*Ibid.*, i. 23–46]
[5] [*Ibid.*, i. 281–94]   [6] [*Ibid.*, i. 17–42]
[7] [*Ibid.*, iii. 169–200, 45–6]
[8] [*Ibid.*, iii. 269–82, 317–18; iv. 353–60, 396; iv. 114; iv. 167–92; iv. 29–32, 309–98]

Surely a man of no very comprehensive search may venture to say that he has heard all this before; but it was never till now recommended by such a blaze of embellishment, or such sweetness of melody. The vigorous contraction of some thoughts, the luxuriant amplification of others, the incidental illustrations, and sometimes the dignity, sometimes the softness of the verses, enchain philosophy, suspend criticism, and oppress judgement by overpowering pleasure.

This is true of many paragraphs; yet if I had undertaken to exemplify Pope's felicity of composition before a rigid critick I should not select the *Essay on Man*; for it contains more lines unsuccessfully laboured, more harshness of diction, more thoughts imperfectly expressed, more levity without elegance, and more heaviness without strength, than will easily be found in all his other works.

The *Characters of Men and Women* are the product of diligent speculation upon human life; much labour has been bestowed upon them, and Pope very seldom laboured in vain. That his excellence may be properly estimated, I recommend a comparison of his *Characters of Women* with Boileau's *Satire* [x]; it will then be seen with how much more perspicacity female nature is investigated, and female excellence selected; and he surely is no mean writer to whom Boileau shall be found inferior. The *Characters of Men*, however, are written with more, if not with deeper, thought, and exhibit many passages exquisitely beautiful. The *Gem and the Flower* will not easily be equalled.[1] In the women's part are some defects: the character of *Atossa* is not so neatly finished as that of *Clodio*;[2] and some of the female characters may be found perhaps more frequently among men; what is said of *Philomede* was true of *Prior*.[3]

In the Epistles to Lord Bathurst and Lord Burlington, Dr. Warburton has endeavoured to find a train of thought which was never in the writer's head, and, to support his hypothesis, has printed that first which was published last. In one, the most valuable passage is perhaps the elogy on *Good Sense*,[4] and in the other the *End of the Duke of Buckingham*.[5]

The Epistle of Arbuthnot, now arbitrarily called the *Prologue to the Satires*, is a performance consisting, as it seems, of many fragments

---

[1] [*Moral Essays I: To Cobham*, ll. 93–100]

[2] [*Ibid., II: To a Lady*, ll. 115–50; 'Clodio' is the portrait of Warton, *ibid., I: To Cobham*, ll. 179–207]

[3] [*Ibid., II: To a Lady*, ll. 83–6]

[4] [*Ibid., IV: To Burlington*, ll. 39–46]

[5] [*Ibid., III: To Bathurst*, ll. 299–314]

wrought into one design, which by this union of scattered beauties contains more striking paragraphs than could probably have been brought together into an occasional work. As there is no stronger motive to exertion than self-defence, no part has more elegance, spirit, or dignity, than the poet's vindication of his own character [ll. 125–32]. The meanest passage is the satire upon *Sporus* [ll. 305ff.].

Of the two poems which derived their names from the year, and which are called the *Epilogue to the Satires*, it was very justly remarked by Savage, that the second was in the whole more strongly conceived, and more equally supported, but that it had no single passages equal to the contention in the first for the dignity of Vice, and the celebration of the triumph of Corruption.[1]

The Imitations of Horace seem to have been written as relaxations of his genius. This employment became his favourite by its facility; the plan was ready to his hand, and nothing was required but to accommodate as he could the sentiments of an old author to recent facts or familiar images; but what is easy is seldom excellent: such imitations cannot give pleasure to common readers; the man of learning may be sometimes surprised and delighted by an unexpected parallel; but the comparison requires knowledge of the original, which will likewise often detect strained applications. Between Roman images and English manners there will be an irreconcileable dissimilitude, and the work will be generally uncouth and party-coloured; neither original nor translated, neither ancient nor modern.

Pope had, in proportions very nicely adjusted to each other, all the qualities that constitute genius. He had *Invention*, by which new trains of events are formed, and new scenes of imagery displayed, as in the *Rape of the Lock*; and by which extrinsick and adventitious embellishments and illustrations are connected with a known subject, as in the *Essay on Criticism*; he had *Imagination*, which strongly impresses on the writer's mind, and enables him to convey to the reader, the various forms of nature, incidents of life, and energies of passion, as in his *Eloisa*, *Windsor Forest*, and the *Ethick Epistles*. He had *Judgement*, which selects from life or nature what the present purpose requires, and, by separating the essence of things from its concomitants, often makes the representation more powerful than the reality; and he had colours of language always before him, ready to decorate his matter with every grace of elegant expression, as when he accommodates his diction to the wonderful multiplicity of Homer's sentiments and descriptions.

[1] [*Epilogue to the Satires: Dialogue I*, ll. 114–30, 147–end]

Poetical expression includes sound as well as meaning. *Musick*, says Dryden, *is inarticulate poetry*; among the excellences of Pope, therefore, must be mentioned the melody of his metre. By perusing the works of Dryden he discovered the most perfect fabrick of English verse, and habituated himself to that only which he found the best; in consequence of which restraint, his poetry has been censured as too uniformly musical, and as glutting the ear with unvaried sweetness. I suspect this objection to be the cant of those who judge by principles rather than perception: and who would even themselves have less pleasure in his works, if he had tried to relieve attention by studied discords, or affected to break his lines and vary his pauses.

But though he was thus careful of his versification, he did not oppress his powers with superfluous rigour. He seems to have thought with Boileau, that the practice of writing might be refined till the difficulty should overbalance the advantage. The construction of his language is not always strictly grammatical; with those rhymes which prescription had conjoined he contented himself, without regard to Swift's remonstrances, though there was no striking consonance; nor was he very careful to vary his terminations, or to refuse admission at a small distance to the same rhymes.

To Swift's edict for the exclusion of Alexandrines and Triplets he paid little regard; he admitted them, but, in the opinion of Fenton, too rarely; he uses them more liberally in his translation than his poems.

He has a few double rhymes; and always, I think, unsuccessfully, except once in *The Rape of the Lock* [iii. 153–4].

Expletives he very early ejected from his verses; but he now and then admits an epithet rather commodious than important. Each of the six first lines of the *Iliad* might lose two syllables with very little diminution of the meaning [further, see No. 114]; and sometimes, after all his art and labour, one verse seems to be made for the sake of another. In his latter productions the diction is sometimes vitiated by French idioms, with which Bolingbroke had perhaps infected him.

I have been told that the couplet by which he declared his own ear to be most gratified was this:

> Lo, where Mæotis sleeps, and hardly flows
> The freezing Tanais thro' a waste of snows.
> [*The Dunciad* (B), iii. 67–8]

But the reason of this preference I cannot discover.

It is remarked by Watts, that there is scarcely a happy combination of words, or a phrase poetically elegant in the English language, which Pope has not inserted into his version of Homer.[1] How he obtained possession of so many beauties of speech it were desirable to know. That he gleaned from authors, obscure as well as eminent, what he thought brilliant or useful, and preserved it all in a regular collection, is not unlikely. When, in his last years, Hall's Satires were shewn him he wished that he had seen them sooner.

New sentiments and new images others may produce; but to attempt any further improvement of versification will be dangerous. Art and diligence have now done their best, and what shall be added will be the effort of tedious toil and needless curiosity.

After all this, it is surely superfluous to answer the question that has once been asked, Whether Pope was a poet? otherwise than by asking in return, If Pope be not a poet, where is poetry to be found? To circumscribe poetry by a definition will only shew the narrowness of the definer, though a definition which shall exclude Pope will not easily be made. Let us look round upon the present time, and back upon the past; let us enquire to whom the voice of mankind has decreed the wreath of poetry; let their productions be examined and their claims stated, and the pretensions of Pope will be no more disputed. Had he given the world only his version, the name of poet must have been allowed him: if the writer of the *Iliad* were to class his successors, he would assign a very high place to his translator, without requiring any other evidence of Genius. [pp. 161–208]

[1] [Probably a reference to No. 70]

128. Warton's *Essay*, volume ii

1782

Joseph Warton, extracts from *An Essay on the Genius and Writings of Pope*, ii (1782). The volume was reviewed in the *Monthly Magazine* in February 1782.

After publishing the first part of the *Essay* in 1756 (see No. 106), Warton delayed the appearance of the second half for twenty-six years. According to Warton's advertisement two hundred pages of the second part had been printed 'above twenty years ago'. Dodsley, his publisher, kept the sheets, and then finished the volume so that it corresponded to the format of the first volume. Later in 1782 Dodsley put the two volumes in a larger format, and shifted section seven from volume two to volume one in order to equalize their length. He thus produced the fifth edition of volume one and the second of volume two. The text given here is that of the first edition, with variants from the second edition given as footnotes. Warton also changed the title, altering *Writings and Genius* to *Genius and Writings*, in answer to Stockdale's objection (p. 469). Joan Pittock has recently concluded that Warton continued to write the second part between 1756 and 1782, but that the first two hundred pages were printed by 1760. She also gives an account of the reasons for which Warton delayed publication: see 'Joseph Warton and his Second Volume of the *Essay on Pope*', *Review of English Studies*, xviii (1968), 264–73. See also W. D. MacClintock, *Warton's Essay on Pope: A History of the Five Editions* (Chapel Hill, 1933). For a brief discussion of Warton's criticism, see Introduction, pp. 23–6.

[*The Temple of Fame*]

... Pope's alterations of Chaucer are introduced with judgment and art; that these alterations are more in number, and important in conduct, than any Dryden has made of the same author. This piece was communicated to Steele, who entertained a high opinion of its beauties, and who conveyed it to Addison. POPE had ornamented the poem with the machinery of guardian angels, which he afterwards omitted.

[pp. 62–3]

[*An Essay on Man*]

IF it be a true observation, that for a poet to write happily and well, he must have seen and felt what he describes, and must draw from living models alone; and if modern times, from their luxury and refinement, afford not manners that will bear to be described; it will then follow, that those species of poetry bid fairest to succeed at present, which treat of things, not men; which deliver doctrines, not display events. Of this sort is didactic and descriptive poetry. Accordingly the moderns have produced many excellent pieces of this kind. We may mention the Syphilis of Fracastorius, the Silkworms and Chess of Vida, the Ambra of Politian, the Agriculture of Alamanni, the Art of Poetry of Boileau, the Gardens of Rapin, the Cyder of Phillips, the Chase of Somerville, the Pleasures of Imagination, the Art of preserving Health, the Fleece, the Religion of Racine the younger, the elegant Latin poem of Brown on the Immortality of the Soul, the Latin poem of STAY,[1] and the philosophical poem before us.[2]

THE ESSAY ON MAN is as close a piece of argument, admitting its principles, as perhaps can be found in verse. POPE informs us in his FIRST preface, 'that he chose this epistolary way of writing, notwithstanding his subject was high, and of dignity, because of its being mixed with argument which of its nature approacheth to prose.' He has not wandered into any useless digressions, has employed no fictions, no tale or story, and has relied chiefly on the poetry of his stile, for the purpose of interesting his readers. His stile is concise and figurative, forcible and

---

[1] *poem of* STAY] *poems of* STAY *and* BOSCOVICK 1782b [Warton refers to Girolamo Fracastoro's *Syphilis* (1530), Marco Vida's imitations of Virgil's *Georgics, Bombyx* (1527) and the *Sacchia Ludus* (1527), the *Ambra* of Angelo Poliziano (1454–94), a Latin verse declamation on Homer, Luigi Alamanni's (1495–1556) *Coltivazione* on agriculture, Boileau's *L'art poetique* (1674), René Rapin's *Hortorum* (1665), translated into English in 1672, John Philips' *Cyder* (1708), William Somervile's *The Chace* (1735), Mark Akenside's *The Pleasures of the Imagination* (1744), John Armstrong's *The Art of Preserving Health* (1744), John Dyer's *The Fleece* (1757), Louis Racine's *La Religion* (1742), Isaac Browne's *De Animi Immortalitate* (1754), and to *Philosophiae versibus traditus* (1744) of Benedetto Stay (1714–1801), who wrote on scientific subjects in Latin verse]

[2] *us.*] ~ ; *to which, if we may judge from some beautiful fragments, we might have added Gray's didactic poem on Education and Government, had he lived to finish it. And the English Garden of Mr. Mason must not be omitted.* 1782b [Gray died in 1771, and his 'The Alliance of Education and Government' appeared posthumously in Mason's edition of the *Poems* (1775); Mason's poem was published in 1772]

elegant. He has many metaphors and images, artfully interspersed in the driest passages, which stood most in need of such ornaments. Nevertheless there are too many lines, in this performance, plain and prosaic. The meaner the subject is of a preceptive poem, the more striking appears the art of the poet: It is even of use to chuse a low subject. In this respect Virgil had the advantage over Lucretius; the latter with all his vigour and sublimity of genius, could hardly satisfy and come up to the grandeur of his theme. POPE labours under the same case. If any beauty in this Essay be uncommonly transcendent and peculiar, it is, BREVITY OF DICTION; which, in a few instances, and those pardonable, have occasioned obscurity. It is hardly to be imagined how much sense, how much thinking, how much observation on human life, is condensed together in a small compass. He was so accustomed to confine his thoughts in rhyme, that he tells us, he could express them more shortly this way, than in prose itself. On its first publication, POPE did not own it, and it was given by the public to Lord Paget, Dr. Young, Dr. Desaguliers, and others.[1] Even Swift seems to have been deceived: There is a remarkable passage in one of his letters. 'I confess I did never imagine you were so deep in morals, or that so many new and excellent rules could be produced so advantageously and agreeably in that science, from any one head. I confess in some places I was forced to read twice; I believe I told you before what the Duke of D—— said to me on that occasion; how a judge here who knows you, told him, that on the first reading those essays, he was much pleased, but found some lines a little dark: On the second, most of them cleared up, and his pleasure increased: On the third, he had no doubt remaining, and then he admired the whole.'[2]

THE subject of this Essay is a vindication of providence, in which the poet proposes to prove, that of all possible systems, infinite wisdom has formed the best: That in such a system, coherence, union, subordination, are necessary; and if so, that appearances of evil, both moral and natural, are also necessary and unavoidable; That the seeming defects and blemishes in the universe, conspire to its general beauty; That as all parts in an animal are not eyes, and as in a city, comedy, or picture, all ranks, characters, and colours, are not equal or alike; even so, excesses, and contrary qualities, contribute to the proportion and harmony of the

[1] [On the confusion which resulted from Pope's anonymity, see No. 80a. Thomas Catesby Paget, Lord Paget, published *An Essay on Human Life* (1734). John Desaguliers, F.R.S., was a popular scientific lecturer]
[2] [See No. 80f]

universal system; That it is not strange, that we should not be able to discover perfection and order in every instance; because, in an infinity of things mutually relative, a mind which sees not infinitely, can see nothing fully. This doctrine was inculcated by Plato and the Stoics, but more amply and particularly by the later Platonists, and by Antoninus and Simplicius.[1] In illustrating his subject, POPE has been deeply indebted to the Theodicée of Leibnitz, to Archbishop King's Origin of Evil, and to the Moralists of Lord Shaftesbury, more than to the philosophers abovementioned.[2] The late Lord Bathurst repeatedly assured me, that he had read the whole scheme of the Essay on Man, in the hand-writing of Bolingbroke, and drawn up in a series of propositions, which Pope was to versify and illustrate.[3] In doing which, our poet, it must be confessed, left several passages so expressed, as to be favourable to fatalism and necessity, notwithstanding all the pains that can be taken, and the turns that can be given to those passages, to place them on the side of religion, and make them coincide with the fundamental doctrines of revelation.

> 1. Awake,[4] my St John! leave all meaner things
> To low ambition, and the pride of kings;
> Let us (since life can little more supply
> Than just to look about us, and to die)
> Expatiate free o'er all this scene of man;
> A mighty maze! but not without a plan. [i. 1–6]

THIS opening is awful, and commands the attention of the reader. The word *awake* has peculiar force, and obliquely alludes to his noble friend's leaving his political, for philosophical pursuits. May I venture to observe, that the metaphors in the succeeding lines, drawn from the field sports of setting and shooting, seem below the dignity of the subject; especially,

> EYE nature's walks, SHOOT folly as it flies,
> And CATCH the manners living as they RISE. [i. 13–14]

[1] [Neoplatonists of the fourth and fifth centuries]

[2] [Leibniz's *Essais de Theodicée* (1710) was the only complete and systematic work published in his life; William King's *De Origine Mali* (1702) is discussed by Mack, Twickenham, III. i, pp. xxviiff.; Shaftesbury's *Moralists: a Philosophical Rhapsody* (1709) was included in his *Characteristics*]

[3] [Bolingbroke's opinions undoubtedly influenced *An Essay on Man*. Whether that influence extended as far as Bathurst told Warton, Blair and others is doubtful. See Introduction, p. 21]

[4] Jonson begins a poem thus: 'Wake! friend, from forth thy lethargy—' ['An Epistle to a Friend, to perswade him to the Warres', *Poems*, ed. G. B. Johnston (1954), p. 138]

2. But vindicate the ways of god to man,   [i. 16]

This line is taken from Milton;

> And justify the ways of god to man.[1]

POPE seems to have hinted, by this allusion to the Paradise Lost, that he intended his poem for a defence of providence, as well as Milton: but he took a very different method in pursuing that end.[2]

[pp. 118–25]

8. From burning suns when livid deaths descend,
    When earthquakes swallow, or when tempests sweep
    Towns to one grave, whole nations to the deep.   [i. 142–4]

I quote these lines as an example of energy of stile, and of POPE's manner of compressing together many images, without confusion, and without superfluous epithets. Substantives and verbs are the sinews of language. . . .

13. From the *green* myriads in the *peopled* grass—
    The mole's *dim* curtain, and the lynx's beam;
    Of smell the *headlong* lioness between,
    And hound sagacious on the *tainted* green—
    The spider's touch how exquisitely fine,
    Feels at each thread, and lives along the line.

[i. 210–18]

THESE lines are selected as admirable patterns of forcible diction. The peculiar and discriminating expressiveness of the epithets distinguished above by italics will be particularly regarded. Perhaps we have no image in the language, more lively than that of the last verse. 'To live along the line' is equally bold and beautiful. In this part of this Epistle the poet seems to have remarkably laboured his style, which abounds in various figures, and is much elevated. POPE has practised the great secret of Virgil's art, which was to discover the very single epithet that precisely suited each occasion. . . .

18. All are but parts of one stupendous whole,
    Whose body nature is and God the soul;
    That chang'd thro' all, and yet in all the same;
    Great in the earth, as in th' ætherial frame;

---

[1] [*Paradise Lost*, Book i. 26]

[2] end.] ~ ; *and imagined that the goodness and justice of the Deity might be defended*, without *having recourse to the doctrine of a future state, and of the depraved state of man. 1782b.*

> Warms in the sun, refreshes in the breeze,
> Glows in the stars, and blossoms in the trees;
> Lives thro' all life, extends thro' all extent,
> Spreads undivided, operates unspent;
> Breathes in our soul, informs our mortal part,
> As full as perfect in a hair as heart;
> As full as perfect in vile man that mourns,
> As the rapt seraph that adores aud burns:
> To him no high, no low, no great, no small;
> He fills, he bounds, connects, and equals all.   [i. 267–80]

WHILST I am transcribing this exalted description of the omni-presence of the Deity, I feel myself almost tempted to retract an assertion in the beginning of this work, that there is nothing transcendently sublime in POPE. These lines have all the energy and harmony that can be given to rhyme. . . .[1]

NOR have we a less example of sublimity in the three preceding lines, which describe the universal confusion that must ensue, upon any alteration made in the entire and coherent plan of the creation.

> Let earth unbalanced from her orbit fly,
> Planets and suns run lawless thro' the sky;
> Let ruling angels from their spheres be hurl'd,
> Being on being wreck'd, and world on world;
> Heav'n's whole foundations to their centre nod,
> And nature tremble to the throne of God.   [i. 251–6]

IT is very observable that these noble lines were added after the first edition. It is a pleasing amusement to trace out the alterations that a great writer gradually makes in his works. Many other parts of this epistle have been judiciously amended and improved.   [pp. 130–9]

[Moral Essays III: Epistle to Bathurst]

20. Like some *lone* Chartreux stands the good old hall,
    Silence without, and fasts within the wall;
    No *rafter'd* roofs with dance and tabor found,
    No *noontide* bell invites the country round:

---

[1] [Warton compares Pope's sublimity with that of the 'old Orphic verse', of which he gives an example]

Tenants with sighs the *smoakless* tow'rs survey,
And turn th' unwilling steeds another way:
Benighted wanderers, the forest o'er,
Curs'd the *sav'd candle,* and *unop'ning* door;
While the *gaunt* mastiff *growling* at the gate,
Affrights the beggar, whom he longs to eat.   [ll. 189–98]

In the worst inn's worst room, with *mat half*-hung,
The floors of *plaister,* and the *walls of dung,*
On once a *flock*-bed, but repair'd with *straw,*
With *tape-ty'd* curtains, never meant to draw,
The *George* and *Garter dangling* from that bed
Where *tawdry yellow* strove *with dirty red,*
Great Vill[i]ers lies.—   [ll. 299–305]

The use, the force, and the excellence of language, certainly consists
in raising, *clear, complete,* and *circumstantial* images, and in turning
readers into *spectators.* I have quoted the two preceding passages as
eminent examples of this excellence, of all others the most essential in
poetry. Every epithet, here used, *paints* its object, and *paints* it *distinctly.*
After having passed over the moat full of cresses, do you not *actually*
find yourself in the middle court of this forlorn and solitary mansion,
overgrown with docks and nettles? And do you not hear the dog that is
going to assault you?—Among the other fortunate circumstances that
attended Homer, it was not one of the least, that he wrote before
general and *abstract* terms were invented. Hence his Muse (like his own
Helen standing on the walls of Troy) points out every *person,* and
thing, accurately and *forcibly.*   [pp. 222–3]

21. Who hung with woods yon mountain's sultry brow?
From the dry rock who bade the waters flow?
Not to the[1] skies in useless columns tost
Or in proud falls magnificently lost;
But clear and artless, pouring thro' the plain,
Health to the sick, and solace to the swain.
Whose causeway parts the vale with shady rows?
Whose seats the weary traveller repose?
Who taught that heav'n-directed spire to rise?
'The Man of Ross,' each lisping babe replies.
Behold the market-place with poor o'erspread!
The Man of Ross divides the weekly bread.

[1] [Warton gives a long note rebutting Warburton's note on this passage

He feeds yon alms-house, neat, but void of state,
Where AGE and WANT sit smiling at the gate:
Him portion'd maids, apprentic'd orphans blest,
The young who labour, and the old who rest. [ll. 253–64]

THESE lines, which are eminently beautiful, particularly one of the three last, containing a fine prosopopœia, have conferred immortality on a plain, worthy, and useful citizen of Herefordshire, Mr. John Kyrle, who spent his long life in advancing and contriving plans of public utility. The HOWARD of his time: who deserves to be celebrated more than all the heroes of PINDAR. The particular reason for which I quoted them, was to observe the pleasing effect that the use of common and familiar words and objects, judiciously managed, produce in poetry. Such as are here the words, *causeway, seats, spire, market-place, alms-house, apprentic'd*. A fastidious delicacy, and a false refinement, in order to avoid meanness, have deterred our writers from the introduction of such words; but DRYDEN often hazarded it, and it gave a secret charm, and a natural air to his verses.[1]   [pp. 231–4]

[*Imitations of Horace*]

No part of our author's works have been more admired than these imitations. The aptness of the allusions, and the happiness of many of the parallels, give a pleasure that is always no small one to the mind of a reader, the pleasure of *comparison*. He that has the least acquaintance with these pieces of Horace, which resemble the *Old Comedy*, immediately perceives, indeed, that our author has assumed a higher tone, and frequently has deserted[2] the free colloquial air, the insinuating Socratic manner of his original. And that he clearly resembles in his style, as he did in his natural temper, the severe and serious Juvenal, more than the smiling and sportive Horace.   [pp. 337–8]

[*Imitations of Horace: Second and Fourth Satires of Dr. John Donne Versifyed*]

63. Two noblemen of taste and learning, the Duke of Shrewsbury and the Earl of Oxford, desired POPE to melt down and cast anew the

---

[1] *verses.*] ~, *well knowing of what consequence it was sometimes to soften and subdue his tints, and not to paint and adorn every object he touched, with perpetual pomp and unremitted splendor.* 1782b.
[2] [Warton has a footnote in praise of Horace]

weighty bullion of Dr. Donne's satires; who had degraded and deformed a vast fund of sterling wit and strong sense, by the most harsh and uncouth diction. POPE succeeded in giving harmony to a writer, more rough and rugged than even any of his age, and who profited so little by the example *Spencer* had set, of a most musical and mellifluous versification; far beyond that of *Fairfax*, who is so frequently mentioned as the greatest improver of the harmony of our language.

[pp. 421–2]

[Imitations of Horace: Epilogue to the Satires]

64. THE two Dialogues, entitled One thousand seven hundred and thirty-eight, which are the last pieces that belong to this section, were more frequently transcribed, and received more alterations and corrections, than almost any of the foregoing poems. By long habit of writing, and almost constantly in one sort of measure, he had now arrived at a happy and elegant familiarity of style, without flatness. The satire in these pieces is of the strongest kind; sometimes, direct and declamatory, at others, ironical and oblique. It must be owned to be carried to excess. Our country is represented as totally ruined, and overwhelmed with dissipation, depravity, and corruption. Yet this very country, so emasculated and debased by every species of folly and wickedness, in about twenty years afterwards, carried its triumphs over all its enemies, through all the quarters[1] of the world, and astonished the most distant nations with a display of uncommon efforts, abilities, and virtues. So vain and groundless are the prognostications of poets, as well as politicians. It is to be lamented, that no genius could be found to write an *One Thousand Seven Hundred and Sixty-one*, as a counterpart to these two satires. Several passages deserve particular notice and applause. The design of the Friend, introduced in these dialogues, is to dissuade our poet from *personal* invectives. He desires him to copy the sly, insinuating style of Horace; and dextrously turns the very advice he is giving into the bitterest satire.

> Horace would say, Sir Billy *serv'd the Crown*,
> Blunt could *do business*, H—ggins *knew the town*:

---

[1] We cannot ascribe these successes, as M. de Voltaire does, to the effects of *Brown's Estimate*. See Additions à l'Hist. Generale, p. 409. [John Brown's *Estimate of the Manners and Principles of the Times* was published in 1757]

In Sappho touch the *failings* of the sex,
In rev'rend bishops note some *small neglects*;
And own the Spaniard did a *waggish* thing,
Who cropt our ears and sent them to the king.

[*Epilogue to the Satires*, i. 13–18]

[pp. 425–7]

I CONCLUDE this section by observing, that these Dialogues exhibit many marks of our author's petulance, party-spirit, and self-importance, and of assuming to himself the character of a general censor; who, alas! if he had possessed a thousand times more genius and ability than he actually enjoyed, could not alter or amend the manners of a rich and commercial, and, consequently, of a luxurious and dissipated nation.[1]

[pp. 438–9]

[*The Dunciad*]

But in the year 1742, our poet was persuaded, unhappily enough, to add a *fourth* book to his *finished* piece, of such a very different cast and colour, as to render it at last one of the most motley compositions, that perhaps is any where to be found, in the works of so exact a writer as POPE. For one great purpose of this *fourth* book, (where, by the way, the hero does nothing at all) was to satirize and proscribe infidels, and free-thinkers, to leave the ludicrous for the serious, Grub-street for theology, the mock-heroic for metaphysics; which occasioned a marvellous mixture and jumble of images and sentiments, Pantomime and Philosophy, Journals and Moral evidence, Fleet-ditch and the High Priori road, *Curl* and *Clarke*.—To ridicule our fashionable libertines,[2] and affected minute philosophers, was doubtless a most laudable intention; but speaking of the Dunciad as a work of art, in a critical not a religious light, we must[3] venture to affirm, that the subject of this fourth book was foreign and heterogeneous, and the addition of it as injudicious, ill-placed, and incongruous, as any of those dissimilar images we meet with in *Pulci* or *Ariosto*. It is like introducing a crucifix into one of *Teniers*'s burlesque conversation-pieces. Some of his most splendid and striking lines are indeed here to be found; but we must beg leave to insist that they want *propriety* and *decorum*, and must wish they had

---

[1] *nation.*] ~ . *We make ourselves unhappy, by hoping to possess* incompatible *things; we want to have wealth, without corruption and liberty without virtue.* 1782b.

[2] *fashionable libertines*] petulant ~ 1782b.

[3] *we must*] I ~ 1782b.

adorned some *separate* work, against irreligion, which would have been worthy the pen of our bitter and immortal satirist.

But neither was this the only alteration the Dunciad was destined to undergo. For in the year 1743, our author, enraged with *Cibber*, (whom he had usually treated with contempt ever since the affair of *Three Hours after Marriage*) for publishing a ridiculous pamphlet against him, dethroned *Tibbald*, and made the Laureate the hero of his poem. *Cibber*, with a great stock of levity, vanity, and affectation, had sense, and wit, and humour. And the author of the *Careless Husband*, was by no means a proper king of the dunces. 'His treatise on the Stage,' says Mr. Walpole, 'is inimitable: where an author writes on his own profession, feels it profoundly, and is sensible his readers do not, he is not only excusable but meritorious, for illuminating the subject by new metaphors, or bolder figures than ordinary. He is the *coxcomb* that sneers, not he that instructs by appropriated diction.' The consequence of this alteration was, that many lines, which exactly suited the heavy character of *Tibbald*, lost all their grace and propriety when applied[1] to *Cibber*. Such as,

> Sinking from thought to thought, a vast profound! [i. 118]

Such also is the description of his gothic library; for Cibber troubled not himself with *Caxton*, *Wynkyn*, and *De Lyra*. *Tibbald*, who was an antiquarian, had collected these curious old writers. And to slumber in the Goddess's lap was adapted to *his stupidity*, not to the *vivacity* of his successor. [pp. 443–7]

. . . In Book iv. the Genius of the schools is made to declare, ll. 150–60, that,

> Words are man's province, words we teach alone. . . .
> Confine the thought, to exercise the breath,
> And keep them in the pale of words till death.

Surely our author, when he passed this censure, was ill-informed of what was taught and expected in our great schools; namely, besides reading, interpreting, and translating the best writers[2] of the best ages, to be able to compose Essays, Declamations, and Verses, in *Greek*, in

---

[1] 'Tis dangerous to disoblige a great poet or painter. *Dante* placed his master *Brunetto* in his *Inferno*. And *Michael Angelo* placed the Pope's master of the ceremonies, *Biaggio* in hell, in his Last Judgment. 1782b adds a note on Brunnetti]

[2] writers] *poets, orators, and historians* 1782b.

Latin, and in *English;* and in some, to write critical remarks on Homer, Sophocles, Demosthenes, *Aristotle's* Poetics, or *Longinus;* an exercise not of the memory, but judgment. And as to *plying* the *memory,* and *loading* the *brain* (see verse 157) it was the opinion of Milton, and is a practice in our great schools,[1] 'that if passages from the heroic poems, orations, and tragedies of the ancients were solemnly pronounced, with right accent and grace, as might be taught, *(and is)* they would endue the scholars even with the spirit and vigour of *Demosthenes* or *Cicero, Euripides* or *Sophocles.*'[2] The illustrious names of *Wyndham, Talbot, Murray,* and *Pulteney,* which our author himself immediately adds, and which catalogue might be much enlarged, with the names of many great statesmen, lawyers, and divines, are a strong confutation of this opprobrious opinion. In Book iv. 211–52 is just such another breach of truth and decorum as was remarked above, in making *Aristarchus* (*Bentley*) abuse *himself,* and laugh at *his own* labours:

> Thy mighty scholiast, whose unweary'd pains
> Made Horace dull, and humbled [Milton's][3] strains.
> Turn what they will to verse, their toil is vain,
> Critics like *Me,* shall make it prose again. . . .
> For attic phrase in Plato let them seek,
> I poach in Suidas for unlicens'd Greek.—
> For thee we dim the eyes, and stuff the head,
> With all such reading, as was never read;
> For thee explain a thing till all men doubt it,
> And write about it, Goddess! and about it.

LASTLY, in this 4th book, the sudden appearance of Annius, l. 347, of Mummius, 371, and of a gloomy clerk, l. 459, make this part of the poem obscure, as we know not who these personages are, nor whence they came. After all, the chief fault of the *Dunciad* is the violence and vehemence[4] of its satire, and the excessive height to which it is

---

[1] *schools*] *seminaries* 1782b Warton also added a footnote: 'What is said on this subject by Quintilian, b. 1. and 2. is as much superior to Locke's Treatise on Education, in strength of reasoning, as it is in elegance of style.']

[2] [Warton paraphrases and quotes from 'Of Education', *Complete Prose Works of Milton,* ed. D. Bush *et al.* (New York, 1951–6), ii. 400–1]

[3] [Warton has 'Maro's']

[4] Which sour the temper of the reader; insomuch that I know a person, whose name would be an ornament to these papers, if I was suffered to insert it, who, after reading a book of the Dunciad, always *sooths* himself, as he calls it, by turning to a canto in the Fairy Queen. This is not the case in that very delightful and beautiful poem, *Mac Flecnoe,* from which Pope has borrowed so many hints, and images, and ideas. But Dryden's poem was

carried; and which therefore I have heard compared to that marvellous column of boiling water, near mount *Hecla*, thrown upwards, above ninety feet, by the force of a subterraneous fire.[1]   [pp. 450–53]

[Conclusions]

THUS have we endeavoured to give a critical account, with freedom, but it is hoped with impartiality, of each of POPE's works; by which review it will appear, that the *largest* portion of them is of the *didactic*, *moral*, and *satyric* kind; and consequently, not of the most *poetic* species *of poetry*; whence it is manifest, that *good sense* and *judgment* were his characteristical excellencies, rather than *fancy* and *invention*; not that the author of the *Rape of the Lock*, and *Eloisa*, can be thought to want *imagination*, but because his *imagination* was not his predominant talent, because he indulged it not, and because he gave not so many proofs of *this* talent as of the *other*. This turn of mind led him to admire French models; he studied *Boileau* attentively; formed himself upon *him*, as *Milton* formed himself upon the Grecian and Italian sons of *Fancy*.[2] He gradually became one of the most correct, even, and exact poets that ever wrote; polishing his pieces with a care and assiduity, that no business or avocation ever interrupted: so that if he does not frequently ravish and transport his reader, yet he does not disgust him with unexpected inequalities, and absurd improprieties. Whatever poetical enthusiasm he actually possessed, he withheld and stifled. The perusal of him affects not our minds with such strong emotions as we feel from *Homer* and *Milton*; so that no man of a true poetical spirit, *is master of himself while he reads* them. Hence, he is a writer fit for universal

---

[1] It is in a valley in Iceland, about sixty miles from the sea; it is called the fountain of *Geiser*. Sir Joseph Banks, our great philosophical traveller, had the satisfaction of seeing this wonderful phænomenon.

[2] Fancy.] ~ . *He stuck to describing* modern manners; *but those* manners, *because they are* familiar, uniform, artificial, *and* polished, *are, in their very nature, unfit for any lofty effort of the Muse.* 1782b.

---

the offspring of *contempt*, and Pope's of *indignation*: one is full of *mirth*, and the other of *malignity*. A vein of pleasantry is uniformly preserved through the whole of Mac Flecnoe, and the piece begins and ends in the *same key*. It is natural and obvious to borrow a metaphor from music, when we are speaking of a poem whose versification is particularly and exquisitely sweet and harmonious. The numbers of the Dunciad, by being much laboured, and encumbered with epithets, have something in them of stiffness and harshness. Since the total decay of learning was foretold in the Dunciad, how many very excellent pieces of *Criticism, Poetry, History, Philosophy*, and *Divinity*, have appeared in this country, and to what a degree of perfection has almost every art, either useful or elegant, been carried!

perusal; adapted to all ages and stations; for the old and for the young; the man of business and the scholar. He who would think *Palamon* and *Arcite*, the *Tempest* or *Comus*, childish and romantic, might relish POPE. Surely it is no narrow and niggardly encomium to say he is the great Poet of Reason, the *First* of *Ethical* authors in verse. And this species of writing is, after all, the surest road to an extensive reputation. It lies more level to the general capacities of men, than the higher flights of more genuine poetry. We all remember when even a *Churchill* was more in vogue than a *Gray*. He that treats of fashionable follies, and the topics of the day, that describes present persons and recent events, finds many readers, whose understandings and whose passions he gratifies. The name of *Chesterfield* on one hand, and of *Walpole* on the other, failed not to make a poem bought up and talked of. And it cannot be doubted, that the Odes of Horace which celebrated, and the satires which ridiculed, well-known and real characters at Rome, were more eagerly read, and more frequently cited, than the Æneid and the Georgic of Virgil.

Where then, according to the question proposed at the *beginning of this Essay*, shall we with justice be authorized to place our admired POPE? Not, assuredly, in the same rank with *Spencer*, *Shakespeare*, and *Milton*; however justly we may applaud the *Eloisa* and *Rape* of the *Lock*; but, considering the correctness, elegance, and utility of his works, the weight of sentiment, and the knowledge of man they contain, we may venture to assign him a place, *next to Milton*, and *just above Dryden*. Yet, to bring our minds steadily to make this decision, we must forget, for a moment, the divine *Music Ode* of *Dryden*; and may perhaps then be compelled to confess, that though *Dryden* be the greater genius, yet *Pope* is the better artist.

THE preference here given to POPE, above other modern English poets, it must be remembered, is founded on the excellencies of his works *in general*, and *taken all together*; for there are *parts* and *passages* in other modern authors, in *Young* and in *Thomson*, for instance, equal to any of POPE; and he has written nothing in a strain so truly sublime, as the *Bard* of *Gray*.   [pp. 477–81]

129. Hayley on Pope's genius and his satire

1782

William Hayley (1745–1820), the last lines and note to Epistle III, l. 475, of his *Essay on Epic Poetry* (1782), *Poems and Plays By William Hayley Esq.* (1788), iii. 76, iv. 211–16. The *Gentleman's Magazine* lists Hayley's poem for December 1782.

> Yet peace—new music floats on Æther's wings;
> Say, is it Harmony herself who sings?
> No! while enraptur'd Sylphs the Song inspire,
> 'Tis POPE who sweetly wakes the silver lyre
> To melting notes, more musically clear
> Than Ariel whisper'd in Belinda's ear.
> Too soon he quits them for a sharper tone;
> See him, tho' form'd to fill the Epic throne,
> Decline the sceptre of that wide domain,
> To bear a Lictor's rod in Satire's train;
> And, shrouded in a mist of moral spleen,
> Behold him close the visionary scene!   [iii. 76]

NOTE XVIII. VERSE 475.

And, shrouded in a mist of moral spleen.] It seems to be the peculiar infelicity of Pope, that his moral virtues have had a tendency to diminish his poetical reputation. Possessing a benevolent spirit, and wishing to make the art to which he devoted his life, as serviceable as he could to the great interests of mankind, he soon quitted the higher regions of poetry, for the more level, and more frequented field of Ethics and of Satire. He declares, with a noble pride arising from the probity of his intention,

> That not in Fancy's maze he wander'd long,
> But stoop'd to truth, and moraliz'd his song.
> [*Epistle to Dr. Arbuthnot*, ll. 340–1]

522

The severity of Criticism has from hence inferred, that his imagination was inferior to the other faculties of his mind, and that he possessed not that vigour of genius which might enable him to rank with our more sublime and pathetic Bards. This inference appears to me extremely defective both in candour and in reason; it would surely be more generous, and I will venture to add, more just, to assign very different causes for his having latterly applied himself to moral and satyric composition. If his preceding poems displayed only a moderate portion of fancy and of tenderness, we might indeed very fairly conjecture, that he quitted the kind of poetry, where these qualities are particularly required, because Nature directed him to shine only as the Poet of reason.—But his earlier productions will authorize an opposite conclusion. At an age when few authors have produced any capital work, Pope gave the world two poems, one the offspring of imagination, and the other of sensibility, which will ever stand at the head of the two poetical classes to which they belong: his Rape of the Lock, and his Eloise, have nothing to fear from any rivals, either of past or of future time. When a writer has displayed such early proofs of exquisite fancy, and of tender enthusiasm, those great constituents of the real Poet, ought we not to regret that he did not give a greater scope and freer exercise to these qualities, rather than to assert that he did not possess them in a superlative degree?—Why then, it may be asked, did he confine himself to compositions in which these have little share? The life and character of Pope will perfectly explain the reasons, why he did not always follow the higher suggestions of his own natural genius. He had entertained an opinion, that by stooping to truth, and employing his talents on the vices and follies of the passing time, he should be most able to benefit mankind. The idea was perhaps ill-founded, but his conduct in consequence of it was certainly noble. Its effects however were most unhappy; for it took from him all his enjoyment of life, and may injure, in some degree, his immortal reputation: by suffering his thoughts to dwell too much on knaves and fools, he fell into the splenetic delusion, that the world is nothing but a compound of vice and folly; and from hence he has been reproached for supposing that all human merit was confined to himself, and to a few of his most intimate correspondents.

There was an amiable peculiarity in the character of Pope, which had great influence both on his conduct and composition—he embraced the sentiments of those he loved with a kind of superstitious regard; his imagination and his judgment were perpetually the dupes of an affectionate heart: it was this which led him, at the request of his idol Bolingbroke, to write a sublime poem on metaphysical ideas which he did not perfectly comprehend; it was this which urged him almost to quarrel with Mr. Allen, in compliance with the caprices of a female friend;[1] it was this which induced him, in the warmth of gratitude, to follow the absurd hints of Warburton with all the blindness of infatuated affection. Whoever examines the life and writings of Pope with a minute and unprejudiced attention, will find that his excellencies, both as a Poet and a Man, were peculiarly his own; and that his failings were chiefly owing to the ill judgment, or the artifice, of his real and pretended friends. The lavish applause and the advice of his favourite Atterbury [see p. 16 above], were perhaps the cause of his preserving the famous character of Addison, which, finely written as it is, all the lovers of Pope must wish him to have suppressed. Few of his friends had integrity or frankness sufficient to persuade him, that his satires would destroy the tranquillity of his life, and cloud the lustre of his fame: yet, to the honour of Lyttelton, be it remembered, that he suggested such ideas to the Poet, in the verses which he wrote to him from Rome, with all the becoming zeal of enlightened friendship:

> No more let meaner Satire dim the rays
> That flow majestic from thy nobler bays!
> In all the flowery paths of Pindus stray,
> But shun that thorny, that unpleasing way!
> Nor, when each soft, engaging Muse is thine,
> Address the least attractive of the Nine![2]

This generous admonition did not indeed produce its intended effect, for other counsellors had given a different bias to the mind of the Poet, and the malignity of his enemies had exasperated his temper; yet he afterwards turned his thoughts towards the composition of a national Epic poem, and possibly in consequence of the hint which this Epistle of Lyttelton contains. The intention was formed too late, for it arose in his decline of life. Had he possessed health and leisure to execute such a work, I am persuaded it would have proved a glorious acquisition to the literature of our country: the subject indeed which he had chosen must be allowed to have an unpromising appearance; but the opinion of Addison concerning his Sylphs, which was surely honest, and not invidious, may teach us hardly ever to decide against the intended works of a superior genius. Yet in all the Arts we are

[1] [See Spence, *Anecdotes*, i. 159–60]   [2] [See No. 62]

perpetually tempted to pronounce such decisions. I have frequently condemned subjects which my friend Romney had selected for the pencil; but in the sequel, my opinion only proved that I was near-sighted in those regions of imagination, where his keener eyes commanded all the prospect. [iv. 211-16]

130. Johnson on 'whit'

1782

Conversation between Dr Samuel Johnson and William Weller Pepys on 29 October 1782, reported by Fanny Burney, *Diary and Letters of Madame D'Arblay . . . edited by her Niece*, ii. (1842), 164-5. Johnson, who was visiting Brighton at the same time as Mrs Thrale, had already argued with Pepys (1740-1825) in June 1781. Ailing and discouraged, Johnson's ill-temper was only too evident to others. Further, see J. L. Clifford, *Hester Lynch Piozzi* (1941), pp. 197, 212, and Boswell's *Life*, ed. L. F. Powell (1934-50), iv. 65n., 487-8.

The sum of the dispute was this. Wit being talked of, Mr. Pepys repeated,—

> True wit is Nature to advantage dress'd,
> What oft was thought, but ne'er so well express'd.
> [*An Essay on Criticism*, ll. 97-8]

'That, sir,' cried Dr. Johnson, 'is a definition both false and foolish. Let wit be dressed how it will, it will equally be wit, and neither the more nor the less for any advantage dress can give it.'

Mr. P. But, sir, may not wit be so ill expressed, and so obscure, by a bad speaker, as to be lost?

Dr. J. The fault, then, sir, must be with the hearer. If a man cannot distinguish wit from words, he little deserves to hear it.

Mr. P. But, sir, what Pope means—

Dr. J. Sir, what Pope means, if he means what he says, is both false and foolish. In the first place, 'what oft was thought,' is all the worse for being often thought, because to be wit, it ought to be newly thought.

Mr. P. But, sir, 't is the expression makes it new.

Dr. J. How can the expression make it new? It may make it clear, or may make it elegant; but how new? You are confounding words with things.

Mr. P. But, sir, if one man says a thing very ill, may not another man say it so much better that—

Dr. J. That other man, sir, deserves but small praise for the amendment; he is but the tailor to the first man's thoughts.

Mr. P. True, sir, he may be but the tailor; but then the difference is as great as between a man in a gold lace suit and a man in a blanket.

Dr. J. Just so, sir, I thank you for that: the difference is precisely such, since it consists neither in the gold lace suit nor the blanket, but in the man by whom they are worn.

This was the summary; the various contemptuous sarcasms intermixed would fill, and very unpleasantly, a quire.

131. Vicesimus Knox on the two parties in English poetry

1782

Vicesimus Knox, *Essays Moral and Literary* ('New Edition', 1782), ii. 186–7.

I think it is not difficult to perceive, that the admirers of English poetry are divided into two parties. The objects of their love are, perhaps, of equal beauty, though they greatly differ in their air, their dress, the turn of their features, and their complexion. On one side, are the lovers and imitators of Spenser and Milton; and on the other, those of Dryden, Boileau, and Pope.

Now it happens, unfortunately, that those who are in love with one of these forms are, sometimes, so blind to the charms of the other, as to dispute their existence. The author of the essay on Pope [Warton], who is himself a very agreeable poet, and of what I call the old school of English poetry, seems to deny the justice of Mr. Pope's claim to the title of a true poet, and to appropriate to him the subordinate character of a satyrical versifier. On the other hand, the authors of the Traveller [Goldsmith], and of the Lives of the English Poets [Johnson], hesitate not to strip the laurels from the brow of the Lyric Gray.

Goldsmith, in his Life of Parnell, has invidiously compared the Night Piece on Death to Gray's Elegy; and in a manner which betrays a little jealousy of a living poet's fame, given the preference to Parnell. There is also a little censure thrown on the elegy, in a collection which Goldsmith published under the title of the Beauties of English Poetry. I remember to have heard Goldsmith converse, when I was very young, on several subjects of literature, and make some oblique and severe reflections on the fashionable poetry. I became a convert to his opinion, because I revered his authority. I took up the odes of Gray with un-favourable prepossessions, and in writing my remarks on them, joined in the censure. I have since read them with great delight, and on com-paring their style, and even their obscurity, with many of the finest pieces of Lyric composition in all antiquity, I find a very great resemblance. I am not ashamed to retract my former opinion, and to pay the tribute of applause to those elegant friends, Gray and Mason. At the same time, while it is easy to discern that they differ greatly from the school of Dryden and Pope, it is no derogation from their merit to assert, that they are the genuine disciples of Spenser and Milton. Such also are the very elegant and learned brothers, one of whom presides, with so much honour, over the school at Winchester, and the other has written an elegant and elaborate history of that English poetry in which himself excels.

APPENDIX A

Pope on versification

1706(?)

Pope to William Walsh, 22 October, *Corresp.*, i. 22–5. This letter is fabricated from one to Henry Cromwell, dated 25 November 1710. Sherburn remarks, 'Evidently he felt inclined to emphasise the influence of Walsh, and had relatively few Walsh letters to print.'

After the Thoughts I have already sent you on the subject of *English* Versification, you desire my opinion as to some farther particulars. There are indeed certain Niceties, which tho' not much observed even by correct Versifiers, I cannot but think deserve to be better regarded.

  1. It is not enough that nothing offends the Ear, but a good Poet will adapt the very Sounds, as well as Words, to the things he treats of. So that there is (if one may express it so) a Style of Sound. As in describing a gliding Stream, the Numbers shou'd run easy and flowing; in describing a rough Torrent or Deluge, sonorous and swelling, and so of the rest. This is evident every where in *Homer* and *Virgil*, and no where else that I know of to any observable degree. The following Examples will make this plain, which I have taken from *Vida*.

> Molle viam tacito lapsu per levia radit.
> Incedit tardo molimine subsidendo.
> Luctantes ventos, tempestatesque sonoras.
> Immenso cum præcipitans ruit Oceano Nox.
> Telum imbelle sine ictu, Conjecit.
> Tolle moras, cape saxa manu, cape robora Pastor,
> Ferte citi flammas data tela, repellite pestem.[1]

[1] [The sources of these lines, in order, are: Vida, *Ars poetica*, iii. 374, 376; *Aeneid*, i. 53; Vida, iii. 425; *Aeneid*, ii. 544–5 (combined); Vida, iii. 422, 423]

This, I think, is what very few observe in practice, and is undoubtedly of wonderful force in imprinting the Image on the reader: We have one excellent Example of it in our Language, Mr. *Dryden*'s Ode on St. *Cæcilia*'s Day, entitled, *Alexander's Feast*.

2. Every nice Ear, must (I believe) have observ'd, that in any smooth *English* Verse of ten syllables, there is naturally a *Pause* at the fourth, fifth, or sixth syllable. It is upon these the Ear rests, and upon the judicious Change and Management of which depends the Variety of Versification. For example,

At the fifth. *Where-e'er thy Navy* || *spreads her canvass Wings,*
At the fourth. *Homage to thee* || *and Peace to all she brings.*[1]
At the sixth. *Like Tracts of Leverets* || *in Morning Snow.*[2]

Now I fancy, that to preserve an exact Harmony and Variety, the Pauses of the 4th or 6th shou'd not be continu'd above three lines together, without the Interposition of another; else it will be apt to weary the Ear with one continu'd Tone, at least it does mine: That at the 5th runs quicker, and carries not quite so dead a weight, so tires not so much tho' it be continued longer.

3. Another nicety is in relation to *Expletives*, whether Words or Syllables, which are made use of purely to supply a vacancy: *Do* before Verbs plural is absolutely such; and it is not improbable but future Refiners may explode *did* and *does* in the same manner, which are almost always used for the sake of Rhime. The same Cause has occasioned the promiscuous use of *You* and *Thou* to the same Person, which can never sound so graceful as either one or the other.

4. I would also object to the Irruption of *Alexandrine* Verses of twelve syllables, which I think should never be allow'd but when some remarkable Beauty or Propriety in them attones for the Liberty: Mr. *Dryden* has been too free of these, especially in his latter Works. I am of the same opinion as to *Triple Rhimes*.

5. I could equally object to the *Repetition* of the same Rhimes within four or six lines of each other, as tiresome to the Ear thro' their Monotony.

6. *Monosyllable-Lines*, unless very artfully managed, are stiff, or languishing: but may be beautiful to express Melancholy, Slowness, or Labour.

7. To come to the *Hiatus*, or Gap between two words which is

---

[1] [Waller, 'To the King on his Navy, in the Year 1726']
[2] [Waller, 'Of a tree cut in Paper']

caus'd by two Vowels opening on each other (upon which you desire
me to be particular) I think the rule in this case is either to use the
Cæsura, or admit the *Hiatus,* just as the Ear is least shock'd by either:
For the *Cæsura* sometimes offends the Ear more than the *Hiatus*
itself, and our language is naturally overcharg'd with Consonants: As
for example; If in this Verse,

> *The Old have Int'rest ever in their Eye,*

we should say, to avoid the *Hiatus,*

> *But th' Old have Int'rest—*

The *Hiatus* which has the worst effect, is when one word ends with
the same Vowel that begins the following; and next to this, those
Vowels whose sounds come nearest to each other are most to be
avoided. O, A, or U, will bear a more full and graceful Sound than
E, I, or Y. I know some people will think these Observations trivial,
and therefore I am glad to corroborate them by some great Authorities,
which I have met with in *Tully* and *Quintilian.* In the fourth Book of
Rhetoric to *Herennius,*[1] are these words: *Fugiemus crebras Vocalium
concursiones, quæ vastam atque hiantem reddunt orationem; ut hoc est,
Baccæ æneæ amænissimæ impendebant.* And Quintilian *l. 9. cap. 4.
Vocalium concursus cum accidit, hiat & intersistit, at quasi laborat oratio.
Pessimi longè quæ easdem inter se literas committunt, sonabunt: Præcipuus
tamen erit hiatus earum quæ cavo aut patulo ore efferuntur. E plenior
litera est, I angustior.* But he goes on to reprove the excess on the other
hand of being too sollicitious in this matter, and says admirably, *Nescio
an negligentia in hoc, aut solicitudo sit pejor.* So likewise *Tully* (*Orator
ad Brut.*)[2] *Theopompum reprehendunt, quod eas literas tanto opere fugerit,
etsi idem magister ejus Isocrates:* which last Author, as *Turnebus* on
Quintilian observe, has hardly one *Hiatus* in all his Works. *Quintilian*
tells us that *Tully* and *Demosthenes* did not much observe this Nicety,
tho' *Tully* himself says in his Orator, *Crebra ista Vocum concursio, quam
magna ex parte vitiosam, fugit Demosthenes.*[3] If I am not mistaken,
Malherbe of all the Moderns has been the most scrupulous in this point;
and I think *Menage* in his Observations upon him says, he has not one in
his Poems. To conclude, I believe the *Hiatus* should be avoided with
more care in Poetry than in Oratory; and I would constantly try to
prevent it, unless where the cutting it off is more prejudicial to the
Sound than the *Hiatus* itself. I am, &c.

---

[1] [*Ad Herennium,* IV. xii]   [2] [*Orator,* xliv. 151]   [3] [*Ibid.*]

APPENDIX B

'The Ballance of Poets'

1745

From Robert Dodsley's *The Museum: or, the Literary and Historical Register*, no. xix, 6 December 1745 (1746 ed.), ii. 165–9.

SIR,

M. *De Piles* is one of the most judicious Authors on the Art of Painting. He has added to his Treatise on that Subject, a very curious Paper, which he calls *The Ballance of the Painters*. He divides the whole Art of Painting into four Heads; Composition, Design, or Drawing, Colouring, and Expression; under each of which, he assigns the Degree of Perfection which the several Masters have attained. To this End he first settles the Degree of sovereign Perfection, which has never been attain'd, and which is beyond even the Taste of Knowledge of the best Criticks at present; this he rates as the twentieth Degree. The nineteenth Degree is the highest of which the human Mind has any Comprehension, but which has not yet been expressed or executed by the greatest Masters. The eighteenth is that to which the greatest Masters have actually attained; and so downwards according to their comparative Genius and Skill. *Monsieur de Piles* makes four Columns of his chief Articles or Parts of Painting; and opposite to the Names of the great Masters, writes their several Degrees of Perfection in each Article. The Thought is very ingenious; and had it been executed with Accuracy, and a just Rigour of Taste, would have been of the greatest use to the Lovers of that noble Art. But we can hardly expect that any Man should be exactly right in his Judgment, through such a Multiplicity of the most delicate Ideas.

I have often wished to see a Ballance of this Kind, that might help to settle our comparative Esteem of the greater *Poets* in the several polite Languages. But as I have never seen nor heard of any such Design, I have here attempted it myself, according to the best Information which my private Taste could afford me. I shall be extremely glad if any of your ingenious Correspondents will correct me where I am wrong; and in the mean Time shall explain the general Foundations of my Scheme, where it differs from that of the *French* Author. For he has not taken in a sufficient Number of Articles, to form a compleat Judgment of the Art of Painting; and though he had, yet Poetry requires many more. I shall retain his Numbers, and suppose twenty to be the Degree of absolute Perfection; and eighteen the highest that any Poet has attained.

His first Article is Composition; in which his Ballance is quite equivocal and uncertain. For there are, in Painting, two sorts of Composition, utterly different from each other. One relates only to the Eye, the other to the Passions: So that the former may be not improperly stiled *picturesque* Composition, and is concerned only with such a Disposition of the Figures, as may render the whole Group of the Picture intire and well united; the latter is concerned with such Attitudes and Connections of the Figures, as may effectually touch the Passions of the Spectator. There are, in Poetry, two analogous kinds of Composition or Ordonnance; one of which belongs to the general Plan or Structure of the Work, and is an Object of the cool Judgment of a Connoisseur; the other relates to the most striking Situations, and the most moving Incidents. And tho' these are most strictly connected in Truth and in the Principles of Art, yet in Fact, we see them very frequently disjoined; and they depend indeed on different Powers of the Mind. Sir *Richard Blackmore*, a Name for Contempt, or for Oblivion in the Commonwealth of Poetry, had more of the former than *Shakespear*; who had more of the latter than any Man that ever lived. The former we shall call *Critical Ordonnance*, the latter *Pathetick*. And these make the two first Columns of our Ballance.

It may perhaps be necessary to observe here, that though literally speaking, these two Articles relate only to Epic and Dramatic Poetry; yet we shall apply them to every other Species. For in Lyric Poetry, in Satire, in Comedy, in the Ethic Epistle, one Author may excell another in the general Plan and Disposition of his Work; and yet fall short of him in the Arguments, Allusions, and other Circumstances, which he employs to move his Reader, and to obtain the End of his particular Composition.

Our next Article answers to that which *Monsieur de Piles* calls *Expression*; but this likewise, in Poetry, requires two Columns. Painting represents only a single Instant of Time; consequently it expresses only a present Passion, without giving any Idea of the general

Character or Turn of Mind. But Poetry expresses this part, as well as the other; and the same Poet is not equally excellent in both. *Homer* far surpasses *Virgil* in the general Delineation of Characters and Manners; but there are, in *Virgil*, some Expressions of particular Passions, greatly superior to any in *Homer*. I shall therefore divide this Head of *Expression*, and call the former Part *Dramatic Expression*, and the latter *Incidental*.

Our next Article answers to what the Painters call *Design*, or the Purity, Beauty, and Grandeur of the Outline in Drawing; to which the Taste of Beauty in Description, and the Truth of Expression, are analogous in Poetry. But as the Term *Design*, except among Painters, is generally supposed to mean the general Plan and Contrivance of a Work; I shall therefore omit it, to prevent Mistakes; and substitute instead of it, *The Truth of Taste*, by which to distinguish the fifth Column. And indeed, this Article would likewise admit of several Subdivisions; for some Poets are excellent for the Grandeur of their Taste, others for its Beauty, and others for a kind of Neatness. But they may all be rang'd under the same Head; as *Michael Angelo*, *Raphael*, and *Poussin* are all characteriz'd from their *Design*. The *Truth of Taste* will, *cæteris paribus*, belong to the first, in the highest Degree; but we must always remember that there can be no Greatness without Justness and Decorum; which is the Reason that *Raphael* is counted higher in *Design* than *Michael Angelo*. For though this latter had a grander and more masculine Taste, yet *Raphael*, with a truly grand one, was incomparably more correct and true.

It is not easy to assign that part of Poetry, which answers to the Colouring of a Painter. A very good judge of Painting, calls the *Colouring*, the Procuress of her Sister, *Design*; who gains admirers for her, that otherwise might not perhaps be captivated with her Charms. If we trace this Idea through Poetry, we shall perhaps determine Poetical Colouring to be such a general Choice of Words, such an Order of Grammatical Construction, and such a Movement and Turn of the Verse, as are most favourable to the Poet's Intention, distinct from the Ideas which those Words convey. For whoever has reflected much on the Pleasure which Poetry communicates, will recollect many Words which, taken singly, excite very similar Ideas, but which have very different Effects, according to their Situation and Connection in a Period. It is impossible to read *Virgil*, but especially *Milton*, without making this Observation a thousand times. The sixth Column of the Ballance shall therefore be named from this *Poetical* Colouring.

As for Versification, its greatest Merit is already provided for by the last Article; but as it would seem strange to many, should we intirely omit it, the seventh Column shall therefore be allotted for it, as far as it relates to meer Harmony of Sound.

The Eighth Article belongs to the *Moral* of the several Poets, or to the Truth and Merit of the Sentiments which they express, or the Dispositions which they inculcate, with respect to Religion, Civil Society, or Private Life. The Reader must not be surprized, if he find the Heathen Poets not so much degraded as he might expect in this Particular; for tho' their Representations of Divine Providence be so absurd and shocking, yet this Article is intended to characterize the comparative Goodness of their moral Intention, and not the comparative Soundness of their speculative Opinions. *Where little is given, little is required.*

The Ninth and last Column contains an Estimate of their comparative Value and Eminence *upon the Whole*. This is greatly wanting in the *French* Author. The Degrees of Perfection which he assigns to *Rubens*, make up a Sum, when the four Articles are added to each other, exactly equal to what he calculates for *Raphael*; so that one, not greatly versed in the Study of Pictures, might imagine from thence that *Rubens* was as great a Painter as *Raphael*. This general Estimate is also more necessary in the present Scheme, as some of the Articles, particularly that of Ordonnance, are applied equally to every Species of poetry; so that a Satirist will be rated as high, in that Article, as an Epic Poet; provided his Ordonnance be as perfect for Satire, as that of the other is for Heroic Poetry. Upon this Account, Justice to the Manes of the diviner Poets requires that we should acknowledge their Pre-eminence upon the Whole, after having thus set their Inferiors upon a Level with them in particular Parts.

You see this general Method is here applied to a few, the greater Names of Poetry in most polite Languages. I have avoided to bring in any living Authors, because I know the Vanity and Emulation of the Poetical Tribe; which I mention, lest the Reader should find fault with me for omitting *Voltaire*, *Metastasi*[o], or any favourite Author of our own Nation. I am, Sir,

Your most humble Servant,
MUSIPHRON.

The Ballance.	Critical Ordonnance.	Pathetic Ordonnance.	Dramatic Expression.	Incidental Expression.	Taste.	Colouring.	Versification.	Moral.	Final Estimate.
Ariosto . . .	0	15	10	15	14	15	16	10	13
Boileau . . .	18	16	12	14	17	14	13	16	12
Cervantes . .	17	17	15	17	12	16	—	16	14
Corneille . .	15	16	16	16	16	14	12	16	14
Dante . . .	12	15	8	17	12	15	14	14	13
Euripides . .	15	16	14	17	13	14	—	15	12
Homer . . .	18	17	18	15	16	16	18	17	18
Horace . . .	12	12	10	16	17	17	16	14	13
Lucretius . .	14	5	—	17	17	14	16	0	10
Milton . . .	17	15	15	17	18	18	17	18	17
Moliere . .	15	17	17	17	15	16	—	16	14
Pindar . . .	10	10	—	17	17	16	—	17	13
Pope . . .	16	17	12	17	16	15	15	17	13
Racine . . .	17	16	15	15	17	13	12	15	13
Shakespear . .	0	18	18	18	10	17	10	18	18
Sophocles . .	18	16	15	15	16	14	—	16	13
Spenser . .	8	15	10	16	17	17	17	17	14
Tasso . . .	17	14	14	13	12	13	16	13	12
Terence . .	18	12	10	12	17	14	—	16	10
Virgil . . .	17	16	10	17	18	17	17	17	16

Bibliography

WORKS

The Twickenham Edition of the Poems of Alexander Pope (London and New Haven), vols. i–x:
i. *Pastoral Poetry and an Essay on Criticism.* Ed. É. Audra and A. Williams (1961).
ii. *The Rape of the Lock and Other Poems.* Ed. G. Tillotson (1940, 3rd ed. revised 1962).
III. i. *An Essay on Man.* Ed. M. Mack (1950).
III. ii. *Epistles to Several Persons (Moral Essays).* Ed. F. W. Bateson (1951, 2nd ed. revised 1961).
iv. *Imitations of Horace.* Ed. J. Butt (1939, 2nd ed. revised 1953, 1961).
v. *The Dunciad.* Ed. J. Sutherland (1943, 3rd ed. revised 1963).
vi. *Minor Poems.* Ed. N. Ault and J. Butt (1954).
vii–x. *Iliad* and *Odyssey.* Ed. M. Mack, N. Callan, R. Fagles, W. Frost, and D. Knight (1967).
The Prose Works of Alexander Pope. Ed. N. Ault (Oxford, 1936).
The Art of Sinking in Poetry. Ed. E. Steeves (New York, 1952).
The Correspondence of Alexander Pope. Ed. G. Sherburn (Oxford, 1956).
R. H. Griffith, *Alexander Pope, A Bibliography* (Austin, Texas, 1922–7).

REPUTATION

AMARASINGHE, U., *Dryden and Pope in the Early Nineteenth Century* (1962). A full and well-documented account.
AUDRA, É., *Les Traductions Françaises de Pope (1717–1825)* (Paris, 1931).
——, *L'Influence Française dans l'Œuvre de Pope* (Paris, 1931).
BATESON, F. N., and N. A. JOUKOVSKY, *Alexander Pope* (Penguin Critical Anthologies: Harmondsworth, 1971). A lively and informative selection from 1711 to the present day, with challenging introductory essays.
CLARK, D. B., 'The Italian Fame of Pope', *Modern Language Quarterly*, xxii (1961), 357–66.

GUERINOT, J. V., *Pamphlet Attacks on Alexander Pope 1711–1744* (1969). Gives essential bibliographical details, and substantial quotations and paraphrases. An invaluable guide to this tangled material.

HARDY, J., 'Stockdale's Defence of Pope', *Review of English Studies*, xviii (1967), 49–54.

HELSZTYNSKI, S., 'Pope in Poland. A Bibliographical Sketch', *Slavonic Review*, vii (1928–9), 230ff.

LA HARPE, J. DE, 'Le *Journal des Savants* et le renommée de Pope en France au xviiie siècle', *University of California Publications in Modern Philology*, xvi (1933), 173–216.

LEEDY, P. F., 'Genres Criticism and the Significance of Warton's *Essay on Pope*', *PMLA*, xlv (1946), 140–6.

LENTA, G., *Pope in Italia e il Ricciola Rapita* (Florence, 1931). Sketchy.

MACDONALD, W. L., *Pope and his Critics* (1951).

MAURER, O., 'Pope and the Victorians', *Studies in English*, University of Texas (1944).

PITTOCK, J., 'Joseph Warton and his Second Volume of the *Essay on Pope*', *Review of English Studies*, xviii (1967), 264–73. (Supersedes earlier articles.)

ROGERS, R. W., 'Critiques of the *Essay on Man* in France and Germany 1736–1755', *English Literary History*, xv (1948), 176–93.

SIBLEY, A. M., *Pope's Prestige in America, 1725–1835* (New York, 1949).

WARREN, A., 'To Mr. Pope: Epistles from America', *PMLA*, xlviii (1933), 61–73.

WIMSATT, W. K., *The Portraits of Alexander Pope* (New Haven, 1965). The authoritative guide to the iconographic tradition. Generously illustrated.

WRIGHT, L. S., 'Eighteenth Century Replies to Pope's *Eloisa*', *Studies in Philology*, xxxi (1933), 519–33: incomplete account. See also Twickenham, ii. 414–16.

Index

The Index is arranged in three parts: I. References to Pope's works; II. Critics and anonymous pieces; III. Important topics and comparisons with other writers.

II. CRITICS AND ANONYMOUS PIECES

III. IMPORTANT TOPICS AND COMPARISONS WITH OTHER WRITERS